D1603687

Champions of Civil and Human Rights in South Carolina

CHAMPIONS

VOLUME 1

EDITED BY Marvin Ira Lare

# of Civil and Human Rights in South Carolina

Dawn of the Movement Era, 1955–1967

THE UNIVERSITY OF SOUTH CAROLINA PRESS

Published by the University of South Carolina Press
Columbia, South Carolina 29208

www.sc.edu/uscpress

Manufactured in the United States of America

25 24 23 22 21 20 19 18 17 16   10 9 8 7 6 5 4 3 2 1

Library of Congress Cataloging-in-Publication Data
can be found at http://catalog.loc.gov/.

ISBN: 978-1-61117-724-4 (cloth)
ISBN: 978-1-61117-725-1 (ebook)

To my beloved wife, Patricia Ann Tyler Lare, April 20, 1944–August 31, 2014.

She patiently shared my time, energy and passion with *Champions*. We both knew that without these volumes the wisdom of countless minds, hearts, and lives would be lost.

Contents

Part 4. Spawning the Movement in South Carolina

Preface and Acknowledgments

First, I must express my appreciation to my late wife, Patricia Tyler Lare. Her skills and experience have been helpful to the project in a myriad of ways, but most important, she kept our personal lives on track and in order so that I could maximize my time for this anthology. Without her patience and understanding, such a daunting task would not have been possible. She and other members of my family have freely gone without my time and attention across the years of this project. I am profoundly grateful to them.

Perhaps the best and most interesting way to provide an overview of this anthology and acknowledge my debts in preparing and publishing it is to tell the story of its origins and development. My anthropology/sociology professor at Southern Methodist University was fond of intoning, "Origins are always lost in mystery!" Fortunately, while *Champions of Civil and Human Rights in South Carolina* certainly has many sources, its origin as a project is quite clear.

In April 2003, as I approached retirement from my position with the South Carolina Department of Social Services, I attended a meeting of the board of directors of the Palmetto Development Group. William "Bill" Saunders was a fellow board member, and when he heard that I was retiring, he inquired, "What are you going to do when you retire?" I gave him my standard joke that I was going to read one third of my time, garden one third of my time, write a third of my time, and travel a third of my time. He went right past the joke and asked what I was going to write about. I replied that I wanted to address some theological issues but that I might write about the Luncheon Club—an interracial, interfaith group that had been meeting since the early 1960s. He said that he had been writing about the 1969 Charleston Hospital strike, in which he had been a key figure.

On my way home from the meeting, I reflected on the fact that the leaders of the civil rights movement, like the subjects of Tom Brokaw's *Greatest Generation,* were rapidly passing from the scene; aging and death were catching up with them. I pulled over to the emergency lane of the interstate and wrote in my notebook, "Anthology of Civil Rights in South Carolina." As I drove on home, I began listing in my mind a dozen or so persons who should be included in such a book.

A week or two later I went to Bill's office—he was chair of the state Public Service Commission at the time—and discussed my idea with him. He encouraged me but insisted that the title should include "Civil *and Human* Rights." Discrimination, he pointed out, was not solely a civil matter but a matter of inhumanity, threatening the very lives of those who were its victims. He pulled from his files the 1955 state legislation that made it illegal for any public school teacher or state employee to belong to the National Association for the Advancement of Colored People (NAACP).

I continued to think and talk with Bill about the project. I reasoned that it was the type of thing the University of South Carolina Press might have an interest in publishing, but I did not know anyone there with whom to discuss it.

Toward the end of May, I took my remaining vacation time for a trip to England and Ireland as a good way to wrap up my employment with the state. On the flight to London, my wife and I sat beside a young British woman, Nicole Mitchell. I was surprised to discover that she was the director of the University of Georgia Press. My heart raced as I thought how I might appropriately broach the subject of my project with her. Finally, I described my "retirement project" and asked if it would be appropriate for publication by a university press. She indicated that it would and suggested that I contact her friend and colleague, Curtis Clark, who had recently come to head the University of South Carolina Press. She indicated that she and Curtis had been associate directors at the University of Alabama Press and had recently taken new positions in Georgia and South Carolina. I then recalled reading an article to that effect a few months before, written by Bill Starr. I contained my enthusiasm and indicated that I would pursue that contact.

Toward the end of the summer I contacted Curtis Clark and, on September 8, 2003, met with him and Alexander Moore, acquisitions editor for the press. We discussed the concept, and they encouraged me to proceed. In subsequent meetings with Moore, he made numerous practical suggestions, including establishing an official connection with the university through the Institute for Southern Studies. Thomas Brown and Robert Ellis assisted me with that.

It was apparent to me that while I had been personally involved in civil and human rights activities for decades, I was not fully aware of what was afoot in South Carolina relative to my proposed initiative. I did not want to duplicate the efforts of others and hoped that what I did would be complementary. Therefore, during September, October, and November 2003, I consulted people across the state to find out what they were doing in this area and ask their advice and counsel regarding a proposed anthology of the stories of leaders of civil and human rights activities in South Carolina. Listed here are those I consulted during this early period, arranged in alphabetical order rather than in the order I contacted them: Jack Bass, College of Charleston; Marcus Cox, the Citadel; W. Marvin Dulaney, College of Charleston and the Avery Research Center for African American History and Culture; Charles Gardner, City of

Greenville (retired); William Hine, South Carolina State University; Robert J. Moore, Columbia College (retired); Winifred "Bo" Moore, the Citadel; Steven O'Neil, Furman University; Cleveland Sellers, University of South Carolina; Claudia Smith-Brinson, the *State* newspaper; Selden K. Smith, Columbia College (retired); and Bernie Wright, Penn Center.

In addition to discussing the content and methodology of the anthology, I inquired about an appropriate "home" for the project: a public or private nonprofit sponsor with which I could work and secure grant funding. The name of Fred Sheheen came up repeatedly. The former director of the South Carolina Commission on Higher Education, Sheheen was now associated with the Institute for Public Service and Policy Research (IPS&PR) of the University of South Carolina. I had previously worked with him on a number of projects and had been impressed with his vision and leadership.

I approached him with the suggestion that the institute might become the sponsor of the anthology project. He said that there were only two things to which he was going to devote the rest of his career. One of those was race and the other was poverty. He agreed to discuss the sponsorship with the leadership of the institute, including its director, Robert Oldendick. A week or so later, he reported that the institute had agreed to be the sponsor.

I proposed that the next step be to hold an anthology colloquium, to which we would invite scholars, community leaders, and advocates to secure their input. Randy Akers, executive director of the Humanities Council[SC], indicated that planning grant funds might be available for such an initiative. We submitted the application and received funding to cover costs related to holding the colloquium.

The concept of the colloquium was to present an overview of the proposed anthology to participants and secure their input as to the overall design, as well as to identify persons and events that should be included. To model the type of entries we desired, I asked three persons to write some part of their stories relevant to the struggle for civil and human rights in South Carolina. Bill Saunders wrote about an attack on the Progressive Club on John's Island; Rhett Jackson wrote about the merging of the black and white conferences of the United Methodist Church; and James L. Solomon Jr. wrote of his experience as one of the first three black students to enroll in the University of South Carolina. These papers were distributed as samples of what the anthology would include.

Eighty persons were invited for the daylong event at Seawell's Restaurant in Columbia on March 19, 2004; thirty-six attended. Twenty scholars participated. Others included nine "activists," four newspaper reporters, and three graduate students. Four were black females, twelve black males, six white females, and fourteen white males. Fred Sheheen and Cleveland Sellers gave overviews of the purpose of the project; I provided a PowerPoint presentation on the proposed framework; Saunders, Jackson, and Solomon presented their papers. Six small group discussions were held in the morning and afternoon with moderators and reporters in each. Claudia Smith

Brinson secured students from her writing class at the university to assist in the colloquium: Elizabeth Catanese, Rebekah Dobrasko, Paige Haggard, and Rachael Luria. Most of these individuals also assisted with the anthology festivals held later that year.

Fred Sheheen and the Institute for Public Service and Policy Research assisted in securing a grant from the Southern Bell Corporation (now AT&T) to underwrite miscellaneous expenses, including holding three anthology festivals, one each in Greenville, Orangeburg, and at Penn Center on St. Helena Island, in May and June of 2004. These gatherings sought to involve probable contributors to the anthology and demonstrate what might be included. There were approximately twenty participants in each of these festivals. It was quite apparent how rich the stories of the activists were, but it also became clear that having them and others write their own stories—even with considerable assistance—was unlikely. This led to the decision to secure oral history interviews as the primary content of the anthology.

Carol and Bob Botsch of the University of South Carolina–Aiken informed me that a specialist in oral history, Dr. Maggi Morehouse, had recently joined them on the faculty. I contacted her, and she graciously agreed to lead a one-day seminar on doing oral histories. We informed our "anthology network," then composed of some ninety persons, and invited them to attend and/or identify upper-level students to participate at USC in Columbia on September 18, 2004. Approximately a dozen attended, about half faculty and half students.

Also, I contacted a number of scholars to explore if they might have graduate students who could assist with the project. Marvin Dulaney suggested Felice Ferguson Knight, an M.A. student at the College of Charleston. We met and identified ten persons to interview from the Charleston area. She conducted the interviews in a very professional manner and provided full documentation, transcripts, and copies of the audiotapes for the anthology. Bill Saunders became the subject of her thesis. Janet Hudson arranged for Andrew Grose, a student at Winthrop University, to do an interview in Rock Hill; and Jackie Brooker arranged for Nathan McConnell, a student from Claflin University, to do an interview in Orangeburg. (The students and their teachers are credited with these interviews where they appear in the anthology.)

I have already mentioned the Humanities Council[SC] planning grant and the grant from the AT&T Corporation that underwrote the developmental stages of the anthology. In addition to these, the Humanities Council[SC] provided a major grant for 2005 to 2006, and a "We the People" grant and a staff grant in 2007. These grants were pivotal to the success of the project not only in the funds they provided but also in the credibility they afforded the project in other circles. Randy Akers and his staff were most helpful throughout the project.

The South Carolina Bar Foundation provided the largest grant awards from its Interest on Lawyer Trust Accounts (IOLTA) fund. In both 2006 and in 2007, the foundation provided very substantial support. The cost of conducting interviews across the state, transcribing them, and gathering archival materials was largely underwritten by Bar Foundation grants. As well as making in-state travels, I went to the University of North Carolina, Chapel Hill; Duke University; the Moorland-Spingarn Research Center of Howard University; and the Library of Congress in Washington, D.C., to secure documents.

The Nord Family Foundation and the Nelson Mullins Riley and Scarborough Law Firm also provided support in 2007 to complete numerous editing tasks. The Institute for Public Service and Policy Research provided in-kind and cash-matching support required by some of the grant sources.

The institute was essential to the implementation and management of the project. Fred Sheheen and Beth Burn, program manager in his office, provided assistance and encouragement. Beth Burn proofread and submitted most of the grant applications. Other institute administrative staff and the services of the USC Grants Management Office were critical to the project's success. Instructional Services in the Division of Information Technology made backup copies of all interviews and audiotape copies that I sent to those I interviewed.

As the interviewing process got underway, I consulted with Cleveland Sellers on the list of activists to be interviewed. We had a list of roughly ninety persons, but as we considered the length of the project, we reduced the list to seven-five or eighty. We felt that one volume of that size would be adequate to cover the subject. However, as I proceeded with interviews, new names kept appearing that begged for inclusion. The scope of the project from 1930 to 1980 demanded that more entries be included from archival materials and interviews from other sources. Felice Knight, in addition to conducting her own interviews, provided me with the transcription of a 1982 conference, "South Carolina Voices of the Civil Rights Movement . . . 1940–1970"—over two hundred typescript pages—which was archived at the Avery Research Center for African American History and Culture. This goldmine of voices, many of those from individuals now deceased, called for inclusion of more entries in the anthology.

I also consulted with Bob Moore concerning Judge Matthew J. Perry Jr. I knew that Bob had done extensive research with Judge Perry, and he had inspired my interest in the anthology project with his stories of Judge J. Waites Waring of Charleston. I discovered that Bob had done twenty or more interviews with key figures in the Civil Rights Movement, including hours of interviews with Judge Perry. He was pleased to make these available to me for the anthology, and I have included a number of them, giving him credit as the source.

Bob mentioned that his niece Lynn Moore, who had recently relocated to Columbia from Vermont, could possibly be of assistance in transcribing interviews. I certainly needed that kind of assistance, so I agreed to give her a sample on which to work. Lynn, with early experience in administrative services at Boston University, a career in social services, and an avid interest in history and justice issues, proved to be a godsend. She transcribed over eighty of the interviews with a skill and accuracy that was unrivaled. Beyond her technical skills she brought a personal interest in teasing out words from difficult-to-hear audio recordings and often researched references valuable to an authentic rendering of the text. While my work as editor has required the preparation of numerous drafts, her initial transcriptions have been invaluable. To avoid redundancy and minimize the size of the anthology, the crediting of Lynn as transcriber and me, as interviewer and editor, with each entry is assumed and omitted. Where others provide those services they are credited with the entry.

Another early resource has been the South Caroliniana Library at USC. Herb Hartsook was director of the library when I started the project. He was most helpful as we explored the interface between the anthology and the roles of the library. That relationship continued as he became director of the university's South Carolina Political Collections. When Allen Stokes returned as director of the Caroliniana Library, the working relationship with the library continued and was formalized. The library would digitize my interviews and make them available as audio documents to the public. In exchange, the library would have twenty of the interviews transcribed for me. Catherine Mann did an excellent job on those, and she is credited for them in the text. Nicholas Meriwether, oral historian for the library, took a keen interest in the anthology project from early on. He arranged for digitization of the tape recordings, making copies for me as well as for the library. We consulted regularly on the progress and plans of the anthology, including securing the appropriate releases. More recently Andrea L'Hommedieu filled the role as oral historian at Caroliniana. She has been most helpful in following through on the commitments with the library.

In the upstate of South Carolina, Ruthann Butler, director of the Greenville Cultural Exchange Center, was very helpful; I maintained a close working relationship with her and Steve O'Neill at Furman University. Steve and Courtney Tollison explored with me ways of securing interviews with key civil rights leaders in that area of the state. Together they taught a summer school session in 2006 on oral history and civil rights leadership. With their students they supplied interviews for the anthology as noted in the text.

Periodically we held anthology consultations in various areas of the state to share our progress and seek further counsel and guidance. Additional persons who joined the growing network through these consultations include, in the Greenville area, A. V. Huff (retired) from Furman University and Steven Lowe with USC-Upstate; in the Charleston area, Tom Rubillo, an attorney from Georgetown, South Carolina; and in Columbia, a number of graduate students. In addition to Cleveland Sellers, others with the USC African American Studies Program were particularly helpful: Bobby Donaldson, Patricia Sullivan, Kent Germany, and Carolyn Sultan.

Melanie Knight, with the South Carolina Department of Archives and History, has been involved with the project since the colloquium in 2004. Besides participating, she volunteered to assist in numerous ways. Most notable of these was her review of the optical character scans of the papers of Judge Waring and his wife, Elizabeth, from the Howard University archives. Many of these, including Mrs. Waring's typescript diary during the *Briggs v. Elliott* deliberation, required very extensive correction of the electronic documents. Also, she transcribed from raw material much of the appendix of biographical information on the interviewees and other persons key to the anthology. Also, Bobby Donaldson recommended Ramon Jackson, one of his graduate students, to assist in compiling the timelines.

The close working relationship with the USC Press, especially with Alex Moore, continued throughout the long process of preparing and publishing the documents that, even with heavy editing, grew to three, then four, and now five volumes.

I hope that this narrative approach has provided insight as to the nature and extent of the debt I and all readers owe to those named here. At a deeper level, however, a "narrative analysis" level, there are still many mysteries of origin. A few that I can identify reveal something of my motivation for this project. My older sister, Norma Lare Wasson, inspired me with her high school declamations on capital punishment and racial justice. James and Phil Lawson, whom I encountered in the Methodist Youth Fellowship and at college, helped undergird my commitment to pacifism and non-violence in the civil rights movement. Glenn and Helen Smiley, field workers with the Fellowship of Reconciliation (FOR), nurtured my interest in peace and justice issues during college, before they left to assist with the Montgomery bus boycott. Bishop Gerald Kennedy and the Reverends Russell Clay and Richard Cain made possible my experience as a pastor of an inner-city, interracial congregation in Los Angeles in the early 1960s. Father Louis Bohler, my colleague and friend, helped make possible my participation in the voting rights march from Selma to Montgomery in 1965. And, finally, there are my colleagues and supporters in Dallas who made it possible for me to attend the funeral of Martin Luther King Jr. in April of 1968.

The list could go on, but as mentioned before, it certainly includes the patience and support of my wife, Pat, and my family, who graciously went without countless days of my "free time" in retirement for this passion.

Prologue

First, I want to express my deepest appreciation to the champions who have shared their stories for this anthology. Society owes all of them a profound debt for their courageous actions and, now, for reliving their experiences for this and future generations. That debt can partially be repaid by the degree to which each reader draws strength and courage to continue and extend the struggle for civil and human rights in our day and on new frontiers.

There are countless other champions whose stories are not included in this collection. We owe them, also, for the part they played in one of the greatest peaceful revolutions in history. Our debt to some of them can also be made visible to the extent that readers are inspired by this collection to search out and record their stories as well. Helping their stories live can be the pursuit of any of us who inquire from family members and neighbors about their experiences; it can be the mission of students from middle schools to graduate schools to research leads found throughout these volumes to help complete the story.

Some champions have already been feted in other works, and others have yet to be fully recognized. I have intentionally not expanded upon many prominent figures, some of whom have already been well described for history. Some of these notables still await the appropriate memorializing of their service and leadership. Specifically, I have not included the various governors of South Carolina who contributed richly to civil and human rights during the period covered by this anthology. I believe that they have or will receive their due in other works. Also, some very prominent civil rights leaders in and from South Carolina receive little attention in these pages, except for brief selections and passing references. It has been difficult to exclude them from fuller coverage here, but again, they are due far more than what the limits of this work can provide. Rather, I have tried to include here stories of those who all too easily could fade into forgotten mystery, but without which we would not stand where we do today.

A word about the scope of this anthology: my focus has been from roughly 1930 to 1980. I have tried to include persons who exercised notable leadership during that period and have divided it roughly into three periods: 1930–1954, "Laying the Foundations"; 1955–1967, "The Movement Era"; and 1968–1980, "Birthing a New Day." This ambitious range was questioned somewhat by some participants in the anthology colloquium that was convened on March 19, 2004, to provide guidance and suggest contacts for the project. The consensus seemed to be to exclude the 1930s and 1940s, there being enough to cover during the period of the 1950s through the 1970s. I resisted that counsel, however, believing that those earlier days were critical to an understanding of the subject and that we stood on the shoulders of those giants of that pre– and post–World War II era. Firsthand interviews for that period have been limited, but I have supplemented those with other firsthand accounts and original documents.

The content of this anthology does not sift out into neat periods. Any given interview may include comments about the person's childhood, such as those of Benjamin Mays, B. J. Glover, and I. DeQuincey Newman, and their comments about recent and even contemporary events or issues, such as Ernest Finney's remarks on the "minimally adequate education" of court decisions and the removal of the Confederate flag from the statehouse chambers and dome. I have exercised my judgment in placing each entry where it seemed appropriate to me, where the primary or most significant contribution of the person seemed to fit in the total scheme of the collection, and even dividing interviews into parts and placing them in different sections.

My approach to these interviews and the oral history they provide has been rather eclectic. At first I had presumed that these champions would be ready and able to write their own stories for this anthology. At the three "anthology festivals" we held across the state, we offered to provide whatever assistance participants needed, ranging from clerical services and assistance to "ghost writers" who would capture their stories, but I soon realized that if it were that easy to record their stories, it would, in many cases, have already been done. Next, I hit on the idea of personal interviews conducted by me and other capable teachers and students across the state. The oral history seminar we held on September 18, 2004, proved quite helpful both for this project and other history projects across the state. The seminar taught and demonstrated an interviewer/questioner approach that is commonly used. I developed the format of a structured interview to assist interviewers, which also proved quite helpful.

However, as I began conducting interviews myself, I became aware of an emerging approach known as "narrative analysis." This approach, I was advised, allows the interviewee to start where they wish, end where they wish, and construct the structure of the interview themselves. The character and nature of the narratives would be revelatory, not only of the stories but of the persons themselves. I found that since the interviewees had been selected because of their visible activity in civil and human rights, they generally were more than ready to share their stories and would need little prompting. As can be seen from most of my interviews, only a few follow-up questions were generally necessary for them to tell their stories amply.

What then is the character of this collection? First, while it contains history, it is not a history. When I discussed the project early on with Cleveland Sellers, he observed that "you are taking an anthropological rather than an historical approach." I agreed. Further, I have come to think of these volumes as literature rather than history, something of a collective memoir, which entry by entry would reveal more and more of the life that pulsed throughout the struggle for equity and justice. While we know in general the outcomes of the stories, we learn more and more of the intricacies and the humanity of each character as they reveal themselves to us. I even like to think of the project as a novel written by multiple authors and collaborators. I think the reader will find this approach exciting and interesting as they come to know, rather personally, each of the characters and see the drama play out.

A word about the editing process: First, I have been blessed with very good transcribers, whom I have credited in the acknowledgments. With the transcripts on my computer, I listened carefully to the recording—generally on audiotape—and perfected the transcript as nearly as possible. Next I modified the text to turn spoken English into written English. That is, I took out meaningless repetitions of "ah," "and," "you know," and other speech patterns that would interfere with reading the text from the page. I endeavored to preserve the particular colloquial speech patterns of the interviewees without letting them become burdensome to the reader. Generally, I spelled out words that in dialect might be shortened, such as "going" for "goin'," and such; however, where it seemed particularly called for, I amended the spelling to reflect the speech pattern of the individual. I sought to strike a balance that would allow the text to read well while revealing the individuality of the interviewee. Finally, I edited for content revelatory to the subject of the anthology—deleting digressions, duplications, and things that seemed insignificant to the story. However, I kept content that reflected the character of the person, even if it was somewhat tangential to the tale. I also divided some interviews into parts to be included in different sections of the anthology along with others on the same general subject.

With regard to grammar and punctuation, I have adapted standard practice to the unique features of the interview and the needs of oral history. The starting, stopping, interruptions, and reflections call for a somewhat different approach than a composition. Edited deletions, short and long, also seem to call for forms that reveal the edit rather than preserve the flow of the narrative. Readers and researchers who seek to read the entire, original transcripts or listen to the audiotapes can find them at the University of South Carolina's South Caroliniana Library and other repositories identified in footnotes. In any case, I hope the reader will find my style appropriate to the text and helpful to reading.

Finally, a word about the volumes of the anthology currently being published, volumes 1 and 2, *The Movement Era*. I have included in them entries that begin in 1955 with the aftermath of the U.S. Supreme Court decision favoring the desegregation of public schools, and that end in 1967 with seminal victories, such as dismissal of Benner C. Turner as president of South Carolina State College. For convenience of size and flow of content, volume 1 deals with early events and broad topics of the era, and volume 2 deals with specific issues and events near the close of that period.

Volume 3, *Laying the Foundations,* will focus on the earlier period, 1930 to 1954. Volumes 4 and 5, *Birthing a New Day,* will focus on the period 1968 to 1980. This non-chronological order, suggested by the publishers, recognizes that the "movement era" is the lens through which the earlier period and subsequent period have meaning and significance.

PART 1

Following the 1954 Supreme Court Ruling: The Setting

The S.C. (Negro) Citizens Committee Press Release

November 6, 1955

(Dear Editor: Due To The Unfortunate Misunderstandings Of The Negro Citizens, We Kindly Request That You Carry This Statement In Full, APW.)*

From: A. P. Williams, Chairman, Interim Committee
Richland County Division, S.C. Citizens Committee
1808 Washington Street
2—9573, Columbia

Current Organizational Sentiment And Objectives Outlined

The Richland County Division of the South Carolina Citizens Committee held its first meeting of 1955–'56 in the auditorium of Allen University on Sunday, November 6 [1955]. Officers elected were The Rev. J. P. Reeder, president; I. P. Stanback, vice-president; the Rev. Arthur T. Fisher, secretary; Mrs. Rosena Benson, assistant secretary; the Rev. John R. Wilson, treasurer; and A. P. Williams, chairman of the interim committee.

Quoted below is a statement issued at the close of the meeting,

"We, the members of the Citizens Committee of Columbia and Richland County, a local unit of the South Carolina Citizens Committee, organized in 1944 to meet momentous problems facing the Negro citizens at that time, and working subsequently in various areas through political action and other civic movements, issue the following statement as to current sentiment and objectives:

*From the NAACP Collections of the Manuscript Division, Library of Congress, Section II, Box C-182, Folder 5.

"Our organization, having a composite representation from various religious and lay groups stands solidly for the respect and observance of all laws—national, state and local. We would have it clearly understood that we include the United States Supreme Court Decision of May 17, 1954 which declared that 'in the field of public education the field of public education [*sic*] the doctrine of SEPARATE BUT EQUAL has no place;' and the implementing document of May 31, 1955. We felt in May, 1954 what time has proved to be true: that the May 17 decision would become precedent for many others guaranteeing the full enjoyment of the various phases of citizenship by all the population groups in America.

As law abiding citizens who recognize fully that either to circumvent or to defy the law is rebellion, and that to join others in so doing is criminal conspiracy which could lead to anarchy, we declare now that as citizens of the United States, of the Commonwealth of South Carolina, and of the County of Richland, we shall in no degree at any time knowingly disregard the law, but shall seek consistently to fulfill all responsibilities and enjoy all privileges outlined in such laws. Therefore, speaking with special reference to the U.S. Supreme Court Decisions mentioned above, we hold any persons deporting themselves otherwise as being parties to a criminal conspiracy and in rebellion against, the Federal Government.

"From 1896 until 1954, Southern Negroes existed and suffered deprivations and indignities under the Plessy v. Ferguson Decision, commonly known as the 'separate but equal doctrine.' But we respected that Decision as the law of the Land. We fomented neither conspiracy nor rebellion, but waited until the course of human events and through legal procedures that Decision was reversed. Now, with continuing proper regard for the law, but pardonable fervor and devotion, we are determined to abide by and to profit by the more recent civil rights decisions of the Highest Tribunal of our Land.

"The apparent crisis in race relations in our Native State has come about simply because some of its citizens, reeling under the perennial disadvantage of pitifully sub-standard facilities and restricted and discriminatory curricula provided Negro children in segregated schools, used the right guaranteed them under Article I of the Bill of Rights to petition their government for redress. The discriminatory and sometimes intolerable conditions against which Negro parents have revolted were common knowledge for decades in every community as not even token effort to fulfill the "separate but equal" claim.

"In their various efforts to force the Negro parents to compromise themselves in the pursuance of the Right to petition, or to force the petitioners into submission or even into starvation, if necessary, certain elements of the population including many prominent men who either know or who have sworn to uphold the law have taken dastardly steps both subtle and obvious. Most outstanding among these is the now well-known and much discussed 'economic squeeze.'

"In the most highly infested areas, exemplified by the City of Orangeburg, the Negro citizens have attempted to meet the 'Freeze' in the only way they know how— through economic boycott. Only time will prove the efficacy of this action.

"We hasten to say that the pain and persecution of the Orangeburg Negro citizens is also our lot. Their fight for constitutional rights is our fight. We stand ready to co-operate fully with them and with the people of any other community in the effort to seek redress under the Constitution of the United States.

"We deplore the deliberate misstatements made in the effort to distort our true objectives, to confuse the public, and to cloud the issues in the vain striving of the opposition to dissipate the strength of Negroes in their struggle for full citizenship. This brash disregard for truth would be most disconcerting if the calibre, background, and connections of the sources of such utterances were not well-known and well understood by this organization.

"The struggle in which we are engaged is neither temporary nor futile. Since the ultimate objective is the proper evaluation of each individual and the proper regard for human dignity, our efforts cannot fail for they must have the blessing of the Master of Men who said, 'I have come that ye might have life, and that ye might have it more abundantly.'"

For this reason, we shall cooperate unceasingly with and fully support any and all organizations which work within the framework of the law of this Land to obtain for all Americans the full enjoyment of their rights and privileges.

Believing that our cause is just and knowing that a just cause cannot fail, and with neither hate nor bitterness toward those who would deny to others the freedom they prize for themselves, we pledge ourselves one to another and in the presence of Almighty God to work toward to the inevitable triumph for good in out lives and in the lives of the children of this State.

The 15th Annual Conference, S.C. NAACP, Press Release

November 25, 1955

Immediate release*
From: Mrs. Andrew W. Simkins, Secretary
S.C. Conference of NAACP
2025 Marion Street, 2–9578, Columbia

To Hold 15th Annual Session of NAACP
Nov 25 1955

The fifteenth annual session of the South Carolina conference of the National Association for the Advancement of Colored People opening in Columbia Friday evening will close on Sunday with a mass meeting at 3 o'clock in the Township auditorium, featuring Thurgood Marshall, chief NAACP counsel, as speaker. Heads of all other state organizations have been invited to be platform guests on this occasion.

Others appearing on the program, with James M. Hinton, conference president, presiding, will be the Reverend Francis Dolan, pastor of Christ the King Catholic Church, Orangeburg; and the Reverend I. DeQuincy [sic] Newman, Sumter, delivering respectively the invocation and the benediction; Harold R. Boulware, Columbia attorney, who will introduce the speaker; and John Bolt Culbertson, attorney, of Greenville.

Widely known as "Mr. Civil Rights" and conceded by millions to be America's greatest constitutional lawyer of this generation, Marshall has won fourteen court [cases] of sixteen times "at bat" before the United States Supreme Court. He turned

*From the NAACP Collections of the Manuscript Division, Library of Congress, Section II, Box C-182, Folder 5.

down the nomination by former President Harry S. Truman to be a judge in the federal courts of the State of New York because of the importance of the school segregation case underway at the time of the nomination.

Among his chief accomplishments before the Nation's highest tribunal are: the end of segregation in interstate travel, the opening of Southern graduate and professional colleges to Negro youth, the unanimous decision of the U.S. Supreme Court against public school segregation, the death knell to the infamous "white primary," the striking down of the "separate but equal" provision of housing and recreational facilities, and the telling blow against restrictive covenants which force segregated housing.

During the opening session on Friday evening, in the Allen University auditorium, Clarence Mitchell, director of the Washington bureau of NAACP, will evaluate the current Washington scene as it relates to political action and civil rights.

Featured as speaker during this meeting will be Mrs. Ruby Hurley, director of the southeast region of NAACP. She will discuss regional activities with special reference to her experiences in connection with the Emmett Till case. These two speakers also will serve as consultants in panels "Mapping Strategy to Meet Current Issues" to be held on Saturday in First Calvary Baptist church, the conference headquarters.

The annual meeting of youth councils will be held Saturday in the Bishops Memorial AME church, 2219 Washington Street, beginning at 9 o'clock. Herbert L. Wright, nation- . . .

Other participants on the panels will be W. W. Law, member of the national board of NAACP and president of the Savannah Branch; Dr. H. B. Monteith, president of Victory

Mrs. Andrew W. (Modjeska) Simkins, the "Mother of Civil Rights" in South Carolina, secretary for the S.C. (Negro) Citizens Committee. Courtesy of South Caroliniana Library, University of South Carolina.

Savings Bank, Columbia; Lincoln C. Jenkins, Jr.,. attorney at law, Columbia; J. T. McCain, associate director, Council on Human Relations, Columbia; the Reverend Francis Donlan, C. SS. R., pastor, Christ the King Catholic Church, Orangeburg, moral consultant; James T. Dimery, Kingstree, and the Rev. Horace T. Sharper, Sumter Branch president.

The annual meeting of youth councils, Leroy Nesbitt, president, will be held in Bishops Memorial AME church, 2219 Washington Street, beginning at 9 AM. Herbert L. Wright, national NAACP youth secretary, serving as consultant for the youth council, will address the Saturday evening session of the conference to be held in the Benedict College chapel at 8 o'clock. The other feature of this meeting will be a panel discussion "Youth's Role in Gaining Full Citizenship For All."

On Sunday morning at 9 AM in the assembly room of the Allen University library "The Role of the Church in Integration" will be discussed by the Reverend M. S. Gordon, pastor of First Calvary Baptist Church, Wendell P. Russell, and Dr. Henderson S. Davis, pastor of Emanuel AME church.

"Hear the World's Greatest Civil Right Lawyer." Flyer promoting attendance at the Fifteenth Annual Conference, South Carolina NAACP, November 25–27, 1955. Courtesy of the Library of Congress, NAACP Files.

At 11 AM, the Annual Conference Worship Service, with the Reverend M. S. Gordon, pastor of the host church, delivering the annual message.

Music during the entire conference session will be under the direction of Mrs. Roscoe C. Wilson, chorister of First Calvary Baptist Church This choir will appear on the opening program of the conference. Music on Saturday evening will be rendered by Benedict College. Mrs. Wilson has planned a program of organ music to begin at 2:30 on Sunday at the Auditorium. Officers of the South Carolina conference of NAACP in addition to Hinton are: Robert A. Brooks and J. Arthur Brown, vice-presidents; Mrs. Andrew W. Simkins, secretary; Levi G. Byrd, conference treasurer; Dr. B. T. Williams, legal defense fund treasurer; A. J. Clement, Jr., chairman of executive board, and board [of directors]; and S. J. McDonald, Sr., Chairman emeritus of the Board, Mrs. A. B. Weston, Youth Advisor.

The public is invited to attend all of the meetings.

Excerpts from Thurgood Marshall's Address, November 27, 1955

Excerpts from address by Thurgood Marshall, NAACP Special Counsel, scheduled for delivery at 3 p.m., Sunday, Nov. 27, [1955,] before the 15th annual convention of the South Carolina State Conference of NAACP Branches.

For Release upon Delivery:

During* the past two and one-half months we have been attending similar state conference meetings in all of the southern states. Our office has also gathered together all of the available information as to the progress that has been made toward desegregation in the southern states. From all of this information we are now able to give a fair appraisal of progress that is being made in this final drive to remove race and color as decisive factors in American life.

We *know* that the average American in the southern states has been moving one way or the other in response to irresponsible speeches of southern governors and other state officers, inflammatory news stories and the horrible record of un-American groups and individuals who have set themselves up above the law of the land. While we have been outraged by statements of public officials, economic boycotts against Negroes, threats and intimidations and murders of some Negroes, we are still determined to chart our course upon the record rather than upon emotional urges.

It must have been expected that governmental officials and private individuals would use any decision of the Supreme Court on racial matters to prey upon the innate prejudices of other human beings. It must have been foreseen that many Americans

*From the NAACP Collections of the Manuscript Division, Library of Congress, Section II, Box C-182, Folder 5.

who live in the South would mistakenly view any change of mores and customs as a challenge to band together to preserve the tradition of the old South. While all of this should have been expected that is no reason why we should permit these forces to decide our future. For a moment let us look at the brighter side of the picture and expose the record of the South insofar as desegregation and non-discrimination is concerned.

First of all, let us recognize that there is no longer a solid South in regard to Negro rights. There is no longer the possibility of reestablishing the once solid South. On one side we have southern states that seem determined not to budge an inch. On the other hand, we have states that are determined, intelligently and as rapidly as possible, to bring about conformity with the Constitution of the United States. For example, Mississippi is certainly not typical of the South for that is possibly the only state that has a state-wide policy of denying Negroes the right to register and vote. Then, too, there are five states of the South that have not at this late date gotten around to admitting Negroes to the graduate and professional schools. These states are Alabama, Florida, Georgia, Mississippi and South Carolina. In all of the other southern states, Negroes are attending public and private universities without friction of any kind and in the truly American manner. It is time that we recognized that while there are a few states determined to maintain their unlawful practices of racial discrimination, these states are in the minority of the southern states.

On the question of desegregation on the elementary and high school level, we first must recognize that of the seventeen states of the south and the District of Columbia, eight of these states and the District of Columbia are desegregating their elementary and high schools. Nine states are not desegregating. So even in this area, one half of the states have already moved toward compliance with the Supreme Court's decision. For example, the District of Columbia has desegregated its public schools and here is the record of eight southern states which have started desegregation:

Arkansas—three towns already on a desegregated basis;

Delaware—21 of the 104 school districts desegregated;

Kentucky—24 of the 224 school districts desegregated;

Maryland—Baltimore plus eight of Maryland's 22 counties desegregated;

Missouri—85 per cent of the total Negro school population attending mixed classes;

Oklahoma—271 out of the 1463 districts with school age Negro children desegregated;

Texas—Between 1 and 2 per cent of the Negro school population desegregated in 65 of Texas' school districts;

West Va—All but 10 of its 55 counties have desegregated.

Now let us look at the record on the other side:

Alabama—No desegregation but rather efforts to get legislation enacted to perpetuate segregation.

Florida—While no desegregation *in* force except at two air force bases, biracial committees are at work *in* one-third of the Florida counties surveying the possibilities of early desegregation;

Georgia—State leadership from the Governor on down bitterly opposed to desegregation with the most recent developments being an action in the Supreme Court of Georgia seeking to prevent the Waycross School Board from even thinking about the possibilities of desegregating;

Louisiana—No desegregation with state policy bitterly opposed to desegregation including an appropriation of $100,000 to hire lawyers to oppose desegregation;

Mississippi—Most violent opposition;

North Carolina—Complete opposition on the state level with much evidence of willingness of local school boards to desegregate if permitted to do so;

South Carolina—Bitter opposition on the state level with considerable support on the local level;

Tennessee—No desegregation except the Oak Ridge federally controlled system;

Virginia—Bitter opposition on the state level with many local school systems publicly and privately in support of desegregating if permitted to do so.

Here is the record. The important measuring rod of progress in this field of social change is whether or not a start is being made. You will find from this record that a start has been made and rapid progress is following in half of the areas involved. It is just a matter of *a very* little time before the most recalcitrant states will most certainly follow the line. No state and no small group of states no larger than nine in number can continue to buck the will of the balance of the country. Once an opening was made in the solid south, the end came into view. The widening breach in the South cannot be stopped short of including the entire South on the side of law and order.

There are two other factors to be considered in looking to the future. The Supreme Court of the United States has recently made it clear that segregation in recreational areas such as public parks is likewise unconstitutional. The second point to bear in mind is that local state and federal courts when required to do so are upholding the legality of local school officials willing to desegregate their systems. Only a short time ago, the Supreme Court of Texas in a case which sought to prevent the Big Springs School system from desegregating its public schools had this to say about state laws which still require segregation in public schools:

> At the threshold of our consideration of the issues in this case we are met with the argument that since the constitutional and statutory provisions requiring segregation in Texas schools were not before the Supreme Court in the Brown case they were not condemned *and we should hold them valid* and enforceable. That proposition is so utterly without merit that we overrule it without further discussion, except to say that Section 2 of Article VI of the Constitution of the United States declares: "This Constitution and the laws of the United States which shall be made in pursuance thereof,* shall be the supreme law of the land;

*The effect of the decision of the Supreme Court of the United States in the case just cited is too well known to require discussion.

and the judges in every state shall be bound thereby, anything in the Constitutions or laws of any state to the contrary notwithstanding."

This decision from the highest court in the State of Texas certainly destroys the myth prevalent in every southern state that the decision of the Supreme Court in the school cases did not apply to them. Of course, it is unbelievable that anyone in South Carolina would attempt to make a lawyer-like argument that the decision of the Supreme Court did not apply throughout the State of South Carolina. Since May 31 of this year, the constitutional provisions *and laws of* the State of South Carolina requiring racial segregation are unconstitutional, void and not worth the paper they are written on.

It is just a matter of time, and a very short time until local school boards in South Carolina will do as the School Board did in Big Springs, Texas and in Hoxie, Arkansas, that is to defy the state officials and follow their oath of office of upholding the Constitution of the United States as well as the Constitution of the State of South Carolina.

Indeed, in the Hoxie, Arkansas, situation we have the perfect example of how far a school board can go in desegregating. The Hoxie School Board desegregated its schools this Summer. White Citizens' Councils and other groups called a strike of the white students and held protest meetings and harassed the school board with all types of petitions and threats. Instead *of* abandoning its position, the Hoxie school board stuck to its decision and followed this by action in the federal courts in Arkansas which brought about an injunction against these groups to stop them from interfering with desegregating. If this can be done in Arkansas, it can be done in South Carolina. We believe that those school boards which desire to follow the law of the land can take heart in the decision of United States District Judge Trimble in which he ruled that:

> I shall not disclose what my personal feelings are with respect to whether or not it would be wise or desirable that segregation of the races in the public schools of this state be enforced as provided by state laws that have been effective since 1875; however, it must be stated that there are no valid segregation laws of the State of Arkansas, for they have been declared unconstitutional and void by the Supreme Court of the United States. Brown v. Board of Education of Topeka, 349 U.S. 294, 23 Lw 4273.

According to the allegations of the complaints in this case the [prosegregationists] are seeking to compel the [directors] to do the very things which the school directors involved in that litigation were ordered not to do.

[Despite Marshall's optimistic projections made some eighteen months following the United States Supreme Court's decision on May 14, 1954, public school segregation continued in South Carolina. It was not until 1963 that "school choice" legislation permitted a few courageous black students to enroll in white schools, and it was not until 1970, some fifteen years after the court's decision, that an integrated, unitary public school system was implemented in the state.]

Annual Message

"The Cry for Freedom in South Carolina"

November 27, 1955

All men* are created equal and endowed by their creator with certain inalienable rights among which are life, liberty, ant the pursuit of happiness, according to the Declaration of Independence, one of the fundamental doctrines upon which the principles of American democracy are based.

[Omitted here are twenty pages, approximately 6,800 words, of this message. It details the state's record and policies regarding education of black students and other injustices of the Plessy v. Ferguson, "separate but equal" era. What follows below begins on page 21 of the original document and continues to the end of the message on page 26.]

Summarily, what has happened in South Carolina in recent months? What have been the reactions to the petitions for school integration by some persons in the dominant group in some counties who operate through Citizens' Councils? A home has been

---

*From the NAACP Collections of the Manuscript Division, Library of Congress, Section II, Box C-182, Folder 5. The author and presenter of this message is unknown at this time. It was filed with the program and other materials of the 15th Annual Meeting of the South Carolina Conference of Branches, National Association for the Advancement of Colored People, which was held November 25–27, 1955, largely at First Calvary Baptist Church, 1401 Pine Street, Columbia, South Carolina. The opening meeting was held at the Allen University Auditorium on Friday evening, and Thurgood Marshall's presentation was held at Columbia Township Auditorium on Sunday afternoon. There is no presentation by this title on the program. It may have been the Sunday morning sermon. It might have been presented by James M. Hinton, president, or the Reverend M. S. Gordon, who was the host pastor. The extensive details regarding the history and current scene of South Carolina would suggest that the presenter was someone from within the state rather than one of the national or regional presenters who were present.

bombarded with stones, bricks, and garbage; a church has been burned; a Minister of the Gospel has had to flee for his life; a business establishment has been blasted; threats of death have been made against some NAACP leaders; credit has been withdrawn and mortgages foreclosed; tenants have been evicted from their homes; jobs have been taken from petitioners and other known integrationists, some of whom have been ruthlessly pursued and repeatedly discharged after pressure was put on the employers by the boss of the Citizens' Council; threats have been made to deprive relatives of NAACP members, particularly petition signers (who are not always members of the NAACP), of jobs; a sum of $10,000 has been offered for the membership roster of the NAACP; families have been separated because of the loss of jobs; there have been refusals to sell products to Negro businesses, especially those close to petition signers; Negroes have been offered money to induce Negro consumers to patronize businesses they now boycott because of the application of discrimination against petitioners; employees have been questioned regarding their affiliation with the NAACP; some school teachers have been asked to sign statements regarding membership in the NAACP and have been told that they will teach what they have been instructed to teach (that is, not to suggest changing the dual system of education but to advise segregation in the community); economic (and other) pressure has been applied against some of those who went to the rescue of petitioners who lost jobs and credit; some Caucasians have been refused the opportunity to work in certain establishments because they sympathized with the Negro and spoke against economic pressure being applied; some Caucasians have been boycotted (with regard to products) because they did not join the pressure group; some white Clergymen have been reported to their ecclesiastical superiors with the idea in mind of having superiors in position punish the Clergymen who acted and spoke in behalf of the Negro group; some white Clergymen have been forced to leave the communities in which they served because of utterances declaring it undemocratic and unchristian to apply pressure against a man because of his beliefs regarding human rights; and a curfew has been imposed in one community in Orangeburg County to keep "the darkies off the street" after midnight, according to public statements made by the mayor.

Some of the above practices are unconstitutional. But do some care about the constitution? Some have openly, boldly, and strongly defied it and the Supreme Court.

Sanctity of homes is disregarded; the right to work is denied; freedom of belief and action is curtailed; privacy is violated. And, hence, papers, documents, and records of the NAACP were destroyed in one city in order to protect innocent people. For the information of all concerned, no one has to answer questions about his membership in a legal organization. He has the constitutional right to refrain from answering interrogations.

In spite of opposition, the NAACP makes the following statements. Freedom-lovers are undaunted. No outstanding social advances have been made without some suffering, although the atrocities would not have occurred if men had respected the personalities and rights of other men; in other words, suffering is unnecessary for reform to occur. Nevertheless, it has occurred because of selfishness, greed, and arrogance. The struggle for human rights has been waged through the centuries; and it will continue to be waged until men begin to live by the Christian way of life, for human beings do not indefinitely submit to tyranny. Historically, champions of the rights of [Negroes have] been persecuted. Persecution of freedom and truth-lovers has taken these forms: ridicule and castigation, deprivation of economic security, exile, torture, imprisonment, and death. On the other hand, the fate of tyrants has been removal, banishment, and death. The champion of liberty is unpopular with the tyrant, and the tyrant eventually becomes unpopular with the people. The masses do not yield to slavery forever. And there is an eventual triumph of freedom.

Humanitarianism requires sacrifices. Castigation accompanies humanitarianism. The humanitarians are remembered. Many [who] have criticized them have fallen in oblivion. But stalwarts of freedom reign gloriously. How beautiful is the word "liberty!" How brilliantly it shines! And if we die in the struggle for human rights, we will die with the word "liberty" on our lips.

The politicians in the Citizens' Councils in Orangeburg County say that they are in a "death grip" with the "vicious NAACP," which must be "weeded out and exterminated by destroying the leaders." Hence, friends admonish as follows: "Don't be in the NAACP; you have too much to lose." "Your life is at stake." "Those who do nothing to earn their rights will enjoy the benefit of your sacrifices, will rock in comfort in palatial homes while you'll not have food to eat. They will even laugh at you and call you a fools."

To this answer: No price is too great to pay for liberty. Life without liberty is not dear. Christ said, "Man shall not live by bread alone, but by every word that proceedeth out of the mouth of God." (Matthew 4:4)

To us the spiritual is important. Eternal values are paramount. Soon we who are living today shall pass from the face of the earth. What heritage shall we bequeath to posterity? Let us not be deceived by trinkets and ephemeral trivialities. Let us think of lasting values, in terms of the more abundant life now and eternally for ourselves and our successors. Let us not have a false sense of values, but let us place the correct appraisal on the things that benefit mankind and promote the world order of peace.

Did not the Christ say, "He that would follow after me, let him deny himself and take up the cross"?

We are dedicated to a cause. Denial means working for the general welfare, thinking not of ourselves, but others; sacrificing ourselves today for the people of tomorrow, with the hope that they will live in a brighter world.

Let us follow the examples of our great statesmen and humanitarians, such as, Abraham Lincoln, Woodrow Wilson, Franklin D. Roosevelt, Harry S. Truman, and Dwight D. Eisenhower.

Will it be a noble or an ignoble place in history? Who reveres Hitlers, Mussolinis, and Perons? Will it be those who suppress liberty to whom the world will look for guidance and inspiration? Lose not the opportunity and the responsibility to have a part in the movement for freedom. Lead and join the oppressed in removing the chains that bind them. To hesitate is to be lost. Though some discomforts may be experienced, sacrifices are necessary for progress. Advancement demands sacrifices.

Let us always remember to be diligent seekers of truth and knowledge. The course is not easy; though arduous, we must not falter in our goal. The firm decision to aid one's fellow man must never be abandoned in spite of opposition. Divine truth holds the answer to the problems of man; unchristian statements open the gates to his destruction. Supreme in all its glory stands truth.

Some real dangers to democracy are intolerance, ignorance, hate campaigns, dictatorships, conspiracies, and suppression of liberty.

Let us not forget that Hitler rose to power through the use of the above methods. Finally, brothers were spying on brothers and sons on fathers. No one was safe. Let us beware of dictatorships and the kind of social climate that gives rise to them. A Citizens' Council boss of one city has now openly criticized the mayor in the street. The mayor and other elected officials failed to assert independence, authority, and responsibility of office to protect all citizens and to enforce the laws in harmony with the liberties guaranteed in the Constitution of the United States. Legislators joined the leader in his totalitarian methods. Hence he now is taking over control of the city. He dictates to merchants about whom to sell to, to deny credit to, to employ, and so on. Very soon no one in the city can be elected to public office without his sanction.

When some Negroes who favor integration were pressurized, they went to the ruler (or he went to them) and asked him (or he asked them) to take their names off the petition, because they did not know what they were signing, are satisfied with the "good" schools that the Negroes now have, etc., instead of going to the NAACP through which the petition was filed [or to the] school Board with whom it was filed. Everyone who signed petitions was conscious of the import of his actions; and it is certain that no one was asked to sign petitions against his will. The act of signing was free and voluntary. Even some of the Negroes who were forced in the embarrassing position of removing their names from petitions did not retrieve their jobs. At any rate, there is a dictatorship. And lawlessness has spread (as it will continue to do if it is unchecked). No one is secure. Now some of the Caucasians have begun to apply to one another the same methods used against the Negro. Lawlessness respects no color. Tyranny grows to such a point that its scepter falls on any man. Eventually, no order exists if tyranny continues to spread unchecked.

Effort is necessary to remove tyranny: it must be combated. Tyranny must be resisted with aggressive action. An individual must fight for his human rights. He must act to protect that which is worth having. The strong efforts of some to deny and withhold freedom from all men indicates the advantages they derive from trampling upon the backs of their fellow men. These strong, selfish motives and actions must be met by counter-action in order that all men can justly enjoy the benefits of democracy and freedom.

To those who accuse the leaders of the NAACP of selfish motivation (specifically with regard to educational integration), the following assertion is made: We have an education (some of us enjoying a superabundance of it). We are fighting for the children who are being educated today and those who will be educated tomorrow. We are working for equality of opportunity to which all human beings are entitled. We clearly realize the importance of education. The alert, educated man who can think, examine, and understand personalities, issues, and events cannot be enslaved. Enslavement is impossible with education. We, therefore, are determined that educational equality will prevail.

Consequently, let those who are approaching NAACP officials for the NAACP roster understand thoroughly the following: There are some things that men of integrity do not do for job, money, nor popularity. We exert every effort to protect those who seek freedom for all men.

Emphatically, we do not accept the idea of Greek democracy that some men are born masters and some men slaves. We accept American democracy of equality for everyone, with our minds, bodies, and hearts.

Tyrants examine your position; it is unstable, unchristian, undemocratic, inhuman, and unsound. It will not stand. An artificial estimation of position is cast in inglorious oblivion when the masses of men discover that of worth and place it on a universal pinnacle. The cry of liberty which rings through the world will not be stifled.

PRAYER

Christ of Gethsemane, Christ of the Cross, Christ of Peace, Christ of Salvation, Christ of Glory, please open man's eyes to the futility of greed, exploitation and denial of opportunity. Show men the necessity of living for others.

Open the eyes of those who live in comfort and luxury while their fellow man hungers and suffers.

Let not men be misled and deluded while connivers destroy them. Have perverters of truth realize that supreme in all its glory stands truth, which reigns emblazoned on the sands of time.

Show those who are persecuted for righteousness' sake that what today seems a malignant obstacle, tomorrow changes into radiant victory. May they realize that the spirit of the good man is indestructible.

O majestic Supreme, hold back the hand of tyranny in our land: Grant to all men understanding and love. Let men realize the full meaning of Christianity, the religion of brotherhood.

With humility, we beseech thee. Amen.

PART 2

The Reaction of Orangeburg and
South Carolina State College

Fred Henderson Moore, Part 1

Expulsion

Felice F. Knight [FK]:* Good morning. Today is September 1, 2004. My name is Felice Knight, and I am interviewing the Reverend Dr. Fred Moore. First of all I'd like to thank you very much for coming. And I know everyone has busy schedules, so this is very important to us that you are able to share your civil rights experience with us. I'd like to start off by asking you biographical questions, because part of the anthology is to give a brief biographical description of the persons featured in the anthology, and then we'll get into your civil rights activism.

Fred Moore [FM]: Very good.

FK: Okay, so, when and where were you born?

FM: I was born July 25, 1934, at Roper Hospital.

FK: Oh, Roper!

FM: Old Roper [chuckles]. Yes, old Roper.

FK: Here in Charleston?

FM: Here in Charleston.

FK: Okay, and tell me a little about your family, your parents. . . .

FM: Well, I'm the last of twelve children born to my parents, the late John H. Moore Sr. and Rosalee Milton Moore. And my mother finished the third grade—fourth grade. And my dad had no formal schooling whatsoever. My dad was a common laborer at one time. Well, he last labored at the navy yard, Charleston Naval Shipyard. And my mother sold vegetables on the street all of her life, for a living. And . . .

FK: What, what street? Was it at the Marketplace or just on the street?

---

*Fred Henderson Moore was interviewed at Avery Research Center for African American History and Culture, College of Charleston, on September 1, 2004. The interviewer, Felice Knight, also transcribed the interview.

FM: She had a pushcart. She wagonned [*sic*] her stuff from the market and the produce houses on Market and/or East Bay Street, and then she would go out into the street and peddle her wares.

FK: Okay.

FM: She participated in many Azalea Festival contests and usually won. Never lower than second prize, first prize or second prize. They called it the "Street Criers Contest." Um, of course the, uh, azalea festival was the forerunner of [*chuckles*] the present Spoleto Festival.

FK: Oh, I didn't know that! Okay, all right. And tell me what it was like growing up in your community and in your family.

FM: Well, it was very, warm, personal. People helped each other. They were real true neighbors. And if one didn't have, the other truly did have. "Let me borrow a pound of sugar or a pound of lard or some bacon or butts meat or whatever." And in that context, many people remember my mother as having fed a village.

For the reason that, as she peddled her wares, usually primarily below Broad Street to the wealthy and well-to-do, they would give her food. And things were very tough during the Depression years and the years which followed, and so, people would just be, literally waiting in line for my mother to come from the city and she would share what she had with them. Um . . .

FK: So where exactly did you live in relation to the city?

FM: I lived, it's a subdivision called Honey Hill, which now butts Green Hill. They are adjacent subdivisions. Green Hill is probably better known today 'cause it's one of the later subdivisions.

FK: These were near the downtown area?

FM: No, that was James Island. That was James Island. My mother was born on Broad Street, coincidentally, next to the Cathedral of St. John's. I would kid some people some time, especially some of these white attorneys, I'd say, "I'm a Broad Street lawyer." [*He chuckles.*] My mother was born right here.

But, that was basically it, and we attended the Grace School at what call—then called Three Trees.

FK: Three Trees?

FM: I don't why they gave it that name, but that was the name of the school. Three Trees Elementary School.

I don't recall whether it was significantly attached to the three oak trees. I know there were oak trees out there. And, well, that institution was born way before me, so I don't know what inspired that name. So I went there from grades one through eight. On James Island. Then afterwards, I attended Burke High School. And I became president of the Honor Society my third year there. And then president of the student body my last year, and I was awarded the Danforth Foundation Leadership Award for qualities of leadership. Also at Burke, I wrote for the *Parvenue* and I always say I lettered in "football." [*He chuckles.*] People always asked, "Well, how did that happen?" [*Moore was crippled since childhood.*]

Well, I would travel with the team, and then the team's captain, who was my class-mate, Samuel Rouse, who still lives here, Sam Rouse was the co–sports editor along with me, but I did all the writing [chuckles]. And so, and the journalism department had [football] letters [chuckles].

Um, then I won three or four scholarships my senior year in high school. After taking the college entrance examination board test wherein Paul Edwards, who now lives in California, Paul and I were the only two blacks taking the college entrances examination board test. 'Cause typically the black universities of that day would ad-minister their own scholarship exam.

And so I was awarded a scholarship to Carnegie Tech in Pittsburgh. But then knowing very little about how college expenses are allocated, I had only received a tuition scholarship. So Carnegie and those were $350. . . . Paul Edwards was going to MIT and he had gotten it together. He got a scholarship too.

But then, my mother—my father was dead by the time, he died around in his seventies, I was the last of the children—could not afford expenses at Carnegie, I thought then. But one of my brothers, older brothers living in Pittsburgh, with tuition paid and room and board at my brothers, all I really needed to do was buy books. But I didn't know. I didn't know. . . . I think it was in fact Mrs. Maudeville, who was one of our counselors a Burke, she didn't think through [or] explain those details to me. And Mrs. D.C. Mason got out a leadership scholarship for me from NYU. And also, took the competitive exam for Charleston County and I placed first in the scholarship exam, and I was awarded a four-year scholarship to South Carolina State College, which paid nearly all of the expenses. So I decided to attend South Carolina State.

FK: When did you graduate from Burke?

FM: Uh, in 1952. June of '52. . . . But there was something significant about my early childhood which ties into my later development and maturity and matters of civil rights.

I questioned my mother early on about why blacks were treated as second-class citizens. That was a common expression of that day. And she say, "Well, son, my grandmother"—who reared her, because her mother died in childbirth—I think this was the third child, what would have been the third child—"my grandmother would always say, chile, the buckra lend nigger lease to live."

And I thought that was so humorous.

So later on then she said, "So you have to remember that the buckra lend nigger lease to live, and some day God will change things. So just keep on praying." So that was a ray of hope for me.

But significantly, and not necessarily ironically, my father became involved in an incident that was triggered by me in some way. I was a child of five years old, and here was this white collector who came to our home on James Island and who was doing his routine collections. And he asked if my mother was home. To use his words, he said, "Rosa home?"

And my father, I think, resented that. And he say, "Rosa not here. She gone to town."

Then he said, "Well, I'm gonna," that is was the white man says, "Well, I'm gonna take all o' the damn things outta the house."

So my father just says, "You go ahead." So this man commenced to go toward our front window, helped himself to one our crate baskets [chuckles]—

You know, the four helpers was gone. In any case, he was about to stand on that to get into [the house] and push the window sash up. So then, I looked at my older brother, Wesley, who still lives here in Charleston, and I said, "I wonder if Daddy's gonna let that white man go in our house?"

And when I said that, my Daddy threw away his—either it was a Bugle cigarette that he was rolling or a Ripple—he threw that away, and he ran up to the window and he jerked the man outta there. And he worked him over a little, then he grabbed him by the seat of his pants and scourged him to the car, open the door for him and stuffed him under the steering wheel, and he slammed the door and he said, "Now you see that road? Now you get!"

And to me it was like, "Right on," you know.

FK: Yes.

FM: But that was a picture of courage displayed. The ultimate display of courage, especially in those days. It's . . . I mean that was unheard of, you know. He should . . . Ordinarily, he would have been lynched. I don't wanna say should have been lynched. 'Cause we had a cousin who was lynched by a white crew. He was flogged, beaten, and he died several days later because of a domestic conflict between him and the white man who shared a relationship with a black woman. Of course, you know, tragically they were both married. And after my cousin beat in a confrontation. Of course, the white fella started the fight. . . . I don't [know] whether it was a few days later or whatever it was—this story was told to me—but, [my cousin] died from the beating. Because . . . Not the beating with the white man [by] himself, but the white man brought back like a posse of other white men and they worked him over real bad. And uh— The lady who triggered that [chuckles], she, uh, took a bus to New York. She never returned to James Island until here in the '80s, I believe. She came back. . . .

Um, so my comparison, you know, "Why was my father spared?"

He went on to court and they talked about the incident. The white fella presented his side. He asserted my father attacked him for no reason at all. He had bruises to show for the encounter. So the judge asked my father to tell his side of the story. The judge, a Judge Royal, whom I learned later on was a Quaker and they tend to be very fair . . . My mother asked to speak instead and the judge allowed her to speak. She said, "John is a very kind individual. He'd do you any kind of favor whatsoever, and he's ever so nice to me and the children. But one thing with John, John got a short stem and his bread ain't done." [He chuckles.]

So everybody laughed. But you know the people in the community, they say, "Well, anybody who would beat up a white man is . . ."—that had to be '40, around, around 1940 or '39, I was, I was five in '39—"somethin' had to be wrong."

But, I later talked—I don't know if you've met Bill Saunders over at COBRA [the Committee for Better Racial Assurance of Charleston, South Carolina]. Bill says, "Fred, there was nothing crazy about your daddy." He said, "You know I think that many black men in that day had made up their mind like he did on an individual basis that if a confrontation came they weren't gonna back off." And he said, "You know, they resented the way they were treated. And he probably resented this incident, resented what the man was trying to do with him. He just stepped up to the plate." *[He pauses.]*

But you see, that created within us—'cause my brother was like that—the desire to resist being taken advantage of. Not to go out and pick any fights, but hey, we weren't gonna stand no confrontation just so.

Um, and I resented riding on the buses. You know they had the typical signs: "Colored passengers sit from center door to the rear. White passengers from the front toward the center door." And one incident really stood out. The driver [said], "You niggers . . ." The bus became crowded, and so as whites came on, "You niggers, get up. Get up and let those white people sit down."

Oh, that just burned me deep within. So I carried those things, you know, somewhat dormant, but yet, a very burning memory of what it presented to me, what it meant. And I later went to Norfolk the last summer I was in high school to stay with my brother, the late Herman Moore Sr., who was in the navy, attached to the Norfolk Naval Air Station. I presented an essay that I had written on "Why I Speak for Democracy."

I guess all of us have a hypocrite residing deep within. And I had it in me. So I wanted to write this article with some flavor that would appeal to the white establishment. So I characterized America as being "the greatest democracy on earth." And my brother . . . First his wife read the essay and she was very proud of it. My brother came home, and she said, "Oh, honey, Fred wrote a essay for a contest. You should see it!" He read that essay, and he tore it to shreds. And his wife was very upset. She cried. I cried, too *[chuckles]*. She said, "Why did you tear up Freddie's essay?"

Then he was still raging mad, and he said, "Look, I'm not angry with you. So don't misunderstand." He said, "Come and sit down." He put his arms around me and he said, "Kid, you don't write lies." He told his wife, "I don't want him growing up being no Uncle Tom."

[He told me,] "Don't write lies. Hey, you're saying America is the greatest democracy, now you don't mean that! You can't mean that." Then he culled a bunch of examples of what we had done during the summer. You know, you're riding your bus to the predominately white shopping area, Church Street in Norfolk, Brother Granby Street, just the opposite, Herman said, "Where did you sit?"

"Back o' the bus,"

"When in the stores, who got served first?"

"Them."

"More especially if you were already ahead of some white and they came in after you, you had to move to back of the line. Go to the United States Post Office in Norfolk, to take a postal exam and," he said. "You know I was in the line"—he was in the line with me, I was just a boy, was sixteen, seventeen years old. And he said, "So where did we stand in line?"

"Behind."

"And then got nearly up to the counter, you remember that, I had to move back to let the white people, you know, take my place." So, he said, "You don't mean America is the greatest democracy. Now you can rewrite this article, but maybe what you wanna say is that America has the potential of becoming . . . but it certainly isn't now."

You know, I did rewrite the article, and I placed in there that it was regrettable that we had not reached that level yet. Of course, I won no prize.

FK: Right. What was the contest for, like the *Post and Courier* or something?

FM: There was a, uh, the Pepsi Cola, I believe it was the Pepsi Cola bottling company. Or some Freedom Foundation, that sponsored it, and out of that, you could win a scholarship. In fact, Mr. Pyatt, Rudy Pyatt, had done a prize-writing essay the year before. And that's what really inspired me. 'Cause Pyatt was just a class editor. Pyatt and one of my brothers were classmates. So then I got elected the student body president and succeeded Pyatt, who had been student body president too. And we both ended up at South Carolina State. And we would later become roommates. And, you know, we shared mutual opinions concerning the white establishment.

And this occasion arose, in which Pyatt challenged the way the track team and the other athletic teams were being handled by the administration.

FK: Was the administration white or black at South Carolina State?

FM: At South Caro–? Oh, it was a black administration. Uh, you know, we had white "overlords." *[He chuckles.]*

So . . . President Turner had indirectly sanctioned Pyatt. The paper was censored. In fact, the lady who was the director, Florence Miller, was harangued about Pyatt writing this article. And he spared no bones about what he would say, written in a very scholarly way. 'Cause I remember, Mr.— Dr. Benjamin Payton, who is now the president of Tuskegee, was student body president before me. And [Pyatt] criticized Payton. He referred to Payton as "the do-nothing, peanut-peddling, president of the student body." *[He laughs.]*

FK: Oh no! *[He laughs.]*

FM: And, oh, Turner hated Pyatt's guts. But, you know, things were fomenting.

FK: And [Pyatt] was the editor of the school newspaper?

FM: Of the *Collegian*? I don't believe he was the editor. I think he was the associate editor or something like that, but he wrote, as I did, write for the *Collegian* the first two years I was there.

FK: Okay.

FM: There was a significant incident our Junior year. A black woman was slapped by a white man over at Snowflake, Snowflake Laundry and Dry Cleaners—She worked there. And she refused to, what was it? Say, "Yes sir" to the boss or something similar, and he insisted that she did. She did not, and he slapped her.

So that triggered a whole lotta dissension and tumult in the community. There were meetings and finally Mr. Payton called a mass rally of the student body. And we were gonna boycott Snowflake Laundry. We were gonna do this and do that. And somehow—because I was the vice president of the student body—he didn't discuss it with me, Payton just withdrew his leadership role, the leadership, and did nothing about it.

FK: Payton called the mass body meeting to boycott the laundry, but then he backed, he backed away?

FM: Yes, he said we'll get details later on. There were no details. Apparently, he was called in by Turner, who was the master of suppression, although he was a black man. Black/white I'd always call him. He looked white. That was still fermenting in the minds of the students.

Then the Supreme Court decision of 1954, the *Brown vs. the Board,* you know, ordering desegregation of the schools, "with all deliberate speed."

The Orangeburg NAACP had some black parents who were interested in having their children attend formerly all-white schools. They petitioned the board for re-dress, the board denied the petition. And not only that, some of the rank and file of the white leadership got together and formed what they called the White Citizens' Council [WCC]. And one of the objectives of the council, I guess the primary objective of the council, if not the soul, was to suppress those blacks who identified with either signing the petition or having something to do with the movement. And such forms of suppression included disbanding credit, denying access to certain resources. Dismissing some from their jobs, and intimidating others. A case that was conspicuous: they had a baby that required a special type of food ration, and they had to go to Columbia and get it, because the drug store told 'em you know, "You don't have an account here anymore."

FK: Oh no!

FM: And so, by the time September rolled around—we didn't go to school till September then—a Mr. James Sulton, who was then president of the NAACP—he's still living—Mr. Sulton somehow was led to come and see me.

[See the interview with James E. Sulton Sr. in this volume.]

FM: I was engaged in assisting with freshman orientation, as it was the custom of the student body president to come up during orientation week, which was a week ahead of the regular school—either a week or two.

And during that time, he came to me and he talked to me about the possibility of encouraging the students at South Carolina State to engage in a counter boycott. Namely, to not patronize those firms whose owners and managers or overseers were identified as White Citizen Council members.

FK: I see.

FM: That wasn't hard to do. Because in those days, everything was wide open, you know. "We'll put these niggers in their place," uh, as it were. So I was always cautioned that as just a matter of polite ethics, I should see the president and see what he thought about it. You know, "We don't want you to do anything to hurt yourself."

In any case, I went to see the president, met with him. And oh, he was furious! He said, "See Fred, I'm not goin' play no damn hero. I have the well-bein' and the welfare of 1,500 faculty staff and students to protect. I will not allow this student body to become involved with the affairs of the community. So do we have an understanding?"

So I just said, "Well, Mr. President, you know, I hadn't really thought about it from this standpoint." And before I could say anything else, he was acknowledging agreement with me as if I were agreeing with him. So then, he got up and he was telling me about how he been instrumental in getting Ben Payton a fellowship to Harvard School of Divinity.

FK: Ben Payton?

FM: Dr. Payton, who is still president of Tuskegee. He was the student body president the year before—

FK: Before you?

FM: Yes. And he said, "You know, I could get you into Harvard Law School." I don't doubt that he could have. Because I have a niece who got a doctorate from Harvard in later years, and she said, there's set asides for alumni of Harvard. The requirements are somewhat relaxed and a place is assured.

So I shared that with Father Dolan and Mr. Sulton. Father Donlan was the rector, the pastor of Christ the King Church in Orangeburg. I had a lot of respect for him. . . . At one point my freshman year, I had a longing to join the Catholic Church, after my association with a young man here from Charleston who was a devout Catholic, the late George O. Miller, who had become very instrumental in this very same movement. And then . . . My mother, she was just wonderfully brilliant—and I didn't realize just how much at that time. I went home and said, "Momma, I'm thinkin' about joining the Catholic Church."

And she say, "You goin' join the Catholic Church?"

And I said, "Well, yes." And I told her what happened. I said, "And they have nice quiet service and everything is very pious. The members are very nice to each other, nice to me. After service, we get hot chocolate and we play ping pong and they serve you donuts." *[He chuckles.]* And you know, what have you.

And she say, "That's nice." She say, "I'm glad you feel that way. They treat you . . . And I can't tell you what to do, but you must remember you met God in the Methodist Church. God is in all the churches, you's-a make sure you have God in you."

On that bus [back to Orangeburg], I felt supercilious. I said, "Man, you know, you're very silly." So I didn't join the church, but I remained friendly with the members. Miller was my friend. Miller had given me the shirt off his back.

So I met back with Father Donlan and Mr. Sulton and them. Father Donlan says to me, "Well, Fred you know, it's not often that a Negro gets a chance to attend Harvard, much less Harvard Law School." He says, "So, you know, we would understand if you didn't accept this role that we'd like to see you assume. So you think about it."

I said, "There's nothing to think about." But, since President Turner had been so acrimonious and insistent on our not doing it, we had to find a subterfuge. I thought about how it would be carried out.

When the regular student body arrived, I counseled with some members of the student council, and then Rudy Pyatt, Charlie Brown, Alvin Anderson, and there was an Andrew Bland Jr. from here [Charleston].

[See the interview with Charles Brown in this section of the volume.]

FM: Charles and Andrew had graduated from Avery the same year I graduated from Burke. And I had met Bland, Andrew Bland, the day following our graduation. The graduation, you know, proceeded to close the school. The principal of Burke said, "There's a young man here to see you by the name of Andrew Bland." And, so, you know, we shook hands.

He said, "Look, I couldn't resist the opportunity to come over and congratulate you on that superb graduation speech that you made."

I was overawed by that, because here's somebody from Avery coming over to Burke to say that. That was a very good class I was in. Because that year the Burke graduating seniors took nearly all of the scholarships. Typically Avery students would win more of the scholarships. . . .

[At State] Isaac Blake, Blake became a sort of, um . . . , mediator, not mediator, but Blake was a sort of emissary for me. Blake kept me informed of what the students were doing, or the students' leader was gonna do that they didn't want me involved in. They did not want me involved in making up anybody to be hung in effigy. Because they said, "If Turner finds out, he's sure to dismiss you, and we can't afford to lose you."

So they kept me informed. And this group decided that the best form for the protest would be an underground newspaper, which we called and denominated "the *Free Press*."

The *Free Press* was published daily. And at the office of the dean of students, the late H. M. Vincent, who was aware of what we were doing, he came in one night when we were doing [the paper] and he said, "Don't be upset." He said, "You know, I'm for you. Just be careful, don't involve me."

We had the students from the business department and—you know I just agonized that John Lawton, who died back in February and did most of the typing, we could not find him for this celebration we had in Columbia for the historical museum. Nobody seemed to know where he was. And ironically, Ms. Adams, who was in our class and taught at South Carolina State, she knew the people in the Registrar's Office and she sought the information from them, but somehow, Mr. Lawton's name was not on the list of graduates. He was an honor grad!

But then, I understand that they had sent a bunch of material to Charlotte, North Carolina, for records to be microfilmed, and that maybe explained why they could not give us an address for Johnny Lawton. And once we got the address, oh, it was actually two weeks later, they said, well, Johnny Lawton died.

FK: Oh . . . Sad.

FM: . . . but after we made these designations and contrived the *Free Press,* which was published every day, and the late George O. Miller was very instrumental in getting the *Free Press* out. Because we were somewhat befuddled as to how we would get it out without notice.

But Miller had been a veteran of the Korean War, and he knew a whole lotta o' tactics. He said, "Gentlemen, don't worry about it, I'll get it out."

So George Miller got the *Free Press* out. And I remembered one way he did it, he would have it under his coat, then he just happened to drop one on the table, and if anybody asked him anything, like something, or "Where'd that come from?" he'd say, "I need to ask you the same question. It came from somewhere, outta nowhere I guess."

But, we were companions in the effort to bring peace in Orangeburg and to right what was wrong. And after the movement gathered all kind of momentum, we were rather surprised how the whites were feeling the pinch.

Limehouse Men's Wear, uh, Renegers Men's Wear—R-E-N-E-G-E-R-S, I believe that's the spelling. Uh—Coburg Dairy Milk, Sunbeam Bread, um, there was some ladies store, the ladies would be more familiar with the stores they were boycotting.

Then, quite happily, the students from Claflin, the Claflin student body, a certain segment of them, joined in. And Denny Moss, who was president of the student body at Claflin, he led a group downtown. He had placards, see, we couldn't go downtown with placards, because, obviously, if you got identified, Turner would throw us out. But Claflin students could do this. Now, I don't know why to this day, and I don't know if I asked Mr. Sulton or if somebody. . . . As you know, Claflin was private and a church school.

Why didn't Jim Sulton go to Claflin? Just an academic question. Pyatt said, "Well, you know, the people in the community knew the leadership at South Carolina State, and that's why we were selected."

And, coincidentally, the movement, the student protest movement, started in the fall of 1954. *[This was a year prior to the Montgomery, Alabama, bus boycott, which ran from December 1, 1955, to December 20, 1956.]*

FK: Okay, and did community members get involved?

FM: Community members, as I recall, were not directly involved. And when they . . . There was a time when there was a support team from the community that provided transportation, food, and what have you for the students when the boycott reached really its highest level and we were engaged in a spontaneous strike of classes. We weren't eating the food. So food was being supplied from the members of the community.

FK: Why weren't you eating the food?

FM: That was to really put an exclamation point to the movement. That was to bring more pressure on the powers that be to relent in suppressing these blacks, and of course in granting our wishes to have integration, to have an integrated community.

FK: So people—the white establishments in the community—provided the food for South Carolina State?

FM: Not the white establishment, the black leadership provided the food. We don't know of any white sympathizers that I could identify in Orangeburg—

FK: No, I meant, when you decided to strike at school and you weren't eating the food on campus, you told me that you did that to put more pressure on those White Citizens' Council members, correct? . . .

FM: Correct, yes. Coburg Dairy, Sunbeam Bread, and I forgot the other institution, they were suppliers for the dining hall and the cafeteria. You see? And we wanted them cut off and this was a direct way of doing it.

Reverend Alfred Isaacs was one of our key advisors. It was no secret. He had been an open-minded, very ardent, and expressive type of faculty member, whose views on the question of integration were well known. So he became our key advisor. . . .

The state legislator, Jerry Hughes . . . Jerry Hughes introduced a bill in the South Carolina Legislature to have South Carolina State College investigated for suspected "subversive activities," being pushed by a subversive element, and they said, "namely the NAACP." And then they had something like, "The NAACP is suspected of being a 'Red' [communist] affiliate." But that was really flawed. Because the only thing the NAACP national office was giving us was moral support. They didn't provide financial support.

[Roy] Wilkins did come down, he was sort of executive secretary. It was like being head of the nation's NAACP organization. And he spoke on unity and commended us for the unified effort that we were engaged in and to keep it peaceful and nonviolent. He said he was very impressed with what we were doing and it reminded him of the unity that St. Paul spoke about in his letter to the church at Ephesus [Ephesians 4:13] . . . about having perfect unity in the body in Christ. And he said, "We do not advocate boycotting. Boycotting is dangerous, but we do fervently hold that in certain situations you have to choose the lesser of the two evils: boycotting/counter-boycotting. And if there's an activity that is fomented to suppress you and boycotting will bring relief, then you boycott." And that was the implication from his speech. That was heartwarming an inspiration for us.

But getting back to [support from the faculty], Dr. Wimbush, she stumbled into [me] one day surprisingly, and she said, "Mr. Moore, I want to have a word with you."

I said, "Yes, ma'am."

She said, "I want to congratulate you first of all for being such a wonderful leader, and we're proud of what you all are doing, because you're doing something that *we* want to do ourselves, but we can't do it, because [we have] various investments to protect and many of us have bought homes and have obligations. So vested interest prevents us from joining in directly. But we're supporting you." And she gave me an affectionate pat on the back. Trudelle. Trudelle Wimbush.

Then eventually after this bill was introduced in the legislature by Jerry Hughes—to have the campus investigated—the governor of South Carolina got on television and radio and [held a] press conference that because of the turmoil evolving at South Carolina State College, he would have SLED [South Carolina Law Enforcement Division] agents dispatched—they are the South Carolina "FBI"—to go and survey the campus. He's ordering surveillance for suspected demonstrations and subversive activities.

At that point the late Reverend Isaacs came to my room and said, "Fred, you have got to answer that. This governor's a bigot, and you've got to let him know. But, but do it in very intellectual terms."

I said, "Well, what should we say?"

He said, "No. See, you're a bright student, and get with Pyatt and those and, you know, formulate a statement."

So I did the statement and Mr. Pyatt edited the statement. And our press release, uh, press conference aired the fact: "We were not a penal institution nor a mental institution, but an institution of higher learning and a free people in a free land. And therefore, we will not tolerate the quartering of troops on our campus and this day we are announcing a spontaneous strike of classes."

So everybody went on strike. Didn't go to class. And the governor got somewhat frightened, and he made a follow-up announcement that he merely said he would have them available, you know, he didn't say he'd send them.

FK: What did Turner think about all this?

FM: Oh, Turner was opposed to what we were doing. Turner would call me in from time to time and try to ascertain where everything was coming from.

FK: Right, because it's obvious. You're boycotting stores, you are . . . now you're striking classes, you're not eating on campus . . . this is huge.

FM: Yes, so he called me in. He wanted to know. . . We marched on him too. The whole student body marched on him. And sang the Alma Mater.

And he called me up, and he said, "Fred, I will not deal with that mob that's out there. You send some student representatives." And he said, "Who's doing this?"

And I said, "I don't know." And I think for a time he believed me. . . . We had been somewhat close as the protocol goes, student body president, president of the university. He knew me. I knew him.

I needed a job on the campus for incidentals. He got me [the] job. He said, "I make jobs." 'Cause the dean of men had told me that there were no jobs available. He said, "Fred, I make jobs." I was working the next day.

He was angry. And all he thought about, I think, was the fact that his job was at stake. After all, remember everything was white. Quite incredibly, Jim Crow had it that everything was white centered and white controlled. The police department was white, the sheriff's department was white. The school boards for black schools were white! Everything was white! So, you know—so it was difficult to confront these giants.

But then you had to think in terms of what happened during the American Revolution. And coincidentally, that had a whole lot to do with a fueling point for our movement. I don't want to call it a rebellion. I don't think it was a rebellion, although they called it a rebellion. We were taking U.S. history, and this brilliant book written by Mussey and Cr– Crochran, *United States History,* and then we took political geography from Dr. Moss, and he would talk about John George Matlin and his concept of who controlled the heartland would also control the seas. And we got very fascinated with these concepts. And said, "Hey, this is in the condition of the American Revolution. We got a right to speak up for our rights and the rights of other people."

And when the news media moved in, the . . . not *Newsweek* . . . *Time, Time/Life* magazine. It was then *Life* magazine, they interviewed. *Time* interviewed us separately, at my room. "What is the movement all about?"

I told them, "We're engaged in a peace movement, one designed to ultimately unite all of mankind, all races and creed, and to remove the badge of suppression and oppression from our people, and to get the board to comply with the '54 decision."

Dean Howard Jordan, who was dean of the school of education, and a very learned man, he called an assembly. Turner had made one of the shrewdest maneuvers during the movement. Everybody liked Dean Jordon. Dean Jordan effectively persuaded us to return to class. Dean Jordan also aired the decision of the faculty council that no reprisals would be taken against the students, and that the committee would meet with the president, as the leadership committee did meet with the president, to address our grievances. No reprisal would be taken. "And, you all have to think about your parents' investment, invested interest in . . . graduating seniors."

That would later make us very resentful of his hypocritical mode, the design of which was just to satisfy administrative, quote, "prerogatives."

So that following Wednesday or Thursday, we went back to class. And it was about a day later that the late William F. Hickson Sr., who lived in Orangeburg and who was on the faculty of the Agricultural Department at the school—his son was one the leaders with me, Bill Hickson Jr., a graduating senior from Orangeburg—his father sent for me. And he said, "Fred, Turner is angry with the faculty council." The faculty council was headed by Dr. Edward G. Ferguson, head of the Biology Department. "Ferguson got the faculty council to vote unanimously that no reprisals would be taken against student participating in the boycott.

"[Turner] went to the governor and they [concluded] the best thing to do—since the trustee board of South Carolina State is the governing body for the institution—they will convene and they are going to convene for the specific purpose of expelling you, 'cause Turner believes that if you're expelled then trouble will be over." Amen.

[Moore chuckles.] So *[chuckles],* so, um, the board convened—you know how word gets around. You know: "Board of Trustees are on the campus."

Somebody knew that Robert Ephraim was engaged to my niece, and we were all classmates. So that evening, the very evening of the expulsion, Ephraim and Rosa Lee approached me and said, "Fred, we got word that they've come to expel you, but if you would call a press conference, apologize to the president and to the board and let them know that you are sorry, and you were wrong in fomenting this movement, then they'll let you graduate." And he said, "I implore you, I beseech you, I beg of you that as a future member of your family, as your high school *[chuckles as he talks]* classmate, college classmate, Fred, get your butt off the hook. Resign."

I just very quietly told my niece and her boyfriend, "Hey, we just called President Turner a moral coward a few days ago, and this whole movement is about our trying to help people. I cannot and will not resign."

She, my niece, got all emotionally upset, and she said, "Dammit, you're trying to play hero, and my grandmother struggled, sold vegetables on the street to send you to school and you're gonna do this to my grandmother! You're crazy!"

I just stood up and reminded her that my mother taught us to do the right thing. I thought I was doing the right thing. It was just that simple.

So then about, it must have been an hour later, they said, "Dean Mitchell wants to see you in a minute."

So Vincent came by to pick me up, and he said, "They want us to come before the board." And he was very emotional. He was already upset and nearly in tears, and he said, "Fred, it'll be a long time before I get over this." He said, "I don't, I don't understand cowardice in leadership." He said, "But how're you feeling?"

I said, "I feel fine." So we met with the board, and the board read all these charges. Then the board had the lawyer, who was a Moss, I think his daddy a Moss—

FK: Moss?

FM: Moss. Yes. Same name as the president, I mean the student body president of Claflin.

And uh, "Mr. Lawyer" was cross-examining me and what the movement was all about and whether I thought . . . I don't know why he asked the question except I think that he may have been implying that we slandered President Turner and the board and the white establishment. He said, "Do you agree that libel and slander are two of the most dangerous forms of boycotting known to man, of communication that is known to man?"

So I said, "I'd have to see the communication first."

And then he called me a smart aleck *[chuckles],* [and] said, "So the ball is in your court." 'Cause I would not implicate faculty members, as I had been instructed not to do so. I don't think I would have anyway. I had that much common sense. Uh, so he said, "Well, the ball is in your court." So after a line of questioning was completed by the lawyer, they asked the dean of men and myself if we would just be excused and repair to the adjoining room.

They'd call us back. Five minutes later they called us back. And Vincent again asked me how I felt.

I said, "I feel fine." By this time, he was in tears 'cause he knew what was coming.

"Mr. Moore, stand up." I stood up. "It is the unanimous decision of this board that you be expelled from the institution."

I said, "Why am I being expelled?"

He said, "You are a bad character, you've been guilty of bad conduct, and you've broken college rules and regulations."

The Reverend Dr. Fred Henderson Moore at the formal apology for his 1956 expulsion by South Carolina State University for his civil rights leadership. March 3, 2006.

I said, "Is a bad character being part and parcel of leading the student body in a just movement under our constitution and the right to free speech and redress for grievances? If I have broken a college rule or regulation, then you cite the rule or the regulation."

He got a little red-faced and looked at me and said, "You've got the facts before you. We're sorry if you don't understand them. You are dismissed."

Then Dean Vincent very tearfully asked the board if I would be allowed to stay overnight, because he said, "The young man has a handicap and needs to get his things together."

So then the board asked Dr. Turner to respond, that is up to Dr. Turner. And then [President Turner] said, "No, I want Fred to leave *now*!"

Then he asked us to leave by an exit door. We had not come in by an exit door. And at the door, when Dean Vincent opened the door for me, there was Maceo Nance, Dr. Nance, the president to be, shaking my hand and palming me with a twenty-dollar bill. He said, "Fred, I'm so sorry about what happened." . . . And Turner probably told Nance to be there to give me the money to go.

[Maceo Nance became president of South Carolina State College in 1967, some twelve years later. A relevant interview with Isaac Williams will be found at the end of volume 2.]

FM: The NAACP president, J. Arthur Brown from Charleston, was in Orangeburg. 'Cause news travel fast. And they had me ushered off to Father Parker's house after I got my stuff together. And I stayed there for virtually the remainder of the week.

Dr. William C. Hine, professor of history and social science at South Carolina State University, championed approval of an official apology to those who received retribution as a result of their role in the student boycott of White Citizens' Council businesses and other related protests. The apology event was held fifty years after the 1956 actions.

I did come home one day 'cause I know my mother was anxious to see me, and there was this white woman saying that Rosa seemed to be defiantly proud of you *[chuckles]*. "She wants you to do what you did, but she doesn't want you to be expelled from school." Well, it already happened.

And the press went to her. Asked her if she thought she was sorry about what, what had happened. She told 'em, "No, I teach my boys to do the right thing. So I guess Fred is doing the right thing." *[He chuckles.]* She didn't know exactly what everything was all about, but she knew I was doing the right thing.

But maybe you remember about Arthurene Lucy . . . they got her parents to say they were sorry? And I don't recall exactly, I think she may have said that she was sorry, but I know her parents said they were sorry, that she should not have rebelled. So, and that was a ploy of the white man during those days and even now, to put us against one another. But that wasn't gonna happen. I had had too many experiences at . . . even in the white community.

I think the one that stands out most is the one I mentioned to you the other day, wherein, I was, I guess I was between seven and nine, and I was a playmate to a young white boy who was a couple of years younger that lived on Lamboll Street. Lamboll Street is below Broad, going toward South Battery. And I think it's about a block from South Battery. Anyway, the higher-ups lived there. And my mother sold vegetables

The May Queen ceremony was canceled in May 1956. Jimmie (Payne) Grayson received her tiara fifty years later.

to Ms. Lucas, and Ms. Lucas . . . somehow they became very fond of me. In fact, they told my sister-in-law, "You know, that's a bright young child. We want him to play with our son." And Lawrence liked me. He didn't wanna play with his white peers. So I played with Lawrence. Here come momma [Ms. Lucas] home for lunch one day, and she said, "Edna, fix a plate for Freddie at the dining room table with Lawrence." Hey, that's pretty specific.

[Edna] said, "I already gotten one fix at the kitchen table." Now doesn't that point up how deeply rooted we were in submissiveness to the white establishment? "I already got one at the kitchen table."

[Ms. Lucas] said, "*I* said fix him one at that dining room table." So, not in defiance, but she was, she was just baffled. And the cook says . . . And she said, "Edna don't you understand me?"

And she said *[chuckles as he talks]*, "Yes ma'am." Then she brought the food for me. I was about seven—

Ms. Lucas proceeded to tell me a few things about table mannerisms, and then she said, "If he is good enough to play with him, he's good enough to eat with him." And then she put her arms around me, she said, "Freddie, you must always remember that there's nobody in this world who is any better than you are."

Alice Pyatt, who was denied readmission for her role as secretary to the student protesters, receives her Certificate of Apology. March 3, 2006.

That sank in.

FK: Yes.

FM: And yes, I seemingly detoured [from] the course when I wrote that essay—which they never got by the way. That was just something that I had privately been chastised about and rewrote it. But then, you know, there's a tendency to break ranks and to seek acceptance. You know, "Hey, let's get along here." I think that's what happened in that context, but then that helped me to keep mind, heart, and soul focused and when you hear a brilliant speech by President Roosevelt, "The only thing to fear is fear itself." So the only thing I had to fear was fear itself. And I was not afraid. I think it was one moment of weakness, and I have to attribute that to my youth and sensitivities.

After I got expelled . . . I forget what the *Times Democrat* said in Orangeburg . . . didn't bother me.

But then I read this, that *News and Courier* said a bunch of ugly things that . . . But then when I read that *[chuckles]*, that headline . . . I saw the headline from the *State* newspaper. Someone brought it to me: "STUDENT LEADER BOOTED."

FK: *Booted!*

FM: And you know—I don't know why—I almost broke down in tears about the headline. Uh, I didn't, I didn't, I didn't like that. . . .

Of course, I got over it too. 'Cause that's a part of the territory that you're dealing with.

And so that, what happened to me, only deepened my determination and my allegiance to the movement. It was that that precipitated my decision to go along with Father Donlan's recommendation that I go to law school. He said, it's good . . .

See, I had a fellowship to study theology from the Rockefeller Brother's Grant, a Rockefeller Brother's Grant, that the same late Reverend Isaacs, uh, Alfred Isaacs, had obtained for me. But I decided that I would go to law school. And so, my only purpose for being in law school was not like some of my enterprising cohorts, to make a bunch of money and be rich. And oh, I can't tell you how happy I am that I never got on that particular train!

[Part 2 of the interview with Fred Moore will be found in volume 5.]

James E. Sulton, Sr., the List

Marvin Lare **[ML]**: *Mr. Sulton, you want to say a few words to make sure we can hear you good?

James Sulton Sr. **[JS]**: Yes, I'm happy to do this interview and hope that I can provide some input into the anthology that [you're] trying to prepare.

ML: Thank you. Okay, and if you need to stop at any point or take a phone call or handle anything, just feel free to. We can just stop or pick up wherever.

I'd like for you to share for the anthology your many experiences and perspectives on the civil rights movement. You might start off just by giving us where and when you were born and then tell your story in whatever way you're most comfortable. I may ask you some questions but I'm going to let you structure the interview primarily rather than me giving you a whole lot of questions.

JS: Well, I was born right here in Orangeburg, South Carolina, just two doors down from where we're sitting now. I went to the public schools. In fact, my mother and father both were graduates of Claflin College, and I finished the last high school that Claflin had and I finished in the class of 1940. We were taught by the same teachers that taught in the college, a lot of New England people connected with the Methodist Church who came down. And we went to school just like the college students did. You may have an eight o'clock class and you might not have a nine, but we went to school until five o'clock in the afternoon, five days a week. We were taught by teachers who had good backgrounds in English and math and in the languages. In fact, I took French and when I went away to college, Morehouse College in Atlanta, I was able to—because of a test that they gave me in French—to pass the 101 [level], getting [into] a grade higher in languages in French.

I stayed at Morehouse until I went into the service in late 1941, 1942. I stayed in the service for almost four years. Served almost one year overseas. In fact, we were

*This interview took place at James Sulton's home in Orangeburg, South Carolina, on November 30, 2004. The transcriber was Catherine Mann, for the USC South Caroliniana Library.

on a ship on our way to Japan. We had reached the Mediterranean Sea [when] we got word of the atom bombing. [We] were turning around. We were so close to the Rock of Gibraltar that we could see it from the ship.

Came back to the states and was discharged in 1945 sometime around November, I think. Anyhow, I went to Tuskegee Institute, where my late brother-in-law was an orthopedic surgeon down there, and I decided I wasn't ready to go back to college at the time, and I stayed with him and worked at the hospital there for almost a year and then I went back to school. I was a pre-med and I had finished most of the courses that I needed to get admitted to med school but I decided after I met my wife and got married, April of 1947, that having been exposed to the field of medicine I wasn't prepared to wait that long, to put in that much time and energy and I just didn't feel that as a physician . . . I didn't see it.

So I came back to Orangeburg to live, and my brother and I opened a service station. It was Esso then, which later turned into Exxon, but we both owned the business. He was an electrical contractor. I worked for him for a year while we were building the station, and I was living with my mother and daddy two doors down and right across the street was our business.

When we got it halfway, got it built enough to open up for business, we had some problems with the local representatives of Standard Oil Company, who thought we wanted to open what they called a filling station. My brother was enraged. He said, "You must be crazy. You would bring us *one* pump!" He said, "We're going to operate a full-service station and I don't have to, in fact, I don't want to even talk to you anymore about it." So he contacted the people in New York, and I guess it was maybe two weeks later when the truck came with the big underground tanks and pumps and paraphernalia we needed to open our business. Of course, they installed them and all. They belonged to them and I operated it by myself for about a year. I used to change oil crawling under cars. The street was not paved at the time.

So when I came back here to live, first thing I did was to join NAACP, and I was in the forefront with the group. Our first mission was to equalize salaries, especially with the college being right here, the public school teachers being paid on a different scale. My mentor was related somewhere down the line to my mother's family, Miss Modjeska Simkins. Also, Reverend [James] Hinton, who was I thought the most courageous man that I ever met. He laughed off all the threats that were imaginable and real. They tried to kill him. And I don't think that the young people now growing up know the sacrifices that were made in the late '40s, '50s, '60, '70s. They have no sense of history, taking for granted the opportunities that are available to them now, behind the blood and tears.

I came from a business background. My folks ran a lumber mill. And I was fortunate in that my father wanted to see that all of his children had homes before he retired from the business. In fact, the business was J. J. Sulton and Sons. My grandfather lived right here next door. My father built that house for him, and my uncle. When I came back in the spring of '46 my intention was to join the business. I knew that I had the ability to meet and greet people, and I thought that I could expand the business. But they came from the old school and, of course, my father had six children. My uncle had three. They didn't want to put anything in writing. He'd been here all those years, and they wouldn't give him anything in writing, how did I think that I was going to get it. So that's when we decided that we would go into business together.

We expanded over the years. Initially we had to put the land in my name so I could get a GI loan, and I was able to borrow thirty-five hundred dollars. That's all we were able to borrow to build this business. Eventually we built it up and got the station. Physically we built where we could give first-class service and saw the need that we needed to expand in that we were contracting out a lot of the mechanical work because we didn't have the facilities to do it. In 1960 we completed a sixty- by about ninety-foot garage, full-service garage, where we could do wheel alignments and full mechanical work on engines.

Then I noticed that there was a need for fuel oil. I contacted Exxon about it and they made arrangements. They had a distribution plant here. I had no storage so I had to buy my oil from them. South Carolina State College at the time had a lot of these old GI buildings that they built after the war for students, these wooden buildings, and all of them had fuel oil tanks in them. Through my personal friendship with the then superintendent of buildings and grounds I furnished the oil up there. We built up an oil business, which I had to run by myself on the cuff. It was a wise move as far as the need and supply, having resources to supply that need. It was a twenty-four/ seven job.

ML: So that was in 1960 when you went into the fuel oil business?

JS: Yes, around the same time that we built the shop. I decided this is running me crazy, so I said we needed to have our own storage tanks. We put up our own fuel oil station. We had a thirty-thousand-gallon storage bay on the back of the shop where I was able to buy my oil directly and have it delivered from Exxon rather than to go through the local distributor here, but I had a good relationship with him and we worked well together. When I would run short of oil, I knew where I could always get it from, but having our own tanks we could buy oil cheaper. And it was about a four-month season [for heating] but we got a lot of sales with the contractors. South Carolina State began to get some money to do some building, and we were able to get contracts to furnish diesel oil to run their machinery, which was a good off-season business.

We stayed in this business, and my brother was kind enough to let me get involved with the NAACP, which took up a whole lot of my time. I worked many a night traveling the county and the state, wherever Reverend [I. DeQuincey] Newman and Matthew Perry decided they needed help. I led the first demonstration they had in Orangeburg when we marched on the mayor's office, the late mayor. He ran an insurance company, and I led that march of the NAACP chapter going down to his office to protest. That was the beginning of what we started. It was really started before [the] Montgomery [bus boycott, 1955–56]. We never called it a boycott, though. Our

James E. Sulton, November 30, 2004. This and all other illustrations provided by the editor unless otherwise specified.

strategy . . . I keep the thing in my wallet at all times so I can show people what sacrifices people made during that time. I went up to Modjeska Simkins's house there on Marion Street [in Columbia]. We had . . . I don't guess you know what a mimeograph machine is.

ML: Oh, yes.

JS: You do?

ML: Yes, as a preacher, every Saturday night I'd have to run the church bulletins on the mimeograph.

JS: Is that right?

ML: Oh, yes.

JS: I try to keep that thing [in his billfold]. We went up to Miss Simkins to print these things and cut them up into slips that we would hand out to the football games and stuff to let the people know that this was, ah. . . .

ML [*reading the slip from Sulton's billfold*]: "These firms are cooperating with the Citizens' Council. Let's fight back by not cooperating with the following firms O N L Y ! Bryant's Drug Store, Becker's, Coble Dairy, Coca Cola, Curtis Candy Company, Duncan Supply, Edisto Theatre, Holman Grocery, Horne Motors, Kirkland Laundry, Lance Crackers, Lay's Potato Chips, Lane's Television, Limehouse Men's, Orange Cut-Rate, Paradise Ice Cream, Smoak Hardware, Sunbeam Bread, Shell Oil, Tom Toast Peanuts, Taylor Buscuit [*sic*] Co., Walt's Grocery, and. . . ."

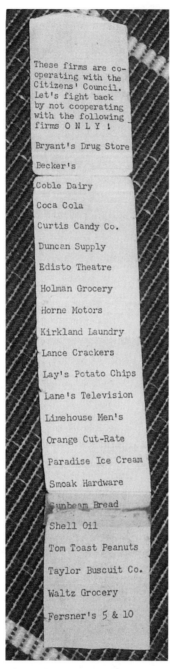

These firms are co-operating with the Citizens' Council. Let's fight back by not cooperating with the following firms O N L Y !

Bryant's Drug Store

Becker's

Coble Dairy

Coca Cola

Curtis Candy Co.

Duncan Supply

Edisto Theatre

Holman Grocery

Horne Motors

Kirkland Laundry

Lance Crackers

Lay's Potato Chips

Lane's Television

Limehouse Men's

Orange Cut-Rate

Paradise Ice Cream

Smoak Hardware

Sunbeam Bread

Shell Oil

Tom Toast Peanuts

Taylor Buscuit Co.

Waltz Grocery

Fersner's 5 & 10

"The List" of white merchants to be boycotted. James E. Sulton carried this list in his billfold since 1956.

JS: Fersner's.

ML: . . . Five and Ten.

JS: F-E-R-S-N-E-R-S.

ML: Fersner's Five and Ten . . . it has here. If you don't mind I'll take a photograph of that. We might include it in the book. I've got my camera with me, and it's amazing how well a digital camera will do these days on things like this.

JS: So we decided that this pitted merchant against merchant. They couldn't understand why . . . In fact, I had these three men come and sit in my den and asked me about why he was on this list and another clothing store manager wasn't. He said, "I know I'm a better person than he is." And, of course, I pleaded ignorance, that I didn't know what he was talking about. He said, "Oh, I know you're running this thing." I said, "Oh, no, I don't have anything to do with it." And I always tried to stay clear of anything that would be printed in the newspapers because they always take it out on . . . You want some light?

ML: No, this will be fine. I'll take it with the flash and without it *["bink" sound of camera focusing]* and I'm sure we'll get it, one way or the other. So, was it primarily on wages you were protesting? *[There is the sound of camera focusing and shutter "click."]*

JS: It was *[sound of camera focusing and shutter "click"]* the only weapon that we really had to fight back. See all this came out of the 1954 *Brown v. Board of Education* Supreme Court decision. We signed the petition asking the district school to implement the decision. And as a result of that, the White Citizens' Council was formed, and everybody who signed that petition was subjected to economic pressure. For instance all our creditors or suppliers quit delivering or cut off our credit. It just so happened that we had some [white] people in town that didn't come out openly, but who would not participate in the agenda that the White Citizens' Council had. The only way you had to fight back was through the . . . what we called "selective buying," and it was most effective. It caused a lot of people to lose their jobs.

ML: Well, you had mentioned before that the first thing you organized around was wages and pay. Was that primarily for the schoolteachers?

JS: Yes, that was the teachers and we got this favorable decision [*Duvall v. Board of Education,* 1945] from Judge Waring. That's where our emphasis was, and then it got to be on voter registration when his decision [*Elmore v. Rice,* 1947] came down. We were able to register the whole county, I mean blacks. It took a concerted effort by the black ministry over the county to make sure that, as best they could, that their parishioners registered to vote. As a result of that we got . . . well, nothing counts like being able to vote, and politicians began to respect the black voice. We know that as a result of that and the reapportionment that Jim Clyburn and I. S. Leevy Johnson were able to get elected to the legislature. I ran for county council. At that time they had at-large [elections], and we didn't have the numbers to win but I wanted to let the people know that we couldn't win unless . . . you couldn't get elected unless you filed and ran. As a result of that we had one person I think that was elected. I ran a good campaign but I wasn't able to win. I knew I wasn't going to win.

ML: What year would have that been?

JS: That was 1964. Earl Middleton was my campaign manager. [Years later] we were able to get Middleton elected to the legislature and then Larry Mitchell. And then through lack of effort, I guess, we messed around and let Will McCain win the seat and he's a Republican.

But we had so many people that never have been recognized who really were the backbone, the people who sacrificed and had their credit cut off, who didn't give in to the economic pressure that the Citizens' Council tried to put on us. Of course, we had the support of a lot of teachers who supported us as they could. In fact, State College at the time had—I've got it somewhere in my scrapbook—they signed a petition supporting us, the NAACP, and came out strong. I think everybody signed that thing except one or two people on the faculty were just afraid to do it. But that "selective buying" started it all, it was most effective. We started hitting the pocketbook.

ML: That was mostly in the '50s?

JS: Mostly in the '50s, yes, that part of it. I might be getting my events kind of mixed up.

ML: That's all right. It's all part of the mosaic, and it doesn't have to be all in order. I was telling Reverend [Nathaniel] Irvin this morning that nowadays a good movie is one where they don't just begin and go from the beginning to the end.

[See interview with Nathaniel Irvin in this volume.]

ML: They have flashbacks and so forth, and that's the way our memories are. We build on one part of our life, and we remember another part. That's fine, we'll just move along.

JS: The foundation was there, and then we had some strong people in the public school system. I don't know whether you have heard about Gloria Rackley.

[See interviews with Gloria Rackley Blackwell and her daughters in this volume and in volume 2 of this anthology.]

JS: She was a teacher in the public school system who now lives in Atlanta. She was a strong leader in the movement, and of course, we were able to get other help. Roy Wilkins was a guest here in my home. He came down and spoke at the Trinity Methodist Church. On one particular Sunday the ministers had all [their people], after the church service, march downtown around the square and kneeled and had prayer. I suggest if you want to see some of the real photographs of that . . . have you talked with Cecil Williams yet?

[An interview with Cecil Williams will be found in volume 5.]

ML: Yes, but I need to get back in touch with him.

JS: He's got pictures of the ministers and all kneeling around the square. Of course, we had pickets and such. As you look at history unfold, you can see some of the mistakes that were made, and you can see some of the dumb things that they did like [Governor] Bob McNair. He ruined his entire political career in 1968 with the massacre, by getting bad advice, *bad advice.* . . . It was absolutely inexcusable the way he handled that situation. And, of course, Billy Turner [Benner Creswell Turner, president of South Carolina State College, 1950–67] had left under pressure. They got rid of him. During the protests, who really needed to keep the lid on things, as far as I'm concerned, letting things really get out of hand was the late Maceo Nance, who was the acting president, who sent the students home.

McNair I think saw the mistake of his ways and knew that in a situation like this, that they were having in Orangeburg and national and international attention it was getting, was not doing the state any good.

But, through Maceo's efforts South Carolina State began to get some money. And I think people don't understand . . . some people don't understand what it takes to run an educational institution. You don't really need an educator. You need a businessperson and a politician. You can always find somebody to teach, head up departments. That's what he did. He had good people who had terminal degrees who were head of the various schools. I think that Maceo must have been president for about sixteen years, I guess, sixteen or seventeen years, and he did a good job. I don't think in my estimation that they have had a president that was able to handle that situation since he left. South Carolina State had the most beautiful grounds of any institution in this state. I mean it was immaculate, and you go look at it now. People are reticent to tell people when they are wrong or when they're not doing things right.

[There is a telephone interruption.]

JS: We had a good turnout for that group. *[Sulton is referring here to the "Voices" bus, which was in Orangeburg on August 9, 2004, recording civil rights oral histories as part of a nationwide tour.]*

ML: I was really impressed.

JS: Were you here for that?

ML: I came down for part of it. I spent the morning down here, and in fact, I have some pictures of you on stage being interviewed. I'll get another picture or two of you now if you don't mind.

. . . You really were leading the NAACP as the local elected person from the late '40s?

JS: During the '50s I was the treasurer of the local branch of the NAACP and came up from the late Reverend McCollom. Do you know about him?

ML: Yes.

[See interview with Matthew McCollom later in this volume.]

JS: Matthew, he was Methodist minister. He was president of the state NAACP, and also, the late Reverend Nelson, who was a Presbyterian minister. You might want to talk to Johnalee, his widow, she lives here.

[See the interview with Mrs. J. Herbert (Johnalee) Nelson later in this volume.]

JS: He was certainly involved and he was, I think, at one time in Rock Hill. J. Herbert Nelson. I don't know how his wife is listed in the telephone book, but I can look it up for you if you want me to.

ML: Okay, that would be good.

JS: I don't know the office that he held in the state NAACP, but he was very active and I'm thinking that his widow would be able to tell you a lot about the Friendship Nine. I think he was pastoring up there at one time. You can get all that information from her.

ML: I'll check with her and see.

JS: It took a lot of hard work. . . . A lot of hard work went into all this thing. I was arrested. I went to the "Pink Palace" in jail. I was put in the penitentiary, all at the time nursing a bleeding ulcer, which later had to have surgery. I don't think that you can talk to anybody about it that wouldn't say that the common man and woman were the heroes of the late '40s and '50s, they were not professional people, they had jobs. Some of them had jobs in the stores that we boycotted. In fact, we got a lot of information from them because our headquarters was the Trinity [United Methodist] Church. We had set up a kitchen there to feed the students and people who were picketing uptown.

Those years, when you look back on it . . . Like Matthew and I were as close as two people could get. When he came back [from the army], he went to the law school. He was the only person I know that was subjected to all that he was . . . but was able to keep his composure. I never saw him get angry.

ML: Yes, he was such a quiet, gentle spokesperson.

JS: He never . . . I mean in public. Of course, we used to have nights. . . . We met every night at churches all over the county, getting the message out, getting the support.

ML: Oh, now you're speaking of Matthew Perry?

JS: Yes.

ML: Not Matthew McCollom?

JS: Not Matthew McCollom, but Perry. [Matthew] Perry was handling the legal stuff. He wasn't going to all these meetings that we were going to. We had a support group.

You really need to include Gloria Rackley. She lives in Atlanta.

ML: I may have an address for her.

JS: You want me to get it for you? I can get it from my cousin that just left out of here.

ML: Okay. That's good. You were speaking [of] the common people, the heroes and heroines that had jobs to do. For instance, you had to keep a business going, support your family and that kind of thing.

JS: Yes, and to give credit you have to have credit and we had an awful lot of credit. But we had people that [cut us off]. Exxon wasn't going to get involved in it, so I didn't have any problem with that. But the local distributor, the late C. M. Dukes, really helped me through it all. We bought our supplies from him like oil filters and tires and all those things.

I was away for a weekend and my brother told me, "Mr. Dukes's been calling, looking for you."

I said, "What did he want?"

He said, "I don't know, I didn't talk to him, he was just asking for you."

So I said, "I'll go down to his place to see him."

Funniest thing happened. As I was driving into his place—of course, he had his storage tanks and stuff that you could buy, he was selling to a lot of independent service stations and so forth. As I was going in there, the leader of the White Citizens' Council was coming out. I said, ain't this something. So I went in there, and I told him, "How long have we been doing business with you?"

And he told me, and he started to interrupt me and I said, "No, wait a minute, let me get through." You got a 2 percent discount on your bill if you paid by the tenth, and even through all the struggles we had, we always discounted our bills because 2 percent is 2 percent. And I told him about the money we had spent there and [said], "Have we ever missed paying you or ever missed discounting our bills?"

"No, no."

"Do you still want our business?"

He said, "You bet I do."

And he never stopped it. He *never* stopped! It was a matter of business, and, of course, my family was pretty well known through business contacts because they had at one time a thriving lumber business.

But the mayor, who later became the mayor, he ran a wholesale [distributorship selling] candy and cigarettes and stuff. And he had the audacity to come out and called me and my brother into the back to the storage room.

"Tell you what I've got figured out," he said, "I'll have Frank"—that was the black fellah who worked for him at his store—"I'll have Frank come by and take your order, and then he'll take the stuff over to his house and you can go by and pick it up."

I said, "You must think I'm a first-class fool. Come in here and let me show you." We took him in the other room and said, "Look on the shelves there." We had more stuff there. People brought stuff down from Columbia, taking advantage of the situation. They came in and they weren't slipping down here, they came in the daylight. We lost nothing as far as the sale of cigarettes and candy and stuff.

ML: See if I understand. So he was going to sell you supplies?

JS: On the sly.

ML: On the sly, but you already were getting supplies from Columbia or from wherever?

JS: Yes. We had a fella, he died during the movement, he was a truck salesman and he'd call on us once a week. I think he lived in Sumter. Anyhow, he'd come by and he sold mufflers and tailpipes and brake parts and stuff, and he said, "Listen, what I'll do, we'll have a full-shelf stockroom down here. He said I'll put all the stuff in here that I think you need or want and every week I'll come by and we'll take an inventory of what you've sold, and you pay me for what you sold and I'll replace it and keep your shelves stocked all the time." And we had one or two other people who did that and did it openly.

But the, we had people who parked right across the street in front of this house right here. Our business was right across the street there, the building is not there now. They were watching who was bringing us supplies. I used to wave at him when I'd come through, coming home for lunch *[laughs]*. I said, "Are you getting everything you need? You need some water or something?" He was just ashamed of himself.

The telephone threats didn't bother me, but they worried my wife. She worked. She had a master's degree in social work. She ended up being head of the social welfare program at South Carolina State for twenty years before she retired. Anyhow, she was definitely afraid and I said, "Don't get excited about this. Nobody can hurt you on the telephone, all the language and stuff, you don't have to listen to that. When they call here, you can tell in two seconds who you're talking to and what they want. Just hang up."

But I used to listen sometimes and talk back. I said, "Why do you have to call as an anonymous call? You know who I am, and," I said, "I like to know who I'm talking to. Would you be kind enough to tell me who you are?" They'd hang up. But all the language and stuff they used, it didn't bother me. But the only thing we had to be careful about was traveling in the county. You'd go to some meeting as far down as Holly Hill, and you had to come back in the night. I tried, *not* tried—I *never* was alone. There was always at least one other person with us if we were driving at night.

ML: You mean more than one person in the car or two or three cars?

JS: No, just more than one person in the car. As I remember, we didn't convoy. We'd attract too much attention.

A lot of people followed the movement around wherever we went. Maceo Nance—he wasn't president then, he was the business manager—he came out from the start and was open with the fact that he was with the group. Nobody messed with him about his job. But, there was a lot of economic pressure put on people. . . .

We had people that would slip downtown and buy from the boycotted businesses. Cecil [Williams] used to take pictures of people you'd see down there. They had a big bulletin board down at Trinity Church where he tacked up the prints, and you'd see people coming down there saying, "I went down there to pay a bill."

"You didn't have money for a stamp? Why did you have to go down there? Shoot!"

Harry Becker, who was Jewish, he didn't know what to do. They had a women's clothing store and did a booming business with the students and the faculty in the public schools. He had first-line clothes and shoes and things. But it [wasn't] worth it. It disturbs me that you could look at the people . . . he sort of got caught in the middle.

I always remember what a politician told me a long time ago, he said, "Politics is the art of possible." He said, "And you have to know when you're just spinning the wheels, but it's important to be out there. You've gotta run for something."

I had a reporter that came out here and she tried her best to—I think she was a freelance writer and she had some articles printed in the *Christian Science Monitor* and she had an article in *the New York Times Sunday Magazine*—she tried her best to get me to say something bad about Kevin Gray [a journalist, community organizer, generally a civil rights activist in the 1960s and 70s]. I wouldn't do it. I didn't think that Kevin was just a burr under the saddle. I don't really know what his mission was, he never really accomplished anything, but he sure tried. Is he active now? I don't know.

ML: I haven't heard anything of him for quite some time. I'm not sure. . . . Reflecting back on the civil rights movement, are there things that you would do differently?

JS: I don't think I could do anything differently. I really don't. I can't go back.

ML: Yes. It sounds like you were an unpaid staff person [for the NAACP] as much traveling as you did and as many meetings you held. You didn't just look out for the interests of the local community, you were in every small town, as far as you could travel, you were there.

JS: Oh yes. I had a late best friend, we went all over the state politically. Like going to Charleston supporting Herbie Fielding, and people like that.

[Interviews with Senator Herbert Fielding will be found in volumes 3 and 5 of this anthology.]

JS: Then, of course, we always helped Jim Clyburn. In fact, Maeco's son works for Jim, Robert Nance. Jim was a student up here during the '60s at State.

ML: What would you say really started you to be an activist? Was it childhood experience or . . . ?

JS: Being in the service.

ML: Being in the service?

Sulton at the dedication of Russell Street as the James E. Sulton Highway, August 30, 2005, Orangeburg, South Carolina.

JS: Being in the service. It started with that, being in the service. . . . In the service, I was a technical sergeant over the maintenance of a trucking company, and we really came in after the fighting in Normandy. We landed at Utah Beach. They had what they called the Red Ball Express that supplied the troops from Cherbourg right on up. We got an assignment of four or five German prisoners of war who were of no danger to help us. One guy was very articulate, and we developed a friendship. He said, "You know, I don't understand *schwärzlich* line."

ML: Don't understand what?

JS: The *schwärzlich* line. *Schwärzlich* is German for black, you know.

He said, "Here you are over here doing all this fighting, and you don't have any freedom at home." He said, "What you fighting for. You're fighting Nazism." He said, "I'm no Nazi. I don't believe in this stuff." And, of course, if you look at it realistically, a lot of the Germans were forced to be in the army. They had no choice. Hitler was the Saddam Hussein during that time.

ML: So that really was what burned in your soul?

JS: That was the desire in me. When I came back, I couldn't, aah . . . I couldn't, aaah . . . I couldn't . . . I just couldn't, couldn't see it. And then the thing . . . I guess the straw that broke the camel's back. In the '50s, here the local hospital was completely segregated, and they had German interns coming at the hospital. Here's a guy that tried to kill me and there you are opening the doors, and you won't let me in the hospital in any capacity.

You came back here and you're segregated and couldn't get the proper care. Those were the kinds of things that just burned me up. I guess trying to . . . to really understand . . . what effect it had on my health was, aah . . . Dealing with a business, a family, the NAACP, and all these various factors, you know, trying to keep everything together and it wasn't eas– . . . put, aah. . . . It just was the cause of my, aah . . . ah, stomach problems that I've had over the years. I've had three stomach operations. I guess those are the kind . . . that happened . . . there has to be a start somewhere. You can't, can't, aah . . . come out and wait for somebody else to do it.

Just like the teacher situation . . . My mother . . . taught school. . . . When I was in high school, I'd drive her down in a little country school where she stayed with somebody in a house that didn't have plumbing and heating and gather wood up . . . take her down there on Monday and go back and get her on Friday. That was the school.

You see all those things that you came through, and you look, you look at what people are coming through and you think, you think that, aah . . . Some people think that their, THEIR, . . . I don't, I don't know where. I don't know what got these black folks to vote for him [President Bush]. I don't understand it. There's probably somewhere that they got a handout from some. . . .

[Omitted here are 342 words of Sulton's comments regarding the administration of George W. Bush, with particular reference to Colin Powell and Condoleezza Rice. These comments are available on the audio recording at the South Caroliniana Library.]

ML: Do you think of anything else now about the movement that we ought to touch on? Of course, we can always get back together.

JS: No, I can't think of anything at the moment. Maybe when you start compiling something you might have some more questions you want to ask. It might come back to me but that's about it.

ML: I certainly appreciate your time. It's sort of like sitting at the feet of a prophet. We've all done some things in our lives but it's just awesome for me to sit with persons who have committed so much over so long a period of time. It's just a wonderful gift to all of us.

[Omitted here are 155 words of Mr. Sulton's comments regarding the appointment of Clarence Thomas to the Supreme Court. These comments are available on the audio recording at the South Caroliniana Library.]

ML: Well, shall we close this off now?
JS: I think that's it.

Charles H. Brown, Effigy of a President

Marvin Lare [ML]:* It's February 1st, 2006, and I'm in the home of Reverend Charles H. Brown. How are you, Elder Brown?

Charles Brown [CB]: I'm doing wonderful, doing wonderful. Retired now. And hopefully we'll stay retired! *[He laughs.]* But we stay busy all along.

ML: Right. Okay. Brother Brown, I take a very flexible approach to these interviews for the anthology for civil rights, civil and human rights, and let people tell their own story and experiences of civil rights in whatever way it comes to them. I may have some follow-up questions and all, but I like people just to share their own thoughts, reflections, and insights.

CB: Okay. While at South Carolina State College in the early '50s, because I graduated from Avery in '52, at a time when blacks in any of the predominantly white schools, at the Citadel, the University of South Carolina, Clemson University, blacks were almost unknown. We decided that many of our classmates at that time, coming from Avery Institute, at that time, decided that we were going to make applications to some of these predominantly white schools, so that we might integrate them. We started our little trek, but were kind of shortchanged because when the authorities found out what we had planned on doing, they found monies to send us to South Carolina State College, and my parents didn't come up with a dime to go, because the County of Charleston paid for it, so as to keep us from going to Clemson, University of South Carolina, and/or the Citadel. Certainly, our training at Avery qualified us for either one of those three schools, but the fact that we received full scholarships to South Carolina State—man! We jumped on it and went on to State College. We did the best that we could. Most of us were—there were about six of us from this area that

*This interview took place in Reverend Brown's home in Charleston, South Carolina, on February 1, 2006.

went to State College at that time, from the class of '52, and while we were there we did the best we could. We engaged in all kinds of activities and what have you.

And it was during that same time that the White Citizens' Council came into being, and they were active in the Orangeburg area. They did some things that were just unquestionably wrong, in terms of holding up the credit of persons, families, that were farmers, depending on credit in order, you know, at the beginning of the season, so that they could do the farming and send their kids to school. And that White Citizens' Council made it difficult for them to even get credit. It was during that time that students at State College, including many of us from Charleston here, organized ourselves so that we might protest that activity of the White Citizens' Council, because it was causing many problems for the farmers who had children in college during that time.

Of course, our activities were not sanctioned by the college administration, to say the least. So that much of what we had do to had to be undercover, kind of offbeat, but we organized ourselves in such fashion that we could continue going to classes, and we never stopped going to classes, never stopped with the activities that we had around. But we also protested the fact that these people were denied credit, blacks were denied credit, even downtown.

One of the first things that we did while we were at State College, during this movement, we boycotted the downtown area of Orangeburg. We were successful in doing that because we were able to shut down two of the major stores down in Orangeburg. Because we wouldn't spend our money down there. We wouldn't even go down there. We stayed at home, I mean stayed at the college, rather than venture into the shopping area of Orangeburg. The result was that a number of stores had to shut down, because they were dependent, more or less, on student activities, students going to shop down there and, you know, get regular things. We decided to get regular things from home. We had kind of a network in Charleston here, with the NAACP, and a number of civic groups got together to assist us, in an undercover kind of way, so that we might be able to subsist while we were there, and while we were going through this crisis, because many of the civic leaders in the NAACP and other organizations and churches felt that we might cause some problems for the administration, and the administration would then take it out on us. And so they supported us. We got food and funds to carry on what we were doing up there at State College, and we hopefully made a difference during that time.

Nonviolence—we didn't engage in any violent activity. I think the most violent activity that I engaged in during the time was to do an effigy, or burned the president in effigy, because he was against our whole movement. And this little item that I have here, I did that myself. I fixed up a little dummy and hung it on the president's tree, right outside his door, at the house that he lived in on campus, and I was going to burn it down. I was going to burn it, but we had some advisors, some teachers, undercover, that couldn't let their identity be known, but they kept the handle on us, so we wouldn't go into violence. It was a nonviolent movement all the way.

The Reverend Charles H. Brown, February 1, 2006.

These instructors that we had kind of met with us during off times and advised us how to continue doing what we were doing, because it was for the betterment of the entire community, and to keep us from engaging in any violent activity whatsoever. So all that we did was to boycott, to voice our protests, even in the cafeteria that we ate—a couple of meals we just did not eat. They fixed the meals for us and we just did not eat the meals.

We had a network in Orangeburg that folk would fix meals and ship them to the campus, and we would go out and get them and feed all the girls, and then the boys would go on off campus and eat. So we were able to subsist during that time, without any violence whatsoever. And that was the key to what we figure was success, a successful movement. Right.

ML: So you did this "dummy," an effigy of Dr. Turner yourself there. Instead of burning it, did you just hang it there?

CB: We just hang it, we just hang it, because it was, you see, it had straw in it, and the straw would have burned real good *[laughs]*. But we were turned around and we just hung it there, so that when he woke up the next morning he had a dummy in the tree, and we took pictures of it. That was one that I kept. Because I did that dummy, I fixed him up *[laughs]*.

Well, the president wasn't giving us any encouragement. More or less, he was going in the direction of the White Citizens' Council. He didn't want students to be involved with the civic activities downtown, and hey! Our education said to us, once you were educated and you're black, you need to get involved in civic activities. And that was one of the reasons we were involved, while we were still going to school, while we're still going and getting our education, we were able to participate in this kind of thing.

It was never properly chronicled because the outcome of our protests, which lasted, I'm not sure how long, was that the president of the student body was kicked out of school. Me and a couple of others had relatives in the school—my sister was there—Pyatt's sister was also there. Pyatt's sister was kicked out, and my sister was kicked out, because they couldn't touch Pyatt or me, to kick us out, because we had both been in the ROTC program for four years, and we were seniors, and we were about to get commissioned. As a matter of fact, the federal government had already located us for our commission to go in the service as first lieutenants, I mean as second lieutenants, and my commission was for the Regular Army. And that was even something that caused, the president was not able to kick me out, so he kicked my sister out.

She had to go to, she went to Claflin for a little while there, and then eventually she just stopped. And she never did go back to get her degree, and that hurt, that really did hurt me, because they couldn't put me out, they put her out. Because they couldn't put Pyatt out, they put Pyatt's sister out. And then they put the president, president of the student body, Fred Moore—I think you know him—they kicked him out completely, because he wasn't in ROTC and what have you, and he was paralyzed during his early years, and so he walked with a limp all the time, just like he does right now.

But they put him out of the school, and of course, he went to Allen University and then he went to Brown, and I think ended up at Howard University, where there were blacks in charge and doing well, and they picked him up, because he was an honor student.

Most of us were pretty good students. I wouldn't say that I was the best, but I tried to keep my average up to par so that when it came time for evaluation for the ROTC and the commission, I believe that I made the highest grade for commission during that time, and I got a Regular Army commission. Unfortunately, I didn't stay in the service but four and a half years, but my commission was R.A., Regular Army, as a second lieutenant. I didn't get my commission until the summer after my class left in '56. I graduated in September, rather than in June, because I had missed a freshman course in chemistry [chuckles], and I had to have that on my record before I got out, and so I took it during the summer. I took that during the summer and became the chemistry lab person who was in charge of seeing that everything was put back in place and all that, as a part of my payment to the school for that particular course. And I graduated in September, with my commission as well, and got my degree. And "he's" in there somewhere [pointing to the wall of honors and plaques], somewhere around here there's a degree from South Carolina State College. We were kind of concerned that this whole thing was not chronicled the way it ought to have been, and all these years it's been *[very emotional tone of voice—near tears]*—it's been a burden—we've buckled down and everywhere we've gone we have tried to do the best that we could. God moves in a mysterious way. He keeps all of us and he has stood by us even in these times. We could have, probably could have made a better life for our families and what have you, had that not happened. Nonetheless, I think the experience of having been in the forefront of what was going on during that time, and then to see the barriers of segregation broken down piece by piece by piece, wall by wall . . . and it was difficult during that time, and it's even more difficult today, to convince our youth that we have come through a long period of anxiety and second-class citizenship. One of the things that I've been trying to instill in many of the young people that I've come in contact with, because I've taught school in two high schools for twenty-seven years, and—that's after coming out of the military, after four and a half years—but to try to let our young people know that we're not there yet. We're still struggling.

We don't have to go to a colored water fountain anymore, we don't have to wait for the right bus to come to get on, we don't have to give up our seats for white folks to sit down, but the struggle is still not over. Because we're still looked at as second-class citizens, and we have to instill in them the magnitude of what we went through to get where we are now. Now it's time for them to step up and do their part.

Because we, my age group—I'm seventy-one right now—my age group is moving off of the scene. Who's going to take the mantle up? Who understands where we came from? And we try to instill in them the understanding, so that they could pick up the mantle, and understand that they still have a struggle to go through, because we're still looked at as second-class citizens. No matter what we do, there's always a hill to climb. Always a hill to climb. And that's essentially where we are.

ML: Are there experiences in your early childhood, or then in the military later, that stand out to you as being sort of watershed events for you and for others?

CB: Well, I never blame anyone for the manner in which I eventually came out of the military. I had a Regular Army commission. But I found when I went into the military that there was still that feeling of second-class officer even, officer. I was a first lieutenant when I came out. Allowing personal things to get in the way of my military career and eventually just kind of giving the whole thing back to them, and moving on.

I'm not proud of having done that, but I figured that it was time for me to move on and so I did. I came out of the service and if I had stayed in, probably would have moved on up, but during that time it was—movement for a black first lieutenant, Regular Army—well, it was a no-no *[laughs]*. They get you there and then they want to hold you there, and I was passed over a couple of times, and I figured it was time to come on out.

And when I did come out, I came on home, eventually, after four years in Washington. I stayed there and just kind of called myself "getting things together." And when I finally decided to come back home, I found Fred Moore, who called me in Washington and said, "Why don't you come home? Why don't you come on home?

We need you down here." And so I came home. I came home on a Saturday. On Monday morning I was in the classroom. Because there was a man named Wilmont Frasier, who was—who was—and just to show you that things hadn't changed that much—Wilmont Frasier was superintendent over the black schools. Okay? And he placed black teachers where they belonged, what have you, and during that time we had more men who were principals, black men who were principals. Matter of fact, all the schools had black principals, and Wilmont Frasier and Fred Moore saw to it when I stepped off of the train that I had a job. And so that Monday morning, I was in the classroom, and I have never looked back *[laughs]*. I just tried to teach the social sciences to the children and tried to work with them so as to bring them to a point where they would understand what the civil rights movement was all about and, of course, get their education so that they could make a difference in the community and what have you.

Another person who was real instrumental in keeping us abreast of what was going on was Doug Donahue of the *News and Courier.* He was the editor of the *News and Courier* during that time. As a matter of fact, I think Doug did some articles in Orangeburg during the time that we were struggling with this boycott and the White Citizens' Council up there. He did some articles chronicling some of the things that— he probably would be a good person to even interview as a part of, because—and he's still a good friend. We get together every now and then and just kind of talk about where we were then and what he's done now. But he's retired now from the *News and Courier,* so—he's chairman, or director, of the Star Gospel Mission now.

ML: It used to be there on Meeting Street.

CB: It's still on Meeting, but just behind the shopping center, at the corner of Meeting and Columbus. It's right in behind there. They have a beautiful facility there.

ML: Can you identify some of the instructors that were supportive there at South Carolina State, now that it's this far after the fact? Would that be betraying any confidences?

CB: Well, one of them is dead. He became the president of South Carolina State eventually, Maceo Nance. He was one of the ones who would pull the reins on us, to say, "No, no, no, we're not going to do that." Or, "You're not going to do that. What you're going to do is something a little different, and it's going to continue to be non-violent." There was another one also, he is of age now, we called him "Uncle Louie," Louie Roach, who was more or less an advisor to the student group, who met with us from time to time, unbeknowings [*sic*] to the administration, of course, because if they had known that they were meeting with us and directing us, their job might have been in jeopardy. But I hold Mr. Roach in high esteem because he did what he had to do in order to keep us from doing what was going to cause the whole thing to blow up, and cause violence to happen. What happened at South Carolina State College some years later—that is, the shooting of students and whatever—couldn't happen during that time that we were there in the early '50s because of those advisors that we had, and they volunteered their services. There was also a couple of men, I can't remember their names right off hand, who were instructors in the ROTC program, and they kind of, you know, advised some of the leadership of the students not to engage in certain things. We had some minds of our own, to do some violent things, but they kept us from engaging in those things, and I appreciate that even to today. Because without their wisdom, we might have, somebody might have died. Somebody night have been kicked out before we were in fact kicked out. And the only ones of us who were involved who did not get kicked out were those of us who were in the ROTC program, and were seniors, and they just couldn't squander the federal government's money that way! *[He laughs.]* So we were kind of on safe ground there, but yes, Louie Roach and Maceo Nance were persons that met with us from time to time and—

ML: Was Reverend Irvin on the staff at that time?

CB: Reverend who?

ML: Irvin. He's down in North Augusta now, Nathaniel Irvin.

CB: Nathaniel Irvin. Yes, he was on the staff during that time. As a matter of fact, I think that Reverend Irvin met with us when we went to Columbia mid–last year, I think it was. We went up there for a forum, kind of a roundtable discussion of the activities of State College during that time, and he was there. Yes, he was there. Rudy [Pyatt] came down from Washington, and many of the former classmates of ours met there. We had a reunion up there.

It was excellent, because even the crowning of Miss South Carolina State during that year was postponed. And the young lady who was voted Miss South Carolina State never received her recognition. We recognized her at that forum that we had, and I'm not sure that she even is still alive, I'm not sure whether—what was her name? I can't remember right off. *[The woman was Jimmie (Payne) Grayson.]* Fred Moore can kick those names out just like that! But I can't.

ML: I probably have it in his records, or—and maybe it's in some of Cecil Williams's pictures.

CB: Yes, because Cecil was around there taking pictures of most of the things. I think that's one of the pictures that Cecil took.

ML: I wouldn't be surprised.

CB: He'd be surprised to see this [picture of the effigy hanging]. *[He laughs.]* But he was taking pictures of many of the activities that we were doing.

ML: And you had mentioned your sister. What was her name?

CB: Barbara Richardson, Barbara Brown at that time. She wasn't married, and she never was able to get back to get her degree, because she stayed at Claflin only a short period of time, and kind of dropped out, because of lack of funds and all.

ML: . . . That was a real, a watershed event and very formative. . . . You went on into the ministry as well as teaching?

CB: Yes, well, I got the call to ministry some years ago, and kind of put that on the back burner, put it on the back burner—until such time as I really didn't have a choice. God put me in a position where I had to say yes, I had to move on, and moving on, at that time I was still teaching, but I needed to get some theological training, and I went to Cummings Seminary in Summerville, while I was still teaching at Burke.

I enrolled in Cummings and took classes in the evenings and taught school during the day, came home just in time to get about thirty or forty minutes of a nap, and then up to the seminary. . . . During the same time that I was in seminary, both—because I was married already—both my wife's grandmother and mother got sick, unto death, and my mother. And we ended up, the two of us ended up taking care of business and taking care of them during the same time. I had to drop out of seminary for a period of time there, but we finally got back. It took me five years to get through the seminary, and once I got the theological training, I was ordained a deacon at the two hundredth anniversary of the African Methodist Episcopal Church in Philadelphia, Pennsylvania, at Mother Bethel. The ordination service, I was supposed to be ordained in our conference right here, but my elder said that he wanted me to go to Philadelphia, and I went to Philadelphia and was one of the two individuals in South Carolina who was ordained deacon in the African Methodist Episcopal Church in the two hundredth anniversary of the AME Church, in Philadelphia, Pennsylvania.

ML: What year was that? Two hundred . . . I should know.

CB: I got a plaque up there somewhere that says what day that was, that's twenty some-odd years ago now. I think I got a plaque or something up here, I'll pull it. But that was a milestone in my life, and when I was ordained deacon I was given the charge of a small church up in Lincolnville. One of the churches that my dad pastored, and my dad—he was down in Florida, he was sick in a nursing home down there, and my wife and I superintended him over a period of time, till he finally passed. But my first charge was a church that he pastored in Lincolnville, where we grew up. And when he went to church, we went to church. Ebenezer AME Church was the name of that one, and then I had five other churches that I pastored before I retired. And I retired about two years ago, I guess, from the pastoral ministry. But I can't seem to get away from teaching. As a matter of fact, I got a call just yesterday to do some training down in Round O, and I'm going to go down there the middle of this month sometime and do some training of members in the church. We stay busy. We stay busy—even though you're retired, you're still on call almost. If the bishop calls or the presiding elder calls, I got to move. And my home church is Mt. Zion on Glebe Street, that's where, when my sister and I were going to high school, my grandmother paid the tuition for us to go to Avery, rather than go to Burke. My brother was in Burke, and my sister and I went to Avery, but they had to pay tuition at Avery, and my grandma paid our tuition, so that we could go to Avery and we eventually graduated from Avery. My class was the class of '52, and there were only twenty-seven of us in that class. Seven fellows and the other twenty were girls. While I was at Avery, rather than trek to Kennedy Street where the family was living, I went to Mt. Zion AME Church and joined up down there, and I've been a member of Mt. Zion ever since. That's where I came out to go preaching, and that's where I am now.

ML: Wonderful. That's quite a history.

CB: Yes.

ML: You and I are contemporaries. I graduated high school in 1952, and I'm seventy-one, and my high school class in a rural area of Ohio was twenty-seven members. Now I think we were more evenly male and female, but nevertheless, it was a public school and all. And I have the same problem, I retire but then things just keep coming up.

CB: They keep coming up, keep coming up. And I've been doing, over the period that I taught high school, in economics, I got to teach economics during that time, and I got into computers. I was one of the first teachers to bring the computer into the classroom to teach the economics class, along with the help of Junior Achievement, their program, and with the help of Buzzy Newton, from Piggy Wiggy [*sic*], and Perlstein, I. M. Perlstein, the liquor man. They helped to finance the computers coming in, and the newspaper in the classroom. The state of South Carolina now has newspapers in the classroom, because there were three teachers in Charleston who made a presentation at a meeting in Columbia, and I was one of those three teachers who presented the newspaper as a means of students in the social sciences getting the most updated information for the day. They could get it from the newspaper, and that started the state of South Carolina utilizing newspapers in the classrooms. So I count that a plus for my endeavors in the field of education, bringing computers in the classrooms, the newspaper in the classroom program, and trying to expose students to all kind of different activities to include the state legislature. We visited with them a number of times during the time I was teaching. And the Model United Nations at Winthrop, and USC. We attended, took students out for those things. And those were days when you could carry students on field trips, and you were in charge. It wasn't but one teacher, maybe two, but those were the days when you could tell a student that this is what I want you to do this day, and they did that, because they knew that if they didn't do that, the next move was to be at their house [*laughs*]. And standing in front of their parents and letting the parents know that you need to straighten this fellow out, because he doesn't know how to follow directions.

But those days seem to have just kind of vanished. The teaching corps today is not what it used to be, in terms of the dedication of those of us who were there and dealing with students. We could paddle the students during that time. Today you can't even speak to them in harsh tones [*laughs*]. We could paddle them in school because the parents, when they brought them to school, or when they sent them to school, they let them know that the teacher is your mama or your daddy today. When you leave here, then I take over again. But that's not the way it is today. We've taken so many things out of the schools—devotions, they don't have them anymore. At Avery we had the same homeroom teacher from ninth through twelfth grade. One of the things we did in the morning when we went to school was to have devotions, and so somebody had to be the chaplain. Guess who that was? Four years running I was the chaplain. They always elected me chaplain of the class, and every morning we had to have prayer and we had to have some sort of scripture that we would read in the classroom. We can't even do that anymore. And that's sad. That's sad. Yes. It puts that extra burden right on top of the teacher, and you just can't do but so many things.

ML: Well, I really appreciate you sharing with me. If you don't mind, I bring my camera along, and I like to get some candid shots of the person in their home or in their situation.

[Brown goes on to recount experiences of his ministry and community leadership. Lare takes pictures of various materials.]

ML: Now, I could perhaps take this [picture of the effigy of President Turner] and make a copy of it and bring it back to you, or what would you rather I do? It may be in Cecil Williams's book.

CB: I'm pretty sure it is. I'm sure Cecil has it. Because I clipped that out of, it was in the Charleston paper, too, I believe, that came out of—*News and Courier,* because Doug Donahue was editor during that time and I just kind of clipped that, and I kept that. That was one of the pieces that I just treasured, because they just would not let me burn that thing! *[He laughs.]* Because I was ready to light him up. But it got his attention.

[Lare takes pictures of the newspaper article, and their conversation continues.]

ML: I need to have you sign a release so that I can use the interview. It's a standard kind of release form there, and I just added the photos that I've taken as being part of the interview.

CB: You have permission to release anything that you think is going to make a difference. And let the world know.

Alice Pyatt, a Summer of Tears

Marvin Lare [ML]:* This is October the 12th, Wednesday, October the 12th, 2005, and I'm in the home of Alice Pyatt, in Charleston, South Carolina. How are you today, Miss Pyatt?

Alice Pyatt [AP]: Fine, thank you.

ML: Good. Do you have any questions about the interview or our project at this point?

AP: Well, I understand what you're doing with the project. As a matter of fact, when Rudy [Pyatt, my brother] and his wife left Orangeburg [for the Anthology Festival in June 2004], they came here.

ML: I see.

AP: And we talked about what had happened there, and then they brought me some information, so I could look through it.

ML: Oh, good.

AP: So I was aware that you're trying to get the wordings from the people who were involved in civil rights issues and whatever.

ML: Exactly.

AP: And with this collection you're putting together a group of writings for the public.

ML: Right. Very good. And I appreciate so much your participation in it.

AP: Well, I hope my memory is as sharp as it used to be *[laughs]*. When this incidence first happened, it devastated me so until I prayed to forget it. And when I was invited to be a part of the panel in Orangeburg, that was the first time I had talked about it in so long. Until it was like I was purging myself.

ML: Yes.

*The interview took place in the home of Alice Pyatt, in Charleston, South Carolina, on October 12, 2005.

AP: Because it hurt so deep. I knew the other people who were involved had their moments but mine seemed not to go away as quickly, even though I was removed from the whole city. It wouldn't go away because each time somebody asked a question, "Where did you start school?," then I had to say, "South Carolina State College."

ML: Right.

AP: While I was at Allen, "Where were you before you came here?" And so that just sort of opened up all the wounds and you start thinking again. Because when I received the letter that summer saying not to return to state college, I cried practically the whole summer. And I am not a weepy person, I'm not a softie. But it hurt so hard, until I cried and I cried and I cried. And I'm a—well—I enjoy food, but during that time I lost my appetite, and by the time school started, for me to enroll in another college, I had ulcers the worst way, to the point where I couldn't eat on campus. I had to eat at a restaurant where they could fix the foods that I could eat, because I had destroyed my—I had destroyed the lining of my stomach—the acids and not eating and whatever, because I was so grieved, it was a terrible loss.

ML: Oh, gosh.

AP: When I graduated from high school, in '55, I graduated with 215 students. Two hundred and fifteen of us marched. That did not include those who didn't march because they didn't have all of their credits.

ML: Yes.

AP: Two hundred and fifteen of us, and we were a close class. Yes, and we still are. And it was like fifty-some of us that went to Orangeburg, to State College. You know, that made you feel good that we're all here.

It was exciting, because you were there with people who you've known for years. And upon entering, you had to take some exams and tests for placement, and whatever, and a number of us exempted certain classes that we didn't have to go to, because we had been taught so well at Burke High School. And several of us in the Business Department did not have to take freshman business classes. We started out with the sophomores. That made us feel so good. As a freshman. And so you know with all these good things happening to you, you're looking forward to a great year and continuation at the college. But then, it was like, not too long after we started college, started school, there were rumblings on the campus about things that were going on in the city. Families and people who were losing jobs and having to move, couldn't get services and all, because of certain issues in the town or in the city that had to do with racism.

But you know, at the beginning, it didn't affect us as freshmen. Because the upperclassmen know things years before we know them. So we're always kept in our place as freshmen, to do as the upperclassmen say to do. But then, it got to the point where we were receiving those flyers, we didn't know from whom, to report to the auditorium for meetings. This is when it started. Now, even though we were going to these meetings, and sessions, and the people who were student council president and government workers on the council and whatever, we still really didn't understand exactly what was happening as far as we were concerned. We just thought it was out there and we're okay here. And it was in fact that it was slowly creeping in to us. Because the president of the student council and the members of the council got together and they decided that they would talk with the president [of the college] because they didn't go along with what was happening in the city, because it affected some of the students, who were a part of the campus, and their families. And President Turner was a—oh—he was a hard person. He didn't move from the right or the left. He only went straight down the middle. And he didn't want to hear that. Because he figured if he agreed with the student body, or the council at least, then it might have some dealings with his position as the president, and as the state would look at him as a leader. So he didn't want to listen to what they said to do. Not to do, but suggestions to sit down and let's talk about this. If the persons who are denying the citizens of the community the right to these commodities and whatever, then we don't think that we should buy their commodities either. Oh, no, no, no, no, no. They don't want to hear that. They don't want to rock the boat. Let everything—

And so we got our first little memo that said, "When you go in the dining room tomorrow morning, we're not going to drink the milk. Meet this afternoon and then we'll talk about it." And so we met, everybody was very obedient, to fill the auditorium, to hear what this is all about. And so they let us know that the company that was producing, that we were getting the milk from, was a company that did not . . . Not only had they fired some of their workers, but they did not want to deliver products to certain stores and people who had milk delivered at home in the town. So we were not going to use their products, the milk and bread and whatever. Now we go to the cafeteria and the breakfast is the best breakfast you ever want to have at a college. And you sit, and when they ring the bell, we stand up and we sing the blessing. That was the normal thing. And then after we got through singing the blessing, we sat and we ate but we didn't drink the milk. And we didn't eat the bread. And we would leave. Well, the president didn't like that. Because this was a waste and we had to still pay for it. So it just got . . . it was not like . . . ah . . . a situation on the campus that was rowdy. It was very orderly. Very organized, very controlled.

But nobody was talking to anybody who wanted to know, "Well, why are you doing this?" I mean we knew bits and pieces, but we looked to the leaders and they gave us our direction. And so it got to the point where the president didn't want to meet with the student body at all, the student government at all, so when they decided to march on his home and we all had to go and sit out on the grass and all around it. Not making any noise, just sitting. He was, oh! He was angry! And then he started accusing different people about who started this and, you know. Well, nobody really knew who started what. We just knew that each time we went to a meeting different people would address the body. And talk about different things. But as to who was sending out the little flyers, or notices, we didn't know. I guess it was Dr. Denighten [?]. Issued in the morning . . . We don't know. And he was so angry, and he said such awful things about the student government and the campus got, we got angry and people hung him in effigy. Right by my dormitory. In a tree.

Then the buzz started on the campus, and the NAACP started coming onto the campus. And it then got from not eating the bread and drinking the milk to not eating the food. Not eating the food. What are you going to do? We had a meeting. They let us know that the community would be bringing dinner on campus to feed you. Don't eat. We went to the cafeteria, to the dining hall, and we said the blessing and we'd walk away. We walked away. Some of us didn't want to leave the food, but we walked away. One boy was caught trying to take some food under his hat. You know what he caught! But anyway, that afternoon people came to the campus with loads of food to serve, to feed you. All who wanted to eat, you know, food was there. You didn't have a good feeling about what was going on, but you couldn't do anything about it. The only thing you could do was to go to school, go to classes. Try to do your studies. Because when I went to State College I had won a scholarship, an academic scholarship, which meant I had to maintain a "B" average or my scholarship would be revoked. So you see, I have to concentrate on my studies.

So one day, Fred Moore asked me, he said, "We're going to see if we can get support from the NAACP. In order to do that we want to see how many of our students will join. And I would like for you to record the names." Okay. So I recorded the names. So a lot of people joined and paid their dues. We all would do this, and I kept a record and all of that. But I didn't really know that that was going to get us in trouble. Because we, you do what you think is best. The NAACP members, or officers, would come and would meet with us to say they are with us . . . and they'd help us in any way they could. And so we want to give them this support since they want to help us. And, so we joined the NAACP.

At school [things] wound down and coming to the end [of the year] the rumors got out that the president was saying if he found out who was responsible, and all the persons who were connected, he was going to send—he was going to expel them from school. I knew my brother [Rudy Pyatt] was on that government board, the body. I knew he was involved in the writing and whatever, and I was really fearful about his not graduating, because he was a senior. And the president decided he was going to expel them, but Rudy was a commissioned officer [through ROTC] and could not be expelled because he was no longer the president's property but he was now the government's property. Because he was commissioned, so he couldn't touch him. So Rudy was okay. Fred Moore was not a commissioned officer, so Fred was going to be expelled. He and some others. But the fellows who were commissioned officers couldn't be touched. Okay? Since they can't be expelled, then he moves to another group. He's going to fire all the teachers who were in sympathy with us. And—now at that time, we don't know anything about the family members. You just don't, you don't know—there's all these things, the buzzing and the whatever. You hear it but you don't know that you are one on the list. Until the end of the school year.

We all went home and—well, before we went home—it was in May that we had this meeting and after the meeting—you understand that Fred had been expelled, and they gave him twenty-four hours to get out of the city. And that—I don't remember how many—teachers were going to be fired. A list of teachers. And that some students who played a major role were going to be expelled because he was going to clear the campus of all of that, didn't want that to go into the next year.

The night that Fred got expelled was an awful night. Everybody was crying and weeping and "It's not fair!" and "What has he done?" You know. And the persons, the people who were on the president's side were angry with everybody who was on Fred's side. I can remember the lady who was over our dormitory saying, "Get back in here! Anybody caught out there, I'll make sure you're sent home if you follow that crowd! Go back to your rooms!"

Well, graduation went on, and those who were commissioned were able to graduate. A number of things that were supposed to be a part of the campus, closing of the campus that year, coming up to May, the president didn't want to happen. It was duked out, stop it. Like May Day, "No, not going to have it." [The May queen, Jimmie (Payne) Grayson, was not crowned.]

And so, during the summer, early on in the summer, some of us got letters, saying that because we had relatives who played major roles in the boycott and the strike and the sit-down and whatever, and caused a disruption to the life on the campus and they could not be dismissed for reasons that were like, because they were commissioned or whatever, that we are asking you not to return. Because you will have sympathy with the cause and want to start it up once you get back here. So we got this letter. When I got that letter, I didn't know what to do. What have I done? I haven't done anything. And nobody wants to talk to you. My father went to Orangeburg because my scholarship was there. And the president wouldn't release it. He said, "Well she can stay out a year and come back. When thing cool down."

Meanwhile, what I supposed to do? That was a four-year scholarship, four consecutive years. You can't just stop and start when you want to. And so my mom and dad came home and went to visit the superintendent of Charleston schools—Charleston County schools—who had given the scholarship, who had signed off for the scholarship, to explain to him what had happened. And he said, "No. No, he can't do that. He can't keep that money. Mrs. Pyatt, I'll see that that money is transferred to wherever you want it transferred. And you tell your daughter, 'Go on and study hard and keep that scholarship.'" So. They came home and my dad said, "Now, I allowed you to select your college the first time. You went to Orangeburg. I'm going to send you to where I want you to go right now. I want you to go to Allen [University]. Because that's our church school." [The phone rings.] And so that's where I . . .

ML: You need to take that, do you?

AP [checking caller identification]: No, they'll leave me a message.

ML: Okay.

AP: And so—that's when I began to weep [long pause].

At State College I had made the choir. I was the only freshman soloist . . . on the choir. I was so proud that I had made that choir, and I had solo parts to sing with my brother, who was a baritone soloist. It just made me feel so good. And all of that was gone.

My sister was next door to our place [at Claflin], who I could visit. I couldn't do that. You know, it just destroyed me! All of my friends and I had to leave to go another school. And I hadn't done anything.

And so I went to Allen. At first when I got there, I didn't want to stay, but I knew that was the only way I could finish school. Because my parents could not afford to send all of us to college. And fortunately, all of us won scholarships. So I decided I was going to give it all I could give it so I could graduate. And I joined the choir there at Allen. I not only sang with the choir, I sang with the trio, the octets, the sextets. And we traveled during the year to sing and do concerts, which was beautiful. It took my mind off what I had lost. And I graduated on time. To get my degree.

I lost faith in people, to some extent. Because—if you promise me something—I think you should follow through with your promise. And the NAACP did not do that. Because when we went to them after we got the letter from Turner, and the NAACP said they could not help me, "I must remember we were fighting for a cause. And in every fight, there has to be a martyr. And I must accept that." Ah—"through the pains that I suffer, somebody else will be better off." And they weren't going to get involved with, with that scholarship. They didn't even say, "Well, we will meet to see." No. Not at all. If it were not for my mom and dad being persistent, I would have lost that scholarship and thereby lost an opportunity to get an education.

And so, not only did I lose faith in the NAACP, I lost faith in the college. Because a freshman student is green, you know. We're just trying to find our way. So how could you suspend—no—how could you ask us not to return as freshmen when we are only moving with the crowd of the campus because the upperclassmen are telling all freshmen, "All freshman, clear the dorms. . . ." You're taking orders from upperclassmen. Nobody is fighting, nobody has caused any harm. We're just talking and trying to negotiate. So why was that so wrong that so many people suffered?

It made me very—well, very strong and also very defiant. After I left there. To say, it doesn't matter what, and it doesn't matter who . . . I am now going to look out for me. Fred Moore came to Allen while I was there, to finish up his work. And the first time I saw him on campus, he said, "Alice, I'm so glad that you are here and we can continue the movement. We're going to get students together and we're going downtown and we're going to ride on the front of the bus."

"No, Fred. I am not going. I have three years to finish this scholarship and that's all that's on my mind right now. I am not riding on the front or the back of the bus, because I'm not getting on the bus. Now if you want to go down there, you may go with whomever will go with you. But as for me, I'm not going. Because once I put my neck on the chopping board, nobody's going to help get it off. And I'm not going to be a martyr the second time. I'm not going to."

So I didn't go. It was important to me to get my education and leave the campuses and try to begin to work for me. And that's what I did.

Now, I don't know . . . I have no accounts of what things happened in Columbia while I was there with Fred and the bus situation, because I just sort of took all of that off my mind. Because right now I'm . . . I've learned through a bad lesson that some-times you've got to move off and be alone in order to accomplish something. Because you get caught up in the masses and you got to suffer the pain.

So I tore up my NAACP card. Never joined since. I have people who have come to me for donations for the NAACP. No. I want to forget all of that. I don't want to be a member. Because I don't think I was treated fairly.

And, after graduating from college, and accepting a job, and teaching high school—I taught high school for twelve years—and then I went into administration. I was constantly telling my students, "Be careful about crowds that you join up with. Make sure you know your way out of it, because you could be the scapegoat." And so it's a lesson learned. If you're not willing to sacrifice, and sometimes sacrifice it all, then back out. Because once you get in it, and you keep going and going, then you are . . . one of it.

And you see, if I had the means to say, "Oh, forget about the scholarship—I don't care," it would be a different thing, but my parents had six children. Five of us won—well, four of us had academic scholarships, which meant we had to use this *[pointing to her head]*. And one had a music scholarship. So you see, we didn't have time to play around in school. We had, we had to stay focused in order to complete those four years. So I said it within myself, "I'll never go back to State College again." But when I went into administration, I was working on a master's at Clemson, but that was too much of a drive. From where I worked to Clemson was ninety-nine miles, and so I changed, went to State College, and pursued the master's degree in education, concentrating in elementary education since I had gone to be an elementary assistant principal.

I got to Orangeburg and I was hoping that things were going to be okay. And after I had completed my master's work, and marched, I received a letter from the State Department [of Education] saying I had not completed the master's work. . . . I didn't take Art Appreciation or something like that. Now I have my [list of] courses—I called the campus, called the college to make an appointment to see the dean—well, the advisor of my program. I went to see him and he told me I had to see the dean of education. So when I got through talking with [the dean], he couldn't tell me anything that could be done to correct [the record]. It was a mistake made and I would just have to [reenroll in] the class! Well—no. Let me talk to the instructor who taught the course. Dr. Triggs taught the course. Not only was I in Dr. Triggs's class as a student, but when we were discussing certain parts of the arts and sculpture and this kind of things—the school where I was working had a magnificent library area where we had all of the artwork and many pictures on display, and sculptures and things. And so I would take things to class. Dr. Triggs remembered that and remembered me very well. But still, the dean of my department had sent in the wrong course title, and he wasn't willing to change it. And I wanted to know from him if the instructor has the record, why can't you write the State Department, and say I made . . . "No, you see when you go changing things, then they'll think you're padding . . ."

"No, no, no, no, no! No, no, no, no! I'm not going to listen to that." Because if the instructor verifies the fact that I was in the class—he has his roll book—that shouldn't be hard to correct.

"No, no, no. We're not—I'm not going to do it." And you know—they wouldn't do it!

I asked to see the president. And so I went to see the president, and the president called all of these people together with me. To say, "Something went wrong. What can we do to correct it?" Dr. Brooks, who was my advisor, [said,] "Well, you see, you go trying to change things and they'll think you're padding reports, and I'm not going to be a part of—it was just a mistake and all she's got to do is just sit in on the class again and—and . . ."

And I declare I just couldn't take it any longer. And so I asked for the floor. And I told them all off. "I thought when you asked me not to come back after my freshman year, it was all done with now. Because I have graduated from college, I have worked five years and working on a master's program. You know, I thought all that was done, but you are still as you were, when you decided that all of us should be sent away." You know—I left there with such a headache—until . . . I didn't know what to do, but when I got to my car the campus police had a ticket on the car!

ML: Ohh! Insult to injury!

AP: I couldn't believe—well—what has happened with me and Orangeburg? I got that ticket—I tore it up into a thousand pieces and I threw it into the air! And he said, "I will write you a ticket for littering." I said, "Do that." And I got into my car and I took off. And I haven't been back there because they made me come back and sit in on that class—I forgot for how many sessions—to do nothing. Just to be there.

ML: So that they could show you were enrolled in that class during that semester.

AP: Yes! So I wondered, "Now, what grade did you give me for just sitting here?" Didn't make any sense. I don't have any fond memories of South Carolina State College. I don't really know that I ever want to go back—to anything. I go next door to see Claflin, because they have grown and last time—well, before my sister died—we went to Orangeburg and rode through the campus of Claflin College, because she hadn't been on the campus since they had done all the work that they have done. And her daughter had never been in Orangeburg, to where [her] mama went to school. So we took that journey there to do that, but State College? Don't have a good feeling about it. Most of the people who were in that room with me have died, but still—I don't care to go back.

ML: Was it the same president?

AP: No, it was a different president. But he didn't take a stand. And that bothered me. And I know an administrator is supposed to support its faculty, but when a faculty is wrong, that administrator who does not want to lose face before his faculty should say, "Miss Pyatt, we will try to resolve this and get back in touch with you." So he wouldn't have to say it to the faculty, "No, you're wrong." You understand. But he didn't do it. It was just a cloud and all I could see is when I was there before and things were wrong and, you know . . .

So. When I accepted to be a part of the panel [at Orangeburg, referred to early in the interview], it was like I, my voice was low because if I got any higher I think I would have just screamed it. Because it was a big hurt. And my brother, Rudy, always felt that somehow he was responsible for my not being able to return, because he played such a big role in the activities and whatever. But I said, "No. Don't blame yourself—because you didn't—you're not the one who told me not to come back. President Turner did that." And that was only because he was a hateful, vicious person. You know, it's his way or no way. And to sit down and just like clean the slate off with students and faculty and whatever—that's evil. Evil! He didn't even have proof. He took hearsay from a student. To think who he thought was—you know— But . . . it was not a happy time.

ML: Yes, I am sure.

AP [after pausing]: The only good that came of that is, I guess, that some of us were able to move on and complete our education and do well, after that time. When others who were not as fortunate, whose scholarships were only to State College couldn't go anyplace. And I feel sad for them. Because they didn't have anyone to pursue a course for them to get back in school.

ML: A number of your friends?

AP: Yes. Never finished.

ML: Left a permanent mark on their life, their experience, their contribution to the community and the state.

AP: Mmh, mmh. But you know, when I look back at it through all that happened, through the boycott, the strike, the sit-ins, whatever we want to call it . . . Ahhh, a lot that we were demonstrating for, sort of fell on the wayside. By that I mean, people just took it for granted after a time and felt, "Well, forget that. We'll move on to do something else." And so you wonder with all the sacrifices, what happened? That it just sort of waned away and now we have so many people who don't even know that it happened and what it happened for. The same day that we were with the panel discussion, we had someone from the audience who spoke, "Why don't we know anything about all of this? We're right here." It's not even a part of history. The only account I— we've seen—is [Ms. Pyatt taps on a book]. And that is not totally all there and correct, because we must remember that the person who did this was making pictures and he was not a part of . . .

ML: The perspective expressed in the book, the book *Freedom and Justice* by Cecil Williams? He was recording the pictures but was not a part of the experience itself?

AP: Right. Because in some of the information that you read there—I know one incident where he's saying that Leroy Nesbitt and Fred, you know this happened and Leroy was—well, Leroy was not a student at State College. He was out. And so, when you are part of something, you can write it because you can see it. But when you are a person, one person on the outside and you're just taking pictures, and then people are telling you bits and pieces and you're trying to write a story, you don't have the actual story. So there's a whole lot to be learned from those who were a part of it, who planned the activities, who went through the daily marches and sit-ins and whatever.

But looking back over it, I know there are a number of things that came as a result of the boycotts and the strikes and the sit-ins. A number of things were made better. But all of a sudden, we're slipping away, going back to the same thing.

ML: You mean now that—

AP: Yes! Yes. And so you wonder—you know—a lesson learned should be a lesson learned. Why are we moving so far [from it] now? [For] those of us who were participating in it, it meant something to us. And even after we look back, some good came of it. But—when you talk to people nowadays, they say, "That wasn't necessary" or "I wouldn't have handled it like that." Because that was a quiet—nonviolent—boycott and strike. But I guess this day and time, we wouldn't ever look at it to handle it in that way. We're going to handle it differently. Because we want immediate results. We don't want to work through a process.

ML: That's a good point. One of the primary purposes of this anthology, of course, is so that those experiences and those accomplishments and their processes are not forgotten, so that they will be the heritage of people who have benefited from them, who may not have any awareness or recollection of those events.

AP: And that's a good thing. It should be made available for all of us to read, because it would surprise you to know the persons who are not aware of so much that has happened. In the '50s and '60s.

ML: Well, do you want to tell me about the rest of your career? You say you went on to teach in high school and then got your master's and [were] assistant principal in elementary school?

[Ms. Pyatt recounts her professional experience.]

ML: Is there any chance that you have that letter that you received from the—

AP: From State College.

ML: From State College. I imagine it ended up about like the parking ticket *[laughs].*

AP: Well—you know, I used to have that letter packed in things that I put in my utility house in Saluda. When I went to move—I was moving from there [to] here—and I didn't remove all the things out of that storage room. Because I figured I'd go back and we could handle that. And then I went back and somebody had broken in and went through things and everything was just in a mess and so . . . I don't have that letter, but you know—when we were at Columbia, at the museum, Barbara Brown, whose picture is in that, in the book with me, she had her *Jet* magazine to show me. And for—more than likely Barbara has her letter. Because Barbara was one who got one of the city scholarships. I got a county scholarship. At that time they awarded ten county scholarships and ten city scholarships.

ML: And that was Barbara?

AP: Barbara Brown. Now Barbara Brown is not her last name is not Brown anymore. Her brother was on the panel, Reverend Charlie Brown. I don't know where Barbara lives right now, but Reverend Charles Brown is her brother, who would know.

You can trace that down. Now Charles Brown and Fred Moore are brothers-in-law. So—that'd help you get in touch with him. Their wives are sisters.

ML: Ah—ah.

AP: I would even call and talk with Alvin Anderson and see if he kept his letter, because he sent me a picture of this picture that's in the book, because mine had gotten destroyed. Alvin did. So more than likely he has his letter.

I'm sure that one of us who was in that group kept up with that letter. I had it and was keeping up with it, I thought, doing a good job, but then all of a sudden I don't have my letter. And I can't get it.

ML: That's the way things happen.

AP: You'll have to get in touch with one of them. I'm trying to—I'm looking it over, looked over all those names of those people. Yeah—that's Barbara. I remember when *Jet,* when they came to our house and Barbara and Alvin came over to have that picture made. One good thing that came out of all of that—my father had a brother who he hadn't seen for many years. When that *Jet* came out, he saw my picture in that *Jet* and he said, "Pyatt. Alice Pyatt." My whole name was in there. He said, "You know, this could be my brother's daughter." He was living in Pennsylvania and inquiring to try to find out where I lived and all of that, it ended up by—well, I guess the next year or so—by the next year or so he had found out where I lived and in some way made contact to the point where he came to Charleston. And met up with my dad again.

ML: A good reunion. It's an ill wind that blows no good, even though it manages to blow a lot of ill in the meantime.

Nathaniel Irvin, Part 1

The Keep Back Family

Marvin Lare **[ML]:*** I'm with the Reverend Dr. Nathan Irvin today at his church. We appreciate very much your taking the time to share with us your life experiences. Tell us about your life and ministry, particularly in relationship to civil and human rights in South Carolina.

Nathaniel Irvin **[NI]:** I want to say first of all, I thank God for you and . . . the University of South Carolina for undertaking this project. . . . You've been a positive influence in the state of South Carolina and in this nation, so I want to commend you for being who you are.

ML: I appreciate that.

NI: And helping us become better people through our Lord and Savior Jesus Christ.

I was born the month of March, the 23rd day, in 1929, which means I'm seventy-five and a half years old as of now. Looking back on the years that I've been blessed, I was born in the suburbs of North Augusta, which is a part of Aiken County. I came up in a very segregated society. I went to a public school that was really just for black people. The fact about it, when I came out of elementary school, there was no high school for blacks to attend in 1945 and '46. [I] went to Central Elementary School in North Augusta, and I had some pretty tough experiences because I was in a family that was not thought to make it. My family was more likely to fail, and we were tagged that way because we were poor and no father in the house. We didn't have any electric lights and no telephone, no refrigerator, only had an outhouse. But we had God and he is the best father in the world you could have. It's better to have God as your father and no earthly father than have an earthly father and no heavenly father. Amen to that.

*This interview was conducted on November 30, 2004, at Old Storm Branch Baptist Church, North Augusta, South Carolina. It was transcribed by Catherine Mann for the USC South Caroliniana Library.

The Reverend Dr. Nathaniel Irvin Sr., the "Keep Back" Kid, November 30, 2004.

ML: That's right.

NI: So my first experience was 1935, in the first-grade class. I was accused of stealing the teacher's daughter's lunch. My teacher was Miss Lillie Grant, and her daughter's name was Jean. . . . Williams sat in front of me. He told Miss Lillie that I stole her daughter's lunch. And because I came from the wrong side of the tracks—he came from the other side of the tracks—she believed him and she whipped me. And God spoke to me in '35, and God said to me, he said, "Don't worry about this whipping. You're innocent. You didn't steal that lunch." And all of a sudden I had relief. I didn't feel the pain. I didn't get angry. I didn't go home and tell my mother about it. I didn't tell . . . Williams about it. It was all over.

So I met Christ at six years of age, and he spoke to me that way. In the school I attended, we were the poor of the poorest people. So our family was kind of looked down upon as not going to be able to make it. Call it "keep back family." *[He laughs.]*

ML: Keep back?

NI: Everybody in my family had been kept back. Mizella was kept back, Leroy, I was kept back. Marie kept back. Delbert kept back, Tony was kept back, my niece . . . and Bertha Belle. No one made their grade on time. I spent ten years in grades one through seven. I didn't really like school because there was not a lot of comradeship and love at that school for us. But we were determined to succeed.

So after ten years there I left that school, went to Augusta to Haines Institute, which is a private school. I had a job in 1943 paying social security. I paid my own bus fare, my own tuition, bought my food, everything. My mother couldn't even write her name, and she inspired me because she couldn't write her name.

One of my experiences in that area was that this white gentleman, a sheriff, came to our house one day because our daughter wouldn't work for him, he wanted to get on my mother. He said, "I haven't slapped a face of a black nigger woman in so long that I forgot how to slap one."

And there I was at twelve years old listening to this white man talk to my mother like that. And, Lare, that inspired me, and my mother said this, she got a knife and said, "Come on, slap this one." *[He laughs.]* He got back in his car and drove back home.

ML: Why had he driven out there in the first place?

NI: My daughter, I mean my sister, was working for him, and she didn't go to work and he got upset because she didn't come to work. He would get after my mother because my sister didn't go to work for him.

But when I went to Haines I was able to pay four bus fares per day. Two bus fares, one from North Augusta to Augusta, [from] Broad Street to Haines, and back. I worked eight hours a day, five days a week, and then two days I worked fourteen hours and twelve hours, on Saturday and Sunday.

ML: How did you have time to go to school and do the forty-hour week and more?

NI: I was blessed. This was a miracle. I coasted into high school. When I got in high school there I was in a different environment. So I was no longer a little old poor boy in a ragged house in South Carolina. I'd dressed properly, clothes on, money in my pocket, and I had a different perspective because there was a teacher at Central made me feel good about myself, Mrs. Franks—a teacher at Central had made me feel good after ten years. She came when I was in the sixth grade class. She said "Nathaniel"— she made my name sound like I'm somebody.

"Nathaniel," I said, "boy, that sounds good. Oh, the first time I heard my name sound with any kind of beauty.

"Nathaniel, take out that trash." Oh, I was happy. "Erase the board." And I began to feel good about myself because I was asked to take out the trash and erase the board and that made me begin to move up. After ten years! I call it Central Prison, not Central Elementary School. Ten years!

But in Augusta I went to Haines and the curriculum, Algebra I, Algebra II, Geometry, Trigonometry, Physics, Chemistry, Latin I, Latin II, French I, French II, World History, U.S. History, Sociology, Old Testament, New Testament. I passed *all* of my classes in four years and missed only three days out of school in the four years.

In my senior year I was given the Most Outstanding Student Award for the school. My brother received it previously, Leroy, my oldest brother, Leroy. He was kind of a pioneer in our family. He was two years ahead of me and he had already preceded me and he made a good record at that school. He'd gone to elementary school in Augusta, Georgia, so he knew the people. So I came in, I followed him. He was the one at school that would bank the money, go downtown with the money. At that time you'd carry a moneybag in your hand to the bank. Not now. And I'd go to the post office and get the mail, and I'd get a paper for the principal, things like that.

But let me tell you now, in 1945 on the bus, city bus, the bus driver said something I didn't like. He said, I was standing near the front of the bus, you know. "Get on the back in the back, you little so-and-so children. Get behind that white line."

And I sounded off on him, which was not normal in those days, in '45. "You drive that bus [and] get your eyes off us. That's your job, drive that bus." I was angry, and I was in ninth-grade class saying that. . . . Got to Twelfth Street, which was two blocks from the school, I pulled the cord to get off and on, when it was time to get off, and I wouldn't turn the cord a loose. I held the cord all the way, and the first stop I still had the cord. "Goooong," all the way. When the bus stopped I still had the cord. "Goooong." And then I swung out the door with the cord, okay.

He got out with his pistol. Put the pistol in my face like this. On the campus, and everybody gathered around—thought I was going to get shot. And God spoke to me, and said, "Turn your back to him. If he shoots you, let him shoot you in the back." I said, "Thank you Lord, hallelujah." I turned around, and he had the gun in my back. [He] walked behind me toward the school talking like that.

But I wasn't afraid to die then, for my rights, because see—I have always . . . I was in danger before [Martin Luther] King, for our rights as individuals of this country. I was not going to be intimidated by a bus driver even when I was in high school. So that's an experience with that bus driver then. However, the principal never called me to the office to find out what I did, and he got fired. He lost his job.

ML: You mean the bus driver or the principal?

NI: The bus driver. I didn't see him on the bus anymore.

So then in the same year, in '45, I was working on this job and my supervisor was Elaine Corbett, a white little lady from Sallie, South Carolina. And she told me I could go to church that Easter Sunday, and I bought a suit to come here to Storm Branch [Baptist Church]. This is my church. I was baptized in this church. In 1943 I was baptized in this church, in 1943, sixty-one years ago, September 12th.

Then, she said, "You can't go to church Sunday. I've changed my mind."

I said, "Well you can't change your mind." In those days white folks don't need you to talk back to them. But I always talked back to white folks or black folks if I needed to *[laughs]*. She couldn't understand me talking back to her. "You can't change your mind."

"Yes, I can."

Long story short, she and I got into it, which is not normal, and she *bit* me, okay. Here's the mark right here! You see it?

ML: Yes. And she *bit* you?

NI: Yes, and if a white lady put your hand in her mouth in '45 *[laughs]*. Been there sixty years.

ML: You have the marks . . .

NI: Like Paul.

ML: Yes, I was going to say, just like Paul, marks on my body. *[This refers to the Apostle Paul, Galatians 6:17.]*

NI: See I was in danger before King. You can't find a black man can tell you that a white lady put his hand in her mouth in '45—you find one, Lare, let me know, hear?—that's still alive.

ML: A lot of them wouldn't have been alive. Was she with the school?

NI: She was the manager of the restaurant where I worked.

ML: Oh, I see.

NI: She was my supervisor. She was in charge of the restaurant.

ML: Yes. Was she objecting to you going to this church?

NI: No, it was just the fact that she wanted me to work on Easter Sunday because they were going to be busy that weekend at the restaurant, so she thought I should work and I had planned to be off.

So I quit and got a job the next week at the drugstore up the street and worked there a month. But up there I didn't get any tips. [Before] I would carry, like fried chicken, to the hotels and motels and I got tips. But carrying medicine out to the people, they said, "Tell the doctor I'll see him the first of the month." They'd drag to the door, and I mean no money, no tips.

ML: At least you had a better wage, but not tips.

NI: And—at the restaurant—I had fried chicken to eat, hot rolls, French fries, when I got there from school. That was quite a treat. But the owner of the restaurant—James Warren Sanford, a graduate of Georgia Tech, he was one of the finest men, and he taught me how not to be prejudice against white folks, okay. He helped me a lot because I've never had a problem with white folks or any kind of folks, and he did a lot because he accepted us just as people, okay. He accepted my brother and he accepted me as just people—he said, "Come back to work."

I went back to work, and she's still there and nothing's said, you know. He would allow us to sit in his car with him, up front, and go to his house and eat at his table. We would pick his peaches, sell his peaches, and there was no feeling of being black around James Warren, of being inferior or nothing like that. He died at ninety-three years of age, and I went to see him in the hospital and he just hugged me. He said, "Nathan," he said, "Nathan," he just cried. I mean, he was just a blessing to us, and his dad was a blessing to us. So that was an episode in that day.

Also, on the bus one day, coming from Augusta to North Augusta, there was a white man who lived in Augusta that was very prejudiced towards blacks. He would sit back in the back of the bus so he'd leave a few seats for us. He'd always get down, that way he would put up a barrier.

ML: As far back as he could?

NI: Yes. So one day Gertrude got on the bus at Thirteenth Street [and] she stepped on his foot by mistake. He slapped her, *Bam!* And a fight ensued. We were hitting each other left and right, on the Thirteenth Street Bridge of the Savannah River, punching it out, eleven-thirty at night, left and the right, left and the right. There was no conversation about what happened, in fact, he just, *Pow!*

ML: Tensions were so high?

NI: Yes, fighting like that. The bus driver's name was Ted, and Ted stopped the bus on the bridge, came back there—quietened [*sic*] us down. One fellow had a knife coming out like this, a weapon. . . . My brother over there, Leroy Irvin, was on the bus, Robert Lee Key on the bus, and others on the bus. But what happened was Ted—he was from Pennsylvania, I think, and I tell you, you can tell Pennsylvanians.

So we got across the river in North Augusta, [Ted] stopped the bus—at eleven thirty. He took the white man by his tie and put him off the bus, got his wife, put her off the bus, got his son, put him off the bus, and the bus rolled on. And we stayed on the bus. He put them off in the darkness of night [with no buses running], and it *cold* [*laughs*].

ML: Oh, that took some courage on his part.

NI: Yes.

ML: Were there other whites on the bus at the time?

NI: Oh, yes, the whole bus was full.

ML: And everybody knew that [the man] was a troublemaker?

NI: Yes. So—I will never forget that experience.

And in 1957 I was driving from a basketball game on Lugoff Avenue in Augusta going to my brother of choice's [*"of choice": a phrase Irvin uses in reference to in-laws and stepchildren*] home and I was attacked by four whites on Park Avenue. There were four of us in the car and four of them, and the driver of that car's name was Julian Reese, a white guy from . . . Georgia, and he tried to push me off the road and I wouldn't let him push me off the road, and he didn't like that. We got to the stop sign. He got out the car. All four of them came to our car, and I let my windows up with my hands quick as I could because he was going to punch me in the face. But he hit the glass and shattered my glass and not a bit of glass hit my face, Lare. Listen, God shielded my face from that glass. *Bam!* Knocked the glass out. And of the four of us, three said, "Let's get out," but I had just begun teaching school.

I started teaching school in 1956 here in Aiken County, and I was a minister and I didn't want to get out there and show myself ignorant, so I said, "No. We won't get out. Get the tag number and when I get to my brother of choice's house, we'll call the police department."

We called the police department, and they came to the house, which is uncommon, and asked, "What happened to you?" I told them, and in twenty-five minutes they said, "We got them. Come down to Harrisburg"—which is a place where blacks couldn't go in the daytime, much less at night, in Augusta.

I went down to Harrisburg that night, and there were four whites down there. Had a line-up down there. Patrol wagon was down there and he said to me—the white policeman, wasn't no black policemen then—"Which one did it?"

I said, "That's the man."

And he wouldn't let him talk. He would not hear the white man. He said, "If he says you did it, you did it," and he handcuffed Julian Reese. Put him in the patrol wagon. At my word, he carried him to jail. That's unheard of in Georgia in '57. So he went to jail quarter till twelve that Friday night. He said [to me], "Be to court tomorrow morning at nine." He stood trial the next day at nine o'clock. What quick justice! *[He laughs.]*

ML: Yes.

NI: So the next morning at nine o'clock I was at the courtroom on Ninth Street in Augusta, and there we were in the courtroom all crowded. . . . And the judge—Lare, listen carefully again, this is God again, so all the things I'm telling you about now, look at God, okay, because they're not common. They're not made by man, so what I tell you today is not of Irvin, it's a higher power, because what happened to me now is not common—the judge never questioned me. Can you imagine? In the courtroom he questioned a white man but never questioned me, what I did, or why or anything, and he found him guilty, and so many days in jail, and was fined.

And a white policeman came to me after that and said, "Look here. Let's go to superior court for aggravated assault," a higher court on Green Street for the same crime. I went to court on Green Street in the bigger court, and there the judge never questioned me again.

And [the defendant] told the judge, "He cursed me."

The judge said that I had said that I didn't curse anybody, he was the one cursing. "He's guilty." He found him guilty again and sentenced him so much money, a fine, and stuff like that.

After that the police came to me again, which is uncommon. They said this is the way to sue him. I said, "No, let him go. Okay?" And that was uncommon in the South, period.

In 1961 where I live right now—we built our house in 1960—and this is in the city of North Augusta. In other words, it's visible. In those days to be living in a visible part [of town] was uncommon for blacks. You needed to be back where "we can't see you." We built our house in 1960, and they tried to stop us from building our house where it is and so forth. We finally built and in July of '61 I came home and the windows were knocked out—my living room windows—the TV was damaged, the coffee table was damaged.

[Irvin is emotional. There is a long pause.]

ML: Deep pain *[long pause]*. It's all right *[very long pause]*. The nerves . . . they run deep, don't they? *[There is another long pause.]*

NI: When I called the police department in North Augusta they cursed me out. What in the . . . this kind of thing . . . They cursed me out.

I went to the FBI in Augusta and they gave me a negative response. Asked him, "What's the next step?"

He said, "Savannah."

Went to the FBI in Savannah and they came out. Ed Collins, who is an FBI agent, he lives in North Augusta now and he and I discussed [this] a few years ago—when I ran for [the South Carolina] House of Representatives he supported me—so we discussed this.

Anyway, a little car came by that night. A little Volkswagen came by, red, and we thought [this] may have been the person who did it. And every Volkswagen in North Augusta was checked out [by the FBI] and he finally found the right one and brought me the names of three whites. One was nineteen. One was twenty. One was twenty-one.

And he said to me, said, "What happened to you is because you're part of Dr. King." The FBI told me this, "These guys are punishing you because you are following Dr. King and moved up too fast."

And they brought these three names in, nineteen, twenty, and twenty-one, and a warrant for their arrest. And I said to Ed, I said, "No, Ed, let them go. I'm not going to put them in jail."

He went to their house that morning. The FBI went to their home and their parents were very, you know, tense, when they came to the door, and he told them that Reverend Irvin has dropped the charges and they dropped their heads.

I don't know their names, where they live. I didn't try to find out their names or where they lived, but I let them go after that. Those are some experiences that we've had.

Dr. King came to Augusta in '63 and I listened to him at Tabernacle Baptist Church. At that time there were not many people who [would] come out, especially those who were in education wouldn't come out.

But let me back up again though. There were a lot of things I skipped over. I'll back up. I went to the army. I went to State College in Orangeburg in 1949 as a freshman, paid my own way, all that. I got drafted in 1950 during the Korean War. Went to the army in Fort Jackson and Fort Bragg and came back in '53 at South Carolina State College. At that time I had my wife and one son. And so at State College I took my education, and really *today*, fifty years ago *today*—let me shake your hand on it—I was a senior at South Carolina State College, *today*, '54 to '55, and see over there on our right [*pointing to a plaque on the wall*]. See *Who's Who* right there? I was in *Who's Who at South Carolina State College.*

ML: Yes, uh-huh.

NI: I made that and I made the dean's list that year, all right, 3.0 average. At that time I had two sons, how do you like that, and a wife, living on the campus at South Carolina State College. That's my senior year there, and I was superintendent of Sunday school, I was president of the Social Studies Club, president of the [NA]ACP Club, and I pledged [Kappa] Alpha Psi fraternity that senior year. So I had a real busy year that year. In 1955 I graduated from with a B.A. degree in social studies.

After I graduated, I applied for a position at South Carolina State College, and also I decided to go to graduate school. President Turner, B. C. Turner, the president of State College at that time, said, "If you go to graduate school, we can't pay you full-time pay to be a full-time student." But they didn't treat me right because they didn't cut my hours but they cut my pay. Over 60 percent of my pay was cut. So I carried fifteen hours of graduate study, but I worked from eight thirty in the morning until five o'clock in the afternoon. I was assistant to the dean of men there, and I was in charge of the freshman boys in Loeman Hall and the veteran boys, but they did not pay me well, but I used the GI Bill that I had to supplement my pay in '55 to '56.

Now [that's when] the civil rights movement really started, you know about that?

ML: Yes.

IN: It started at South Carolina State College. The first demonstration by students in America against the administration [regarding civil rights] started at South Carolina State College, headed by Fred Moore, the president of the student council, which you are already aware of that period of time.

ML: This afternoon I'm interviewing Jim Sulton.

IN: All right. Good! He was part of that.

ML: He was the president [treasurer] of the NAACP chapter in Orangeburg that contacted Fred Moore to see whether the students would support their boycott of the white businesses that were persecuting the NAACP members. Is that not right?

NI: That's correct.

[There is a telephone interruption.]

ML: We were talking about the student demonstrations against the administration that year at South Carolina State. That was about what year?

NI: 1955 to '56. The mayor of Orangeburg was Jennings, and Mr. Sulton, as you know, was president of the NAACP. Sulton issued a manifesto, that you know about, and if you signed the manifesto you [were] liable to lose your job. Well, I signed it and I realized later that I was fired. I didn't realize I was fired till later because my contract was not renewed. Normally, as college staff they would allow you to make a decision on whether you're going to come back or not. But I signed the manifesto.

The problem was, they wanted to use the bowling alley—you know about the bowling alley—and Mayor Jennings owned the bowling alley. He owned Coble Milk. Coca-Cola belonged to Mayor Jennings and Sunbeam Bread. He had everything. We said to the president [Turner], don't buy any more Coca-Colas, no milk, no bread, and if you do buy it, we're not going to eat it. The students wrote on the grounds, "Uncle Tom, go home!" at night. They had an underground communication system.

Dean Benson and I were on the side of the students. So we didn't tell the [administration] anything. I had to be up at night. I lived on the lower part of the campus, but my job kept me into the evening time, eleven o'clock at night. I'd be in the dormitory, and the kids were throwing the trashcans down the hall, down the stairs, and all that.

I had to go to the cafeteria to watch them. I knew they were going to have a demonstration in the cafeteria, and they came in and they said their grace and all this fried chicken on the table and everything, and they just put their hands in the food and pushed it on the floor and walked out of the cafeteria. They didn't eat that fried chicken. Had lettuce and tomato and potato salad, ice tea.

And they came outside, and there hung from the tree [an effigy of] George Bell Tillman, the governor of South Carolina, hanging in the air. When you do that on a state campus . . . *[He laughs.]*

ML: Pouring oil on the fire, is it?

NI: I'll never forget it. *Jet* magazine covered that story. Had it hanging in the air. The kids walked out, and Dr. Turner fooled the kids that they were going to be all right. You can go back to school. You can go back to class. And when they did go back to class, then he just—*whack,* he hit the hammer—and fired some of the teachers. Dr. K. K. McMillan lost his job. Alfred Isaac left. Annie [last name is uncertain] was expelled. Libby Little was expelled. Fred Moore was expelled. My contract was not renewed. Things like that happened. That's *real* experience in the civil rights struggle. You had to go!

In Elloree the public school principal got fired. There were a lot of hard feelings, hurts and pains during '55 to '56, just an enormous experience.

ML: There wasn't really much of a national movement at that time. There were the law cases, the NAACP lawsuits, and so forth, but no mass movement.

NI: That's right. No movement at all. There was the law case led to establishing the Law School at South Carolina State College. Finney, Judge Finney, who was a student there because he couldn't get into the University of South Carolina, they started that school. *[The South Carolina State Law School graduated its first student in 1950. Ernest A. Finney, Jr. graduated in 1954.]* Ended up being [Chief] Justice of the [South Carolina] Supreme Court, how do you like that? *[He laughs.]*

ML: I interviewed him a couple of weeks ago.

NI: Isn't that a blessing? We went to school together. His dad was a professor [dean] at Claflin. We were in school together. . . .

[Dr. Irvin continues to describe his career in education and ministry. The second part of this interview will be found in volume 2.]

PART 3
National Leaders from South Carolina

Septima Poinsette Clark, Ready from Within

[Among the champions of civil and human rights in South Carolina, Septima Poinsette Clark (1898–1987) is one of a few towering figures whose life and career span the entire period this anthology includes. Included here are portions of two interviews appropriate to the "Movement Era" covered in volume 1 of this anthology. Other materials will be found in volume 3. The excerpt below appears approximately 1,900 words into the transcript.]

Dismissed

Grace McFadden [GM]:* You taught in the public school system of South Carolina up until what . . .

Septima Clark [SC]: I was teaching at the same time, until '56, and in January 1956, the state of South Carolina decided that no city or state employee could be a member of NAACP. There were 736 teachers in Charleston County, and we sat down at one of our meetings and wrote letters to them asking them to protest that thing. . . . the letters went to them, and *only* twenty-six answered. I can understand why. The system was that you didn't have work in those black ghettos. And they didn't want to lose those teaching jobs.

So anyway, twenty-six of them answered and we had a meeting with the twenty-six, and then what we decided to do was go down and see the superintendent. Mr. Rogers was superintendent at that time, that was in '56. When we got ready to go to see the superintendent, five of us went down to his office. It was on the corner of

*Grace Jordan McFadden was the first director of the African American Studies Program at the University of South Carolina which began in 1971. Among her many accomplishments in that field she conducted a series of path-breaking oral history interviews in conjunction with South Carolina Educational Television. This is a transcription of the audio from her video interview, conducted in 1982.

St. Philip and Moultrie Street at the time. . . . Anyway, we could be dismissed because there were only the five of us who wanted this kind of a change.

So we had three judge court hearings and thirty-one teachers from Clarendon County came in, and eleven from Charleston County, and they had the hearing. And Judge Anthony Williams, he's dead now, he said that he didn't know enough about—didn't have enough facts and he asked the [attorneys] to go back. . . . [They] came down to represent the teachers here, from New York. And he asked the lawyers to go back and file new briefs, and the very next day, after they went back and said they would need another month's time, the very next day the big headline came how the legislature was calling for another session, a special session of the legislature, or the senate . . . meanwhile, what happened . . . they changed the ruling. No city or state employee could be a member of a list [of "subversive organizations," including] the NAACP. The next year Jessica Brown listed her affiliation and she was dismissed, but she didn't push her case.

At the time, when they dismissed me, I was the only teacher who had had forty-one years of teaching, and I [qualified by the number of years] in teaching . . . to have a pension, but they didn't give me a pension at that time. The money that had been taken out of my money to put into the pension fund was given back, but they wouldn't give me what the state was supposed to put in. That's what I'm fighting today for, for the rest of my money [chuckles]. So it's been twenty years now and there should be thirty-six hundred dollars a year, for twenty years, which makes the state owing me seventy-two thousand dollars. I'm looking forward to get it! [1982]

GM: You were dismissed when you were how old?

SC: In '56 I was fifty-eight.

GM: So what did you do, Mrs. Clark?

Highlander Folk School

SC: I went to Highlander Folk School. Highlander Folk School was anxious to get me, and they made me director of education. I started that first college workshop, and got those boys, Stokley Carmichael and John Lewis and [the Reverend James] Bevel, and the rest of them into a workshop up there. And a Dr. [James] Jackson, who is now down [inaudible]. . . . After we got together up there, Ella Baker, who was seated on Saturday night [at an SCLC banquet], came in and organized them into the Student Nonviolent Coordinating Committee. And they started Freedom Rides and the other things.

GM: Where was Highlander Folk School?

SC: It was in Tennessee. It was a school for problems, a school that helped people get rid of problems. It started with the labor movements—I can remember down in North Carolina, the eastern part of North Carolina, we tried to help labor union people, and then it came to some parts of South Carolina, when they had trouble with labor unions there. And then they went on to Tennessee with the strip miners and the people who worked with the [inaudible]. . . . But it's really a school for problems.

And when it got to the blacks here, we had to eliminate illiteracy, because we had twelve million people who couldn't read nor write in eleven Deep South states. So I sat down night after night at Highlander and worked out a program called "Citizenship Education Schools," teaching these people how to write their names, how to read, how to send off money orders for what they wanted, and things of that type.

GM: How long did you remain with Highlander?

SC: Four years.

GM: What caused you to leave and where did you go?

SC: When I left Highlander—Dr. King came up in 1957 and wanted the program, but Highlander was closed because we catered to blacks and because we catered to blacks, they [the State of Tennessee] closed up Highlander, and we [continued] . . . to teach but we went to another building. Nevertheless, Dr. King said he would love to have our program because it would expandthe Southern Christian Leadership Conference, which he did.

Southern Christian Leadership Conference

SC: And they sent me to Atlanta then, to do the work with the Southern Christian Leadership Conference, and I started holding workshops at a place in Liberty County, Georgia, and black people from all over the South piled in buses that brought them to this center in Liberty County, Georgia, and taught them. People who could read, ... write legibly came and they learned how to teach others, and when they learned how to teach others about their government under which they were living, how to write their names and about the crops and things they were growing, then they were able to go back and teach.

They held schools in their kitchens, under the . . . trees in their yards, if it was summertime, in beauty parlors and the like. And we would go and visit them from one place to another, to see if they were doing the thing right, and then we would go down with these people to the [voter] registration office. Most of them were afraid to go to attempt to register their name. See, that was a dangerous thing to do. A man in Selma, he said, "I've lived dangerously all my life. I tried to resister three times." He said, "Lord, that's a dangerous thing to do." And it was, because the White Citizen's Council killed three of our people coming from northern Virginia all the way to eastern Texas, while we were registering voters.

GM: What were some of the painful experiences of that whole . . .

SC: When I was arrested and they tried to put the hammerlock on me in Tennessee, because I was teaching about twelve whites and sixty blacks in one room, and they didn't like that. And so they [threw me in jail], but you know, two white [missionary] teachers came about two o'clock that morning and paid five hundred dollars to get me out of that thing. And as soon as I got out [of] there and I went back and did my workshop again, that next morning.

Another thing was the White Citizens' Council, when I was in Natchez, Mississippi, a fellow came and kicked one of the white fellows working with me and I just went to the telephone and called Washington, and it wasn't too long before the chief of police sent protection for the men, for the people who were at the courthouse with the people wanting to register and vote.

And then when I was in Grenada, Mississippi, we were having a court trial and it was a prosecuting attorney [who] came over to me and he wanted to make me somebody else. He said, "Aren't you—?" The woman who used to work with the NAACP.

GM: You're thinking of Ruby?

SC: Ruby Hurley. "Aren't you Ruby?" I said, "No, I'm not Ruby Hurley." But I wouldn't tell him my name. I just wouldn't tell him. So anyway, he was real angry and when he went back, and I sat there. I wouldn't let him see that I was nervous about it. Because just that night before, we were having a meeting in the church in Grenada, and you know what happened? We stepped out of that church, and about five minutes after we stepped out, that whole church burned up. And we don't know how those men got in there to put those things in every corner of that church while we were still sitting in there. . . . That's what they did.

Successes

GM: What do you think were the greatest successes of the Southern Christian Leadership Conference?

SC: Today I see the fruits. Saturday night and Sunday night there were 350 seated young people, they were mostly young people, who worked in the Student Nonviolent Coordinating Committee who had come to honor Ella Baker, who was the [first] executive director of the Southern Christian Leadership Conference at that time. That was never shown on the pictures. And those young people are carrying [things forward], wherever they are. No end of it. Marion Barry, the mayor of Washington. Jim Forman, working with the [SNCC] group. Charles Horwitz, with the [the Freedom Information Service and others] in Washington, D.C. I just . . . *[inaudible]* . . . richest foundations of New York City. And on the West Coast there was Harriet Temsley *[uncertain],* from Los Angeles. There were over fifteen or more states represented and for those young people to be carrying on this flag of the Southern Christian Leadership Conference, I call it the fruitful success of the Southern Christian Leadership Conference and the civil rights movement.

And if America is going to be the America that Dr. King spoke about, if we are going to redeem the soul of America, then we must think of every nationality, the Puerto Ricans, the Mexican Americans, the Spanish-speaking Americans. If you . . . *[inaudible]* . . . they all have their rights. And this is the kind of thing that I think we need to consider as we work and vote.

GM: Thank you very much, Mrs. Clark.

Du Bois, King, and Clark

[This portion of a different interview with Septima Clark is excerpted approximately 1,400 words into the transcript. Portions of the earlier part will be found in volume 3 of this anthology.]

W. E. B. Du Bois

Jean-Claude Bouffard **[JCB]:*** . . . You met with W. E. B. Du Bois?

Septima Clark **[SC]:** I had a class under him in 1937 at Atlanta University, "Interpersonal Relationships," and I was very happy that I had the chance to . . . because I got on a trolley car, they didn't have buses then, and a young woman came in with a baby in her arms and a little boy, and the little boy sat in the front of the car, and she was so worried.

She said, "Come back here! Come back here. You can't sit there."

And he said, "I'm Mama's little man. Why can't I sit here?" He didn't understand.

So I told Du Bois that in the class, our class met at four o'clock in the afternoon, and he said, "Later on, you're going to be able, when you are able to register and vote, to sit in the front of the bus." The book that he wrote around 1903 *[The Souls of Black Folk]* I see coming to pass now, the things that he said in that book way back in 1903. Then again I met Du Bois. I went to New York and was fundraising for the Highlander Folk School in '57, and I went over to his house. He was in Brooklyn at that time. And he was about to make a trip to Massachusetts, and had just come back from China. I had a chance to speak with him personally again. That time I had been dismissed from South Carolina schools.

JCB: For your activism?

SC: For my activism in the NAACP. The state said that no city or state employee could be a member of the NAACP, and most teachers said that they were not members,

---

*Jean-Claude Bouffard, a visiting professor from France, conducted the interview at the College of Charleston, Charleston, South Carolina, sometime between July 20 and August 5, 1982.

and I didn't feel as if I could live with myself if I [denied it], and I told them that if white teachers could be members of the White Citizens' Council and the Ku Klux Klan, I should be able to be a member of the NAACP. Otherwise, I said, they'll tell me what church to go to, what committees to attend, and so I was dismissed. And not only that, my pension was taken away from me. I'm still fighting to get my current pension back. Yes.

JCB: What sort of a man was Dr. Du Bois? I've read some of his work, but you're the first person I have come across who . . .

SC: Studied under him?

JCB: Yes, and actually met him personally and had a chance to come to close quarters.

SC: I felt as if I never could have the *feeling* that he had. I don't know if you know, when his first child died in Atlanta, Georgia, he didn't want to bury it there. He felt as if he didn't want the soil, the Georgia soil, to cover the body of his baby. He was just so *extremely* angry with the system that he found living there and working at that institution. I've never felt that way about people. I always had a feeling that they were reared in one culture and I'm in another, and so I can't have hate in my heart. I thought if I have hate in my heart it's going to hurt me. I felt that he had a little bit too much hate in his heart. He died in Africa the night before we had the march. *[This was the March on Washington. Du Bois lived from February 23, 1868 to August 27, 1963.]*

JCB: Yes. Well, I was going to try, since you knew both men, Dr. Du Bois and Dr. King, if you could tell me more about . . . You said Dr. Du Bois had this hatred of the system—

SC: That's true.

Martin Luther King Jr.

JCB: Not so, apparently, Dr. King?

SC: Not at all.

JCB: This man was absolutely incapable of hatred, from what I've heard from people who knew him.

SC: That's true. That's right. Well, I sat on the front seat in Birmingham, Alabama, in 1963—it must have been '63, before he went to Europe—I went to Europe with him.

JCB: For the Nobel Prize?

SC: That's right. I was in Paris. I don't know if you were there in '64.

[There are technical problems with the tape.]

SC: A Nazi came up and slapped him in the face, and he dropped his hands just like a newborn baby and didn't try to fight back. And he called Rosa Parks—she was on the front seat—and asked her to get this man a bottle of Coca-Cola because he felt he needed something cold to drink *[laughs]*. I knew that [King] had this stab wound over his heart, and I said to this man, "Don't hit him. Don't hit him. Hit me instead."

He had just had an examination for that stab wound. He was altogether different. Then I was on the plane coming from Montgomery to Atlanta, and a Nazi, too, a big tall fellow, came up and stood over him, Dr. King, and said, "You're reading about yourself, aren't you?" He was reading the paper. He said, "I'm reading the news." He drew back to hit him but there was a man on that plane as a steward instead of a stewardess, and he grabbed this fellow and put him in the back. You know, he got up again and tried to hit Dr. King, but that time they chained him in the back seat—this was a little Southern plane. When we got out of that plane, Dr. King was just laughing, saying, "Nearly got me, didn't he?" He didn't feel a bit angry.

He really helped me to change my ideas, too, about things like that. My mother was altogether different. If you didn't do things just like she did, if you weren't just like her, then she couldn't like you at all. My father was real nonviolent. He came out of slavery nonviolent, and I'm glad that I got more of him, because he gave wood to those soldiers, and water, when the Yankees came to free him, down there on that Battery. And for his work in that Civil War, he refused a pension, up to his death in 1927, of eight dollars a year *[laughs]*. And my mother couldn't stand it. She said, "Just take it and go buy your peanuts and sit down and eat them." She didn't like it at all. She was different.

But you know, I'm glad for her courage though. She had a schedule. We didn't play until Friday afternoon. Then we could go to our aunts' and play with their children, on Fridays. All the other days she had your work cut out for you when you come from school—washing and ironing and cleaning and something. She really had a real schedule. Three meals a day, hot meals in the wintertime for eight children, and two hot meals in the summer, with a cold supper. I felt that she was really a wonderful person, and when I was surrounded by the Klan in Natchez, Mississippi, and arrested in Tennessee, my mother's courage helped me to feel that these people aren't too bad, but they're doing this to try to prove a kind of a system.

And the reason why I said that was because two white women, two missionary women, in Tennessee, the mountains of Tennessee, came, two o'clock in the morning, to take me out of the prison. They had a check that the man would not receive. They had to go back and get cash dollars, which they did. Wherever I've been in the eleven Deep South states, I've found warm hearts in some of the white people around me. Not all of them, though. You know . . .

Highlander Folk School

JCB: You have a certainly. . . . In what circumstances did you come to know Dr. King? Do you recall?

SC: Oh, yes. I was teaching at the Highlander Folk School, in Monteagle, Tennessee, and Mrs. King was coming to Chattanooga to speak. I went down there to hear Mrs. King speak, and while there, Dr. King came.

JCB: Can you recall approximately the year when this was?

SC: Fifty-seven, early '57. I went to Highlander the latter part of '56. That's when I was dismissed from the public schools here. And so Dr. King came, and I'm going to tell you how funny black people are. People seeing me at Highlander, you know we didn't dress up—I still don't—and a woman rode about twelve miles, coming up on top of Lookout Mountain, where I was staying for that night, to ask me if I had a black dress that was suitable to stand in line with Mrs. King and to meet Dr. King. Otherwise she didn't want me to stand in that line *[laughs]*. There are materialistic people that want you to dress up all the time.

JCB: Dr. King, therefore, was some sort of a celebrity already?

SC: Oh, sure. He was preaching then at Montgomery, back and forth, though.

JCB: Dexter Avenue Baptist Church?

SC: That's right, yes. I've been there.

The Future of the South

JCB: What [were] your first impressions of him? [And] when you came to know him at somewhat closer quarters?

SC: Yes, in August of '57 Highlander celebrated its twenty-fifth anniversary, and Dr. King was the speaker. It took about two years to get Dr. King to come—he had so many things. Anyway, Dr. King came. Aubrey Williams, of the Southern Regional Council, spoke about the South was playing with fire. That was his subject, and he painted a terrible picture of decadent whites from the South. Dr. King came behind that, and he spoke about a look to the future, and he pointed to all the wonderful things that he recommended that would happen, and it's really coming true. Integration, the desegregation, and unionization. Those were the three things that he talked about. And there were people from Alabama going all through the library, looking at books and talking to Myles Horton. The people at Sewanee, the seminarians, were up there for their one hundredth anniversary, and they all came down that morning, and that yard around us was just filled with people. We had loud speakers all out there. It was a wonderful morning for me, and I was so glad that Dr. King could come behind Aubrey Williams and . . . was there also. I was so glad that he could come behinds them and let them know his feelings. He said if we could survive slavery, we can come through with this. It was a great speech, really. I felt that this was the man we need to follow. This was the person that was going to help you to make thing come right.

JCB: Later on I would imagine you came to know him at closer quarters, more personally.

SC: Oh, yes, because I worked with him.

The Private Person

JCB: What were the differences between the public figure and the orator, the man who could hold the crowd enthralled and spellbind them by his oratorical gift, and the private person? This is something with which I have difficulty grappling, because as a private person he's almost not known.

SC: Yes, that's the truth. And as a private person I worked with him, and we were establishing citizenship schools all over the eleven Deep South states. We had about 195 schools. Well, I came into South Carolina and was going to a little town called Wagener to give these people who were going to have classes—to teach them how to read and write so they could register and vote—and when I got back to Atlanta that Monday morning, Dr. King's secretary came to me and wanted to know, did I say anything about Dr. King while I was talking to these people?

And I said, "Well, sure. I let them know that Dr. King is the man who's head over all this thing." Although the Marshall Field Foundation was giving us money to open up all these schools, still the spirit of Dr. King was the thing that I talked very much about. And I was surprised to find out that he felt that everywhere you go you should always mention it. I thought that was a sort of a selfish spirit.

JCB: Would you repeat that please?

SC: I felt that was a sort of a selfish spirit.

[There are sounds of others coming into room, unintelligible. Apparently, introductions are being made, including Sophie.]

SC: And Sophie is at my house practically every day. We're good friends. It's a bit cramped [here].

JCB: Would you like me to turn the seat? Or you'd be more comfortable because I . . .

SC: That's all right. Okay.

JCB: That's a bit better. If you'd like to rest your legs perhaps?

SC: No, I'm all right. That's fine.

JCB: You know, it's very impressive for me to meet somebody who was there such a long time.

SC: Long time. Oh, yes! And I was so . . . Well, I was talking about Dr. King.

JCB: Yes, ma'am.

SC: And there was another thing that I found. There was a worker with me, Dorothy Cotton, and she found out that when you worked in the church that they wanted every organization to be headed by a King, and she couldn't take it, so she decided she couldn't work with the man. Well, she's still in Atlanta, though, working with Mrs. King.

He Felt He Had to Go

SC: We had a big meeting with members from all over the South, and the men were talking and they felt that Dr. King should lead most of the marches, and I said, "You're going to kill your leader. You don't need him to lead every march. After you have been developed, you should be able to go into Albany, with a guy there from Albany."

JCB: That's true.

SC: Yes. And lead some of the things.

JCB: Are you talking about Dr. Anderson? Was that Dr. Anderson?

SC: No, it was a Reverend, and I can't think of his name.

JCB: Conrad?

SC: No. Another guy from Albany, Georgia. I know who it is. Charles Sherrod [SNCC activist in southwest Georgia], that's who it was. I saw him the other day when I was in Atlanta. Anyway, just before he got ready to go back into Memphis, in '68, I said to Dr. King, "No!" I wrote him a letter—and I asked him not to go, because I felt that Andy Young was over there, and James Bevel, and why shouldn't they lead the march? He didn't have to go and lead a second march. Well, they had a meeting and he read this letter that I sent him to the group, and of course everybody was laughing at me for trying to save Dr. King. He didn't want to save himself, he felt that he had to go. So anyway, I spoke to some of the secretaries and asked them to talk to him, too, and you know, not one of them would open their mouths at that meeting to say what I said to him. And just before he went, I was in Washington working with the American Friends Service Committee for seven days, talking to representatives of the nine southeastern states, and I heard about him going into Memphis, and about the people who—how the boys in the back of the line [of the march] were smashing [windows]. So *again* I tried to say something to him about not going to Memphis, but he felt that he had to go there, and that he had to lead the march, the second march, and it had to be a nonviolent march.

[On] the Sunday before he went he had dinner with his mother, and he told his mother he thought this was going to be the end. That Monday morning when he went down to the plane there was a bomb threat, and he waited there, and went on. And then that Thursday was the time he was killed. Well, I was back here by then, back from Washington, and right at my house that Sunday night when I came back, Lyndon Johnson decided that he wouldn't run for a third [*sic*] term. I don't know if you remember him saying that his daughter said, "Daddy, why does Robb have to go?" That was her newlywed husband. And so he decided that he wouldn't run for a third term. He thought that the war in Vietnam, we thought too, was just an unjust war. Anyway, the fireman came to my house, and I said, "There's no fire here." He came rushing in, and I had my grandchildren and great-grandchildren, and then a little bit after that, that same Sunday night, here come the policemen. They heard there was a fight here. But, "There's no fight here." And I thought there's something spreading around that I knew must have been happening everywhere, and that Thursday, that's when Dr. King's death came.

When I heard of his death, there was a young man here working, Farris, and he'd been working with SCLC. He was here and he decided he'd go on to Atlanta. Well, a German woman called me all the way from Germany that night—she'd heard the news. A fellow from Holland called me that night too. There was a man that lived down at Sheldon, South Carolina, and his wife was an Englishwoman. He came up with his wife and two children. They slept on this floor that night. They were nervous, you know, very much so. And a cousin of mine, also. So we spent the night, that whole night, talking and working here. Dr. King was due in Denmark, South Carolina, and on to Columbia that day, but he decided he just must go into Memphis. That was something he couldn't keep away from.

JCB: Did you have any premonition that he was going to meet his death in Memphis?

SC: Oh, I felt it a long time ago because I was at Richmond, Virginia, when a group came up there and they were so angry, just so angry. His mother just cried that day at that meeting. It wasn't too long before. And then I went to another place, wasn't Virginia this time, and they were— Oh, it was a new politics convention in Chicago, and blacks and whites just paraded through those aisles, with all of those placards. "Down with King. He's too nonviolent." All kinds of things. I just couldn't see how he could live much longer. We got him on a plane that night back to Atlanta, before he could get hurt.

JCB: In Chicago.

SC: In Chicago, yes.

How He Evolved

JCB: How did you see Dr. King evolve over the years from this young, newly famous preacher that you met at Monteagle to the world figure that . . . and down to Memphis? How did he change personally?

SC: To me, I think he must have been brought up as a highly middle-class boy, because his mother had so much money. She schooled the father, and then here comes Martin Luther and the other boy and girl, with all of the materialistic things around them. Then I saw him—well, you know—he went to school, and coming back from school, he said that he studied about Gandhi, and he felt that he had to follow the teachings of Gandhi, which he really did.

And when he received his fifty-four thousand dollars there in Europe, he stood on that stage and said that he would not keep one penny. He said, "I'm on the top of the mountain now, but the people in the valley have been the ones who have put me up here. I must go back to them and I must give all of this money to them." So when he came back to New York, you know, they had the red carpet out, and all the limousines, and we marched around to the courthouse down there, and he made a speech. Then that afternoon at the armory—no, it wasn't at the armory that afternoon, it was at the Waldorf-Astoria Hotel—we had all of these famous actors and actresses in line, talking to Dr. King. And then that night he went to the armory, and when we went to the armory, those boys who were murdered in Mississippi. . . .

[Three Congress of Racial Equality (CORE) field workers were killed in Philadelphia, Mississippi, by the Ku Klux Klan in response to their civil rights work during what became known as "Freedom Summer," dedicated to voter registration. They were James Chaney, a twenty-one-year-old black man from Meridian, Mississippi; Andrew Goodman, a twenty-year-old, white, Jewish anthropology student from New York; and Michael Schwerner, a twenty-four-year-old, white, Jewish CORE organizer and former social worker, also from New York.]

JCB: Schwerner, Chaney, Goodman?

SC: Yes. Their father—Chaney and Goodman, and what's the other one? Schwerner?

JCB: Schwerner.

SC: Their parents were there, and they all talked, and Dr. King stood up on that platform and gave away every penny of that money. I can't forget Mrs. King. I was sitting behind her.

She said, "We have children. He should be thinking about our children." He said, "Our children will be taken care of, even when I'm gone."

JCB: By Harry Belafonte?

SC: Who?

JCB: It was Harry Belafonte who made sure that Dr. King subscribed for a large life insurance.

SC: Is that so?

And then Harry Belafonte came there one day and Mrs. King was having trouble with the children running in and out, and he said he would pay for her to get a helper in the house, and he did. And then, too, when Dr. King was killed, he and his wife came down and took over the house with the children. He did a wonderful job.

JCB: How did you see Dr. King, as a person, change over the years? The early years were marked by significant successes, in Birmingham certainly, and at least on the national level brought about the Civil Rights Act, and there was Selma, and the Voting Rights Act, so there was a sort of attention, and then Dr. King goes to Chicago and—and apparently he gets [rebuffed]. And then he comes out against the war and alienates a large number of his fellow leaders, and also [he] becomes persona non grata in the White House. How did this have an impact on him, so far as you saw him?

SC: Well, in Birmingham I saw him being arrested, and I saw the policemen putting the hammer [hammerlock] upon him. In those years, at that time— What's the man's name who runs that motel?

JCB: Bull Connor?

SC: Oh, yes, Bull Connor was the head of the police department, but there was a man who ran a motel.

JCB: Gaston? J. P. Gaston?

SC: Gaston, that's right. We were right here when he came up, and those policemen were very rough. He went up to— Dr. King didn't try to fight back or move.

Marches

SC: Now, when we were in Selma, the first time we marched across the bridge, it was really terrible.

JCB: You were in that first march when John Lewis was beaten up?

SC: That's right. And the second time we had so many people who came with us, nuns and Catholic fathers, and a lot of—well, 250,000—and I was walking from that hospital to Selma, in front of . . .

But before I got to march the end of the week, I had a busload of people coming from various parts of Alabama, taking them into Georgia, and I taught them non-violence, and then we came back that Thursday morning to march to Montgomery. I brought my busload of people, and we were supposed to only be guarded until four o'clock that afternoon, and they were so late with that program, when that clock struck four and we were standing down there in front of the church—I knew those soldiers were going to turn on us and they did.

Now I'd lost two of my people off the bus, and I sent the secretary to look for them, Miss Harper, and she couldn't find them, so I got out, and I think on account of my gray hair I was able to go through that crowd [laughs]. They didn't try to kill me but they ran the girl back with their swords. And I went all the way to the church, and I found those two and I brought them back and got them on the bus.

By the time I got [back] to Georgia, there was a crowd of whites there, just as angry as they could be, and I said—I had one or two whites on the bus with me, from Georgia—I said, "Don't get out of this bus, because if you get out of this bus I'm afraid they're going to get on you." So he stayed on the bus and he didn't try to get out to get anything from the luncheon counter that they had over there. But while we were in the march, Father Kelly from Charleston was marching beside me and somebody else, and there was a white fellow on the sidewalk and, oh, he was terribly angry, and Father Kelly wanted to go over and speak to him. I said, "Father Kelly, if you leave this line"—we were in the middle of the street, you know—"we'll never find you. He'll take you into a side door of one of those stores, and we'll never find you, so you better stay with us." And he did—he didn't go. Dr. King was happy, though, that so many people joined us in our second march in Selma.

I told you about the march in Detroit, and in Chicago.

[The interviews of Jean Claude Bouffard with Septima Clark continue for over seven thousand words. Some portions will be found in volume 5. Marvin Ira Lare, editor of this anthology, went to Selma after the first and second marches were turned back. He participated in the successful march to Montgomery. His account of the experience will be found in the appendix of volume 3 of this anthology.]

James T. "Nooker" McCain, Field Director, Congress of Racial Equality

Grace McFadden **[GM]:*** I'm Grace Jordan McFadden, talking with Mr. James T. McCain, a native of Sumter, South Carolina, an educator, a civil rights leader, a former field director in the Congress of Racial Equality, and one of the great citizens of this state.

Mr. McCain, we might begin by asking you, what was the Congress of Racial Equality?

James T. McCain **[JTMC]:** The Congress of Racial Equality, I think, changed. It really was a splinter organization to begin with. It was founded by six students in Chicago University in the early '40s. It was an organization that fought discriminations on all levels. The first group that started the CORE was a group of students who could not live on campus. These were four white students and two black students. They could not go to the bowling alleys, the skating rinks—that's the way it started. That's the conception of it. Now it was a part—at that time it did not have a national image as such, and as [the] students left the University of Chicago, those affiliated with the first founding of CORE tried to organize splinter groups in the community where they went.

Now the purpose of CORE when I started working with CORE, and started out, was to try to eliminate discrimination on all levels. Of course this was in the late '50s. Later on, CORE changed because of the whole civil rights movement. The whole impact of the total civil rights movement in the late '50s and the '60s changed the very foundation of all, not only CORE, but I think all the civil rights organizations . . .

*Grace Jordan McFadden interviewed McCain, Videotaped in the South Carolina Educational Television studio, c. 1982.

CORE was . . . known as a *direct* [action], nonviolent organization. In other words, we attacked the discrimination directly, through confrontation. That was the early way CORE got started.

GM: You became aligned with CORE in 1950 . . . ?

JTMC: Fifty-seven. In the fall of 1957, I was hired as a field—what we called at that time a field secretary.

GM: What exactly was the function of a field secretary?

JTMC: Our function was to go into communities and try to get people, black people, black and white, to come together and do something tangible about discrimination in their areas. At that time, CORE had never been south. The furthest south CORE had ever been was Baltimore. It had chapters out in St. Louis, Los Angeles, and other areas, but it had never made any impact upon the South, because southern people had never heard about CORE.

So after I became the field staff person, and because I was a southerner, I was given the opportunity to see, could we form CORE groups in the Deep South, and we were fortunate. Some of the "areas," they were all black. Some of the other southern "areas" there were white and black. But might I say, at that time, it was a risk for white people, in certain of these areas, to even work with blacks in any relationship, because in even the Council on Human Relations, in the state of South Carolina, many white people were pressured because they came to meetings by the Council on Human Relations. Just to sit down and talk about the problems. So it was really pretty bad when it first started out, but this condition kind of relieved itself as time went on.

GM: What do you think were some of your major accomplishments as field director of CORE?

JTMC: I think that some of the major—the major is to see that these places were open. I think the greatest thing, because of this, in 1959, Jackie Robinson came to Greenville to speak for a conference of NAACP. When Jackie Robinson got off his plane in Greenville—it was Greenville-Spartanburg airport—they refused him admittance to come through the *white waiting room!* He told us about it at that meeting that night. Reverend J. H. Hall, who was a Baptist minister, wanted to do something about it, so they wrote the national office and asked that I come down, and I went to Greenville. So what we did, we got all the ministers in that area together. They didn't want to have confrontations with the whites so they were kind of reluctant, but they did come together, because we told them we wouldn't do this. So what we did, we planned our strategy for Emancipation Day, which was January the 1st [1960]. What we did, we said we were going to drive out to the airport and confront the airport officials.

The mayor of Greenville didn't want it to happen. They tried to compromise, so we told them we wouldn't do that. "Go ahead. We will not give you a police escort out to the airport." The airport was about ten miles from Greenville.

To our surprise, when we got to the emancipation program, about 150 cars left, and sure enough, we had a police escort. So when we got out there we had state highway patrolmen to help park cars. But the most, I think, alarming thing that I had ever seen, going up to Greenville airport you had to go up a hill, and when we started up that hill, there was a mass of white people in front of the Greenville airport. You couldn't hardly see it. They were just strung out, about three hundred of them. No white person had ever been to a meeting of ours. We didn't know what this was for, because the papers had played it up and everything else.

So we had to kind of regroup our forces, because it caught us off guard. We didn't know what to expect. So Reverend Hall, his wife and I, we marched three abreast. We were the leaders. Reverend "Quincey" Newman [I. DeQuincey Newman], NAACP officials were right behind us. When we got up there, to our surprise, Mrs. Alice Spearman, a white lady who was director for South Carolina Council on Human Relations, she had a group of three hundred whites who were in favor of us, and they helped us sing songs. We presented a petition to the people up there at the airport, and in less than three weeks they desegregated the airport.

GM: What were some of your most difficult missions with CORE?

JTMC: Some of the most difficult missions that I encountered was in the state of Mississippi. The three kids that were—I don't know that they call it lynching—killed in Philadelphia, Mississippi, those three young men were working under me. And I had just talked with them about three weeks before they were killed.

GM: Who were they?

JTMC: Schwerner, Goodman, and Chaney.

GM: Right.

JTMC: They were working for CORE at that time. They were students. During the summer, white and black students would come and work for us, during the summer. They got twenty-five dollars a week, and free room and board, just to help get other students in the South in the area where they were working to do something themselves. That was why . . .

Another one of the most difficult encounters I had was in Jackson itself, during the Freedom Rides, or after the Freedom Rides, when they were on trial. At that time, when you would come back into Jackson from wherever you were—because you'd been on a Freedom Ride as far off as California—you had to come back to Jackson [for the hearing]. We could not get anybody to pick them up. We couldn't get taxis to pick them up, or no one. And I had to go before the chief law enforcement officer and demand that they give us the opportunity to pick people up, because if I were to pick you up, and you were white, especially a white lady that had to come back, I would be arrested.

GM: You mean at the bus terminal?

JTMC: At the bus terminal, or at the airport. Because we had just as many whites who were arrested on the Freedom Rides as we had blacks, and if you were, especially, and I were picking you up, but we did clear that, and I would go out and pick them up with someone and bring them back, because I was responsible for getting them back to trial.

They'd try two a day, one in the morning, one in the afternoon. And the judges' charge to the jury was just like a record, the same thing over, over. They didn't change words from the very first trial until the last one.

GM: What were the Freedom Rides?

JTMC: The Freedom Rides were a group that left New York City, and at that time—that was . . . before the Supreme Court decision that [segregated] interstate bus transportation would be done away with. White and blacks—CORE chartered a bus—for white and black students and adults that started in Washington, came through Sumter, but some of them stayed here, because this was one of the local points. They stayed about two days to wash up, getting their clothes and everything rewashed, and they went on. And the bus was burned one Sunday morning out of Birmingham, Alabama.

GM: So they were riding . . .

JTMC: They were riding together, black and white students and individuals riding that bus together, and they burned it up. But they finally got another bus and went on to Jackson. Jackson was the destination, but the very minute they got into Jackson, they arrested all of them.

GM: Were you ever forced to leave an area?

JTMC: No. I never was forced. I was told that if I didn't do certain things, if I was caught, what would happen to me. The only thing they would say to me, "We'll put you in jail."

One of the scariest things that happened to me—I'll tell you this. We were in Canton, Mississippi, we had been to a meeting that night in the black community. At that meeting, at that black church, white deputies were in every window. So they arrested several young, teenage black boys. And we had taped their conversation, from them, what happened while they were in jail. How they were tried with force, and they would snap a pistol [at their head], that maybe didn't have anything in it, to tell them, "If you don't tell us what's going on. We'll. . . ." They didn't tell them. So we taped [their accounts].

One morning after some trouble in Canton, we were leaving Canton in two cars, one station wagon and one sedan—one white young man, and four of us. Soon as we got outside the city limits of Canton, the police stopped us, and when they stopped us, they took two of the young field staff persons and arrested them, and put them in their patrol car. They left three of us, didn't say anything to us. So they searched the bags. They asked me whose bag this is.

"Mine." They knew me.

So when they finally got to the tape recorder, that we had taken recording of the [accounts]. So the police asked us questions, "What are these?"

. . . I didn't say nothing. I didn't tell them what they were. For the simple reason I got scared, because if they had found out what was on those tapes I thought we might have had trouble.

So he took them out of the case they were in and that's when . . . You couldn't guess in a million years what this policeman said about those things. That's when I found out that they would do anything.

GM: What did he say?

JTMC: He said, "Good God, you all use more Scotch Tape than anybody!" *[He laughs.]*

He thought the tapes were Scotch Tape! And he gave them back to us and I put them back down in there, and when he said that, I said, "Well, the mentality of this person that didn't know what kind of things they were . . . they'd do anything to you!" So they pulled off from us in two patrol cars, with the car that they had our two staff people in the middle of them. They didn't say anything to us.

Well, I was afraid. I said, "If we pull off and go, they'll say, 'You're escaping.' They'll do anything they want."

So a young man asked, "Mr. McCain, what do we do?"

I said, "We're going to follow them to the police station." We went to the police station behind them, stayed down there almost an hour and a half, sitting around in the office.

Finally I asked the chief, I said, "Are we under arrest?" He said, "No, you all can go." And we left and I went on back to Jackson.

Then we had trial, and I was accused, because I was working in the New York office, I was accused of being a "Northern Yankee pusher," who came down to raise disturbance. And when the judge asked me where my home was, when I told him Sumter, South Carolina, it almost killed everything, because I was not from New York.

GM: During your duration with CORE, who was the national director, or who were . . .

JTMC: James Farmer. James Farmer was the national director of CORE, because shortly after Farmer left, I left CORE also.

GM: Do you want to discuss the change in strategy of CORE, say from the Farmer years . . .

JTMC: Well, the strategy was that the majority of people in the CORE chapters, other than in the South, the majority of CORE members were white. It had been like that from the very inception of CORE. They were white, white liberals who were to do anything to help you. After the riots in New York, the Harlem riots in New York, and after Watts, things started changing, and blacks wanted to assert themselves. So blacks started taking over. In other words, then it became a power struggle for the director of national CORE. See, the director of national CORE, for many years, was Charles Odoms, from St. Louis, who was a white lawyer, but then the blacks wanted to get in, let us say, at the top level. Many of us didn't think this was going to do right. We're going to phase out, because blacks were just going to take over the organization, but they weren't the ones who were funding the organization.

And this is what happened. The strategy changed, and when what we called the "militant blacks" at that time came in, and came to the convention and started voting all the old timers out, who had kept CORE together, then it was time for us . . . Then funds started falling off. It was time for some of us just to bail out, and Farmer was the first one.

GM: What year was this?

JTMC: I left CORE in '66. Farmer must have left in '65. But what I did, when I left CORE, I left to start working with SEDFRE *[pronounced "sed-free"]*.

GM: What is that?

JTMC: SEDFRE is the Scholarship, Education, Defense Fund for Racial Equality. SEDFRE was a part of national CORE . . . from the very beginning. SEDFRE was the fundraising agency, something like the Legal Defense Fund for NAACP. It had its own board, its own fundraiser, and it was tax exempt. So what happened, if they wanted me to do a certain project for them, through the Department of Education, they paid for it. And when CORE started dividing itself, SEDFRE pulled out completely and formed its own organization, and I worked for SEDFRE for seven years.

This is when. . . . it changed because they call it citizenship education, but it was political education. I came throughout the whole South and tried to get blacks to run for public office, try to get blacks to register, forming political organizations within a community. That was the seven years I spent with SEDFRE.

GM: What were some of the successes of SEDFRE, when you left CORE?

JTMC: Well one of the successes of SEDFRE—what we did in SEDFRE, we even got government contracts. We worked with the federal government as trainers for the Head Start program, trainers for parents who had children in school, and these kind of things. My job—SEDFRE did not have a big staff—but they hired me because they wanted to do something about registration in the South, and that was my job, to come south and do that. That's what SEDFRE did. SEDFRE was not an organization that's going out to fight discrimination per se, like CORE did.

GM: They dealt more with voter registration?

JTMC: That's exactly right. I mean, that's the job I had. But they also worked with, as I said before, with government programs, trying to help the lower-income farmers, help organizing co-ops, and that kind of thing. They did something like that in Louisiana and in Georgia. So they weren't the direct action, they didn't have the direct action philosophy like CORE had.

GM: In the '60s, Mr. McCain, it seemed as though there were so many civil rights organizations trying to do what might have ultimately had the same goal. I'm not sure. But how do you assess the role, and were there conflicts?

JTMC: I imagine there were conflicts. I'm positive of conflicts. But as long as King, Dr. King, was living—Farmer was with CORE, Whitney Young was the Urban League—was living, the NAACP with . . .

GM: Roy Wilkins?

JTMC: Yes, Roy. And John Lewis with SNCC *[pronounced "snick"]*. I think at the heads they were all going towards the same thing. Now they approached it entirely differently. NAACP approached it from the legal angle. They did not believe in non-violence to begin with, not direct action. Whitney Young had, I mean, the Urban League was not that kind of organization [either]. Martin, I think we know, Martin, the Southern Christian Leadership Conference, under Martin Luther King, we know his was totally nonviolent. And SNCC, I think, was an organization just to supply the manpower, in many instances, because it was students, and they had to have students, because the majority of people in this movement were not older people. They were younger people at that particular time, and they were college students.

GM: So there were differences. Was there any time when each of these groups might have worked together on a particular mission that you were attempting to . . .

JTMC: Well, Farmer was down in Alabama when King led his movement. We lent our support to try to get people to join marches, together, like you had your March on Washington, that Dr. King led. We worked very closely. CORE financed people to come to it, and everything else. We did the same thing with the Poor Peoples' Campaign in Washington, although I was working with SEDFRE then. And what we did, the part that SEDFRE played, was to train and have institutes on nonviolent activities for marches. If people start attacking you on a line and you're marching, there are certain things you don't do. In other words, we had the persons—we called them the lieutenants—who were supposed to do this. [If] you were going down the street and people start heckling you, there's certain decorums [*sic*] you had, certain things you wouldn't do.

GM: Why did you believe that nonviolent direct action really would work?

JTMC: That's a hard question to answer, because I knew nothing about nonviolence. I hadn't even practiced nonviolence, until I started working at CORE. Because I imagine this was one of the things that was in the minds of the people when I was hired, whether or not I could follow that philosophy. But after I got into it, they gave me material to read, and I thought at that time, as far as I was concerned, it was just a strategy to get things done.

GM: During your tenure with CORE, I believe that you kept an extensive diary.

JTMC: I certainly did.

GM: Does the public have access to it?

JTMC: As far as I know, the University of South Carolina—the librarian, Mr. Johnson, came over here and got every piece of material that I had and carried it back to the South Caroliniana Library.

GM: A lot of young people today take so many things for granted. If you were to say something to them, what would your message be?

JTMC: My message to young people today is to improve themselves to the best of their ability. Try to excel. Believe in excellence. Have confidence in themselves that I want to be the best there is, in whatever profession I'm in, whatever I'm doing, and not take second best. Say I'm all right as long as I'm in the upper ten. *No.* Now you may not be the first person, but as long as you believe in yourself, you can excel. I think you can. And stop taking things for granted and stop killing so much time. And not looking back on the past. Stop criticizing some other group for your failures, but do something about your failures yourself.

Ida Mae McCain, the Home Front

Lorin Palmer:* . . . and then that's a little booklet, . . . the one that Rudy pulled together.

Marvin Lare [ML]: That's great.

Lorin Palmer [LP]: Isn't that great? Now let's look at this and see what this says. There's some pictures I wanted to show you that . . . Rudy Lombard. And you know, when I brought them here they were grown men, and so "Nooker" [J. T. McCain] looked at them, but I don't think it really dawned on him who they were. So we pulled the picture and we said, "Now Nooker, this is Rudy, as a grown man." These were young people when he worked with them, because you know, children led that movement.

ML: Yes.

Arnette. [AE]: Look at . . . there.

LP: But he used to . . . Well, he's the closest thing to a grandfather that I ever knew, because he could walk to the funeral home and check on me. . . .

LP: Speak very loudly.

ML: Yes. Mrs. McCain, I'm so pleased to be in your home today.

Ida Mae McCain [IM]: Why, thank you.

ML: Today is Monday—a pretty good day for a Monday—May the 22nd, 2006. I'm with Mrs. J. T. McCain and her daughters, and Lorin Palmer has been good enough to bring me by to see you today. Mrs. McCain, I understand that you've talked with a lot of people who've been interested . . .

IM: And I don't hear well.

ML: Yes. You let me know if you're not hearing me, but I'll try to speak up. Are you hearing me now?

---

*Ida Mae (Mrs. J. T.) McCain was born in 1912 and died in 2009. The interview was conducted in her home in Sumter, South Carolina, May 22, 2006. Others present and participating were Lorin Palmer, Arnette Ellison (Mrs. McCain's eldest daughter), and Joyce Doty (Mrs. McCain's youngest daughter). The audiotape begins with Palmer in mid-sentence.

IM: Yes.

ML: Very good. You have a lot of remembrances of your life and the life your husband. I'd be pleased for you to tell me some of the things that you remember, that meant the most to you across the years. I'll ask some questions if you want me to, but I like to let people tell their own story in their own way, so what would you like to share with us today? . . .

IM: I kept house. I stayed home and kept house. McCain paid for this house, and he just wanted to do what he did, and he was happy. . . . He had over a hundred awards. A whole room full back there. I don't know what I'm going to do with it.

ML: When we finish I'll take my camera and I'll take some pictures of the awards and recognitions. With us today—and they may chime in a little bit, although they're being a little bit reticent—are her two daughters. Are you both from Chicago?

[JD]: Yes.

ML: Both daughters of J. T. McCain.

Mrs. McCain, do you remember when your husband came home from the school and found that his new football equipment had been taken by the white school?

IM: What did he say? I can't hear.

ML: As I have heard it, that was the last straw, that set him on the path of the civil rights movement and led to the, his becoming the first field secretary of CORE, the Congress of Racial Equality. Tell me some of the things that you remember and that you treasure about your husband and your life together.

LP: What do you remember about how Nooker became involved in the movement? What was it that started him in civil rights?

IM: Well, at first he was the president of the [Sumter] NAACP, and he was at Morris College during that time. Whenever anything came up that would help the students, he was always there to help them out. It started off back in nineteen, about forty, when he was dean out there at Morris College, and he left Morris College and got a job down at the Mullins, South Carolina. He worked there about two years and he wanted to come closer home, so he came to Summerton down at Scott's Branch High School. He worked there but he wanted to have a "Judge Waring Room" put on at Scott's Branch [High School]. You know Judge Waring was one of the persons that came out for civil rights.

[A major section on Judge J. Waites Waring and his wife, Elizabeth, will be found in volume 3.]

IM: They fired him, and then he got a job with the NAACP, not local but kind of South Carolina. From there just one thing led to another. In fact, he got these jobs [offers], and whichever one that he thought he could do best, those are the ones he accepted. He just enjoyed it.

JD: Mother? Mother, when he left down there, is that when he went to CORE? When did he go to CORE?

IM: Right after he left?

JD: When he was fired down there?

IM: No, not when he was fired. He got other jobs. He was with the national branch of NAACP, and then he met this Jim Farmer and . . .

LP: He met him in New York? He met Jim Farmer in New York?

IM: Yes. They hit it off pretty good and during the Freedom Riders— Oh! In the meantime he was sent with different ones, and he would go to Florida and they would set up . . .

LP: Chapters?

IM: Clubs.

ML: The local groups, yes.

IM: Yes. He did that for a while and of course some of the younger people were kind of hotheaded. They didn't want to do what they should do and they wanted what they wanted, and he wanted them to be calm and eventually the other side would see the blacks' side [of things]. He worked like that for several years and then— Oh yes! During the time when the three fellows—one, the Jew, the white one, and the Negro—were lynched.

LP: They were shot.

IM: And he sent them. Before he died, he wondered if he did right. That was on his death—just before he died. That's one of the things he wondered if he did right by sending those three boys out and they were lynched.

LP: In Mississippi.

ML: In Mississippi.

IM: He said he didn't know whether he did right or not. That was one thing he didn't . . .

Well, I remember they came through here one night, Freedom Riders, and Jim Farmer was among them, and some of the other heads and they got lost. Some of the travelers got lost in Rock Hill, South Carolina, and Jim Farmer got on the telephone in there and called Robert Kennedy and told him that they had lost these boys and he wanted him to find them. Well, sometime— It wasn't so long before Robert Kennedy called him back and said these boys were in Rock Hill, South Carolina, in jail. And he told the people here who had stopped to wait of them, "Let's go." So Jim Farmer and some of the rest of them went up and got these boys out of jail.

That's where the Freedom Riders came in, and they all caught this bus and went to Montgomery, Alabama, and of course you must have read the papers and know what happened. But whatever happened, eventually it paid off. But his job was to calm— don't let them upset you, and if you don't you'll see the other side. And that happened. That was his job. His job was to keep these others calm. And of course it's written in most of these things what happened during that time.

He met Rudy Lombard and those when they were in with the Freedom Riders.

LP: You also want to share about [how] he was committed to voter education and voter registration.

IM: Oh yes.

AE: . . . which was a point of contention during the movement, remember? Because there were many that did not want to go that way.

IM: Yes.

AE: And so he eventually won his argument about the importance of it, taking on that level and the strategy . . .

ML: That's when Judge Waring stood out and he stood up for the Briggs petitions.

IM: Oh! He— You know, Judge Waring decided that teachers were not getting equal salaries. He [McCain] was one of the ones that sued the state, and they got it. They got equal money, you know, equal money for each.

ML: For blacks and whites.

IM: Yes.

LP: Didn't Nooker lead that movement?

IM: Yes, he did. Yes. That's what I was looking for. I had it the other day, but I can't find it. I meant to put it someplace I could find it, but . . .

Well I stayed home and kept house.

LP: You were an educator also. You taught school for many years.

IM: Yes, and took care of the children.

LP: Were you ever afraid that Nooker wasn't going to come home?

IM: No, somehow I wasn't. No, because I knew he was calm and he thought things through before anything happened.

ML: You had a lot of trust and confidence in him then?

IM: He wasn't a bully, he wasn't . . . Frank Robinson was— You know his son is back here now.

LP: I didn't know. We need to make sure we speak with him. We need to speak with Frank Robinson's son.

ML: Yes. Very good. These two daughters, are they your only children? Did you have other children?

IM: I had a son. I have a son. He's a manager at UPS in Atlanta, and he's able to retire now. He's fifty-two, and he's able to retire. And he says he doesn't know whether he wants to retire, says he likes his job and he feels good. He doesn't know what he wants to do. I don't know what he's going to do.

ML: Well, how old are you now?

IM: Ninety-four.

ML: Ninety-four! Okay. And your husband, before he passed, how old was he?

IM: Ninety-eight. Yes, he was ninety-eight that June.

AE: No, that March. March. He died on their sixty-eighth wedding anniversary, June 5th.

ML: Yes. What were some of the happiest days you remember? What were some of your happiest days?

IM: When he came back home *[laughs]*.

ML: You may not have thought you were worried about him, but you were mighty happy when he came back home. I'm sure he had to travel a lot, didn't he?

IM: Oh yes! He told me when he came home and I retired, "You can go anywhere you want to go, I don't care. There ain't nobody else got nothing to do with it. I traveled all over the United States, and if you want to travel, travel!" And I did it!

LP: Did you always know where he was? Did you know where he was in the movement when he would be traveling?

IM: He contacted me, and he came home periodically, took care of things at home, and left out again.

JD: One of the things I need to say is that he left instructions for others to take care of his family while he was gone. People like my grandfather, others . . . Is that what you told me? You told me that he left instructions for certain people to make sure his family was all right when he traveled.

IM: Yes.

ML: Who have been some of your best friends across the years? Who are your best friends?

IM: Who are my best friends?

AE: How about Edmund Palmer?

IM: Yes. Oh, Ed, yes! And Dr. Jones, and B. T. Williams. And the Sampsons. The Sampsons were railroad men. They all lived on Oakland. The Boatmans were railroad men, and they rode the train from D.C. to Sumter. Mailmen. They did very well and graduated several doctors, of their sons.

AE: Yes. Dr. B. T. Williams lived right in that house across the street. The Boatmans lived next door—her neighborhood of people close together.

IM: I was hoping Bubba McElveen would put in the paper how prominent these Sumter [families], with a small place like Sumter, produced so many doctors. The MacDonalds had four doctors.

JD: My dad's first cousins, MacDonalds, all four of them were doctors.

LP: When you go to Greenville, Sampson's an important name.

ML: Where were you born and where did you grow up?

IM: I was born in a place called Tignall, Georgia.

ML: Tignall?

IM: The Chenaults!

JD: She's been to her family reunion . . .

IM: At Camonir. c-a-m-o-n-i-r. When the gold train—they sent this money— the money was borrowed from France, and they sent the money and they got the money at the Civil War. They got this money and they were on their way to Savannah, and they stopped at this Chenault plantation, and they robbed them. They robbed the gold. They don't know where the gold went. But my daddy said they buried that gold in the graveyard, because you're not supposed to bother a grave. And he said that's where that gold is. And people come from all over looking for that gold, but they won't let them go in that cemetery. So that's where my family—Washington, Georgia . . .

AE: Tignall is out of Washington, Georgia.

ML: Oh, okay. I know where Washington is, but I've never heard of Tignall before. How were things growing up?

IM: My grandfather was a smart man. He was a carpenter. I forgot what they called him. There were four brothers—they're on here somewhere *[referring to the Chenault reunion T-shirt she is wearing].* And each one had their own farm, because they were slaves, my grandpa and those. They were slaves, but they were treated very well, because their bosses were well off. So I grew up on my grandfather's farm, but my mother thought that I'd have a better education if she moved to South Carolina, so we moved to Anderson, South Carolina, and I finished high school there as a work student. Then I went to Morris College as a work student. I got along all right.

ML: What year did you go to Morris College?

IM: Nineteen thirty— When I went there? Thirty-two, I graduated in '36. I went to Morris College, as a work student, but I graduated in four years. Then I got a job teaching.

JD: I think she . . . Didn't she do the Teacher's College at Columbia University?

ML: This [certificate] says Temple [University].

AE: Temple. Daddy went to Temple. Didn't you go to Temple, or where did you go?

IM: Yes, I went to Temple.

JD: Yes, that's what I thought. And Nooker went there also.

AE: Yes, Daddy got his master's from Temple. . . .

This is the story Daddy told us. We went up to S.M.H. Kress, the dime store, and I wanted some ice cream, and they wouldn't serve it to me, and I asked him why. He said he couldn't explain to me at five [years of age], why I couldn't have ice cream when I knew he had money to buy it, and he said he decided then he would try to change the law, to make things right.

ML: "And a little child shall lead them."

AE: Yes.

ML: So when he couldn't explain it to a five-year-old, he decided it was wrong.

What do you remember of your father's work? How old were you when he was working for CORE and . . .

JD: I was in high school, and I know he would never let me go anywhere with him, because he said I was too hotheaded and he didn't think I would just sit there and not retaliate, and he said he also didn't have time to do his job and worry about me.

ML: And be a parent, too.

JD: So I didn't get into the movement until after I finished college, moved to Chicago and became involved with— It was Operation Breadbasket then, with Jesse [Jackson]. Just the little things but no involvement when he was with CORE.

In fact, we didn't know, and those newspaper articles will tell you, we didn't know until many years later the things that Daddy was doing. I do remember once that the Attorney General's Office called here and he wasn't here at the time, and they were just calling to find out how to contact him. I happened to answer the phone, but I don't know where he was at that time.

ML: What year was that in Chicago at Operation Breadbasket? That would have been after your college?

JD: Sixty-five, yes, '64, '65.

ML: I spent a month or two in Chicago in '60—well, actually, January and February of '66, at the Urban Institute, which was a training program for clergy.

JD: Yes. I think Dad came up there in Chicago for that, at the University of Chicago?

ML: I don't know that it was associated with the University of Chicago, it wasn't on the campus—gosh, that's been so long ago—I think most of the sessions were held at a church, and while we were there is the first I heard of Jesse Jackson. While we were there, Martin Luther King was speaking at a church. That may have been when . . . King lived there in Chicago—

JD: In Chicago, over on the West Side.

ML: Yes, over on the West Side for a while. That may have been that same period of time.

JD: But we didn't find out a lot of stuff until after, you know, reading about things about him. None of us knew.

ML: Children hardly ever know much about—they're just their parents. They don't know about that until years later and then wish we knew more.

JD: Exactly.

ML: Is your sister older or younger than you?

JD: She's older.

ML: I'd be glad to ask her what some of her experiences were. Do you have other recollections and experiences that you think would be helpful?

JD: No, he was just Daddy. He was here with me. I think it was Jim, my brother, that really missed out when he was gone, because—let's see, I graduated from high school in '59.

Wasn't Daddy home when I graduated from high school? Arnette, in '59 was he with CORE, when I graduated from Mather? [Yes], he was with CORE. You see that was a boarding school, in Camden, South Carolina.

AE: We both went to that school.

ML: I remember Mather, I visited there before it closed. I moved to South Carolina in 1969.

JD: I had that similar experience at Cut Rate. ReeRee, Marie, that grew up with our family, took me down there, and I was small, and I wanted a drink of water, and of course she knew what was coming. So she looked at me and she said, "Oh, you don't want any of that old nasty water. You don't want that water, it'll make you sick. Come on, let's go." So that was another way of dealing with a response to segregation.

ML: It was a real challenge for parents to explain, or how they were going to interpret that.

AE: Yes. [I remember] Mother telling us stories about how— I think there was a store uptown called Sumter Dry Goods. And it seems that she said we were coming down the stairs and a white lady was talking to a clerk and she had a child and she pointed out and said, "Look, a n——," and pointed at us. Mother said the clerk didn't say anything, but she laughed, so [Mother] went home and she told Daddy what had happened. Daddy went back uptown—it seems that he was very well respected in Sumter, even though he was black—anyway, it seems that he went up there and reported what happened. They didn't say anything in front of him, but actions were taken against the clerk. . . .

My daddy was here . . . because I'm so much older. I had left. You see, I was born in '30, so when Daddy was involved, I really was away from home most of the time, because after I graduated from college I left home and went away to work, so during Daddy's tenure, just these two, my brother and Joyce, were here with Mother, because Daddy was gone all of the time. Other than what I hear I don't know he . . . But he was always here in presence, you know. We always knew that if anything went wrong where to go. Very quiet, very quiet, but took care of business. Yes. He was a wonderful father, wonderful human being, humanitarian. He'd do anything for anybody, but he didn't want anyone to know. Very humble.

JD: A very humble man, the most humble man I've known in my lifetime. He didn't want any accolades. It was just—and I think he was for right. There wasn't any gray area. It was either right or wrong.

AE: That was it.

JD: And he raised us that way.

AE: It has been said one of the reasons Daddy . . . Most of what Daddy did in the civil rights area was behind the scenes because he feared for the family. He didn't want anything to happen, so by many not knowing the things he was doing then there was no threat to Mother or us. In fact, many of the things that Daddy did we didn't know about till after he died. When people came to tell us various things, we said, "He did! He did!" We were amazed at how many lives he had touched. Because he never talked about it, never.

ML: Was he teaching then, when you were young? Was he teaching?

AE: When I was a girl he was dean at Morris College, and when I was little—Mother was still in school out there, and I was about maybe four or five—Daddy used to take me with him and they had a hole in the fence out at Morris College, and we would go through that hole and Daddy would take me and leave me with Mother in the dormitory. I can remember running up and down, back and [forth]— That's right. He would take me. . . . Now why we would go through that hole in the fence I don't know. I guess it was—

Mother, do you remember that? Remember when Daddy used to bring me out there to the dormitory? When you were in college? And I used to run up and down that hall, and when you and "Sip" and Daisy and all of them were at Morris, in school.

JD: She didn't hear you. [Mother], did you hear Arnette?

IM: No. I hear but I don't know what you're saying. I'm just half deaf.

ML: She was asking if you remembered when she was little and she'd come to the college and run up and down the halls.

AE: . . . and Daddy would bring me out there, and "Sip" and Daisy and you—I don't know what floor, third floor—and Daddy would bring me and leave me out there with you while you were in college.

ML: Daisy and the others? Friends? So she had to live in the dormitory in order to be a student?

AE: Yes, she lived in the dormitory, right. Well, at the time, Daddy and Mother were not . . . I'm a child from a former marriage. Of course, she's the only mother I have ever. . . . My mother died when I was two. I don't even know her. But anyway, that's why Mother was in the dormitory, and Daddy was on the faculty, so they weren't married at the time, but then after she graduated they married.

JD: She's the love of his life. They were very romantic toward each other.

ML: Yes, I can tell from the pictures.

AE: Oh, I'm telling you, anybody you ask can tell you, he thought the world . . . Anything we ever wanted, we went through Mother to get it from Daddy. "Go ask your Mother." Or he'd say no, and we really wanted it, we'd go to her, and we'd get it *[laughs].*

But my brother said, at Dad's funeral, that he believed God gave Dad so many years because [they] missed [so many] years [together], so God gave him more years so that they could be together to make up for that. He said he also had heard that she was such a "fox" that he made sure he outlived everybody, so that they wouldn't pursue her *[laughs].* And he said after the funeral was over, somebody told him, "Your mother was a *stone* fox!" And he said, "Uh-oh, Daddy, you missed one!" *[She laughs.]*

LP: But Mrs. McCain has always been a very feisty, independent go-getter in her own right. I don't know if she heard me, but that's the truth. Do you agree with me on that?

AE and **JD** *[together]: Definitely.*

AE: That's why we have [to take] so much time trying to find somebody to be with her, because she lives alone and refuses to let anybody come in here.

ML: I think they're telling on you now.

IM: I bet they are *[laughs].*

AE: And that's called selective hearing *[laughs].* She heard that!

LP: So you were married for how many years, do you remember?

IM: Forever!

JD: I think it was—sixty-eight years.

IM: Yes.

JD: Because I think Daddy was with her just before their anniversary. Their anniversary was June 5th and he died June 5th, the morning of June 5th.

LP: She said she was never afraid during those years. Isn't that amazing?

JD: Like I said, I think I was away and [Mother] and Jim were here. I was right over at Mather, and then I went to West Virginia to go to school. Dad had organized a CORE group in Charleston, West Virginia, and that's why I went away to school in West Virginia, because he wanted me to go to an integrated school. It was the only state school in West Virginia, and it's like reverse integration because the campus was just about all black, and the white students came in from Charleston and other places around, but not too many of them lived on campus. So that's how I ended up . . . She wanted me to go to Spellman. So that's how I ended up there in Institute, West Virginia. Because he had organized that CORE group there.

ML: And he had good connections there for you.

JD: Yes, right.

ML: Can you think of other things you'd like to share for the book? Was your childhood happy, or did you have some problems with people when you were a child? . . .

JD: It was the same with us. We knew— We'd go and look at the water fountain and it'd say "White Only" and "Colored Only," and we'd go to the "White Only" and drink out of it and then run out of the side of the store.

I remember the theater up there where the opera house is now. The blacks had to go through the alley, upstairs, so we were not allowed to go to the movies, because Daddy said if we had to go up the alley we weren't going. And we didn't go to the movie until they built a black theater over on Liberty Street, and that's when we went to the movies. So it was the way it was.

The story was when we lived at my grandmother's house around on 12 North Salem, and that's the family house, Mother told a story—I don't know if she remembers—she said when we built around here, Mr. Brody passed by one day and asked Daddy why we hadn't moved in, and he said because there was no furniture. He had gone to the bank and from what I understand, the house was even paid for then, and the bank wouldn't loan him any money. So Mr. Brody asked him how much [he needed]. Now he was a Jewish guy, and he had some stores uptown, and Daddy told him what he needed, and he went up to the store and gave Daddy the money, and Daddy bought the furniture and we still didn't move in here until he had paid Mr. Brody back. So I was in second grade when we moved around here. That was just the type of person he was. And if I had listened to him about saving money, I'd be a millionaire!

LP: He was an investment king. He would always give me advice on an aggressive investment portfolio.

AE: Yes. That's it.

ML: Well, I'm glad that you all, you girls were here when I happened to be over here today.

JD: Yes. We're leaving in the morning.

[There is further discussion of arranging a companion for Mrs. McCain. Photos are taken of Mrs. McCain and of various documents and awards Mr. McCain received.]

James E. Clyburn and Bobby Doctor, Inspired Students

Cecelia Cunningham, Charleston Jr. NAACP, Moderator:* Without further ado, since we are on a time schedule, going to hear from you first, Jim, okay, hear from Jim Clyburn. Let's welcome him, please.

James Clyburn [JC]: Thank you very much, Cecelia. I am always pleased to get back to Charleston for whatever reason, but this particular trip is of great significance to me. . . .

As a bit of background, I've asked Bobby Doctor, who is to be on the program this afternoon, to join me in this presentation today, so that we can make sure that we give you a comprehensive viewpoint of exactly what the student movement at S.C. State College was all about, because Bobby and I were of the seven students who originally met—four from S.C. State College, and three from Claflin—to organized what became, eventually, the student movement.

I don't know where Bobby's impetus came from for all of this. Mine was in a very early experience that occurred when I was thirteen or fourteen years old.

My little league baseball coach was J. T. McCain, who walked . . . [I] had known [him] very well, [he] was also principal of Stone Hill Elementary School in Sumter, and as was the practice, J.T. put in his annual order for equipment for the next year. And when he put in his order, he arrived at school one day to find that the equipment had been delivered. The only problem was that the equipment, the new equipment

---

*This discussion took place on Saturday, November 6, 1982, as part of a conference in Charleston titled "South Carolina Voices of The Civil Rights Movement: A Conference on the History of the Civil Rights Movement in South Carolina, 1940–1970." The transcripts are archived at the Avery Research Center for African American History and Culture, College of Charleston. The original transcripts were prepared by W&S Typing and Letter Writing Service. The selected segments presented here are from pages 202–23, and were scanned to text for this anthology by Kent Germany, African American Studies Program, University of South Carolina.

that he ordered, had been taken to the white elementary school and the equipment that they had had, [had] been removed and brought to Stone Hill. J.T. refused to accept that equipment, and was promptly dismissed from his job as a principal.

[See interview with James T. "Nooker" McCain above in this volume.]

JC: It was that experience, at that age, that started me to thinking and pondering and wondering all about exactly what segregation meant. And I've never gotten over that experience. So, when I got to State College, that [feeling] was here, somewhere *[probably pointing to his heart or head],* waiting to come forward. And when, on February 6, 1960, the opportunity presented itself for us to express our frustrations with the way of life in South Carolina, it seemed just natural for me to be in the forefront of that. . . .

I'll never forget. Going to bed on February 5th, planning on how we were going to move on Orangeburg Square the next day, I had all kinds of nightmares. And that morning when we woke up, there was a little patch of white hair, right here, that I was vain [enough] to pluck out, and to this day, no more hair has come.

So we, in all of that anxiety, we still felt it our duty to move. The atmosphere, very few people realize today, because no one wants to talk about it. I chatted with Jim Sulton outside before we got started. Here is what we were operating in at S.C. State College. Number 1, the NAACP had been outlawed on S.C. State campus. Number 2, the president of S.C. State College, at that time, had banned all gathering for the student body. We could not get in any kind of unity, for any purpose. And number 3, the only way that we could meet was to do so on the Claflin campus. *And* in order to stymie that—we hear so much talk about the Berlin Wall—in order to stymie that, a high, barbed-wire-topped fence was placed between those two campuses to keep from going on that campus. . . .

I think that the sobering experience came when we decided to move on Orangeburg Square and got down to find that every single plan that was made and finalized at 2:30 a.m. that was already presented, *[addressing a member of the audience]* Brother Blake, to the powers that be. We were baffled, really baffled, as to how all of that took place. . . . But even though they expected us and were prepared for us, that that day, as you know, resulted in 368 arrests. The jails were packed. . . .

And when we finally got to jail that day, we were one of the fortunate ones to be crammed into a cell for six. . . . There were more than sixty people crammed into that cell. And I'll never forget. We had to take turns standing. You just worked your bodies so that the leaking radiator, which leaked hot water, we had to take turns as to who would stand under that radiator. It was that kind of an atmosphere. . . .

We finally got out of there, and I talk about this day because it was the day that had a profound impact on me, not only was it a day that we had started in the coaching for the case . . . which eventually led to *Edwards against South Carolina,* which revolutionized much of our Constitution . . . we went from that campus up to Columbia, and this arrest of 182 or 180—I can't remember exactly which—led to the *Edwards* case, but it was that evening when we were all herded into the courthouse to be bailed out, and it took a long time to get us bailed out, and we were hungry.

[An account by Matthew J. Perry of the Edwards *case follows in this section under the title "A Pearl of a Case."]*

JC: We had not been fed, and I'll never forget, Bobby Doctor coming over to me and saying, "Are you hungry?" And I said, yes. He said, there's someone out here with a hamburger that will like to share it with you, and I didn't ask any questions. I went out and there was Emily England with this hamburger, whom I never remembered seeing before, and it was that hamburger I always credit with saving my life, and in return for that, I went on to marry her. . . . We decided that here was a new energy that had to be harnessed, and that meeting eventually led to the weekend of October 10 and 11, the day I met Jim Blake, when he was still at Morehouse College. We met down at Atlanta University that year, and formed what became known as the Student Nonviolent Coordinating Committee [SNCC]. I sort of became the ambassador, I was given the job of traveling around the country to the meetings. Bobby's job was to carry out the activities there on the campus.

And for that reason, I want to defer at this moment, to Bobby, who will talk a little more in detail about that, and hopefully we can bring all of this together during the question and answer period. Thank you so much.

[The audience applauds.]

BOBBY DOCTOR: That hamburger was not a "Big Mac Attack." It was a "Little Mac Attack" and Emily certainly corralled him.

I think that it is important that we understand that power concedes nothing without force or pressure. It never has and it never will. Power responds to power, not sentimentalism or emotionalism, but power. Now power comes in different forms. There are all kinds of power. There is all kinds of force. There is violent force, and there is nonviolent force. And the kind of force and the kind of pressure that we instituted back in 1960 is of the nonviolent category.

I wanted to be here because history is being recorded. History is being recorded. But, more importantly than that, the historians are taking part in the recording. I wanted to be here because there are a number of persons, to my way of thinking, [who] represent the conscience of South Carolina. There are a number of persons in this particular program who in some way represent [an] alarm clock for justice and equality in South Carolina. There are a lot of folk on this program, in this audience today, who represent the "agitator of a washing machine." And it is important that we understand the historical significance of this particular program. I happen to serve as the regional director of the U.S. Commission on Civil Rights.

The student sit-in movement in South Carolina started on February 6, 1960, in Orangeburg, South Carolina. It started on the heels of the student sit-in movement in Greensboro, North Carolina, which started on the 1st of February 1960. I very clearly remember that less than a week later, we had initiated a student movement in Orangeburg, South Carolina, and in many ways we were encouraged by what took place in Greensboro.

There were several persons who were the original initiators of that particular action, and I would like to name those persons for you, two of whom I've since forgotten, regrettably. There were four from S.C. State College. Their names are Lloyd Williams, Clarence Duke Missouri, Jim Clyburn, and Bobby Doctor. We had three from Claflin. That particular contingent was headed up by a fellow named Tom Gaither. Tom went on to become one of the top officials at CORE and did quite a bit of work and made quite a few sacrifices down in the Louisiana area.

Charles McDew, who later became, perhaps, the chief spokesperson for that particular movement in Orangeburg, came in a little later. There were many, many organizing efforts, as Jim has indicated, the strategy sessions at night in the music hall, or the music room, I should say, over at Claflin College, the numbers of meetings, mass meetings, student meetings, and other meetings, there were a number of marches which took place. Most of which, or at least a couple of which, resulted in arrest, but there were also some marches which did not result in arrest because we really never got downtown to sit in. We were met with fire hoses, in some instances, and in every instance, we were met with law enforcement officials who were obviously intent on blocking our way.

I guess the most significant thing that comes to mind when I talk about those experiences is the opposition. And obviously there is opposition which might be understood because there were persons who obviously, white persons, who were hell bent on protecting the status quo. But interestingly enough there were also some blacks who were hell bent on protecting the status quo. Some of them are still at S.C. State College.

I recall very vividly the law enforcement officers on that particular campus radioing downtown, and I think when we talk about why and how the people downtown who knew what was going on during those days we had campus police cars, and they had radios in those cars that were obviously hooked up to the police radio system downtown. They would call down and tell the officials down there that we were coming. They would, obviously, give all of the details, as to how many— They would obviously give the details as to who the leaders were, and all that sort of information, which is why we had to devise different kinds of strategies from time to time.

I recall on one occasion meeting a group, a small group, downtown, initially, to sit in at a drugstore, which was on Orangeburg Square, to try and divert attention away from a large group of students who were coming down from a different direction. Needless to say, we were arrested and dragged out of the drug store. I'll never forget this big, burly police officer who must have been about six foot six and weighed about three hundred pounds, and they put six of us in the backseat of a police car. He and a smaller officer, and [they] threw us in, then they got in, and there was no screen between us. Obviously, if we wanted to do them some sort of bodily harm, the six of us, I think, could have overpowered the two of them. But we had no intentions of doing that. But after they got us in, the two of them looked at each other, and the big one decided that, "Maybe we should search them." So, we got out of the car again, and they threw us up against the car, and searched us, and this one, big officer, literally begged me to run. Literally begged me to run, so he could shoot me. Obviously I wasn't about to do that. But we ended up being placed in jail, and, of course, the large group came down later on.

We obviously went to court. I think it was a day or so later, or a few days later. One of the most disheartening things that I have ever had happen, we sat there and we observed officials from S.C. State College on the witness stand *testifying against us.* That was one of the most disheartening experiences that I have ever had. I know the guy's name, and—Jim—I've talked to you about it, and I have some very bitter feelings towards that today. I recognized that obviously the officials, who were black at South Carolina State, needless to say, were instructed to take a certain course of action in dealing with us. I have no problems with that. That was real, and that was reality back then, but I guess I take some exception and hold some bitterness over what I perceive to be the joy with which a lot of that took place. So, when I talk about opposition, I'm not always talking about white opposition, but also talking about black opposition.

The Orangeburg sit-in movement . . . student sit-in movement evolved into the state sit-in movement. We obviously conducted a number of different demonstrations in Orangeburg, but we also went to Columbia, South Carolina. We also went to Rock Hill, South Carolina.

I recall on one occasion a part of our group was up in Rock Hill demonstrating up that way, and Tom Gaither was one of the leaders up that way at the time. And Tom was singled out. As a matter of fact, [he was] put in jail, there is a little state prison farm, just outside of Rock Hill, up there. If I'm not mistaken, Tom spent some weeks—I don't recall the exact number, but three comes to mind—for some reason or other, three or more, three weeks in confinement in that particular institution for simply attempting to get the system in Rock Hill to become more responsive and obviously to become less racist and discriminatory.

We also went to Columbia, my hometown, and had some rather bad experiences up there. It was always standard operating procedure during that particular time not to have the student stay in jail for more than a day. We went to Columbia and obviously they were not as well organized there as we were in Orangeburg, we assisted them in pulling together their efforts up there, and we were to stay in jail, I think, a few hours. The few hours turned out to be, I think, something like three days!

I'll never forget the experiences that I had during those three days in that Columbia jail. They literally fed us out of dog pails about that [motions with hands] in diameter and about that deep, where they would put maybe two or three inches of grits on the bottom. A cold hunk of cornbread, and a sardine, or a piece of fatback. I didn't eat for three days! The last day, and if I had known we were going to get out when we did get out, I ate one sardine off the top of that bucket, about two to three hours before we got out, and that's all in the three days period.

I also had some rather disheartening experiences. I ran into a lot of friends I had gone to high school with and grew up in the projects with who were in jail, obviously, having committed crimes. It was interesting but when I walked into the cellblock, I had on a suit. Back in those days we tried to have the opposition believe that through our cleanliness and immaculate dress, that somehow or another, we were much more acceptable. Obviously that didn't make any difference to them. But be that as it may, we always did dress like that. . . .

But, to make a long story short, it was an interesting experience. It obviously was an experience that had a great impact on South Carolina, and I am sure at some point or another, during the questions we'll get into, we'll get into some of the more detailed information that I may have left out. Thank you.

[The audience applauds.]

JC: Thank you very much, Bobby. Before we get into questions, I might add that the movement into Columbia that Bobby spoke of was in the spring of the year of 1961. Sort of very historical to the movement for two reasons. It was those arrests in Columbia that led to the *Edwards against South Carolina* case that revolutionized the Constitution insofar as peace is concerned. It is also the first time in the history of the movement in South Carolina that a white person became conscience stricken enough to join the march, and was arrested with us that day. I recall, of course, that they did not keep him in jail. After beating him up pretty bad, they took him straight to the bus station—I think, [he was] from New Jersey or something—but that, too, comes to mind. . . .

We went to Rock Hill together, we stood in Doug Broome's together, we went to Bessinger's together, Bessinger's in Columbia, which at that time was called "Piggy Park," also in Charleston, that became a focal point in Charleston in 1963. In between all of this, I was the one designated, along with Chuck McDew, to sort of travel the countryside, going to Mississippi and Alabama, and it's interesting that Clarence Mitchell III, who is now state senator, and he serves in the legislature, Delegate Assembly in Maryland, so when I met him—not only that, Marion Barry, who is now mayor of Washington, D.C.—was in that October meeting of 1960 and it is amazing sometimes, David Rogers, who eventually came in and John Lewis—David Rogers is now the administrator of Washington, D.C., but better known as—you know Bobby Doctor—played a funny kind of role in all this. [Bobby] introduced me to my wife, and David Rogers ended up marrying [Bobby's] sister.

We've been . . . all of this ties us closely together, and to make it even more interesting, yesterday, for an hour, I was on the phone with Clarence Mitchell III. I just got, the earliest part of this week, a card from Jean and David who were visiting Japan as part of a special three-week tour with city managers from all over the world. We all still stay close together. And we still, in some way, have a network going. And every now and then, as this past Christmas, when I was in Washington for a week with my brother John, who came into the movement during this time, and we got together, Marion and I, and reminisced about October of 1960 and what that weekend really meant to us. It is hard for me to explain what we still feel when we pick up the newspaper or pick up a magazine and see the picture or the names of one of those people, or when we go somewhere and see each other. It is something still with us, as Cecelia [Cunningham] said earlier, it will always be with us, and hopefully that in what we do, in whatever areas of responsibility that we have. Hopefully this thing will live on and on forever in our children and in our children's children, and hopefully in this entire country, whichever walk of life you may have come from, and whatever it is that you might walk into in the future.

Now, if there are any questions, [we will] gladly try to answer them.

QUESTIONER: As I talk to people who were involved on a number of campuses during the spring of 1960, some seem to have a remembrance of that time, "something is happening right now. I want to be a part of it," you know, an urgency that was very immediate, and some seemed to have that same urgency, but a knowledge that this is happening *again,* and this time we want it to stick. Some knew of things that had happened in Oklahoma during the '50s and in Washington, and in Chicago, I want to know if either of you have any recollection of being of one school or the other, if you felt that this was new at the time, or if you knew that this was sort of starting again, or if it was a continuation of something that was happening?

JC: That's interesting. Exactly right, There was that "warrioring" school of thought, and I think that Rev. *[referring to the questioner]* said it so well. Some of us thought we were doing something new, some of us knew it was not new. I had, I don't remember where I got it from, but vivid recollections, not of only the J. T. McCain thing that I spoke about earlier when I was about thirteen, fourteen years old, but I have recollections from studies of sit-ins from the 1940s, led by A. Phillip Randolph.

Many of us knew that, and I think it was that kind of history that made the thing hold together. Most of that came, quite frankly, from students who were on State College's campus, and I think Jim Blake probably had more of this, because at Morehouse you had students coming from a broader area, and you had all of this. And I remember Harry Botenellie coming into the movement, who had this knowledge. He was not only a veteran at the time, and well-read fellow, we still stay in touch, he's now in Washington, D.C., and John Scott, who was—I think—from Toledo, Ohio. These guys came into the movement, and they had a much broader picture than many of us had.

What we had, quite frankly, was just more guts. They knew it. But these guys were really scared, because they were coming from the North, and they were just scared of the South. For some reason we were not afraid. And when you put those two dynamics together, it worked well. And I think you're exactly right.

Those warrioring . . . the factors were there. So much so, I'll never forget that in 1960 when a lot of people failed to realize that there was a big gap between Montgomery of 1955 and '56, and what happened at Albany [Georgia] in 1960. In that four- or five-year period, [the movement] came close to dissipating, and the issue—the big issue—was whether or not Martin Luther King Jr. was expected to practice his preachings and we were going to jail.

All of a sudden Marion Brad came in one day and says, "King leads us to jail. We ain't going anymore." Really, because it was getting rough. And I'll never forget, that it was at that Atlanta meeting, it was just after that meeting, that was in the Morehouse campus, that was one of the most remarkable experiences that I have ever had. That was the day that Martin Luther King Jr.—we were standing at the door, Jim Blake, myself, Marion Brad—and someone said, "There he goes there," and I turned around and looked, looking for this, this *giant* of a man, . . . and he passed *under my chin!*

This is when I really began to get a feel for the dynamism. All of this happened right on that campus. We left that campus and went to Albany, and convinced that it was that meeting that the eventual march in Albany—where Andrew Young came into his being, who has now gone off to be ambassador. Andy and I, as many of you know, remained fast friends throughout all of this. . . .

It was that meeting that changed the course of history, because had it not been for that, had it not been for Albany, the telephone call that the Kennedys made to King's wife—and every poll in the country showed up unto that point that more than 50 percent of that vote *[inaudible]* in large made to Archibald Kerry, an AME from Chicago, who supported Nixon in the Republican ticket in 1960 and then turned around that weekend on that phone call, and eventually he stood ended up having 28 percent and changed the whole course of history. . . . and why I'm saying, during the questions, you can really flesh this thing out. You really can't do it too well in fifteen to twenty minutes. . . .*

[The following selection is taken from later in the presentation.]

JC: I close with this, Cecelia, that's quite true. I remember when we had our first meeting with Matthew Perry, trying to decide how we were going to present our court case. When they started trying to determine who would be best to testify, I remember the biggest consideration was where did your mother and father work, because everybody knew that the moment you took that stand, somebody was going to lose a job back home, and one of the reasons why, my brother John and I were so far out in the movement, was because my mother was a cosmetologist and my father a minister. She wasn't fixing those white people's hair, and my father wasn't preaching to any white people, there wasn't anything they could do to us, so I became the star witness. It didn't have anything to do with Jim Clyburn being anything else, except insulated from this system.

[Other selections from the conference will be found elsewhere in this anthology.]

---

*The reference by Congressman Clyburn is to the influence of the Chicago Daley Machine in securing the 1960 Presidential election for John F. Kennedy. Archibald Carey, a powerful leader in the Chicago community, played a pivotal role. Consult pages 154–55 of Dennis Dickerson, *African American Preachers and Politics: The Careys of Chicago* (Jackson: University Press of Mississippi, 2010). Thanks are owed to Prof. Bobby J. Donaldson of the University of South Carolina for assistance in locating this information.

Matthew J. Perry Jr., Part 1

A Pearl of a Case

Robert Moore **[RM]:*** Do you remember about demonstrations by State College students in 1960?

Matthew Perry **[MP]:** I certainly do . . . There were perhaps a thousand students who marched the streets of Orangeburg on that day in March of 1960. Some 380 of them were arrested. They were arrested and charged with the crime of breaching the peace. I was still practicing law in Spartanburg. Reverend Newman had called me to find out if I was going to be in my office. He didn't tell me what they were going to be doing. He had a strong sense of the propriety of not involving me as the lawyer for the organization in the active demonstrations.

RM: He knew the demonstrations were going to take place. Was it simply a matter of his knowing it, or had he helped organize it?

MP: I have no doubt that Reverend Newman and other persons active in the organization were mindful of the fact that the students were going to speak out. I believe it *[laughs]*.

RM: Was the NAACP's role to shape and make more effective what was going to happen anyway, or did they foster something that wouldn't have happened otherwise?

MP: I'm not sure I can give a definitive answer to that question. I know that Reverend Newman and others, to include people like Reverend Matthew McCollom, who died some years ago, [and] Reverend J. Herbert Nelson, these were people who advocated a nonviolent, very orderly approach to challenging the existence of racial practices at that time. Whatever their involvement was, whether they urged the students to

*Robert J. Moore interviewed Judge Perry (1921–2011) at his office in Columbia, South Carolina, on December 27, 1995. The interview was transcribed by Larry Grubbs of the University of South Carolina, South Caroliniana Library, Modern Political Collections. This selection begins on page 23 of the original transcript and runs to approximately page 29.

do it, or whether having discovered that there was a disposition by the students to do it, they attempted to give proper leadership, I hesitate to state definitively. They were indeed involved in counseling the students to refrain from any odious conduct of any sort, and to at all times to conduct themselves as ladies and gentlemen. This stood us in very well in later appeals. All of the evidence, even on the part of the police, was that the students conducted themselves in an orderly fashion.

RM: So breach of peace was hard to prove.

MP: That's right. Having been notified now that they had nearly four hundred students in jail in Orangeburg, I'm sitting in my office up in Spartanburg, get in my car and head out. I called other lawyer colleagues, Lincoln Jenkins, W. Newton Pugh in Orangeburg, Jack Townsend, also a lawyer in Orangeburg, and Willie Smith of Greenville. We all descended into Orangeburg. The students had been arrested for three hours by the time I arrived. I had developed a sense, in my various interactions with Thurgood Marshall and others, to be sure and cover yourself. Get your clients to authorize you acting in their behalf. So we had them all brought into the Orangeburg courthouse, and I drafted out a little statement on a piece of paper. "We hereby employ and retain Matthew J. Perry, and such lawyers as he may wish to associate with, to represent us in respect to the pending case, and we authorize Matthew J. Perry to do thus and such, and to take any and all means necessary to vindicate . . ."

The matter then was getting them out on bail. One of the things that we had to do was to get the bail set. The bail had initially been set, I think it was a hundred dollars a person. Senator Marshall Williams helped, and persuaded the then-magistrate to reduce the bail to some more manageable figure. Then, we had to fan these lawyers out, and all these ministers who were interested, to get interested citizens to sign the bonds. We got bond forms. We got all of these young people out of jail, and of course the trial proceeded. We had several different trials, and they were quite the occasion at that time.

RM: They were duly convicted?

MP: They were duly convicted.

RM: You wanted to tell about the trial. I don't want to cut you off from that.

MP: The trials were interesting. The police officers who testified concerning what they were doing gave some very interesting testimony. I recall, for example, that one officer testified that he encountered this group of students walking toward the center of town, coming toward Amelia Street. Amelia Street is a street that proceeds from the railroad corner towards the center of town in Orangeburg. He said, "They were walking, generally in columns of twos, and I went to the head of the column and I said, 'Halt, you may not proceed further. Return to the place from whence you came,' or words to that effect. The students looked at me, and those at the head of the line seemed to confer with some behind them. They decided to disobey my order, and they continued to walk. I said, 'You are all under arrest.' There must have been two hundred or so in that line. I said, 'You're under arrest, follow me. I marched them all to the county jail.'"

Here he had no other policemen helping with the operation, and he led them all and they all followed him *[laughs]*. On cross-examination, he was asked, "Did the students say anything in response to you?"

"No."

"Were they profane in their language in any manner?"

"No."

"Did they commit any other acts of disorder as far as you were able to observe?"

"No."

"Were they blocking traffic?"

"No." *[He laughs.]*

He said some of them were carrying signs, saying, "Down with Segregation," "We want the city officials to honor our rights as citizens."

We developed all of this on cross-examination, and the record was just perfect as a freedom of assembly, freedom of speech case. Similarly, the officers who encountered some of the others going down other streets gave testimony not inconsistent with that. On that occasion, they brought out the fire department. There was a much larger group who was marching down Russell Street, but they were orderly in every respect. When they refused to disperse, they turned those fire hoses on them.

RM: Oh, they did?

MP: Yes. Wet them down. We eventually won all of these cases on appeal.

RM: They were tried in small groups, is that the way it worked out?

MP: Yes. I believe the first group consisted of around fifteen students. Everybody attended, it was a major event.

Now you had the emergence of the "Matthew Perry" persona in the legal community, because the press now is focusing heavily upon me and my every move.

Either that day or the day after, you had the arrests of the sixty-five people in Rock Hill. That later became *Henry v. Rock Hill.* We represented those people. You had the young people, twenty-five or more of them, who were arrested in Sumter, in a case called *Randolph v. the City of Sumter.* At the trial levels in every instance, these young people were convicted, and they were appealed. It wasn't until the following year, in '61, that 187 were arrested marching around the State House. That case later became *Edwards v. South Carolina.*

RM: Tell me about the appeals in the Orangeburg student case. Those were separate from the *Edwards* case.

MP: But *Edwards* became a national treasure, because the judge who sat on the appeals in the Orangeburg case was late getting his decisions. *Edwards* came along, they were tried and convicted, and the Supreme Court accepted that case, and decided that case *before* we were able to get the Orangeburg cases. Thereafter, we won the Orangeburg cases, not in a grandiose opinion, they said for the same reasons we said in *Edwards v. South Carolina,* these convictions were reversed.

RM: We'll start with that case then, *Edwards.* This was a case of students marching around the State House. Were these Benedict and Allen students, or State students?

MP: Many of them went to Benedict, many went to Allen, some were from the Orangeburg campus. You had some ministers. I remember there was a Reverend Carter who was a pastor of a church in Newberry. There were people from around the state.

Once again, Reverend Newman ascertained my expected whereabouts on a certain day. I tell you honestly I didn't have any idea in the world what was going to happen, but I had come to know Reverend Newman, and had come to realize that something was going to happen *[laughs]*.

Lo and behold, I get a call that afternoon. I'm still at Spartanburg, I'm now contemplating my move to Columbia. This call came from Lincoln Jenkins, saying that they've got nearly two hundred students down here in jail. I get in my car and come to Columbia.

He and I used somewhat the same procedures we used earlier in Orangeburg. These cases were tried in four separate groups before then-Magistrate Frank Powell. He later became the sheriff of Richland County. The testimony was that the students were orderly, they were marching in columns of twos, they were carrying signs. The state legislature was in session, and they wanted the members of the legislature, according to the testimony of the trial, to know that the black citizens of South Carolina were dissatisfied with the manner in which the law impacted adversely upon them, and they wanted the legislature to do something about it. Perfect freedom of speech, perfect First Amendment concerns.

The city manager of Columbia and the then–chief of police both testified concerning the conduct of these students. They testified, "Yes, they were marching around, they were in columns of twos, they were singing, some of them were singing patriotic songs, "The Star-Spangled Banner." Every now and then they would sing a Negro spiritual. Finally, we decided after they had had long enough, after they went around a second time, I told the chief of police, 'Time to stop it.'

"The chief of police went to the head of the column, and he said, 'Stop. You're in violation of the law. You must now disperse and go back where you came from.'

"At which time this minister began to speak loudly and began to harangue the crowd with religion, and with patriotism, saying, 'I'm a citizen,' and all of this kind of thing."

"We said, 'You're all under arrest,' and marched them all to jail."

That is in essence the testimony *[laughs]*. We argued that before the South Carolina Supreme Court. Frank Powell convicted them all. . . .

RM: The appeal to the South Carolina Supreme Court, how did that . . . ?

MP: They affirmed the conviction. So, now we filed the petition for certiorari.

RM: This is *Edwards*?

MP: This is *Edwards v. South Carolina*. Jack Greenberg, then the director counsel of the NAACP Legal Defense Fund, argued the case before the Supreme Court on the trial record.

He called and he said that he had argued and handled cases from all over the country, and he said, "I just want you to know that trial record is a jewel. It was a pleasure to argue it."

I was there with him when he argued it. The Supreme Court rendered its decision, reversing *Edwards,* all those convictions. That case became one of the *pearls* in First Amendment jurisprudence.

RM: I have a quote from Justice Stewart. "The circumstances in this case reflect an exercise of rights in their most pristine and classic form." That must have really made you thrilled.

MP: Oh, it did. If you read the opinion, you will see the footnotes are references to my cross-examination of the witnesses. Many of these were fact intensive. You've got to develop your facts.

On the basis of *Edwards,* all of the other cases were reversed, *Henry v. Rock Hill* similarly. They were all based on *Edwards.*

RM: Was anything unique about the Henry case that you'd like to comment on?

MP: They were all excellent exercises by the citizens of the various communities of their concerns about racial practices locally. In the Rock Hill case, there was a very fine Presbyterian minister confined to a wheelchair, Reverend Cecil Ivory. It was my pleasure to represent Reverend Ivory, and all of the various people that were involved in that incident.

[Moore conducted approximately seventeen hours of interviews with Judge Perry. Additional portions of those interviews will be found elsewhere in this anthology, and much of the material is included in the book Matthew J. Perry: The Man, His Times, and His Legacy, *edited by W. Lewis Burke and Belinda F. Gergel (Columbia: University of South Carolina Press, 2004).]*

Cleveland Sellers, Part 1

From Denmark to Destiny

Robert Moore [RM]:* This is an interview with Dr. Cleveland Sellers, in his office on January 30, 2003. I appreciate your willingness to talk with me this afternoon, Cleveland, and I wanted to start out by letting you identify who you are by telling us just a skeletal history of your life.

Cleveland Sellers [CS]: Okay. Cleveland Sellers, I'm a native of South Carolina, grew up in Denmark, South Carolina, which is in Bamberg County. That's in the southwestern part of the state of South Carolina, on the border of what is referred to as the lowcountry.

I was educated in Denmark, secondary education in a unique situation, and that was the state of South Carolina, in order to maintain segregated schools and not have to build a facility in Denmark, worked out an agreement with Voorhees College in which it paid Voorhees College a tuition for all of the local secondary educational students in that district. And so the experience was that we ended up, ninth, tenth, eleventh, and twelfth grade, housed on the campus of Voorhees College, and actually the faculty and all was a part of the college faculty, so it was a very unique educational experience for us.

RM: Funded by the state?

CS: Funded by the state, absolutely.

RM: And you were born what year?

CS: Nineteen forty-four, November of 1944. And I was born at home, which is still the home place in Denmark.

RM: Is that where you still live?

CS: I still live in Denmark. I lived in the old home place up until about 1995 and moved out of there then, but we still maintain the home place.

*This interview was conducted by Robert J. Moore in Cleveland Sellers's office, African-American Studies Program, University of South Carolina, Columbia, January 30, 2003.

Cleveland Sellers at Penn Center, assisting in planning for this anthology with the Civil and Human Rights Anthology Festival, June 2004.

RM: Okay. And then after Voorhees?

CS: After Voorhees—well, Voorhees is I guess a unique turning point. The school was built around the philosophy of the Tuskegee educational system and it was influenced by the Booker T. Washington tradition, because the woman who founded Voorhees, Elizabeth Evelyn Wright, was a protégé of Booker T. Washington, and was actually sent out from Tuskegee at a very young age to build an institution and to educate rural blacks, and she ended up coming from Tuskegee to—First she went to a place around Ehrhardt, South Carolina, and she started on the creation of a school and it was burned down, and so she moved from there to Denmark and she started that process over again, and was fortunate enough to get much of the school up and running before she, at a very young age, became ill with—it was either malaria or some disease—and succumbed to that disease. But the college was built in—let's see, it is 102 years old so it was built in—1898, I think, is the date that she started working on it, and she died probably about six or seven years after she got it going.

So I'm saying that to say that the experience in the college community and in a Booker T. Washington–oriented institution was somewhat different from probably most of the other educational experiences because what it did was it brought us in contact with many of the blacks who had achieved: the Mary McLeod Bethunes, certainly Elizabeth Evelyn Wright, Booker T. Washington, Du Bois, and so it was that kind of institution. Those institutions generally were set up with that Booker T. Washington orientation but they had the teachers coming from Hampton [Institute], and so they brought in a little different teaching methodology also, and so you got the best of two worlds. It was certainly focused on the experiences of African Americans. We talked and celebrated Black History Week at that point, many of the figures that we were talking about would be figures that we would be discussing at various and sundry points during the session. So there was a level of, I guess, confidence that was built, and the fact that people were pursuing academic excellence and scholarship was, I think, unique and made that particular experience very unique.

Being on the college campus in 1960, when the sit-ins started in Greensboro, North Carolina, it wasn't but a couple weeks before the fervor actually comes down what is now I-85 and I-77. Actually the sit-ins arrive in Denmark, and this was actually organized by the college SGA [Student Government Association] and some of the students there, and they actually became involved in the sit-ins, so being a high school student during that particular period of time, it gave me an opportunity to be very much involved in organizing the sit-ins, even though the college students, men in particular, were the ones who actually went out and sat in, or attempted to sit in, at a drugstore in downtown Denmark. It was a united effort at the campus to develop strategies and to work out details and get communications out and do all the kinds of things that were necessary to make those demonstrations successful.

So I had an opportunity to be involved in that, and then at the same time, was one of the founders of the youth chapter of the NAACP at Voorhees College, and at that point it was Voorhees School and Junior College, is the way it was labeled. So we had a joint chapter and there were high school students as well as college students who made up the chapter. And so we were very much involved and enthusiastic, and I think that is one of the areas in which the consciousness raising occurred, where we were aware of what was going on in the fledgling movement, and that there were issues and commitment and the idealism that kind of permeated the movement. [That was] the kind of discussions and the kind of involvement that I was afforded, primarily because we were at the campus all the time, twenty-four seven.

So that's, I think, the kind of experience and orientation that led me to become involved much earlier than some in the civil rights movement.

RM: Did you go on to college right after that?

CS: When I graduated from high school, I went directly to Howard University. Again, for the institution it was expected that every student who graduated would go off to college or would go off to school of some type. The option would be for some to go into the military so they could generate funds through the G.I. Bill in order for them to go to college, but it was expected that you would go to college, and so a large percentage of my high school graduating class did end up in some college or technical college or a university or in the service so that they could generate funds so they could go to college.

And so I went off to Howard University as a student in mechanical engineering. One of the reasons why I was particularly interested in Howard University was because Howard University was a renowned institution for African Americans, had a tremendous history, and I had concluded that if in fact Voorhees, which was a much smaller institution, had the kind of civil rights commitment and activities that it did, that if you would go to an institution like Howard University, you would find a much broader and much larger group of activists and activities to be involved in. I was rudely awakened very shortly after I got to Howard because what I discovered at Howard University was that Howard University had a very middle-class orientation, they were very, I guess, what do I want to term that? "Job conscious." And very much involved in emulating as much as possible the status quo, and the young men would—on some occasions they had shirt and ties that they would wear to class, they would sometimes change after lunch. And they were really kind of antithetical to the movement, and to the fledgling movement so—I did, however, find a number of friends and acquaintances, or those who had become friends and acquaintances, and joined a very small group of students, activists, called the Nonviolent Action Group, or NAG, at Howard University. It was a very powerful group and it involved a lot of very dedicated and committed individuals of whom Stokely Carmichael was one, and Ed Brown and Muriel Tillinghast, and the list goes on and on and on, many of those who achieved success at later points in the civil rights movement and then later in the educational community at large.

RM: The name of that organization was?

CS: NAG. N-A-G. Nonviolent Action Group at Howard University, and it had the impact on the movement that many of the student groups might have had. For an example, early on the students out of Nashville, out of Vanderbilt, James Lawson, and John Lewis out of American Baptist Institute, and Marion Barry out of Fisk, formed a kind of nucleus, and the initial stage of the movement in terms of the philosophy of nonviolence and the introducing of that was done by that Nashville group.

And then later you have the influence of the Atlanta group, and this is Julian Bond and Lonny King and a number of others there, and they were more in terms of nonviolent direct action. "Let's be involved, let's be organized, let's attack segregation where we find it," primarily Atlanta and the urban area. NAG was a more urban-oriented and urban-conscious group, so we were involved in issues that centered around the securing of the engagements of people like Bayard Rustin, who, because of the taint that was attached to him in regards to his being a Socialist, at that point the university was very reluctant to having Bayard come and speak. And Malcolm X was almost a no-no, almost completely. And through a struggle and organizing internally at the school, through the SGA and many of the other organizations that we were able to infiltrate and influence, we were able to get the Lyceum Program to in fact bring both Bayard and Malcolm to Howard University.

Through that effort, we became even more conscious, and then had an opportunity, before and after each spoke, to sit down and talk with them. Bayard Rustin, about some of his experiences, and with A. Philip Randolph and his experiences with In Friendship.* That was a group in New York with Ella Baker that actually assisted the Montgomery bus boycott movement with resources, and I think it was Bayard who initially introduces Dr. King to the philosophy of nonviolence. It's Ella Baker who talks about the importance of organizing, and it's Ella Baker who also is influential in getting Dr. King and those leaders that emerge through the Montgomery bus boycott to come together to form the Southern Christian Leadership Conference.

So with that kind of history, it gave us an opportunity to sharpen our skills and to challenge and to be challenged by discussions with Bayard about organization versus the issue of mobilization, philosophical issues on nonviolence, the difference between organizing in the South and organizing in the North, and those kinds of things. That relationship with Bayard would lead to our—and this is the NAG group—being much of the "cannon fodder" for the March on Washington. We were the "grunts" who went about making the seventy thousand cheese sandwiches, and the eighty thousand posters, and dealing with the logistics and running errands and putting all—I mean, we were the ground troops that made the arrangements on the ground for the crowd of 250,000 to have a successful march on Washington!

Howard University was that kind of experience for me. I had the opportunity of working with Gloria Richardson in Cambridge, Maryland, at the point where they started local demonstrations over the issue of segregated Cambridge, and Cambridge then went under martial law for a period of a year. And so we were very much involved in doing that, and that's where we sharpened our organizing skills and understood what's required in order for you to organize communities. And working in Cambridge, Maryland, we were in the North and we understood the kinds of pull and take. In Washington we ended up organizing a rent strike, and we were involved in organizing protests against the bus system —in D.C. it was segregated—and that all led to the beginning of the process of organizing home rule in Washington, D.C.

We were all on the cutting edge and very much involved in those kinds of activities. [I] stayed at Howard University for two years, was involved, as I said, in Cambridge and in the March on Washington. The church bombing in Birmingham had, I think, another tremendous impact on me. And, we were talking in our group about making a much larger commitment. Bob Moses and SNCC ["Snick"—Student Nonviolent Coordinating Committee] were proposing the Mississippi Summer Project. The challenge came to us to organize that. We felt like we could be very influential and be a part of that so we made efforts to organize students from other campuses around the Washington, D.C. area. We got some students from Morgan State, we got some from the University of Maryland, and we took them to Oxford and then [out across] Mississippi. I think about thirty-three students all told for the Mississippi Summer Project.

*For more information regarding In Friendship, see the Web page "Martin Luther King and the Global Freedom Struggle: In Friendship," http://mlk-kpp01.stanford.edu/index.php/encyclopedia/encyclopedia/enc_in_friendship.

RM: And the "we" is the NAG group still?

CS: NAG group. The NAG is a SNCC affiliate, and so we were interchanged between being SNCC and NAG, but for the purpose of identifying us as not being on a payroll for SNCC, we were the NAG group at Howard University. That's the "we," yes. And the group, again, consisted of a lot of folk who ended up at various and sundry stages in the movement. H. Rap Brown, during the spring of 1964 had come to Washington. We began to work on assisting him in enrolling in Howard University and brought him into the NAG program. He was the brother of Ed Brown, who was a student at Howard University and one of the original founders of the NAG group. We had Mike Thelwell, who is an author and educator now, and it consisted of a large number of very interesting young people. From there, the summer of 1964 I go into Mississippi. I go to Oxford first, and while we're in Oxford assisting in preparing the students and recruits to go into Mississippi, Mickey Schwerner picks a volunteer, and he and Chaney return to Mississippi. They get a call there's a church bombing. For project directors, any kind of activity that was a bombing or a strange murder or arrest or those kinds of things, would usually be checked into by the project director.

He goes back and shortly after he gets back in Neshoba County, he goes out to Philadelphia and comes up missing. All three of them.

After about three days, we had concluded that something tragic had occurred. They understood the importance of communication, they understood the priority of communication, and therefore we concluded early on that they were probably dead. But what we did was we gathered a group of eight, with four cars, and we sent them out to Mississippi to see if we could locate Schwerner and Goodman. I ended up in that detail, going into Philadelphia, Mississippi, for a period of three nights and I think it was four days, in which at night we would actually search the woods, the ravines, the riverbeds, or whatever it was that people might have thought that either bodies were stored or people could be held as hostages.

Farmers would go out pretending to hunt and they would draw maps of these places and they would pass these maps along, and at night we would go in and actually check the places out. After it appeared as if our cover was going to be lifted and we might be discovered and create some problems for the people that we were staying with, we decided to withdraw. We weren't having success in locating Schwerner, Goodman, and Chaney.

I go from there to Holly Springs, Mississippi, which is the northern part of Mississippi, and we ended up with a twelve-county project area, probably one of the largest projects in Mississippi that summer. We're in the Delta and the Delta is the black belt, and so we have our work cut out for us. We're preparing to organize the Mississippi Freedom Democratic Party which would, in August, go to the national Democratic convention and challenge the seating of the regular Democratic Party.

We also organized freedom schools in which we actually taught the basics: reading, writing, arithmetic. And we introduced a reader, which was African American history —one of the first primers or readers exclusively geared toward African American history. We also worked with setting up community centers, recreation centers for young people in the communities, in which we'd bring them and have activities, and put together organizations and do recreational kinds of activities, and just a place where young people could gather.

I stayed in Mississippi for probably eighteen months and [then] was elected the program director of the Student Nonviolent Coordinating Committee in 1965, and moved to Atlanta, in which my responsibilities became assisting with collecting, inventorying, and disseminating resources. At this point, there is a "Sojourner Truth Motor Fleet." We have almost a hundred employees in the Student Nonviolent Coordinating Committee—

RM: How many?

SC: Almost a hundred. The Student Nonviolent Coordinating Committee never in its entire existence went over 120 employees. Part of the reason for that was that many of the students and volunteers that came down for the summer, after the summer was over, they wanted to stay, and so we did make provisions for many of those, which created some tension within the organization because going into the Mississippi Summer Project SNCC was a predominantly black organization.

So we were beginning to spread our wings. We had become full-fledged civil rights workers at that point, and that was a struggle, just to get in. Certainly the March on Washington and the lesson we learned there made it an imperative that we understand our principles, that we stand on our principles, and that we recognize and empower ourselves to recognize that we should have voice in the civil rights movement. That was a struggle for a long time. The attitude was that we were young and naïve and the old-line professionals had all the wisdom, all the knowledge, and so we challenged that.

At the March on Washington [all] the speeches were submitted to those persons who were heading up the March on Washington. John Lewis's speech, which talked about going through the South with demonstrations, antisegregation demonstrations, "like General Sherman . . ." created some anxiety and so we spent most of the day, before John Lewis spoke, trying to negotiate that through. Eventually A. Philip Randolph spoke with Courtney Cox and Jim Forman and John Lewis. . . . He did not want any kind of disruptions, but he wanted us to be a part. And so we agreed to change some of the language of the speech. But that was a hard pill to swallow.

But it was a process of growing up, because never again would we allow folk to dictate to us how we felt and how we articulated what we felt, so as an organization that was a growth process and we became mature after the 1963 March on Washington, and became a legitimate civil rights organization in and of ourselves.

. . . I probably represented the first of the program directors in SNCC and, like I said, the responsibility was about a million-dollar budget and about a hundred and some employees, and a fleet of almost thirty-three automobiles, and you name it, we had it. We had a national office, we had friend groups, we had fundraisers, we had concerts, and trying to coordinate all those things and make them work.

RM: Where'd you get the million dollars a year?

CS: Well, we got that from fundraising activities. On occasion we would have major concerts in New York that would be organized for us by Harry Belafonte and Sidney Poitier and Diana [Diahann] Carroll and Bob Dylan and Jane Fonda, and a number of others would come in each time to assist with that. So we had major concerts, and we had a professional fundraising group that sent out the invitations. I mean, it was professional each time. We had a fundraising office in Los Angeles, we had one in Chicago, we had one in New York, and that's the way most of those funds were raised. Then we also had the foundations, the Field, the Taconic, and other foundations that would assist, or Voter Registration would also—V.E.P., Voter Education Project—would also on occasion fund some voting programs . . across the South. . . .

[Relevant interviews with Richard Miles and James Felder will be found in volume 2 and with Armand Derfner in volume 5.]

CS: We had a first-class research department headed by a gentleman by the name of Jack Minnis, who was a trained researcher, and so we were able to exchange information with the press, with other organizations. . . . Through that effort it was Jack Minnis who discovered that in Alabama you could actually organize a county party, and that rule was put in way back during the Civil War era, and we were able to do that to organize the first Lyons County Freedom Organization, which was separate from the Democratic and Republican Parties, and it was an effort to organize the disenfranchised blacks in Alabama. That organization, the Lyons County Freedom Organization, is the birthplace of the Black Panther Party.

The Lyons County folk identified and adopted the panther as a symbol. Now the symbol for the Democratic Party in Alabama was a white rooster that had, on the top, "White," and on the bottom, "Supremacy Forever." And so when we were organizing the party to make it consistent with political parties, we asked those folk in Lyons County what did they want to represent them, the symbol, and they put out all kinds—a giraffe, the lion, the bear—and we told them what the symbols were for the Republican and the Democratic Party, and the Democratic Party in Alabama, and they suggested that we use the black panther. It was sleek and cunning and sometimes it frightened people, and that was okay, and it kind of represented them. I mean it was cunning in the sense that was a very powerful, kind of assured of a certain self-assurance that the pride and all those kinds of things, and so they wanted the panther as their symbol.

We were able to go to Green County and Dallas—Dallas County is Selma—and Lyons County. . . . When it came time to vote—this is after the Voting Rights Act of 1965—we asked young people from the urban areas to come down and help us do the G-O-T-V [Get Out The Vote], get people out, transport them and all that. So folk came from New York, Chicago, Philadelphia, and California, and when they went back to talk about their experience, they talked about it in the context of this Black Panther Party in Lyons County, Alabama. Bobby [Seale] is on record as saying that when he and Huey [Newton] were trying to name their new organization they remembered the Black Panther Party. So they took the Black Panther Party [name] because of many of the things it was doing: organizing people, trying to empower people to register to vote, and that other kind of stuff. But, they said for the urban areas we will add "for self-defense," and so that's what they added. But the origin of the Black Panthers is in Alabama. Very unique kind of thing.

So the Lyons County model was the model that comes out during 1966 with "Black Power," and certainly after the position against the war in Vietnam, the suspect cry for "fight for democracy in Vietnam." The economic adventure that we thought was in fact the enticing reason for America's involvement in Vietnam . . .

So even after the Mississippi March, Dr. King invited Willie Ricks, Stokely, and myself because he wanted to really understand Black Power, and he knew that we were the architects of it. Ricks was the person who came up with the term. He just said the term worked. That was his job, that's what he did, and so he told Stokely to use the word, and then define it, but define it very loosely. The point was that Dr. King invited us over to his house and he wanted us to talk about it, and then he talked about some of the reasons why it was going to be difficult for him to embrace that, but he said essentially that he respected our idea about Black Power and he was still committed to nonviolence. We all agreed that we weren't trying to impact [the nonviolence], that we were just trying to move on in terms of our development.

The same thing happened with him over the Vietnam War. When we came out against the war, Dr. King and all of the other civil rights hierarchies, said, "you all are cuckoo," and they kind of pushed us out. "You all have to fend for yourselves. We're not going to be sympathetic to that." But one of the things that it did was it pushed Dr. King, I think, even further, to the point where he recognized that he could not restrain himself anymore. He had to take a position against the war in Vietnam. And I think that was the good part, and so that's the wholesome and healthy part.

You know, people talk about differences in strategies and differences in terms of philosophy, but I think that the unique part about the civil rights movement, the thing that made it successful and last as long as it did, was the competing ideas, and the struggle through that. On the bottom line that people got upset with one another but it wasn't the kind where you'd lose a friend. I mean, you just— "I'll walk down the road if that's what you want. I'll go down the road with you, but I'm still thinking that this other thing might work better." And so you have that kind of thing. So you see a clip, for an example, on the *Eyes on the Prize,* where Stokely and Dr. King are walking down the road together, and the reporter goes, "And that's Dr. King." And Dr. King says, "I'm committed to nonviolence. I will be committed to nonviolence. I won't change from nonviolence." They go to Stokely and Stokely says, "I'm not committed to nonviolence." And they keep on walking down the road together.

I mean, you have to understand how those dynamics work. And it was about disagreeing on strategies and tactics, not disagreeing on your commitment or your dedication or any of those kinds of things, and I think people would probably be shocked to know that they maintained a very cordial relationship all the way through to Dr. King's assassination. And matter of fact, when Dr. King, in 1967, which is some time after the Black Power supposedly was snafued [*sic*] and split people up, Dr. King called Stokely up and invited him to his church when he was getting ready to announce his antiwar [position]. Said, "I want you there. I want you on the front row." We didn't get on the front row but we were there, in the front, and I tell people that because I want people to understand that that relationship was like that. I mean, he would call and say, "Stokely, I need you over here. I got something—I want you to be there when I deliver it." And Stokely would say, "I'm there."

And this was the same kind of thing in relationship when he goes with the Poor Peoples March up to Washington, and he goes and he says, "Stokely, I'm trying to do this thing. I'm trying to coalesce and build and organize poor people, black, white, Hispanic, Native American, whatever they are, and put the pressure on the government to address the issue of the poor in this country." And he said, "Now I can't do it if I have a lot of people, young people, coming in and challenging [me] about the tactics and all those other kinds of things." So he says to Kwame *[a reference to Kwame Turé, the name Stokely Carmichael later took]*, "I want you to help me keep the other groups from coming in and taking the focus off by trying to discredit nonviolence," or whatever it was.

And Stokely said, "I agree," and essentially told folk that "If you don't want to support the march, fine, but don't go out there. Stay where you are. And for those who want to go out, go ahead. And we're supporting it, but we support it because of Dr. King's commitment to raise that particular issue about poverty."

And at that point Dr. King was talking about redistribution of wealth. He was talking about against the war in Vietnam. He was in the process of assessment and reassessment and reanalysis, so where he might have ended up, I'm not sure, but certainly that was a transitional period and he felt strong enough about the relationship between he and Stokely that he could call him in and they could discuss what they were trying to do and Stokely would help where he could.

RM: So everybody was growing by that clash of ideas.

CS: Oh yeah, everybody was growing. It was, like I said, like a university. There were always new ideas. We had Frantz Fanon and we had—what's the book? Oh, my goodness. Silberman? I can't think of the name of it. *[The book by Charles E. Silberman is* Crisis in Black and White *(New York: Random House, 1964).]* And you had to read this stuff.

RM: Silberman. Yeah.

CS: And it would be almost like each month there would be a new book, a new perspective, a new—'Introduction of Philosophy' and those kinds of things.

So I stayed around Atlanta until my term was up as Program Organizer, and it was about that time that I decided maybe I needed to retool, go back to school, and decided to come back to South Carolina and address the issue of completing my education.

Cleveland Sellers, president of Voorhees University.

In the fall of 1967 I come back to South Carolina, and I know that Denmark is probably much too small, and I wanted to think about, and I had considered the possibility of going to South Carolina State and I began to try to work through that. I had worked along with students when they had a protest activity down there called "The Cause," which was in 1967, and so I knew some of the faculty, Roland Haynes and a couple of the other professors there, and I indicated—

RM: George Thomas?

CS: Yes. And I indicated that I probably would try to go to school there. I was stepping out of the mainstream of this commitment and tensions, and so it seemed to be inviting for me to do that. And so I came in in November of 1967. Things went pretty smoothly. School was out the first of December and I came back around, I imagine it was the latter part. . . .

By this time the president of the NAACP youth chapter there at South Carolina State was interested in the bowling alley, which had a sign "White Only" in the window, and that was like a red flag, and so they wanted to go down and protest.

RM: What was his name?

CS: John Stroman. And so I am in the process of transitioning and I'm not going to make commitments to protest activity and protest campaigns. What I have done is,

I am interested in organizing student groups and getting them involved in a kind of African American history, the history of Africa, the self-determination, knowing who you are, and at the same time beginning to tie those student groups into the patriarchs like Esau Jenkins, and Modjeska Simkins, and all of the folk who were around—the movers and the shakers, the attorneys, and at this point [some] of the people were Matthew Perry, and Pugh, and Finney up there in Sumter. These folk had been very much involved in civil rights and even McCain, who became the national director of the Congress for Racial Equality. He's not back in Sumter that early but I kind of thought that he would be coming, and he would be the kind of person that I'd want the students to know and to sit down and discuss and talk about their involvement and how they develop the consciousness and the commitment and those kinds of things. So that's what I was involved in.

[Part 2 of this interview will be found in volume 4 in the section on the Orangeburg tragedy.]

PART 4
Spawning the Movement in South Carolina

I. DeQuincey Newman, How Beautiful upon the Mountains

Grace McFadden **[GM]:*** I'm Grace Jordan McFadden, with the Reverend I. De-Quincey Newman. Reverend Newman is an eminent theologian, politician, and civil rights leader in the state of South Carolina. In the late 1950s he served as president of the State Conference of Branches of NAACP, and during the decade of the 1960s, he had the awesome responsibility of serving as state field director of the State Conference of Branches of NAACP, when great strides were made in this state. Reverend Newman, thank you. It's a pleasure to have you here.

I. DeQuincey Newman **[IDN]:** It's a pleasure being here, Dr. McFadden.

GM: We might begin by having you recall your earliest recollections of growing up in South Carolina as a black person.

IDN: Quite early in life I realized that there was something amiss in South Carolina. I did not take long to find out just what it was, and the thing that was amiss was the complete and absolute segregation as a way of life in South Carolina, and the prevailing condition of black people having no rights that a white person was bound to respect. This was most disturbing, but as a child there wasn't anything that I could do about it. Black adults had been thoroughly intimidated and for the most part had resigned themselves to accepting segregation as a way of life. Few were the times that even token efforts were made towards challenging segregation, or black people standing up for their constitutional rights.

They were dangerous times. There was the ever-present threat of the Ku Klux Klan. Blacks were without friends in the various governmental frameworks, from the

*Newman was born in 1911 and died in 1985. Interview conducted by Grace Jordan McFadden on videotape. Videotaped in the South Carolina Educational Televisions studio, ca. 1982. Archived with the African American Studies Program, University of South Carolina. The subhead here ("How Beautiful . . .") is taken from Isaiah 52:7.

governor's office on down to the office of the lowliest magistrate in the state. There was no governmental agency toward which blacks could turn for redress of grievances. Governmental agencies, including the courts, there was no place for blacks to redress their grievances. And it was just the way of life, and it was not until the early '40s that blacks began to speak up loudly enough to be heard.

GM: Is there anything, Reverend Newman, that sticks out in your mind, that you can recall as a youngster, that was a painful experience that dramatized the segregation that existed within your community?

IDN: Yes, I remember one occasion. As a small boy, my father sent me to the post office. As was his habit whenever he sent us on errands, he timed us, gave us so many minutes to go and come, and I was sent to the post office, and I ran all the way to the post office. On the way back I got tired and sat in a chair in front of the fire department to rest. The fire chief, of course he was white, came out in a rage, red as a beet, cursed me for everything he could think of, and told me what he would do to me if I didn't get out of that chair. That was a white man's chair, and no nigger was allowed to sit in that chair. He frightened me nearly to death. I'd never had that kind of experience before. This was in Kingstree. We had not long since moved to Kingstree from Anderson County. Up until that time I didn't know that there was a race problem. I knew nothing about segregation. What was a black man's place or a white man's place.

And there was another experience equally as traumatic, or more so. We lived not far from the convict camp, the stockade, where prisoners were kept, and there was a man, a black man, who had been arrested, I don't remember what the crime was, but he was locked into a wooden calaboose, I believe they were called, with iron bars at the doors and windows. That night the Ku Klux Klan visited this lockup where the black man was held, saturated the kerosene or gasoline, and set a fire. And the man began calling for help in the middle of the night. "Help. Help. Help."

I was awakened and went into my father's room, shook him to awaken him, and asked, "Pa, ain't you going to go up and help the man?"

My father [said], "Go on back to bed, boy."

And I was insistent, and I shook him, and I said, "Pa, go and help the man."

But he didn't. I kept that in my heart for a long time, and I held it against my father. There was a man being burned alive, and my father wouldn't turn a hand to help him. Of course, I've learned since then, had he gone to give help to this person in distress he would have been shot down. He'd have been killed. My father knew that, and knowing, or learning the facts of life since then, I could appreciate why my father did not go to help this person. Any number of people in the community knew what was happening, but everybody was afraid to do anything to help this man out who was being burned alive. I've never forgotten that. It was a bitter experience.

It was an experience that lives with me today, and even now—and that's been over sixty years ago—that kind of experience causes me to be very careful, very careful, and to walk a tightrope when I'm in areas that I'm unknown or where I don't know whether I've got any friends or not.

GM: Do you feel that these experiences impacted on your involvement in civil rights?

IDN: I'm sure they did, perhaps in a subconscious way, because I've never failed to lend a helping hand, and all effort towards the uplift of black people, and to strive for equal rights for black people, and to champion black causes. I'm certain that those experiences had a great deal to do with motivating me toward becoming a civil rights activist.

GM: When did you get involved as a civil rights activist?

IDN: As a student in college, when the first NAACP college chapter was organized to serve students at Clark College and Gammon Theological Seminary, in Atlanta, in 1936.

GM: And that was your initial involvement?

IDN: Yes, that was my initial involvement. I had been involved in peace movements prior to that time, through what was known as the Student Volunteer Association, which later fell into disrepute and turned out to be a front for Communists. But the NAACP was the first handle that I had for working in civil rights.

GM: Reverend Newman, you're known in the state of South Carolina as an eminent theologian, really the "Boy Wonder," a lot of people have called you. Do you feel that the clergy in South Carolina, the black clergy, has historically been at the vanguard of the civil rights movement?

IDN: Yes. You see, for many, many years, the only professions that a black youth could aspire to was that of teaching school or preaching. So they were the only sources for educated leadership, or leadership of any kind, the clergy or the teaching profession. Teaching was a sensitive profession because the school superintendents and the school trustees were all white, so that black teachers were inhibited. They were not free to give, provide leadership, civil rights leadership for black people. So that the clergy alone, with the exception of the few independent black business people we had, an undertaker here and there, were the only sources for leadership for black people.

I'm proud to state that the black clergy did provide, they did take advantage of the opportunity they had to provide leadership. The fact is, the black church was the only institution controlled by black people. It was the only place that could provide a forum for the discussion of black problems, and even today, the black clergy plays an important role, although now the efforts have been augmented by black lawyers. We have good black lawyers in South Carolina, thanks to the NAACP, through the court action that was taken. We have black lawyers. We have blacks who are in politics. We have, I think, some three hundred black elected officials in the state of South Carolina, town and county council persons, black mayors, legislators, school board members. All resulting from efforts that were made in behalf of black people beginning early in the 1940s.

GM: So in the 1980s we see great strides.

IDN: Yes.

GM: Now you served, Reverend Newman, as president of the State Conference of Branches of NAACP in the latter '50s, and as field director in the decade of the '60s. What stands out in your mind as some of the major achievements during that era?

IDN: Of course, the desegregation of the University of South Carolina and Clemson University, the secondary schools, the Civil Rights Act of 1964, the Voting Rights Act of 1965, are the milestones of the civil rights movement during the 1960s. And of course, prior to that time, I think the most outstanding achievement was, in 1947, when the white Democratic primary was outlawed as the only meaningful elections in the state of South Carolina. It was in that year that Judge J. Waites Waring ruled that the doors of the Democratic Party had to be open to blacks.

GM: Do you feel, given that, that in 1980, the decade of the '80s and decades to come that black people have a responsibility to assume a major role in the whole political process?

IDN: Very definitely. There could be a reversion in the race relations pattern. We haven't progressed yet to the extent that we can take our freedom for granted. We have to be very vigilant, very vigilant. And we've got to be on the defensive. There is an element in the majority race who resent the progress that black people have made, and if they could turn the clock back, they would. Make no mistake about that. We're not out of the woods yet. There is a veneer of goodwill, a veneer of goodwill. It's in the best economic interest of the state to indicate good race relations, but among the majority, we feel that we're getting along as well as we are now because of the protection of the image of the state, rather than stemming from the heart, or because from the Christian viewpoint it's right. It's right to have brotherhood, regardless of race, creed, or color. I wish that this was what our race relations stem from, but that isn't the case. Still the most segregated hour of the week is eleven o'clock on Sunday mornings.

GM: Reverend Newman, do you feel that progress was made in the state of South Carolina in the field of civil rights without overt hostility? Do you feel that there has been progress that was made without hostility between the races? I'm thinking of the kinds of problems that occurred in Mississippi and in Alabama, when the news media was filled with examples of confrontations that existed, but it doesn't seem as though South Carolina had that kind of open hostility.

IDN: Yes. We were fortunate in South Carolina to have eight governors to come upon the scene of appreciable enlightenment. While Governor Ross Barnett was governor of Mississippi, and Governor Wallace was governor of Alabama, and Governor Vandiver, I believe it was, was governor of Georgia, all arch-segregationists, we had already had, in South Carolina, Governor Hollings, a racial moderate. And then Dr. Russell, the former president of the university, a moderate. And Governor McNair, then Governor West, Governor Edwards, Governor Riley. South Carolina has been blessed with a number of moderate governors before the states of Alabama and Mississippi began to have moderate governors or moderate people in control of their respective legislators.

Then too, another factor that enabled South Carolina to come through the civil rights crisis with a minimum of bloodshed is the fact that South Carolina produced its own civil rights leadership. It did not have to bring in professional civil rights leaders from elsewhere to provide leadership for blacks in the state. These homegrown leaders were familiar with the lay of the land. They knew when to strike and when not to. They knew in advance, they had ways of finding out when it was the best time to have a demonstration and when was a bad time to have one. Because South Carolina, as you know, is a small state and if you've been around for a good while, whites get to know blacks and blacks get to know whites, and they are able to communicate with each other. South Carolinians are very reluctant to accept civil rights or political leadership from the outside.

GM: Reverend Newman, you're certainly one of those civil rights leaders who came from within the state, and who contributed hours upon hours of hard work and dedication to make civil rights work in the state of South Carolina. Thank you very much.

IDN: It's a pleasure talking with you, Dr. McFadden.

Anne Newman and Emily Newman, a Family Affair

Marvin Lare [ML]:* I was saying, off tape, before we started recording that as I've talked with people around the state and they mentioned your husband with such high regard, but they also say, "Well, now, don't forget his wife. If she hadn't kept the office for him, if she hadn't kept the home front going, well, he wouldn't have been able to do what he did." . . .

Anne Newman [AN]: Right, right . . . Well, I guess Spartanburg would be the best place to start because that's when he decided to become field director for the NAACP, and like I said, the Methodist Church had this committee that was social—what is it, social concerns?

ML: Christian Social Concerns?

AN: Christian Social Concerns, and he just said, "Well, Anne, I guess this is a good start for me to at least pull out so that all the help I've been given in these churches, but I have more to give than just that." And that's when he was asked to become the field director for the NAACP. And that is the beginning of the life of our civil rights movement. . . .

ML: What would be a—I don't know whether to say a "typical day"—but what were some of the things that stand out in your mind?

AN: I can give you a typical day with Reverend Newman. They were tough days in the '60s, but I had no problems with people, and of course I was thrusted [sic] out in the front a good bit because of that. And of course he would be out of town a lot, so I had to look—I learned—there would be different people that would come in our office, and of course I opened the office for the state NAACP here in Columbia. And we couldn't find anyone who would let us have materials, typewriters, or anything,

*Anne Newman (1925–2009) was interviewed at her home in Columbia, South Carolina, on February 23, 2005.

and so there was a nice young Presbyterian minister who was just starting with this new business that was moving to Columbia, and he came by one day and I was talking with him that I can't get paper, no pens, no pencils. "What can I do? I need something to work with."

And he said, "Well, I'll tell you, I'll get you everything you want."

And I said, "Well, I'm able to pay you. We can pay you whatever it is."

And he did. He stepped out and—you would have thought R. L. Bryan would have let us have everything we wanted, but this man, whatever this company was that he was working for, he brought me typewriters, pencils, everything I needed. And then I started to opening up my office, and we paid our bills. I saw that our bills were paid on time just like I do for my family, I pay them on time. And after then I had no trouble, Lorick and all these other companies that would come in, they would have me for machines and I could use anything—and that's how our office got started. Nobody knows the problem that we had, but I must admit, Reverend Lare, as long as he would stay away from me, I could get what I wanted. You know, as long as they wouldn't see him [laughs]. Which is terrible, isn't it? Isn't that terrible? But that, you must remember, now that was back in the '60s, and a lot of times I couldn't even keep the salesmen to keep coming if they knew that he was involved in it. And we went on from there.

But the worst experience I think I've ever had with Reverend Newman was when I got a chance to buy a house here on Chappelle Street, the first house—being a Methodist minister—we ever owned. We'd always lived in somebody else's parsonage, but we never lived in our own place, and the first chance, I got a chance to buy the—you know, when they build a house for you, they let you stay in there for two or three months to sort of see if anything's wrong with it. And so we bought this brand new house on Chappelle Street and closing day came—you don't want to hear my story!

ML: Oh, yes, yes!

AN: The closing day came and two or three days before that I said, "Reverend Newman, don't forget, we're supposed to have our closing on the house such and such a date."

And he said, "All right."

And each day I would remind him, but the day came for us to close and up there on the corner of Gervais Street and Main, in that building used to be a lot of lawyers, right across from the capitol, and [when] the time came—I went. I was there with everything they needed and everything on time, and then wait for Reverend Newman because he had to sign the whole thing. So we waited, and we waited, and one lawyer went to the window and looked out and said, "They're marching around the statehouse!"

I just felt like my whole life had just gone on before me, and so I got up and I said —the kids from Claflin, and State, and Benedict now and you know—and I said, "Well, I can tell you right now, we won't sign any papers today."

So it just happened that the contractor said, "We'll wait till tomorrow."

But when they arrested all of them and put them in jail, all of them, *all* of them, and I went down to the jail and I said, "Didn't I tell you today was the day we were supposed to sign the—"

"Well, they're all lawyers. They can bring the papers down here. I'll sign them." *[She laughs.]* And of course we had to wait till another day. I think that was about my worst day. You have these ups and downs, but we had quite a few close calls though, in those days, quite a few.

ML: In retrospect, being arrested . . . seems like that was such a common kind of thing but it was bound to be just heart-stopping every time.

AN: Right, right.

ML: Regardless of the situation, because you really never knew how it was going to work out.

AN: That's true. Like the integrating of the state parks—he was caught down there at Myrtle Beach State Park, and it just happened he wrote my phone number on a little piece of paper and gave it to the man. He didn't know the man, he didn't know whether the man would use the number, but it just so happened that the man called me and of course I had to call lawyers. So I guess that's why we called it "a family affair," because there were so many close calls, and they had to just pass—and if you could get it to me, I knew where to send it, but back in those days you couldn't trust many people. . . . When he integrated the state parks they put him in prison down there in a little jail of some kind, and this man did call me and said, "Your husband said you know what to do."

First I called Mr. Perry, then I just started the ball a-rolling, and I called New York and got them alerted, and then it was out of my hands. There wasn't any more I could do, but I knew how to get them started doing that. Yes. But he made it out of there okay, he really made it out okay. But that was a scary time for him because if it had not been for the jailer that was holding him, they would have killed him that night. But this jailer kept them off and so that he could get to his car and get out of Myrtle Beach, and that's how he got out of Myrtle Beach. Mmmh, those were rough days when you sit down and think about them.

ML: So, basically did the New York office handle the bail bonds and so forth?

AN: That's right. They did all the money, along with attorney Perry.

Emily Newman [EN]: And there was one source here, Manning Baxley.

ML: Manning Becksley?

EN: Baxley. He would front money for . . .

ML: Was he a bail bondsman or just an individual?

EN: He was a very—he and his wife were very community minded. Mrs. Baxley was a Satterwhite, that was her maiden name, and the Satterwhites and the Baxleys had stores that serviced the black community, small community stores. And so they were among our more affluent members of the society, much more so than the doctors and the lawyers of that time, and they just both came from families that understood noblesse oblige. So he was one of those people that quietly funneled the money, and there was one arrest in Orangeburg where he was the sole—he came up with a half a million dollars. . . .

Mother talked about the experience as far as getting out of Myrtle Beach. The sheriff was the one who aided Daddy in getting away that particular evening, and they created a distraction out in front so that Daddy and the other people with him could be taken out of the back and allowed to [get to] their cars, and the sheriff said to him, "I can escort you to the county line, but after that you're on your own."

Daddy said that they drove as fast as the Mercury would go. We're talking about 110, 120 miles an hour. And when he got back he did not talk for several days. He said it was a very frightening experience for him. . . .

ML: Emily, do you want to share some of your childhood memories, or some of your memories and experiences along the way, too?

EN: The first thing that I remember, and I think the two things that sort—or maybe three things that sort of established my personality. The first thing that I remember very vividly is the Klan coming to get Daddy in Spartanburg, and they rang the doorbell. We lived in a two-story house at Silver Hill United Methodist Church—it was the parsonage—it was a very large parsonage, and instead of the stairs rising from the front door up, they rose from the back door up, and so I remember going to the door because it "ding-donged" and looking out, and about that time my mother realized who they were and came and grabbed me and pulled me behind the stairwell. Her father was alive at that time, and my grandfather was one of those kind of people who had grown up in a time when certain people could do whatever they wanted to and get away with impunity, and he was one of those kind of folks, so he pulled his double-barreled shotgun out and shot them off the front porch. About that time the police came, and you could hear the sirens and whatnot, but they did not respond until there was a counteraction. So that's one of the first things I remember.

A little bit later—this really made me not be a "public figure," not ever be interested in being a public figure—Medgar Evers was the equivalent of Daddy's position down in Mississippi, and he was invited by Daddy to lead several of the voter registration and movements towards getting people to join the NAACP, both of those movements. So, of course, things were segregated and he stayed with us in our house on Chappelle Street, and I saw him every morning for breakfast, and they'd go out and do their thing, and he left our house on Friday and got killed in his front yard on a Monday.

That was a very traumatic experience. Because all during this period Mother would get death treats every night, *every* night. Not some nights, *every* night. And we lived—I don't know if you—well, Chappelle Street is in Columbia North, and we were at that time surrounded—we were an island of the black bourgeoisie, surrounded by the white community. . . .

I have a distant cousin who experienced the same thing as far as the school integration was concerned, and that's Millicent Brown, she was J. Arthur Brown's daughter—well, she is—and she and I've discussed and compared notes about what that was like.

[An interview with Emily Newman and Millicent Brown will be found in volume 2.]

The Reverend Isaac DeQuincey Newman, the first African American to serve in the South Carolina Senate since Reconstruction. Sketch in Senator Kay Patterson's office. Reproduced with permission of the artist, Ron Chapiesky. Photographed by Marvin Ira Lare.

EN: When I went to elementary school I was manipulated into doing that, as far as the change was concerned . . .

ML: Following Reverend Newman's tenure with the NAACP, he continued to serve in a lot of ways. What are some of your recollections and some of the experiences?

AN: His Christian social concern with the state. After ten years we left the NAACP and he went to work for then—was it Governor West?

ML: Probably would be.

AN: Yes. Rural Development, and he started him another trend of audience. He was always able to get them together. I don't know how, but he always had a lot of people who really respected him. And then he got on subjects like people had community problems, no water, unpaved roads, just things like that. He was still doing his church duty, to help them get those things, and he made all the contacts. That was partly what Rural Development was. And of course he was—I forgot how many years he stayed with Rural Development—

ML: I think at least until the late '70s or maybe—

EN: Later than that. It would have been probably— I think he retired from that to run for the senate. I think probably '82, '83. It would have been after Governor Edwards.

ML: During Dick Riley's . . . ?

AN: And Mr. [Alex] Sanders was retiring [from the state senate] to go to [be president of the College of] Charleston.

You know what I think? He went up to have a conference with Mr. Sanders because he had made up in his mind that he was going to run for that office if it ever came up, or he was going to run for the senate whenever there was a vacancy. And those two people hit it off real well. Mr. Sanders thought that was a grand thing for him to do, and he would not stand in his way one bit, and he didn't one way or the other.

Reverend Lare, I have never had to shake hands with so many people! At night when I'd go home, I'd have to put my hands in Epsom salts water to get them healed again. I said, "Please, don't put me through this." For one thing, I didn't want him to go into anything else. I thought he had really done enough for people, and you know how you feel people don't appreciate what you do for them? I was just about to get to that point. But all these organizations and the white folks would have him, and I'd have to go, but some people don't know how to shake your hand. That's why I'm reluctant to stick my hands out today. I couldn't even close my fingers. They—you know how people squeeze your hands? Anyway—what was I saying?

EN: You were talking about the fact that you had to go to so many meetings. . . .

AN: And he had no problems. Now he had problems with the black race, because some of them wanted the office, but other than that he was the first black since Reconstruction to serve in the state senate. . . .

MaeDe Brown and Millicent E. Brown

J. Arthur Brown Jr., a Man for All Seasons

Marvin Lare **[ML]**:* Please say a word or two, Mrs. Brown and Millicent, so that I'll make sure whether I'm getting a pickup here.

Millicent E. Brown **[MEB]**: Okay. Millicent Brown, Charleston, daughter of J. Arthur Brown. Third daughter.

ML: Third daughter, okay.

MEB: And third of four children of J. Arthur and MaeDe *[pronounced "May-Dee"]* Brown.

ML: And Mrs. Brown?

MaeDe Brown **[MB]**: MaeDe Esperanza Meyers Brown *[laughs]*.

ML: . . . Your late husband was such a standard bearer in the field. I don't know where we would be without him and others like him.

MEB: Did you ever know him?

ML: No. What year did he die?

MB: 1988.

ML: 1988. I may have crossed paths with him, but I was focused mostly in Columbia until '86. Then I worked with Jim Solomon, Dr. Solomon, with the Institute on Poverty and Deprivation statewide, so our paths may have crossed but I'm not really aware of it.

MEB: And by the time Daddy died—Daddy died quite unexpectedly—but by that time, by the '80s, he was no longer holding a specific office with NAACP. When he died he was actually working as a consultant with the City of Charleston, with Mayor Joe Riley.

*J. Arthur Brown lived from 1914 to 1988. This interview was conducted at MaeDe Brown's home in Charleston, South Carolina, on June 27, 2007.

Millicent Brown and her mother, Mrs. J. Arthur (Maede) Brown.

[An interview with Mayor Riley will be found in volume 4.]

MEB: What was it? Human Relations Specialist?

MB: No, it was something else.

MEB: Liaison?

MB: Liaison, for the mayor's office and the community.

MEB: I think it was an interesting position. It was something actually created by city council, at the urging of the mayor.

MB: Because they knew about the type thing he did. He was always involved in civic things.

MEB: I think his work for the city was a way of saying that here's a government entity that recognizes that you need people doing this kind of thing, above and beyond a regular ombudsman that would handle city matters. But you needed somebody like Joe Brown, who could talk to people and who was trusted, and so it was a way that the structure, the infrastructure of the city was allowing him to do the work he loved, that he's always volunteered to do, is what I'm saying.

ML: That's so valuable because an ombudsman, I always think of as being fairly reactionary, somebody brings a problem and then they deal with it, whereas to be proactive, encouraging, and facilitating, and building communications, whether there's a big issue or not, building understanding and not waiting for there to be a problem to be dealt with.

MB: One thing significant I've always heard him say that people would look toward him for answers to certain things. They'd contact him and he'd always say, "Well, if I don't know the answer, I can put you in touch with somebody who does." Almost on any subject.

ML: Yes, yes.

COBRA

ML: I believe Bill Saunders mentioned to me that he had worked with Bill at COBRA [Committee for Better Racial Assurance], too, for a while. . . .

MB: Yes, he was with . . .

MEB: He was one of the founders with COBRA.

MB: I used to tease him and say, "People goin' to call you a street man," because he wasn't satisfied just to sit behind a desk all the time. He would use the office sometimes to make calls but he actually got out in the community. Trying to touch people, you know.

ML: That's a very valuable role, but it sometimes creates family stresses as well as appreciation. Do you have any reflections on those days and particular events?

MB: Oh, yes, quite a few. During the civil rights era when he'd be gone away from home so much, especially when he was state president of the NAACP. He was first president of Charleston branch and then he moved up to the state. A lot of times he didn't even try to keep in touch with us, we didn't know where he was. So that was very stressful. And his mother, she was always supportive of him, but she had a very bad heart and it was sort of a strain on us with him out in the field like that, and the danger at that time, involving himself in all the sit-ins and the drive-ins of—I was thinking about Edisto Beach when he went down there. We didn't know for two days. He couldn't contact us. Then finally when he said something about Reverend Newman . . . they were traveling together, but he didn't know where Reverend Newman was. So it was a stressful thing.

Then we had several bomb scares in our basement. Firemen had to come in and clear the place to find out just what it was. We left the house but it was . . . then there was a fire, a smoldering fire.

I served for five years as president of the Charleston Branch of NAACP, I served for five years as president of the State Conference, which was ten, hard, rugged years during the '60s, when it was dangerous to even be affiliated with the NAACP. I have to be very grateful to my family who stood by during these times, nights when we were disturbed, on several occasions when crosses were burnt on our front doorsteps, we stuck it out because we knew there was a job to be done.

[Source: "South Carolina Voices of the Civil Rights Movement: A Conference on the History of the Civil Rights Movement in South Carolina, 1940–1970," p. 73. Archived: Avery Research Center for African American History and Culture, original transcriptions prepared by: W & S Typing and Letter Writing Service, 1982.]

Klan Crosses

MEB: The Klan burnt a cross on . . .

MB: Oh, well, we had about three crosses, different times, burning on— And all this was so stressful. As I said, his mother had a bad heart, and we wondered about how it would affect her. But she got through it pretty good. She lasted several years after the big things. But the cross burning was very upsetting.

MEB: One of the times—the crosses would be burnt on the sidewalk in front of the house.

MB: Very close to the steps. The steps came out to the sidewalk.

MEB: And it ignited the awning of the house, and so that was the time we particularly remember. It was in the middle of the night and fortunately somebody was still on the street and was able to . . .

MB: They rang our bell with vehemence. I could hear him saying, "Mrs. Brown, your house is on fire!"

ML: It could easily spread into the frame and everything.

MB: That's right.

ML: Did the fire department come and put it out or was . . . ?

MB: I was amazed how my mother-in-law stood all this. She always appreciated what he did for the community.

When we first got married I didn't realize he was—I knew he was always a person that involved himself, even in college—he was two years ahead of me in college. I noticed that he was active in various things that were going on around, but after we got married is when I really noticed how he would involve himself with—actually it wasn't NAACP at that time, it was civic things. Anything civic he would involve himself. . . . He was just an active person. He had an active mind. Then, of course, when he got into the NAACP, I perceived a different type [of] involvement.

ML: Where did you go to college?

MB: South Carolina State.

ML: About what year was that? A lot of great leadership has come out of that school across the years. Are there things that you particularly recall or reflect on?

MB: He finished in '37 *[pauses]*. Not in school particularly, but after we got married. As I said, I just noticed soon after we got married how he involved himself, and I just went along with it and joined the crowd *[laughs]*.

Ace Up His Sleeve

MB: Then of course when our children came, they just automatically followed in their daddy's footsteps, wanted to be a part of things, you know. And then when my little daughter—the school suit was in her name, and that's Minerva—and it was so long in getting straight with the whole ordeal, so she graduated from high school and nothing happened, and went on to college. So Millicent just automatically—now that's something! My husband, he kept a lot of things from me. He thought I would worry, and the activities that they were doing like signing the petitions and so on. Even though I'd signed the petition, I didn't know he was going to involve my children! *[She laughs.]* But each one of them had a part in the struggle. And so Millicent's name was [substituted on the petition]. They didn't tell me until the morning that they were going out to Rivers School to . . .

MEB: You mean to the school board?

MB: Yes, the school board. That's right. Before you went to Rivers. That's right. They didn't tell me till the morning, and they were so secretive about it, I thought

Originally we started our school desegregation efforts with my middle daughter, Minerva. We were told at that time that we had to exhaust all of our remedies and our remedies were that we would have to carry the person to the school. . . .

(1) We took Minerva to Burke School. The principal told us no, he would not take the transcript to [transfer] from another school.

(2) Then we had to check with "snooperintender" [superintendent] of education to see what he felt about it. And,

(3) Then we had to go to the school board to see what they felt about it, District Twenty.

(4) Then we found out that District Twenty was a subordinate of the county board.

(5) So we had to go to them.

Had we missed any one of these steps, according to the legal realms of the law, we could have been thrown out of court. . . . What they were doing was playing a delaying game to let Minerva go along so far at Burke School that she was ready to graduate, and it would be a moot case.

So, this was when we got smart with them, and my young daughter, Millicent, had about three more years in school, so we switched the case on over to Millicent.

[Source: J. Arthur Brown at the 1982 conference, "South Carolina Voices of the Civil Rights Movement," 74.]

she was dressing to go to school. And I don't know whether you told me or your daddy told me, "We've got something we have to take care of." *[She laughs.]* It was afterward that I . . .

MEB: What he told you was, I remember this, "Dress her up nicely."

MB: Oh, yes *[laughs]*.

MEB: He said, "Dress her up nicely." And I didn't know where I was going either. And that's when he said we were going down to the school board meeting. And this would have been probably '60—

MB: Sixty? When did Minerva finish high school?

MEB: She came out in '61? She was a senior when they made the switch. Because the suit stayed in my name for three years before there was any action. So I was going into the seventh grade when this happened that morning.

ML: Gosh. But already you could see that it wasn't going to go through in time for her, so they substituted your name on it.

MB: Yes.

MEB: They wanted to dismiss the case, saying it was "moot." And so Daddy always used to laugh about how . . . He said he had an ace up his sleeve *[laughs]*.

ML: And you were it, huh?

MEB: Yes, yes. Because he had this third daughter that he could put in there.

ML: So was it '63 then that you finally . . . ?

MEB: The first [public school] deseg [desegregation] in the state of South Carolina was in Charleston in 1963, nine of us in the Charleston schools.

Bennett Belles

MB: Now in the meantime, going back to . . . the oldest daughter was in college during the demonstrations and she was a part of the college—what do you call it—"resurrection"? She involved herself. She was in North Carolina, she was at Bennett College in North Carolina, and she became secretary of the student NAACP chapter for North Carolina. And then she involved herself in several things. So all three of them were quite active.

MEB: Because she was in Greensboro when the first sit-ins took place in 1960, when the A&T students sat down. And a lot of people don't give credit to the Bennett girls, just A&T students, but Bennett girls . . .

[See the interview with Gloria M. Jenkins (Sumter) in this volume.]

MB: They did a lot.

MEB: Right across the street. The campuses are very close. And a lot of people like Joenelle, my sister

ML: Gloria [Montgomery] Jenkins from Sumter called them the "Bennett Belles."

MEB: Yes, that's what they were called.

ML: And then your youngest child of the four?

MB: Is a son . . .

MEB: He's twenty years younger than I am.

MB: We adopted him.

MEB: But his name . . . tell him about how you all named him.

The Horton Legacy

MB: Oh. Do you know . . . heard of Myles Horton?

ML: Yes. Oh, yes.

MB: Well, we had a very good relationship with him. During the summers the whole family used to go to Highlander. And we had a very nice relationship with Myles Horton, and so when we got this little boy we said we'd name him Myles. And that's how he got that name.

MEB: Myles Gregory Brown.

ML: Is the "Gregory" for Dick Gregory, or is it another . . . ?

MB: We just liked Greg.

ML: How did you get involved with Highlander and Myles Horton?

MB: It might have been through Septima Clark. Septima Clark and Bernice Robertson, when they had the [freedom] schools. Daddy had the relationship then with them, and then from time to time he would take the family. In fact, he would take the three girls before I . . . before I even got up there, and then eventually I went to some of the conferences.

The court case *Brown v. School Board District Twenty,* included . . . I think, thirteen real plaintiffs. My name was used, but there were thirteen of us on that first day back in 1963 that marched into several local schools, some elementary schools, and some high schools on the peninsula. And I never, never like to take credit, if you will, without remembering that there were a whole group of us that went through similar kinds of experiences on that first day. . . .

I think it's important to have a little bit of understanding of who I was going into that situation. Obviously growing up in J. Arthur Brown's household, with all the very rich experiences that that afforded me, I had been to Highlander, and I had met Guy Carawan, and Candy, and Myles Horton—and Septima Clark was very dear—and all of the other folks who had been so involved nationally and internationally in the struggle. I had had the privilege of being exposed to folks like that, even since I was very young. You know, Mike King was Mike King, before he was Martin Luther King, and I think that that was such a very, very rich background to have had that made a big difference on me when I did go into Rivers [School] that first day. But, nonetheless, that kind of experience did not prepare me adequately, because when I thought about it, other than the Guys [Carawan] and the Myles Hortons, I did not know *any* white people, I had not really been around any white people

(continued)

(Continued)

other than like that. I certainly was still very unprepared, because I did not know that they didn't know anything about black folks and I didn't know *anything* about them!

[Source: Millicent Brown at the 1982 conference, "South Carolina Voices of the Civil Rights Movement," 92–93.]

ML: That really played such a pivotal role. It's just so interesting. I think I've got an invitation or notice of their seventy-fifth anniversary.

MB: Yes, that's right. Came the other day, yes. What was that you all went to a few years back?

MEB: We went to a memorial tribute when Myles died. It was really exceptional. I went with my sister, Minerva. Did you know we both went?

MB: I was thinking all three of you went.

MEB: I don't know if all three of us went but I know that Minerva and I went, and I had a chance to take my son, who was only about—he might have been only six or eight, maybe eight, at the time. But that was just a phenomenal experience, to take him. And I was able to . . . I had talked to Myles shortly before he died. I talked to him from Charleston. I think I talked to him, telling him that Daddy had died.

MB: Oh, yes.

MEB: Yes. We called to tell him, and so I was talking to him. I said, "You may not know this, Myles," I said, "because we've lost touch with you, but do you realize that J. Arthur has a son, and we named him Myles after you." And so what he said was—and we talked at great length about this—he said, "Well, there is one thing I would love to see happen and that is I wish somebody would put [me in touch with] all of the kids who have been named after me . . ."

MB: Is that right?

MEB: ". . . because they come from all over the world. They're from every country." And he said, "I would like to see . . . wouldn't it be wonderful if they could be put in touch with one another, just so they could understand why they were my namesake."

When we went to the memorial for him when he died, I was able to announce that to the group that had assembled, and I have to admit I started doing some things towards it, but if I could ever retire like you and have some time, that would be a project I would love to pursue. Because all he said was just that they would talk to one another, knowing that they came from different cultures and nationalities, and just that they had that in common, that their parents had something that they found about Highlander and about him.

ML: That would be great . . . "Namesakes" or something like that. "Namesakes Society."

MEB: Myles Horton Namesakes Society.

ML: He played such a pivotal role.

Freedom Schools

ML: I didn't realize it until I got into this a bit, that he spent a good bit of time down here on the islands.

MB: Yes, he did. I think that's when he met Septima.

MEB: No, no. Septima went up there.

ML: And then she or others got him involved down here in the freedom schools.

MEB: Mr. Esau particularly. Esau Jenkins on Johns Island brought him down.

MB: When you think about it, all the great guys years ago . . . I can't say they're all gone because there're probably some great ones now we don't know about, but it's just nice to look back and see accomplishments of these. Like Esau, a man of very little education. What he did with voting and trying to see that other people got their education.

[There is a pause. A WPAL radio interview with Esau Jenkins will be found in volume 3 of this anthology.]

Dining Out and In Jail

MB: I was always at home—not always but most of the time—when my husband was gone so much and sometimes later on when the kids started going to the various things, I was always at home. But I got involved about the midway of the struggle, being arrested and all. Three women, three of us, went up at the Fort Sumter Hotel, because several people had been arrested trying to get in there to be served a meal. We didn't pay any attention to that. We decided we'd go, and as soon as they saw us coming . . . they . . . locked the door, and it didn't bother us. There were rocking chairs on the piazza and the three of us just sat there and rocked, and we were dressed to kill, too. We were going out to eat dinner! Finally someone unlocked the door and came to the door and said, "You know you're trespassing." I don't think we even answered him. We just continued rocking, and then finally, the next thing we knew, a police car had come and hauled us off to jail.

MEB: Do you remember who you were with?

MB: Yes. Ruby Conrad, James's grandmother—what was her name?

MEB: James Blake's grandmother?

MB: Yes. She was very active. And Marjorie Amos[-Frazier]. No, there were four of us. What's that other person's name? I can't think of her name now. But anyway, there were four of us, and the most exciting thing about the whole thing—we knew that they were going to get us out of jail so we went on, they put us in these cells among some very hard criminals, you know, people screaming out and "going" on right next to us and all. But the four of us were together so that was all right. Finally, after several hours—oh, I guess it was about five or six hours, toward morning—the organization got the

We remember very distinctly when we were told back in those days that we were to stay in our places. Then the question came to us, "Where is my place?" Back in those days when we boarded the train we went to the North station. We had to go up to the front of the train. When we got on the buses, we had to go to the back of the buses. We went to the Gloria Theater, we had to sit upstairs. If you caught a boat going to New York, you sat downstairs. So where was your place? Up? Down? Cross? And back? We felt it was the wrong thing to do and we struggled against it.

[Source: J. Arthur Brown at the 1982 conference, "South Carolina Voices of the Civil Rights Movement," 73–74.]

right papers to get us out on bond and they didn't have my name on there, and so the other ladies said, "We're not going to leave you here by yourself. We'll refuse to go." And so the jailer said, "No, you've got to go. We've got papers here . . ." And so there I was by myself and people screaming all around there and like that. It was about . . . they found out that they had spelled my name wrong. They had the papers made out for "Mrs. J. Arthur Brown." When I went in there and they asked my name, I said, "MaeDe Brown." But they knew. It was just to harass you, that's all. And so I guess it was very close to daybreak before they finally got the papers. They had to go to town and get the lawyers to make up another set of papers. And that time I was really frightened. I didn't like being there alone. As long as we were doing this thing together it was all right. But that was one incident . . .

As I said, from time to time we had exciting things happen. But it was remarkable, I think about it now, we were so calm about it, it didn't bother us, because we knew it was a cause, and we were willing to be a part of it. I never got nervous about anything. The only thing I got nervous about was when I didn't know where my husband was, on these various trips.

MEB: These little tiny towns all over . . .

MB: Yes, that's right.

MEB: Daddy went to every nook and cranny in South Carolina, places that you just had never heard of before, and a lot of times, especially after he got that Volkswagen, I was his traveling companion, and I don't know exactly why, but . . .

MB: You weren't going with him to Edisto?

MEB: No, I went there, too. I was there for a lot of the demonstrations, but I'm talking about when he was just going, on weekends he was just going for speaking engagements. He was trying to encourage— He would be the guest speaker. I always thought I was in Alcolu or Silver. I mean these *tiny* towns. But I'm just saying, I always went with him, and I don't know if he just wanted a traveling partner, but I was with him a lot of times. I'm saying not the demonstrations only, but he was called on so much when he was state president to be out there to encourage people. . . .

MB: Especially with the voting, too, and registration. He worked on registration a good bit. He did a beautiful job on getting people registered.

The Cheerleader

MEB: But see, my recollection, I remember very vividly that going into communities where he had to try to convince people. That's what you had to do. I mean it's not like just going and signing people up. I mean it was the psychological, having to reinforce that it is time, and things are going to change, and they're not going to change automatically, but you have to do something in order to *make* things change. And I just know even as a child I knew that the hardest part, it seemed, was to go to these churches where people are just *broken down* and just don't feel— That's just the way the white man is, and just accepting it. . . . It looked like he was just like this big—what was it? King was called the "Drum Major"? Daddy was like a *cheerleader*. Always having just to kind of lay it out there. But you have to change people's minds psychologically before you can expect that they're going to do anything specific like voting and everything. He would answer questions afterwards, after he'd spoken, and people wanted to know, "Aren't things going to get worse?" And, "What's going to happen to us?"

MB: "If I register . . ." Simple things . . . "What would happen to me if I register?"

MEB: And people trying to see, is the NAACP going to back us up? Are you all going to be there? And I think that's why Daddy tried so hard to work with an organization that he felt could be trusted, that would be there as long as people were doing things legally, then . . .

MB: During the sit-ins I remember when a bunch of students went to Kress and sat down, and of course they were arrested, and Minerva was one of those.

[See Harvey Gantt's account of the high school students' sit-ins in this section.]

MEB: The first in Charleston, for the Charleston sit-ins. That was '60.

MB: The first in Charleston. And they were put in jail for five days and six nights, something like that. But anyhow, coming back to the stress of the thing, finally when they got straight with the bond and so on . . . they were getting their money, getting people all around, even though they weren't taking part in actual demonstrations. People were putting up their property and all for bond money. When they finally got them out of jail, there was another meeting, we had a mass meeting. They had it at one of the churches, and we were all there waiting, because we got word that they were going to get them out [of jail], and they were coming to the meeting. When I saw *my child* walk in there! She was so thin. For five days they couldn't eat the food, and I guess the stress and all . . . I got so full when I saw them walk in there, and she looked so thin.

MEB: She wasn't a small person. The more robust one of us.

MB: . . . to see her look like that, all pale and . . . So there were some stressful times, but as I said, we didn't fear. I don't know of any fear with people that took a part.

MEB: When we would talk to Daddy and say things, Daddy would just say, "MaeDe . . ." when they would call with these bomb threats, remember what Daddy would tell you?

MB: Yes, yes. "Wait now . . ." He'd always have a answer for everything.

MEB: Had an answer or a joke and everything. What he told you about if people were going to bomb your house . . . ?

MB: . . . they wouldn't tell you about it. . . .

MEB: He was convinced of that. Now that doesn't really make a whole lot of sense. That's not true. But at the time we believed him *[laughs]*.

And Joenelle had us trained, my oldest sister, she had us trained how to answer the phone.

MB: Yes, that's right. Don't give them the satisfaction of arguing with them.

MEB: They would call us and disturb us in the middle of the night, and Joenelle would just make sure that we would always answer, "Hello?" As if they had just called in the middle of the day.

MB: Yes. Don't show fear in your voice.

MEB: . . . or that you've been even inconvenienced. As far as you're concerned, everything is going just fine. It wasn't that this was funny, this was serious business, but you had to keep humor, had to keep your spirits up.

MB: That's right.

MEB: And you can't accomplish anything if you're frightened all the time. And so we just maintained a sort of bravado that we established. "Oh, they want to arrest us? Okay, fine. Well, here we go."

MB: . . . and always singing. All groups were together, they always had a song that would get their spirit up and pass it on one to the other.

On my side of the family I had a disturbing thing. My younger sister had a son, he's dead now, who had hemophilia, and they were so cautious about him, in Orangeburg, as to proper treatment, like the milk and all he had to have, and various things. And Orangeburg was so bad that they cut off all—his father was a bricklayer—they cut off all the jobs for him and the milk company stopped delivering the milk. There was just so many—and he was hit bad. But they survived it, got through. And that was a time when Orangeburg was like an army center. . . .

I'll tell you what boosted us up, too, through the various years. We had a relationship with Thurgood Marshall. He and my husband got to be quite close, and he would come on various [occasions] ever since the teachers' case . . .

MEB: The equalization of teachers' pay.

MB: Equalization of teachers' salaries. Ever since way back then.

ML: Yes, that was way back in the '40s.

MB: That's right, that's right. They had a relationship over those years, and I think that's what boosted a lot of people, that we had the comradeship of everybody, with people in high authority, and they encouraged us so. And Bob Carter from the [national NAACP] office.

MEB: And Connie Motley. She was my lawyer. She and Matthew J. Perry were the ones assigned to the Charleston school case.

MB: Matthew Perry, he was a terrific man, and he's a South Carolinian, you know. It wasn't just the national people. And [Harold] Boulware. Boulware did his part too.

The Home Front

MEB: Let me ask a question, Mama. Tell us what kind of conversations you and Daddy would have had. I mean he's gone a lot, I know, but then when things were really getting hot, what was he saying to you?

MB: That we had to do it. I never resisted because I was just a part at the time too. I wasn't at first and . . .

MEB: Did he let you know that he appreciated that?

MB: Oh, yes. And he mentioned to several people, "MaeDe's taking care of the home front. She knows what I'm doing and she's taking care of the home front." Because he had a real estate business and a good bit was on me.

MEB: Because we would have gone to the poorhouse otherwise, because Daddy was not taking care of any real estate. . . .

MB: And you know what was bad about that. They were saying . . . I think they even wrote him up in the newspaper, "If he would take care of his own business . . ." It said if he used more time taking care of his business than going out beating the bushes and getting people to register. And that was really a slam on us. I don't know what he did about it, but . . .

MEB: And he had helped somebody to get the job with the Housing Authority, and it was this person who wrote Daddy up *[laughs]* for being an absentee landlord, which he really was.

He was always on the road. The main means of support was the real estate business, houses that he had inherited from his parents, and we lived off the rent that was collected from these numbers of places, all in Charleston. I can remember people coming to the house saying, "Mr. Brown didn't come to get the rent this month. . . ."

ML: Yes. Well, quite an adventure.

MB: Yes.

MEB: Where did you think Daddy got all that inspiration?

MB: I don't know. I said he always involved himself in campus activities along in college, but it wasn't till I'd say about a year or so after we got married that he became involved in civic things. And then his association with certain people. I don't know if you've heard about Mr. Bob Morrison. He was the owner of a filling station. He and Dr. Jones, and all those older people. He always liked to talk with them and he got involved in civic things through them.

MEB: And there is this legacy of that kind of activism here. People from the turn of the century. In many cases it was, like you said, the dentist, Dr. Jones, but Mr. Morrison was an independent black businessman and that independence is what made all the difference in the world. And John McCray, who was here before going to Columbia with his newspaper. I just think Daddy came along. . . . I think of myself as coming along at such a rich time, in the middle of the movement, but when I

I think I first became involved with thinking where segregation was concerned, when particularly in high school, I lived on Ashley Avenue, not but so far from the Citadel where I could hear the taps and the revelry from my bedroom. Yet my parents who were taxpayers in this community had to bag me up and sent me off to school where I lived four or five blocks from a state-supported institution, at that time I can very vividly remember, as looking at this audience, there were five Japanese boys attending the Citadel. They all rode together in a little blue Chevrolet car. You saw one, you saw five, and they were able to come from Japan to the Citadel when I go four blocks to the Citadel. And I think I took the position then that if I ever got a chance to hit it, going to hit it hard.

A disturbing fact was that several years back it was brought out that one of the captains in the Japanese Army was fighting against America, was shot down in a plane with a class ring of the Citadel on his finger. They were able to bring him from Japan, educate him here, and he went back and fought against them in the army, and yet we, who are taxpayers, were denied. So we have come a long way, been a great struggle.

[J. Arthur Brown at the 1982 conference, "South Carolina Voices of the Civil Rights Movement," p. 76]

look back at my father being born in 1914, he also was born into an environment with a *lot* of activism. He went to Avery, you see and Avery was . . . what about Halston? Would he have known Halston when he was president of NAACP?

MB: Oh, no, that was before his time.

MEB: That was before him. Daddy was born in 1914, but the Charleston NAACP was founded by a local . . .

MB: Artist.

MEB: Artist, yes. Edwin Halston.

ML: Yes, I recently saw the display here at Avery, and it really was eye-opening to find out about his story and his activism that early.

MEB: And I just think *[inaudible—possibly "Woos" or "Prouse"]* was aligned with Avery, and the teachers . . .

ML: Equalization of pay?

MEB: Not just equalization. Even earlier. Septima Clark was at Avery teaching, when the big challenge . . . black teachers were not allowed to teach black students on the [Charleston] peninsula. Those folks who were surrounding Avery, including Septima, were a part of that legacy, and Bob Morrison . . . and Daddy going to Avery . . .

MB: He did have very strong values . . .

MEB: And he loved older people and he knew what stances they had. He loved Mr. Morrison, and Bob Morrison was fiery. He was not even—he was a *real fiery* . . .

MB: He was a historian too.

MEB: He was. . . . There's a whole history or paper trail of the kinds of letters to the editor that he was writing.

Daddy had good role models, is what I'm saying. He didn't come out of nowhere with this stuff. He had a rich tradition right here that people don't associate with Charleston often. It's not been played up a lot, but that's why the books on Avery are very good. The ones by Lee Drago, Edmund Drago. He talks about the Avery legacy and it doesn't include only civil rights activism, but he does give credit to how much of that activism was a part of the Avery legacy as well. *[She speaks softly after a long pause.]* Bob Morrison. And it just seems as if Daddy was going to take his cues, he had lots of choices, but he went with the ones that had been doing things and were articulating it. Daddy liked to talk.

MB: Yes, he was a talker *[laughs]*. He listened, too. . . .

Septima P. Clark 1898–1987: In 1919 I came from the islands and felt, well, there was an artist here, Edwin Halston, who told us about a thing called the NAACP. I thought that was a good thing to join, and I did join. When I joined up, I heard about black teachers not being able to teach in the city of Charleston, so I took my class that I was teaching at Avery Normal Institute and went from door to door to see if black parents wanted their children to teach black children in the city of Charleston, and I found that they did, so we got their signatures, some of them on little pieces of paper bag. And after getting those signatures, we gave them to the president of State College in Orangeburg—Tommy Miller. He took them to the Legislature and in 1920 we got black teachers in the school, and in 1921, they got black principals in the schools in Charleston.

[Source: *Southern Change*, 10, No. 2, 1988]

MEB: He could listen, but I think he was a wordsmith. He liked fancy phrases. He enjoyed listening to how Thurgood spoke. You know what I'm saying? So when he got . . .

MB: He would sometimes repeat the speeches verbatim!

MEB: But you know who else?

MB: Mays.

MEB: Exactly. Benjamin Mays.

MB: Dr. Benjamin Mays.

MEB: . . . who was an educator and an activist, and Daddy was very influenced by him. Benny Mays would come to speak at South Carolina State. . . .

MB: Every Easter.

MEB: Okay. And I'm thinking that was when you all were in college, right?

MB: Yes. Yes, he was so interested, that's what I say, he involved himself in serious things.

MEB: He had those kinds of role models that he was exposed to, and I'm talking about orators. I guess that was the word I was searching for. Daddy had a love of oratory, not just talking for the sake of talking, and not preaching because . . . Was he ever interested in being a minister?

MB: No, but several people thought he was *[laughs]*.

MEB: Yeah, he talked like ministers did. But he didn't have any calling for the cloth.

MB: And then they accused him of being a lawyer too. He was either a lawyer or a minister, they thought.

MEB: But I'm thinking that in addition to the substance of what he heard from the Thurgoods and the whoevers, there was also just this, I think this love of how to craft ideas and how to craft speeches, that you could be as influential as you possibly can with just that turn of the phrase. And he used to sometimes—I mean I have it—I'm long-winded like he was. I had to undo a lot of that when I went to get my doctorate. I had to really learn that flowery speech isn't always the best speech, but I'd gotten that from Daddy. I thought you had to dress everything up. But he had grown up listening to people like Benny Mays who. . . .

MB: Oh, he was a big admirer of Benny Mays.

MEB: These were people who were not just good speakers. They were speaking about racial uplift, personal responsibility. He took it to heart. . . .

ML: So, let's see, you say that he passed in '88, so he was what then? Seventy . . . ?

MB: Seventy-five.

ML: Seventy-five. Yes. People still miss him, I know.

MB: It's very uplifting to hear people even today, after all these years . . . A couple of weeks ago, a man came for something else—I've forgot the man's name now—but anyway, he said, "You know, we certainly miss your husband." He said, "He was the man we just looked up to." And it was nice hearing that after all this time.

MEB: A few years ago Minerva and I had gone to visit a woman who had really been involved with every phase of the movement, mostly in North Charleston, Miss

Dr. Millicent Brown speaking at the thirty-fifth anniversary of the African American Studies Program at the University of South Carolina, October 12, 2006.

Mary Lee Davis. We had gone up to Highlander with her and everything. We were visiting her in the nursing home. . . . She put something in perspective that I had really not given much thought to. She said, "You know, your daddy could have been a rich man." And Mary Lee knew Daddy well enough, she knew all this property that he inherited, land out here on James Island, those houses, and had he been a different kind of person we could, we could have been a wealthy family. We were that fortunate to have had that kind of grandfather who had bequeathed all this to him. But she said, "But you all were just as poor as we were." *[She laughs.]*

MB: So busy fighting other people's battles.

MEB: Yes, and just dedicated to doing the work that he was committed to doing . . . Daddy ended up working—he liked the work he did towards the end of his life, but he worked because he needed to keep insurance.

MB: That's right. So Mary Lee was right when she said . . .

MEB: She knew. She knew, and she knew our grandfather. She knew that those decisions he made came at a very high price. And I said that as segue just to tell you for the record, Marvin, that in honor of Daddy and all of his legacy . . . we managed to hold on to one final tract of land over here on James Island, and we are now in the process of developing it. As opposed to selling the property we're actually building a housing development, and [our family] is committed to it, and the development is called "Heritage Oaks," and it's really . . .

MB: We've got an oak tree that is . . . it's between nine hundred and twelve hundred years old. It's really a focal point on the property . . .

MEB: But I brought that up because in thinking about Miss Mary Lee Davis's comment, basically he ended up in the end of his life selling off properties to live on, just to . . .

MB: But this we kept, eleven acres of it. . . .

MEB: Daddy has been talked about as somebody who kept thinking. He didn't become stale. A young person said this about him, right as he died, "J. Arthur could have still talked to young people and hear younger ideas."

He didn't get so jaded and say, "Well, the way we used to do things . . ." He shared what he'd gone through with people but he wasn't stuck in time. To the bitter end he . . .

MB: He was always somebody you could always go to. He's always been like that, ever since we got married. So I remember one time saying, "Joe, you're going to be so tired trying to take care of other people that you don't have time," because that's when I started to say, "you don't have time for your own family."

So he said, "Well, I'll always believe that as I do for someone . . ."

"Oh!" I said, "You don't know what's going to happen to us." That's when he started the traveling.

He said, "I'll always believe that as I help people that somebody's going to help you . . . help my family." He always said that, that we wouldn't go to waste.

ML: That's such a rich heritage, and so many people are so busy grabbing and grasping and holding on to what they have. They think that will be their security but the real legacy he gave to the children and the community was far richer than money.

MEB: I really do believe that, building on what you just said, coming up in that household, there's not one of us that doesn't aspire to the kinds of principles that both [our parents] showed us. Mama being so supportive taught us very early that this is what you do. There wasn't any friction about she wanted us to go one way and he wanted us to go another way. We didn't even have those moments of wondering what our role as citizens really should be.

. . . I was at Burke High School, I was very happy, . . . and at fifteen, you know, skinny as I could be, and whatever, but I was beginning to evolve into a young woman, I was going to start dating pretty soon, I was popular, I had friends, and to go from that to absolute zero, because from the day that I walked into Rivers High School, none of that popularity or my plans for being a regular teenager *were ever to be realized.* . . . Nothing hurt me more than this one experience that I will share with you, that will go with me to my grave, and that was the first time I went back to Burke High School, went to a basketball game, and black students rejected me, they told me I was trying to act white. And here was just a nonentity nobody wants you . . . I will say, of course, that I had many friends that stuck by me through thick and thin, but those first words were really pretty hard to swallow.

Again, another sense of confusion came about—and I dealt with that very poorly—I was doing very well in my course work. I had had a very strong background from the black schools I had gone to all those years. So I was a pretty good student. Then I began to sense that the folks at Rivers were saying, well, fine, if they can *all* be like Millicent Brown, but that just always struck me as being ridiculous, and I felt almost guilty that I was doing well in my academics because I was giving this picture that you can be acceptable, if you come packaged like this. If light skinned, that helps, and if

(continued)

(Continued)
you're smart. And I saw immediately
through this, but I cannot say that I
knew how to deal with it. . . .

[Source: South Carolina Voices of the Civil
Rights Movement . . . 1982, pp. 94-96 Ibid.]

ML: I've come across in the 1982 conference at Avery, I think it was "Voices of the Civil Rights Movement," *your* description of the loneliness of . . .

MEB: At Rivers school.

ML: . . . of being the only black and how the whites shunned you and would scatter from you in the hall, and things like that. It's really a powerful image.

Millicent Brown at the 1982 conference "South Carolina Voices of the Civil Rights Movement"

MEB: Not only my own experiences but I continue to talk and meet others who were the first into those situations. It's a major research interest of mine. It's what I'm doing now, a project trying to get at those "first children." I've realized that people have various forms of support, but more and more we identify ourselves as coming from homes where there were parents that took stances, and when you come from that kind of a house, you see . . .

MB: It stays with you.

MEB: It stays with you.

ML: Yes, that's for sure. Do you have many materials that would be of interest? You spoke about the letter to the editor and things like that.

MEB: Daddy's stuff is at Avery, the J. Arthur Brown Collection.

ML: Oh, yes, that's right. In fact I've got that on my list to do, is to go through his materials there.

MB: He was more action than anything else.

MEB: Yes, much more action and didn't keep records. We don't have anything. Everything we find we pretty much put in the collection. . . .

MEB: When he was working with the city, one of the biggest projects that my father worked on, not too very long before his death, was the area of our homestead, the land that his grandmother had out there on James Island, which is where we ultimately built a home So we're back on our family property that's been in the family for six generations now. The effort with the city was to incorporate that into Charleston. . . .

MB: On his own he'd take petitions around to all the people in that area, saying it'd be better for us because James Island was taken piece by piece so we want to be a piece of the city, too. There are benefits to us.

MEB: But I'm saying it goes back to him trying to convince people. I mean he was doing . . . I saw him do it when I was little, with the NAACP stuff, but I saw the same thing as a much older child watching him trying to still get out there and convince people that to become incorporated was certainly better. And so to the bitter end he's the same community person. . . .

MB: Yes, because his end was very quick. He was on his way to the podiatrist, had a ten o'clock appointment, and he came through the bedroom. I fixed a light breakfast for him, and reminded of the time, and he got as far as the family room and just slumped. Actually it wasn't until later on that I realized what happened. The table and chairs had turned over from his weight. . . .

ML: Was it a stroke or a heart attack or . . . ?

MB: Stroke. And then what happened, I kept saying to myself on the way to the hospital, "This is a stroke, I realize it, but so many people survive with therapy and so on like that." I kept saying that, and "If he's going to be a semi-invalid or something we can manage." But what happened, after we got to the hospital he had another one, and I think that's it. He was deteriorating then. Within three days he was dead.

ML: Oh, gosh. That's a real shock.

MEB: But we immediately said, what Mama? *[She pauses.]* About Daddy going like that?

MB: Oh. That's the way he would want to go.

MEB: You said it, Mama. You said he would have been miserable if he had. Not that life doesn't have value even if you are incapacitated, but J. Arthur would have been so un . . .

MB: He was so used to moving, moving . . .

MEB: On the go all the time.

ML: Well, I wish I had known him personally.

MB: That's what I told my minister not too long ago. I said, "Every now and then you hear me talk about my husband. I just wish you had had a chance to know him."

He said, "Well, from what I can hear, I wish I had too." *[She laughs.]*

ML: Well, we'll hope that this anthology project will help people know him.

MEB: There weren't a lot of twists and turns in Daddy's life. What Mama's described, that was how they lived.

ML: How long were you all married?

MB: Forty-seven years.

MEB: He was devoted to NAACP, and Omega Psi Phi . . .

MB: His fraternity.

MEB: . . . his fraternity. You know we talked about that, he and Reverend Newman were fraternity brothers.

MB: And his church.

ML: Which church?

MB: St. Mark's Episcopal.

MEB: That was always trying—Episcopalians being not directly or not very openly involved in a lot of the civil rights movement, that was a issue for Daddy, trying to convince his church. You know how Episcopal churches are, and he was always just trying to prod people in the church to . . . Here these mass meetings are being held in all the AME churches, all the Baptist churches, and trying to say to St. Mark's . . .

MB: Don't forget the one he sponsored at St. Mark's. He had . . .

MEB: Because people had been complaining, some of the youngsters had been saying, "How come we go to everybody else's church but yours?"

MB: "You should have it at *your* church." So he sponsored it. He didn't have too much trouble convincing them, but they had the best turnout in that church, better than almost any church they had, other than Emmanuel.

MEB: Yes, because it's a big church too.

MB: This is an Episcopal church.

MEB: He felt better that finally—and again it didn't happen often but he just said he told the vestry, he was on the vestry and he told them, "How can I face people and I can't bring these serious issues to our own congregation?"

So they probably just did it to appease him. Again, it wasn't a church that's ever had much of a history of activism, but he pushed it.

ML: I think in Episcopal churches it varies a good bit with the rector. Some Episcopal clergy were really out front, and then others were not holding back but they just weren't in the forefront in terms of mass appeal.

MEB: But at the time you also understand you're talking about *black* Episcopal congregations, and there are fewer, way fewer, of those, and so it was just an interesting struggle for him, but one he was adamant about. Because he was a lifelong member and very supportive of that church but he was a blended person. Like I said, he had this rich background of someone who had some means. He wasn't a child of poverty, okay?

MB: But he understood . . .

MEB: But he was not so much middle class that he could not relate to other people and to other circumstances, so he was not somebody that felt he had to be in one camp or the other. He had his feet planted in a number of these . . .

ML: A "man for all seasons" in a way.

MB: That's right.

MEB: He really was. He really was.

ML: Well, I've got the standard release form for you all to sign.

MEB: You want to turn your recorder off? Because I don't think you need to . . .

Harvey Gantt, Part 1

High School Sit-In'ers

[The interview is in progress.]

Robert Moore **[RM]:*** Tell me a little bit more about the sit-ins. Were you engaged in any in addition to that one when you were arrested, when Matthew Perry came down?

Harvey Gantt **[HG]**: Never got involved in a single additional one.

RM: And that was at Kress's or . . . ?

HG: I went to jail and it was an S. H. Kress's. Twenty-six of us, twenty-seven of us. We did it—and didn't tell our parents because we thought that they would prevent us from doing it that close to graduation. It was the spring of the year.

RM: Who organized it?

HG: Oh—it's been years. Student leaders.

RM: Not NAACP leaders?

HG: Yes, student leaders like myself and some other people.

RM: Student Council of the NAACP.

HG: We did it on our own.

RM: But Reverend Newman didn't come down and say, "You guys do this."

HG: We didn't have any adults. They didn't even know we were going to do it. In our Youth Council meetings, we were just in awe of these students who in February had sat down at Woolworth's in Greensboro, and saw it spreading across the country and said, "Why aren't we doing the same thing? If we believe in this movement, we ought to do something about it."

We got some information from national NAACP headquarters about nonviolence and how you've got to be prepared to cope with the kinds of things that possibly could

*This is the first of four parts included in this anthology. The interview took place at Gantt's office in Charlotte, North Carolina, on October 27, 1999, and was conducted by Dr. and Mrs. (Meribeth) Robert J. Moore.

179

happen to you—sitting on a stool, people don't want you there, call you "N," people calling you names and throwing racial epithets, and maybe even doing violence to you, pouring ketchup on you or hitting you. So we went through sensitivity training on our own to try to teach ourselves how to be as stoic as we possibly could, and to hold our ground and not to be cooperative if they were having police remove us from the scene.

And then the three leaders decided that we wanted to make sure we kept it a secret, we wouldn't tell our twenty-four other peers the day we would do it or when we would do it. We would just have a meeting and then say, "Okay, guys, let's go." And that's exactly how we did it.

RM: Is that right?!

HG: It was decided and we went there, and then of course, like we said, our parents were shocked when they were told to come down to the jailhouse to pull us out. They didn't know that we were the ones. My mother had no idea that I would be involved in something like that.

RM: So you and two others organized it? Can you tell me their names?

HG: James Blake, who is an AME official in New York City —I wouldn't even know how to reach him—and the other person was Cornelius Fludd, who lives in Austin, Texas. He's an assistant athletic director at the University of Texas. But we were the leaders by right of being the officers in the Youth Council at that time, and I guess we didn't think of it as being such a big deal, as much as we were motivated to act and if we were going to be leaders we had to have something to keep our membership engaged.

Meribeth Moore **[MM]**: What happen when you walked in? They weren't expecting you—

HG: They were not expecting us. They were very surprised. The people who were eating quickly got up and left.

MM: Were there twenty-seven students?

HG: Yes, we had already counted the students.

MM: You knew that you could take the whole counter.

HG: And we knew that those stools that were now occupied that people were going to be gracious enough to get up and let us have it *[laughs]*. Southern hospitality, huh? As a matter of fact, they would even leave some of their food there for us to eat—so we all got to sit. We all knew that we were going to be able to sit because we'd counted the lunch counter stools.

The waitresses immediately were instructed, and you could tell that they had been trained to do this, simply said to us, "I'm sorry, we cannot serve you. Will you please leave?"

So we were equally trained just to ignore it and to ask for a menu to get service. It seems so silly now—it really does. I mean, I tell my kids about this all the time. How casually we can go up to any lunch counter or do anything, stop at any fast food, and nobody thinks about it, nobody pays attention to it. In fact, they were surprised that we were doing such things back then, but it was a big deal. It really was a big deal.

MM: [What] did you see in their eyes when they told you? Hatred or fear or kind of, "Oh, God, I don't want to say this but I've got to say this"?

HG: I don't think I saw that. I think I saw that—what I saw —other people may have seen different things—I saw an excited person who probably never thought we were going to do any physical harm to them but that this was a dreaded moment and it's going to happen. They weren't smiling when they told us we can't serve you. They were being southern and very polite, but they simply said, "We can't serve you. Will you please leave?"

Then they withdrew from the scene, and they left us to sit there. We sat for a long period of time. The police did not immediately remove us. If you recall, the sit-in tactics were such that you sat for a while, and then I believe they had to close the store, had to have some legal right, way to get you to move out, so the store was now closed, and the manager would come and tell you that, and of course if you don't leave, then they can officially invite the police in.

RM: You're trespassing.

HG: You're now trespassing on the property, and our crime was trespassing, not the issue of whether or not they denied us service *[pauses]*.

But the white people in the store did not come up and harass us. Perhaps had we stayed there for a long period of time they might have, but as I recall it we probably spent no more than an hour, an hour and a half or two hours before we were hauled out to police cruisers amidst a big crowd of people that had gathered around. They'd heard about these kids.

But I always remember the reception I got at the police station. They were very jovial about it, almost as if our kids, *our* kids, are down here and certain people recognized certain of the people there. I heard them on the phone calling up. They didn't put us in a jail. They hauled us into a courtroom where we were under guard, and eventually our parents came and picked us up *[laughs]*.

Someone bailed us out. I think the NAACP, the adult chapter, was prepared for this kind of thing. They were surprised, too *[laughs]*.

RM: J. Arthur Brown didn't know?

HG: We must have sat in the courtroom for, oh, I think it was late evening by the time we all got out of there, but I guess we really knew we weren't going to stay in jail.

To put that in proper perspective, it was courageous to do what we did, I suppose, now I look back on it, but in our heart of hearts we probably knew that the police chief or the community was not going to put a bunch of high school seniors, many of whom were honor students, in jail or consign us to bread and water, just to think of jails at that time that's all you'd get to eat.

So we knew that we'd be bailed out because that had been the pattern across the South. Kids would be bailed out, and this was one more case that was going to ultimately find itself adjudicated in the Supreme Court, which is precisely what happened with a series of cases. They got collected together. And we had this trespassing record—my mother kept saying, "Well, you know you've got a record," even though we weren't going to Clemson at that point *[laughs]*. "You've got a record because you've been arrested. Now you can't say you've never been arrested!"

I said, "Mom, I was arrested for a *good* cause. I'm proud to put that down." And finally the Supreme Court did clear us, sometime long after I'd gone to Clemson.

RM: The trial was what, a week later or when?

HG: I don't remember a trial. We never went to trial. What happened was we had scattered to the wind by the time the trial occurred, and I can't even remember what the legal maneuver was, but we never sat in a courtroom as a group.

RM: I'll have with talk with Matthew [Perry] about this.

HG: Yes, he ought to tell you exactly how it went forward. As I recall it, I knew that I was somewhere in Iowa State University going to school, and I never had to appear in court for that. Unless I'm just drawing a mental blank, I don't remember ever going to trial. I remember hearing about the case, and I certainly heard about it when they said that group of sit-in cases were thrown out of court by the judge's ruling on a whole bunch of them. What was happening was that the NAACP and other lawyers took those cases into federal court, and so they became a class-action suit, I think. I know they never went to Charleston municipal court.

[Parts 2 and 3 will be found in volume 2, and part 4 will be found in volume 4.]

Beatrice "Bea" McKnight, Modjeska Protégé

Robert Moore **[RM]:*** This is an interview with Beatrice McKnight, and it's on November 7, 2003. We're at the Tillis Family Life Center, and we're really happy that you're willing to talk with us, Beatrice. Are there any stories about your experiences with segregation or discrimination that come out of your childhood that you'd like to tell us?

Beatrice McKnight **[BMCK]:** Well, as I think back, I think about growing up near the Valley Park community. . . . I often noticed that the park always had "No Trespassing" signs, and we were not able to use the facilities there. That just concerned me, that we were not allowed to go near the park. We had to either play in our backyards or either somewhere on the sidewalks or in the street, while we had the Valley Park within two to three blocks for me from where I was living at that time.

There were other things that—when I would ride the bus, I often wondered why did we have to go to the back of the bus. Well, of course, I realized later why we were doing this, but I always wondered. We didn't have transportation in my home at the time so we'd always have to use the public transportation, which was the bus here in Columbia. . . .

RM: As the civil rights movement was bubbling up a little bit in the '40s and '50s, do you remember what attitude you had toward the movement? Were you excited about it or did you think it was a fruitless effort?

BMCK: Well, at first I guess, thinking back, I'd heard about the situation down in Alabama with the bus situation there and I kind of got concerned about it, but I guess I thought about it a great deal when I could see that after Rosa Parks decided that she was not going to get up, and I began to notice that people weren't going to ride the bus.

*Bea McKnight lived from 1939 to 2010. Robert J. Moore conducted this interview at Barhamville Road Community Center, Columbia, South Carolina, on November 7, 2003.

They would carpool. I thought that was great, that people would be walking to their work, they would pick up, they would share. It was like they were united behind one particular cause, and they were going to work toward bringing about the change. Of course, I was quite excited when I heard that they had won the case and persons were able to ride anywhere on the bus. And so that really struck me.

Opening the White-Only Primaries

Even prior to that, hearing about the situation with George Elmore, way back. *[The case* Elmore v. Rice, *1947, involved the right of African Americans to vote in the Democratic primaries.]* His son was my classmate in school, in fact, we started in elementary, right at Waverly [School], and on to Booker Washington [High School]. But I remember Mr. Elmore and his five-and-ten store right there on Gervais Street. He decided that he was going to take on this situation about voting. They really, really, really—I would say they ostracized the man, because he almost lost everything. He lost his house, his wife had a nervous condition and she was later placed into the institution here for a number of years, and I could tell that had a real effect on his children. He would take pictures, he was a photographer, and he later was driving a taxicab.

RM: This is the son?

BMCK: No, this is the father. This is Elmore himself.

RM: And you say he lost his house?

BMCK: Lost his home, yes. After he decided that he was going to stand up and he was trying to fight for persons to get the right to vote and he did, but a lot of people didn't come to his rescue and he lost quite a bit.

I do recall that Modjeska Simkins tried to help him as much as she could, and a few others, but he just about lost everything. And in his business, I think they didn't supply him with the materials that was needed, so therefore he lost.

RM: What business did he have?

BMCK: The five-and-ten-cent store over here on Gervais and Oak Street.

RM: So he lost that, and he had owned his house and lost it?

BMCK: Yes, on Tree Street here in Columbia, and he lost that as well.

RM: I didn't know that story.

BMCK: Oh yeah, he was the one to kind of break the barrier as far as trying to help people to vote, African-Americans to vote here in Richland County. And so it was pretty rough during that time. These are some of the things I remember as a child coming up. It just struck me.

RM: I knew *Elmore versus Rice,* I knew the case. I just didn't know what happened with Elmore, the punishment, in effect, that he got. You think the black community didn't rally to his support as much as they might have?

BMCK: Or as much as they should have.

RM: They should have.

BMCK: Yes, yes, yes. Because here was a man putting his life on the line and because of this he suffered a great deal. But he didn't give up. I mean, he just carried on, and he's just one among many who felt that if this was a cause that they wanted to fight for, that they stood up for this cause, and regardless to what happened.

And we can relate back to the situation down in Clarendon County and Summerton with the situation where you had the Briggs, you had the Reverend DeLaine and Mr. Pearson, and there were others down there just to try to get their kids, just to get a bus to attend school. Out of that originated the *Brown versus Board of Education* in Topeka, Kansas, but it started here. It started here. It started right here, and people lost jobs, they lost all kinds of things down there, but they fought on. Yeah.

RM: Do you remember when you got involved in the civil rights movement?

BMCK: Yes. In the '50s. It was between the latter part of '57 and early part of '58. Yes, I do recall.

RM: And what are your memories of the early involvement in the movement? Are there some stories that you might tell me?

BMCK: Okay. We had meetings, Monday evening meetings, and in fact, the church was located just across the way here, Second Nazareth Baptist Church. That was where the meetings were being held.

[See press release, November 6, 1955, in "The Setting" section at the beginning of this volume.]

BMCK: The Richland County Citizens Committee would have these Monday night meetings, and so I decided that I wanted to attend, along with a friend of mine. We decided okay, this is something we wanted to do, so we did go out to the meetings to find out exactly what was going on, and when we got there, her cousin, who was A. P. Williams Sr.—A. P. Williams II, I should say—was really involved. And so he wanted us to come to the meetings, and so we decided that this was what we wanted to do, so on Monday evenings we'd try to make it to the meetings. And from that they got involved with a number of issues. We started involving ourselves as well.

Employment and Business Opportunities

BMCK: They were talking along the lines of trying to establish businesses or trying to establish a company here to help some of the blacks find employment. I do recall the Muslim community coming in and trying to really get involved with this, and they wanted to try to start some type of business here, and I believe they tried. Wasn't too successful but . . .

RM: That was as early as the '50s?

BMCK: Oh, yes. Oh, yes. Back in the '50s. At the church we had this meeting and we were trying to see—at Reverend Bowman's church, William McKinley Bowman's church at that time —and we all were there at the meeting, trying to see what can we as a race do to try to help with the employment situation here for our people. We did get, I believe—I'm trying to think—I think Mrs. Simkins started a quilting company, as I recall, and they were able to hire a few persons, but the Muslims decided they would have a little restaurant, and they'd have a place around here to try to hire some people, and we started looking at the various businesses. Where can we send people to work? Of course, the Town and Tourist [Motel in the 1200 block of Harden Street, Columbia, South Carolina] was just about to open up. We were looking at some of the other places around. So that was kind of the first effort, and after that time we started looking closely at what was happening on the national level, and so we decided that we wanted to look at the stores, look at the bus, look at the schools, but as time moves on we just decided to work on one issue at a time, trying to move into those areas. We were able to accomplish quite a bit.

RM: I want to get back to that, but before we get away from the Town and Tourist, tell me a little bit about that. Was that the only black motel in town, or one of several?

BMCK: There were a few, yes, there were a few. Mrs. Simkins, of course, had what was called Simbeth Lodges that was out on [U.S. Route] number 1. She had a little motel out there, and when persons would come in, of course we didn't have that many facilities, when persons would come in they would usually stop there. I do recall her telling me that she met James Brown and some of the other entertainers, they would stop right at her facility there. But yes, in the city we had the Town and Tourist. It wasn't until later that we had another one here, around on Two Notch Road. But Town and Tourist, and I'm trying to think of another place around here. That was kind of the location where people would come and have meetings, and we did have the A&B House that was up on Harden Street. That was a kind of eating facility. And we also had the College Inn. College Inn was right next to it.

But the Town and Tourist was the place around here at that time. . . . There were other little places kind of around, but Town and Tourist was the only one in the heart of Columbia that people, whenever they would come in, speakers, whatever, that's where they would stop.

RM: I recall there were a lot of meetings, whites and blacks, and that was one of the places they could meet.

BMCK: Yes, that's correct. That's true, that's true.

Modjeska Simkins

RM: Okay. Back to the Citizens Committee, Richland County Citizens Committee. Mrs. Simkins was a leader in that, and is this when you started your association with her?

BMCK: Yes.

RM: It's been a rich association ever since, right?

BMCK: Yes, but years prior to that Mrs. Simkins spoke at my home church, Bethel, on the corner of Sumter and Taylor Street. There was a meeting—well, it was a program. The ushers had this program that night and Mrs. Simkins was the speaker, and I was there as a member of the church, and also as a member of the junior ushers, and she really impressed me. I was, I think I was in high school, kind of early years in my high school, and when she spoke she really struck me, and I went up to her and I said to her she was good. I kept kind of close. I mean I would watch her very closely, and

Modjeska Monteith Simkins as a young
woman. Courtesy of McCray Collection,
Manuscripts Division, South Caroliniana
Library, University of South Carolina.

Modjeska Monteith Simkins in later
years. Courtesy of South Caroliniana Library, University of South
Carolina.

so after about the latter part of the '50s, I really got to know her, really got to know her, and we kind of formed a bond that lasted some thirty-five years.

I really gained so much from her. She had so much knowledge about a little bit of everything. I mean she could tell you things that you never knew about, but she could go back in history and talk about so many things, and relate you to this, that, and the other, and as she traveled I would travel with her and we would go places around the state, out of state, and she would talk about so many different things and what happened back years ago and coming on up to the present time. So oh, yes, it was never an experience like that. I don't think I'll ever have an experience with a person of Mrs. Simkins's caliber again. I don't know, she was just a different woman, and a woman of so many great contributions she's made, so many great contributions. So I was just happy that I was able to get to know her, understand her, learn about her, and so there's just so much I gained from her down through the years. I guess I was able . . .

And the voting process, she would talk about the strategies and what we should be doing as far as dealing with situations in the community, whether it was the hospital with the black employees or the patients. She would work with that, as well as with the integration situation with her niece, Henrie Monteith, enrolling in University of South Carolina. She was really behind that, and also having meetings at the various places, and her involvement with organizations in Alabama and other national organizations.

She would often tell me in her travel how she and Fred Shuttlesworth, who was at that time with SCLC, and Ralph Abernathy and, of course, Martin Luther King, how they would, various meetings would be held and she would tell me the Monday night meetings in Birmingham and Montgomery—this was just something different. I mean when they would have the meeting scheduled for, say, six o'clock, the church would be packed, and she would often tell me how the things were going on and how they would really be getting themselves ready and when time for Dr. King to approach, the church was packed, overflowing everywhere. And so she would often talk about that and her involvement.

RM: What role do you think she played in the race situation in Columbia? Was she a sort of burr under the saddle for the establishment the whole time, or was she able to push far enough but not too far, or did a lot of people think she pushed too far? I mean, what's your assessment of sort of how she fit into the movement? She was a bit more far out than some people in the movement.

BMCK: Yes, very aggressive, very aggressive. There's no question in my mind. I think when she spoke and when she attacked the issues, they listened. Her approach might have really upsetted [*sic*] some people. There's no question about that, from the governor on down, but that was her approach and she didn't hesitate one bit. She would come on and she would deal with whatever issue that she felt needed to be dealt with. She did just that. If I could just say it, "the power to be" didn't particularly like her but she didn't back down from them. She felt that this was something that she wanted to do and that's something she did, and her slogan was always, "She can't be bought and she wouldn't be sold," she was so determined. . . . I'm not talking about whites now. I'm talking about blacks too. She would call all of them on the carpet, and if they didn't like it, they could come to her, but most times they didn't, and she would just say it just like she felt it.

Even with the NAACP, when something she didn't like, if they weren't doing what she thought or felt that they should be doing, she would call them on the carpet. I mean she would just let them know. So it was nothing or nobody that she kind of missed if it was something that she felt was needed. There's no question about it. I do believe that there were a lot of them around that felt that she, they didn't particularly like the way she handled some things. . . .

RM: Were there some blacks who were opposed, feeling that they were going to rock the boat, that they were going to destroy their little bit of a relationship with whites and little bit of advantages they had from time to time? Were there a significant number of blacks who seemed to feel that way?

BMCK: Yes, I would think so. I felt that back when they organized this Relations Council [the Greater Columbia Community Relations Council], I believe it was, some felt there was an established relationship there, and there were times when Mrs. Simkins just didn't go along with a lot of those things, but they felt that they were in there with them and they were sitting down and trying to make some changes. I don't think, though— I believe it was Lester Bates was the mayor at that time.

[A section on local government will be found in volume 4.]

BMCK: When things were happening in other places, like Birmingham, Mississippi, and other places, they didn't want these things to happen in Columbia or the state, because they just felt we're not going to have that kind of image [here]. There were blacks who were in there, and they felt that she was just a radical and they were trying to smooth things over and work with them, and whatever they said, they were going along. She felt they were going along with whatever was said. . . .

Black Churches and Politicians

RM: I remember her saying some not so nice things about pastors that she thought were kind of selling out, not wanting to press the issues, and sometimes trying to be politically active, and she thought [they were] selling out to politicians who paid them to get the vote out and that sort of thing.

BMCK: Right. Absolutely. She was very much concerned about that because she said that the politicians would come into the black churches only during the election time, and at that time they were trying to give money to get the vote out in that candidate's favor, and she just thought it was wrong, that the ministers shouldn't be selling the black community out, because after all, that was a gathering place for blacks on Sundays, and she felt that they shouldn't allow their pulpits or their churches to be used for candidates to come in and tell them to vote, and how to vote. They were getting the money and trying to tell the candidates they could deliver so many people to them, and oh!

She was really, really upset about things like of that nature, and she talked about the preachers. . . .

RM: Were there any particular ministers that she pointed out? You want to name any names?

BMCK: No, I don't want to name names [laughs]. I don't want to name, but there were some. But I don't want to name them. No, I don't want to name them. You see, she would name them, but I wouldn't name them.

RM: My impression is that she was fairly critical of many aspects of organized religion, yet I found her to be a very spiritual person.

BMCK: She was.

RM: She didn't go to church much, did she?

BMCK: No, but she was a member of the Second Calvary Baptist Church, and what happened, it was an incident at the church. A young lady in the church became pregnant, and she said that there were members of the congregation that felt that she shouldn't be a part of the church, and that really did it for her. . . . She said, they just ostracized the young lady, and she felt that was wrong, and you shouldn't be pushing her out but helping her and bringing her in and talking with her. And from that time, she said she was really . . . she didn't want anything else to do with that, especially her church. That's not to say she didn't go to church, because she did. . . .

South Carolina Council on Human Relations

RM: You mentioned the South Carolina Council on Human Relations. As a matter of fact, I think that's where I first met you, at those meetings. What is your assessment of that organization? Was it very useful or was that . . .

BMCK: Oh, yes. Oh, yes. Oh, yes. I got involved during the time when Paul was there, Paul Matthias, and Paul and I talked, and in fact, we were able at the time, because I was involved with an organization that was called "Welfare Rights [Organization, or WRO]," and Paul and I, we would sit down, and out of that originated a handbook to pass out, it was a booklet, pass out to people in the community to inform them on their rights and other things. And they were very involved in the community, and had a number—did a lot of research, a lot of research, and I think a lot of key issues originated out of the South Carolina Human Rights.

[An interview with Paul Matthias will be found in volume 5.]

BMCK: When I say that, the welfare situation in this state was deplorable years ago, and they had, as I recall, I think John Delgado, and there were several other persons involved with that, and I think they did a great job, a great job. There's no question about it. And Alice . . .

RM: Alice Spearman?

BMCK: Oh, yes. Oh, yes. Alice Spearman was a wonderful woman, learned so much from her, and Alice was really involved in the organization, and I was sorry because some things happened after Paul left, and things seemed to . . . I felt that it was going to kind of continue, but it went downhill, downhill. And that was unfortunate. It happened, but the council was doing great things, and you had people coming from all over the state, and they were involved in many different issues, and that was a good relationship there because you had blacks and you had whites. I felt they did a wonderful job. I know that I think—what's his name? I talked about John. Mazie Ferguson. I know that [Dick] Harpootlian worked there as well, and Arthur, Arthur. . . I can't think of Arthur's last name. *[She is possibly referring to J. Arthur Brown.]* Quite a few of them were involved there.

Then you had the American Friends [Service Committee], with Hayes [Mizell]. Hayes was upstairs [in the same building], I believe it was.

All of those persons made great contributions to this community. They did wonderful things, and I think a lot of things happened. You were able to get some legislation passed. You were able to do various things. So, yes, they played a vital role in this community. There's no question in my mind they did.

Roles of Civil Rights Organizations

RM: What do you think was the most effective civil rights organization in South Carolina?

BMCK: Well, we could say, if we look at changes, you have to say the NAACP. However, after a period of time the NAACP started, I believe, kind of moving away from a lot of the key issues, at certain points. Now there were changes in a lot of issues, but I think the NAACP played a good role, but the Richland County Citizens Committee played a *great* role, because when we approached them [the NAACP] on several issues, it was like they were stand-offish. I mean they didn't deal with a lot of the issues that we felt that they should have dealt with. With the marches downtown during the civil rights period, we had young people coming from Allen University and Benedict College. This was put on by the Richland County Citizens Committee.

RM: Sit-ins?

BMCK: Yes, yes. And demonstrating in front of the stores as well. We would have students come to Bethel [AME Church], right there in the heart of Columbia, right there on the corner, and a lot of times we knew that the president, especially of Benedict College, Dr. Bacoats, didn't want the students to come, and so during the period they said they would come, either lunchtime, or they would come if they had a break in between [classes], so what we would try to do is prepare them some meals right there at the church, and would come and pick up some of them who were marching. Right in front of the store they would come and we would have the placard ready for them to go on, and then when they returned they would have a sandwich or we would have something prepared for them, and they would come. And, of course, Allen University students would come. It was kind of like they'd come at different times.

But the NAACP played a major role, but at the same time we did, too. We, meaning the Richland County Citizens Committee. Because the issues, when we would bring it to the attention, like, as I said, the mental hospital situation, where blacks were being paid less than the white employees, when the black patients were being treated less than the white patients. And then there were other issues. We were trying to get Martin Luther King here in Columbia. We, meaning the Richland County Citizens Committee, and there were a few of us. We did meet with Bernard Lee at Leevy's Funeral Home. That's when Mr. [I. S.] Leevy himself was alive, and Bernard was there and we had meetings with him, and also with Benjamin Mack, who was the aide here in Columbia, trying to prepare for different activities with SCLC. Well, of course, the NAACP didn't sanction that. They really didn't want King to come in here, and we had some difficult . . . but we had a few ministers with us, we had a few people, and others with us. So it was like they were saying he was a troublemaker, he'd cause all kind of problems. We couldn't understand why the NAACP was fighting this, but we were determined to try to bring him here, and he was coming during the time that he went to Memphis, Tennessee. He was scheduled to come to Columbia.

RM: On the Poor People's March [1968].

BMCK: That's correct. And he decided that he needed to go to Memphis, and we were hoping that after that period that he would still come. But of course, you know, he was assassinated and he didn't get here. But he did go down to Kingstree. That was back . . . We were trying to . . . I think he was down on several occasions to Frogmore, down there at Penn Center. That was like his little retreat. But we really wanted him here for a big, big group—big gathering. But a number of persons fought him coming here at that time.

RM: There's talk of the NAACP just not wanting SCLC to come in, thinking it would take away from their membership and influence in the state. So you think that's it?

BMCK: Yes, that was it. That was it. I think the SCLC at that time was motivating people and getting people really going, and NAACP was kind of laid back at that time. King, of course, had people really going, so it's no question in my mind. I do believe that they felt that SCLC would take away from them. And CORE [Congress of Racial Equality] was here but CORE was—Mr. [James T.] McCain in Sumter was involved with CORE—but CORE was not as visible and vocal as SCLC and NAACP around here. With CORE, I didn't know too much about some of the things CORE was doing, but we didn't really get SCLC going here in South Carolina. It was here but not that great. I mean NAACP was the thing. They wanted to be the thing around here.

But Richland County Citizens Committee, we were able to do a lot of things around here that NAACP did not do, and the NAACP was not involved even with the integration of the schools here in Richland School District One. We were the ones to get out and recruit about forty-five parents to try to get their children to go to the schools here in Richland County, and we had several meetings on Sunday evening. We got to the church and we had about twenty, as I recall, about twenty-six parents who said, yes, they would make sure to take their children to the school the following day. And I do remember, because they recognized Miss [inaudible], the Urban League did, the other night, that she had two kids to go to Rosewood Elementary. She carried them there. She had two to go to Hand Middle School, I believe it was one or two to Dreher. She walked with them, she took them. And we had the Frasiers, two kids. We also had the Wheelers—the Wheelers had about four, I believe, to integrate the schools. But the parents decided, yes, they were going to take their kids, and they did. But this effort was through the Richland County Citizens Committee, and we called on the NAACP, but for some reason they didn't assist us, so we said, well, we're going ahead. We're going ahead with this, and that we did. So that's how . . .

Marches

RM: What sort of personal involvement did you have with sit-ins and that sort of thing? Were you doing any of the marching or were you organizing behind the scenes, or what's the story there?

BMCK: Oh, yes, no question about it. I marched, and I was organizing as well. Oh, yes. Oh, yes. I marched downtown, Columbia, marched . . . We had a big program at Sidney Park CME Church, and we were getting people together, marching from the church to the capitol and coming back around. I was a part of the organizing effort, but I was marching and singing at the same time, so yeah, there's no question about that. The marches that were held around here, I do recall the march that we had down in Edgefield, when the late Senator Strom Thurmond did not want to sign the Voting [Rights] Act bill for renewal, and we got together and did a lot of planning, along with Jesse Jackson, and went to Edgefield. So we were organizing, getting ourselves together there. We marched from the Strom Thurmond High School all the way into the heart of the city, so I was leading the singing of the march and getting them together and getting them worked up, and we traveled on in, and by the time the marchers got into the heart of the city, then I was there leading the songs and we were getting people together.

So, yeah. Oh, yeah, marches around here, I wasn't always out front, but I was behind. I was involved with getting things kind of together, and they would always want me to lead the songs, and as we would go along we . . . And, of course, we would have the persons that we called . . . I'm trying to think now . . . I can't remember [now what we called them] . . . The last big march we had here was in 2000 about that flag, and they had me as the coordinator for getting the persons to direct the march. *The marshals*—that's what I couldn't think of!

RM: Marshals. I couldn't think of it either.

BMCK: The marshals. So that's kind of the role that we played in that, organizing marshals and trying to make sure people were moving in the direction they were supposed to, and having people at certain places there, the Capitol grounds and whatever. But the marshals, usually I would try to get them together, and we got it straightened out. Most of the marches that have been held around here I've been pretty much involved with it, pretty much involved.

RM: I remember your leading the singing very capably. Terrific.

Leaders

RM: If you were to list the five most important or influential black civil rights leaders in South Carolina, who would you name?

BMCK: Oh, of course, Modjeska would be number one. Matthew Perry, who was the attorney. Matthew handled most of the cases around here during that period. And, of course, I didn't agree all the time with I. DeQuincey Newman, but he would be considered one. Septima Clark, down in Charleston.

RM: Did you know her?

BMCK: Didn't know her personally. Met her, though, but didn't know her personally. And I want to tell you somebody else that I thought played a major role, and they don't really look at her now, and that's Victoria Delee. Victoria DeLee, to me, played a major role in the struggle around here.

RM: Is she still alive?

BMCK: She is alive. I'm told she lives still in Ridgeland. She is alive, yes. Yes. There are others but these are some key people that I would think made some outstanding contributions around during this time, around here.

RM: Did you know McCain? James McCain, the CORE person?

BMCK: I didn't really know him, but he, too, played a major role. I'd seen him on several occasions, but I did not know him. There are other persons, but these are some of the keys.

RM: You've named five.

White Leaders

RM: Were there any white persons who were important in the movement?

BMCK: Oh, yeah. Howard McClain—

RM: Howard McClain, with the Christian Action Council.

BMCK: I'm trying to think of some of the others around here during that time. All of you, all of you. You [Bob Moore] and Seldon [Smith] played a major role. Major role!

RM: Not very major, but . . .

BMCK: Well, I mean, we were involved in several things together. You know, we had to have some of *you*. We had to have you! *[She laughs.]* Yeah!

Well, of course, Alice Spearman. As I said, organizations like the Council on Human Relations played major roles here. I'm trying to think of some others here that really, really took a stand, and they were really with us during that time.

RM: How about James McBride Dabbs?

BMCK: Oh, yes, yes. He was in Aiken, right?

RM: Mayesville.

BMCK: Mayesville, okay. Yes, yes. Oh, yes, I remember him well. Yes.

RM: Were there any white politicians who were helpful in your view?

BMCK: Now I think Hyman Rubin. Hyman was on the city council. Hyman was involved. I know that Barbara Moxon, Barbara was involved with that League of Women Voters. I'm trying to think of some others, too, at that time.

RM: Would you put John Bolt Culbertson in that category?

BMCK: Oh, my goodness! Why wouldn't I think of him? Yes, oh yes, no question about that. Yeah, yeah. John Bolt was up there in Greenville, yes . . .

RM: What's your assessment of the mayor?

BMCK: Lester Bates?

RM: Yes.

BMCK: I think, and this is just the way I see it, I think Lester was trying to make sure that Columbia, South Carolina, would not be like a Montgomery or Birmingham. I think he was, I think he was. While I don't know all of the ins and outs, I think behind the scene he did quite a bit. . . . Yes, I think he played a major role during that time. And at least we didn't have the dogs and all these other things that were going on elsewhere, yes.

Orangeburg Massacre

RM: What is your assessment of Governor McNair?

BMCK: During that time with the Orangeburg Massacre, and I want to say to you now, I was down there. We went late one night, Modjeska and I, along with a Mr. Griffin. Mr. Griffin drove us down there at that time. We met with Cleveland Sellers, and there were a number of others that we met there, in Dr. Roland Hayes's house.

RM: Haynes.

BMCK: Haynes, that's right. Down there in Orangeburg. We talked with them, and they were telling us exactly what happened, that those kids wanted to use the bowling alley, but after a period of time, seems as if things start developing. They could tell that violence was just about to take place. I don't think, because the kids didn't have weapons, they only wanted just to demonstrate, and when the order was passed down to them, to my knowledge, Pete Strom, who was the head of SLED [State Law Enforcement Division], and he—I'm not saying that he gave the order in any way. I'm not saying that. But to me, because several people, even Modjeska herself, was trying to call the governor, McNair, to ask him to try and stop the effort as far as that situation. Not to shoot those kids and to try to hold off on several things.

But it seems as if nobody was listening to anyone and they just went ahead, and I don't have any hate or anything of that nature, but I don't look on him favorable, not as a governor. And I believe that he didn't run for office because of that. That really did a job on this state. It really, really tarnished its image, and this state really suffered as a result of that. But I think in later years he realized, while he never has openly admitted it, I think that he realized that what had happened, what he did . . . [Governor] Hodges, he did touch on it, and in so many words he apologized, and that, to me, makes a man bigger in my sight, that a mistake had been made. After all, you've got African Americans here who felt that this shouldn't have happened, and things did happen. In my book, [McNair] doesn't look too good. Doesn't look too good.

Movement Accomplishments

RM: What did the movement accomplish? What kind of successes has it had?

BMCK: I think it accomplished a great deal. I think, one, with the Voting Rights Act, which allowed people to vote, especially African Americans. As well as the civil rights legislation wherein it allowed us to go to use places we were not able to use before, whether it was hotel facilities, whether it was public accommodation, whatever it was, and it did allow us to use these places, which it had not been done before, and it wasn't because it was the good graces of people. We had to put forth the effort in order to accomplish these things.

Also the school integration. I think Henrie [Monteith] going to the university, Harvey Gantt going to Clemson, it opened the doors for so many others. . . . We just want a chance to take advantage of these various things. After all, this was a state-supported school, or state-supported schools, and we have a right to take advantage of these opportunities just like anybody else.

And there were many other things that occurred around here. Right now, look at the housing situation. Housing has been kind of bad in this city for a long time. When I say bad, it has almost been that blacks have been on one side and whites on the other side. I think now, with the Fair Housing Act, that it allows people if they can afford it, they can move places that they have never been able to move before. While I may not want to leave my community, there are those who would, and so you have people moving in different places if they can afford it. It also gave African Americans in particular the opportunity to advance themselves, whereas they weren't able to advance years ago.

But I'm afraid that we have allowed, we've got ourselves caught up in situations that we have not reached back, we have not done a lot of things that we could do. Sometimes they have felt, "Well, I made it and I don't have any right to reach back and help somebody else because I've made it." And they don't see where people struggled, people died, to make things possible for them. We didn't have a lot of elected officials years ago. We have a lot of elected officials now that we didn't have, and somebody paved the way, and it just didn't happen overnight. We had to work toward trying to get those three blacks elected back in the '70s, I. S. Leevy Johnson, James Felder, as well as Herbert Fielding in Charleston. So there are so many things that we've accomplished, but now I think we're just so complacent. We're not fighting like we used to fight, we're just not concerning ourselves with the issues. . . . We had problems years ago but we were more united then, and we're not as we ought to be today.

But did the civil rights movement accomplish? *Yes!* A great deal, a great deal. But those accomplishments will only last when we decide that we want to make sure that we continue with our history. As long as we let things slip from under us, we're going to move back rather than move forward.

RM: What are some of the failures of the movement, in your view? Were there some things that didn't get accomplished that should have been accomplished?

BMCK: Well, I think, yes, we had some failures, we had some failures. We didn't do enough, as I see it, enough to help our people understand what it is that they ought to be doing. I think what happened was that we didn't do enough educating them on the total picture, because so many times I hear now that "I think integration messed us up."

And I'm saying, "How in the world did integration mess you up?"

"We had our neighborhood schools," they would often say to me.

I'd say, "I understand that."

"We had our neighborhood stores."

"I understand that too."

"And now all of that's gone."

And they felt that they had a closer-knit or closer contact with their children before they were able to go over to the other schools. That, I've heard, as some of the failures in what has happened.

And, "Yes, we can go anywhere," they tell me now. "Yeah, we can go anywhere to eat, and we can go to this place and go to that place, but why is it we don't have some places in our *own* communities that we could go to? We had the Town and Tourist years ago, we had the College Inn, we had the Alban, but now we don't have those places."

So they look at that as a failure, and while I don't totally agree with them, there are some failures and things that happened to us that maybe if we had done it a little different. . . .

And then they say, "While we were out there marching and planning, others were preparing their children and things were happening in this country against us that maybe we weren't aware of."

That's possible, because, as some have said, we left the [Confederate] flag up there back in the '60s. It remained there until 2000, and it was only supposed to be up there during the Centennial [of the Confederacy] period and then be removed, and now we have it directly in our face. Well, there was a negotiating part, people were there sitting at the table. I wasn't there so I don't know exactly what happened, but at the same time, they first said they wanted to put it in a museum. It's not in a museum, it's right on the capitol grounds, and that to me is really hurting the state in a lot of ways. . . . I don't think industries want to come into a state with a lot of problems.

I think, though, we need to work harder on building a better relationship, and then at the same time we see there's a lot of racial profiling going on. There's a lot of other things that's happening. [The] employment situation right now is worse than in years gone by, and people are losing jobs. There's more crime. Crime is on the increase. Drugs in our communities. So we failed somewhat. Yeah, we have failed somewhat. But we still have a long way to go. We still can work toward making some changes.

Booker T. Washington High School

RM: Related to that, you went to Booker T. Washington High School?

BMCK: Yes, I did.

RM: And all I've heard from other people is a very positive experience. Did you have a very positive experience at Booker T. Washington?

BMCK: Oh, yes, very positive. Yes, yes, I did. Booker Washington was the first African American high school around here. C. A. Johnson High School came along back the latter part of the '40s. And we had very good teachers, teachers who were concerned about you, and there were activities at the school that you could get involved with, and there was just some closeness there. It was almost like a big family, and when the school closed it was really heartbreaking, and I do recall we had a meeting with the then–Dr. Guy Vaughn, who was the superintendent of schools.

We had heard the rumor—we, meaning Mrs. Simkins, A. P. Williams, there were about three or four others of us—had heard that the school was going to eventually close. In the community around Booker Washington you had a lot of established, well-known African American families. On the Blossom Street you had at that time Salters, Shivers—there's a church that's located right over here now, Jones Memorial [AME Zion]. You had a lot of churches over in the community right around the school. We were able to—there were a lot of plays we had there at the school. Families lived nearby, within walking distance, and you just had a pretty good relationship. We had families up on the hill that later the university took over the property there, and families had to move out. A lot of families lost homes up there. The Cannons, I do recall—oh, a lot of families up in that area.

There were a few families who were determined that they were going to stick it out, like Fannie Phipps Adams, and by the way, Fannie was assistant principal at Booker Washington High School. A wonderful woman, wonderful woman. Fannie was there, and also you had outstanding teachers. I do recall a man by the name of Gilroy Griffin, who was a chemistry teacher—a fine man, lived around the corner from me. And you had a lady by the name of Miss Annie Washington. She would come to my home, she was a member of my church, and history teacher—fine woman, fine woman. She lived over on Barnwell Street. Some of them now I do recall. Margaret Walker—oh, just a number of teachers around. Very, very good teachers, a good experience. Ethelyn Nance. Just wonderful teachers, we had good teachers and accomplished a great deal.

RM: That must have been a wrenching sort of thing that made you wonder maybe about the trade-off, losing a place like Washington and getting integration, and yet losing something of that community.

BMCK: Yes, yes. There's no question about it.

RM: And you said there are some people who are saying that we'd have been better off—

BMCK: Yes. I don't know what happened, but we were trying to tell them that the school district was going to turn Booker Washington over to the University of South Carolina, and that happened. And people start looking strange and start saying if it wasn't for that, we would have perhaps had our school, but changes do come, and we could see signs of changes coming about because they were building several things at the university at that time. . . .

You could see things happening because they started moving people out. Some stayed up in one section though, and it was right there, the housing community. But I guess it was something that was going to eventually happen, and because it was right there, and then when the university started expanding, then things just start happening. It just started happening.

RM: Enveloped the Booker T. Washington area.

BMCK: Yes, yes.

RM: But so many black schools were closed or demoted from high schools to middle schools. It must have a been a distasteful—

BMCK: It was hard, hard. It really hurt too. I know that there were other schools around that were closed. Well, Waverly was my elementary school, and the Waverly Annex is still there but it's not a school. But I think it really hurt with Booker Washington, it really hurt, and we did all we could do to try to keep it open, but it just didn't happen.

The Movement Years

RM: When you look back on the '50s and '60s, what sort of feeling do you have about those years? Is it a feeling of satisfaction or despair or bitterness or sadness for lost opportunities, or do you look back on them as pretty glorious years, because you were accomplishing some big things?

BMCK: I guess it's twofold. There were joys, there were accomplishments. On the other hand, there was sadness, because, as I said, some things happened around here that you would have to think about. But as far as the movement is concerned, I would say those were great days, they were great days. I just wish some of those days were around, maybe in a different way, because we had more unity then. I forever will say that. We realized what our goals were, and we tried to fight for those goals. We may not have accomplished a lot of things, but there were some key things that we did accomplish.

On the other hand, there were some things that sadden, you're sad about. But overall, as I look back, I think they were years that I was part of and I shall never forget, and it was just a time in life, that historical events were taking place, and that they will forever be with me. They will forever be with me.

And the friendship that was established, the relationships, and I will forever remember Modjeska, and so many times I think back on things that we have done, how we used to laugh and she would tell all kind of stories and do all kind of things, and well, naturally, when you look back—and people who played a major role in different things. You think about all those things and life itself, and it's just something to think about. But, oh, yeah, they were good days. Those were good days, but as I said, there were some sad days as well.

RM: Exciting times.

BMCK: Exciting. Very much so, very much so. But we were able to live through it, but as you think back, it was a blessing that you were able to live through those days because so many tragedy things happened, so many things happened. I remember they wanted me to go to Selma, but I couldn't go at that time, and when I heard about the killing of Mrs. [Viola] Liuzzo and that other young man [Jimmie Lee Jackson], it just hurt. I mean you just think about it. And also when you think about those three, Schwerner and the other ones in Mississippi . . .

RM: Goodman.

BMCK: Goodman and Schwerner and—I can't call the other one's name. That was something. And to hear about Medgar Evers being shot right there on the side of this house there, right there in his driveway. These were sad times.

And, of course, Martin being killed. I remember I was in the kitchen, we were talking, and the news flashed and said that Martin Luther King had been shot, and oh my goodness! That was just something to behold, and later it was announced that he had passed, and so I thought about it. Later I called Modjeska and we'd start talking, and I said, "You know, something tells me I want to go to the funeral." I start calling around to see . . . Mr. Wheeler said that he would go, and then I found out later he said he couldn't go. So anyway, I said, "Oh, yes, I'm going, I'm going." So at the time I was talking with some other people, nobody seemed to want to go. So finally I asked my husband, and he agreed to go, so we drove to Atlanta, and I did go there.

We arrived that afternoon, and that night as people were going around, in front of me was Ralph Bunche. I'm trying to think—there were several others. I saw Wilt Chamberlain. Coming out of the church, I turned and there was Richard Nixon, so I was able to see a lot of people, and saw Sammy Davis Jr. So that was quite an experience, that was quite an experience that night.

As we were leaving the church I heard someone saying that Jackie Onassis was coming in, and I didn't see her but later that night on the news, I could tell as the news flashed you could see her going. There were a lot of people there that evening, but they just had it roped off and you just could go on around, and I was able to witness that.

And, of course, the next day with the service, the gathering, and then traveling, getting the horse and putting the casket in, and traveling over to Morehouse for the final rites, and then that was something as well. So I'd gone, I'd gone down there. I said, "Well, I will go, because after all this man gave his life." And so that was an experience.

RM: Well, you have a lot of great memories.

BMCK: Oh, yes.

RM: Are there some questions that you think I should have asked and haven't asked?

BMC *[laughs]:* No, I think you've covered about everything. I think you've covered everything. I don't know if I've answered everything, but you have covered.

Childhood

RM: You don't remember anything else from your childhood? I'd really like the stories about specific things in your childhood, other than the park and the back of the buses.

BMCK: Growing up in Columbia, I remember coming around this area, because I lived over in here in this area when my parents were alive. My mother died when I was seven, and then we had to move in with my grandmother over on Pine Street. It was a time in my life that—well, of course I missed my mother a great deal, and trying to adjust. The following year my father died. So it was kind of a blow to me as a child, but I had a wonderful grandmother and an uncle and aunts, and I have a brother.

We grew up in a community that I would think was close knit. My teacher at the time lived right across from the Chappelle Memorial AME Church, and she would often boil eggs, maybe during the Easter time, and she would come by my house and she would drop them off. And there were other people in the community that I was kind of close to, so that was kind of developing at that time.

I guess, thinking about my mother, or thinking about my parents in particular, that there was a kind of void there. I mean I missed them, but we had wonderful relatives that cared for us. And then as I moved on from my early years into the high school years, they were very good years. I'm moving on.

But getting back to my childhood, that was kind of the way we grew up. My mother would walk from—we lived on Allen Benedict Court right over here—walk from Allen Benedict Court to Waverly [School]. She would take us back and forth when she was alive, and they didn't have hot lunches at that time when we were there back in the '40s, I think it was '45 to '46, my mother would always prepare the meal, prepare a lunch for us and we would take the lunch at that time. There was a cafeteria there at Waverly but there was no hot meal. But I do recall my mother preparing the meals, our little bags, and we would take them. And I was in plays and singing. My mother would take me round to different churches to sing. I do recall that, when she was alive. . . . And I was in a lot of plays at Allen University, and I kind of missed those things [when she died].

RM: Yes. Did you go to movie houses downtown?

BMCK: I went to Carver Theater. That was across from Allen University. As a child, coming up. Yes. I did go to that. I didn't go down to the Capitol [Theater]. The Capitol was down there on Washington Street, but I did go to the one right there across from Allen.

RM: Did you go to any of the so-called white ones and have to sit in the balcony?

BMCK: No, I never did go. We knew what was going on there: you have to sit up in the balcony. Lot of times people called it the "buzzard's roost." Go up there and whatever. But I didn't go there. No, I did not go there.

RM: Well I thank you so very much. This has been . . .

BMCK: I enjoyed it.

RM: Well, it's been fun.

BMCK: Yes, I enjoyed it.

J. S. Wright,
Come on to the Meeting

Marvin Lare [ML]:* This is Monday, October the 31st, and I'm in the home of Reverend J. S. Wright. Say a few words, Reverend Wright. We'll make sure that we're picking up your voice as well.

J. S. Wright [JW]: What are you most interested in?

ML: I think we're good to go now. I'm interested in your own very personal perspective and experiences. As you were saying, earlier before the tape was picking it up, there's not been very much written about the history and the story of civil rights and the leadership in South Carolina. It is usually just a footnote in what is written about the movement. I'd like for you to share your experiences in your own way. I'll follow up with some questions if there are things that are not clear to me.

JW: I had experience under President Hoover's administration. I mean personal experience. Under his administration. I think President Roosevelt. He followed him. From Hoover's administration on up to now, I have had some experience, and it was kind of difficult there in the middle and late '20s on. So far as our people surviving in any decent economical way. It was sharecropping and . . . I'm talking about in the '20s now, on up to the middle '30s. At least that period. The boll weevils were really bad and we—when I say we, I mean my people—were not able to buy the poison to put on the cotton. But the other folks could buy it. And that meant that many years, or seasons, we didn't make enough cotton to pay the bills. And they came and took everything we had, so far as the cattle and the mules and what little corn we raised. Occasionally they would leave a cow, and that meant we had to—let's use a common statement—root, live hog, or die.

*Marvin Lare interviewed J. S. Wright at his home in Augusta, Georgia, on October 31, 2005. The interview was transcribed by Lynn Moore.

And we didn't have but about three months of schooling in that time, the '20s and '30s. And that was in, I guess, a building about as large as this whole house or maybe a little larger. From first to seventh grade, one building. I'm sure you heard about that. And so we moved from there, gradually kind of moved out. And particularly when President Roosevelt came.

During Hoover's time and early in President Roosevelt's administration we had to go in their cotton fields and scrap what they left, for surviving. You see, and I think it was two, two and a half cent per pound after we scrapped it. And that was where we looked forward to for all that calling Christmas of gifts. And that was the few months that we were in school. That gradually picked up, some, particularly when President Roosevelt came in. He had a whole lot of different common labor works that just cut the side of the road, et cetera, and that made it a little different economically for the folk that could do the work. But at that time we were just scrapping the cotton—out there—and my mother raised a lot of chickens. She had everything, chickens, ducks, turkeys, guineas, geese—you name it. That was particularly . . . and the cows. We grazed them on the hedgerows. I survived on that. I'm sure you've heard about some of that.

ML: Yes, but describe it anyway, as you remember it.

JW: And in that category I worked until '39, in South Carolina, in that low part. And I left—in '39 I came to Scofield-Aiken High School, in the seventh grade. I'd just finished seventh grade. I went there four years and I did my high school there. That's where I began manhood. . . .

But really what I was interested in was the clashing with the other group. That really came about, personally with me, after I married. Because I saw how badly my parents were treated. You see, they took everything we had, and Daddy had to walk four and five miles a day to a sawmill to get enough something to buy groceries with. I didn't forget how we were treated, and so I said to myself, and I talked with a peer about, I said, "If there's anything that I can do, at least let them know that I'm a human being, I'm going to do that." So in 1942 I married and I started preaching in '41.

And I don't know just how I made the inroad but I got in contact with Dr. King, because I was pastoring then in Denmark, and living there. And I began to have meetings —I invited him down to the church, to give insight of, really, what he was doing and what he could do to help us. Oh, two, three years he would come down at least twice and sometimes three times a year, until he got it where I could handle it. The whole Bamberg County. And some of it reached into Orangeburg. That was a time that the fire sure enough got hold of me.

My wife had finished school. I worked and sent her to college. After I finished high school, then she got her senior year—I continued to work and pastor, and I did my seminary work. She started teaching. Of course, at that they didn't get but forty dollars a month, the teachers didn't. That was big money.

So unfortunately, when I got the community kind of together to really see where they wanted to go, where we *should* go, I ran into [re]percussion with some of my own people. There were about five of them, and I wouldn't dare think about their names, but there were two of them and three of us. Didn't want me to go in the direction that I was going. And fortunately again, my wife was blessed to get a job—she could walk there in five minutes, from where we lived. And she worked there about ten years, while I was working in the community with Dr. King. They sent me word, "Don't let him come back anymore." This group, five of them. I was boiling like a pot. I told them that if they wanted that, what they had, I'd take care of the church. And I didn't stop.

The end of that year, when it began to boil, they fired my wife. Without any confrontation or counseling with her. Twenty days before school closed. She had not received a contract for the next year. So the principal called her in his office and said that she would not get a contract because of her attitude. Well, they hadn't said any more to her about her attitude you can . . . and that's her picture up there [gesturing above the couch]. So I knew that was fishy. I began checking around. That was in Bamberg County. They went to Allendale County, Orangeburg County, Barnwell County, and Aiken County and told the superintendents of those counties not to hire her because I was a little Martin Luther King. Well, we . . . [drumming fingers on the table] . . . we just didn't. . . . Fortunately she and I were in high school together, and we just tried to be honest in every respect, and we kept in closest friendship with the principal there, and she made good grades, and that's the year that the special education came out. And that was her major subject. The second was English. They couldn't find another teacher but her, so they hired her. And that was in Denmark, and she had to drive to Aiken. She did that for about a year and a half, about two years. Fortunately.

And that superintendent in Aiken told her just like they told him. That I was a little Martin Luther King and not to hire her. But he told her, "I'm not hiring your husband. I'm hiring you because you're qualified to do the job." That was in 19— No, I move up here [Augusta, Georgia] in '65. That must have been in 1962, '63, somewhere. . . .

Anyway, came here. She commuted but I did not stop. I did not stop. They sent me word that if they catch me at night I'd be a dead duck. I wasn't anything but pastoring and visiting the members and et cetera, et cetera. At that point we had begun to get—maybe about one—of their buses occasionally to help get some of our children. That was moving off. [He drums his fingers on the table.] I wasn't worried about that too much because I had started. But the main interest at that point was the theater and the drinking fountains. We couldn't go in there, only to clean them.

I kept having meetings and built up my attendance because I was determined to make some adjustment—or they could just knocked me out of the way. So I got them, enough of my folk, to work with me—that was in Denmark, and we lived in Bamberg County—to go down to the county seat. One afternoon as they stand in the door and watch, I go to the fountain and drink. I guess about twenty-five or thirty of them in down there. They stood around the door and looked.

Somehow the news got around that we were coming. When we walked in the front door, the mayor was over here and the sheriff was over there, and they asked if they were gonna go to the fountain." All the folk had come to stand with me was at the door. We didn't make it congested, but we just were there observing. When they came, I walked straight to their fountain and drank some water. I heard them say, now it's the word they used, "That's a crazy nigger, ain't he?"

I didn't think it over. . . . I just went on and drank the water and came back. Well once one drink it, they can't doubt it then. So they had no more trouble going in there drinking water.

The next drive was integrating the theater. We had a little pigeonhole upstairs, and we could go up there and watch the show, but they had to go down here. I kept working. I'm just giving you the main issues. I'm not talking about the other little petty things we ran into. These are the main ones.

About a month after that—I kept on working—one Saturday morning one of them—their race, not my people—they didn't call me. [But] one of them called me. Said, "Preacher?"

"Yes, sir."

"How long are you going to be home?" I'm just using his words.

I said, "Well, I'll be here a while." My children were across the field, playing.

He said, "Well, I'll be out there. I want to talk with you."

That's the only time I got a little afraid. My discretion—if a negative statement would come in, I did it with my wife, I didn't do it immediately though—because that doesn't pay off. I went on just like nothing was happening. Even in pastoring. I told my wife, "I'm going to invite him in. If he does not come in, I guess he going to ask me to go into the car. I'm going. You watch, just to see what happens."

So he drove up out there in the yard, and I said, "Won't you come in, sir?"

"No, you come out here and sit down."

So I went on out there, and he was sitting in the car, right under the steering wheel, in the front, and I got on the opposite side. He was by himself. So the two of us, after I got in, he said—now these are the exact words he said—he said, "Preacher."

I said, "Yes, sir."

He said, "I'm the deacon at First Church here, and I know you're going to hear it and I want to tell you myself." He said, "For two years we've been trying hard to get you to kill you." And these are his words, if I ever said it—he said, "But we couldn't get to you."

See, I didn't stop my visitation in the service of the church and the community, but I would not go by myself. And they were looking for me, following the car to see if I'd be by myself in night. They'd knock me down, and nobody knew who, what, and what. But they'd find me dead. But the Lord did lead me in that direction. Never to go out by myself.

So anyway, he said, "I knew you would eventually hear, but I wanted to tell you myself." He said . . . "We were wrong," he said. "We were wrong! . . . If we had ten more men in the city like you . . . it would be better off."

I never did discuss the situation with anyone but me, my wife, and the Lord. And he couldn't get nothing I said. But these are the words he said. He said, "I was wrong. We were wrong. I came back here this morning to ask you to forgive us."

I said, "I'm not angry with you." And I wasn't. So he went on talking. I said, "I'm not angry."

He said, "I want to ask you a question."

I said, "What's that, sir?"

He said, "Now, on Wednesday of this week you're going to integrate the theater, aren't you?"

I said, "Yes, sir. We plan to go anyway."

"He said, 'Well, would you mind if me and my wife, you and your wife would be the first four and go in there together?'"

I said, "I don't mind. Be glad to have you go."

So that Wednesday you couldn't get into town, in and about the theater. We walked on in there together.

ML: Mmmm. Mmh!

JW: And that was it. We didn't fuss no more.

Those were some of the main issues, but other little agitations and things happened all the way out. But I said to my wife—and she was with me, she was a nice girl, working with me—I said, "Now, let's keep what I'm saying here and tell the Lord about it. Because it doesn't matter what kind of friends we have, they're not going to tell it like we told them. The Lord's going to fix it." Whenever I meet anyone I tell them, "Come on to the meeting." That's all I'd do, kept on having meetings. So that Wednesday we were there and the—that's the only thing we had to do. When one goes in, the gate is down. . . .

But fortunately, or unfortunately—I don't know—I got called here [to Augusta]. My wife found a job right over there to Aiken in two year time, and that's where she retired. So I came here in 1965 and I've been here ever since.

Those are some of the main things. There are so many that I experienced, but the way I saw them treating my Daddy, I never shall forget. And the way we had to come up. But I thank God for my experience. He has been good to me. Good to me, you see. Out of all the children . . . but I'm the only one that lived. The only one that lived. But she [perhaps meaning his mother] had a statement that I shall never forget. She said, "You all just pray and regardless of how people treat you, you treat them right. One day that bottom rail is going to work to the top." I won't forget that.

ML: The bottom rail?

JW: *The bottom rail's going to work to the top.* So I've had to beg for bread. I've had to beg for bread. He's been good to me. And I've learned to love people because I can't pray to God if I've got any hatred in my heart. Regardless of what happened. He said, "Vengeance is mine. I will repay." And he'll do it. I've seen it off and on. Off and on! . . . My wife and I were married for sixty years. She's been dead going on three. I haven't had to beg bread, and I thank God for what he's done. And I walk the street with my head up. Yes, sir. I thank God. I've had some unusual experiences, and sometimes the very person you think ought to give you a lift will do this to you [motions down]. But God sees all we do and hears all we say. And I declare he'll fight your battles. Just take your burdens, just take your message to him. And leave it there. Yes, sir. So that's just a little bit of what I've been through.

ML: You're almost ninety years, right? When's your birthday?

JW: April. The 25th. . . .

ML: What's the name of the church here that you came to pastor in 1965?

JW: Macedonia. Baptist Church. In 1965.

ML: And what was the church you were serving there in Denmark?

JW: I served Rome in Denmark for eleven and a half years, and I served Thankful in Bamburg for nine and a half. Baptist churches. And I served Nazarene in Fairfax, Allendale County, for five years, before I came here.

ML: Yes. When you were bringing people together, what was the name of the organization?

JW: It was NAACP, and of course, Dr. King had his own name for his . . .

ML: The SCLC [Southern Christian Leadership Conference]?

JW: Yes, SCLC. It was interchanged—I mean some of them didn't like—I mean some of my people were scared of the NAACP. I said, "Well, let's get SCLC." We worked them together.

ML: So, it was pretty much sort of interchangeable . . . There in Denmark, did you know Cleveland Sellers?

[Interviews with Cleveland Sellers, the youngest of the three generations, will be found in this volume, volume 4, and volume 5. Also, Sellers interviewed Victoria DeLee. That interview will be found in volume 2.]

JW: Oh, yes. He was my trustee and I baptized his children. I baptized Cleveland Sellers. The old man's Cleveland's grandchild.

ML: I'm working very closely with Cleveland. He's at the University of South Carolina now, as head of the African American Studies Program.

JW: Smart boy.

ML: Yes. Fine fellow.

JW: Well you see, he was there then and so much went on, and some just stuck with it. [But] he just had to stretch out.

ML: Yes. He took it and ran with it. I'll remember you to him. I'll see him soon again, and I'll tell him that we spoke.

You talked about the water fountain, the theater, and buses—how about on voting rights?

JW: That was the main issue. Voting. In 1944 my brother and I and two more fellows sued the mayor in Denmark. There was an attorney, I think it was Mr. Waring, I believe, lived in Charleston.

[A major section covering Judge J. Waites Waring and his wife, Elizabeth, will be found in volume 3.]

JW: He was backing us up. We sued the mayor in Denmark, and he gave us permission to go to Bamberg and register to vote. We had to read the Constitution before we could register.

ML: The whole thing or just a part of it?

JW: About two-thirds of it. When I finished reading it, bless his soul, he asked me, "Where do you teach?" I said, "I'm sorry, sir. I don't teach. The Lord just blessed me enough to read it like that." That's the only way we could vote. That was '44.

ML: And pay the poll tax.

JW: Yes, sir.

ML: How much was the poll tax?

JW: I've forgotten how much it was, but it was some extra money than just your property tax. I can't remember now what it was. We had to do that.

ML: Voting in 1944 was very, very early. Ten years at least before Martin Luther King came on the scene. Ten or twelve years.

JW: Yes, sir. It put a stake, if I may use that term, on me, on us. Me and my brother growing up, the way they treated us. So we just had to start doing something. So we got together and decided we [were] going to vote. And we talked to that judge out of Charleston. Judge [J. Waites] Waring. I guess he's gone on home now.

ML: Yes. He died about 1968.

JW: He backed us up. He gave us a written statement. We carried that in there. And he looked at it. He didn't want to do it, but rather than get shamed in the public about that, he gave us permission. So seven of us went on down there and read a part of that Constitution and voted. Then we started gaining ground.

ML: With only three months of school a year, at least starting out, it's quite a challenge to read and to get an education. You came on over here, was it to Augusta or where for your schooling?

JW: To Aiken. It's about forty miles from here. When I came to the campus from Denmark, I didn't have five cents. But I was determined to get a little bit of training. I came there, I joined a quintet. Worked in the kitchen. I cleaned three rooms, and I rang the bell for the changing of the classes.

ML: Was that at Voorhees?

JW: No, that was Scofield, in Aiken. That was my work, worked my way through. I was there for four years. I'd get up five o'clock every morning and go there and—at that time they had a woodstove. There were about 250 on the campus, and they had them big old grits pots to put on there. I forgot the lady's name now that did the cooking. I put on the water and she had that time. I also was a waitress. I'd go there and make up the fire in the stove, throw on the water, and about that time she'd be coming in. Then I'd go over and dust the rooms, classes. I cleaned them in the afternoon, but I had to go there and dust them out in the morning. I go back and dust then. Then I'd go by my room and change clothes and go back and serve the food while they're eating. But I made it. I was determined to make it. I was convinced, and I am now, you can make it if you try, and put God ahead. Yes, sir.

ML: You spoke about having a letter from Judge Waring. Do you have copies of that, or of any of the old documents or anything that might be interesting?

JW: No, sir. My oldest brother, he's gone on to be with the Lord now, he and his wife, chances are might have had some, but I don't have any. He was really nice to us, and he was successful. It's just—I'm not going to say discouraging—it's sickening to see how many of us were treated, and it's not over yet. And we all are human beings. I can't help but at intervals mention this correlation in my messages sometimes. The Israelites—you know how they got over, how they were treated. So we are the Israelites in America.

ML: Yes. Hewers of wood and carriers of bricks and so forth?

JW: Yes, sir. We came over here on the boat. Whatever it was. As slaves from Africa, and the Israelites were carried down to Egypt, slaves. But God fixed it. And God has fixed this. I'm not discouraged. I'm concerned about people, but I have concluded and I'm just as satisfied as I am sitting in this chair, that if it's in a person, he can make it if he try and put God in it. You can't mess around now. You have to scuffle and talk to God. There'll be some snags, but you can overcome it. You can overcome it. Yes, sir.

ML: That's a good word to end on, but we don't have to stop there though, either. I'm really glad that Reverend Irvin referred me to you.

[See the interviews with the Reverend Dr. Nathaniel Irvin in this volume and volume 2.]

ML: I've got the address for Reverend A. C. Redd. . . . I'm going to drive by there and I'll see if it will be convenient for me to see him.

[The interview with the Reverend Dr. A. C. Redd will be found in volume 3.]

JW: I didn't mention him, but he was with me. When I was in South Carolina, we were God's team. Redd was. Yes, sir. I know him personally.

ML: Again, thank you.

Samuel Hudson and Sarah Hudson, Dreamkeeper

[Mr. Hudson* had suffered a stroke and had great difficulty expressing himself but was fully alert and aware of the conversation. Mrs. Hudson provided most of the comments with Mr. Hudson's assent. "SH" is used for Mr. Hudson. "MH" is used to indicate Mrs. Hudson.]

Marvin Lare **[ML]**: I'm in the home of Mr. and Mrs. Samuel Hudson in Georgetown, South Carolina, today. Why don't you say a word or two, Mr. Hudson and Mrs. Hudson, and I'll make sure I'm picking up your voices on the machine.

Sam Hudson **[SH]**: Okay.

Mrs. Hudson **[MH]**: We're delighted to have you here today. We hope that this project will mean something to the state and to the world, and . . . we'll have it recorded for posterity. So many of our young people do not understand, or do not know about our struggle, even though we tell them. They cannot understand that we would have allowed such a thing to happen, as to not drink at a water fountain when you were thirsty, or not have a sandwich at a counter when you were hungry, or go to the back of the bus. I looked at the story the other day of Rosa Parks's life and it was interesting—I had never known this—to note that you came to the front to pay your fare, then you got off and went to the back! That blew my mind. And I suppose if I had been like her, I suppose I would have been too tired to move, too, that day. It shows you that we have made progress, but there is still so much to be done yet. We're still in the process of overcoming.

ML: That's quite true. Can you say a word or two, Mr. Hudson, also? Then I'll check to make sure we're picking you up.

---

*Samuel Hudson (1921–2006) was interviewed in the Hudsons' home in Georgetown, South Carolina, November 8, 2005.

SH: I know it's picking up some of it.

ML: We'll just check that. Okay.

Mr. Hudson, don't be embarrassed *[he is trying to speak].* We'll just take whatever time we need to for you to get it out, so don't be embarrassed or hesitant in the least.

MH: I think he may need some prodding, so question him to get him to . . .

ML: Let me ask you, Mr. Hudson, where and when were you born?

SH: I was born in 1921, in this county.

MH: What was the name of the community?

SH: Kent community.

MH: So now, you were born in 1921, how old are you now?

ML: About eighty-four?

SH: Eighty-four years old.

ML: Lewis Burke at the Law School at the University of South Carolina referred me to you. I wonder if you know why he would have suggested you as being one of the important civil rights leaders in Georgetown.

SH: Let's see. Maybe I could tie it all together some. Burke was a VISTA worker [Volunteers to in Service to America, sometimes referred to as the domestic Peace Corp].

MH: He's one of the VISTA workers you brought to South Carolina? Was he ever in Georgetown?

SH: He was in Georgetown. And there's two others.

MH: Brenda and Hank are here now. Brenda and Hank Stroop are here now.

SH: That's right.

ML: Were you with the Office of Economic Opportunity ["War on Poverty"] here in Georgetown?

SH: Yes. Burke was a VISTA. He was a student . . . he sort of shifted— *[inaudible].*

MH: What did VISTA workers do when they came here? Did the community welcome them?

SH: No.

MH: The community said, they're changing our way of living?

ML: Was that in the middle or late '60s?

MH: Well, no, it must have been early '70s, because you took over in '69. So that would have to be in the '70s, perhaps, that VISTA workers came to this county. The EOC [Economic Opportunity Commission] was composed of three counties: Georgetown, Horry, and, finally, Williamsburg, wasn't it?

SH: Yes.

MH: Three counties comprised that, and he was the director for about, I think, twelve to fourteen years.

ML: Let me go back to Hank Stroop for a moment. Is he the Department of Social Services director?

MH: Yes. When I looked at your letter, I said, "Well, he knows Hank!"

SH: Yes.

ML: I retired from the Department of Social Services in 2003, and I was in the Planning and Research office, but I knew Hank.

MH: Hank has retired though now, hasn't he?

SH: I don't know whether Hank retired or not.

ML: How did you get from your degree in electronics to the Office of Economic Opportunity, the War on Poverty programs?

SH: It's not such a long story. Burke . . .

MH: You want me to help you remember your story there about that?

He graduated in what they call Mechanical Industries Applied Electricity, and he was chosen by the Marshall Plan to go to Liberia, West Africa, to open a school in radio and electricity. We went and stayed for a year there, and his brother died, so we came back home. His brother had this business on the corner, a garage and filling station. He was the only brother left so he came back to Georgetown after a stint in the Marines, and after coming back to Tuskegee, he came back here. So he did a little bit of everything after that. He did real estate. He dabbled in housing construction with Sam Bonds and Nathan Brown. They developed the Virginia Heights housing project out here in town where David Drayton lives.

[An interview with David Drayton will be found in volume 2.]

MH: David Drayton's people owned that property. He became assistant director of the CAP agency [Community Action Program, another iteration of the Office of Economic Opportunity and War on Poverty] and William Capp was the director.

ML: How do you spell that?

MH: Capp. C-A-P-P. He was executive director, and William evidently retired after he'd been there about two years, and Sam became the director. And he was there from '69 until '81, as director. And, of course, he traveled all over the country representing the agency. He was involved with all of the local offices in the state. He moved that agency from—I think it's in there [the Dreamkeepers Program]. From how many thousand dollars to so many millions of dollars. He did all kinds of things.

ML: Were you all the ones that started Head Start in the county?

SH: Yes.

MH: OEO started Head Start for the children. They did repairs of homes of low-income families. All of those kinds of things. They did that. He did that until '81, I believe it was. That agency closed down. They had a process where, I think they said, at the end of the fiscal year, all the officers would resign, before the new officers were reelected, and at the end of '81, [he] was not reelected. Someone else was elected to take that position.

So he's had a very varied life. He's done real estate, he's done insurance, he's helped to plan housing developments, he's helped with his church develop an apartment complex. He has worked with so many young men here in the streets, helping them get started, trying to show them the way to go. Do all those kinds of things.

"Dreamkeeper," portrait of Samuel Hudson at the Dreamkeeper Museum, Georgetown, South Carolina.

He had his first stroke in '76, and he bounced back like everything, and in the last two or three years, I think that old stroke has come back to haunt him, and he ended up with a heart pacemaker.

When you go to Mr. Drayton's, you will see all of those pictures of those winners [Dreamkeepers], previous winners. About seventeen or eighteen of them are already dead.

He received a Dreamkeepers Award—when was it?

ML: This program is 2001.

MH: Yes, that's the year he received it.

ML: Okay. Where were you from, Mrs. Hudson?

MH: I'm from the upper part of the state, Union County, Jonesville. We met at Tuskegee. We were "state-ents," and we got married there. This December, God willing, we will have been married sixty-two years. We have four children, two boys and two girls, and the older son —the young man there on the left *[referring to a family picture]*—passed in January. He'd been suffering from lung cancer for about three years. So he passed. Our younger son was a deputy attorney general, deputy attorney general with Medlock.

ML: Travis Medlock?

MH: Yes. Where is Travis? Is he still in Columbia?

Mrs. Samuel Hudson with her husband following his stroke, November 8, 2005.

ML: Yes. I see him once in a while . . .

MH: Our son was working with I. S. Leevy Johnson, and they said he was such a good lawyer that Medlock wanted him, so Medlock took him. And now he's with SCANA [utility corporation]. He works with SCANA. James. That's our second son. We had two.

The eldest was an electrical engineer. And his son is an electrical engineer. These are the four Samuels *[referring to a family photo.]*. Those are the four Samuels.

ML: That's a lovely picture. So four generations of Samuel Hudsons!

SH: Yes.

ML: How did you get to Tuskegee?

SH: Well, let's see. I blame that on my mother.

MH: His mother sent him away from Georgetown. I think he was courting too hard here at Georgetown, so she sent him to Tuskegee to get him away from girls, not knowing that there were girls at Tuskegee! *[She laughs.]* And so we met as 'state-ents,' people from the same state, and so . . . We met in '41 and in '43 we were married. He went to the service in '44 and stayed until '46, Marine Corps. Went to the Pacific,

Okinawa, and Saipan, and those kinds of places. Then he came back to Tuskegee and taught from '46 to '51. Then we went to Liberia, stayed there a year, and then came back here, and we've been here now for about fifty-two or fifty-three years.

ML: Yes. In terms of the civil rights struggle, what were some of the major events here in Georgetown? How did you bring about change?

SH: Georgetown was a typical southern community. We . . .

MH: You will note from that article that he traveled extensively in Georgetown, Horry, Williamsburg Counties, registering people to vote and to do those things. He served with the Progressive Democrats, he attended . . . What meeting was that you attended on the national level when the Mississippi delegation walked out? Was it Mississippi delegation?

[According to Wikipedia, the Mississippi Freedom Democratic Party was an American political party created in Mississippi in 1964, during the civil rights movement. It was organized by black and white Mississippians, with assistance from the Student Nonviolent Coordinating Committee.]

MH: That was the same year that they saw Bill Clinton, Bill Clinton spoke? And your board chairman, Catherine Lewis, said he's going to be a president one day? Catherine Lewis was librarian.

SH: Yes. *[Mr. Hudson assents to this.]*

MH: So they've done quite a bit to get rights and positions, leadership, that had not been afforded to them before. They worked with the highway patrol to be sure [black] highway patrolmen were hired. All those kinds of things. Definitely got a lot of people registered to vote.

ML: Did you run into much opposition in voter registration?

SH: In voter registration, opposition was . . . *[He is unable to express himself.]*

MH: You had to pay a poll tax? *[Mrs. Hudson seeks to prompt him.]* They didn't have to read and write, did they? Interpret anything during that time, did they?

I don't think we had it as bad here with registration as they did in some places, where they'd make you take these tests over and over, and flunk you. Now just before we came here, there was a hanging in Georgetown. Tom Rubillo, one of our local lawyers, has written a book about it. I was thinking maybe he was one person you should talk to too.

[See Thomas J. Rubillo, Trial and Error: The Case of John Brownfield and Race Relations in Georgetown, South Carolina *(Charleston, S.C.: History Press, 2005).]*

ML: I'd be glad to. Tom Rubillo?

MH: He's a lawyer. White lawyer here in town. Let me see if I can find my book and give you the telephone number.

ML: Good. So I guess it was about like night and day to come from Liberia back to Georgetown and find you had to start all over in terms of voters' rights and everything else.

MH: Yes, because in Africa you knew . . . It was a feeling of freedom that you didn't have in this country, and especially in the area where we were. Everybody knew it. But you come back here . . . I know when we were getting ready to go to Africa, I don't know whether this happened in Florence or where, but we were booked—the Phelps-Stokes Fund out of New York had booked us transportation to New York on the train. We thought we were going to be in a coach with overnight facilities. When we got there we found out that we weren't. Blacks didn't have those kinds of facilities, you know. And as a teacher I have a—I keep it—a law passed by our state in '56 that said if I were a member of the NAACP, I would be fined and all of that, you know. I said, "Golly gee . . ."

ML: That's something.

I see *[from the Dreamkeepers program]* your involvement with the radio station. Do you know Bill Saunders with WPAL in Charleston?

SH: Yes. I know Bill very, very well *[alert, immediate response]*.

ML: Bill and I were the ones that got the idea of this anthology started.

MH: Yes, I saw that!

[This refers to the article from the State *that Lare had provided them. Written by Claudia Smith Brinson, it appeared on August 16, 2005.]*

ML: I thought that you probably would know him.

MH: All righty. Sam Bonds and Mr. Drayton have a world of information over there about the blacks and all the people who've been so vocal in the struggle. There's a girl here who runs the funeral home, Barbara Hughwell, Wilds' Funeral Home on Merriman Road. I just talked to her a little while ago today and I started to mention you to her. . . . I know she has a funeral tomorrow. But now she is responsible for the center, basically one of the main workers in getting that center that Mr. Drayton now runs, the Committee for African-American History Observances, so perhaps she would have a lot to say.

ML: Okay. So it's the Committee for African-American Observances?

MH: History Observances. The CAAHO. Committee for African-American History Observances. CAAHO. And Mr. Drayton is now running that. He's the person in charge of that office.

ML: What year was it you came back to operate the family business there?

MH: In 1952. We've been here since then.

ML: What was it like to be in Georgetown and be a black citizen, if you could call yourself a citizen?

SH: Yes *[chuckles]*.

MH: It's a typical Southern experience. The different water fountains, colored waiting rooms, white waiting rooms. You'd go to the doctor, you'd have to sit in a little nook, while they'd have the fancy waiting rooms. When you went to buy clothes, especially hats or things that came in contact with the body, they would want you to put a rag over your head, or something like that, you know.

When you think about it, you wonder how civilized people could have been so insensitive to other people. And these were the same people who went to church on Sundays and sang and prayed and read God's word.

ML: Were there marches and demonstrations or boycotts here? What was the main methodology to get some change? Or was it more just as a result of national policy?

MH: It was more national policies, plus—I know with the school boards, the Justice Department, I think the NAACP brought the Justice Department in to look at the situation here. There were certain things that they'd have to do, as far as the Justice Department was concerned. When was integration fully . . . ? Integration down here didn't take place until around —let's see—Pat graduated in '73 from Winyah—and when he went there, must be about '69. It was about '68 or '69, I believe, before integration started taking place.

ML: Your career has been in teaching, Mrs. Hudson? What ages did you teach?

MH: High school, basically. However, I was certified on about four levels, home ec, biology, general science, and elementary education. I had a master's degree when I came here.

Sometimes when we look back at integration, this is what we thought would make life better for blacks, but sometimes we wonder whether we lost more than we gained in the process, as it related to discipline of our children and the teaching of our children. Because black teachers were determined that a black child would learn, and I know that there are good white teachers, but there were teachers who didn't care whether the child learned or not—just don't cause me any troubles. My sister was telling me the other day, she said she had a little student, she was trying to get him do to something, he said, "Miss Good, if you don't cause me no problem, I won't cause you no problem. So leave me alone and let me do what I want to do." I don't know.

We've come a long ways but there's still so much to do. Our jails are still full. Police brutality. I don't know whether it's brutality or whether it's the person being accosted. I looked today at them trying to arrest somebody today, and it looked like four or five policemen were trying to arrest one man. I heard them say he was drunk, but . . . I don't know where we're going to end up in this world. It seems that everything the Lord is showing us, that time is winding up and we have to get ready.

ML: Did you teach here in Georgetown when you came back?

MH: Yes, I taught here. I taught here at Howard for a while, then we opened a new school out in the county, in Georgetown County, for blacks, a segregated school. Kelly Squires was the principal, and I taught there about twenty-four years. Then when integration, so-called integration, came, they sent me up to Pleasant Hill, a basic white community, to integrate the schools up there. I stayed up there for four years, then I came back to Caupe, and I ended up retiring from Georgetown High School in 1986. They'd gotten rid of Howard and finally gotten rid of Winyah. Those two schools had merged as Georgetown High School. I retired from Georgetown High School in 1986.

ML: Were those two schools one black, one white that were merged together then?

MH: Yes. Howard and Winyah.

ML: Bill Saunders has given me a copy of this law that you shared with me about . . . *[Under the law, NAACP members could not be teachers or state employees].*

MH: Oh, he has?

ML: Yes. But that's one of the first things when we were talking about this project. In order to keep your job, you had to keep a pretty low profile as far as NAACP was concerned?

MH: Yes, and you had to lie. I was thinking as I pulled that out today, I thought about the Christians of "The Way," how they used to be persecuted because of their beliefs. Blacks were the same, being persecuted the same way if they were members of the NAACP. Someone was saying at some meeting where we were that they would slip and pay their membership, and they'd be secretively given their cards at night, or something like that. When you think about it, you wonder. What did people think? They were mistreated, and these were the same people who were taking care of their children, cooking their food, doing all those things.

ML: Did you have a chapter of NAACP here in Georgetown, or was it in the county?

MH: Yes, we had a chapter here in Georgetown. We had a president here who was very good working with us, Herbert Williams. He was one of those [Dreamkeeper] winners there. He was very good with the NAACP, and we've had several other presidents since then. Morris Johnson is now the president of the branch. He's not too well, and I don't think he's doing too much now, because most of the strength of that organization has been in the older ones of us and we're getting so we can't carry it on, and the new ones—the younger people, a lot of them—don't seem to feel that there is a need, because it's so easy to do things now, but we know that it has not always been this way.

ML: That's right. Was your business here pretty much in the black community, or did you depend upon the white community, too, for your business?

SH: Let's see —I was in the middle . . .

MH: Basically, though, it was blacks. You would have white customers.

ML: And white suppliers, white supply companies you had to deal with?

MH: The supply companies would be white, all the supply companies were white.

SH: The workers were black of course.

MH: He was appointed to serve as a county commissioner, and for how many years you were chairman of the library board? His name is on about three libraries in the town. He was a library board member, and he attended the White House conference on the library. What was it? White House Library Conference? I've forgotten now how it was worded. They went to Washington several times to that.

But you know, in spite of the segregation, people who wanted to succeed were able to do so. There was a drive. I often think about my father, who would not allow us to—we lived on a farm—but he would not allow us to work with the white man. Go in their homes nor do work for them. And we were always supplied with reading materials, however. Both my mother and father were teachers in their early days, and they saw that we aspired to education.

ML: That was in Union County?

MH: Union County.

ML: I'll be seeing Bill Saunders in a week or so, and I'll give him your regards.

SH: Please do. *[He is quite adamant about this.]*

MH: He still has his radio station?

ML: He was chairman of the state Public Service Commission, but then he left that—or they left him I guess you would say—along in 2004. He's working in Charleston with the organization that he established, COBRA, Committee for Better Racial Assurance.

You may have also known Willis Crosby's up in Greenville, with SHARE, the Community Action Agency there. Did you know him?

SH: Yes. I know him. I know COBRA and . . . we put together the . . .

ML: We'll ask him about that, something that he worked on with Bill.

SH: Yes.

MH: Did you know Dr. [De]Quincey Newman? I. Quincey?

ML: Oh yes. Not long ago I interviewed his wife and daughter, Ann Newman and Emily. . . .

Mr. Hudson, if you don't mind, I'll take a picture or two of you and your wife, and maybe some of the pictures of your family here.

MH: Okay.

SH: Okay.

ML: And this Dreamkeepers Award, I'd like to get a copy of that, or make a copy.

MH: You can have that one. You may take it. I think I have another one, so you can have that one.

ML: Okay, that's wonderful. *[There is a lengthy pause.]*

NOW this copy—Bill gave me a copy of the original document [the legislation prohibiting teachers and state employees from belonging to the NAACP] but this is . . . You've been carrying this around all these years, haven't you?

MH: Yes. That's my little keepsake.

ML: Yes, I know. I bet that got passed out around the schools sort of surreptitiously?

MH: That's right.

ML: In fact, we were talking about Newman. Ann Newman told me about how teachers would slip her a little bit of cash, you now, very behind the scenes.

MH: That's right. Behind the scenes.

ML: Mr. Hudson, do you mind if I take a picture of you?

SH: Well, no.

ML: Mrs. Hudson, would you mind sitting there beside your husband? I got a picture of him and I'll get a picture of the two of you.

MH: Let's stand here now.

ML: A handsome couple all these . . . How many years?

MH: Sixty-two in December. If we live to December the twenty-second. . . .

MH: Now where are you from?

ML: I was born and raised in Ohio.

MH: What part?

ML: Near Canton, Akron. Northeast Ohio.

MH: My daughter worked in Summit County, as a social worker.

ML: That's only twenty miles or so from where I grew up.

MH: She went to Mount Union [College].

ML: You're kidding me! I went to Mount Union too.

MH: Oh! *[She laughs.]* Isn't that something!

ML: Mount Union was eight miles from where I grew up, so I didn't get to go off to school. Well, small world.

SH: Right.

MH: She graduated there in '70.

ML: And her name again?

MH: Whyllys. W–H–Y–L–L–Y–S. Whyllys Byrd. And she's a substance abuse counselor for the army at Fort Hood.

ML: Give her my regards. I got a call just last night, I got a phone call from Mount Union College asking me for my annual fund contribution *[laughs]*. . . .

MH: Have you met Lucille Whipple?

ML: Yes. She was at a meeting we had in Orangeburg, and I need to get back together with her. They have a whole lot of her information at Avery [Research Center for African American History and Culture at the College of Charleston] but I want to get her story in her own words as well, and then sift that down, because that'd make a whole book in itself.

MH: Yes, yes. Her son-in-law is my pastor here in town.

ML: Oh, really?

MH: It's a small world. Networking is powerful, isn't it?

ML: Yes, it is. That's right. People who care and are committed, you find a lot of the same folks. Thank you so much for giving me some time and your stories and materials.

MH: Sure. I hope we've been a little bit of a help.

ML: Oh you have. You really have.

MH: Now who's going to do all the transcribing?

ML: The South Caroliniana Library is going to do some of it, and then I'm just talking with a woman [Lynn Moore] to have her do some of it.

MH: Have you been able to get good grants?

ML: It's slow and tight. I've gotten some money from the [South Carolina] Humanities Council, some from BellSouth, and I've just put in an application to the Bar Foundation, but I . . . didn't know. They were sort of skeptical whether this fit their priorities or not, but I hope so.

[The South Carolina Bar Foundation provided two very generous grants that were critical to the completion of this anthology.]

ML: Yes? It's coming along. It's a labor of love, because I'm not getting paid much of anything for my time. I'm starting to get a little bit of money for my gasoline, but that's all I've gotten out of it so far—and an awful lot of satisfaction!

MH: I bet.

ML: I tell people it reminds me of the days when I was pastor of a church, and I'd go and visit in the homes of people and sit down and so on, so it reminds me very much of pastoral visitation, you know?

MH: Yes, that's true.

ML: I get to know so many people and get to know their stories.

Samuel M. Bonds, Bitter Experience

Marvin Lare [ML]:* I'm in Georgetown, South Carolina on November the 8th, 2005, and I'm talking with Mr. Sam Bonds. How are you today?

Sam Bonds [SB]: Wonderful.

ML: Good. Mr. Bonds, in these interviews about civil rights in South Carolina, I like to let people just tell their own story in their own words. I like to let people begin where wherever they want to and cover as much as they want to. The focus is civil rights, racial justice, ranging over a period of time from about 1930 up to 1980. A lot of people go back before that time and have comments after [that period], but I've tried to identify people who have taken some real leadership and initiative in that field during that period of time primarily. Tell us a little bit about you and your life and experience.

[Sharen Mapp comes home.]

ML: We can interrupt any time we need to. That's just fine.

SB: That's my daughter.

ML: Hi. How are you? I'm Marvin Lare.

Sharen Mapp [SM]: Sharen Mapp.

ML: Nice to meet you.

SM: Nice to meet you too.

ML: Ms. Mapp, you know that I'm interviewing your father concerning civil rights in South Carolina? I'm working on an anthology of civil rights in South Carolina, and that's not writing a history—that's collecting original stories, original experiences and perspectives. We'll publish it in a book, but also save all the materials and information in the archives for future generations to have.

---

*This interview was conducted at the Bonds home in Georgetown, South Carolina, with Sharen Mapp and Harolyn Siau also involved, on November 8, 2005.

Sam Bonds, his daughter Sharen Mapp, and Harolyn Siau at their home in Georgetown, South Carolina.

SM: Okay. And where's this archive?

ML: Most of it will be at the University of South Carolina, in the South Caroliniana Library. I'm also working there with the African American Studies Program and Cleveland Sellers, and other people there. Then, in the Charleston area, it'll be archived at the Avery Institute, which is associated with College of Charleston. In the upstate, some of it will be archived [at Furman University] in Greenville. They'll be linked together so that people who want to do future research and studies can have access to it just about anywhere.

SM: Oh great! That's good. And you said you're writing a book?

ML: Yes. And when I say "write," I should really say "editing" a book, because your father and others like him are the ones who're "writing" it, in the sense of telling their stories. I'm focusing first of all, of course, on the people who are still living, because there are a good many who have passed on, so I'm trying to reach all the folks across the state who played a significant role in those days. In a few months I'll begin working more in the libraries and archives to find posthumous accounts, from folks who've passed away.

SM: That should be interesting. Do you mind if I sit in?

ML: Not at all. I'll be glad to have you.

SM: Okay.

ML: And if you would like to add comments or anything, I'll be glad to have it, too. Does that give you enough of a framework?

SB: Yes.

ML: [Mr. Bonds], what would you say was your first awareness of racial justice issues and concerns?

SB: Back in the '30s. I had some bitter experiences back in the '30s. The first bitter experience that I had, a group of white men attacked my father one Saturday night and beat him up. That was the first bitter experience that I had. I guess I was about eight or ten years old, but I've never forgotten it. As the years rolled on, in my teenage, I'd become active in the civil rights movement. One of the experiences was a black man was electrocuted. His name was George Thomas. That happened in the latter part of the '30s. The next experience I had was another electrocution, a black man. He was electrocuted. I'll die and go to my grave saying that he never committed the crime. He died, I feel, covering up for the act and crime that a white man committed. But he died for it. He was electrocuted. His name was Arthur Waites. His alias was "Fat Eye."

I was always active in the civil rights movement. As a teenager, there was a man by the name of Glenny Pouchè, who was one of the pioneers, a fearless individual. He was a poor man but he was a brave man, and he wasn't afraid to speak out about the injustices of the times that he lived in. He came to Georgetown. His home was in Georgetown, but he ran away and came back. He came back in the middle '40s, and he organized and was active in voters' registration, because he knew that's where the power was. If we could change the system, change the laws of voting, we would be recognized, and we were fortunate in having the laws changed, carrying South Carolina to court.

Judge Waites Waring presided over the case, and [Waring] was treated so rudely by the citizens of South Carolina, whites, until he was ostracized because of the fact that he made a decision beneficial to the blacks. He was interested in justice for all, but I'll always believe that that decision—he never was a popular man after that decision, and he died for making that decision—I'll always believe that that decision shortened his years.

I had quite a bitter, bitter experience when I was in my twenties. I operated a little business, a poolroom, and one night the fellows broke in the poolroom, and it was on the other side of town, and I lived on this side of town. My business was on the west side of town, and I wasn't married, but I had a grave responsibility. I raised my sister's children. I raised three boys and one girl. So I would be occupied all the time and busy, because I was largely the breadwinner of the family. All of my sisters and brothers left town, but I stayed to care for my sister and mother, and the family.

And doing that, running the business, someone broke into the business on the weekend. I would normally open on Saturday, so that Saturday morning, gathering up the stuff for the business, I was told that my business was broken into, and I went across there to see—I'm trying to think what year that was. It was in the '40s. Anyway, I went to the business to investigate. All of the doors were open, and I reported it to the sheriff. The sheriff came and he asked me a few questions, to try to frighten me, because I never had any fear of white people. Never was, and that was because of my father. I saw him ridiculed by white people, and I made up in my mind that my life wouldn't reflect that, and I wouldn't take what my father took. I'd die before I'd take it.

What brought me to that point was, I was about eight or nine years old. I would follow my father on the truck. He would carry me around with him, and I saw a white woman stand over my father and talked to him like she would a dog. That thing hurt me to my heart and I've never forgotten it. For many, many years I hated white people. That turned me against white people. I hated the ground they walk on. It made me bitter. But as I grew older, I had a Christian mother, and she taught me to love, and to love others and care for others, and what would happen if you continued to hate. "You mustn't hate. You must love." She drilled that into me, and I grew out of it. But the hate never got out . . . the thoughts lingered with me.

In 1939, it was in the '30s, I went into plumbing business. I ordered a book from Sears Roebuck, and I learned my trade out of a book and set up a construction company, building and construction company. I learned it out of a book, and the practical side of it I learned from a black fellow who was a plumber. He later died, and I took over the business. At that time I was the only licensed black plumber in town, but I had a very good friend, a Jew, by the name of Abe Fogel. I could always go and talk to him and tell him about the problems black people were having.

He would always tell me, say, "Aw no, Sam, you need to forget about that. It isn't like that anymore."

And I would tell him, "Abe, you're white. You're rich. I'm black. I'm poor. You don't know what in the hell I'm talking about. In order for you to learn, you have to listen to me."

And he would listen. For multiple years him and I grew to be good friends. He was a merchant on Front Street, and not an agency in this town would lend me a dime. The banks would laugh at me, the loan officer would laugh at me. They wouldn't give me no consideration whatsoever. It's useless in going to a bank. They would just about run you out there. They wouldn't talk to you. I'll never forget, there was a banker by the name of Tab Porter. He ran First Citizens. I think he was the president of First Citizens. I went down there to him multiple times to get a loan.

These were the answers he would give me: "I will take your application." "We have too many applications. We didn't get to your application." "We have it under considerations until the board meets again."

One day I met an old white contractor by the name of Bill Thompson. He was the leading contractor in town, white. And I told him, I said, "Captain Bill."

Well, anyway, I was having problems all over, all because of my color. I went in the hospital and I stayed for years, in and out of the hospital. They had a program, the Rehabilitation Association, that set black people up in business and gave them aid. I went to the man and asked him for some help. The man laughed at me. His name was Campbell, never forgotten that name. And he laughed at me. He turned me down.

[Harolyn Siau comes in. She excuses herself to the adjoining room and the interview continues.]

SB: . . . He turned me down. I told him I wanted to open a business. He came by the house, but he laughed at me, and went away. I never heard any more.

But that didn't stop me from pushing on. I got me a little boy, and I started selling cosmetic products, selling junk iron, anything to make a dollar, I'd do it. And I would work. I couldn't get tired. At one time I worked for three days and nights without stopping, to complete a job, and when I completed the job and drew my money . . . Upon completing the job a policeman—someone told the policeman I was a plumber, that there was a black man working up there, plumbing a building and black plumbers were scarce, and they all but ran me out of Myrtle Beach.

I started my business over there, I would receive calls and I'd go to do the job, and they would say to me, when I finished the job, "Tell your company to send me the bill."

I would tell them, "The business belongs to me," and they wouldn't ever call me again. I would never receive another call from them. That happened multiple times. I would go to white people's house to do their work, and they would think that I'm working for somebody else and they wouldn't hire me. I could do the work, but they wouldn't hire me, all because I was black.

This thing of racism runs deep in America. The problems and the hell that Bush is catching now is a hangover from slavery. A lot of the hell that Bush is catching over there in [Iraq] is the sins that America has committed to its citizens. And it's still going on. America needs to clean up their house and stop going around trying to clean up the world. There's a lot of injustices going on in America. I see it every day. I see it *every day!* There's not a day hardly pass that I don't see some type and kind of injustices. But the thing is, I have learned to live with it, to use it to my advantage. But I could write a book on some of the things that I went through. I don't even tell my children.

But I teach all of my children this: "Get and be educated." And I always taught them this: "The best people in the world grow up in my house. The best people in the world. They ain't nobody else in the world better than you." That's right. I teach them so that when they go out they will have the guts to stand, because I have already learned what's awaiting them outside. And a lot of times, black people don't understand. They live so far away from the problems, until they don't understand. And when they see you pursuing avenues that they sometimes fear to tread, they ridicule you, criticize you, because they don't understand. Because they live under a cloud of, a cloud—I had the word to bring out, but I lost it. They live under a cloud of prejudice, and it's so dark till they cannot see the light. And a lot of times, businesses I have opened and ran and did well in it, and the white man couldn't get to me, so they put the black man on me. Do you see what I'm talking about? So you had to fight two. You had to fight the black community and the white community, and you had to be strong, and if you wasn't strong, they would crush you.

I have a business right now, the biggest recreation building in the county, the largest the black community owns, and they closed it. And [the community] need it. They don't have no place to go, but they closed my place. But they don't understand and see the injustices they are doing to themselves, because they can't hurt me. You see? I'm [only easing up], I don't need the business. But they need it. You follow me, what I'm talking about?

ML: Yes. What kind of grounds did they close it on?

SB: Closed it on the grounds of the zoning. And to show you how prejudiced they are, in the same block, right across the street where my business is, they grant a license to another person to open up a business. Right across the street. I'm on this side and they're on that side *[motioning with his hands]*. Whenever you see a black man made it to any height of success, you can call him a giant. Because he had two armies to fight: the black army and the white army. That's right.

ML: Were you ever in the military?

SB: No, I had polio. They wouldn't accept me in the military, and I went to Southern Craft—that's the biggest industry in Georgetown at that time—and they told me they wouldn't hire me because of my condition. I made up in my mind that, damn it, you wouldn't give me a job, and all you had to do is ride a bicycle and carry the mail to the offices. They didn't have automobiles to pick up the mail then. They had bicycles to pick up the mail, and then [after] the bicycles they bought a car to pick up the mail. But I wanted to ride the bicycle to pick up the mail, but they wouldn't give me a job, said I would be a liability to the company. So that thing stayed in my mind for more than twenty years. I never forgot that thought, and I never forgot that feeling that I had when I walked out of that office.

Twenty-five or thirty years later I was elected to city council, and when I was elected to city council, I said, "This is my chance to uncover the injustices International Paper did to me." And I fought them tooth and nails about the injustices and the prejudice and the advantages that they took of poor people, in paying taxes. They're still not paying the taxes that they should pay, but I'm not on city council now. I was an advocate for justice when I was on council all of those years. I lost a lot of business. I was ridiculed a lot, not only by white people but by black people. Sometimes I feel that the ridicule from the blacks was more bitter than the ridicule from the whites.

ML: Yes.

SB: I don't want to talk you all night now, because I could just go on.

ML: That's all right. You mentioned about, was it Glanny? Glenny? Pouchè.

SB: He was a giant for civil rights.

ML: He worked on voter registration and so forth in the '40s?

SB: That's right. In fact, him and I and Sammy Hudson worked all over the state organizing black people to vote.

[See the previous interview with Mr. and Mrs. Samuel Hudson in this volume.]

SB: That's right. We went day and night, talking to them and teaching them how to vote and the advantages of voting. We had to meet—we had a white fellow—I forgot—I had his name just now *[snaps his fingers repeatedly]*.

ML: It'll come back to you.

SB: He was a civil rights man and he was afraid to stay in the hotel, because they knew his purpose, fighting for justice. We'd go all—there was a man, he was a Georgetonian—he was a doctor, he went to Meharry Medical School and he came back to Georgetown. He taught in Georgetown for two or three years, and then he went on to Florence and opened up in Florence. He was a giant for equal rights and justice. There was another man, he was a preacher, Herbert Williams. He recently died, about five or ten years ago. He was a man always attaining for equal rights and equal justice.

ML: Did you all work mostly with and through the NAACP or other groups, local or . . .

SB: We had a chapter, the NAACP chapter, and we would go all over the South. I was offered a job one time, that's when I found out that you didn't have to be trained to work for the FBI. They wanted to give me a job. My job was to penetrate the crowd and take notes, and report back to the FBI. I said, "No! I don't want that job!" *[He laughs.]*

My son was about six. He hadn't started in school yet, and the civil rights and racism was raging then. I was in it and I would go all over the state. Many nights I would not get any sleep, attending meetings and following up the movement. But the young people today, they don't know the price we paid for the things that they enjoy today. Like going— I went to the airport one time. I was taking a flight for Christmas, and I carried my nephews with me, and I purposely went in the airport on the white side, so that they could get the feeling of racism and prejudiceness [*sic*]. I don't know if they remember, but when I went in there, they told me that, "You can't come on this side, you going have to go on the other side."

And I walked right on in the restaurant, where all the white people were, and the white woman walk up to me and told me that "you can't eat in here. You have to go downstairs and eat."

And another experience I had—my kids. I was divorced. My wife and I wasn't together, but I would always keep up with my kids and keep in touch with them, so I would pick them up and ride them out on Sundays. On the weekends I would always pick them up. And my boy brought tears to my eyes one Sunday. I'll never forget this. We were riding down the Strand and my son said, "Daddy, I want to go over there to play." I got so full I couldn't answer him. And I never did answer him, and I kept on down the Strand and went into the colored beach.

ML: Atlantic Beach?

SB: Yes. But that experience . . . and that hurt, I never forgot. And the week that the Supreme Court issued the decision to outlaw segregation, that Sunday I crashed the Mammy's Kitchen on Myrtle Beach. I had two or three fellows with me, they were so scared *[laughs]*, but I didn't care *[laughs]*. I walked right on in and they kept telling me, "Patty, you can't go . . . " *[He laughs.]* They ah . . . "Patty, you can't go . . ." And we went on in there and sat down. Them other two fellows, they were so nervous they couldn't eat. But I ate, and laughed at them. . . .

ML: But they served you?

SB: But they served me. Because the court said they must serve me. That's right.

Man, they would call you all kinds of names but I had—the black teachers before segregation ended, they had a way of calling you "nigger" so our teachers in our schools [would] say, "All of the citizens of Niagara Falls are 'niggers.' Don't be ashamed when they call you a nigger, because they're ignorant. They don't know the basic English language and the words as they're described."

They went on to explain to us the word and where the word came from, but the southern white man was ignorant and they used the word "nigger" to ridicule you, but we were taught to ignore the word. And they would . . . they would . . . a few black folks would get mad and want to fight, but the most of them just ignored it. But by the time I got twenty-one, if one called me a nigger I'd knock them in the nose. I would fight, because of the past bitterness that I absorbed through the years. You hurt a child and that child would, it'll make that child bitter and it will scar his mind, and it never would leave him for many, many years. Time will have to weigh it down. Yes. This country here . . .

ML: You mentioned about your father being so mistreated and being attacked and about this white woman talking so badly to him, but when you started to talk about . . .

SB: Her name was—I remember the woman's name vividly, and I'm looking at her right now. I can visualize her right now. Her name was Birdie Condon, a wealthy white woman. The house still stands. Every time I pass the house I see that. That thought runs through my mind.

ML: You mentioned about him being attacked besides with words, but . . .

SB: My father, he was attacked and beat up by some white men one Saturday night.

ML: Did they have— What was their reason? Just to be mean or did they feel he was getting out of line or what?

SB: They would catch black people and just beat them.

ML: Yes, because that was the sport?

SB: That's right. That was a sport for them. And they'd get in a crowd and say, "How much a niggers you beat last night?" They would say things like that. That's right.

ML: And the men you said were electrocuted . . .

SB: Was George Thomas. His son lives right across the street. Paducah.

SM: Oh yes?

SB: [His] daddy was electrocuted.

SM: You're kidding!

SB: That's right.

ML: He was in prison? I mean, he was condemned to death and executed?

SB: He went through the system and condemned to death and was electrocuted. I remember that just as plain as it happened yesterday.

Another man—I just heard about this one—another man was on a plantation, that's about six miles out of town, and a man ran the plantation as the superintendent, and the superintendent, I was told, was going with a black woman out there, and he would go out there to see this black woman, and the man told him, "Don't you come back 'hoat [out] here no more." And they never knew what happened to the man. That's a natural phenomenon, for black men disappearing.

ML: The Hudsons told me today about a book that Tom Rubillo wrote telling about the lynching of a man, something about the barbershop and so forth? Do you know about that?

[See Thomas J. Rubillo, Trial and Error: The Case of John Brownfield and Race Relations in Georgetown, South Carolina *(Charleston, S.C.: History Press, 2005.]*

SB: Yes, yes. That happened before my time. The lynching of a black man. There were several lynchings before my time.

ML: In your work, besides voter registration, going around and teaching and helping people to learn to vote, did you have any demonstrations or marches locally to change things, or was it pretty much just individual action and that kind of thing?

SB: No. What we would do— If a store did something to a black person, the blacks would give them the silent treatment and don't trade there no more. Just wouldn't trade there anymore. That's right. And they would eventually go out of business.

ML: They had to treat you right if they were going to have your business.

SB: That's right.

ML: In the NAACP, who were some of the other leaders that you remember or that you worked with, or people that inspired you?

SB: Herbert Williams, Glenny Pouchè, Marcus Richardson, Dan Prelou, James Prelou, there was a minister, Reverend Jackson. Those are a few of the names that I can recall.

ML: I appreciate that.

SB: But there were many more than that. . . . John—I can't think of it—I know John like a book, but he had a [newspaper], a powerful paper.

ML: Oh yes, I know, and I know his widow. McCray.

SB: John McCray. That's it.

ML: *The Lighthouse and Informer,* at least, was one of his papers.

SB: That's right. And the white man didn't stop until he put that paper out of business and put John in the gang, in the chain gang. Yes, sir. And Hudson, Sammy Hudson, Nathan Brown, and I—he came to Georgetown, penniless, and Sammy Hudson, Nathan Brown, and I gave [McCray] the money.

We had a movement. If a black man was on the run—you heard about the Underground Railroad? There's a building in Georgetown now, still stands, and my parents told me about that house served as a station for the Underground Railroad when the blacks would be traveling north. The house still stands. It's on the corner of Meeting and Front Streets.

ML: Okay. Just a sidelight—you know, I told you I was born and raised in Ohio, and about three great-grandparents back, the Baldwins, had a house that had a big central chimney in it, all the way from the basement all the way up. Of course the chimney got smaller as it went up, but behind those panels is where they used to hide the runaway slaves. One day the slave masters came, because they had the right, if they could capture the slaves, they could take them back with them. Anyhow, my great-great-grandfather [Richard Baldwin] was sitting on the rail fence across the road with his rifle on his lap, and these folks came by and they told his father [Moses Baldwin], "If you'd tell that grey-eyed devil to put down that rifle, we'd see if you had any of our slaves around here."

SB: I started to tell you, the railroad still exists. You don't have it now, but about five or ten years ago a fellow was on the run, black fellow was on the run, and if a knock come on your door three times, three or four o'clock in the morning, we would answer the call. That individual would come in. You feed him, and give him what funds you have *[thumping the table]*, to go on to the next station. But they're a very secretive in who they tell. . . . *[Details omitted at request of Mr. Bonds.]*

ML: Do you have any other thoughts or reflections?

SB: Plenty more. But it'd take it till in the morning to tell you. That's right.

ML *[addressing Ms. Mapp]:* Do you have any thoughts to share or questions of your dad?

SM: I do remember . . .

Harolyn Siau [**HS**] *[from the adjoining room]:* I have something to add about the "nigger" story. My daddy is eighty-nine years old and he knows a lot. But anyway, just the one story that came to mind while Sam was talking, he was about fifteen—a man around here, a local man named Mr. Polk, had drove up in the yard. Daddy was waiting to be paid, so Mr. Polk drove up and said, "Walter, how you like my Model T?" Or "my Cadillac," whatever it was.

He said, "I like it fine, Mr. Polk."

"You niggers will never see the day that you own one of these, because we keep the money out of your hands."

So we had all grown up and gone to college, and we didn't move far from home, but all our cars was in Daddy's yard, and he said, "My Lord! Oh, I wish Mr. Polk could look at my yard!" *[She laughs.]* Because we all had cars. . . .

SB: Tell them about Pyatt.

HS: Oh yes. The land that the high school is on was owned by a rich woman named Miss Pyatt. A black man who used to live on our street by the name of Johnny Graham used to work for her. So he wanted to get a piece of land to build a house on. Because, you know, she liked him.

She said, "I'm so sorry, but I don't sell land to niggers."

So, one day I was riding him beside the school, he said, "Daughter, I sure wish Miss Pyatt was here to see these *niggers* on her land!" Because the high school, and the black folks own the land. He had lived long enough to see the worst times [turn into] this time. He hadn't forgotten that one, not one thing.

[Daddy's] grandfather was the last slave freed by the Siaus in this [county]. . . . I've thought about that thing, I wasn't but three or four generations from being a slave.

That's scary! My great-grandfather was the last one. And he was the son of old man Siau, who died here around the time my mama died, about twenty years ago. So the only thing strange about our family is we're the only black Siaus, which means we know where we came from. . . .

ML: How do you spell that?

HS: S-I-A-U.

ML: And your father's name is?

HS: Walter.

ML: Walter. Okay.

HS: Senior. He has a son too. . . .

My grandfather moved to Mullins and so the majority of them are there. They don't spell that name the same way because they probably couldn't read or write, so they spelled like it sounds, C-E-O. So my daddy said, "That's all right, Daughter, let them stay there and we are here. We got ours spelled right." *[She laughs.]*

ML: Let me go back, Mr. Bonds, to about the folks who'd hire you as a plumber and then—would they pay you for what you had done, even though they wouldn't contract with you the next time?

SB: They would pay me. I never would tell them that I owned the company until I got through working. Then they'd tell me, "You can tell your boss to send us a bill."

I say, "You can give me the check now because I own the company. You're talking to the boss."

They'd go in the office and write me the check, but that would be the last time I'd get a job. A few of them . . . but they have a network. I did it quite a few times, but they have a network and they'll find out, and when they find out I own the company, no more jobs.

SM: That still goes on today. My brother came down here. He owns a house on Pawley's Island, excellent plumber, learned from his father, worked with him all his life. Had to move back to Atlanta because all those jobs, all those houses being built on the beach, he can't find work up to his standard of living. They won't give him the contracts. He has to work for somebody else in order to get the contract.

SB: That's right. You know one thing? I don't know how I made it. Sometimes I laid down in bed—and I believe in God—if it wasn't for the grace of God and His guidance, I never would have made it. That's right. Because some of them white people—I never was afraid of them. I cussed them out when other blacks would run from them. I'd stand right up in their face and talk to them.

And they'd call me, they'd say, "That's a dangerous nigger."

That's what they said when they put me in jail, try to make me admit that I broke in my own place.

ML: So that's what happened about the pool hall? The sheriff arrested you!

SB: Yes, said I broke in my own place. That's right. And put me in jail! And the jail was high up, and I was to the window and I saw a black woman coming from the white folks' kitchen that day, and I hollered down and told her to go by and tell

Mama I was in jail. And my mama came around there, and the sheriff cursed us to my mother, "Tell her she better get her goddamn ass out the jail yard."

I was three story up and I heard when he told my mother that, and I hollered back downstairs, I said, "You [inaudible] motherfucker. If I could get my hands on you I'd beat your ass." That's what I told the sheriff.

And he took me downstairs, and there were three of them in the room, and told me, "Nigger, you may as well go on and admit that you stole that money."

And I told him, "You can't make me say a damn thing. I told you I didn't do it, I don't know nothing about it, and I'm still telling you that."

The sheriff grabbed his billy [club] out his case and started to me. And I started to him, with my fists up. And I told him, "I'll make you shoot every goddamn bullet out this gun if you hit me." I told him just like that.

The high sheriff told him, he said, "This is a crazy nigger here. We better carry him back." That's right . . .

ML: "Carry him back"—did they let you go or . . . ?

SB: Yes, they let me go. But the reason why they let me go: my sister was working for the clerk of court, and my mother and my sister went to the clerk of court and told him I was in jail, and they picked me up. The clerk of court called the sheriff and told the sheriff that he'd better turn me out and turn me out in a hurry.

The sheriff told him about a bond, and he told the sheriff, "I don't give a damn how much it took a bond out. You turn him out!"

I never heard any more about it. That's the kind of experience black people had. That's right.

ML [addressing Ms. Mapp]: Have you heard any stories you didn't know? Have you heard any of this from your father before?

SM: He didn't tell us these stories [reserved laughter].

ML: This is what I find so often, is that children in the same family . . . we keep things in. Now my kids don't know a lot of my experiences. But . . . so hopefully this anthology will be a way of passing it on, helping people know.

SM: He always protected us and shielded us. My only experience with having . . . when we'd go to the beach every Sunday evening, a white beach, and a black beach. That type of thing. I'd go to the doctor's office: the white side and the black side. But that's my only experience.

SB: But all of them had a good life. They never experienced the things that I had. And I wouldn't tell them all, because I didn't want them to grow up with all of that hate. I'd tell them and teach them how to be strong, so that they could be respected. I never would allow them to take anything from anybody, ask anybody for anything. I kept everything in abundance around them. They never had to ask anybody for anything. But I was a *workhorse*.

ML: Yes, I can tell that. If it wasn't for workhorses, pioneers like you, we'd still be dealing with a lot of that. We still have enough to deal with, but at least . . .

SB: I'll tell you another experience. One time . . . That was in *[long pause]* 1947. I'd just got out of high school, and the insurance man would come by the house to collect insurance, and my mama had insurance of, I think, for twenty-five or fifty cents. You remember that? I came in the house and when I walk in the house, I heard when he told my mama—hollered at my mama—about her insurance, and tell her, she was lying, she wasn't sick.

I flew at that man. I remember the words I told him. I remember vividly what I said to him. I said, "You get your goddamn ass out of this house and don't ever put your fucking foot back in this house again. My mama don't need no goddamn insurance. I'm her damn insurance. And get your ass out of the house."

And he never put foot back in there no more. That's right.

My sister and them tell me, "You run that man away. That man's scared to come back." *[He laughs.]*

ML: I guess so.

SB: To the house. That's right. I protected them. After I got up, I got grown, because there wasn't enough hours in the day for me to work. That's right. And that's why I can't work now. I get up every morning and try, but . . . *[There is a long pause.]*

ML: I'd better go now. But, if you think of other things to tell, you've got my phone number on that sheet. . . .

SB: Boy, you're going to make money off us *[laughs]*.

ML: I'll be lucky if I get my gasoline.

SB: You can send me one of the books.

ML: I will. And before that I'll send you a copy of this tape in the next few weeks. And if you don't mind, I'd like to take a picture of you.

SB: Okay. Could you snap all of us?

ML: Sure, and I'll get you a copy of the picture too.

SB: And when you gets rich, send me a little check *[laughs]*. Because I know it's going to sell.

ML: Well, I tell you, a friend of my wife, she was having lunch with her the other day, and she told her—a white woman—and she's been a schoolteacher all of her life, and my wife mentioned about what I was doing, and she said, "That's too bad. Who on earth would want to read about that?"

SB: She'd be surprised.

ML: That's right. But that's part of that attitude we still are dealing with.

SB: Some people are still living in . . .

Lottie Gibson, the Bridge
That Brought Me Over

Marvin Lare **[ML]**:* This is Tuesday, May the twenty-third, 2006, and I'm in Greenville, in the office of Mrs. Lottie Gibson at Greenville Tech Central Campus. How are you today?

Lottie Gibson **[LG]**: I'm nicely, thank you.

ML: Very good. You were just asking what the project is about, and as I mentioned, we're focusing on civil rights in South Carolina in the mid-twentieth century, from about 1930 to 1980, and as I had said, you certainly qualify as being a significant person in that history and that leadership. We'd like you to share with us your experiences and perspective on that era for this and future generations.

LG: Well, certainly it has been a very difficult period. It has been a real struggling period for many of us who've felt like we needed to fight for what we perceived to be freedom for us. We made some advancements during that period and just about the time we thought we were about to overcome, we realized that there are many challenges yet to experience and many challenges to overcome.

Mine was more than an opportunity and privilege in that I was married to Dr. W. F. Gibson, who was a real activist for justice for all people. [He] supported me in my efforts so that I would not have to go into the workplace at that time, and I could concentrate on how we could benefit [moving] forward.

He passed away in June of '02 and there's been a real void in the community, and I think in the state, the region, and really at the nation, because we get lots of telephone calls telling us and saying if "Doc" still lived, as he was affectionately called, he would certainly attack things that are happening now.

*The interview took place in Lottie Gibson's office at the Greenville Technical College Central Campus in Greenville, South Carolina, May 23, 2006.

Threats

LG: He was fearless, and that provided for me and for the family not to be frightened about things. In our home we had been threatened that it would be burned, and crosses would be burned in the yard, and people would come at night and remove either he or I or both of us away from the children, and all kinds of frightening kinds of statements [were made]. But we learned early on that when people call you and tell you that they're going to do something, most likely they're not going to do anything. If they're going to do something they'll go on and do it.

And it was just, I guess, a miracle that Dr. Gibson was self-employed and had a good business and did not have to be dependent on anyone for a living for us. He came from parents who worked in their own way in the state NAACP, and in their community, to bring about justice for all people. And we had the support of my family, feeling that if we felt that this was something that we needed to do, we must go forward.

I guess we have attended, either together or separately, so many marches that you could hardly remember to recall them and recall what happened during them. But I'm thoroughly convinced that a force of people can make a change, and we have seen it happen during that period. Dr. Gibson took time off from his office and closed it during the integration of the schools, went from school to school to try to talk to not only the administration but the students who were having a difficult time adjusting to the new law.

If you have specific incidents or specific kinds of things that you would like me to speak on, I'll be happy to try to do that.

ML: I generally like to let persons tell their own story in their own way, beginning where they want to and ending where they want to, but I do follow up with some questions. Tell us about your career and involvement, and we'll also get further into your husband's life as well.

Voting

LG: We learned early—and I say, "we," because we worked as a team—that registration was an important—and voter education and voter participation—was a very important tool to work with in overcoming some of these ills of society at that time. So we began going to the various neighborhoods after blacks were allowed to vote in the late '40s and into the early '50s. We were trying to get people on board. Me just coming out of college here in Greenville—and having worked with the NAACP youth chapter, and having been a founding member of that chapter in West Virginia, where I attended college—I was able to come here and begin to tell my people that voter education was very important and voter registration was even *more* important, and that we had to be in touch with those people that was offering for public service and seeing what their platform was and what they would do for us as a people who were struggling so at that time just to be equal.

Jobs

LG: Jobs in South Carolina, particularly in Greenville County, where we lived, for black people had been very difficult because they could not work in the mills, which was our main textile industry, not even *as janitors* or *maids*. So to find employment we more or less had to go through what few jobs were at the schools, and some industries would work black people. That was a challenge. So training people to try to have some kind of entrepreneurship where they could have some income on their own through services.

I remember as a developing girl many people worked in private homes for whites in Greenville County. Some of those whites were nice to those people in trying to help them secure housing, either to live in until their demise, or [a house] to be given to them as a token of appreciation for their services. Many black folk worked to take care of white kids. Many black families did laundry, did the laundry and all. And then there were black women that would go into white homes on certain days and do sewing and make clothing for . . . maybe they would have a week's schedule where they worked at one home getting the children's clothing or the adults' clothing ready for the upcoming season. In addition to that, a lot of the men worked as chauffeurs and cooks.

Then in private businesses we had barbers and beauticians and dressmakers and tailors, in small shops and, of course, restaurants in various neighborhoods throughout the county. Employment and the management of your finances was always a challenge because there was so little of bit money going into black homes.

But once we learned that we had to struggle on through and get a better education through not only high school, but college, then we were in a position to provide a better service, and we were able to get better jobs. I have friends, I guess, that work in almost every walk of life now and it's really a real privilege to see them do this, because there's always room for improvement. And because of my advocacy for justice and peace and equality, lots of people call me about their problems, and that's how I get to know about a lot of problems.

One of the main problems that we're facing now, it wasn't during that period, but on the threshold, right at the end of the '70s and into the beginning of the '80s, this community was introduced to *drugs,* and of course we already had a lot of mountain-made liquor that people participated in selling and drinking and all, that created social problems that we didn't really need.

Willie Earl

LG: I know that you heard of the killing by the Yellow Cab Company people of Willie Earl in the late '40s and, of course, they didn't get their trial going until, I think, about '48 or '9, if my memory serves me right. I remember staying out of school and going to that trial, which was really supposed to not happen. My parents were adamantly opposed to us going, but some group of us attended that trial at the courthouse, and of course, we always had to sit in the balcony at the courthouse or movie theaters or any place like that. If we were black we had to sit in the balcony. And we saw those people exonerated. They had killed that man, drug him, and abused him. . . . It was just awful. But they all were free from doing that, and that was certainly a shock to the community, and a fear in many homes. I graduated high school during that period, so I had an opportunity to sort of observe and know what was going on.

I've always had an appetite for justice and freedom and equality for all people, and I've tried to work through *Christianity* to achieve that, but it's been very difficult and, even now, challenging because there are so many *mean-spirited* people, and it's just really very difficult. But we have made some advances, and we've overcome some obstacles, and we've had some people that have really been dedicated to making life better.

Leaders

LG: We had a young minister to come to Greenville from the lower part of the state, Marion I think it was, and he led a group of teens and all into the demonstrations in the late '50s, and was able to make an impression on the majority community that black folk was really tired of being treated so badly and worked so hard for the menial kinds of livings that they had. So they'd still respect Reverend James S. Hall and his wife, Elizabeth, for their leadership. They went to Springfield Baptist Church, and they did a really, really yeoman's job in that.

The Springfield Baptist Church, Greenville, South Carolina, was the center for much civil rights protest training and planning. Photograph from the South Carolina NAACP Annual Conference Program. Courtesy of the Library of Congress, NAACP Collection.

So out of fear and disbelief for a lot of things, we have grown a lot of civil rights leaders. Reverend Jesse Jackson is a Greenville native son, and he works even today across all state lines and all in various communities. Where there is an ill or an injustice he's there, and people can say what they want to. He's been a force for justice and a force for freedom, and he is someone who needs to be respected, in my opinion. He's going to be with us this Thursday, as you know, and it would be good if you could interview him, because he can tell you his feelings as a boy and a young, developing man, how he came up.

But we have others that have worked and lobbied in the arena of justice. We have a woman here whose name is Leola Robinson. She was a young person who marched and fought for freedom and justice and equal opportunity. You have had an opportunity to talk with her?

ML: Yes, I have. She spoke for the anthology festival we had here in Greenville in 2004.

LG: Well that's good, because she has a real story, and I can remember her working at the USO, where we would have some of our meetings, and where we would fix snacks and all. When they were going on a demonstration, we would try to give them a little snack, so if they got locked up at least they wouldn't be hungry when they got to the jail, because they didn't know what time they would be getting out. And of course I named Mr. Horace Nash, who is now deceased. He was a real force working with her. She probably named him in her remarks, because they worked very closely together.

And of course there are others, like Hattie Smith and Margaree Crosby and Joan Madison and Doris Wright. I'm looking at some of them and can't call their names *[pauses].* The list goes on. I'm sure that in some writings those names would be in some of the papers.

But please know that freedom, justice, and equality in Greenville County has come *veery slow.* Now we did—you said you'd talked with our former mayor, Max Heller. He was a force for trying to bring about some level of equality in Greenville County, being of the Jewish race himself and having felt so many ills and been so disrespected. But because he was a man of justice and stood for freedom and equality, he was able to get a lot done for the city of Greenville.

We had had a mayor, Kenny Cass. I remember him as a mayor—it's my understanding he still lives and he's in a nursing home—during the twenty-eight years that he was the mayor, I don't think we had any progress in Greenville. At least I can't name any. That was a long period of *"I stand for nothing." [Lare chuckles.]*

But life is difficult. It really is.

Education and Career

ML: You said you graduated in West Virginia? How did you get there?

LG: West Virginia State College. I have a cousin that had graduated from there, so I knew about that college, and of course, my mother had graduated Benedict College, and my father was not a college person. But I knew that I had to go somewhere to school, so I figured if I got far enough away from home, I wouldn't be home every weekend, and I would have opportunity to meet people from other places that would give me a different view on what life could be, and it was a good experience. I still am in contact with some of the people that I met there, and we still see each other at different meetings and national conventions and programs and all. While in college I served on the student council and several other organizations at the school, so I had an opportunity to meet and learn a lot of people.

ML: Before we went on tape here, you were speaking about packing up your office here, after thirty-one years!

LG: Oh, my office is . . .

ML: Tell me about your thirty-one-year career.

LG: Well, my first job out of college was with Phyllis Wheatley Community Center as a woman and girls worker. I did programs. My major in college had been drama and English, and of course, I started work the summer. . . . I was very lucky because I graduated and came home in May, and I started work at Phyllis Wheatley in June, because a friend of mine that had held that job had gotten married that Christmas—I had been in her wedding—and she was going on, moving with her husband, and I was recommended for the job, so I was very happy.

After working there for almost two years, I was accepted at Atlanta University School of Social Work, and that is where I did my graduate work. So when I returned to South Carolina from grad school, I worked for the Department of Social Services. Well, actually, I had worked from the Department of Social Services about six months before I went to grad school. So then I worked for the Department of Social Services. I worked in Spartanburg. I did child welfare. I did foster home studies, institutional studies, and adoptions. So I got a little taste of that.

Then I started working for the USO, the United Service Organizations, here in Greenville. We had Donaldson Air Force Base. I was the director of the USO for eight and a half years, and during that period I had an opportunity to meet and know a lot of people. And then the civil rights movement started, while I worked for the USO.

And of course that was my real appetite. I was ready to work and serve in that because it provided for me an outlet for meeting people and going places. We would go different places for marches—Columbia, Atlanta, Myrtle Beach, Conway, Boston—and Gib, of course, went to more places than me because by then we had started our family, and I had to stay home to take care of the children. But to interact with people from all over the state, and then he became very active with the state and national NAACP, so that gave us another . . . In fact, I was just with Congressman John Conyers out of Detroit, and he had visited our home in the late '50s, before we got the restaurants and all.

Integrating Restaurants

LG: We were just getting the restaurants integrated, and of course, that's the whole story by itself—how six black people and six white people had met on a week-to-week basis just to discuss how we could have black folks eat in public restaurants *[laughs]*.

But we had a plan, came up with a plan, and there was one group of people that had been designated as callers, and then they were given names of other folk that would go that day. So we were notified in the neighborhood of twelve o'clock, and we had to call our people in our group, have them ready for two-thirty to go to the restaurants. And they were going to tell, the managers of the restaurants was going to tell their staff at two o'clock that black folks would be served at two-thirty and if they couldn't serve them, or felt bad about it, they needed to leave work before two-thirty, because the people were going to come in, and they did not want to inherit any suits from any mistreatment that people had. So, anyway, our little group—it was five of us, two men and three women—we went to Eckerd's drugstore in Terrace Shopping Center, and I remember we went in and sat down, and, of course, we had sort of reviewed what we were going to order so that we all would have something different. You know, like, one may have ham and cheese, one may have a cheeseburger, someone else may have pastrami on rye with cheese and all. And I remember this one man, when he made his order, he'd say, "I like two 'nana splits and a Pepsi." You ever heard of *two*? *[Lare laughs.]* And the lady looked at him and he say, "You heared [*sic*] me, I goin' eat one here and I'm goin' take one with me." So we teased each other about that for years and years and years. "Goin' out tonight? Goin' out today to eat? Don't get no two 'nana splits and a Pepsi now!"

And then that night, we went out to a restaurant. Said we weren't going to let it just end for lunch in the day, and we went that night. And when the waitress was taking the orders for the beverages, my husband, who had worked as a waiter on Miami Beach while he was in dental school, he ordered Sanka and the lady next to him said she liked Sanka too.

I said, "Well, I'll have hot tea with lemon."

And the next man said, "Make mine Maxwell House."

You ever heard of anybody ordering a brand coffee? *[She laughs.]* Well, maybe they would do it now . . . but he said, "Make mine Maxwell House." And of course, we had that for a joke for a long time, never heard of ordering . . .

"Gosh," she said. "All we have is the house coffee. We don't have Maxwell House."

So through it all . . . I guess I shared those little things with you to say that through it all we were able to raise our heads and get a little laugh or a little smile out of it, and to go forward.

Some groups were told on their day when they went to a restaurant, "We don't serve niggers here."

And, of course, they had to say, "Well we don't eat 'em. Make mine . . ." so and so. And they'd order something, pay for it, and not eat it, because they figured they'd poisoned it or something.

The next day I went to the YWCA where they served meals. These are the "Christians," now, that I'm dealing with, and I went in and I got my tray, and I got my food and I paid for it, and of course, the *devil* stepped in and said, "Go to the largest table in here and see how many people will join you." Well, I'll have you know I sat at that table with about nine other chairs and nobody joined me, and I ate very slowly and finally, while they stood around the walls holding their trays, when I finished I left and I said, "So sad, that we live so distantly, and yet we fill the churches up on Sunday morning."

Since then we've had different incidents at different kinds of restaurants, but once the word passed down that we *will* have integrated eating in the restaurants, it just sort of went.

Greenville County was slow to implement integrating the schools, but they were told on a Friday to have it integrated that Monday, and of course, it finally went through. It finally went through.

ML: Tell me about—you say you'd have a group of six whites and six blacks—what was the arrangement and who were the people that stood with you?

LG: They were supposed to be the leaders in both communities, the leaders in the white community and the leaders in the black community. My husband was chosen as one of them, and he had two attorneys, and I think it was two ministers and one insurance guy, who still lives in Columbia. His name is Harrison Reardon.

ML: Oh, yes. I know Harrison.

LG: You know him?

ML: I know him well.

LG: Okay, well, he was a part of that group. They went, maybe two nights a week, to the chamber of commerce and sometimes other places, and met and discussed how they would implement the integration of the restaurants. Of course, when the plan finally came into floration [*sic*] it was just from then on. We tried to go in at least twos, if you could get somebody to go with you, everywhere you went, until they really got really used to it, but once they found out that our money spent just like everybody else's and it helped them to be a little more wealthy, it went smooth after that. Wasn't so bad after all. Windows where we had received hotdogs and other kinds of sandwiches suddenly opened their doors.

County Council

ML: Are you on county council now?

LG: I am. I serve District 25. I've been there fourteen years, and I have two more years on this stretch, and depending on my health and my memory and a whole lot of other things, I'll make a decision whether I'll continue or whether I need to give it up.

ML: I interviewed Xanthene Norris so . . .

LG: You did?

ML: Let's see. It was probably early last year.

LG: Oh, okay. She's a better councilperson now than she was then, so maybe she needs to be reinterviewed! *[She laughs.]* She would kill me if she knew I'd said that!

ML: I understand there's a—I regret I won't be able to go to it—but I understand there's a fundraiser for her . . .

LG: For her tonight, yes. I'll be going.

ML: Give her my regards.

LG: I'll take your check, too *[laughs]*.

ML: I already gave a check to Ruthann Butler today!

LG: You did?

ML: Yes.

LG: For Xanth?

ML: Well, she was saying about the cost of things, and the Jesse Jackson event on Thursday and so forth, and I know that Intercultural Center has a real struggle, too, and she's been very helpful to me for quite some time, and so I gave her a check, but I might have to send Xanthene another one.

LG: I was just kidding you. I didn't really have no . . I had no right to say that, but I just said, as I carry this message . . .

ML: That's all right.

LG: . . . but as I carry this congratulatory message, I have a little something to back it up with. But I think she'll do okay. That is a good group, sponsoring group, and so by the time we dig down in our pockets and do something, we'll be okay. She'll be okay.

ML: Well, was it primarily the NAACP that was the organizing effort here, or were there various groups?

LG: Well, actually the NAACP, who worked so closely together with the churches, was the force that brought about the implementation, not only in Greenville but throughout the South and, of course, South Carolina being a part of that. A group of us were talking last week, saying that if we had the leadership in the churches dedicated to justice as we had at that time, we would perhaps be so much better off. But I guess "to everything there is a season" [Ecclesiastes 3:1], and we've reared two or three generations of "nonbelievers," because things were beginning to be so easy for them. But all in all, I never give up. And I hope I won't *give out* soon. So I feel like things will get better—they got to. *Can't* get worse. I know I've had two calls this week—well, actually had one was last week because it was Saturday—and then I've had two people to call Monday, saying that the Klan was meeting up in Travelers Rest, and that one of our people that's offering for office was there and participating with them. So, you know, you can't control people's mind or heart. They got to do and feel for themselves. I got so I don't even worry about it.

ML: Well, how long have you been with the Tech system here now?

LG: With Greenville Tech? I've been here thirty-one years. Well, actually it'll be thirty-one years next month. I call myself retiring at thirty years. I've been leaving here since January the first. Every week they say, "Stay another week. Wait a little, we've got to get somebody." But they finally got somebody last week to take my place, and of course, that means that I got to sure enough get seriously busy and get this stuff out of here. I think when I dump some of these boxes that we've emptied out, it won't look quite as bad. And then we can get started in these other boxes. Some of them boxes I packed up over five years ago, so I doubt that they have much stuff that needs to be saved. . . .

ML: That's great. Tell me of your husband's childhood and experience. What made him sensitive to these issues, or was it just being a professional person?

LG: I'm sure that his mother and his father was a great force. His father was a brick mason, contracting brick mason, by profession. He was very good, so even white folk who may have not liked him respected his craftsmanship in what he could do, because he had a contract. . . . He worked on the Charleston Naval Yard, and then he worked on the base for the marines in North Carolina, that marine base in North Carolina. I can't think where it is right now. But his mother was a teacher, and she believed and worked secretly with the NAACP. So he grew up observing and seeing how all kind of incidents down there in Darlington and that area, killing people, and when you know these people, and they've been so brutally killed for what perceives to be nothing, it's a challenge. So by the time he got in college, he was already a little young rebel-riser [*sic*].

At his funeral, it was funny, one of his colleagues from Meharry Medical School said that they had worked in New York for the summer, and they had just passed that railroad law where if you were going from one state to another, you could sit in any of those coaches. You didn't have to sit up there close to the smoke or in the back, you could sit anywhere. So Gib had told him, "I'm going to try it. I don't care if they lock me up. I'm going to try it."

So he said he was on the train and the conductor came to them and told them, said, "You *boys* need to move up there to the first coach."

And so Gib said, "No, we're going to enjoy it back here. We're back here behind the nice restaurant and everything, and we'll just stay right here."

So [the conductor] went and got somebody else, and they came back and told them they needed to move.

Gib said, "No, we're going all the way to Nashville, Tennessee. We'll just stay on here."

And this guy, Dr. Spurgeon [*uncertain*], said, "Now Gib wasn't scared and he was ready to go to jail, but I was so nervous I was trembling!"

But he sat on there with Gib, and they never did really put them off or call. Said they would stop and they would be sitting there, sort of nervous, saying, "Is the police going to come and get us? They going to lock us up here? How will we tell people where we are?" Blah, blah, blah. But they never did really lock them up, but they just threatened them, and then the train'd pull off.

So he got really involved in what was right and what was not right in college. Then by the time he did his internships in New York and all, he came here to Greenville to work. He was ready to really work through the NAACP and get some positive things done. So he started out as a chapter president, and then he moved to the state and he was the state president, then he moved to the national board. Gib, as I look back on his life, he had vision about what needed to happen, and he had a real appetite for contacting those presidents of corporations and businesses and getting commitment from them on justice. And he was well read, so he knew what kind of conversation to have. He could talk to them about what was right and what wrong, and what the law was. So he was a force for change and people give him credit for that, even still.

ML: We all miss him. He stood out. Everybody . . .

LG: Yes, and then, you know, [they] accused him of overspending NAACP money, which was a *total* misunderstanding, because he said he never counted any money, never was around any money. Anything he ever used in terms of money was strictly from what was budgeted through the board. People who know him know that he lost money working with NAACP, because he got so he would go—I remember when he sat the whole time in court with Merlie Evers, your know, her husband had been killed, he sat with her. He was the only board member that sat with her the entire time, until the verdict was read. And she seemed to have thought that . . . *she* . . . she offered against him, and became the president of the national board, as he had served for about eleven years.

But I had told him, "Ain't no road that it ain't no end, and everything comes to an end." And, you know, "What goes around, comes around?" You just have to live every day for what it means to itself. Eventually you will have peace of mind and all. "What is for you will be for you." I believe that strongly. I surely do.

Family

ML: Well, tell me about your family and what . . .

LG: We have four children. All four of them are in Greenville now. My oldest son is a used car dealer, and he has a detail shop connected to it, so he does that. In fact, today he's gone to an auction to get some older cars to sell.

And then the next one, he has a problem staying on any kind of job. He likes giving excuses on why he can't work. Very smart, too. I just don't know what his problem is. The people at church said, "Well, he's just so mannerly, and he has just such good manners."

And I said, "But we're talking about *job skills.*"

Went to Benedict [University] three years and just quit. Been trying to get him to go back but he has not or will not do that.

And then, of course, my third boy is a lawyer. He graduated West Point Military Academy. He served three and a half years in the service, then he had taken the LSAT because he thought that he was going to get to go to law school through the military, but that was the year that they got rid of fifteen thousand officers—they were cutting the budget that way. He had served in Saudi Arabia eighteen months, and he had served in—all his service was done in Third World countries, because he spoke four or five languages, so when he came home from Saudi Arabia, he got that discharge, and he applied and immediately got in Georgetown Law School. So he graduated Georgetown Law School and he practices here. He practiced first with Jones, Day in Atlanta, because that's who he had done his internship with, and then he decided he didn't like that and he went to a law firm in Miami. Supposed to be the largest law firm—Jones, Day is the largest one in the United States, but this one was right next to Jones. Anyway, he didn't stay down there too long, and then he came here. He worked at Reibold, Carlisle for a while and then he's on his own, practices on his own.

And my daughter is a magistrate judge, and she's at the detention center. She works there and she can decide who stays and who goes home. She does that. So we're all here in Greenville, and while we have some things we'd like to do better, we're all doing something. So that's a blessing. I'm glad to have them all in Greenville, for a change, because at one time I didn't have any of them here.

ML: Grandchildren?

LG: Yes, we have nine grandchildren. My oldest boy married a girl that he had dated some years before—he spent a good bit of time in jail. He had a real drug problem. And none of these drug treatment centers could help him, because Gib and I both spent *real* money trying to get him—he went to that place out from Charleston when he was a young boy, then he went to two places in Georgia, then he went to Morris Village in Columbia, went up there to this Appalachian thing up in Asheville. None of that helped, so he went to prison, which was about his second or third time, because they kept paroling him out—he's a good talker. And he said he woke up one day, and he just said he wasn't going to fool with drugs no more, so he's been straight now about six or eight years. But he married a girl that had two daughters and then they have a little boy. He'll be four in August.

Then my next boy, he married a girl that has two kids. They're very smart, one of them's got a full scholarship to the University of North Carolina, Charlotte, in medicine, and the boy, he'll be a senior next year. But they live with their father in Rocky Mount, North Carolina. Their father's an engineer and he's had them since they were little. They have equal custody, so they're back and forth, but they need to stay where they're going to go to school and go to church, but they come a lot here.

And then my third boy, he has two girls, eleven and twelve, and then he has a little boy nineteen months.

And my daughter has one little boy.

So I got five blood grandchildren and four step-grandchildren, and they're just as nice as they can be. They're just as nice to me as they can be. Of course, they're the older ones and they're a great source of help. I do pretty good.

"Retirement"

ML: Well, when you get moved out of this office now, what are you going to do?

LG: I'm still on the county council and I think that's . . .

ML: Keeps you mighty busy.

LG: Oh, tell me! See, I don't just serve people in my district. I serve all over the county, because I found out some of those white council people won't serve them black folks. They don't think about them. So I serve the white ones [who] just can't get no help and the black ones. So I don't know—they just say, "I hope you don't leave."

I said, "Well, I'm leaving it to my health. If my health's not good, ain't no need of me dragging on."

ML: . . . such a critical problem now in terms of race and justice and equality and opportunity?

LG: I think we have one that's bigger than race, and that's alcohol and drugs. I'm on a mission with them, trying to get the county council to see that they need to build a drug treatment center in Greenville. Over 80 percent—we've taken, since I've been on council, we've taken three surveys, done three studies, and each time the people being held at the detention center on a daily basis is over 80 percent . . . at one time it was up to 92 percent of the people in the detention center's crimes were drug or alcohol related. Now that says something to me. It says that we don't need a bigger jail—we need a hospital. We need a drug treatment center to get these people back on foot, and get them out into the world of work so they can become taxpayers instead of tax receivers. So I'm on that mission. I serve as the liaison from the county to the Alcohol and Drug Commission—in fact we meet tomorrow—and I'm just sort of hoping that, like I said, nothing stays the same. Everything must change. Maybe these hard-hearted people who think that, who don't envision that alcohol and drug is a disease, and will decide to treat it instead of punish it. See, we pay forty-five dollars a day for every day that they're in jail, and they're just overcrowded. This guy called and told me—I think it was Friday—he said, "Mrs. Gibson, you know, we have nine hundred and something beds but we have fourteen hundred people. We have out all our mats." And he can't seem to get law enforcement to realize that.

Of course, I'm not saying, "Don't take a look at who's breaking the law or don't do anything to them" but I just want another way to treat them.

ML: Yes. I just heard the statistics yesterday that the United States has the highest rate of incarceration in the whole . . .

LG: . . . world!

ML: Yes.

LG: California tried this new—I was reading that—you read it? About them trying this new way of alternatives to prison? And they have improved thirty-something percent. That's pretty good.

ML: That is. That's excellent.

LG: That's pretty good. That's the main . . . I'm going to be working with that, and as a developing child I grew up very close to the church, and very involved, and I have not been involved in the church other than just going and sitting in the pew, paying my dues, really in the last thirty years, which I know my mother and father turns over in their graves about. I just . . . We got a little minister—I can't let him send me to *hell* [laughs] but he's doing a good job of it and I'm just going to try to do better in the church. I'm going to do something at the church. I've been praying on it, trying to see what I really would be better in, to serve people. I got plenty to do.

ML: Our church, and a number of them, have Stephen's Ministry, in which lay persons, but that are trained and professionals like you, make themselves available to people in the congregation or the community who have troubles that need counseling and support and nurturing and all.

LG: Well, I do that all the time. Yesterday I . . .

ML: Maybe you could train some other people to make a Stephen's Ministry corps or something like that.

LG: We have a good many professional people in our church, and that's how come I wonder why we're so *stupid* that we can't get rid of this preacher. They keep praying and telling me he's going to be better, and I don't think so.

ML: What church do you go to?

LG: Springfield Baptist.

ML: Oh, okay.

[The telephone rings.]

LG: Would you please excuse me?

ML: Sure.

LG *[speaking on phone]:* Lottie Gibson. A girl that worked for me for along time. She's . . . Where were we?

ML: We were talking about the church and you finding a role there.

LG: Yes, I'm to seek for that, so I think I'll be busy. A real mission for me has been to try to work with people coming home from prison, and keeping them from returning. And I used to have a weekly meeting with a group, with several groups, through the years. Lasted a long time. And the Department of Corrections stopped allowing people—some of the Department of Corrections—to come and talk to people about what it's like to be in prison, and also to come and sort of help us keep the work and all going. We had a pretty good little thing going. We had cooperation from the sheriff, and the chief of police, and Probation and Parole was working with us, but some kind of way this one guy that was sort of very, very interested in it, they wouldn't let him come anymore and we sort of stopped. But I have still . . . I work very closely with the Parole Board now. I know five or six of them personally, and I call them about different cases that people call me about, and then I try to have a support base for people when they come out of prison. Some that don't have homes and all, I've been able to get in the Salvation Army, and different other places, until they can work and get on foot. I do that a lot. So I got a plenty to do.

Inspiration

ML: I'm sure. Let me wrap up with asking you who has been the biggest inspiration to you, and who do you really admire most in terms of . . .

LG: Well, I guess my mother. My mother was a real force in my life. She wasn't a loud person, or an aggressive person, but to me she was a very common-sense person, and she was a teacher, so she was equipped with the knowledge. She believed in choices, and she believed in circumstances for those choices. My father supported her well, and we did pretty good. My oldest brother still lives in Arlington, Virginia, and we talk weekly, sometimes once a month.

My mother, I guess, has been the biggest force, but I've met some real leaders along the way, including my husband. He was a force for strength, and like I say, at times when other people wanted to speak out, they wouldn't, because they had their job security, especially teachers. And you had to be either a teacher or a preacher. And so he always said, "I got your back." So that's good to know. And I have been able to work . . . now Gib would contact corporate and business people and folk that made decisions, but when it came down to that day to day getting things done, like helping people get housing, and food, and childcare, and stuff like that, even jobs, he would tell you that was my job. So that's the work. That's the real work. But of course, "Dr. Gibson got it *done!*" *[She laughs.]*

ML: . . . even if his wife did it for him.

LG: "He got it done!" *[She laughs.]* But it's been an interesting life. Yes, it's been an interesting life, I tell my children. I've had a lot of experiences other people haven't. It's been a real full life.

ML: I appreciate you sharing with me today, and . . .

LG: Oh yes! I hope your information will come well.

ML: Thank you. If you don't mind, I'd like to take a picture or two.

LG: Oh my goodness! Let me get on this coat right quick.

ML: Okay.

LG: Well, lord, you going to take it in this?

ML: We can see the prints of where all of your plaques and pictures and so forth were on the wall *[referring to the faded wall around where the plaques and other items had hung].*

LG: I had over two hundred. I got them in some boxes back there. I'm going to take them home. Some of them I'm going to send to Ruthann [Butler].

[Lare takes photos.]

ML: . . . I'll send you a copy of the photos, and I'll get this tape copied in a week or two and send you a copy of it. It'll be a good while before I get the transcriptions done and all that, but you'll be on the list for a book when it comes out. . . .

LG: Have you talked with Reverend James Hall up in Philadelphia?

ML: No.

LG: He was a real force for change. Hand me that purse right there in front of you. I'll give you his telephone number.

ML: Okay. I may have him on my list, but I haven't contacted him yet and I'd like to have that.

LG: Now I tell you what. He made a real difference, because he had the ability to . . .

ML: So he's still . . .

LG: . . . living, and doing well. He spoke at the State Baptist Convention thing in Columbia last week. He was their banquet speaker. . . .

ML: Okay, great.

LG: And of course, I guess you know how to get in touch with Reverend Jesse Jackson.

ML: Yes.

Mrs. W. F. (Lottie) Gibson,
May 23, 2006.

LG: And I'm going to tell him that you're going to be calling. He'll be here Thursday. We wouldn't have this holiday [Martin Luther King Jr.'s Birthday] here in Greenville if it hadn't been for Reverend Jackson. He came here to mobilize these people, went around to the press and talked with the editorial board and all, and got them working, and different things. People . . . they can give credit to whoever they want to, but they better give it to him—he's the one that got them started. Of course now, the ones who really got it going was the ones who voted for it. And we're going to be honoring them Thursday night.

ML: Let me give you my card and my cell phone number, I'm writing it down here. I don't think I sent you some materials about this project, did I?

LG: You spell this L-A-R-E. You pronounce that Lare?

ML: Lare, just like "care." Here's a copy of a brief description, sort of a progress report and plans of the project.

LG: This is nice.

ML: Here's a copy of a news story that they did in the *State* last year about it. Everybody has been so cooperative and helpful. When I went to retire in May of 2003, I was in a meeting with my friend Bill Saunders, from down in Charleston, you probably know Bill, and we were talking about what we were going to do and I said I was going to be doing some writing, and he said, "What on?"

LG: I saw that—writing, gardening, reading, travel— What you got in that garden?

ML: My wife thinks I'm neglecting the garden. And I've got a release form here for me to be able to use the interview, because the USC Press always wants you to get permission to . . .

LG: You know Miss Modjeska Simkins? I don't know if anybody talked with you about her efforts.

ML: Oh, yes.

LG: She was a real force for justice. I remember one time she came up here when we was going to march at Bob Jones. She drove up here, eighty-eight years old, by herself. Got out the car down there, and Gib said, "Now you're not walking anywhere."

"Oh yes, I am. I didn't come up here to sit around."

ML: I'm working closely with the Modjeska Simkins Center there. I don't know whether you know Catherine Fleming Bruce, who's the director of it, or not.

LG: I think I know that name but personally, no . . .

ML: Okay. I'll add on [the form] here "and the photos" I took. If you come across some things, materials, you think that should be included . . . let me know.

LG: One thing, one weakness black folk have is they don't have a real history, written history, and they don't take a lot of pictures through the years. I can think of lots of things. . . . I can think of when we marched in Edgefield. We had a *river* of people, you couldn't even see . . . back for a long, far as you could see, just people. That was for voter registration. And I can remember when we marched, that was on a Sunday we marched down there, we filled that place up.

ML: Do you know, I don't have many names of people in Edgefield and Abbeville and down that way. Do you know of some contacts yet? Down there? Do you remember some of the folks who've been with it?

LG: Have you talked to them people over there at the NAACP office?

ML: Yes, but I have . . . and Ike Williams gave me a real good interview and some contacts.

LG: Oh yes, Ike. But now Ike wasn't on the Edgefield march. Nelson Rivers in our national office in Baltimore, I think he was with us on that march. Nelson Rivers knows a lot of stuff.

ML: Yes, I have talked with Nelson, then with Lonnie Randolph mostly on this education, "Corridor of Shame" education activities, and I've just started some work at the Library of Congress, on the NAACP records there. I've just got a little ways into the books from 1919 to 1939, including the organization of the South Carolina Conference of local chapters.

LG: Yes, my secretary, her daddy was Mr. Johnson—he was one of the organizers. Mary Johnson Brockman. He was the treasurer . . . no, that little man that went with him was the treasurer. What was his name? Let me get some information on him.

[She dials a number and speaks on the telephone]

LG: Hey! What was that little man's name used to be with your daddy all the time that carried that money?

Levi Byrd. B-Y-R-D. Yes, he was good. And your daddy's first name?

Mr. Frank Johnson.

They used to come on the bus from Cheraw to Columbia to the meetings, and he used to bring the money in a little suitcase. Wasn't that something? In a brown bag. Bless his heart. He was cute, too.

Okay. I didn't get Leola. I'll try her though after a while.

Bye.

[Sho hangs up the phone.]

LG: Mr. Levi Byrd, he was one of the founding members.

And then they organized [locally] in the Springfield Baptist Church here in Greenville. I think late '39 is when we came on board. Of course, we don't have any of those people still living. I can't think of a one of them that's still living. But this James Hall came here and got this community moving.

Jackie Robinson

LG: And it all started from the . . . Jackie Robinson came here to do a speech, and they wouldn't let him sit down in the airport. Isn't that stupid? One little seat. I mean, for a man that had bathed that morning, and probably the night before. Wasn't like a nasty person coming in! I still can't believe it. And I remember when we had the march at the airport. I didn't get to march. Gib marched but I was doing the meals. See, they wouldn't let us use the restaurants. Now, this is part of the *history.* You'd better turn that [tape recorder] back on for this, because this is *good.*

ML: Okay. It's on.

LG: When we had the march on the airport because of the Jackie Robinson situation, he had come here to speak for our state convention in Greenville, and when he got ready to leave they went to the airport and they wouldn't let him sit down—told him to go around to some little back place. Reverend Hall was with him, and Mrs. Hall, and Mr. A. J. Wittenberg, which you probably have heard his name.

ML: Yes.

[See other accounts of Jackie Robinson's visit in this volume by J. T. McCain and Xanthene Norris; in volume 2 in the interview with Millicent Brown and Emily Newman (with photos) and Ambassador Richard Miles; and in volume 4 in the interview with Mayor Joseph P. Riley Jr.]

LG: And they couldn't believe that they didn't want the man to sit down in the waiting room, so they said, "Hu-aah, we're going to march on this place." I think that was shortly after the first march had started down in Alabama. So we got to talking about it, and we said we would do it New Year's Day . . . one second please.

Jackie Robinson addressing the closing meeting of the 1959 South Carolina NAACP Conference at Municipal Auditorium, Greenville. Courtesy of the Library of Congress, NAACP Collection.

ML: You were saying—

LG: So anyway, we began to plan, and it was going to be statewide, and we'd see what kind of cooperation we got from other communities. Well, we had people to come from everywhere. And we had five or six hundred, maybe a thousand people—I don't know because all those people weren't from out of town. I see a lot of local people. And they marched and all.

But my job was to provide the food, and I was director in the USO and, of course, accustomed to feeding two and three and four hundred people, because the guys would come in and bring their families for different kind of . . . Sunday meals and holidays. I had me a little crew and we fixed, at the church and at the USO. We had food for everybody. Of course, we didn't let the majority community know we was feeding them down there at the USO. I said, "If I get fired, that'll be all right." *[She laughs.]* Anyway, we had just the greatest success, and Reverend Hall can tell you all about that, because he led that effort.

And then another march that was in my memory that I wanted to share with you, and seems like I've just about forgot what that was. The marches pay off—*they pay off!* It brings people, and then they talk to other folk that they know, and the word goes out and it goes on. It's a *loud song*. We had a successful day the day we marched on the airport, and Springfield Baptist Church was the host church, right there on McBee

Anniversary of the Supreme Court school desegregation decision. Families of those who had signed the original Clarendon County petition gathered on May 17, 2006, at the South Carolina State House for passage of a joint resolution recognizing the day

Avenue. That church burned since then and we have a new church, but the spirit of organizing and giving and serving is still among some of the members. *Surely right.*

That's all.

ML: Okay. I appreciate so much . . .

LG: I know you're tired of me!

ML: No, not at all.

[The tape pauses, then resumes.]

LG: . . . Speaking of things to do, I'm just back from Detroit to that national convention. I always do a workshop for them, and I'm in some community groups. I never forget NAACP—*that's the bridge that brought me over.* So it's a plenty to do, and I work very closely with Rainbow/PUSH and Reverend [Jesse] Jackson. I'm planning on going to the national convention there in June, in Chicago. So it's a plenty to do.

ML: Yes.

LG: It's a plenty to do.

ML: I just hope you have the health and strength to do it.

LG: Yes, thank you. I need that.

ML: And to enjoy it too.

LG: I've had a spell of sickness, so I appreciate that. And thank you for coming, and I wish you luck and success with your book. I believe it'll be a good seller for our people, to tell the story . . .

Have you dealt with any of those people that helped with the case down in . . . it wasn't in Williamsburg County, was it?

ML: Oh, Clarendon County and the *Briggs v. Elliott?*

LG: Clarendon County, yes.

ML: Yes. In fact I was just with them just last Wednesday, which was the anniversary of the Supreme Court decision, May 17th. They had a joint resolution passed at the statehouse, and they had the families of all those folks [who signed the petition] there for it. Judge Finney spoke, Lonnie [Randolph], and [house members] Cathy Harvin and David Mack, and others, and it was a very nice time.

LG: Yes, May 17th was it. I remember I was in college, in grad school in Atlanta, Georgia, and the lady whose daughter was one of the lawyers, Mrs. Smythe. I'm trying to think what the lawyer's name was. She left me in charge of her house and her car, and they went and sat in the hearings and all. And I had carried them to the airport and went back and got them when they was coming back, the mother and father of the female lawyer [pauses]. She had a sister that lived here, Mrs. Thomas. There are lots of memories. *Lots of memories.*

ML: We wouldn't be where we are today without . . .

LG: The March on Washington—I remember it coming through and people living in our house. We had a couple and another guy, fixing food and all, and how the Christians over at the YWCA had told us we could use the "Y" on Bernie Street and then told us the day of we couldn't use it, and it poured down rain. We carried them to the ballpark and water was just falling in the beans and potato salad and on the chicken and stuff, and the people was hungry. I tell you, it was criminal. *It was criminal. It was criminal!*

ML: I appreciate so much your time on this . . .

Xanthene Norris,
a Passion for Kids

Marvin Lare [ML]:* Your name again.

Xanthene Norris [XN]: Xanthene Norris, X-A-N-T-H-E-N-E, Norris, N-O-R-R-I-S.

ML: Okay, Mrs. Norris, I'm Marvin Lare, and in my retirement, if you can call it that . . .

XN: I'm the same thing, okay, my retirement.

ML: . . . one of my projects is working on an anthology of civil rights and human rights in South Carolina. I'm pleased to share with you that Ruthann Butler gave me your name and recommended that I contact you. I would like for you to share with us your experience, your background, where, how you came to be involved in civil rights, just to tell your story however you would like to tell it.

XN: Okay, well, I grew up in Greenville, South Carolina, born in Winston-Salem, North Carolina. Moved here when I was about three years old. And so I attended the public schools during the time of segregation, of course, until I graduated in 1946 and went to Atlanta to go to college. My experiences in Greenville were I guess typical of most kids who grew up during the time of segregation. However, I did have some personal experiences that were rather baffling to me and that I didn't understand at the very beginning. There were only two of us, two daughters in my family and my mother and my father. And my father was the—I just loved him to death. At that time we would either walk to school or sometimes my father would take me and then sometimes I would ride the public transportation that we had at that time, which was a bus. Really the public transportation we had then was much better than we have in Greenville now. But anyway, that's what I did and went back and forth to school.

*The interview took place at the home of Xanthene Norris in Greenville, South Carolina, on January 27, 2005, and was transcribed by Catherine Mann, for the USC South Caroliniana Library.

One time I was riding the bus in Greenville—I would say it was probably around '43 or '44, and at that time we graduated in the eleventh grade, not the twelfth grade, but I got on the bus and put my money in the little slot that they had to drop it. The man accused me of not putting the money there. I had put a coin in there, exactly how much it was. Anyway, he finally told me to get on to the back of the bus and slapped me. And so ooh, it just, you know . . . I went on to the back, and I was just horrified that this man had done this to me.

When I got home I was waiting for my—I told my mom—but I told my daddy, knowing that he was going to do something about it, you know. But when we went the next day to confront the conductor that was on this thing, you know, he let my daddy have it and told him some of the same things, you know, and what he would do to him! And my father, I noticed, kind of stepped back, didn't say a lot and all, and it just hurt me so bad that he was not able to do that. So I think that was the time that I really realized all of the problems in the infrastructure and everything that was involved socially with segregation at that time.

I cried all the way home, and my daddy tried to talk to me and tried to let me know that "was the *system* and that we had to *live* with that." I had always done well academically in school, and so it didn't affect my grades. I didn't ride the bus all the time, all that often so I tried to make up that I *would not* ride the bus because . . .

My mother was a teacher. She had had two years of college, and she taught up in the mountains. That's when we had county schools and city schools, and so she was working in the mountains, which meant that she went to that area in the Travelers Rest area. She went up there on Monday mornings and stayed there until Friday. What we would do is pick up my mom, so quite often my daddy would pick me up on Fridays, and then we would go and get my mom. Of course, with my sister, all of us would ride up there. During that time I stayed with my grandmamma and my daddy through the week.

My grandmother had a lot of Indian in her, had beautiful hair that went to the wave, and back then she would what we called wrapping, wrapping her hair. I don't know if you've ever heard that, but you just take black cloth that she had gotten and this is the way she wore her hair, wrapped. *[She shows her own hair wrapped up.]* On the weekends she would take that a loose and would have all of this beautiful hair. So she wrapped my hair, and so the biggest problem I had back then was telling my mom, "Ooh, it's too tight," you know, when she would do my hair.

But anyway, but I had a beautiful time living as far—you know, we didn't know we were poor. I know you've heard that a thousand times. We were poor. My father was able to, he came from a large family so they would kill hogs at a certain time during the year, so we had plenty of food. That wasn't a problem. The only thing we didn't have was good fish, and would go with my daddy quite often would go to fishing. Salmon was a novelty for us to have. But living up was pretty—it wasn't bad.

The only other thing that we had a problem was with white males driving through our neighborhood. They would quite often ride and show their penis and have it exposed and, you know, try to get us to get into the cars. So quite often my family, my father and then other men who lived in that community, would threaten these men and, of course, they would run and, of course, you know, and when they would report, take the license plate, we never did hear anything from it. So consequently, you know, but that was always a problem.

So all of this put a lot of fear into especially the girls and, of course, the young men would sometimes and the boys would often join the men, and they would just kind of monitor and watch out. So you got to know certain cars and what cars were coming through and at what time. So, you know, that was very traumatic for me at that time. But my parents would not allow us to play outside the gate of our yard because they were very concerned about that. So where we went most of the time, we went together, maybe all of the girls and some of the boys. Like if we would go to a movie, my father would take us to the movie and come back. So we had a very closed situation in that we had to fear whites, you know. So it was the trauma of that and living in that situation.

However, since I was very academic, I had a lady that was very good to me that my daddy worked for. My father at one time worked for the railroad, and back then black men who worked for the railroad made a fairly good living. But, of course, he was hurt, and so he lost his job. So that was it. I lived near the railroad station, and so I tell everybody now I say, well, that's one reason I talk loud because we had to learn to adjust talking over the loudness of the trains because they ran by, you know, coal and all of that and made a lot of noise, plus you had all this smoke and all of that.

But we lived in an area where we had a lot of people that looked out . . . I lived next door to a lady that she and her husband were Presbyterian, and he was a minister and she was our piano teacher. So I was able to get a lot of things that a lot of people don't get. I was able to get piano lessons from her at a very cheap price. I also attended her church, and often in the summer I would go to Harbison. I think it was a college. It was probably a junior college, in the summer, so I got to get some of that because of that. So, in a way, other than just the trauma of being afraid of white men and what would happen to us, you know, but as far as having some of the things that a lot of my friends did not get, I was able to get them because my mother and father were able to provide that for us.

So it wasn't that bad from a cultural point of view, because I learned music, learned how to play the piano, and knew a lot about music. Sang fairly well in the choir and in school, and when I got to college, I sang with the philharmonic. So all of this really helped me, and I was able to get a lot of things that other people didn't. But other than that and the fear of living within Greenville County, but while I was gone to college my parents wrote and told me they didn't know whether or not they wanted me to come back because I think it was [Willie Earle] that was lynched in Greenville, and, of course, that was very traumatic at that time.

I was in college and happened to be about the same age as Martin Luther King. He was at Morehouse, and I was at Clark and it's now called Clark Atlanta University.

Back then it was Clark University. Since then they have merged with the Atlanta University, which is a graduate school. So the two of them have merged. But anyway, I went there so he pledged Alpha fraternity, and I pledged Alpha Kappa Alpha. Met him, didn't know him that well, just remembered that, you know, we were all lined about the same time. So we got some of the experience that was happening in Atlanta, which helped us to understand a lot of things.

Of course, Atlanta back then was the Mecca for blacks, other than going to Howard in D.C. If you could be in D.C. at Howard or if you could go to Fisk, these were all good schools that blacks could attend. So I was very fortunate in that I was able to get a scholarship, and I was able to go to a good school. Plus my parents said if you work hard and you have a good average, we will do whatever, so I ended up valedictorian, so which meant that they came forward, and the lady that I was going to tell you about that was also one of my mentors. She worked at one of the buildings, had owned one of the buildings on Main Street, and my father worked there for her. And so she gave me, made sure that I did receive a Coca-Cola scholarship. Wrote some essays and all of these gave me money and, of course, when I got ready to go she gave me, picked up some clothes that I could go. So, when I got to Atlanta, although I didn't have what most of the young ladies had in Atlanta, that was one reason I didn't want to go to Spelman because I felt like that I would not fit in because I did not have the . . . and back then girls who went to Spelman, and Spelman was, as you know, the president was a white lady so it had a little bit more than Clark had, so I thought I could fit in Clark better. So that was the reason I chose Clark rather than to go to Spelman. But had a wonderful time in Atlanta.

One thing I still realized, that I was still in the South. There was a young man that was in my class by the name of Nehemiah Cooper, and he was from Africa. And we would all look out for each other so when we get ready to go, come back home during, we only came home during Christmas, didn't go home all the time, so we always rode the train. So everybody from New York all the way down to Atlanta, we would end up having most of the coaches, so we would have a great time coming back and had a wonderful time. But this one particular time, when I first met Nehemiah Cooper, we were going to the station, the railroad station in Atlanta, and he was sitting at the "wrong place," we thought. We were sitting in the place that said, blacks only, you know, or "Colored." Back then we said, "colored." Oou, Lord, I forgot about we used to say "colored" all the time. But anyway, it said "Colored Only," so we went over there and nicely told him to come out. We said, "You're in the wrong place."

And he said, "No, y'all are in the wrong place."

He let us know that he was from Africa, and he was in a different status. He said, "Y'all are slaves, y'all from slaves. I'm not a slave, and therefore I can go where I want to go in America."

So that was another reminder again you had to come back down to reality and realize that here we are in Atlanta, thinking we're doing a great thing and things were great, but then he reminded us, hey, you know, y'all are not full-time citizens. You know, you can't go places. And then we kind of started watching him, and he went anywhere he wanted to go. All he had to do was have that accent and talk about that he was from Africa. So, we realized that we could be anything but a black, a colored lady, or a colored man in America then you had second-class citizenship.

So constantly, even though I was able to get a lot of amenities that a lot of people didn't have, I soon realized that there was a place, that I needed to realize that's the way it was, you know. But then you start becoming bitter about the whole situation.

The civil rights movement didn't really get a hold then because I was in Atlanta from '46 to 1950. But you began to realize things that were changing. I remember in Atlanta it was entirely different, but when I got back to Greenville I was shocked, and I looked up on the billboard at Church Street and I saw these black women. That had not been before—they had black women, there were ads about cigarettes and all that, but before then black women did not have any beauty. We were not considered to be beautiful. That had been built up in me in Atlanta that I was just as beautiful as anyone else. And my mother had a lot to do with that. You know, you're not second class. So she had a lot to teach me to do that, so although I had these experiences I felt good about myself. I really did. So it made me smile when I looked up when I came home and looked up on the billboards to see that black women were being able to do ads, advertisements and all that we had not done before. So that made me feel great.

But in Greenville—and I decided to come back to Greenville to live. Now, why I made that decision I don't know, but I think it was basically because I loved my parents, and I realized that they had made a lot of sacrifices for us. I wanted to come back to make sure that we'd get a house that was kind of livable, you know, and so that's what I did and came back. So we set up so we could have, you know, better heat in our home. So that's what I did, and I came back to Greenville, so I guess it's one of the best things. So I got stuck in Greenville. I really did.

But the biggest part that I dealt with in the civil rights movement was in the '60s in Greenville. I happened to have belonged to Springfield Baptist Church, which in Greenville was the seat of the civil rights movement. Reverend J. S. Hall was my pastor, and then you had also working with him was Reverend A. J. Brockman, who just died. We're getting ready to have his funeral. And then also Reverend C. Mackie Daniels, and of course, these were the people in Greenville. We also at that time started working with A. J. Wittenberg, who was a part of it, and he belonged to my church. He was a trustee. So his daughter Elaine [Wittenberg Boise] was the one that kind of more or less opened up and started the suit against Greenville County and the school district about [the integration of] the schools in Greenville.

[See the interview with Elaine Wittenberg Boise in the section "Public Schools—'Freedom of Choice'" in volume 2 of this anthology.]

So I was able to get involved in all of that from the mere fact since I was a teacher now at the high school from which I had graduated, which was Sterling High School, I was able to work with the students in a kind of advisory thing to try to train them about nonviolence and all of that. So that's what we did within our school, although during that time there was, it's always something that makes you come back to reality. Sterling was burned and, of course, part of it's still up there. I don't know whether you got to see that or not.

ML: Yes, I did.

XN: Okay, so I was in the building the night that that burned. *[Telephone rings.]* Can you cut that 'cause I want to see if this man is coming to pick up my car?

[The recording is paused while Mrs. Norris takes the call.]

XN: . . . it was a training mode in that I was able to work with these students. I taught some of the people like Peterson and Margaree Seawright [Crosby] and Joan Madison all that who first sat in the library to open up the library. That's what we started with first, okay. And so we worked with that.

[An interview with Margaree Seawright Crosby will be found in volume 4.]

XN: Jesse Jackson, I also taught him. Jesse was in school at that time, so he came back and joined us during the summer to be a part of that to go into like Kress and Woolworth's and all of that.

And I had gotten married and my husband ran a barbershop, which at that time was a pretty good pay because it's a service job, so he made pretty good money. So what we did, we provided food to make sure—and gave them money to make sure that when they went places they had the money to go in. We also joined and, of course, the attorneys did the legal work. But we all had our places, and we had our roles to play. Mine was not, I was not involved other than walking like we walked for Robinson when he came here. I think it was Robinson.

[See the interview with Lottie Gibson above for a list of other accounts of the Jackie Robinson visit contained within this volume.]

ML: Jackie Robinson?

XN: Jackie Robinson. He came here, and of course [he could not use the waiting room] at the airport. We were in that march because he was discriminated against and had to go into the colored part of the airport.

We marched against that, but as far as the sit-ins are concerned, that was a movement of students, college students and high school students. High schools students were lively, high school and college students for the sit-ins in the places. So we kind of provided, we provided the money for that, so ours was advisory.

But at that time, as I said, was the time that Sterling was burned. Reasons were given other than they said it was not arson. We, however, feel that it was and also my church burned, Springfield was burned. So where we are located now, which is on the corner of McDaniel and Washington Street, it was given to us by McBee and the street is named after them. The McBee family gave us that building to try to . . . I guess a lot of white folks felt terrible about it because our church was burned. They say that basically that it was a problem of wiring and all that, but *we know that* [arson] *was the reason.* So, two places that I love very much, Sterling where I had attended school and I was working at that school, and then there was also my church that I love very dearly, grew up in that church. Although I had gone a lot to the Presbyterian Church I think I told you about, Springfield was my church because my father was a deacon there. So my roots are basically with the Presbyterian Church and with the Baptist. But when that church was burned, it really took a lot out of me. It really did.

So, as you go through all of these problems that we had at that time, it can make you very bitter. But the struggle is still continuing for me. That was one reason when my husband died I decided that I would run for county council. And, of course, I'm on county council, and as you know now we are still struggling because a lot of the whites who live over in the other areas of the county, Greenville, the city of Greenville, is different from the county. And so you have these people who cannot vote for a Martin Luther King holiday, or they went on to still say that he was a man that did not support the [Vietnam] war, that he was a man that also was a womanizer. They won't even talk about him winning his Nobel Peace Prize and all of that. That doesn't make any sense to them and they want to talk about all these [other] things. So it's been a very bad struggle. It's been about eighteen years that we have been struggling with that process.

So we've had a march here in 2002, I believe the spring of 2002 with Jesse [Jackson], and that was a very good march, but of course, everybody disappeared. The whites disappeared so as we marched it was mostly just blacks. There were a few whites there. So I think a lot of people still are in denial about, you know, the rights of our having justice and equal rights. That's hard. We helped build America. A lot of us fought in the war[s], a lot of the men did. But they cannot even—they still have all of these things about—and that came out in county council when we had people coming in, whites coming from almost everywhere with the flag, the Confederate flag, you know.

I realize now that it's still a struggle and probably will still be a struggle until some of this . . . So what I did—and mine has always been one where I use what I could to negotiate—what we did this summer is that we worked on getting rid of some of those Republicans that were on county council. So we were able to—I guess you've heard all of this—we've been able to disqualify . . . three people did not win their *reelection.* Although we didn't have any Democrats to win that we were able to get *moderate* Republicans to win. So seemingly now we might be able to make some strides. Hopefully we'll get the Martin Luther King holiday [recognized] because we're the only county that's probably left in the state of South Carolina with not being able to do that. So mine was one—I taught civics lessons during the time that we were getting this election—I taught people that you can go in and ask for a Republican ballot. You don't have to ask for a Democratic ballot. They didn't understand that so I had to teach that to them and Lottie and I, Lottie Gibson and I, I don't know if you talked to Lottie or not . . .

[See the interview with Lottie Gibson above.]

ML: Not yet, but I . . .

XN: Okay, okay, and so we were able to go in and work with them and do that and we were able to. . . . So you might have to sometimes use what you have in order to get where you want to get and so that's what I did.

I went to Boston as a delegate [to the Democratic Convention] for South Carolina. Came back and I realized that we had a lot to do in South Carolina and that even with people like Inez Tannenbaum that I thought was a great lady, I felt like that when we got back because, it was not there. I *knew* it was not going to be there. *[She is referring to the votes for the Martin Luther King Jr. holiday.]*

But I worked for the summer. Edith Chew and I were roommates [at the convention], and Edith is a white friend of mine. We're very good friends. So Edith and I did a lot of registration. We walked the streets. We encouraged people. We went to a lot of the senior citizens to make sure that they were registered and would have rides. So that's what we did, and then Lottie and I went in the area of the three [county] districts. and we worked hard with those people to let them realize that this is your right. You can do this. . . .

Lottie was a grassroots person across the years. She and others have worked through the NAACP. I joined the NAACP but Lottie was here and worked at it. Her husband ended up being national president of the NAACP, so consequently hers was much more involved than mine. But mine was more intellectually with the students that I had that admired me and I admired them. So I was able to do the training, which to me I am happy that I was able to do it.

Also, I was on the board of the YWCA, which was an organization that really worked during the time of integration. So we started about six or eight months before [integration of the schools] to make sure that we would have not a lot of turmoil during the time of integration. So I was working then at Greenville High School, at the end of segregation and the beginning of integration. I went to Greenville High School and now was a counselor, ended up being head counselor, so I have those counseling skills that have been a lot of me.

So, I want you to realize is that mine has been one of advising, of working with students, then also helping them to get into college, to open up their horizons that the lady had done for me, Mrs. Finley had done for me during the time. So I served for a catalyst for a lot of students. "You can do it." "You can go to college." I'll make sure that this is done, do their financial aid, still doing it.

I had thirty-four years in the school district, ten years with the Greenville Urban League, and with the Urban League my position was working with Talent Search. So what I did I provided SAT and ACT training programs. I carried kids on college trips. I went to places that would give them a break like Berea College and a lot of colleges in Alabama that I knew that they could go there cheaply. So that's been my role basically, so when I served on the board of the YMCA, I was able to make some roads there, some inroads that we were able to do a lot of things for the children.

So in my small way I have been able to—it's because of the struggles that I've had, knowing how you feel and how people can make you think that you are little but that you can rise above that. That's basically the role that I have played, not only with students, but also this summer I did it with adults. So that's where we are in the struggle, and it's going to be a long struggle.

I tell my little boys, I have six grandchildren, three girls and three boys, and I have two great-grand boys. And so I take care of them in the morning and take him to the nursery school. So the Lord has blessed me. I'm seventy-five years old and the Lord has blessed me, and so I'm still able to move around, get up and walk in the mornings and get my exercise and, you know, that's where I am and that's what I've done. Got any questions?

ML: Yeah, we'll fill in just a few blanks. You mentioned about Springfield Baptist Church as being a center for organizing in the civil rights movement. Was it primarily the church or the NAACP?

XN: Through the NAACP, and we had the student NAACP. One of my daughters, they sent her during the movement to learn about student rights, so my daughter was a part of that. But it basically because of the NAACP that this was done. The Urban League plays a different role. It's not a grassroots organization. I worked at the Urban League and it's a fine organization, but it was really the NAACP. So you had people like "Quincey" Newman and all of them that, you know, worked. It was because of the NAACP and getting the students involved, that "You can do it," "I want you to be a member . . ." Horace Nash and Leola Roberson were, Leola was a student of mine. I had known Horace and he was relative of mine. So because of them they got the NAACP youth movement moving, and that was why my church was known at that time—because J. S. Hall was a mover and a shaker during that time. . . .

ML: How did you decide to run for public office? Tell me about that experience. When were you elected or when did you run?

XN: I was elected in March in 1997. My husband died in December '96, and my husband and I had talked about it and he had told me, "I don't know whether or not you . . ." and he was retiring at that time so we said, we need to be together and enjoy life some, but on the morning that he died, on the morning before he died, he died that evening, he said, "Are you still thinking about running?"

I said, "Well, you know, we talked about it and . . ."

He looked at me and said, "Well, maybe you better think about it, you know." And then he asked—my husband loved money—and then he said, "Don't you get paid for it?"

I said, "Yes, but not that much."

He said, "Well, maybe should look at it."

And that evening he died, you know.

ML: It was like him giving you permission, encouraging you.

XN: Encouraged me to do it, so after that . . . I had a lot of friends. . . . I've lived in this neighborhood since the early '60s. . . . So a lot of the people who live in this area, and a lot of them I taught them when they were at Sterling, so they came around, so they said, "Maybe you need to run. That will give you something to do."

I said, "Oh, I'll find a lot of things to do," but I kept thinking, listening to them, and so it has been a challenge, but I've truly enjoyed it because again, you know, I'm able to work things out and then able to do things.

Lottie had worked some before me, and the year I came in—no it wasn't, it was in 2000—I made the motion to have a Martin Luther King holiday. So she and I joined together to try and work this out. So that's when I made up my mind. And so everybody says, how did you get into it? It was because of the death of my husband that I ended up doing that. . . . My children have been very supportive of it, and the grandkids are real proud of me. "Grandma, I see you on TV."

I say, "It's more than that . . . ," you know, but they enjoy it and so they're very supportive of me. . . .

So, you know, it's been a joy for me. It's been a pleasure and I'm doing what I want to do. Passion, I have a passion for children and kids, so that's where I made my greatest contributions. So now what I'm doing, I'm doing scholarship programs. I'm getting ready in March the 31st to have the UNC, I'm the chair of that.

ML: UNC?

XN: United Negro College Fund, UNC. So last year was my first year with that. I was the gala chair, and so we raised $150,000 there. So this year we're going to have a little bit more because I already have about that much already. I also work with the J. E. Sirrine Scholarships within the school district. I'm able to do this because I've had a lot of experience in financial aid. Used to do the financial aid forms, FASFA and all of those, so I'm still doing that. And then at my church I'm chairman of the college ministry, so I have a thing that I do there. My kids that I have in church I was able to give them four-hundred-dollar book awards in December for them to go back to school, and that's not counting the scholarship that I plan to give at the end. So I'm into a lot of scholarships.

I also do the Miss South Carolina pageant. I have a franchise that's called the Palmetto Franchise, so I work with young ladies to help them to get that training and for the scholarships. A lot of times they say, "But it's a beauty pageant."

I say, "Not for me. It's a scholarship program." So what we do is try to provide scholarships—for the top one is fifteen hundred dollars, [second] eight hundred dollars, and [third] six hundred dollars. They can take that, they can buy books, and help them in school. So I'm still doing that, all involved in the passion of helping kids to better themselves, so that's what I'm about now.

ML: Yes, that's wonderful. . . .

XN: Yes, so I've done three terms [on county council]. What I did, I ran for Fletcher Smith's seat when he went to Columbia. So I ran and was elected in March of '97 because they went ahead and just immediately went ahead and installed me. And so then I ran again for my own term. So this is my third term, but the first term was not a full one.

ML: Do you have programs and things like that?

XN: Yes. This is March '97. That's when I was first installed . . .

ML: Are there any other community leaders, black or white, that stand out in your mind as really having made a difference?

XN: Yes, of course. There was, you know, Attorney Sampson, and Attorney Willie T. Smith. All of them worked during that time, Fletcher's son, but it was mostly, you know, those two gentlemen that provided most of the leadership for us during the time of the struggle. And then, of course, there was Leroy Shelton, who was a person who also went, and he was the one that, who was the bondsman that provided, you know, getting the kids out of jail. He was an entrepreneur in Greenville during that time.

Willie T. Smith, he became a judge, family court judge. And then, of course, there was Mitchell, that used to be a senator.

ML: Theo Mitchell.

XN: Theo Mitchell. And, of course, A. J. Wittenberg, who was the, he was the president of the local Greenville NAACP. And so, as I said, his daughter Elaine was the [court case] for the integration in Greenville County schools. Let's see who else. There were different times then later on in elections. . . . Lottie and Dr. Bill Gibson continued their work with the NAACP, not only with that, but also in the election. I remember they were very instrumental in getting [Richard "Dick"] Riley to become the governor, and we continuously worked with them. So, you know, those are, I would say . . . S. T. Payton, who now works with Institutional Resources, which helps to build the schools, and he worked at that time also for GE [General Electric]. During the time he was working for GE, and then, of course, he's retired there now. He's working with Institutional Resources, which are the persons responsible for the building of the schools. I know I'm missing somebody else. Oh, there's—and he was very good—and his name is Sam Zimmerman. Sam was very good. He started out in the school district, and he worked a while with the school district and then he went into, he finally ended up as a journalist with the *Greenville News.* So you had people doing things at different levels, you know. They had people in journalism and they had, like I say, attorneys, and you had all these people that were providing services for during this time.

Our pastor died, no, he didn't die. He left Greenville and went to Philadelphia, and after that we had Reverend D. C. Frances, who ended up being the person that continued to struggle at Springfield Baptist Church with civil rights.

ML: He followed Hall?

XN: He followed Hall, yes. So this is our church after our church was burned. This is the picture of the inside of our church when we were able to have a project done on it, so after that.

ML: Did Reverend Corbett follow D. C. Francis then?

XN: Yeah, he did. Reverend D. C. Francis died, and Reverend Corbett came. Reverend Corbett is more or less low key. His forte has been within the National Baptist

Convention, he and Reverend A. C. Cureton. Reverend A. C. Cureton also he served as, Corbett served as the dean for the national conference. . . . We've had a long struggle with Bob Jones too.

ML: Oh, yes. Making any progress?

XN: Well, I don't know. *[There is a telephone interruption.]* They're the ones, we don't all have the same philosophy. As you said, we don't have the same philosophy about education and a lot of the things. So it's been a big struggle, and it's infiltrated Greenville County Council, and these men have also put the ones that we have on county council, they have infiltrated the boards, many of the boards that we have like the disability board and, you know, GTA, Greenville Transit Authority. So you have all this philosophy that has kind of gone in, and it makes it very difficult to get things done. And so that's a problem for me. . . .

ML: I greatly appreciate you sharing your story for the anthology.

XN: Okay, it's been nice meeting you.

ML: Likewise. It's so encouraging that people keep up the struggle.

XN: Yes, right.

ML: It seems like—we're lucky if you take two steps forward and one back.

XN: Yes, and it's going to be a struggle for quite a while, it is. Hopefully, we might be able to pull something through within the next week, but I'm not sure. If not, it will be April before we get anything done with the Martin Luther King holiday. But we might be able to do something next week. We have a strategy that we're trying to do right now.

ML: Well, best of luck to you on it. Well, thank you so much.

[The holiday was approved the following week, February 2, 2005.]

Matthew Douglas McCollom, Peace, Peace, Where There Is No Peace

Grace McFadden **[GM]**:* I'm Grace Jordan McFadden, with Reverend Dr. Matthew Douglas McCollom. Reverend McCollom is a native of Lee County, South Carolina. He is a United Methodist minister, past president of the South Carolina Conference of NAACP. He is currently campus minister, serving the Orangeburg community.

I'd like to begin by asking you to just give a brief historic background of Reverend McCollom.

Matthew McCollom **[MM]**: Well, I don't know what you mean by brief. When I begin to talk about myself, I just go on and on and on. Actually, I am the son of a United Methodist minister, so that we moved all over South Carolina with my father and throughout my own ministries, I've lived in most sections of the state, and have had pastorates in Greenwood, and in Orangeburg here, in Charleston, and then was a district superintendent of the Walterboro District. Currently I am campus minister here in Orangeburg, director of the Wesley Foundation, a United Methodist ministry to the college community, so to speak, sort of minister-at-large to the college community.

I have been involved in the civil rights movement, particularly here in Orangeburg. I was pastor here from 1950 to 1962, during which time I served as president of the local branch of NAACP, at the time when the 1954 school desegregation decision was handed down by the Supreme Court. I was local president of the NAACP, so that that catapulted me into the limelight, as well as into a lot of danger. But as time went

*Grace Jordan McFadden conducted the interview with McCollom (1912–1980) on videotape in conjunction with South Carolina Educational Television in 1982. It is archived by the African American Studies Program of the University of South Carolina. This is a transcription the audio of that interview. The subtitle for this interview ("Peace, peace . . .") is taken from Jeremiah 6:14.

by, my position as president of the NAACP here opened doors to membership in the Southern Christian Leadership Conference—I'm a charter member of Martin Luther King's organization—and to any number of other involvements and organizations. It's been a challenge and a privilege to have participated in all of these.

GM: Reverend McCollom, when you were with the NAACP in the 1950s, following the 1954 decision, you mentioned that there was a lot of danger and adventure. What did you mean by that?

MM: One can be even more than literal in referring to that because prior to the announcement of the decision, on May 17, 1954, our local NAACP presidency was a very ho-hum, innocuous kind of thing. It carried with it no prestige or notoriety or anything else, but when the decision was pronounced, immediately the reaction of the white community brought NAACP officialdom into very open scrutiny.

We were the "enemy of all civilization," as it were. "Here you are, trying to integrate our schools," and "This is the worst thing in the world, and we're not going to have it," and "You're the ones who are pushing this, you and some outsiders that we can't identify." And so all of the efforts that must be marshaled to prevent integration must be aimed at the NAACP leadership.

Hardly any one of us, especially in towns where the movement really warmed up to the boiling point, hardly any of us expected to be *alive today.* But the challenge was there and the opportunity was there, and you knew that something significant was happening, and it needed leadership, and you couldn't just turn tail and run, so you stood your ground. And at times you had to say, "You can kill me but you can't stop me!"

It got just exactly to that point, and there are many of us who believe that the one reason we did not get killed, assassinated, was that it would have reflected too badly on the white community, so they spared our lives, to save their own sense of shame. It really came to that.

GM: The black church serves more than as a religious institution.

MM: Oh, by all means! A place of social gathering—only in the last ten years has the black community had access to the black school. Have you ever heard of a civil rights rally being held in a public school? Not at all. The lodge hall isn't large enough to hold a public gathering, so where do black people go when they need to hear about freedom, and about progress, and about full citizenship, and about manhood and womanhood? They go to the church and they listen to the minister. There is no other place that was open to us.

The black church has by and large been the focal point for social activities. In my youth, I remember black magicians coming around, and they would have their thing in the church. I remember the Williams Singers, and the Fisk Jubilee Singers, and the —Johnson Singers. When they would be on tour, they would come to the black church. I remember, for instance, down in Kingstree when my father was pastor . . . You say your husband has some roots down that way?

GM: Yes.

MM: I remember an occasion on which one of these outstanding groups came to sing at our church, and there were *white* people sitting in the best seats in the place. I recall asking my father, I must have been twelve, thirteen, "What are these people doing here? They don't belong to our church. Why have they got the best seats in the house?"

My father could not answer. All he could say was that, "Well, they're our guests, and I'll explain it to you later."

His explanation was never really satisfactory. It may be that my concern for that kind of discrimination and pushing the black aside so that the white might have some privilege, that my thinking was beginning to solidify, even as far back as that. In going around trying to get a job in the tobacco warehouse, we black youngsters always had the meanest jobs, and you could go and cut somebody's lawn, but you were always eating your lunch on the back porch, or on the steps. You were going around to the side door if you wanted to buy something. You always had to go to the back door if you wanted to approach a white person's house. This kind of thing. I could never understand why that should be, and nobody was ever able to explain it to me.

It just may be that my interest in civil rights, and my involvement in it, began way back there, because none of those explanations were ever satisfactory to me. There was never a black policeman. One black fireman, as I recall, because he knew how to fix the fire truck when it broke down. But in all of these public places of position and privilege, there was never any black person, and I always wondered why that was. Nobody could ever explain it. We had to sit way upstairs in the theater, in a "buzzard's roost" to see a movie in Kingstree and in Camden, where we lived, and in Orangeburg when we came here and I was a high school and college boy. I could never understand that, and nobody could ever explain it to me. "Oh well, that's just the way it is."

So that I've always had an interest in that kind of thing, and it seems to me that it was kind of natural that I should react as I did when things began to warm up here in Orangeburg in the mid-'50s, even though by that time, I was in my mid-thirties.

GM: What was your father's name?

MM: He was S. M. McCollom, Reverend Samuel Marion McCollom.

GM: Reverend McCollom, when you were mentioning that in your father's church when the group came, the white people were sitting in the best seats. It seems that, historically, black churches have been open to white people. White churches have been closed to blacks. How do you assess the whole notion of what David Walker called in the 1920s, "Jim Crow Christianity"?

MM: That seemed such—to the people of the time—that seemed such a natural thing that hardly anybody questioned it. I would suppose that somebody, some young adult, would say, "Well, he can come over to your church and preach, Pop, but how is it that he never invites you over to his church?" Or something like that.

But there was never any answer. And always on the marquee out front of the white church there was a sign saying, "Everybody Welcome," but somehow or other we just knew that it didn't mean us, so that we never made any move toward going there to worship. So that we sort of sublimated the thing, or rationalized it, to say that, "Oh, well, white preachers can't half preach anyhow. They just get up there and read some poems and tell some jokes—and many of them do—and they don't half preach anyway so we wouldn't enjoy it so we may as well stay in the black church where we know there's some *real* preaching going on."

But we knew all the time that that was about as hypocritical a way of practicing Christianity as anybody could. There is no way in the world for rational people to practice Christianity on that level, without blocking out of their minds so much of the true heart-meaning of the Christian faith. Like an incident that was related by a girl in Summerville. She said that in her Sunday school class they were talking about Christian love, and she finally had to ask, "Well now, all right, you say love everybody"—this was a white girl—"love everybody, let's love everybody. Well, love people of Africa?"

"Oh, by all means."

"And love the people of all the nations of the world?"

"Yes, by all means."

"And love the England people?"

"Oh yes."

"And love the yellow people?"

"Yes."

"And love Martin Luther King?"

"Are you out of your mind!"

You know . . . this kind of thing. Only by considering what prejudice really means can you begin to understand how they could do this.

GM: Reverend McCollom, in the 1890s the great abolitionist and freedom fighter, Frederick Douglass, observed that if the Christian church were half Christianized that there would be a cry up to heaven against the wrongs that had been perpetrated against black people. Then you observe, more than fifty years later, that the Reverend Martin Luther King Jr. maintained that it was the responsibility of black Americans to make the ideals of American democracy operative. I wonder how you assess this observation.

MM: Well, the statement is true, as far as it goes. The difficulty with it is that you're calling upon the powerless people to move the powerful people. It's almost impossible. It has happened. We have done it, but it's been a miracle all the way, and there have been frustrations and setbacks all the way.

From the time that Reconstruction ended there was a deliberate effort to turn back the clock to as near slavery conditions as possible. The separate-but-equal doctrine and that sort of thing. The black codes, so far as voting was concerned. To be sure, what we experienced in the political arena was also true of the area of religion. How people could pronounce such things as are pronounced in our Declaration of Independence and the Constitution and Preamble and that sort of thing—how they could stand up and say these things and then live daily the absolute contradiction of them is more than most of us can understand. There is no way of rationalizing it except to say that while we say all of these things, at the same time we are really selfish human beings, self-serving, self-seeking, and we build up myths, and we resort to clichés and stereotypes in order to get our own way, in order to create advantage for ourselves, and it is this kind of pride and arrogance and self-seeking and self-serving that permit us to live such contradictions, such hypocritical lives.

I had the occasion to read very recently Frederick Douglass's Fourth of July speech. It's a marvelous thing, you know, the kind of thing I had been saying without reading it. I had read it previously, of course, but to find him saying things and expressing such contempt for the kind of hypocrisy that has been exhibited in—quote-unquote—"the white man's sense of democracy and freedom and justice." Disgusting! There are hardly any words—we don't know the words with which to characterize such contradiction, such hypocrisy—so that for a while we tried to roll with the punch and say, "We're not looking for social equality. All we want is justice." Well, the one would imply the other. We're not looking for social equality. All we want are equal schools. How are you going to have equal schools if the white people are in charge of all the decisions, all the money, all the school lines, the textbook commission, the tax commission, which assesses all the taxes and that sort of thing.

People now talk about going back to neighborhood schools. Back? We never had any neighborhood. . . . There were some schools placed in our neighborhoods, but we never had any control over them! And there were clichés that we used which were altogether out of harmony with the truth, but we used them as if they were true. And we just went along and hoped that nobody would rock the boat.

Happily enough, the NAACP came along in 1909 with a concern for not only the fact that blacks were being lynched at more than a hundred a year without any redress, but that the old separate-but-equal thing, which by that time was only ten or twelve years old, was touching every phase of black life. The NAACP was organized to address all of those inequalities, and if you have any sense of the history of the fight for equal schools, or the fight for justice in the courts, or the fight to eradicate lynching, or the fight for equal job opportunities, or the fight for public accommodations, or the fight for the right to vote . . . "All men are created equal," you know, and "the right to vote shall not be abridged by any state, et cetera, et cetera." And yet I had absolutely no right to cast a vote until I was in my mid-thirties!—1948 or '9, along there. Judge Waring [helped see to that].

It had been the implication on down across the years that blacks have no rights that whites have to respect. In regards to voting, let's have a political club and we'll call it the Democrat club, and we'll elect public officers and they will be the officers over a whole population, and they'll assess the taxes and they'll be the mayor and they'll be the sheriff, but of course, only our members can vote, and even though the sheriff is going to arrest this black person, who had no say-so in his election, that's the way it ought to be. So the old *Dred Scott* decision. . . . And in public education, in South Carolina, in many school districts, out of the school dollar, they spent ninety cents on the white child and ten cents on the black child. There was nothing wrong with that. The old *Dred Scott* decision, you know. Who cared and who could do anything about it?

People lived with these contradictions, and when we went as high as the Supreme Court, it is found that not even the Supreme Court was willing to address such basic constitutional questions as to whether the *Dred Scott* decision was still operative in America. And what we had only yesterday, in the [proposed] Mottle Amendment. Here was an opportunity, so far as he was concerned, to turn back the clock to 1857, *Dred Scott*. You're talking about the rights of black children to equal protection of the laws, but these rights of black children must fall in the face of some white people's comfort and desire and whim. The black rights must fall by the wayside if some white person has something that he greatly desires to place over against it. And happily not. The house summarily and soundly rejected the Mottle Amendment on yesterday, and I laid awake all night last night thanking God for it!

Only little by little, by organization with the intelligent approach of attacking the whole system and its legal roots and its ideological roots, could it be hoped that we could get rid of that kind of invidious segregation that kept us out of every meaningful thing, except that when you got in your own house at night you could lock the door and feel some of the togetherness with your family, feel maybe you have something to say about what happens in your own house, except that then the Ku Klux Klansmen might put on their bed sheets and ride down and intimidate everybody. I remember those rides. You'd pull down the shades, turn off the light, and hold your breath, literally, in fear of some stupid atrocity that those otherwise intelligent people made in the image of God might perpetrate against the black community.

I think all of this is the same thing—Christian people, they do this! Ku Klux Klansmen do this because they're Christians, and the rest of the white community puts up with it because they're Christians, and that's the way they interpret Christianity. *Peace* between the races, and separation between the races. This is perhaps the most overriding factor among the "Christian virtues." How it could be elevated to that point, none of us can know, but that's the way they think and that's the way they feel, and they can find scriptures to back up such foolishness.

GM: So then the burden of making the ideals of American democracy operative rest upon black people.

MM: They have rested upon us because if you look at it plainly, you will have to admit that at no point in American history has our leadership, our federal government, made a solid commitment to justice and equality for minorities. Not at any point! I had hoped that at the point of the Bicentennial we would have made a commitment to make America really free, by 1976. But nobody even thought of it. In NAACP we tried to put the idea, but our national leaders didn't take the bait. "*Really* free by '76." "Out of this fix by '76."

"No."

So that when progress has taken place, it will be discovered that people have moved only as far as we have been able to push them. And we have been able to push them only as far as we have been able to marshal our intelligence and our will, our desire for freedom. To marshal this and to show them up and to bring their own laws into court, into their courts, to show them where the justice ought to be and where the inequity has existed, and what you ought to do about it. There are still some basic questions which must be addressed by the Supreme Court.

GM: Is there a need for a theology of liberation?

MM: There are many who think that there is such a need. Actually, in the black church, for a long time there was the need to let off some steam, to equalize the situation between the races. There are many things of which we suffer now, many deprivations, but, "One of these days, in heaven we're going to have milk and honey, we're going to make up for all the things that we have suffered."

So that a lot of the preaching dealt with that kind of subject matter. There are many people who think that it was unnecessary and just so much hot air, but actually, without an opportunity to blow off steam, emotionally and otherwise, in church, you would have had chaos. If people couldn't get up in church and shout and sing and release some of their pent-up frustrations, they would have released those frustrations in fighting and wrangling and in disrupting society, so that as long as these preachings [*sic*] and worship services were carried on in a context of promoting moral, spiritual values, Christian values, this was good.

However, as time went by, and we became more and more possessed of the necessities of life, were less and less deprived of some of the necessities and have some of the amenities, actually, there is less and less a need to live with one foot in heaven. Some of us really never had it so good. We have money in the bank, and some of the comforts, so that the emphasis on heaven is no longer necessary, not viable.

But even those who escaped some of the economic deprivations continue to suffer politically. The fight for equality in the public schools, for instance, has been almost like a step-daughter, so far as legislation is concerned. "How can you not love yourself?" This is liberationist theology. Because you are born in the image of God, you have inalienable rights. Not because our Constitution or Declaration of Independence would say that you have these rights, but unalienable rights, *God given*, because you're made in his image. This is where the church stands.

So often when I hear a young person say the church doesn't mean anything to him, I have to remind him that from the beginning in America, the church is the *only* agency that has been saying to you and about you, "You are a child of God. You're not a *thing*. You're not a thing. You're not something to be used and abused and taken advantage of and proscribed and disfranchised. *You* are a child of God." The church has said this about you. Now you treat yourself this way. And if the church didn't do anything else, if it only stood there and proclaimed every day, "You are a child of God. You're a *somebody*," it would fulfill its basic functions. That's what the church is all about. To make people know that they belong to God, and He belongs to them. And that's why they have rights and value and worth.

Gloria Rackley Blackwell and Her Daughters Jamelle Rackley-Riley and Lurma Rackley, Part 1

Roots of a Storm

Growing Up

Gloria Blackwell [GB]:* When I grew up, there was no other church and no other denomination. Mother was not the type—because she was a minister's daughter—it wasn't as though this is the *only* way and all that kind of foolishness, but we were Methodist. That's what we were.

So we went to all the conferences and all the meetings, everything. I was the only girl and she would sit in the conferences and really entertain me. I don't know if she was doing it consciously or what. *[She whispers much of the following.]* She would tell me all the little things. . . . That's so and so . . . His son is . . . And not gossiping but like, you know, his son is . . maybe at Gammon now, studying theology. He was the first president of the Methodist Youth Fellowship. . . . And that's so-and-so's wife, and . . .

Marvin Lare [ML]: It's a wonder that she didn't marry you off to a Methodist minister *[laughs]*.

Lurma Rackley [LR]: She might have had that planned. She didn't have a very willing daughter.

ML: Mind of your own.

---

*The interview took place at the home of Lurma Rackley, daughter of Dr. Blackwell (1927–2010), in Peachtree City, Georgia, on January 17, 2005, and was transcribed by Catherine Mann for the USC South Caroliniana Library.

GB: As a little girl growing up, I think that my interest in . . . I guess now we could call it civil rights, but it was just natural growing up. I was a Methodist. My mother was a Methodist minister's daughter, and I have always thought of—maybe just because of the perspective or the background that she brought to the church—I've always thought of the Methodist Church as being an organization for social concerns. I really think that's what Methodism is. Of course, Christianity is there and that's the base, but we are supposed to be in . . . The commission [in the church] that I always chose—I always went to the Commission on Christian Social Concerns because I just thought that was really what it was all about.

And so in the church and through the church you did the things a Christian was supposed to do, you know. You visited the sick. My mother was a teacher and she was always— Somebody is sick, we're going out to feed someone, or we're taking some clothes or whatever was necessary, and those were the things that we did. And teaching—for Mother, teaching was certainly not a way to make money. I think they worked for script sometimes in the '30s. She taught because she truly believed that that was a mission, that people needed to learn. She was very, very serious about that. In those days, if you didn't learn, you might have gotten a spanking! Right? *[She laughs.]* You didn't just get a scolding.

So, the church was the center.

Now Daddy, it was Daddy more—not that Mother was against it, but Mother was so busy in those things. It was Daddy who took me to NAACP meetings. I remember being young and going to Columbia and listening to [Reverend James] Hinton speak. I can't remember when that was, but we went to NAACP meetings where there were big rallies in South Carolina. Big might have been very small. . . .

ML: But as a child it would have [seemed] . . .

GB: Yes, and we were going a long ways. Columbia is eighty miles from Little Rock [Dillon County, South Carolina], so that was a big trip and we would go over to the NAACP meetings. I can remember, Hinton was just a very important person and a very important name. That was just something, to being doing those things.

And my uncle was very involved in that also, but I can't remember that being significant to me. That was my mother's uncle, her mother's brother. I can't remember that having any importance to me. But, I remember getting that magazine all the time too.

LR: *Crisis?*

GB: Yes, it seems to me that we got the magazine, but I can't remember being aware then of Du Bois, but just the whole idea of what the NAACP was. We were getting memberships earlier, and then later—this was after Lurma was born I guess—I remember coming back home after a divorce and living there at home for a while and going around the chapters and dives. I was going around all in the "highways and hedges" and cotton fields and everything getting memberships to revive the NAACP chapter that was pretty strong when I went away from home. We were trying to get a strong chapter in Dillon County, South Carolina.

It was always there. I don't remember any time when we were not socially conscious and socially active, and I don't remember that as being anything different. That was just like brushing your teeth.

ML: Who you were.

GB: Yes, things that you did. That was just what you did.

Watershed Events

ML: What are some of the things that really stand out in your mind as being the watershed events both in your own experience and in the things that you led?

LR: Maybe during the actual Orangeburg movement, the demonstrations and so forth.

GB: Yes, because I don't recall, like Bennie Mays remembers, of somebody being lynched when he was young. I don't remember any trauma like that when I was young. Things were going along pretty well it seems to me. Now, we certainly lived in the segregated South, and things were ugly all the time just as a part of the fabric of South Carolina, but as far as our personal lives, it seems as though everything was all right.

The thing that precipitated the Orangeburg situation was that we were members of the NAACP and Matt [Reverend Matthew McCollom] was the president at that particular time. We were always doing NAACP things and so you just go. You're part of the NAACP, whether they have any big thing going or not, you go and do your memberships and talk about issues.

In Orangeburg we had, among other things, a hospital that was . . . the regional hospital for the counties, and black people had almost no—they had accommodations but as I understand it they were down under the hospital. I don't know if that was a real basement or what it was down there, but they say that it was just truly horrendous and unsanitary, that you could go into visit someone and the examining gloves that had been used could be lying around in a chair. It was just awful.

We had two colleges in Orangeburg and the faculty members and . . . almost anybody who needed medical care tried to go up to . . . the campuses and use the infirmaries because we would not go to *that* hospital. I never went. I really don't know what that facility was like because I never visited that hospital. We just knew it was a terrible place. But some people had to go for emergencies, and we were trying, through the NAACP, to get someone who went there to serve as a . . .

LR: Plaintiff?

GB: Yes, a plaintiff, around whom we could build, if not a case, to sue, or at least take some action to talk with the administrators.

LR: Do you remember what year that was, the late '50s?

GB: Late '50s and around '60 because that's what precipitated this matter.

You can't get . . . we found it *wryly* amusing, that you really can't get a person to sue the doctors who you are going to—who are in the process of operating on them or treating them, right?

ML: Yes.

GB: So the people we needed were the people who were least able to put up a fight or start a fight. So we would write letters to the hospital, and they would ignore the letters. That was one of the things we were doing. We were also writing to the Citizens' Council. We had a White Citizens' Council in Orangeburg, and all those little organizations making statements and doing things that were very, very negative and really incendiary, making statements about what black people should or should not being doing and what they were doing and how there would never be integration. . . . We're trying to address these things and they're ignoring us or maybe occasionally writing some sort of answer that was more insulting than silence or no answer.

So Jamelle, the daughter who will come in later, was in high school and hurt her finger. I was teaching in an elementary school there, and their father was teaching at South Carolina State. . . . She was playing in the gym and hurt her hand, dislocating her finger and it had to be reset. My principal at the elementary school came over, came to my room, and told me that Jamelle had been rushed to the hospital. He was sending a sub to my room, and he wanted me to rush over because she was not responding well to whatever was happening. They needed me to get over there right away.

I rushed over, and when I got to an examining room, she was hysterical. They had given her a sedative or whatever they do and, you know, sometimes they have an adverse reaction. Anyway, she was just carrying on so I rushed to her and was soothing her. She quieted down and they took her upstairs for, it wasn't really surgery, but she had to go to surgery to get this thing done because they had to knock her out.

We were left in the emergency room, and I was so drained from this thing. A woman said, "Oh"—she's so nice and started picking up our things—and she said, "You know, you can't stay in here because this is an emergency room, but you can go down in the waiting room," and did her hand like that *[waving toward the right]*, but there was nothing out there. There was just a hallway and a Coke machine or something, some vending machines, and some crates around it, and the crates were sitting on end. I think there may have been some persons sitting on one of the crates. But I recognized, even though I was drained and emotionally upset from Jamelle, I recognized that that was not a waiting room, and I just assumed that this woman had made a mistake. I knew better, but I say that I assumed that she had forgotten right from left. She motioned this way but she probably meant that way *[motioning toward the left]*. And so I went the other way to the waiting room.

There was a nice waiting room. There was leather furniture and everything. I went and sat, and that resulted in my being arrested. They came and got me and took me way, took me to jail.

Jim Sulton came. He was treasurer of the NAACP. He came rushing down and posted the—I didn't have to go into a cell or anything. By the time we got there, shortly after . . . I got there with the two plainclothes policemen, a police car in front of me and a police car behind me, taking me to . . .

ML: Dangerous person *[laughs]*.

Gloria Rackley Blackwell.

Orangeburg Movement

LR: But you know, Mama, the movement was already going by the time that happened.

GB: Oh, yes.

LR: I thought you were suggesting that that was what kicked off the Orangeburg movement, but you understood, Mr. Lare, that the movement was already in full swing by the time that happened?

ML: Yes, although things don't have to go exactly in sequence.

LR: Right, the movement itself with the kids picketing and stuff on the campuses started in the late '50s.

GB: Yes, . . . by the time we as a family got involved, they had already had that *major* thing with the [fire hoses], because you were not involved when the first group of kids were put behind the fence. We might have been out in Oklahoma or somewhere, but something had happened before we physically got out on the street and started picketing. I don't remember. I don't think we were on the street when the hospital thing occurred. We had already been on the street.

LR: Yes, that's why you were such a figure. That's why they had all those police cars.

GB: Why they were scared, because they knew my name already.

LR: Yes, you were already in the movement by the time that happened.

ML: They thought that this was really a test case, and all it was, was that you were with your daughter there.

GB: Well, we were happy it was a test case now. We were really happy and even when a woman came up and said, "What is this?" Because we were kind of weary about this, and I asked them, "Do you want to handcuff us?"

Jamelle Rackley-Riley.

They said, "Come this way," these two plain[clothes police], and they said, "Oh, no." And they were so nervous they would not even touch me or anything. They didn't want anything against them.

And Miss Hallie Thompson, I think her name was, took Jamelle with her to take care of her so that I could be taken on to jail. She was just someone, a black woman in the hospital, but actually she was an NAACP member and was being careful and sure, you know.

We were not setting anything up. They set it up, but they were wise, I guess, to be very, very careful, and when we got to jail, the man at the desk said, "What's the charge?" And nobody said anything. They said, "Who is the arresting officer?" And neither of them would admit to being the arresting officer *[laughs].* They had no arresting officer so we had to stand around, and finally they called the chief, and he came out and he said, "Okay. I'll be the arresting officer," and he hadn't even been there *[laughs],* you know, but somebody had to be.

Later, way later, to jump way ahead, when Matthew Perry came down, we tried three times to have a trial, and it was never "time." We'd go down and they'd say, "We aren't ready." Or, he would tell me and I would try to get off from work and then he'd call back and say, "No, we aren't doing it."

So we went down the third time and they said—I can't remember that little fella's name, a little attorney, and Matthew said, "Well, counselor . . ." They had a very friendly attitude between them, the two attorneys.

LR: The prosecutor and Matthew?

GB: Yes, he and Matthew Perry.

The prosecutor said, "Well, counselor, I'm afraid we can't do it today."

Lurma Rackley and childhood friend Luther Battiste at the dedication of Russell Street as the James E. Sulton Highway, Orangeburg, South Carolina, August 30, 2005.

You know Matthew Perry, and he was always so correct in his speech and correct in his stance, and he said, "Well, and what is it this time?"

"Well, they can't decide what the charges are."

So they still didn't know what to charge me with. So Matthew said—and I thought this was so funny, nobody else seems to think it's quite as funny—he said, "Well, you can charge her with 'murder.' It doesn't make any difference. It doesn't make any difference anyway." And he said, you know, sort of "ha-ha-ha."

And the fella said, "Now counselor, are you implying that we don't have justice in our courts."

It was a big joke. And Matthew was saying, you can charge her with murder or anything else. All we want to do is to get through here, get it on the books here, because he was going to appeal, and go somewhere where it would be, ridiculous as it was, and get justice. Because we really did believe—and that might have been stupid of us—but we really did believe that we would find justice in the upper courts. I don't know if we would be able to believe that today in the Supreme Court, but the other fella evidently thought so, too, and they threw it out. We never had a hearing on that, I don't think, but they did get a ruling, you know, from that case. They ruled the hospital open to all.

ML: So they dismissed the charges, but they changed the policy of the administration?

GB: Yes. I think at one time I went up there to pick up a deposition, but I don't think I ever had to come for court on the hospital case. I had to come to court on a lot of other cases but not that one.

Trinity United Methodist Church, Orangeburg, South Carolina, where Reverend Matthew McCollom was pastor from 1950 to 1962.

Family Council

GB: But we sat around the table when this was happening and the students were already—I think they had already been enclosed. We were away in school. Jack was studying for the doctorate, and I think it happened when we were away somewhere.

LR: When the students got fire hosed?

GB: Yes. We came back and all this was happening, so we sat around our table like this, two girls, my husband, and I, and talked about this and said we feel that we just have to do things and everybody was vulnerable. Jack was working for South Carolina State College, and I was teaching in the public schools, so we probably would get fired, or other things could happen, and the girls were little girls, so that might change our way of life and our income and a whole lot of other things. We wanted to tell them [the children] that if we decided to do this, there may be consequences. And there were. Can you remember that?

LR: I don't remember there ever being any real question whether we were going to go. I remember walking up on the South Carolina State campus before we even started walking downtown.

GB: Yes, well, they [the girls] said, "Yes," they tried to be serious. We never thought anybody was going to say, "No," but it was like we were committing ourselves and understanding what could happen. And so everybody was sure, sure, sure, sure we can do it, *yes*.

Jamelle was old enough to picket, but Lurma was too young and we tried to get the little kids, we had lots of little kids among the adults who were involved, Charles Thomas's children and Matt McCollom's son. He was not quite as young as you [Lurma], okay. Some were old enough to march with the pickets, but these little kids, we thought, just shouldn't be up there on the street because we didn't know what the other side might decide to do. So we asked them—we stationed them—we didn't have to ask because the grown-ups were in charge. Somebody was directing this, the college students, so they were positioned in front of the South Carolina and Claflin Colleges, and they were supposed to picket out there and wear their signs saying, "Don't Shop Downtown" and things like that, which would discourage people, all of the other students who were not participating and grown up, from going downtown to shop, but they weren't going to leave and go downtown.

The children did that for what—a while, a little while, but they didn't like that at all because there were no arrests and no real excitement. They didn't like that, so they came back and reported, saying they had to go, they wanted to go downtown with the others and they wanted to picket in front of the stores and all that and so they did. There was just a big number, over fifty, right, or maybe more.

LR: Little kids, and the younger [youth]?

GB: Yes, in your age group, just a whole pile of them. All of these were the students of professors and doctors and people, I mean everybody upstanding parents, just fine children, a whole pile of them Methodist, though not every single one. Some were from [Reverend J. Herbert] Nelson's [Presbyterian] church and others, but just a whole pile of fine young kids. Most of them never missed a day in school. They were good students, just fine children.

LR: Probably nobody younger than ten, maybe ranging in age from ten to sixteen, I would think.

GB: Yes . . .

Training and Discipline

GB: We would meet at the basement of Trinity, and sometimes it might be Matt, Reverend McCollom, but most times it was a teenager, a college student, because we had articulate, beautiful college students, mostly men. We had some girl leaders who could lead the songs and get the mood going and everything. But it was serious. There was never any ruckus or anything wild. They understood what they were doing, and they would go over that again and say things like, "Now we want we to check your pockets." The boys had to check their pockets to make sure they didn't have a penknife, and the girls didn't have anything to be construed to be a weapon.

They always prayed, and they always went with the understanding that we were doing a Christian service. We always met at that church, in the Methodist Church, and they were doing something that was correct and right and Christian. They might be met with [hostility], they might be misunderstood, and they might be hated for doing it, but they weren't supposed to hate back.

[Jamelle enters, is greeted, and joins the interview.]

Jamelle Rackley-Riley **[JRR]**: . . . I apologize for not being down here earlier. I had a class that I was doing and it's from one to two. Had to go ahead and do my class. Can I have a peanut butter . . . ?

ML: *Almond* butter. It's very good.

JRR: It's one of my favorites.

GB: And so the good thing about those children, these were younger Jamelle was older, she was two years older so she could be in the older group—when the [younger ones] got arrested they couldn't be held. We had already filled up . . . The college students were filling up the jails. We had overrun the little jailing and facilities that Orangeburg had to offer.

ML: The "pink palace"?

GB: Yes, they'd overrun the "pink palace," and then there was some other place. There was a jail and then there was the pink palace, it seems to me, and so they opened up the Armory. They turned the Armory over, and that was the jail where the college kids, the college girls especially, were held, in the Armory. So when these little kids marched downtown, Lurma and those, they would get all the way down, and they could just sign their names, and then they would dismiss them, theoretically into the custody of their parents, and that made them just "delinquent children."

"You know, now. If you come back again, you know . . ." something might happen, that kind of thing.

So they went down and signed in and went out, and they would rush back to the church, form a new picket line, and go again. They were so delighted because that gave a look of more members than we actually had *[laughs]*. But it just seemed that we just had kids coming from everywhere, and they couldn't hold them.

Lurma finally— I believe Lurma could talk about that, your experiences there. She finally got arrested. They let all the other children go and didn't let Lurma go because she was "Rackley," and they were already very, very angry at me and what they thought I was doing.

Reluctant College Student

GB: . . . when it first got started, in the fall, in the early fall—Jamelle joined the picket lines. We were just doing little things, going to restaurants and sitting in the shops and things like that, and Jamelle was old enough to do that. You can tell about that. Then she went away to college after her one arrest. Right? One incident?

JRR: One incident. I never got arrested because I went off to college before the movement got to that point, where people were being arrested. Actually I called home—I was a freshman at Bennett College in Greensboro, North Carolina—I called home and said I wanted to take a hiatus from college because I wanted to be involved with the movement.

I didn't appreciate being isolated from my mother and my sister while they were up there in harm's way, and I didn't know what was going on. Part of it was because I wanted to be there with them because of the perceived dangers, and a part of it was that I wanted to be involved with the process. I felt left out. And so I felt that, I was just a freshman, I had just started college and knew nothing. I could not imagine my mother saying, "No. You can't come home." This was some historic stuff that was going on here. But she didn't. She *didn't* say, "Yes." *[She laughs.]* So I had to stay.

GB: But you were involved in the restaurant thing.

JRR: Yes, my incident was that in one of the sit-ins. I was bodily brought out of a restaurant. That was kind of— Looking back on it, I don't remember feeling afraid. I was only fifteen at the time, or perhaps I'd turned sixteen already, and probably weighed ninety-nine pounds, so that could have been a traumatic event. But because I don't remember it in that way at all, obviously it *wasn't* traumatic. Probably because of all the . . . coaching that we received from Reverend McCollom and my Mom and all the other leaders about always coming from a point of love.

When you come from a point of love, no matter what happens, no matter what the other person is doing, your reaction to that is not based on what they're doing but based on how you're feeling about what they're doing, and the love that you're generating back to them.

I missed out on a lot of the "fun" part and a lot of the "not so fun" endangerment part because I was away in school.

ML: Your mother would not let you come home.

JRR: Would *not* let me come home! *[She laughs.]*

ML: Your business was college.

[Part 2 of this interview will be found in volume 2.]

Johnalee Nelson,
It Was the Popcorn

Marvin Lare [ML]:* You say you're from New Hampshire. That would be after my wife's [Patricia Tyler Lare] own heart. She grew up in Richmond, but her mother was from New Hampshire.

Johnalee Nelson [JN]: What part of New Hampshire?

ML: Near Newmarket, not very far from Durham. She spent almost every summer . . . Her father was in the military and in the reserves and so he would be off on active duty, and so my wife's mother and she would go to New Hampshire and stay with the aunts and the uncles and the grandparents. Where in New Hampshire are you from?

JN: I lived in Portsmouth, New Hampshire, which as you probably know is about fifty miles from Boston and then, you know, near the beaches.

ML: Yes, well, you might be interested to know that on the Haines side of my wife's family her great, great, great . . . anyhow, about twelve generations back, I think it was 1635, he was on the ship [the *Angel*] *Gabriel*. It was anchored in the harbor there, and a hurricane came through and sank the ship, but he was washed ashore with nothing but his mattress and his Bible in his mattress. He was one of the founders of the church right there on the town square in Portsmouth. His name is on a plaque there yet, Haines.

JN: Very good, very good. I was born in Beaufort, South Carolina, but my mother had followed directly and indirectly her brother who left Beaufort on a ship and ended up in Portsmouth. I don't think that was the destination that was set out. Then he encouraged her to come to Portsmouth, and she went and she liked it and decided that, well . . . and I was with my grandmother in Beaufort at the time. So the two of us moved to New Hampshire.

*Marvin Lare, with Nathan McCollough, a history major at Claflin University, conducted the interview with Mrs. J. Herbert (Johnalee) Nelson at the Nelson home in Orangeburg, South Carolina, on December 8, 2004. It was transcribed by Catherine Mann for the USC South Caroliniana Library.

ML: Well, in these interviews I let people tell their own story, and then if I've got questions and comments I'll inquire, but I'd like to hear about your life and the work that you and your husband pursued across the state.

JN: Well, he is the one now, so you know, any questions that you wish to ask if I can answer them I'll be happy to share that information. I was the one who was the supporter and that sort of thing, and he was really the one who was out there doing the work.

ML: Well, the perspective of the home front is always so important . . .

Growing Up In New Hampshire

JN: Well, you see growing up it's true that I attended school, first grade in Beaufort, and at that time families and individuals across the board were blinded to the point that, as a child, one really did not know about segregation and that sort of thing. And when I went to New Hampshire I was the only *brown spot* in the school, but at that time that was not a conflict because I imagine the rules and regulations and individuals just hadn't given race a thought. We lived in not an exclusive part of town by any means, but we were not in the same neighborhood as the majority of Afro-Americans. It wasn't a matter of being across town. I didn't hear that word "across town" or "across the tracks" until I came to South Carolina.

Walking was the main source of transportation and we could go, everyone was privileged to go to whatever church they wanted. I know that during the Easter season and special seasons during the year for some unknown reason I just had the desire to visit [other churches], and naturally there were teachers and schoolmates, classmates who were members of those churches. But that wasn't a big deal. I mean that wasn't something that you made something over. A special program is going to be at such-and-such a church regardless of whether it was Methodist, Congregational, Episcopal, or what, and everyone is invited. The word "ecumenical" became a part of my life, not a part of my vocabulary, but a part of my life without my even recognizing it at that time.

My stepfather had a café and it was in the area of town where businessmen . . . they would go and they would have lunch there. Then he was also a caterer, and as a result he catered for a lot of weddings and Christmas parties and that sort of thing. So I became familiar with cleaning lobsters and didn't even have a taste or a desire to eat one *[laughs]*. When I came here and folks were talking about how great lobsters were and how expensive and that sort of thing, I said, well, if I had just a nickel for every one that I tried to open and clean out, you know, pull the meat out and that sort of thing, because lobster salad was the going thing. Whereas we talk about potato salad in the South, it was lobster or crab salad there.

Going South

JN: So that's the kind of . . . and I graduated from high school there. My desire was to go into nurses' training. It happened that my grandmother died my senior year in high school, and my saying that I wanted to go to nursing school came at a time when things were just not smooth and easy, and yet not difficult. But you have to get the papers and everything in order, and when I wrote to the hospital . . . I had to take a test. By the time that had gotten clear . . . it was too late for the September class. So Mother, having kept her connections with individuals who were her friends and her classmates, called Edith Waterman at State College, and Edith was registrar and asked if I could come for *a semester,* and the answer was, "Yes, send her on."

When I came for the semester, southern hospitality and culture, the whole nine yards that I had not really been exposed to— So I just stayed for four years and thoroughly enjoyed it.

Then I guess my junior year— I never did go home for the holidays because that was two days travel, I mean two days going up and two days coming down. But there were always friends. The first two years I visited in Beaufort, which, of course, was hometown. The third year I visited in Anderson, South Carolina, and the fourth year I visited in Sumter. By the junior year we had decided, a group of us had decided, that we were going to be roommates, and it so happened that the roommate from Sumter asked me about coming early because they always have a going-away party, and I did and as a result I met the young man. Of course, that was just, you know, meeting another young man, and he came down to several football games because he was at Johnson C. Smith, and Johnson C. Smith and State College, they were rival teams, and the friendship, I guess, just grew into a relationship.

ML: Yes, yes. How many years were you married before he passed?

JN: Thirty-nine.

ML: Thirty-nine. Well, the role of a pastor's wife is interesting in and of itself, as well as the civil rights years. What were some of the things that stand out in your memory?

JN: Well, you know, the amusing part about it was . . . I won't say it was the first, maybe the first *real* conversation we had after we had been introduced to was the common questions, "What do you plan to do? What are your dreams?" He had said that he was either going to be a mortician or he was going to be a minister.

I just let it fly over my head. I knew that this was not the person for me because, number one, with the morticians I was scared to death of the deceased. I had not had the experience. You know how some parents take their children to every funeral . . . not so much *take them,* but because there were no babysitters they took the children with them to the funeral. But I had never had that experience because where we lived in Beaufort—we went to a Baptist Church, which was a good two blocks down the street where you go to the corner, and you could look down and see—so there was no problem with my grandmother leaving me at home, and all of the neighbors didn't ever go to the same funeral anyway. So it was a matter of [saying to a neighbor], "Well, I'm going and look out for Johnalee." And that's what was done. And in New Hampshire I remember when a classmate and a neighbor died at the age of fourteen. She and I were very close friends, and she had a rare condition and as a result she passed.

Mrs. J. Herbert (Johnalee) Nelson, December 8, 2004.

Well, that was a shock to me, but then at the same time now I didn't view the body. Really the first body that I viewed was my grandmother's, and of course, that was a time when they did not take the body to the funeral home and keep it there. They embalmed in the home, so she never left the home until it was time to come south, you know, to bring the body south. But coming here, coming to South Carolina, it was common to go to funerals and to meet persons that you really, you thought a lot of just on first sight, and then something would happen and that person would pass, and of course, you'd go to the funeral.

But that was not my cup of tea, and then, when he said, "A minister," I'm no, no, because my stepfather was the senior deacon, and of course, everything that went on at the church we were there. Not that I was there all the time but I knew what it was, and then every Sunday when we had visiting ministers they came to *our house* for dinner, and I was the one that had to do the cleaning up and would *help* with the cooking. I mean I didn't ever cook anything, but when it came to preparing the vegetables, washing them and getting them ready and so forth and so on, Mother had me doing all of that. So, "Huh-uh, no," you know [laughs].

But anyway, it's amazing how and I know now—I did not know then but I know now—that by *divine guidance* things change and they change, and I would say if you had been brought up in the right manner, then you accept the changes if they don't seem like they are something that is foreign and off the wall. So we got married and he went to the service, and when he came back, his youngest brother was just finishing his undergrad work, and they had decided that they would go to seminary together, and so that's what happened.

Ministry

JN: The younger brother, Dwight, had been working on the railroad, and James Herbert was working in the North during the summer and teaching with his father during the winter. But they decided and so they went to seminary, and of course, the story begins and ends with that as far as ministry is concerned. But he felt that that was his calling. His father was a minister. He had an older brother who was a minister and an older brother who was an educator. The brother ahead of him became a minister, but he became a *Methodist* minister. And of course, the younger brother was a Presbyterian minister also. There were five boys and four of them were ministers.

ML: That's quite a lot of religion in one family!

JN: Oh, yes, oh, yes, and of course, our son is in the ministry. He is founding pastor of a Presbyterian church in Memphis, Tennessee, having spent twelve years or eleven and a half years in Greensboro, North Carolina, pastoring. So, you know, ministry is a good field.

ML: What seminary did your husband go to?

JN: Johnson C. Smith, and Johnson C. Smith, the seminary at that time was in Charlotte, North Carolina. Since then they have moved it to Atlanta, and that's where our son went to school. He went to Johnson C. Smith.

ML: So what year was it that he came back from service? Was he in World War II or the Korean War?

JN: World War II.

[The doorbell rings. The Claflin student arrives and the interview continues.]

ML: . . . the more the merrier and we can work it all together.

Nathan McConnell **[NM]**: Yeah, that's even better when you work together with somebody else towards doing something.

ML: That's right, and we'll make sure that you get as much as you need for your class project so you can get a good grade on it, okay?

[Dr. Jackie R. Booker, associate professor of history at Claflin University, had been consulted regarding the anthology project and participated in the Anthology Festival at South Carolina State University on June 11, 2004. He assigned one of his students to interview Mrs. Nelson, and coincidently Marvin Lare arrived for the same purpose that day.]

NM: Yes, sir.

ML: Nathan, why don't you mention your name for my tape?

NM: Okay, my name is Nathan McConnell, and I'm a college student at Claflin University. I'm a senior in history/political science.

ML: Very good. Why don't you go ahead and proceed now.

NM: Okay, Mrs. Nelson, I'm going to start off by asking you when and where were you born and where did you grow up?

JN: I was born in Beaufort, South Carolina and I attended first grade in Beaufort, but second grade through high school, my mother was in Portsmouth, New Hampshire, and I was with my grandmother in Beaufort and we moved to . . . she had us to come to Portsmouth. So that's how I got to Portsmouth, New Hampshire.

NM: Homebody history! . . . meaning that you grew up in Beaufort *[laughs]*. What was your childhood experiences regarding blacks and whites?

JN: I did not have the experience that most folks that grew up in South Carolina had because, as I said earlier if you listen to his tape, as a child the time was of such that individuals, everyone loved each other, everyone, and everyone was willing to help everyone. Beaufort was not a big city, so as a result there was really no, as far as I was concerned—and you're asking about me—I knew nothing about segregation.

NM: So it wasn't as if . . . seems like it might have been a big transition from being from New Hampshire and moving down to South Carolina.

JN: That was the transition. The transition was when I came to South Carolina State for college, for a semester, and then got caught up in the culture and the hospitality, southern hospitality, and stayed. I will say that possibly changing trains in Washington, D.C., should have had more of an effect on me than it did. But, you know, it didn't because you see getting on the train in Boston, Massachusetts, I could sit anywhere I wanted to sit.

NM: Oh, really?

JN: But when I got to Washington and changed to come from Washington to Orangeburg, then that was where the difference was made. But here again we were not exposed to the hullabaloo about black and white. So when you're moving with your own group then you're "moving with your own group." I mean and to me it really had no effect. I mean I'm moving with the people who are moving . . .

NM: In the direction you're moving.

JN: Yes.

NM: It's hard for me to believe, I mean not hard for me to believe, but it's strange to find out, like, in Boston and, like, those New England states, because I know Boston might have, like, a whole lot of racism during that time, and I've heard Beaufort up to the present time is not as bad, but it was kind of bad during that time for blacks in Boston.

JN: Not really. Not really. My parents had friends who lived in Boston. And as you say, I was totally, I mean if you want to say *totally* ignorant, I was totally ignorant of segregation until I came to State College.

NM: How was your life affected by discrimination and injustice among the races?

JN: I don't know. How was my life affected?

NM: . . . and not even your life, from looking on the outside, your husband's?

JN: He came up in . . . he grew up in the South, and as a result he was more aware of the negativity of life than I was. I was brought up to treat everybody the same, to treat everybody . . . and you see whereas at that time, maybe not now but at that time, where it made a difference if you were black and somebody was—the other person was white—having gone to school in New Hampshire, having been the only Afro-American in the . . . the schools are in districts, not districts, but in the community, and therefore, wherever you lived, then you go to that school and that's what I [experienced in] elementary, junior high, and it wasn't until I got to the high school that there were others who were Afro-Americans. So, as a result the relationship between black and white, as far as are you asking about me, it was "A okay."

So when I came south—and even right now—I mean I've had rapport with individuals that I know. I've always had rapport because it's easy for me to say, "Good morning. How are you?" "Good afternoon, you having a nice day?" I was brought up to do that, to say that to everyone. So the effect came from the fact that my husband had grown up in the South, so it had more of an impact on him.

It Was the Popcorn

JN: To tell you the truth, I think in my estimation, that which really lit a ball of fire in his life was when we would go to New Hampshire for the summer to see my parents. It was a matter of our daughter enjoyed popcorn, and it was no problem to go to the store and go in a store either downtown or wherever the popcorn stand was and get a bag of popcorn. Well, all right, in Sumter, and that's where she really grew up, in Sumter . . . I mean she was just a toddler. We were on Liberty Street. Well, Liberty Street in Sumter was the area that on Saturdays individuals always had to go to town, you know, you go to town in the morning, and you get back home in the late afternoon because you'd see folks there. Rural towns, you know, everybody coming from the rural areas, you'd see folks there that you hadn't seen all the week or maybe two weeks. So it was a matter of she asked for some popcorn, and even though there was a popcorn place right there where the car was parked, it was a matter of *we couldn't buy popcorn.* So I think that really lit a big fire inside her father, and one thing led to another. And then, of course, there was the school, because he was responsible for leading the movement to sue the county, Sumter County, for segregation of schools. [The suit was lost], and he was [fined] for ten thousand dollars . . .

ML: That was a lot of money!

JN: . . . but the church, the Presbyterian Church came to his aid and sent him a check for the ten thousand.

NM: Yes, ma'am. It's good that he had like a good religious base, spiritual base, thing, and he was able to go to the church and they were able to help him.

Advice and Counsel

JN: Well, it was a matter of . . . you see here, Nathan, as a young man coming along, I say to you and I say to other young people, you have to be friendly with individuals and whatever your job is, you make your job. Enlarge, you enlarge yourself in your work whatever it is and get to know the people and have the people to know who you are. You will find that, yes, segregation is going to always be present, but if you associate with the right individuals, then you won't have any trouble. Don't let the negativity, those who do not have the same privileges you have, don't let their negativity . . .

NM: Discourage you.

JN: That's right, discourage you or get into your system and you start thinking, "Oh, my goodness, I wonder if so and so . . ." Let them say what they need to. If you have a conviction you're doing the right thing . . .

NM: When did you first become involved in civil rights activities?

JN: Well, now "Johnalee" did not become involved *[laughs]* . . . did *not* become involved. When I say I didn't become involved, I know I was involved because my husband was involved, but I was the one who stayed at home.

NM: But you still played your part, even in the smallest form.

JN: I stayed at home and took care of our daughter, and whenever he would come back home I would be wondering, you know, "Where in the world . . . what is happening?" But that's basically what happened.

Now I'll say this, when our son came along, his dad took him to the marches and whatnot and, of course, he was up on the shoulders of . . . well, not Jim Clyburn, but the undertaker, can't think of his name. It will probably come to me.

ML: In Charleston?

JN: In Sumter, because he ran the funeral home there. *[It was Robert Palmer.]*

NM: I know this is really not a question for you, but the activities that your husband was involved in, where did they take place?

JN: Well, they took place in Sumter, and then when we came to Orangeburg it was just a matter of picking up the pieces and bringing them on over here, so to speak.

ML: What year did you move from Sumter?

JN: We moved from Sumter in '63. He got the call, and we did not really move our residence here until '64 or '65 because they did not have a manse for the church, St. Luke. It was down on Lowman Street where the bus station is, that area down there where the church was, and they did not have a manse, and there wasn't any place that we could find, regrettable, you know, a three-bedroom, and that's what the desire was to have a three-bedroom . . . a house with three bedrooms in it. But the church had on the drawing board the plans for a manse, and so that was built, and then that's when we actually moved here. But now we were back and forth two and three times a week, four and five times a week.

NM: I know you gave me a description of, like, Sumter is, like, a rural area. Can you go, like, a little more in depth about the description of Sumter, like, what it was like during that time?

JN: Well, when I said it was a rural area, you know, most of our towns in South Carolina at that time were rural areas. Cotton was the—not in Sumter—main source of income, definitely for blacks and as well as whites who really had the plantations. And of course, there were schoolteachers and undertakers.

NM: What issues and concerns and activities were addressed by you and your husband?

JN: Education.

NM: The role that you and your husband played in civil rights and human rights activities were more, like, trying to desegregate the schools?

The NAACP

JN: Thinking in terms of justice, of peace and justice and harmony and love for each other. You see when James Herbert . . . James Herbert was an active member of the NAACP. The NAACP at that time was a very strong organization. He held office in Sumter. He held office definitely in Orangeburg. During the . . . I believe in 1960 was when Orangeburg had that segregated seating at the lunch counters, and State and Claflin students were involved in that. So that was really the beginning of his activities here in Orangeburg. We came to St. Luke in '63. In '63 he also became vice president of the state NAACP, and then later on, I guess two years later, he became the president. So you see when you speak of *areas* you think in terms of all the areas that the NAACP was involved in.

NM: You said that he was, like, initiated locally or coordinated with the state and national efforts with the NAACP in the state, and as a whole [he would] go places and speak. Did he find allies and support from other groups and organizations?

JN: Very definitely. The church that he pastored, the two churches in Sumter County were very supportive, *very supportive*. They were rural individuals who like today, you have to teach individuals, and James Herbert enjoyed teaching, and in his messages he brought the congregation on board. And then you made mention of the fact about going places speaking. Well, and I'm not saying it because he's my husband, but there were very few high schools who held their graduations or their, what is it, Sunday convocation, who held their services in June, in May or June, that didn't request him to come and speak. And he spoke from his conviction regardless of, you know, whose toes . . . I mean it was kind and gentle and pastoral with the scriptures as the background, but he spoke. Of course, there were some principals who felt that maybe his message might not be the best message. He just said it up front, you can't tell me what to say now. So if you feel that I'm going to do you more harm, and your community more harm, and your students more harm than good, then feel free to get someone else. I mean you haven't hurt my feelings at all because I have a message to give, and the message is for all of us to be together because God created each and every one of us, and he's in charge. We're not in charge. . . .

ML: His messages were primarily in terms of justice and civil rights and to stand up for their rights?

JN: Uh-huh, with love and harmony and peace.

ML: So he used the forum of those school baccalaureate programs to get the message out to be active in the movement?

JN: That's true.

NM: Who else was involved in these activities and what roles did they play? You said it was the church.

JN: Okay, I made mention of the church. When I say *all,* it's generally speaking. When I say the Greek-letter organizations, you know, the fraternities and sororities, and he happened to have been an Omega man and played a key role there, but you had those people who really garnered and who really enfolded that which he would think. I say it with love, I really do, there are very few people that during that particular time that if you said, "James Herbert Nelson," they knew exactly who you were talking about because he made it a point of being open and loving to everyone.

NM: What was the response to the activities of integrating the schools in Sumter? What was the response from the black community and the white community?

JN: Well, you see the thing about it, the black community had very, very little to say to a certain degree now. Understand me now. If you do some research, you will find that in the Elloree school system, there is no question about that. If you were a teacher, you could not belong to the NAACP. In Sumter if you owned a business, and we had very few owning businesses, I'm talking about filling stations. I'm not talking about clothing businesses. If you were an entrepreneur in any form, you could not belong to the NAACP. And if you did, you lost, *you lost* your business. The teachers at Elloree they just could not . . . You wouldn't know him, but Reverend Frank Everett, Francis Everett—he is in a nursing home now—he was principal of a school in Elloree, and Frank just had to really not say anything.

NM: By public officials or was it . . . ?

JN: Public officials were slow to show their hands. You know, you, you . . . we have to bring up the Ku Klux Klan. You see, it was nothing unusual to have a cross burned on your yard, and, you know—I just thank the Lord—when I say we, we didn't have the experience. All right, in Sumter there were key persons. There was—he's a bishop now, James, F. C. James—he's in Columbia. The dentist McDonald—S. J. McDonald Sr. was truly a pioneer—then his son came along. His son was a dentist. Then we had a Baptist minister . . . *[She pauses, thinking.]* I said Fred James. But those were persons . . . and there are other persons now, but you know you always have to have some persons who really stand out in the forefront. When it came to Pawleys Island, opening up that resort down there, James Herbert and Fred went to the meet . . . Oh, I. DeQuincey Newman, because I. DeQuincey Newman was in Sumter at that time. So you had those three persons really standing toe to toe and doing what needed to be done. Oh, we come to Orangeburg, and we think in terms of Jackie Davis from Williams Chapel. We think in terms of I. DeQuincey Newman again. We think of John Currie to a certain degree. John Currie was not on the front lines per se, but John Currie was pastoring Trinity and that's where the meetings were held. Any time they wanted to have a meeting it was held at Trinity United, it was United then, Methodist Church.

NM: How did the media and other groups, how would they respond?

JN: Well, you see the media was always ready to write an article. James Herbert's thing was, you tell the media only what you want the media to know. You don't tell the media everything. You've got to weigh your words and whatnot because the media is not going to print the exact words that you had said. They would put a flair to it, and it may not be the right thing, so he was never willing to meet with the media.

NM: What were the results of these activities? The activities he was involved in towards making it more positive, what were the results?

JN: Nathan, I think the same thing happened then that is possibly taking place now and that is that you . . . Those of us who really feel that God is in charge and really, really believe that, you feel that some measure of success is made. But when you get asked the question what were the successes, my answer is, "It depends upon the individuals." You deliver the message that you have to deliver, keeping in mind that these are words that the Lord has guided you to give. Now naturally, you know, the messages were received with a standing ovation. But you see that isn't what you're asking. That isn't what you *should* be asking.

NM: I guess you can say, like, you can do positive things when God is . . .

Get on the Boat

JN: Even though individuals appreciate and respect what is said, you can't say that that's a big success, and that's why when you raised that question, that's a question that I don't know that anyone could really answer positively, answer and say, yes, this is this, this is this. No, it wasn't like that. I feel as I said that the message was delivered, the message was heard, and well, we know that it could not have been a great success across the board because look where we are today. Look where we are today!

I sometimes really wonder if some of the . . . all of the motion and the action and so forth and so on, if it was really—I won't say if it was worth it—but was it time wasted from the standpoint that those persons who really set the pace, who picked up, in other words . . . naturally James Herbert, Newman, and that group, they were not the first ones that got on the boat. There were persons, maybe you can't even call their names, don't even know who they were, but there were persons who were on the boat. All right, this group got on the boat and they did their part. That first group got on and did their part. And now we have *not* had a group, another group that has been similar to either one of those two groups or three groups to *get on board* and to follow through and do the same thing.

NM: *[His words are inaudible.]*

JN: Yes, but in doing something, I'm not concerned with them doing something different. We're talking about carrying the thread, extending the thread. The thread has not been extended.

ML: You're saying that generations after that have dropped the ball?

JN: . . . become lackadaisical, they've become lackadaisical. You see, number one, individuals became powerful. Economically they became powerful, and as a result they did not, many of them did not have to go through what we went through. You see, I mean when we came through, and I put myself in that bracket, when I was in Beaufort everyone didn't have lights, electricity. Everyone didn't have running water.

But now you see, when I went to New Hampshire, everyone had it but it was a different, you're in a different part of the country. You understand what I'm saying.

NM: I can kind of relate to it, too, because my mom, she grew up and she went through the same things like not having running water, like having to tote water from a well and not having lights and having outhouses.

JN: And then you see education wasn't advanced. You see the average, I mean there was that period of time even when I started teaching that the students did not have nine months of school, or if they had nine months of schooling they couldn't go to school because they were on Mr. Charlie's farm, and whenever it was time to do whatever was needed to be done, they had to be out of school for that. So, you know, but now you see you have a group where all right, all of that has moved and shifted. We don't have to worry about that anymore. But now where are the people who are as dedicated to continuing to keep the boat, or to keep the thread, moving? These people have said, "Well, I don't want to be bothered. Let somebody else do it."

ML: They sort of got theirs and have forgotten the rest of the people.

JN: And, you know, that's life! I mean, you don't hold anything against them. That's life and everyone has a choice. Every individual, God has given each and every one of us an opportunity to make a choice.

Convictions

NM: What happened to you and your husband during these activities and as a result them?

JN: Well, the only thing I can say is that we stuck together, and we were supported. We had strong support from our peers and from the elders.

James Herbert had, he just had a strong conviction and he followed his conviction in the church and in the civil rights movement. I feel that, I know that God was with us and I feel that things came out the way they were designed . . . not maybe truly designed, but I know when our daughter went to Clark and when the Atlanta—not so much uprising—but when the Atlanta situation broke, she was a part of that when the students from Clark and all the other colleges really gathered.

[An interview with James Felder will be found in volume 2.]

JN: Our son went to Johnson C. Smith, and he was a leader of a group for civil rights. I mean, you know, as parents and as the mother, undoubtedly we tried to do the right thing because, as I said, the kids came along and they followed.

Herbie went to—his first call was in Greensboro, and he was there for eleven and a half years, and he had the struggles with the church, but then he was the leader of the K-Mart conflict. You say, well, what success came out of that? Well, I feel that, number one, here again he was following his convictions. Apparently he saw what his dad had done and felt good about that, and I know that his going to the Labor Department in Washington . . . he was sent there for six weeks or longer just to sit in and to listen and to offer suggestions. So, you know, these little things that come . . . but we don't make a big deal about that. That was just another training. That was just another part of what the Lord had in mind for him to do.

Laying the Foundation

JN: Since he's been in Memphis he really ran into racism there in the church, not in the church that he pastors but . . . you probably don't know this, but the Presbyterian Church was divided into two parts, more than two but definitely two. There were the Southern Presbyterians and there were Northern Presbyterians, and there were the Northern Presbyterians who came south and started schools and [James Herbert's] father was principal at Goodwill in Mayesville. It's not in Mayesville, it's near Dabb's Crossroads, started a school there. And, of course, Mary McLeod Bethune started to the [Presbyterian] school in Mayesville. Those persons were the pioneers, and as a result all of this has been built, they have been the foundation. One generation builds on another generation.

NM: How do you feel about those activities now that he was involved in?

JN: Well, I have a pride, a sense of appreciation that he did what he could while he was here and that the Lord felt it was time to call him home, he called him home.

NM: If you had to do it over again, how do you think you would have done it differently?

JN: Well, you know, you think in terms of your coming through high school. You've finished high school and are now in college. If you had to go back, you see, the thing about it knowing now what you did not know then, would there be a difference? Would you do something different?

NM: Big difference, a big difference!

JN: Well, I think we all have that same feeling. If we had to go back again, I mean it would be totally . . . but you see you can't. I mean and that's a good thought question, but all I'm saying is that it's good that we can't go back, knowing what we know now. There would be changes, and I'm sure that we would have an insight where we definitely would do things differently. But now, you know, I really wonder would everyone be on the same accord, you know. Nothing is going to be perfect.

NM: What impact did your civil and equal rights activities have on the rest of your life as a person?

JN: I would say that it opened the doors for knowing who people are, learning the personality of individuals, really sitting back and really evaluating some of the situations that took place, some of the expressions that were made, really finding out who people are. It gives you, it gives to everyone, and it certainly gave me an opportunity to be able to understand that individuals are individuals who really make their own life. We have individuals who have negative thoughts, and if you follow them through, that negative thought that they give for each and everything is not something [snapping her fingers] that just came at this particular time.

NM: There is always something that leads to it, that it grows out of.

JN: That's right, and of course, you know the Bible tells us that the Lord in making us, the Lord made individuals so I feel that when I see someone who is mean spirited, well, we just have to pray for that person because that's what that person, that's who that person is, and unless that individual has a choice to change, that individual is not going to change.

NM: You just kind of talked about this a little bit, what are your current views on what has been accomplished?

JN: Well, I feel there's been good work done in some instances. I'm disappointed that there is a lackadaisicalness or "don't care" attitude. But I guess this is what comes as you grow older and generations are younger. There's no question about it. Individuals really don't care about each other now, and we're talking about the younger generation. They really don't care about whether the elderly get along or not. I mean, you know, they rush by you. And see this thing of opening doors and helping people, there is not, for the masses, this is not going on. Now naturally there are persons who are still there on it, and there are young people who are very gracious and very kind.

NM: I was raised the same way, like, to respect older people . . .

JN: But you see what we have now we have children having children, and before they can get a solid foundation on what should be done . . .

NM: They're having children.

JN: Yes.

Education

NM: What are your largest concerns still to be addressed towards the education system?

JN: Oh, let's not even mention that. You know, I was in the classroom, and when I come in contact with what's going on in the classroom now it hurts me. I mean I could just shed tears because our children, all of the children I feel are not getting that which they should get. And that's not being negative. I mean there's too much going on in the classrooms that did not go on. They took prayer out of the schools. All right, I grant you that could very well be a part of it. But then maybe at the time that it came out, maybe that was a good thing from the standpoint that just to be going through an exercise, I just don't believe in that. As I think back of years that I was in the classroom prior to their taking, say maybe a year before they said we're not going to have devotions in the morning, you either had something that was silly and foolish or something that, "Okay, well, that's Johnny on the P.A. system. That's Johnny. Well, I don't want to hear Johnny." And so as far as the classroom setting was concerned, it didn't make any difference what Johnny was saying. You understand what I'm saying?

NM: Yes, ma'am.

JN: Whereas I've been in a classroom where everyone is focused on what's going on. And then it seems as if they're teaching for whatever test, the PAC test *[snapping her fingers]* or whatever test is going on and children are just really not learning. Now

I'm working with a student, and it boggles my mind when, you know, "Oh, we don't have teachers that do that." How can you do "B" if you don't understand? How can you do "C" if you don't know "A" and "B"? One event leads into another! . . .

Friends

NM: Do you have any other reflections on your experiences of the civil rights activities?

JN: . . . we thoroughly enjoyed life and we have friends that were there for us. I can remember when James Herbert went to jail along with Jackie Davis and several persons here, Gloria Rackley and that group, when they went to jail, Dewey Duckett [Sr.], who was a medical doctor from Rock Hill and was the godfather of our son—in fact, he delivered Herbie—he drove down from Rock Hill that Sunday morning and came back here to the house and said, ". . . what has happened? What are you doing?" and "I just came to see what's going on. I heard . . . that J. Herbert was in jail. . . ."

And Dr. Young, the Young brothers from Anderson . . . we just had a core of people and see they were all persons who were working in civil rights. They may not have been on the front lines but they were there. The lawyer[s] out of Columbia, used to call people by nickname, and it's difficult to come up with their real names.

ML: Matthew Perry?

JN: Oh, yes, Matthew Perry was definitely . . .

ML: . . . and his law partner, Lincoln Jenkins.

JN: Yes, and of course, [Ernest A.] Finney [Jr.]. Finney and J. Herbert were . . . in fact, we were neighbors in Sumter and very close friends. So, I mean, as I say, we really were surrounded by individuals who were there for us, and those friendships still remain.

NM: I'm going to say personally, for myself, I'd like to thank you for sharing your experiences with me. Just coming from Claflin and being caught up in the hustle and bustle of trying to pass these finals, it's comforting being in your presence and speaking with you.

JN: Thank you, Nathan, I appreciate that and, you know, I thought about it this afternoon, just prior to Mr. Marvin coming, it is as if it was by divine order . . . He called me, must have been about twelve-thirty or one o'clock something like that, so I had no idea that he was going to be coming here. So that's why, when you called, I said, "What in the world is going on. All these people wanting to know about the civil rights movement . . ." *[She laughs.]*

ML: I'm just glad that it all worked. I didn't know that somebody had been assigned to contact you, but James Sulton said, "Be sure to see Johnalee Nelson."

I said, "I have her on my list."

And he said, "Well, you go see her right away."

I interviewed him about two weeks ago.

JN: That's what I say, it's by divine order.

Ten Thousand Dollars

ML: Let me ask you a couple of follow-up questions on things that you mentioned. You mentioned about the ten-thousand-dollar fine. Your husband sued the school district, but then they ended up fining him?

JN: No, he didn't sue the school, James Herbert. That group did not sue the school district. They simply were asking for the desegregation.

ML: . . . and the school district sued him for . . .

JN: Well, the thing about it was this. The officials, there were county officials. There was a judge—and I'm not going to call the name—but he owned a lot of property down where James Herbert's father pastored. And the [judge's] dad was right next door to the school and to the manse and to the church, Goodwill Church. Of course, it was not their desire for integration. So it was a matter of the judge . . . would just *[snapping her fingers]* slam the fine.

ML: For disorderly conduct?

JN: Well, you know, for the whole thing . . . disturbing the peace, yes.

ML: Was it the local congregation or the denomination that paid?

JN: No, it was the denomination. Now the congregations were willing to . . . they put money into the pot too, but someone from the denomination came down and did the interview and that sort of thing.

ML: Yes, that sort of leads into a broader question, the Presbyterian Church in America?

JN: No, Presbyterian Church U.S.A.

ML: U.S.A., yes, that's right.

JN: At that time it was the United Presbyterian Church, U.S.A.

Legacy

ML: But the denomination was very supportive and really helped stand behind him to be out front?

JN: And of course, Nathan, he had worked to the point that he had established himself, and that's why I'm saying to you about you have to *enlarge* your territory with the right kind of people because when you do that, then when you get in a bind, they are there for you. Because this is really—I mean I can't tell anything but the truth—this is really what happened, and I have worked in the church with women's work, with youth work, and have gone to all the meetings and, you know, you go on your own. You don't wait for somebody to send you as a delegate. And therefore my having worked and this young man *[pointing to a photo]*, having worked, then, our son is reaping the benefits of what we have done and, you know, he goes somewhere and they say, "Listen here, are you Johnalee's . . . What connection do you have with Johnalee?"

"That's my mother!"

" . . . what you talking about!" *[She laughs.]*

And I'm not saying that egotistically. All I'm saying is that that's the way things really happen in life. We see it happening on the other side of the coin much more so than we see it happening in our own culture. Are you able to understand?

NM: Yes ma'am.

JN: Because the legacy, it's the legacy that's set not only here *[tapping her fingers on the table]* but it was set with his father. . . .

[The conversation fades in and out as Mrs. Nelson is sharing documents with the interviewers. Marvin Lare makes arrangements to borrow some of the documents to reproduce for the anthology.]

JN: Oh, this is Cecil Ivory. He was from Rock Hill and Cecil was one of our close friends, and he was a part of the civil rights movement in Rock Hill. Are you familiar with some of those incidents that took place there?

ML: A student at Winthrop [Andy Grose], interviewed Reverend [William "Dub"] Massey. He was one of the nine "jail, no bail" students. He just sent me his term paper, the transcript of his interview, and he tells about being in solitary confinement and all. But I need to get more on Reverend Ivory himself because I don't have much of that yet.

NM: I'm going to have to leave. I have another test to take. Is it okay if I come by to see you some other time if I give you a telephone call?

JN: You do that. Do that.

NM: It was nice meeting you.

ML: Nathan, best of luck on the test, and if you need any reference or recommendation on the interview, I'll be glad to give it.

NM: Okay.

JN: Yes, indeed, but as I said, it's by divine order.

Courtney Siceloff, Penn Pioneer

Marvin Lare [ML]:* This is January 16th of 2005. My wife, Pat, and I are in the home of Courtney Siceloff in Decatur, Georgia. We've just been catching up on some of our Texas roots. But when and how did you get to South Carolina.?

Courtney Siceloff [CS]: Well, let's see, it's many decades ago. I was a conscious objector and I was in civilian public service, alternative service. Then I went with the American Friends Service Committee overseas. I was very anxious to get involved in overseas work and worked with the refugees from the Spanish Civil War down in south[ern] France. After the civil war in Spain many of the refugees had left and settled in the south of France because of a very common heritage along the Mediterranean coast. The Service Committee had a project working, trying to give trades to these . . . a number of them had been schoolteachers in Spain and came over and they couldn't use their skills that way and so we had a retraining program that we set up. So I worked with that for several years and, you know, very interesting.

ML: How long did you spend with that and is that what led you to Penn Center?

CS: It was a couple of years with the Service Committee there and then came back and went to Haverford College. They had a program where one would live at Pendle Hill, which is a Quaker adult study program near Swarthmore. Several of us who were in that program would drive over to Haverford and work there after college. I was interested in returning to the South, and there was an African American professor, Dr. Ira Reed, sociology at Haverford, and he made a study of Penn School at the time. Penn was a school established by Quakers, Unitarians, and abolitionists during the Civil War. It carried on as a private school with a lot of Quaker backing, and it continued up until '51, 1951, when it was turned over to the county and they weren't quite sure what to do with the property.

---

*Courtney Siceloff (1922–2014) was interviewed in his home in Decatur, Georgia, by Marvin Lare and his wife, Patricia Tyler Lare. The interview was transcribed by Catherine Mann, for the USC South Caroliniana Library.

Courtney Siceloff, executive director
of Penn Center, 1950–68, January 16,
2005.

They were looking around for someone to come down. . . . At the time it was established there were no schools for blacks on the islands in Beaufort County. So they set up a boarding school and then they required the seniors—even those who lived on St. Helena—to come and spend a couple of years in the dormitory. They wanted to make sure that it was more than just education.

Penn felt that they could no longer continue the school itself, and they turned it over to county. The county was using the buildings, but they were planning to build their own school, which would be much larger. That's when we went down there, and the idea was to find out what might be done with the property.

Basically we had a twofold program. One was a conference center. At that time there was no place in the state where, this would be 1951, where blacks and whites could meet together, so we organized a conference center. The groups who used it most were African American groups. The group that had been using it before I came were the midwives. The state health department gave a program training black midwives at Penn. So then anyway, we converted the dormitories into a conference center and continued having biracial groups there.

ML: So you went there in 1951 or so?

CS: Right, and was there twenty years, very interesting period to be there. Obviously change was coming, but there was a lot of resistance to it and the very fact that we—the only place that blacks and whites could meet overnight, live, sleep, eat together, in the state. The black colleges would have day conferences for interracial groups, but they—you know, the dormitories—they weren't able to accommodate people overnight, so ours met a need there.

A work camp from the American Friends Service Committee came to help renovate some of these buildings. They were very rudimentary buildings by any commercial standards. It became, of course, very controversial, the fact of biracial young people, high school age, living together, going out . . . couldn't go to the state parks, which were segregated, but went out to the river beach to swim and . . . you know, exciting period.

ML: Yes, yes. What kind of leadership was there, and how did the policies and priorities get set? Was there a board to lead as well as your vision and initiative? How did all that work?

CS: It mainly was Quakers and Unitarians back in 1861–2 when they set up the school itself, but it became mainly a Quaker organization. By the time I was hired they drew on a number of . . . they had a South Carolinian who had been a state legislator who was on the board, and he felt very much that rather than it just being a Philadelphia, northern organization running a southern operation, that there should really be local people involved. And so he was very helpful in getting other trustees on a local basis, and he became chairman of the board. He was in North Carolina then and had a number of South Carolinians who became very active with the board. The whole matter of outsiders in the South was very controversial. He was quite good in having that base, and we were able to get several local people in the county to become members of the board.

ML: Who are some of the main names?

CS: Well, there was a Dr. Keiserling, a Jewish family that had come from Russia, and Herbert was a member of the board. His brother Leon Keiserling was on a Council of Economic Advisors to President Truman, I guess he was a very prominent economist. But the family had grown up in Beaufort. The parents had come over from Russia, and several Jewish families had settled in the Beaufort area and Herbert was a trustee. He was a physician at that time. African Americans, we had an Episcopal minister. It still was regarded as a very controversial group.

As I say, we set up a conference center. . . . The only place that interracial groups could gather would be at a place like Penn, so a very exciting period.

Dr. King and the SCLC came down several times. Great deal of publicity whenever they came down. They always felt he's going to be leading demonstrations there in Beaufort. They expected all sorts of things to happen. He just wanted a quiet place to meet. But there was a great deal of publicity and anticipation of disruption. They weren't interested in setting up a movement there in Beaufort. I felt very fortunate to be a part of it.

ML: Well, how many staff did you have, and what kind of roles did they play? You became more and more actively involved in the community and with some the desegregation in the community then?

CS: We had a community development program, and we had a training program where we would bring in people from different states in the South. Bring in local leaders, go through and find out who were active in their own communities and bring them for our training program that lasted several months. Letting them know what the government programs were that they could take back to their local communities, how to organize, how to operate within their own communities. So this was one of the primary activities.

We [also] trained Peace Corps volunteers. A number went over to East Africa and West Africa. They felt it was an advantage—Penn still was a remote area. We were able to place the volunteers with local families, black families, and this was an experience of a number of the volunteers had not had. Planning to go over to Africa to work in the Peace Corps, they felt it was a good experience for them.

ML: So it was an introduction to a different culture, dealing with acculturation, even though it wasn't Africa, nevertheless it was a cultural shock to many of them.

In terms of the community development, did you work on specific issues?

CS: Primarily what we tried to do was to get small groups in different parts of the county organized so that they could look at their own communities and find out what the needs seem to be.

We also had a marketing cooperative that we established there. There was quite a tomato growing area, and ordinarily the people who were raising tomatoes would just take them by the box to the packing houses, whereas we were able to organize a cooperative packing house so that we got our own packing shed and marketed the tomatoes, so that rather than just selling them by the box, they got the market price.

ML: They took the middleman out of it?

CS: Yes, right. It made a big difference in terms of what they . . . because ordinarily they would be ungraded and everything, whereas when we set up our own packing houses they were graded according to [quality], and you'd get a different price on each one. And people realized the need to improve their own—how they picked them and grew them. One of the problems was that people, since they were small farmers, got their plants all sorts of places, and we tried to standardize those so that we had a fairly standard agreement, as to which plants they would plant. In terms of the buyers, apparently that made a big difference rather than having different [varieties of] tomatoes.

But it was an opportunity that they were able to be in charge themselves and learn what the market forces were and had the control. They no longer just took the boxes down and turned it over to the packinghouses for them to pay a very small price.

In terms of the conference center, having interracial groups that had no other place to meet, no commercial facilities that would be available to them . . .

Patricia Tyler Lare [PTL]: How did Penn Center happen to not fall under all the Jim Crow laws that the rest of the state had?

CS: Well, we had our own trustee board. . . .

ML: Since it was a privately owned, church-sponsored organization, you could set your own rules. You didn't have to follow Jim Crow traditions, you set your own . . . ?

CS: It wasn't a Quaker operation although Quakers were probably the most prominent members at the time . . . a very strong Quaker connection and Philadelphia

Quakers. One of the persons who became a member of the board was a local lawyer, South Carolinian lawyer, and then a legislator, and he felt it was very important for South Carolinians that it not be seen as a northern operation.

ML: Who was that? Do you remember his name?

CS: There was James McBride Dabbs. He was an author. You know him?

ML: Oh, yes, very prominent.

CS: Who was the other one? . . . It's been a few years since I was there, but he was a very South Carolinian lawyer and he knew the way—he had been in the legislature— and it was very interesting. When he became chairman of the board . . . I believe I indicated the people from Philadelphia pretty much turned things over to the county, whereas he felt that it was important that we put it on the different foot. If you wanted to use the facilities, then you had to negotiate with us on what basis they would be used, rather than accepting the terms of the local [county] people. We would have our program and if they would care to participate . . .

One of the programs—the daycare program at that time—we were able to get the contract for that and upgrade daycare throughout the county. Whereas before it had been strictly a white operation in which the African Americans were not involved in any way to speak of. His influence was very much that this is our property, and we could make the terms. If they would agree, we could contract with them on that.

One of the important aspects of it, too, was our training for Peace Corps volunteers. They first subcontracted with a college up in Vermont for training, and then we began our own training for the Peace Corps volunteers and [were] able to place them in homes in the community. Since most of these were going over to Africa, it gave them experience that they might not have had elsewhere.

ML: It sounds like that the burden of maintaining the property and programs and facilities and so forth was beginning to become onerous for the board in Philadelphia, and they were looking to turn it over to the county but with local leaders . . . ?

CS: No local county officials, local people who were very progressive within the state. That was one of the things that the county had hoped that they could take over the property, but the trustees from Philadelphia felt it very important that that not be the case, that the principles on which it had been organized for African Americans, that those interests should be primary rather than just being a local[ly] operated county facility.

Then as I indicated, when they started—not long after we moved down there— South Carolina passed what they called an equalization tax, sales tax, which was to equalize [black and white] schools, which never got to that point, but at least they began to make an attempt at it. And so we felt that it was important . . . they would like to have taken over the facilities there at Penn, but we housed the high school for that community for a number of years. Penn had had a high school, and in fact, they'd had kindergarten through high school. Very small but it was only reaching a small number on the island even. They had two or three buses. When the county came in, they were able to provide transportation and cover the entire island and several adjacent islands, and therefore our facilities were inadequate for that.

Under the state equalization program, one of the first schools built under that sales tax that they passed was a comprehensive elementary, junior high, high school a few miles distance from our campus. We were not interested in having the campus itself become the property for such a facility. So at that point we turned to the conference center and let the county take the school operation entirely off our campus into the new buildings, which were much more extensive grounds and facilities, which never could have happened there within the limited area that we had.

So we then turned it entirely into two phases. One was the conference center, and the other was a local community development program, which we had in addition to that, which dealt primarily within the county itself. We had several field persons who went out and worked in the communities, finding out what needs the people would like to work on within their own communities, helped them organize, and assisted them in achieving those things.

PTL: Describe the money flow, who paid your salaries, who kept up the buildings and . . .

CS: Well, the trustees. I indicated there had been a small trust under the Penn Community Services, which was the Quaker-backed organization. But then we did fundraising. We got foundation grants in order to supplement whatever could be done with the Quakers, so it grew much larger. I mean the funds from the Quakers became a very small percentage of the total funds raised then. We just went to foundations and got support for the programs.

PTL: And no local government money?

CS: No, we never had any. One of the activities under Penn School when the school was there—I guess they called it Decoration Day—in which there was a National Cemetery in Beaufort and the Penn students would march through town and decorate the "Northern" graves that were in the national cemetery on Decoration Day, and that didn't exactly endear themselves to local residents.

I guess part of it was that they felt at that period that there was no support locally for the school. They always regarded this a northern operation. I don't think there was much attempt in terms of the trustees, Penn trustees, to involve local people. Whereas when you got a South Carolina chairperson who came on after I'd been hired, we felt it was very important that the local community get involved.

There were Head Start programs that the local school system didn't want to touch because of being federal money that we contracted for and then would place them in the school system. The school then found out that they wanted to get in on it, too. They realized that it was income producing, and so they expanded it much larger than when we were able to do it just in our own operation. But we primarily had to do it outside the county facilities until they saw that this was something that they could get involved in. There were several other programs that they wouldn't want to touch, the federal programs. I've forgotten the names of the retraining programs that the government had during that period.

ML: Job Corps or was that before Job Corps started?

CS: Before the Job Corps but there were certain grants that were made available for training, and although Beaufort County had several military bases at Parris Island, Naval Air Station, Naval Hospital, so it was heavily federal money involved, yet officially the school system and the county government didn't want to touch the federal money directly because of the strings that were attached. But then they realized in terms of the programs that were available for the schools, it was something they were missing out on, and so they then got interested in taking over those programs and were able to have it much more widely spread than we were able to on our own.

So we were very glad, you know, that they took that responsibility. But they were very reluctant to get involved with anything federal with the climate at the time. . . .

ML: During your tenure at Penn, things shifted a lot from just community development in terms of economic development and meeting basic needs to activism and a challenge of civil rights and things of that type. Can you describe how that worked out? There must have been a lot of stresses and strains within as well as without.

CS: [I became a] consultant with the U.S. Commission on Civil Rights—and the term "consultant" was a part-time employee—which had responsibilities at one time for eleven states, southern states that organized groups, advisory committees, for the U.S. Commission on Civil Rights. I had been involved with the state committee [the Human Relations Council of South Carolina] as well from its inception. . . .

ML: How did the voting rights and school integration proceed? This march through town on Decoration Day, did that lead then to other protest marches, was that a precursor to them or a model for that?

CS: There were community meetings that would be held. We didn't have the demonstrations like going through town as they once did to decorate the graves at the National Cemetery. But there were programs in which we primarily concentrated on what monies were available to communities that they could avail themselves of, that they were very anxious to be a part of. But there were likewise local protests in terms of employment opportunities for African Americans because no African Americans were being hired in the retail stores, and so quite a campaign and boycott ensued. Local merchants found out—because the population was substantial[ly] African American in Beaufort County—they realized they were missing out.

ML: It sounds like then that Penn Center by doing community development across the county . . . then it was these local county groups that were most visible and out front in presenting challenges rather than in the name of Penn Center?

CS: It was locally organized. That was the whole idea. We had a grant that enabled us to bring people in from different states to do this same thing in their own communities. We had a training program that ran for a number, I guess about four months' period, and then we'd follow them up in their own communities so that they could do it. But then they also had the model of what was being done there in Beaufort, and we were involved in that as well.

ML: So you must have had a good bit of staff then to follow up these people as they went back to their states. Who were some of these people?

CS: We didn't have a large staff. We only had about five people in that program.

ML: Who were some of those people that stand out in your mind across the years?

CS: One of them is Everett Gale, who still lives in this area. He's a Baptist minister. People locally: we had this fellow named Tom Barnwell that lived on Hilton Head, just a great organizer. And then we had a person who had been a Peace Corps volunteer, Joe McDomic, who had lived in Louisiana and joined the staff and became a . . . got elected to the board of directors for the county later on. Our carpenter there on the staff, his father had taught at Penn going back decades, and then he became quite a skilled carpenter, Leroy Browne, and he became the first [black] elected official in South Carolina [since Reconstruction]. He became a member of the board of directors for the county and the first for the entire state.

PTL: He was Leroy Browne?

CS: Leroy Browne. He's still alive, and he's still an interesting person.

PTL: He still lives on . . . is it Lady's Island?

CS: On St. Helena. Lady's is in between.

PTL: That's right. How many did the Quakers send down with you originally? Did you have anybody else that came with you?

CS: No.

PTL: Just you?

CS: My wife and I. We had only been married about a couple of years, and we met on a trip to Scandinavia, led by a very good friend of ours. Then I'd gone to Pendle Hill, a Quaker organization outside of Philadelphia, and while there we learned about the opportunity at Penn and a number of the trustees of Penn were living in the Philadelphia area. So that's the way we made our connection, really through Philadelphia and the Quakers. The school had been closed down at the time we were in Philadelphia, going to Haverford, and they weren't sure what to do with the property, and it was at that point that we were hired to go down and see what could be done.

ML: You were real pioneers.

PTL: Where was your wife from?

CS: She's from Charlotte.

PTL: So she was a southerner?

CS: Oh, yes, more so than I. I was from Texas, so she was more of a southerner. Lived in Fort Worth a while where the motto was "Where the West Begins." Some people didn't consider it really southern but had a lot of southern attributes so it was very southern.

PTL: Well, was she hired also, or did she just go as your wife?

CS: I guess I was hired and then she became the secretary, and just the two of us began the program. She continued working in the office, but she had much more responsibility than just the office. We were raising a family.

PTL: So you had your children there then?

CS: Our children were born there. We visited it before we were married. I was courting her, and this was an opportunity that came up, and we both went down to look it over together.

PTL: It's a beautiful area. I bet you fell in love with it.

CS: Yes, the first night we were entertained by local community people. They had a very small living room, and they were singing spirituals and talking about what was going on. Just a different world, you know! Wow!

There was no question in our minds that this is where we wanted to be. As I say, I was from Texas, and she was from North Carolina. We both wanted to return to this area and work in race relations. This just seemed to be a pretty good opportunity.

PTL: That was a nice fit then.

CS: We were very pleased. It came along at the time we were ready and they were ready.

[*While the audio tape was being changed, an inquiry about the Sicelofts' retirement to the Atlanta area was asked.*]

CS: We felt very fortunate. We lived at a place that now is called Inman Park. It's a very active community in Atlanta not too far from here. . . . It was a changing neighborhood, and a number of people questioned the safety and everything else. It became a very well-established neighborhood. We were very fortunate to live there.

PTL: It's wonderful when it's possible, isn't it?

CS: Yes, to be in the early part of the . . . sort of the pioneers of that community and the changing neighborhood. We became very active.

PTL: It fits your life's work.

CS: Yes.

ML: What year did you leave Penn Center then?

CS: Sixty-eight.

ML: Did John Gadsden follow you then?

CS: That's correct. We'd been wanting to do something overseas, and we both were Quakers and we hoped something would develop with the American Friends Service Committee, which we'd been involved with, but nothing seemed to be open then. And then we trained Peace Corps volunteers at Penn, and there was an opportunity to go to Afghanistan with the Peace Corp and so it was a great experience. We had our two children at that point, and it was a great experience for all of us to do that.

PTL: What were you hired to do in Afghanistan?

CS: What we tried to do was to organize local communities within that country to work on community projects, something like we'd been doing there at Penn Center. We didn't even know where Afghanistan was. We had to look it up on the map.

PTL: Nobody knew then.

ML: What area, near Kabul or out . . . ?

CS: Yes, we were based in Kabul.

ML: We just read in our book club—maybe you know the book—*The Kite Runner.*

CS: Oh, yes.

ML: The setting that he gives, which he draws a lot out of his own life and experience there, would parallel some of your time there. How long were you there in Afghanistan?

CS: We were there three and a half years. We really enjoyed it.

PTL: When did the Russians come in?

CS: No, that was before.

PTL: Was it pretty stable in Kabul?

CS: Oh, yes. But it was still considered pretty wild.

PTL: . . . run pretty much by the different tribal factions?

CS: Yes, but they had a strong king then. He had been educated in France, and his children had their fingers into everything. So there was a great deal of criticism of the family, and how they had profited from his being head of that and then he was overthrown, of course. But it was just happening about the time we were already scheduled to leave, and the Peace Corps pulled out soon after we left. The time we were there it was peaceful and everything, and it was a very good period and it was great for the kids to have that experience as well. . . .

My son was at West Town Quaker School outside of Philadelphia and took a year off between high school and college and traveled around on his own, and it was just a great experience for him. The Peace Corps would enable the [children], students to come over every summer, so he is quite a world traveler. The process of coming over several times and then taking a year off and spending it just traveling around.

PTL: What an experience! Especially when it's a peaceful place, a happy existence and not a fearful one.

CS: We just thought it was very fortunate for our family to have had that experience.

PTL: Did they provide housing for you?

CS: Well, yes.

PTL: Did you live in the community?

CS: The USAID often contracted houses, which were pretty much American-type houses in developments, whereas the Peace Corps allowed you to go out and select your own, and we found one that was very much Afghan, so we were fortunate that way, too.

PTL: You lived as the Afghans?

CS: Yes, it was just a very large compound, nice garden already there, had asparagus growing.

PTL: Did they have the amenities that we are used to with a kitchen and . . . ?

CS: It's a different-type kitchen and everything, but sure.

PTL: Inside bathroom?

CS: Yes.

PTL: Everything that we are spoiled with?

CS: But there were several little out-buildings and we began making wine there. It's great wine country there. Great grapes and so forth, and there was an UN viticulturist that was helping local farmers. He was anxious to make wine, and so we used his expertise. It was just a great experience for all of us.

ML: Let's see, I'm bringing greetings from a number of your friends, including Hayes Mizell and Keller Barron, who was just in our home Friday night for the birthday party of Bob Moore's wife, and so Bob sends his regards as well as Keller. And you mentioned about Joe McDomic. I interviewed him a few weeks ago as well as Frieda Mitchell. Tell me a little bit about Frieda. She seems to be such a fireball.

CS: Oh, she's such an able person! She was working for the Agricultural Department there in Beaufort County as just a secretary, but she became our secretary, and then of course, she branched out and developed her own program, and she was a very capable person. And so you met her recently?

ML: Yes, and her daughter. I'm not sure I can call the daughter's name, but one of the daughters [Muriel A. Hawkins, Ph.D.] is at the University of Wisconsin at Oshkosh as assistant dean for student affairs or something of that type, lovely person.

CS: Wonderful.

PTL: Isn't that wonderful that the next generation can have those opportunities?

CS: So great. I'm trying to think how much [education] Frieda had gone through. I guess she went to Tuskegee. Did she go to Tuskegee?

ML: Well, she went to Mather, there in Beaufort. I think she did take some work elsewhere as well.

CS: She didn't graduate, I don't believe from college. I'm not sure.

ML: I'm not quite sure. Mather was just a high school then?

CS: Right. A boarding school.

ML: Boarding school, uh-huh. But I think she went on for some advanced work. I understand she did a good bit of work with daycare centers. Is that the same thing that you were referring to, setting up the daycare centers throughout the . . . ?

CS: Right, she was contracting for that I believe. A very capable person.

ML: I just mailed back to her the program where the Rockefeller Foundation honored her in about 1978 or so. They recognized her, and I think they sent her to South Africa to model or to share how the daycare centers were set up and things of that type.

Now, Dr. Gatch and Senator Hollings and the concern about parasites, I guess that all came to the fore just about the time you were leaving?

CS: Oh, we were there. Yes, he was considered very controversial. People tried to make out that he was saying the situation was much worse than what it really was. They tried to . . .

ML: Tried to put a good face on things.

CS: Yes. I think he had a hard time. . . . I'm trying to think whether he was admitted, allowed to practice in the Beaufort Hospital or not. There was some controversy about that aspect of it. I think he took his patients to Savannah rather than to Beaufort. But he was very much one who indicated the intestinal worms, and people kept denying it and he led a group of reporters around and made headlines. People really realized they couldn't ignore it any longer. He had gotten so involved with it.

ML: Well, was he doing that just as a private physician?

CS: Yes.

ML: So he wasn't in public health service?

CS: No, he had his own practice but he was just . . .

ML: Just concerned and committed.

CS: He was a very good publicist. He knew how to reach the public through the newspapers, and so he became very controversial because it was very clear that the local health authorities were ignoring this and were feeling that's just the way things are. But he was very able, contributed a great deal.

ML: Were there times that Penn Center was under any threat with racist groups like the Klan or the White Citizens' Council or things of that type, or were you always just sort of preparing people for the front line instead of being on the front line of those kinds of controversies?

CS: Well, early on there had been a rally on Lady's Island of the Klan, of which Penn was the focus, but nothing, we never felt threatened personally. It's also interesting, we had a Sheriff, McTeer, that was there for years. He was almost blind, but he had a driver that would drive him around. He believed in keeping law and order, and I think that was very helpful in terms of our own need. He did not want to see anything happen that would . . . I know there was a situation in which a black person actually was in a training program, not run by Penn but it was situated at Penn, in which he had been accosted by several white people who were sitting drinking in a car. They came after him and he turned around and killed, I think three of them, two or three of them. They were local people. Great deal of feeling at that time, here one black man killing several white people. The sheriff whisked him off to Columbia. I was very concerned, soon after we came, at what could result from that, but he was smart enough to anticipate. He was considered a very fair person. He certainly didn't want to have any racial incidents happening there.

PTL: So was the whole area of Beaufort and the islands pretty free of incidences?

CS: I don't recall any large racial incidents.

PTL: The things that were controversial just stayed at the verbal level?

CS: Well, the boycotts of the local businesses that were taking place, that was . . . they had the nightly meetings asking for changes to take place. But one of our staff members, Leroy Browne, was the first person elected in South Carolina to public office. He became a member of the board of directors of the county, and it was predominately a black electorate. But the very fact that he offered his name and ran against a white incumbent who'd been there for some time, he became quite a state figure, that aspect—a very quiet person. So I think people had a lot of confidence in the leadership within the black community, and I think they were able to negotiate a number of things that took place.

[An interview with Leroy E. and Corinne J. Browne will be found in volume 3.]

People realized, I think, that there had been situations in other counties where there had been a great deal of trouble, and there had been the freedom rides, in which there had been some violence taking place. So I think the county basically, and the sheriff—you have to give him credit for that—felt this is something we didn't want to have. Also, another aspect of it was Hilton Head was being developed at that point, and they didn't want to endanger that economic development. So I think there was a general agreement, which was very fortunate—people felt they were not going to let race become an issue within the county. They were quite anxious to head off anything that would disrupt the community.

ML: When Leroy Browne was elected, was there a majority black vote for him, or did he draw a pretty balanced vote?

CS: The area—you ran within your districts—and his district was predominately black so he had no problems at all winning that. But the fact he was the first one to have offered in the state for that office—he became quite a spokesperson then for black elected officials, although he's very retiring.

PTL: By that time they were actively voting?

CS: Yes, right. No one had really challenged . . . none of the blacks had offered themselves for office. He was really the first one to do so, and his being very successful the first attempt was very encouraging I think for others.

ML: I believe that Frieda Mitchell said that she was the first—she and Alice Sherman—were the first [blacks] elected to a school board in the state as well. There were other blacks who had previously been appointed because many school boards were appointed, but not elected.

CS: I'm glad you got to meet Frieda. She's such a lovely person.

ML: We have such a rich experience doing these interviews. . . . As well as these interviews and pictures, we're including written first hand accounts. We've invited people to write their stories, tell about specific incidents, and we're also trying to recapture original documents and things of that type. Are there things that occur to you that you particularly would want us to include in the anthology? Would most of those records from Penn be in the archives there at Penn, or what would be the best way to assure that we reflect the story not only in our interview but also through other documents and materials?

CS: Well, I think we sent up most of the documents to the University of North Carolina. So whatever records there are I think . . . that was one of the things that our chairperson, Marion Wright, felt important to do. Although he was an alumnus of University of South Carolina, he saw that the University of North Carolina had a much better file on civil rights. He was the one who indicated, although South Carolina would like to have had the records, he felt North Carolina was better organized for such historical matters. I'm sure you'd get those papers into the North Carolina archives.

PTL: That's Chapel Hill campus?

CS: Yes.

ML: Any other thoughts that you have for this initiative?

CS: I just know we felt very fortunate to have had this opportunity. It's something that we didn't think about. Things work out, things one could not even plan for, timing and everything. We just felt very fortunate. Truly, it was the high point of our life, that period at St. Helena, just a great period for the whole family. Our children look back at this as a very important period of time. It was not easy for them at the time often.

PTL: Did they go to the island school?

CS: They didn't go to the black school.

PTL: It still wasn't integrated?

CS: Hadn't started desegregating until later, and they were already involved in their schools.

PTL: Back in the town of Beaufort?

CS: Yes, there were buses that went into Beaufort. Probably could have made a case about since they were closer to a black school to apply, but they were doing well in school we felt like we should be the ones to make that decision for them.

Interesting, when John went on to West Town School, a Quaker school outside of Philadelphia, and he came back and visited schoolmates here in Beaufort and they were really quite interested in what he was doing.

PTL: What's he doing now?

CS: He's now with Bill Moyers, the PBS program, he's executive director, executive producer of it.

PTL: Oh, my goodness. Oh, yes, we watch everything Bill Moyers does.

CS: Yes, he's just very fortunate to work with Bill. I guess he's sort of taken over that program now.

ML: That's right, Bill Moyers has stepped down now. Is he replacing Bill?

CS: No, not on the camera.

ML: Not on the camera but in terms of the producer.

CS: The program itself.

PTL: And your second child?

CS: Mary is out in California. She runs a gallery there, an art gallery, very interested in movies. It's in a very remote area and so they don't get many movies, and so she shows movies there. She lives out on a very remote area right against the mountains and just loves the area.

PTL: It's hard to believe California has any remote areas left.

CS: Right against Nevada, against the mountains there, and so she just loves that area. She had gotten involved in films and that took her to L.A., and then when she saw this opportunity to go up to the place in the mountains she jumped at the chance. We go up annually and visit her there.

PTL: And are they practicing Quakers?

CS: Mary and John? John is active with the Quakers but she's not. I don't think there's a Quaker group up there. She went to West Town School, which is a Quaker School. I think she had as much Quakerism as she wanted [laughs].

ML: Well, we can stay in touch. You'll probably wake up in the middle of the night and say now [snapping fingers], why didn't I tell Marvin about such-and-such.

CS: And, if you think of something . . . in the middle of the night . . .

ML: We can stay in touch, and of course, it's a fairly long process. I'm trying, though, to fast-track it as much as possible. It's very ambitious but I've gotten so much support, I mean encouragement from people, saying oh, yes . . . And some people like Frieda Mitchell said, well, I was always going to write a book, but I never got around to it.

CS: She should.

PTL: Have you done any writing? Too busy being active?

CS: My wife was a pretty good writer. She never . . . not anything was published. She wrote beautifully, and everyone said she should write. It's one of those things that she just not ever got around to it.

PTL: Is she here?

CS: No, she died about ten years ago.

ML: Has it been that long? I wasn't personally familiar, but people mentioned that she had passed. But it was ten years ago now?

CS: Yes.

PTL: You spoke of her in the present tense, and I thought she was here.

CS: Yes, she's so much a part of my life still. It was fortunate she was never here at this place. I don't think she would have liked communal life.

ML: Tell us a little bit about "co-housing." I was familiar with that term but only vaguely so.

CS: Well, you own your own house, but then the property is owned by the community. We have a "common house." We have common meals several times a week, and the work that's done is done by people in the community. You sign up [to help] for meals or for landscaping or whatever. There are certain things we contract for, but most of the work is done by . . . There are monthly meetings in which they make the decisions, rules, regulations, and planning and whatever else, things involved with the community. They have this garden out here. We sell some of it. What we do is buy it ourselves, and then they open to the public. We hire a gardener who is responsible for the planting, and we assist with that. So it's a very well-run community.

PTL: And it works? Not a tremendous amount of controversy?

CS: Well, there's always . . . these meetings get pretty long at times. But we don't have any hired personnel except the farmer and everything gets done. It has to be done by people here in the community, the cooking, the cleaning, the gardening, and whatever else. It's a good community. . . .

PTL *[referring to a photograph]:* . . . This is you or this is your son?

CS: That's my son and his son, my grandson. *[He refers to another photograph.]* Elizabeth and daughter Mary.

PTL: And she looks a bit like her mother, beautiful red hair. Now Siceloff, is it German?

CS: German. It's been spelled several ways. One of the ways is C-E-I-S-L-O-F-T, western part of Germany.

PTL: Did your wife have some Scotch blood to pass this red hair down?

CS: I'm not sure where she came from. She grew up in Charlotte, North Carolina, and her parents came from South Carolina, Abbeville.

PTL: I went to Queens College in Charlotte. From Virginia, I went to Queens. I grew up in Richmond. My maternal side, my mother's family is from New Hampshire.

CS: New Hampshire?

PTL: There's some Quaker villages there. There's one in Concord, between Concord and Manchester I think.

CS: I did alternative service as a conscious objector in New Hampshire.

Joseph McDomic, from Peace Corps to Magistrate

Marvin Lare [ML]:* This is December 22, 2004. At Joe McDomic's satellite magistrate's office . . .

Joe McDomic [JMCD]: . . . on St. Helena Island. We've been here about twelve or fourteen years, I think now, but we only come over on Wednesday afternoon. We spend four and a half days downtown in the central office in Beaufort.

ML: Joe, I really appreciate you taking some time out of your busy schedule to share your life experiences, particularly as related to the civil rights movement and things that led to it and led from it.

JMCD: Well, it's good to be a part of such a movement. I reflect back on those days. They were some trying times, but it was certainly good to be a part of it and be involved in it. So it's something that the children and grandchildren I hope will be proud of their daddy and granddaddy for. Whatever little, small contribution I made towards the movement, I hope that they will certainly be proud of it.

ML: When did you first become aware of the racial discrimination and injustices?

JMCD: I think back in the late '50s when I was in school. We started the boycotts and stuff back in '59 and '60. We organized the classes in our school and protested and got involved, and I've been involved, I guess, ever since that time. We marched down on the state capitol and went down to the drugstores, and, as I said, back then it was something that we just felt like somebody had to stand up and say, we've got to do something here. Some of the people in Southern University, I was at Southern University because it was a predominately black school at that time. LSU was down further, but we didn't have any blacks at LSU during that time. We just felt that we needed to

*The interview was conducted at Joseph McDomic's magistrate's office on St. Helena's Island, South Carolina, and was transcribed by Catherine Mann for the USC South Caroliniana Library.

Magistrate Joe McDomic, December 22, 2004.

do something to bring attention to what was happening to us. So I got involved as a senior in college, and I've been involved ever since that time.

Left Baton Rouge and joined the Peace Corps because they were drafting a lot of folks back then. They didn't have the volunteer army. You had to be drafted. And so during my senior year, they were calling up people, and I went down to be examined and came back with "1A," and I was trying to figure out, "Now wait a minute, I don't want to go fight nobody, what can I do here." And so time I got out of college President Kennedy had started the Peace Corps, so I said, "Well maybe. . . ." It was a deferment, those who joined the Peace Corps, so I applied to the Peace Corps and I joined up in '61. So that kept me out of the service for a couple of years. I went over to South America and worked as a volunteer with the Brazilian Agricultural Extension Department.

I came back to the United States in December of '63 and at that time they were not drafting people as fast, but they finally went to the all-volunteer army [1973]. I said, "Well, now that's a savior for me because I'm not going to volunteer. I don't want to go." So in '64 we had a career educational bulletin that we circulated among return volunteers for jobs and openings. Penn Center had an advertisement for a "Field Supervisor" and I applied. I didn't know much about Penn Center at that time. Didn't know what their objective was all about, but I read a little bit after I got here about it, and it said, "One of the first schools for blacks in this country." That's interesting. I think I'd like to be involved with this.

Came up for an interview in November and they said, "Would you like to stay on now? We'll hire you as a supervisor."

Now they had closed the school, but they were doing community organizing at that time, and I thought that would be right up my alley because that's what I was, you know, looking forward to, getting out there and getting involved. So I came up in '64 and joined the staff at Penn Center. Courtney Siceloff and Everett Keel, Tom Barnwell, Frieda Mitchell, Leroy Browne, Jesse Mae Warren, and we were the staff.

[See the interviews with Courtney Siceloff and Frieda Mitchell in this volume and with Leroy Browne, to be found in volume 3.]

They gave me an assignment to go out and organize about five different communities in the Beaufort County area. And so I said, all right, that sounds interesting to me. So I got out there and got involved with the people, trying to see who was who, who were the power brokers in the community and who made the decisions and stuff of that nature. We got involved with the folks and we started organizing around certain issues, and it certainly turned out to be one of the best things I think that ever happened to me, my coming here and getting involved with Penn Center. Boycotts, sit-ins, and all those kinds of things that continued as part of my work.

ML: What were the primary issues you were addressing at that time?

JMCD: We were looking at housing, water systems, daycare centers. We were looking at jobs. They had the Job Corps as a component of one of the programs that Congress had put out, and so we were trying to get kids who had dropped out of school to further their education and try to get some skills so that they could, you know, try to do something to better their community and themselves. We were trying to get people interested in Job Corps. We were trying to get them in the Peace Corps. We were trying to get water systems, trying to organize daycare centers, healthcare, and all those things. We had a wide variety of things that we saw after we sat down and talked to the communities about what are some of the needs that they felt that they needed to get into. We took off with water systems. We tried to get running water up and down the area. We tried to get daycare centers.

We found that a lot of people in the area had to go outside of their communities to try to find decent jobs and stuff. A lot of people were going to Hilton Head, Savannah, and all these other places, and what was happening, the older people would leave and they would have to leave some older kids home to stay with the children because they didn't have anywhere to leave the younger children, because they weren't old enough to go to school. They couldn't take them with them, so they had to take some of the older ones out of the classroom to stay home. So we felt like a daycare center would certainly meet one of those needs if we could get daycare centers in these areas to try to help out. We were involved [in establishing] a number of daycare centers throughout the area.

Penn Center had one of the first daycare centers in the state, I believe. They started way back then, for the teachers who had to teach at the schools so they could leave their children at the daycare center at Penn Center. So we felt that out in the community we ought to have something similar to that as well.

Another thing, like I said, was housing. A lot of the people were out here doing farming, but very minimal kind of farming at that time because farming was on the way out. People just couldn't make a living doing that, so it was kind of a subsistence kind of thing. We tried to get some housing programs through Farmers Home Administration to improve the housing in the community. We worked pretty closely with the Farmers Home Administration to try to do things of that nature.

Then we had to do a lot of sit-ins and boycotts too. I remember one of the first things we tried to do was to get better jobs at some of the stores downtown. It was strange. We had all these department stores, and nobody wanted to hire any clerks, black clerks, at anything in these department stores. So we went and talked with them and said we're coming to ask you about your hiring practices and see if you can't get some of our local people as cashiers. We had to organize, boycott, and do all that kind of thing before people would really listen to us. But eventually it worked. It did work! I guarantee you. When you start affecting the pocketbooks of people, people will start listening to you.

ML: Merchants were glad to have your money, but they didn't want to employ you.

JMCD: They didn't want you to work in their places. I remember one of the first places we went to was Edwards Department Store. They had a big department store downtown, and we asked them about hiring some blacks as cashiers, and they said, "We're not going to let anybody tell us who to hire," and all this kind of stuff. Okay. So we organized a bunch of folks and put them around and picketed the place. Where the bottom line stops, people said okay, we'll take a couple. We'll try a few. So we started with one or two stores and especially the ones that we did a lot of shopping at, because we felt like those are the ones that would feel it the most if we withdraw some of our monies from them. They started putting in one or two here and one or two there, and eventually it kind of opened up the avenue for a lot of people. But somebody had to start somewhere.

I know we had to organize a Welfare Rights Organization. I don't know if you're familiar with that group. We organized a group that went downtown to the welfare department and said, "Well, 75 or 80 percent of your people are blacks that you work with, but you don't have any social workers that could identify with the people that you're working with. So why not hire some black social workers?" Fella said, "Ain't nobody going to tell me who to hire."

"Okay, sir."

So we got eighty- and ninety-year-old people and put a fence, picketed all around the place, and we're going to stay there until they decide they're going to listen to us. They had a few of them arrested, now don't think they didn't. So we had the lawyers ready to go get them out of jail once they got arrested.

After about a month or two they gave in. They decided that we look like we're not going anywhere, so we might as well listen to them. So that was one of the other things that we finally got some social workers and eventually got a director of the Beaufort County Welfare Department, Social Services now, a black person as the director.

ML: Who is that?

JMCD: The first one was Fred Washington. No, I'm sorry, Al Gardner, and then we got Fred Washington, as the head of the department. I said, "Now, that's making progress!" That was really making some progress, so we were pretty happy about that.

But we didn't stop there. We went to all those places where we felt that there was unfair discrimination taking place, and we tried to address them. Eating establishments, we went to the restaurants. The *first day* I got here we went downtown to a restaurant, it's call Javista, fabulous restaurant downtown. In December 1964 we went down for lunch, went down and a little girl came to the door and she said, "We haven't started serving colored people here yet."

We said, "We haven't started eating in here yet." *[He laughs.]*

"I got to talk to my supervisor." That's all she said.

I said, "Okay."

She went in the back. Supervisor came and said, "We don't serve colored people."

All right. So we filed a suit against him. We were the "bad guys." The FBI came down and talked to us. We were bad fellas because we filed a suit against these folks. They came down and interviewed us for days at the time. "Where y'all came from. What you all doin'?"

I mean, it was rough! But eventually they sent us a letter saying that the people had agreed to serve people regardless of their color. If you have any problems, let us know. We go right back down there. They decided that they weren't going to discriminate against us by refusing to let us in, but what they would do is make us wait a long time before they served us. So, that's okay. "We're going to stay until you serve us." So that was another milestone, we thought. We got them to open up their doors to people regardless of who they were.

Another instance I can remember very vividly was when I first went down to register to vote. This was when I was in college. They wouldn't let you vote until you were twenty-one back then, so after I got twenty-one, I said, well, senior in college, you know, "They are *going* to let me register."

I went down there to register, and the lady said to me, "What do you want?"

I said, "I came to register."

"Register for what?"

I said, "To vote.

She said she would go down and see. She [came back and] pulled out a piece of paper, and said, "Read this for me."

I said, "Okay." Part of the Constitution, I read part of the Constitution.

She said, "Now explain that to me, what you read."

I told her what it meant.

She said. "No, that's not what it says."

I said, "What do you mean, that's not what it says." I said, "What does it say then?"

She said, "Well, I can't tell you."

I said, "I don't think you can read it." *[He laughs.]* Ooooh!

"Well, you're not going to get to register."

I said, "I'll be back."

Had to go back a second time. Same lady, she said, "You're back again?"

I said, "Yes, ma'am."

She gave me a different part this time and said, "Read this."

I read it.

She said, "Explain it to me."

I explained it to her.

"Well, I guess you're all right."

But all those kinds of things we had to go through before we could register.

ML: Now was that registering here in South Carolina or was that in Louisiana?

JMCD: That was in Louisiana.

ML: Did you do that just on your own, or was there a voter registration initiative?

JMCD: There was a voter registration group.

ML: A group?

JMCD: Oh, yeah, right.

ML: Primarily from the college or . . . ?

JMCD: No, no, no, it was in the community. Oh, yeah, it was a community group, absolutely. But we were threatened. I mean all kinds of violence threatened towards us, but that didn't deter the folk. I've got to give credit to a lot of the older folks who stood up and said regardless, "We're going to stand." And they did. It was really amazing.

ML: Tough days.

JMCD: Oh, yeah, oh, it was tough.

ML: But exciting too.

JMCD: Exciting, and at times it was kind of scary, too, because, you know, you had to have a lot of nerve to step out there then. It was scary at times but we had to do it. We had to do it!

Hold that just a second, let me see about this lady.

[A woman has come into the magistrate's office. There is a pause.]

ML: Well, was the leadership from the churches, from the community, from civil rights organizations, or a combination, or both at the various stages?

JMCD: Yes, in the beginning, there were a few of the pastors who would get involved. Some of the churches were afraid. They felt that they couldn't get involved because of the separation of church and all that stuff. It was a good excuse back then for some of the folks. But there were a few ministers who stepped out and joined up, were a part.

Same thing with a lot of the educators, there was a few, very few of them back in the '60s who were willing to put their jobs on the line because you see a lot of those folks were afraid that they were going to get fired if they got involved. You had only a very few of your educators involved with the civil rights movement, especially on the local level. They were terribly afraid and the people threatened them, "If you get involved, we'll fire you. You're going to lose your job."

And not only educators, in a lot of the other jobs, people had jobs where they couldn't get out there and show their faces and protest and stuff because they knew they would lose their job. They would fire them right on the spot. Absolutely.

But you had some of the people like the NAACP who were always out there. That was part of their job. So you had a few organizations like SNCC and all those folks who, you know, young folks back in those days. They certainly would jump out and head up a lot of the movements. You found a lot of young people involved in the movement because young people, I guess a little radical, didn't know anything about fear too much. And so you found a lot of the young.

I know when we started the boycotts downtown, we had a lot of the school-age kids who would come out. They would get out there on those lines with us and picket. I mean it wasn't a problem for them. A lot of the adults, they would get behind and they were afraid to get out there, but those kids were really, I tell you they would really jump out there.

ML: Kids felt like they didn't have anything to lose and everything to gain.

JMCD: Absolutely, absolutely. But a lot of the grownups were really afraid to get out there because of their jobs, and as I said, people were fired right on the spot. I remember when I came here one of the extension agents for this area who went to school at Penn, his bosses told him that he couldn't go to a meeting at Penn. Now he was one of those fellas, he didn't care what. He said, "They're not going to tell me where I can't go. I went to school here. All of my education came through Penn Center. They're going to tell me I can't go to a meeting at Penn?"

They told him he couldn't go to the meeting because we're supposed to have been radical folks over there. Some of them even labeled us as *"Communist"* folks. But it didn't matter. That was part of our job. It was part of our job.

ML: Of course, folks note that Martin Luther King, much of the leadership the SCLC, and other groups met here from time to time. Was that before '64, when you came here, or did they come after that?

JMCD: They had been here before '64, and after I came here as well. Yes, they had been here in the early '60s and a number of times after I got here.

ML: This was sort of their retreat center?

JMCD: Oh, yes, this was their retreat center, absolutely. But, you know, it's kind of like . . . you could not publicize, "Martin Luther King is coming out to Penn Center." It was kind of quiet, a secretive kind of thing because of who he was and the hatred of Martin Luther King that was going on in the country. So when he would come, we would have to usher him in under real strict security and get him back out, you know. He'd come in and address the group and get back out. But yes, he came a number of times while I was here. It certainly was a troublesome time back in those days. Went through a lot but it's all worth it.

ML: When did you begin to see things change?

JMCD: After the passage of the Civil Rights Act, I think. People were slow to change. People didn't want to but the law was there on the books, and people were pressing for the law enforcement people to enforce the law. So it started changing in '65, '66, '67.

The schools probably didn't change massively until about '68–9, or somewhere . . . '70. Some of the schools were opened up, but it was a slow, slow process. I know some of the kids who went to the all-white schools, they were spit on and they were called all kinds of names and everything. It was tough for those kids, the few that ventured out. I know the first group that went out to Beaufort High, about three or four of them, and they were called all kinds of names but they stayed. They stayed right through it, and after a couple of years they made friends and they found out that they weren't so bad after all. But it took a while.

ML: Do you remember the names of some of the key ones?

JMCD: Oh, yes, Craig Washington, oh, yes, those fellas went. There were only about three or four of them that went the first time around. But it was tough. My kids weren't old enough at that time. When my kids got old enough to go, everything was quiet. Matter of fact, my son was president of his class at the school. But those first, '64, '5, no '65, '66, '67, it was really something.

ML: Seems like to me it was in '70 before . . .

JMCD: That was about '70, right. It was about 1970 [before full integration]. But all that time more and more blacks were beginning to go because they saw that the first group made it through. Then a little more the second year, the third year even more.

But in that whole process I think we've lost a lot of the control that we had over the kids and stuff. I know when I was in high school, when the teacher said they were going to send you to the principal's office, that's one place you didn't want to go. They didn't send you home, they'd send you to the principal's office. The old prof, he had something there for you if you went to his office. I mean he had something for you. You didn't want to go back there. But he could control those kids. He could control them.

Nowadays if the teachers just talk mean to them, kids going to talk back to the teacher and tell him all kinds of things. "I'm not going to do this," and "You can't do this." You just didn't do that. I mean we lost a lot of respect. Of course, I don't blame that on the children. I blame that on the parents. . . .

ML: Besides the discipline of the parents, why do you think that is? Do you think that the economics of the family or the leadership of the family or the churches . . . the community?

JMCD: Well, it's a combination of things. Certainly you've got parents, you got a lot of single parents out there who are trying to make a decent living, who a lot of times they get up in the morning and go to work and kids still sleeping. They come back in the afternoon, late at night, and don't have time to spend hardly with the kids. Kids are raising themselves or some are being raised by other kids out in the street or something. A lot of times parents just don't have the time.

The other thing is that it seems like for some reason we can't reach the kids down on the level that they need to be reached. We've got so many different groups of kids in the schools nowadays coming from all walks of life, and that makes it really tough. They need the kind of experience with all these different groups, but at the same time it makes it difficult for you to control all these different segments that you have in the school system now. . . .

Yes, sir . . .

[He speaks to a man coming into the magistrate's office. There is a pause.]

ML: Reflecting back to your youth and childhood, who were the people that inspired you the most?

JMCD: I had a grandmother that raised me. She took me from my mother when I was about three months old. This lady was born in 1882 that raised me from a baby up until I went through high school. Couldn't read or write but she had really common, common sense, and she taught how to be respectful, how to respect other people, how you got to try to get a decent education, how you got to try to treat everybody right. And from being brought up very, very poor, I mean we didn't have anything. We didn't have lights in the house. With that old lady teaching and inspiring me, see I was reading and writing letters for her because she couldn't read, so every time she got a letter I had to read it to her and answer it back for her. She inspired me to get up, go on to school. Go to school. Regardless of what happens, go to school. I worked all the ways through college. Didn't ever get a dime from my parents. I worked during the day and night I studied.

Then I had an agriculture, FFA teacher, Future Farmers of America, when I was in junior high. He would come out and visit with us, come by the house, and try to get us involved in little projects and try to make a little money and stuff. He was an incentive to me. I looked at him, and I said one of these days I'm going to have your job. I admired him. He was always clean cut, clean pants, shirt. I said one of these days I'm going to have his job. So that inspired me. When I went to high school, I had another agriculture teacher who was very good at trying to help kids to get ahead. I looked at him and I said, "Well, between the two of y'all I'm going to have one of y'all's jobs one of these days." And they tried very hard to keep us involved in little projects so that we could make a little money from them. And I had a little chicken project, pigs here and there, that we would take to the fair and got little money from them. They were incentives for me. I had it real hard and I had to work. I remember when I used to work for a dollar seventy-five or two dollars a day, and to me that was incentive enough for me to try to go to school and try to get some education so I could at least make a little bit more money than that. So those were incentives for me.

See nowadays—this is what I think is happening to our kids nowadays—the children don't have anything to inspire them to want to do better because we pay them to do nothing but go to school. . . . See, I had to work in the morning. I had to milk the cows, feed the hogs and chickens before I'd go to school. Had to cut wood. Had to do all that, go get water. We didn't have any running water. Had to do all those things when I came back from school. Those were incentives enough to say to me you got to stay in school and try to get yourself a pretty decent education so that you can get beyond this. But nowadays kids have got everything at their disposal. . . . They need to learn what it is to earn their own money. They need to know that.

ML: Our economy now, though—you can't go out and pump the gas—we're such an automated society. Kids can have tasks around the home. . . .

JMCD: You can find something for them to do. You got to find something for them to do. . . .

ML: What year did you graduate from high school?

JMCD: Fifty-six.

ML: Fifty-six. I graduated in '52 so we're pretty much contemporaries.

JMCD: Absolutely, it was tough but back then I didn't know. You know, I thought that was just the normal way of life. It was the normal way of life.

ML: It's what everybody did.

JMCD: Yes, it's what everybody did, absolutely. But it was interesting but we had it tough, but we didn't realize how tough it was. But I'm glad I had to go through that. I really am.

ML: Tell me more about the Penn Center and some of the other folks you worked with. Did you have different tasks, the different workers?

JMCD: Yes, Tom Barnwell and I, we were the supervisors at that time, going out doing organizing. Then 'round about '68, '66 to '68, we got a grant from the Ford Foundation to do community leadership training, and we brought in people from other states to Penn Center to look at our model that we had going and train them. It was a fourteen-week training program. We went out and asked the leadership in those different communities to elect somebody and send them up for training. We did the leadership development training for two years with a grant from the Ford Foundation. We sent them back into their communities, and a lot of those folks ended up on county boards and some of them even in the legislatures from what we trained here at Penn Center. We trained them from Louisiana, Mississippi, Alabama, Georgia, South Carolina, Tennessee, North Carolina, all those different states. After we trained them, we would go back to the communities with them and spend some time with them, getting them set up in their communities so they could organize their own areas.

So after two years we were not able to get it funded for the next round, so we started doing some other things here in Beaufort and Jasper Counties and up and down the coastal areas. We organized what we called a "Land Program," trying to get people to take a look at some of the reasons why we were losing so much land in these areas.

ML: Heir's property?

JMCD: We started looking at the heir's property situation as to what was causing some of these problems and why. If blacks owned at the turn of the century 5 million acres of land, in the South mostly, why in the '70s had we lost down to about 2.5

million acres? What were some of the reasons why? So we tried to address that issue at Penn. We were one of the first agencies in the country to address the heir's property situation, and we felt that we had to do something because it was just mind boggling to see, with all the education that we have nowadays, how blacks were losing so much land! And even today, it bothers me when I see every year so much of the land still going up for delinquent taxes.

ML: Was the heir's property loss primarily because of the division with the family and then somebody would sell out their share?

JMCD: Well, the problem . . . yes, the problem was we'd have the heir's problem when our people didn't make wills, see. They bought the land and they left it [to their heirs without a will], and I thought that it was a good thing that they did this because if they hadn't done it that way we would end up with much less land than we have today. With the heir's property, at least it's going to take you much longer before you can get a clear title to the property. See, if you buy out one of the heirs, then you still have to go through the court system. You've got to put the other heirs on notice and try to get the clear title to the property, and that's going to take you a while and it's going to cost you a lot more money. But people who—developers—they don't mind that because they've got their own lawyer, and they've got money to burn. They don't mind doing that.

But certainly the older people did not make wills because they felt that if [they] leave this land here for my children, they can set them up, any one of them or all of them, on the property. They can build a house on the property wherever they want to because it belongs to them. But what happened was a lot of those children left and went off to big cities and decided they're not going to ever go back. And so if someone came up and offered them some money for their interest, they sold it out and that's what caused the problem. When somebody decides that they want out, sell it to someone outside the family.

ML: So, could that new owner, could they force the sale of the property?

JMCD: Oh, yes, absolutely, that's exactly what they did. What you call a "partition sale." In other words, they'd go to the court and say, "Look here, I can't get the rest of those folks to sell to me, and we can't agree on which piece we're going to let each other have. I'm one of the cotenants now in this group, and I want the court to put it up for sale. Sell it to the highest bidder." Now the court takes the position that we can't divide the land on an equitable basis because one piece is going to be more valuable than another. You see what I mean? The court said, "But I can divide the money so everybody can have their equal share of the money." So it's sold to the highest bidder, and that's what has happened. . . .

ML: That's the developers, I guess.

JMCD: And you can't outbid them because they've got the money.

ML: Now, did you all ever get that changed? I know when I came on the scene addressing those issues, one of my first visits to Penn Center was talking about heir's property.

JMCD: They never did change that. What we were hoping would happen is that they would pass a law that would give the heirs a first-refusal right. If someone bought out one of the heirs, then they had to come to the rest of the heirs and offer to sell it back to them, and if they couldn't afford to buy it back, then they could go ahead with the partition sale. But you had to buy it back at a reasonable price, though. You see what I mean? . . . But that is not the case, so they still have it where they sell it to the highest bidder. They put it on the auction block and sell it to the highest bidder.

ML: So that's still happening?

JMCD: Right. So the thing that we've got to do is try to get the heirs to stop selling out their interest. If they want out, offer it to the rest of the heirs first. You see what I mean? Let them have a chance to buy your interest out. So that's the thing that we have to try to counteract not having the law passed.

ML: That's a lot of education.

JMCD: It's a lot of education.

ML: A lot of communication.

JMCD: Absolutely, absolutely. But that's what caused a lot of the problems. And the other thing, a lot of people just don't have the money to pay the taxes because these taxes go up so high now. I mean you put up a big development right next to my little piece that I'm using to live on, it's going to cause my property value to go up too. You see what I mean? So they're going to tax you on the highest [and best] use value of the property, as opposed to taxing you on what you're presently using it for. I'm using it for a home site. They ought to tax me as a home site. But they're going to say, well, you can take that site there and sell it and get millions of dollars and buy you another piece somewhere else.

ML: Still no protection though for the owner, the long-term owner, so the tax sales are still gobbling up the land?

JMCD: Oh, yes, tax sales. Every first Monday in October, they have a big tax sale. People come with millions of dollars to buy up property.

ML: As you said, Penn Center pioneered that concern for all over the South, and yet it still is not really . . .

JMCD: It's still not taking hold like it should. It really should take hold.

ML: The election of more blacks and the appointment to judgeships and so forth, has that improved?

JMCD: I think certainly we need more black legislators, need more people to make the laws, no question about it. And we are way, way short when it comes to equal representation in terms of the legislature, in terms of black judges. We are way, way short, even on the county level, state level, and national level. We certainly need to have people who are sensitive to those kinds of needs and those kinds of problems. . . .

Michael Figures, he was a student at Harvard and he came to work in this area one summer and he was working with the land program, about '72, I guess, '72 or '73, and he was really . . . he was a lawyer. He came through from Harvard and spent the summer down here with us. He was from Alabama. After he finished law school, he went back to Alabama, got in the legislature, and eventually got into the senate, Alabama Senate. And he got a law passed in Alabama, one of the few states that had the first-refusal rights for the heirs when their property is sold. He got it passed in Alabama, and we were hoping that we could get something like that in South Carolina, but we haven't been able to do that at this point. That certainly would be a big help to a lot of people if we could get that first-refusal right passed in South Carolina.

We really do need to have some protection for people who lived on the land and do not want to go anywhere else as opposed to one of their relatives who's gone up North and got a little apartment somewhere and decided they're not going to come back, and sell out. So we do need some protection for people like that.

ML: Has that bill been filed in recent years?

JMCD: It hasn't been filed, no. We've talked to several legislators about doing that.... It's certainly something that's needed. Well, Marvin, I'm done talked out.

ML: Any other thoughts in conclusion?

JMCD: Have you talked to Leroy [Browne]?

ML: Not yet. I want to make sure I have his phone number before I leave.

JMCD: Leroy is certainly a person that I think you ought to talk to. Like I said, he was the first black elected official in South Carolina since Reconstruction. He was elected in 1960.

ML: Was it at-large or single-member districts?

JMCD: From this area, St. Helena. That's why he was able to get elected because there were enough black people registered to vote back then, he could get elected.

ML: Well, I really appreciate it, Joe.

JMCD: All right, Marvin, my pleasure.

ML: Likewise. It's really good to do this with you.

Frieda Mitchell,
Fireball for Freedom

Marvin Lare **[ML]**:* Today is the 22nd of December 2004 in Port Royal, South Caro-lina, and I am visiting with Mrs. Frieda Mitchell and her daughter, Dr. Muriel Hawkins [Muriel A. Hawkins, Ph.D., assistant vice chancellor, Division of Academic Support, University of Wisconsin, Oshkosh], who is visiting from Wisconsin for the holidays. How are you today?

Frieda Mitchell **[FM]**: Fine, how are you?

ML: Good. Mrs. Mitchell. I really appreciate your sharing with us today your expe-riences throughout the civil rights movement and other experiences of your life. Can you tell us where "you discovered America," where and when roughly? Now, you don't have to say when.

FM: Where was I born?

ML: Yes.

FM: I was born in Sheldon, South Carolina, which is a rural area of Beaufort County, northern Beaufort County. You need the year?

ML: No, we can skip that. Thank you. From your childhood what are some of the first things that you may remember, both positive and negative. The warmth of com-munity as well as were there some injustices, things that weren't quite the way they should have been. What are some of your childhood reflections?

FM: My childhood was very pleasant. I grew in a community and a family where we were very close knit. I learned at an early age, though, that race made a difference. *Kitty . . .*

[Her cat jumps onto Lare's lap.]

*The interview was conducted at Frieda Mitchell's home in Port Royal, South Carolina, on Decem-ber 22, 2004, and was transcribed by Catherine Mann for the University of South Carolina's South Caroliniana Library.

ML: Don't worry about it.

[Her daughter takes the cat.]

FM: . . . We grew up in a rural community, property that my mother owned, it was in my mother's family for many, many years, and I grew up with my sister. There were four of us.

ML: When in your life did you begin to experience that there were racial injustices and inequities?

FM: Very early, even though I probably didn't realize the full effect of what race meant, but things happened that I resented even at an early age. For instance, my mother did the laundry for the white family who lived on the property across the road from us. And one of the things I remember vividly, when they would bring the laundry in a huge wicker basket, instead of them bringing the laundry in the house, my mother would have to go out and bring the basket in, and I've always wondered why they didn't bring the basket in, why would she have to go out. So that was one thing that I remembered, and I guess even as a child growing up there were things that happened that I resented and I didn't know why, but I just knew that I didn't like some things that I saw.

Muriel Hawkins **[MH]:** Like what? . . .

FM: Oh, okay. The farm where the white folks lived that we took in the laundry, we would go over and help her. I think this was after I had gone away to boarding school. In the summer when I was home, we'd go over to help her babysit, and we never went in the front door. Because it was a huge plantation house and the house was right on the waterfront, but we always went to the back door. So I really never knew what the front part of the house looked like. But the one thing I remember vividly, my mother would always say to me, "Whenever you go in the Campbell's house in the back door, you step over my mother's grave."

When the plantation was established, there was a burial ground for the blacks, who lived in that area, and so they leveled all the graves off and built their plantation home on the waterfront. And my mother always said, "Whenever you go into Helen Campbell's house, you step over my mother's grave."

And, you know, things like that stayed with me. I always wondered and it sort of bothered me, but there wasn't anything I could do about it because my mother never really told us in a negative and a hateful way, but she'd always say that. She'd always tell us those things.

ML: You said you went away to boarding school?

FM: Yes, I did. I went away to boarding to Mather School [Beaufort, South Carolina] because in the rural areas the schools for blacks only went to the sixth grade. My sibling, my older brother, went away to boarding school, Penn School, which is now Penn Center—you probably know the history of that—and my older sister went to Mather School, where I went. Yes, Mather School for Girls, that's where I went.

MH: I went there, too.

FM: Yes, you went there, too. And my second sister went to Penn School, and my brother went to Penn School, and my older sister and I went to Mather School for Girls, and my daughter went to Mather also. If we did not go to those boarding schools, we would never have gone beyond the rural community school at the end of the fifth grade. So my mother's parents made great sacrifices so that we could go to those private schools.

ML: Were they pretty expensive, of course, to have the children . . . ?

FM: Well, we worked. All of us worked. We were allowed to work part of our boarding costs.

MH: The school required all the girls to work. You never knew who there was paying full price or who was on a scholarship.

FM: Right, at Mather. Some of the best experiences of my life were at Mather. And I'm still in touch. I'm on the alumni list. It was just a really great experience there.

ML: What particular teachers stood out to you?

FM: All of them. Most of the teachers were white. They were from the American Baptist Home Mission Society. Most of them were northerners, Boston, they were really, really . . . the best years of my life as a child growing up were the years I spent at Mather, and I'm still in touch with friends who went to Mather. It was really wonderful.

ML: When did you first become involved in civil rights activities?

FM: Oh, my goodness. I remember very well when I first heard . . . I was working as a school clerk at the elementary school where my sister taught. The principal there was really involved—as much as blacks were involved in civil rights—and I heard Martin Luther King speak at . . . was it the March on Washington? I don't remember whether it was the march . . . but anyway we listened at Dr. King, and I guess that's when I really became interested in being involved—because I knew that I wasn't happy with what was going on because I realized at that stage in my life where discrimination and racial prejudice had a great impact, a negative impact on African Americans, so I was ready to be involved. When I heard about the March on Washington and I heard Dr. King, that was when I really realized that I had to be involved.

It was around that time that a position became open at Penn Center, and I left the school as a clerk and I went to work at Penn Center and that was where I met Courtney Siceloff. I don't know if that name has ever surfaced.

ML: Yes, I talked with him.

FM: When did you talk with him?

ML: Oh, on the telephone maybe a month or two ago, and I'm planning to go down there [Atlanta].

FM: . . . I would really be interested in knowing how he's doing. The only thing I know is that his son said he's in a care facility, and I hope he's okay. I hope his memory is up to . . . that he can give you . . .

ML: As I say, he returned my call.

FM: You talked with him and he was quite lucid?

Frieda Mitchell at her home in Port Royal, South Carolina, December 22, 2004.

ML: Yes, we didn't talk long other than to say that I would call and arrange a time to come down.

FM: Very good.

ML: So he had a position open there at Penn Center. What was the position?

FM: Yes, a secretary position, but I was not restricted to just that and that was the one thing that I remember very well because a lot of things were going on during that era, and we were involved with community activities and tutoring and I was not just restricted to typing his letters, although I did that. His wife was there also. She worked and she did a lot of his personal correspondence. But I did, you know, a lot of typing and filing and clerical work. I think the one thing that was most interesting, a lot of groups came to Penn Center for conferences, and we were always involved in their activities. One experience that I had, and this may not be relevant to this, but I'll just share it with you. A conference was held, an international conference, and I'm not sure whether it was Baptists or American Baptists. I know it was a religious conference, and this was during the height of segregation. People came to that conference from all over the world, a whole week or maybe two weeks at Penn Center. And they realized that segregation was the law of the land, so three people from that conference decided that they were going to witness and attend church services in Beaufort. I remember there was a very heavyset black minister and a white minister and a white woman . . . They went to worship at . . . it must have been the Beaufort Baptist Church.

They went to visit to worship, and they stopped them at the door and told them that the two white people could come in but the black man could not come in. And I will never forget as long as I live, they came back to the campus, and we were in a worship service all the rest of the day. They were so upset. They were really upset, and we all moaned and wailed and worshipped and prayed that they were turned away from the house of worship because of that black man. That's one thing I'll always remember, yes.

. . . But Penn was the best years of my life because I got to know the Siceloffs and I got to meet a lot of people and I got to . . . We were not restricted to whatever our work was. We were involved in whatever was going on at Penn.

ML: So you worked as a team?

FM: Yes, worked as a team . . . of course, Penn Center was the Mecca for the civil rights groups. Dr. King came. I'll never forget when the word got out that Martin Luther King was coming to Penn Center, crosses were burnt, not the upright crosses, because it wasn't convenient for them. But they would pour the gasoline on the campus in the form of a cross and light the gasoline. And we were all, gosh . . . we were not afraid but it was just— *That cat wants to be outside.*

There was a young man, and I don't know whether Isaac Richmond is still in Ripley, Tennessee. Did that name ever, did anybody ever mention that name to you?

ML: I don't think so. Isaac what?

FM: Isaac Richmond in Ripley, Tennessee. Joe McDomic may know [where he is], but Isaac Richmond was very, very active in the civil rights movement. He worked with Penn Center, but he went beyond his job at Penn Center and he really challenged the local system and did some things that were unprecedented. As a matter of fact, I think Courtney, at some point Courtney was kind of wishing, "I wish he wouldn't do that." But he would go downtown and we'd picket, you know. We did a lot of picketing. We marched in the stores and—*Cat!*

ML: *He's all right.*

FM: Courtney would want him to not do it, but he didn't say "Don't do it." I think Courtney was not afraid but, anyway.

ML: It was a real stress.

FM: Yes, it was very stressful for him because he didn't want anything to happen that would affect the activities at Penn or throw a bad mark on the agency and the organization and the students. But Richmond organized the Beaufort community and challenged what . . . He did some unprecedented things. He was a brave young minister. And I guess as a result of his being here gave a lot of us courage to do things. We'd picket in the stores. Cleve Sellers, have you met Cleve? You know Cleve Sellers.

ML: Oh, yes.

FM: Cleve was one of the active, Bill Saunders, Cleve Sellers, James Jenkins, and all those people who you have already talked with. They'd come to Penn. We'd have meetings, overnight and weekend meetings and rallies. Penn was sort of the hotbed of activities in the civil rights movement. What else can I say about that?

ML: Was Isaac Richmond on the staff?

FM: Yes, definitely. He was a minister. He was definitely on the staff, and I think at some point, of course, he was unstoppable, but I think at some point Courtney would become concerned for his safety because Ike was really brave, you know, and he was not afraid of anyone. He was small in stature but very big in his ambitions as a minister.

ML: Now, was he black or white?

FM: Black, black, he was black. There was another white person there at that time, Everett Gill. Did that name surface?

ML: I've heard it.

FM: Everybody called him Buddy, Buddy Gill. . . . Everett Gill was there, too. John Gadsden because John was the director at one point. . . . Have you talked with him?

ML: Not yet, but he and I are getting together. Well, when did you get involved in politics and on the Board of Education?

FM: Okay, let me refer to the notes. These notes were given by my deceased friend [Alice Sherman]. She and I both ran [for the school board] at the same time. . . . *[She refers to notes from Mrs. Sherman.]* In 1964 we organized the Education Committee. We knew that school desegregation was imminent, that it was going to happen. So we wanted to get the black community prepared. We never thought about what the white community was going to do, but we wanted the black community to be brave enough to integrate the schools when the order came. We called it the Beaufort County Education Committee.

And that was what we did, and that was how we got [elected] first time around. I didn't sacrifice. My daughter did not integrate, but Mrs. Sherman's son did.

MH: Karen [Hawkins Ulmer] was trying to integrate the schools.

FM: Karen did not go to Beaufort High.

MH: Yes, she did go up there and integrate the schools. But, first she went to a traveling community school.

MH: It was an experimental school.

FM: And then after she left there, she went but initially she did not go . . .

ML: So you and Mrs. Sherman ran for the school board in the '60s?

FM: Right, we ran for the school board. . . . But first, we organized the committee to prepare the kids to transfer, because we had to encourage black kids. The first kids who transferred were only from two families. They handpicked the first black kids that transferred to the white schools were from three families. They handpicked a civil service family, and this was a neighbor, the Smith family. And then the Washingtons, Charles Washington was a black attorney. And they handpicked those students who were brave enough to go to the white schools and all this is in this article that I think I gave you *[Beaufort Gazette,* October 5, 1997, p. 1D].

ML: So it was the Smiths and . . . ?

FM: The Smiths, and the Washingtons. The kids from those families were handpicked to go into the white schools. I'll give you those articles. Good, okay, that will give you the full account of what I'm trying to say because I'm not going to remember all that so accurately.

ML: Well, let me try to hear, were you on the school board when that occurred or . . . ?

FM: No, not then. We were elected in 1968, okay. After we had set up all these activities to prepare the students to transfer, then Mrs. Sherman and I ran.

We knew we were going to be elected because we both ran from predominately black districts. I ran from the Sheldon Township, predominately black, and she ran from the St. Helena Township, and we were guaranteed that we were going to be elected. So that was when we ran and were elected in 1968.

ML: How were you received? Did they accept you, and did you feel like you had a voice in the school board meetings?

FM: Oh, definitely, we had a voice because whenever the school board met they had to move the meetings from the designated place to the auditorium, because the blacks always came to the meetings in droves to give their support to Mrs. Sherman and me, you know. So we always had a crowd at the meetings.

At one time Mrs. Sherman and I convened a meeting. We researched the school board policies, and we had a young attorney, Charles Washington, the father of the two young men, who would tell us. He did the legal research, and we found in the school board policy that any two members could convene a meeting and would be an official meeting! And I guess they never in their wildest dreams thought anybody would have done that. But Mrs. Sherman and I convened a meeting and I chaired the meeting. It was held at the black school, the black high school—standing room only. I think the board members were afraid there was going to be a riot. But that was what we did. We convened the meeting and we set the agenda, and anybody could speak that we wanted to speak. Boy, that was some meeting I'll never forget. That meeting must have lasted most of the night because we had black families lined up to speak.

ML: What issues were they addressing?

FM: They were addressing their concerns about what was going to happen to their children, what kind of protection they were going to have. You name it, everybody said whatever was on their mind. They wanted to be reassured that there was not going to be a bloody riot and their kids get killed.

But the one thing that I'm thinking about, okay, when the school board went to Washington to meet with HEW [U. S. Department of Health, Education, and Welfare] to present their case, of course, Mrs. Sherman and I were not invited to go, but Courtney and I went anyway. Courtney Siceloff and I went, and I'll never forget this. They boarded the flight in Savannah, the superintendent, Dr. Trammell, and the other board members who were going, they boarded the flight in Savannah. Yeah, and Courtney and I got on in Charleston, and when we walked in they were sitting in the first-class cabin having their cocktails. And when Courtney and I walked through, Dr. Trammell could have eaten his butt, he said, "Frieda, I didn't know you wanted to go to Washington to this hearing." *[She laughs.]*

And, of course, Courtney was there with me, and when we got to the hearing Courtney and I sat on the side with the government, with HEW. We did not sit with them. We sat with HEW and we testified. I will never forget that. I got my courage from Courtney because he was brave, you know.

And the other thing that happened that was funny, maybe not relevant to this discussion. But the woman who, and I told her about you. I don't know whether you contacted her or not. Her name is Rosa Wiener, W-I-E-N-E-R. She was a person assigned to work with our school district, so when she came to meet with the school board she didn't stay in town the whole time. She stayed at my home. I lived in Sheldon then and she stayed at my home. When she packed her things to leave, she forgot a pair of shoes so I sent her shoes by Mr. Trammell, the superintendent. When he went back I sent her shoes by Trammell to give to her. Boy, that was something. So he knew then of the connection.

So then he said, "The person was assigned to work with the school district got involved with the black militants."

That was me *[laughs]*. Me and Courtney, we laugh about that, but "the official HEW official got involved with the black militants." So I sent her shoes by him. I knew that he would use that. That was really funny. But anyway, she and I are still friends. In fact, she comes to visit me.

ML: Is she in Washington?

FM: She is in Washington, D.C., and I told her that I was going to be talking with you. She'll probably be glad to talk with you also. If you want to interview her, I'll give you her number. I was rambling.

ML: That's okay. So from '68 on up through, how long were you on the board?

FM: I was on the board sixteen years, four terms. Couldn't get off. Mrs. Sherman didn't serve. Mrs. Sherman got off, served three terms, but I stayed on.

ML: That's a lot of meetings.

FM: It was not easy.

ML: I've always admired people who serve on school boards.

FM: Oh, really? And during that era it was . . .

ML: It takes so much time even now, but I can't imagine what it would have been like then.

FM: You cannot imagine what it was like then because whenever the school board met, my only support was from the black community. Whenever the school board meetings were held, there was always standing room only. I think they probably frightened . . . the black community intimidated the superintendent of the school board whenever we met. . . . Those were some hot days.

ML: Well, what did you accomplish and not accomplish in that process?

FM: I think the one thing that we accomplished was the ability or the opportunity to speak and to be heard, because prior to that, blacks were just . . . we were not even given the opportunity in public meetings to express our concerns. But in an open forum like that, and we were elected so we had all the same rights and privileges that our white counterparts [had], and that within itself gave us the opportunity to express ourselves and they couldn't shut us up.

ML: And for the first time for most whites heard articulate and adamant . . .

FM: Right, yes, and determined blacks to demand their rights. I know we intimidated a lot of folks, and I think for the first time in the history of this area, when Courtney Siceloff came to Penn Center and the civil rights movement became active in this part of the South, I think it brought in an influx of people who had been seasoned since the movement began. Bill Saunders and those from Charleston, Cleveland Sellers came, and, you know, a lot of things were going on. We were picketing for jobs, job opportunities. We were not just demanding the rights in schools and all that, we were demanding rights, equal opportunity for employment, fair employment practices, legal rights in court. It was a whole. It wasn't just one issue . . .

ML: And you were employed at Penn Center throughout this time?

FM: Yes, I was employed at Penn Center. I was a secretary, but I was not restricted to that. We did what we needed to do. Courtney is one of the most remarkable persons that I have ever met, he and his wife. His wife passed away a couple of years ago. . . .

ML: Were there other people who were particularly supportive?

FM: Local people? Oh, yes, there were lots.

ML: Yes, local people or from across the state.

FM: From across the state, Penn Center was like a Mecca for civil rights people. They came. Conferences were held there and they came there. It was the place to be, safest place I guess, and of course, the Ku Klux Klan burnt some crosses but that didn't intimidate anybody. They didn't burn the upright crosses. They burnt the image of the cross and lit the gasoline.

ML: On the ground?

FM: Yes, and they had some rallies going out of town, but nobody paid them any attention.

ML: What about the police and law enforcement, SLED [State Law Enforcement Division] and others?

FM: They were there but they didn't try to intimidate us. You know, they never interfered. They were just there. . . . We were really ready because we were not allowed to picket in the stores. But some brave folks like Cleve and those would go. I remember he went. I think it was Cleve or one of those guys went in the store and the policeman said, "You're not supposed to be in the store with that sign."

He said, "I'm in the store with the sign."

I think they intimidated the police. But it was peaceful, all the demonstrations. I give them credit. They did not bother us. In fact, we would plant the . . . *Be careful of that cat. That cat gets carried away sometimes when you pet her.* We would plant the members of our group because the blacks were afraid. Look, a lot of blacks were very much afraid, and they were afraid to go in the stores. So, what's his name, Lawrence Washington, Wesley Felix, these were all local men, they'd purchase huge bags of flour or rice or whatever would make a lot of mess, and they would go in, give it to certain ladies to go in and purchase these things that would spill out a lot, and then they'd walk up and split the bags and all the rice and flour would scatter all over. And that would frighten the blacks because a lot of blacks did not like what we were doing. Some of the black intelligentsia, so-called intelligent blacks who did not want us to [boycott and picket], they would go in and shop, and they were the ones that we would target to slit their bags. We'd get somebody from our group to go in along with the R.W.'s and the M.S.'s *[initials only are used here at the editor's discretion]* when they'd go in and say, "I don't know why those black folks don't just leave, go away and stop doing . . . disrupting this community."

So someone from our group would go in with them and pretend that they were shopping but they'd have their flour and rice in bags, and we'd go up and we'd go up and slit their bags. That would frighten the do-gooders away. There were some silly things, but I guess it accomplished a lot. You really had to do some things.

ML: Some of that sounds like sort of Saul Alinsky kind of organizing. Did you all train under any particular disciplines or persons?

FM: I don't know.

ML: Both nonviolent as well as.

FM: Yes.

ML: Did you have nonviolent training sessions?

FM: Yes, we did. SCLC would do that, would conduct a lot of those. . . . Dorothy Cotton was one. Dorothy Cotton. Are you familiar with the Blue Ridge Institute up in, an Institute that's held up in the mountains in North Carolina?

ML: Yes. Somebody else mentioned it, but I'm not real familiar with it. I believe it was Highlander.

FM: No, this was Blue Ridge. I'm familiar with Highlander, too, but this was Blue Ridge up in . . . I haven't been there in about three or four years, but the last time I saw Dorothy they would get her to come as one of the resources.

ML: . . . So you pioneered in terms of being elected. Were there other elected officials then?

FM: Not black. Sherman and I were the only, first in the state to be [elected to a school board]. There were some appointed ones, but of course, you know that didn't mean that they were the right ones. But Mrs. Sherman and I ran, and those two districts are still predominately black. Well, they're both very polluted now because you know what's happening on St. Helena Island. You know, the water.

ML: Resort development and all?

FM: Yes, and Sheldon is still a predominately black area, and you probably know the issue now, that the high school is being proposed. Are you familiar with that?

Quite a controversy because they're fighting, and the school board itself is really disgusting. You know, they do not want to invest the money to build a high school down in that area because they say that the student population is not sufficient, and the projection doesn't warrant building a high school and all these excuses and it's just been such a . . . You're probably familiar with that.

ML: Somewhat, but not as much as you would be at the local level. Well, I think we've covered a great many things. Are there any other activities besides the school board? Of course, that was such a major issue.

FM: I know it was.

ML: It affects the whole community and future generations.

FM: Did I mention that one of the activities that Mrs. Sherman and I engaged in was . . . I can't really find words to describe the unrest and the fear and the intimidation and what was going on in the black community when those children were like the sacrificial lambs, the ones who were going into those schools like those Washington kids.

I was just reading how one of them, I think it was Craig, said that he was afraid. He knew that every day he was going to be punched by the white kids. He was drilled. Can you imagine a child being taught not to . . . because their natural response is if somebody hits them they're going to fight back, but we told them, "Do not respond to any curses, anything the kids do to you. Just keep moving." And so he said in one of these articles that he was prepared every day, that when the kids smacked him he would just keep on walking and not fight back. Those were brave children.

ML: Yes, it took lots of courage.

FM: Yes, it really took a lot of courage.

ML: I see the date on this paper. Oh, this is a retrospective on it ["'Freedom of Choice': Beaufortonians Remember Desegregation," *Beaufort Gazette,* October 5, 1997, p. 1D].

FM: Because this is where we are quoted, "Frieda Mitchell, left, and Charles Washington speak with Gazette photographer Jim Littlejohn in 1965." You have that?

ML: Yes. . . .

FM: I was one of the honorees.

ML: Yes, yes, I saw your name in that list.

FM: That was really a pleasure. That was a good thing.

ML: Yes, Ike Williams had a lot to do with that.

FM: Yes. How is he?

ML: He's doing fine. I ran into him just last week, and I'm setting up a time when Representative Clyburn is home for the holidays to get together with him.

FM: Yes, all of those are my good friends. Jim was just like my own son and his wife Emmie . . .

ML: Are there other strings that we need to follow up on too? How long did you continue to work at Penn Center?

FM: I worked at Penn until I retired really.

MH: No you didn't. You worked at UCCD then.

FM: Oh, yes, the organization, the daycare center . . .

MH: You worked at Penn for how many years? UCCD celebrated its thirtieth, twenty-fifth . . . ?

FM: Thirtieth [anniversary].

MH: Okay, so thirty years ago you left Penn. And she founded UCCD, United Communities for Child Development. It's the agency that my sister now runs that began at Penn Center. My mother mentioned that you weren't restricted to just your job that you were hired to do, so she was able to work with the children's development project and founded an agency. Why don't you tell him about that, a community . . .

FM: Oh yes, that's another story. My life's work was working with children, and we organized an agency, United Communities for Child Development, which was a statewide agency for nonprofit organizations that provided quality childcare, state supported and federally funded childcare centers for working families.

That was actually really the biggest part of my life's work. And there's a building that Senator, my dear friend, Fritz Hollings—I'll never forget him. He was able to write into the appropriation bill a grant of half a million dollars to construct a state-of-the-art childcare facility in Beaufort County. And the way it was written, our agency was the only agency in the state that qualified, met the criteria, so we were able to get the half million dollars and the building now is, you can drive by it. It's the Frieda R. Mitchell Building, and it's still providing childcare under a lot of financial stress, not like when I was working, because money was not a problem then. But that's the building that's still providing childcare for working families.

ML: And your other daughter works there?

FM: Yes, my other daughter.

ML: And this is primarily a daycare program?

FM: Yeah, child development. . . .

MH: The Kellogg project, tell him about the Kellogg project.

FM: The Kellogg, oh yes, I didn't talk about that. I was commissioned by the Kellogg Foundation to travel to southern Africa to replicate the program that we had established here. We took our model and our strategies to Mutare [Zimbabwe] in southern Africa for the people there to set up their daycare centers based on our model. That was quite an accomplishment.

MH: And they paid for the fellow to come back here to visit. And we were supposed to go to Johannesburg but things were pretty . . . we went but that was during the uprising.

ML: Well, I'm glad I asked you what else you've been involved in.

MH: Tell him about the Rockefeller.

FM: Rockefeller, yes, Public Service Award, yes. I was the recipient, one of the recipients, of the John D. Rockefeller Public Service Award. . . . I won this even before Marion Wright Edelman. So we share that.

ML: In high cotton!

FM: I'm telling you. Sophia Bracey Harris and I shared. It was a ten-thousand-dollar award that you got, but Sophia and I shared so we each got five thousand dollars. That was quite an experience to get that because I went to Mutare.

ML: That was in 1977, I see *[looking at a copy of the program]*.

FM: And then the people from [Africa] came here, and I took them around to visit projects in Alabama and Georgia and South Carolina. . . . There were seven people from the continent who came and I took them around in those states that I mentioned, and then I went back with them to visit places where they were going to establish the centers that were replicated based on our model here. That was quite an experience.

ML: Oh, yes! Well, any other thoughts? . . .

FM: Well, I hope I've given you enough information for your project. We've talked a lot about a lot of different things.

ML: You've been very helpful. We want it to be interesting so that people will read it. You've given lots of local color and perspectives.

MH: And when the project is completed, will you give the contributors a copy?

ML: Certainly.

FM: . . . Did I tell you that we had a tutorial project for the kids who were going to transfer?

ML: You mentioned it but in no detail.

FM: Yes, we did because that was a big thing we did. We really had to beat the bushes and encourage those black students to transfer when they did that, what we called the *in mass transfer*. Because the ["freedom of choice"] admissions were only those handpicked blacks. Remember I told you from the professionals, the Washington [family], the civil service folks, and whatever the other group was.

But when the big group came [for integration] . . . we did a lot of things to encourage those people, and we tried to set up the tutorial program for the kids who were going to transfer. Surprisingly, I think I told you this, *white* families brought their kids, too, because they were equally concerned. We set the tutorial program up at our black school, Robert Smalls, and when we opened it up, surprisingly all these white kids came along with the black kids because their parents were also concerned. It was such a success that Randall, the superintendent, when he saw the white kids going, he ran us out of our own school, but Mather School came to the rescue and allowed us to have the tutorial program at Mather. So we were able to continue that effort and the white families came to Mather also. So that was a good thing that happened. That was really good. You have turned off the tape recorder so you don't have that.

ML: No, it's on there. I hadn't turned it off yet.

FM: Okay. That was really something that's noteworthy, that those white families were equally concerned.

ML: And this was both in tutoring and human relations, getting along.

FM: Yes, warm bodies sitting next to each other.

ML: As well as academic or . . . ?

FM: Exactly, we did some academic. The main objective was, we wanted those kids to be prepared so that the black kids would have some allies when they got over there and all the white kids weren't going to snub them. But it was really good. And Mather provided the bus to pick the children up. And then the other thing that, and this may not be a part of your [project], but what I thought was worth mentioning, Emmett McCracken, white, who was, was he the deputy superintendent . . . Mr. McCracken was this really nice white man, I'll never forget. He was, he was really a good Christian man, and he wanted things to work out so he would provide opportunities for the black kids who didn't know anything about a Chamber of Commerce or anything, any of the municipal part of the government, so he provided tours to take the black kids to show them, this is the seat of your government, you know, this is so and so and so.

ML: Various civic . . . ?

FM: Yes, civic rights, so he really was a nice person.

ML: Were there any local clergy, black or white, that were particularly outstanding in their . . . ?

FM: Not that I can recall. The black ones were outstanding because they supported the efforts that we were involved in.

MH: Do you remember any of their names?

FM: Oh, goodness. See, black ministers didn't always live, come from [the community], they were sent in from other areas. They were not local people.

ML: Yes. Well, if you think of any . . .

FM: I will. I'll tell you if I think of any.

ML: Okay, we'll go ahead and stop the tape unless you've got anything else . . .

FM: I didn't realize it was still on.

ML: Oh, that's okay.

MH: And you will send us a copy of the tape?

ML: I certainly will. Thank you both, so much.

Willie T. "Dub" Massey, Jail, No Bail, the Friendship Nine

Andrew Grose [AG]:* The first question I want to talk to you about, when and where were you born and where did you grow up?

Willie "Dub" Massey [WDM] *[laughing]:* I was born July 25th, 1942, Rock Hill, South Carolina. The old St. Philip's Hospital . . . That's a long time ago.

AG: Okay. What were some of your childhood experiences regarding the treatment of blacks, and blacks and whites here in the South? . . .

WDM: Well, early on I didn't have a clue because I lived in the black community. I was on what we called Carol Park, it's now Carol Street, that's off Crawford Road in Rock Hill. Um, I guess boundaries would be near Clinton College not too far from there and near [Highway] 901. All of our families in that area were black. I had some cousins that lived in that area as well.

We were there for, I think, until about my third birthday, until I was three years old. And my granddaddy purchased some property on Freedom Road, 112 Freedom Road, and built a house there, and that's really where I grew up. 112 Freedom Road, which is near what is now South Dave Lyle Boulevard, just a block away.

AG: Okay. So, so you really didn't have much interaction with whites?

WDM: No. We were segregated. We had, you know, southern Rock Hill, and then we had a couple of pockets—Sunset Park, Flynn Hill, and Boyd Hill—where black people lived. So there wasn't any contact or involvement with any other race.

AG: Okay. Did you have really any firsthand experiences with discrimination or injustice? I know you said you didn't really live in an area near whites but did you . . .

WDM: Right. Now this, of course, was at an early age because, you know, as I said we moved to Freedom Road right after my third birthday. As I got older and became

*The interviewer and transcriber was Andrew Grose, student of Professor Janet Hudson, Winthrop University, and the interview took place on October 21, 2004, at Winthrop University, Rock Hill, S.C.

a young teenager attending Emmett Scott High School, which was all black, and Emmett Scott being on Crawford Road, and we had to walk to school. I was less than a mile away, so I had to walk. Couldn't even ride the school bus. We realized that there was another high school in Rock Hill—Rock Hill High School. We used the same stadium, but we would play on Thursday night and they would play on Friday night or, if they were out of town, we would get to play on Friday night, in the stadium. We knew that we were segregated, and we knew that our school . . . was inferior.

There was some of the things that we had would come in, like books, would have Rock Hill High stamped on it. And of course, we were Emmett Scott High School. So we understood what was happening. . . .

AG: When did you first start becoming involved with the civil rights movement from your earliest memory?

WDM: All right. Well, it started once I graduated from Emmett Scott High School in 1960. We graduated in that spring and we knew that the students on Friendship College campus were involved in some activities downtown Rock Hill, but we really didn't pay close attention to it. We didn't have a TV, so we couldn't watch it on TV, and the radio really didn't have very much to say about what was going on. The newspapers, really, didn't play a major part [for me]. I think they figured if they didn't get too involved with it, it would probably go away.

So upon graduating in 1960, and enrolling in Friendship Junior College as a freshman, that was my first real glimpse of what was going on and what had happened, in fact, in the spring of 1960. . . . Friendship Junior College being a two-year [school, there were only] freshman and sophomore years. Those who graduated the end of that spring were pretty much leaders in demonstrations downtown. And they were—they had picket signs as they marched in front of the lunch counters, and even going in to sit down. They even had a, a protest somewhere near city hall. But, I remember two names, Arthur Hamm and Abe Plumber, I would kind of recognize as leaders in the movement. There were students from Rock Hill who were students at Friendship as well during that time, but those two names were pretty prominent—I remember them. And so they actually got things started. . . .

But I went in as a freshman not really being too aware of what was happening and not really interested in getting involved because I felt sort of secure in my family situation, where I was one of few students with an automobile.

AG: Oh, really . . .

WDM: Yeah, most kids didn't have automobiles, so, yeah, Granddaddy sent me to college with an automobile. So I felt sort of privileged in that sense. But it was later on, a short while, that I found out that the students' intent was to either desegregate the lunch counters or shut them down.

Everything was sort of following what happened on February the 1st, 1960—obviously in Greensboro on the East Coast. . . .

What happened to me and my personal involvement was there was a young man out of Great Falls, South Carolina. His name—Tom Gaither, it's Dr. Tom Gaither now, he's a professor at Slippery Rock University in Slippery Rock, Pennsylvania. Tom Gaither graduated from Claflin College and took on a position—after being really, really involved in Orangeburg—took on a position as field director for the Congress for Racial Equality, CORE. Jim Farmer was a leader of out of New York. And so Tom, after graduating from Claflin, came to Rock Hill disguised as a student from the North, from New York I think he, he told his tale.

And, ah, he sort of a hung around the campus. He made contact with other graduates of Emmett Scott who—fellows that I knew, and one, of course, a relative and others were friends. And partnered with some of the fellows. I remember Robert Mc-Cullough and Jim Wells, who is an attorney in Florence now, and a couple others, um, um, James Wells, and who else do I want to mention, John Gaines. John Gaines is an attorney in Florence, Jim in Rock Hill. And they started meeting and talking about continuing the efforts that the students at Friendship had started, and they would go out and try to recruit other students get involved.

And, of course, when they approached me I told them, "Well, you know, I'm too busy, I got my social life and my academics and, you know, I really don't need this. I don't know what you're talking about or what you're doing—I really don't want to be involved."

But anyway they continued through September, and I guess it must have been about October, it's ironic that you're doing this interview in October, that I went to one of the meetings. In the meetings they discussed, nonviolent protest—following King and Mahatma Gandhi, and even mentioning Jesus Christ. Well, that kind of triggered me because with Granddaddy being a minister, Grandmother being a minister, and—my mother eventually became a Minister—I was kind of "churchy" anyway, so, ah, it sort of tweaked my interest.

I went to the meetings and they were doing training on nonviolent protest, and I became interested, um, got heavily involved, got motivated, charged, and excited about what was going on. And we would go downtown and would picket with the signs and would sit at the lunch counters. Not just the group that I was a part of—these were day students 'cause we were having meetings in the day student area of Friendship—but also the other students on the campus. Many of them would go down and—I think the school capacity might have been three hundred kids, and I would say the vast majority of them actually participated. So we continued the training and continued going downtown and sitting.

Police would come in and threaten us with arrest or something, and we would get up and leave. We'd get back for awhile, you know, and we'd progress to—probably what, what got your attention [laughs].

AG: Yeah. Which—just so we have it on tape—what were the particular places you were targeting in downtown Rock Hill?

WDM: Right . . . we hit Tarleson, Neal Drugstore that had a lunch counter, Mc-Crory's, obviously dime store, Woolworth had a dime store, Smith Drugs had a large counter, and Good's, I believe, believe those were the ones. Good's Drugstore, that had a large counter.

AG: Well I believe it was in the research I have done, starting around 1960, 1961, the city of Rock Hill had adopted a policy of no bail. What was it, "bail, no jail," or there was some sort of no bail, yeah, "jail, no bail" policy. Let's talk a little bit about that.

WDM: Okay. Well, not the city of Rock Hill.

AG: Okay.

WDM: But Tom Gaither.

AG: Oh . . . okay.

WDM: What happened . . . we would go down like I said and they would arrest us, and threaten us, and many times take us to jail, wait until it gets dark, and then they would release us.

AG: Ah ha.

WDM: Well, see, that was non effect after awhile. You know how it is trying to get young folk to do what you want them to do. After you use all of your threats and then what are you going to do after that? And so the months [got] down to November, and so Tom Gaither it was—mentioned those words. And it's actually "Jail, no bail."

AG: Okay.

WDM: It had been discussed with the Student Nonviolent Coordinator Committee [SNCC]. In particular, their leader named Diane Nash. Quite an outstanding young lady, still outstanding today as, as she's quite a speaker. I love to hear her speak as we had the anniversary a few years back—couple years back I guess it is.

But, Tom told us . . . , "When we go down and police arrest us and take us to jail they'll charge us and everything, and they let us go." Tom said, "There's something else we can do."

And so we were listening. "Okay, fearless leader." I called him "Moses," and we, we kind of gave him that name. And, [he was] 'bout your size, and I think he had a beard then—or not, somehow I really think that but—you sort of remind me of Tom.

But anyway, soft spoken, he said, "Jail, no bail." He said, "You're going to be arrested, and, we're not—we're going to refuse to leave. They lock us up, they're going to have to deal with us."

So, end of November, you know, we had Thanksgiving—everybody went home still thinking about this thing—the end of November. And, of course, December comes around, you know, we had the break, you know, Christmas break. So, as we went back in school, first of January, we actually set a date. It was going to be January the 16th, 1961. "Jail, no bail."

So, word got around, and I don't know how that happened, and some of the professors on the campus, Dr. Diggs, and some of the others, said, "Listen fellows, we've got registration coming up. Might be wise that you register before you go. That way you'll still be students if you do follow through on this."

You know, we really had doubts, so we said, "Okay, no problem."

So we rescheduled to January 31st, and that became the actual date of the "Jail, no bail" test in downtown Rock Hill. And sure enough, on the 31st of January, 1961, we showed up with our toothbrush and, toothpaste [but] very little of anything [else] because we knew what was going to happen. So we went, down to Woolworth and sat at the lunch counter.

We had to talk the other students out of going because the girls wanted to go with us, and we said, "No, no this is pretty serious."

There were ten of us originally, a young man out of New York, think his last name was Smith, Charles Smith, I think. I don't remember a whole lot about him. He was on a football scholarship. I really didn't know him but the rest of us, other than Tom Gaither, were formerly students from Emmett Scott High School—we graduated together. So, and, and, like I said, one of them my cousin, David Williamson Jr., so, we all were familiar with each other, with each other, because we went to school together, and played ball, and, and whatever.

So, anyway, um, we went down and Tom said, "You know, don't fight back. You know, don't say anything. Just be totally quiet. Sit at the lunch counter and order."

We sat there, we ordered, they refused us, they called the police, the police came, and they arrested us . . . and took us to jail. They said loud, "We're going to have to charge you because you've been doing this repeatedly." Here we are after Christmas and a New Year, "We're going to charge you with trespassing during breach of peace." And he said, "We'll give you a trial but, if you're found guilty you're going to have to either pay a hundred-dollar fine or spend thirty days in the York County Prison Camp," which was known as, quote, the "chain gang." The chain gang!

So, again we were committed. And in a way we had our big trial, and they brought in the NAACP attorney who tells this same story if you can catch up with him. He's retired now, but Judge Ernest A. Finney, who became the first black chief justice of South Carolina, stepped down and retired a few years ago. Ernest A. Finney came up to defend us, and he lost the case [laughs]. He lost the case even though he did become the first black chief justice of South Carolina.

As of 2007, eight of the Friendship Nine are living.

Robert McCullough, died on August 7, 2006.

John Gaines

Thomas Gaither, a field secretary with the Congress of Racial Equality (CORE), was the only one of the nine who was not a Friendship Junior College student.

Clarence Graham

W. T. "Dub" Massey

Willie McCleod

James Wells

David Williamson Jr.

Mack Workman

Umm, and so, anyway, 2nd of February, I guess it was, somewhere around there, they loaded us up in police cars, and they drove us out Highway 5, to—it's a new building they're putting up there now, the Moss Justice Center replaced what we were in [laughs]. We didn't get to stay in the [new] thirty-million-dollar Moss Justice Center. There was a little white concrete building next door on a hill there, and it was segregated, black on one side, white on the other side, big hallway in the middle, and then the cafeteria, and then solitary confinement. But we ended up spending time in, in solitary confinement as well.

AG: What did they put you in solitary confinement for? The reasoning?

WDM: Oh, yeah. Well, we, we actually were put in there several times. One was, we wouldn't stop singing. Yeah, we'd sing, you know, a, a *[sings]* "before I'll be a slave, I'll be buried in my grave, and go home and be with my Lord. . . ." and, "Free at last, free at last. . . ." Something to that effect. Or we would sing, "We Shall Overcome," or anything that would upset [the guards] while we were working, you know. We even got, um, kind of "bluesy" and did, ah, Sam Cooke's "Working on the Chain Gang" *[laughs]*. So, we'd upset them and they would put us in solitary, solitary confinement.

One instance, they put us in because of "obstinateness [*sic*] and belligerence" because John Gaines, the attorney in Florence, pulled a muscle in his shoulder—he couldn't work—and we were shoveling topsoil. So when the guards got on us about it, got on him about not working, we threw our shovels down as well, and protested. They took John to York and put him in the city jail on Liberty Street. We thought that, you know, they were really going to do something to him. But we, you know, we stayed to our task, and they put us in solitary confinement. So, any refusals that we gave them, the punishment was solitary confinement.

It was supposed to be on bread and water, cornbread and water, but we wouldn't touch it, but then there was something to that as well. There was a clearing of about two inches underneath the door, a heavy door, and the room maybe about twelve by fifteen, a window that you couldn't see out of that was very high off the concrete floor. Two receptacles, a commode and a sink. They would shove in the bread and we'd shove it back out. But then we had a prisoner, [he] would slip crackers and candy bars from machines to us . . . and, that's what, we would eat, 'cause, the guards didn't have a clue.

AG: Was there ever any time when you were in solitary that you thought that it might have been a little too much, or did you . . . were you ever scared you might break or anything like that?

WDM: No, no, no . . . it, it was a group thing. We were together, we humored each other and we told jokes. We made fun of one another. We sang together, we prayed together . . . maybe even quoted a little scripture 'cause, let's see, am I the only preacher in the bunch—I might be the only preacher *[laughs]*, and I was probably more hard-core *[laughs]*. Ah, but, no, we, we would humor each other, and really it, it wasn't that big a deal. There were threats, um, threatening situations, but you know, we didn't, we didn't allow that to get to us.

AG: Did you ever have anybody back out of the "jail, no bail?"

WDM: No, only one at the beginning, when I mentioned the young man out of New York. And he said later on, the reason he did was because he was afraid he might lose his scholarship, which I thought was kind of shady—because, you know, we didn't lose anything. In fact, we gained as a result of the experience.

AG: What was the, the university's official policy towards this? What, what was their stance on the, the nonviolent protest?

WDM: Friendship Junior College, at that time, it was still . . . we are trying to get the building back, in fact I'm, I'm involved in that as well—Friendship was a black, Baptist college. Okay. Now, pretty much, and this is probably true with all ethnic groups, not just African Americans, but you have to be supportive of young people because without them you don't have a school. Okay, so, all the professors were saying, "Well, we really don't want you to do this," even the president of the college, "but if this is something you must do, we're behind you 100 percent." Okay. That was the attitude they had to take. Because if they said, "Well, you take this time off, you're going to lose credit for the second semester. Okay. So don't even count on it." They said take the books with you, you know, do some prep time, and when you come back we'll try to catch you up. So there weren't any reprisals.

AG: Okay. Now you mentioned some other, other people that were involved in this. What was the kind of some of the response that you saw, while actually doing the sit-ins, of the white community?

WDM: Oh, boy. They were mixed, I would say the majority of the people were there just to see. There were a number of so-called "white hecklers." Young, white males who thought that it would please other persons if they heckled us. For instance, there was one [who] threatened me with a knife, me and a young female. In fact, I had maybe ten females, and I was walking along the lines to kind of protect them, and this young white male came up with his knife and said, you know, "We are going to cut somebody's throat," or something like that.

I took a sign, as the "aggressor" *[laughs],* and knocked the knife out of his hand. But by the time the police got there, there was no knife in sight, but I held my sign.

Matthew Perry came up this time [to defend me]. I don't know if Ernest Finney was with him this time or not, but I know Matthew Perry came—who is a very prominent judge in Columbia. Military Court of Appeals, I believe, if he hasn't been changed from that position, Military Appeals. So, anyway, I kept the sign so when Matthew came up to defend me, the sign was there. It had a nice, sharp, slash in it, which would indicate that there must have been a knife somewhere, so we actually won that case. So the assault charge was dropped from me.

John Gaines, the attorney, in Florence, right, wondered if I had gotten hit on the head like he did if, maybe, my plight would have been different. But anyway, John was hit in the head with a half-brick and knocked to the curb, bleeding profusely. But, "no wears and tears," he's fine *[laughs].* Those two I remember, others I don't. I don't remember any of the others. . . .

AG: What was some of the response you got from the black community that you saw?

WDM: Support and fear. Those who were supportive—one of the main ones that was terribly supportive, *frighteningly* supportive, the Reverend Cecil Ivory, who was the pastor of the Presbyterian Church, Herman Presbyterian Church on Dave Lyle Boulevard. The building is still there . . . owned by, Bobby *[inaudible].* He would tell us—and he was president of the NAACP—"If you boys have a problem, give me a call." Not only that but he rolled his wheelchair up to the lunch counter during the time and asked to be served.

And the lady said, "I'm sorry, I can't serve you."

He said, "Well, I'm sitting in my own seat—thought your objection was us sitting on [your] stools!"

So there was a lot of publicity about that. I think either *Afro American News* or some of the newspapers got that article with his picture in that wheelchair. In fact, a picture of it might be at the, at the New Herman Presbyterian Church that's on Dave Lyle Boulevard, not Dave Lyle but [Route] 901 near the railroad track that leads across the road.

There were others of the NAACP, Dr. Duckett, Dr. Laney, these were physicians. My granddad was a treasurer of the NAACP, Plato Massey. So, there were a number of others, Dr. Hogan, teachers, just, you know, members in general of the Rock Hill branch.

In fact, they had just shut down the bus service because of, ah, ah—I think her name was Ms. Austin—who refused to give up her seat. And, that was, I'm thinking it was maybe about a few years or so after Rosa Parks. So that happened in Rock Hill, and we *still* don't have a *[laughs]* bus service in Rock Hill! But the NAACP was very active during that time. I remember, in fact, they offered to pay our fine to get us released from jail. Of course, we refused it.

AG: When you were being arrested and in the farm prison and going through trial and everything, what was your impression of the public officials at the time?

WDM: Oh, they were very nervous, very upset. I remember them, and—some of them are still living today. Very nervous. They didn't want anything to happen to us, but they wanted to try to scare us and teach us a lesson. But we were too determined, we were too committed, and I think eventually they saw that so it was up to them to try to *protect* us.

They would talk harshly, but none of them gave any kind of physical abuse to us. We got threats when we got to the prison, but nobody laid a hand on us. I would say, and I've said this before, if we were in other states—Alabama, and even Georgia, even Tennessee—I don't know if we would have come out the way we did. That's again, you know, this was the first test of "jail, no bail."

AG: Now, it got a significant amount of coverage in the news and even nationally. Did you know about that at the time?

WDM: Not a clue, not a clue. And, and you got to realize that most of us didn't have TVs. Okay. And the radio, of course, would select whatever they wanted to put on the air. But, no, no, we— Let me, let me say this, after this was over and we came back and we protested—even when I transferred from Friendship and went on to Johnson C. Smith [University], the protesting was still in progress.

But now the only problem was I was from Rock Hill, and they didn't have a clue who I was. None of those students up there had been involved and engaged except for one, and he wasn't really a student at that time. He had finished up, Charles Jones, in Charlotte. He is quite a fellow. Charles, I think may have a law degree and, ah, was ordained a minister, I believe. But anyway, Charles was a part of this group, the Student

Nonviolent Coordinator [*sic*] Committee, with Diane Nash. So he was already in the Charlotte area, and I didn't know him and didn't find out until later that Thomas Gaither called them, I believe they were either in Tennessee or Georgia, and told them that "jail, no bail" had been challenged in Rock Hill.

So, four of them came to Rock Hill, Charles Sherrod, Charles Jones, Ruby Smith, and Diane Nash, sat down at the lunch counters, were immediately arrested and charged, and the two ladies were sent to York, placed in jail—Diane Nash and Ruby Smith—and then the two gentlemen, of course, Charles Jones, Charles Sherrod—I know Charles Sherrod is a minister now in Virginia—they were placed in the same prison where we were, and we didn't know that *[laughs]*, we didn't have a clue.

So, if you ever have the opportunity to talk to Charles Jones, 'course it takes about four hours, but, get ready!

But, anyway, going to Smith, they didn't know who we were, and two of us out of the "Friendship Nine" went there, to Johnson C. Smith, Jim Wells and myself. So we were students at Smith, and of course we didn't get involved there because it was like a different world to us. And we graduated and went on to different careers.

AG: Now after all this, after graduation, were you still involved in civil rights, and what year was it that you graduated? Did you participate in any more activities?

WDM: Graduated in 1965. Got drafted, got drafted! You would think that somebody with a jail record wouldn't get drafted, but I got drafted because it was during the Vietnam conflict, and did two years in the military, thirteen months in South Korea. So in 1967 I came back to Rock Hill, and a cousin of mine was a principal, Wiley Walker, the school in York, Jefferson Elementary. He brought a contract to my house and said, "Time for you to go to work isn't it?"

And I said, "Yes sir." *[He laughs.]* So I got my first teaching job in York School District.

AG: Now that was after, you know, civil rights was still, was still kind of . . .

WDM: . . . and the lunch counters were still closed! Even in '67, whereas in Greensboro, after the protests and everything, they opened the counters up. And they may have opened as early as, before 1960 was out—some months later. But Rock Hill was tough, Rock Hill was *tough*. They shut them down and left them closed and, as best I've heard from people talking about it that, it was after 1967 before they opened, you know, for all people, all races, to sit at the lunch counters. So, that was the case in Rock Hill.

I must have gone maybe, about one year—I was just kind of getting my feet on the ground again—and, probably about 1969 I became a member of the NAACP and became active *[laughs]*, and the first position they gave me was chairman of the Political Action Committee. So I *[laughs]*, I became a political force and ended up in city hall, and complaining about at-large elections and blacks not having a fair shot and pushing towards single-member districts.

AG: Let's talk about your political career. How, how long, how long did that continue? I mean how long were you involved in . . . ?

WDM: I was, I was actively involved until—oh, boy—I guess about, off and on, I guess until about '90, about '94. Um, we had some issues with leadership, and I decided it was time for me to step down. I really haven't been that involved since. Now, I always get people that ask me my opinions or thoughts and things of that nature, but that's about all.

AG: Looking back now, several years later, looking back on what you went through with Friendship College here in Rock Hill and in the area—how do you feel about it now? Looking back and reflecting on it.

WDM: It's, it's probably one of the best decisions I ever made in my life because, you know, how else would I have been a part of history? I mean nobody cares that you go to college, you get educated, you get out and get a job, you teach a lot of—some of my members here at this church—are my former students. But really that, that really doesn't have an impact on change. I like what King talked about with change, "If you live and you don't have an impact on change, then your living is in vain." I sort of keep that in mind, and I feel good about the fact that I did stay with it.

I was probably least likely to be involved because I didn't have to go out and try to seek any attention. I was already getting it. And probably didn't have to do a whole lot towards getting ready for a future because it was already planned. But for that opportunity to present itself to where I could put a dent in history along with the others, walking away from that I would have been sad.

AG: Now who would you say was probably one of your biggest influences in the civil rights movement at those times when you were coming up?

WDM: Probably King. The little that we heard about him—obviously he was committed. He could have gone off with his degrees and earned big bucks—pastor great churches, but he forsook that to try to bring this country closer together, um, in a nonviolent way. . . . I think that was most impressive for me.

I did look at Stokley Carmichael *[inaudible]* and some of the others because I was closer in age. And I thought what they did at the time, perhaps, was necessary to get some attention. Even though it was, you know, looked upon as being criminal. But nobody was paying attention to anybody. Everything was segregated, our jobs were tough to come by—you could be as skilled as possible, but because of your skin color, your pigmentation, you would be discriminated against. It was real obvious. That's one reason I, I pushed so hard for a single-member district in Rock Hill and in school board, the school board as well as city council. I don't get as much ink about that anymore because *[laughs]* those were hostile times that I would stand flatfooted and call them racists to their faces. Oh yeah, and, they don't forget, so *[laughs]* some of them speak to me now, some of them don't—but that's fine.

AG: Were there any kind of rivalries between some of the different African American groups like, that were involved trying to—because I know people had different ways about going about things or maybe had different opinions? Were there ever any kind of internal rivalries inside the civil rights movement here in Rock Hill?

WDM: Oh, definitely. Yes, yes . . . definitely. When I became disenchanted it, it was because of some leadership matters, and I went public with it. There are some folks now who still feel that I should not have done that. But I did what I felt I had to do. I wasn't happy with the leadership, and I was first vice [president] and I let it be known . . . When they were getting ready for elections . . . some people in there had not been really active to vote on the next leadership, the Rock Hill branch NAACP. That was in 1994, and I said, "Wait a minute, who are these people?" And sure enough, there was a coup involved, and the president came out to be the person who would serve as secretary—and I walked away.

It, it probably had something to do with my style which was really assertive, aggressive, and they were trying to get a different tone. That may have been the best thing, I don't know. I, I know it took longer to get things accomplished, but then it probably gave me a time, a time to get back to my family, 'cause I had, you know, small kids at the time, and I spend more time at home and to get into the [ministry].

I was licensed to preach in 1972 and had really taken over a large pastorate in a small place where I grew up. I was pastor there for three years but had kind of walked away from there. I became really involved as a civil rights activist, and that's basically what I was. Then I said what I felt needed to be said, and I didn't mince words and people knew me that way. Probably still think of me that way, but I'm, I've mellowed out now *[laughs]*. I'm putty.

AG: What was one of the biggest results you saw here in Rock Hill, your legacy?

WDM: Over the years, I think the single-member district was, was absolutely. Now of course, the school board hadn't been assembled long, and I ran for an at-large seat against the chairman of the school board *[laughs]*. I didn't, didn't stand a chance. He beat me, I think, twelve thousand votes to five thousand, but the five thousand votes were the largest number of votes that any black person has ever gotten in Rock Hill—in the history of Rock Hill! So, ain't nobody said that about "Dub" Massey *[laughs]*. So I, I still hold that dubious distinction, but I got whipped good.

Anyway, I ran because there were two black districts, majority black districts, and two incumbents on that board. Ann Reid, and Mildred Douglas were running, and they were, sort of speak softly, throughout our various speaking engagements. I'd come through, you know, "We don't have enough black teachers, black administrators, black coaches," you know, I would, I would just, just spell it out. That's a real serious problem because if you happen to be a parent of a black kid, you want them to sit down and be coached and talked to by somebody that look like daddy . . . *[laughs]* and they didn't handle that very well *[laughs]*. Obviously. But I enjoyed it, and it gave me a platform.

AG: Well, if you had to do it all over again, go back to 19—, late 1950s, 1960s, would you do it again and why?

WDM: I would do it again, and the reason is, I was raised in a household of ministers who believed in the word of God, who believed in eliminating fear, who taught the word that *love has no fear.* And if you believe that, then you operate on that premise.

"Greater love has no man than this that a man would lay down his life for his friends" [Gospel of John 15:13]. So we quote that. Say, why would you study the Bible and quote the Bible if you don't live the Bible. So, I was not just a Bible-toter. I lived it. And, and I have those expectations, so I felt that God would take care [of me] and I still feel that right now.

The only, my only regret is that when I went to the campus of Johnson C. Smith that I didn't get involved with the group there. I felt so much not a part of the group, and then I felt upset that they didn't know who James Wells and Willie Massey were, they should have known that. But they didn't know. And, in fact, they acted as if they didn't care. So *[laughs]*, so, that's probably something that I never told anybody before, so it sort of alienated us. If I had to go back, I would get involved.

AG: And what years were you at Johnson C. Smith?

WDM: I was in for three years, '62 to '65.

AG: And when did the single-member district issue come up?

WDM *[laughs]:* Oh gosh, that's a tough one for me. We must have started working on that one with the school board . . . Well one of the things I left out was when, in 1970, when Emmett Scott closed, the new high school was supposed to be Emmett Scott High School. We were told that by the then-superintendent *[inaudible]*. But then, in fact, they named the new high school Northwestern. So I was involved then, so when the students walked out of Rock Hill High, around 1972 or so because they were upset with . . . literature, and being treated as second-class citizens. . . . I was called as political action chair of the Rock Hill branch of the NAACP, to try to get them back in school because they had been suspended, and all downtown [they] broke out windows, lights, et cetera.

So I met with them at the hall along with Brother David Boone and some others, and we did get them reinstated but not many concessions. That gold stripe going down the uniform of Rock Hill High represented Emmett Scott *[laughs]*. They were still having that gold stripe. They brought up a team from Columbia, and one of the members of the team was a gentleman that I looked up to, Moses Rabb Jr., from Rock Hill. [He] was working for a task force down at the campus of USC that came up and kind of talked us down—to calm the situation. But, I thought it was a travesty, and it really didn't help the students at all. We continued during those years, I was still actively involved. I was working in York, the superintendent there threatened to fire me if I didn't stop my involvement in Rock Hill, and I turned in my contract [with] York School District. They backed off from firing me, so *[laughs]*, in fact, I resigned my job over there in 1972, as a matter of fact at the end of the year.

[Then in] '73 to '74 I was a full-time—one of the first black full-time students—at Winthrop. Earned my master's in counseling, continued on, and in '76 earned my EDS in public school administration. So, did three years of straight studies pretty much. . . . They hired me back in the district, believe it or not, in '74. Went back to work with them there and then earned my EDS in two years. But still actively involved in the NAACP. I never did break that involvement until we had some internal situations.

AG: Well, I think that's about it. I think the only thing else I was going to ask you about— How would, how would you compare where we are now in our South, in the southern society, compared to where we've come from? Good, bad?

WDM: I would say . . . it's hard for me to say *good.* I would say we're close to being *moderate.* And that's kind of tolerance because, there's still inequality in, in most of places in South Carolina, including our area—York County, Rock Hill—but it's no blame to those in power because for people to be in a community and not empower themselves so that they can share a part of what's going on, it's their fault. Nobody's closing any doors now, saying you can't come in, you can go in, but then you have to prepare yourself to go in and get involved, and stick with it. I think that's a part of the black community . . . if I had all the black people in York County in one building, I'd say something to the effect of, "You're hurting yourselves. You need to get real, get some skills, get some education, and stand up for yourself. It's not about skin color now, but it's about effort. If you're not making the effort to be who you want to be, you don't have anybody to blame."

AG: Well, I think you've about covered everything I was going to ask you, Reverend Massey. I just want to thank you again.

Charlie Sam Daniel, Once I Get Grown

[Daniel is speaking as the recording begins.]

Charlie Sam Daniel **[CSD]**:* . . . and they say that's kind of a little hard to detect, a thing like that.

    Marvin Lare **[ML]**: Yes, it can be, especially when you have lung cancer and it doesn't show up because of not smoking and all, it's very insidious.

    CSD: I noticed she had a cough, started it back in September of last year, and she kept telling and saying to the doctor, but it started to kind of go away. That was some of it you know.

    ML: I'm in the home of Charles Sam Daniel in Saluda today, on Tuesday, April the 18th, 2006. Please say just a word or two, Mr. Daniel, and I'll make sure we're getting a good sound recording level.

    CSD: Well, it's a beautiful day outside.

    ML: That's right.

    CSD: Yes, sir.

    ML: Okay. I think I may have picked up a word or two at the beginning when you were talking about your wife's passing, just what—the end of February was it?

    CSD: Yes, sir, the twenty-third of February, Yes, sir.

    ML: Well, you certainly have our sympathy and our regrets as well.

    CSD: Thank you, sir.

    ML: It's a hard time, I know. A number of people, including Miss Logan, Delores Logan, have recommended that I talk with you about the civil rights movement here in Saluda and your personal involvement and experiences in it. . . .

*The interview took place at the Daniel home in Saluda, South Carolina, on April 18, 2006.

Charlie Sam Daniel struggled to regain family property in Saluda, South Carolina.

CSD: Yes, sir. I guess that I would start off from . . . I'd say when I was a small boy, I tell you, I assume that I couldn't have been over three years old. I know it. I remember the Depression, what you call the "Hoover Days," and I was born in 1929. My father, he owned approximately two hundred acres of land, and I remember when they came down to repossess—you know, people lost their property. We were moving from where I was born and all of my siblings were born, about a mile and a half I'd say, across the woods, and going over there. And of course I remember we going in the wagon and carrying the chickens and different things like that. And of course back then, as I say, it was rather rough coming up.

Once I grew up, and being over there and we had to go back across the property that my father lost to a country school—crossing the property going to the country school. My father, I believe that he might have gave the land—it wasn't but about two acres—for the school. I always, when I think about that, well, if I have to say, you know . . . But back at three years old . . . I remember the white people coming and getting the stuff, but I didn't just understand all the different ramifications of it. Once I found out the ramifications of it, it was just in me to want to really one day possess that land again, which—that was in 1929 *[big sigh]* . . . so I think the Lord allowed me to really get it back, and which I'm proud of that.

Thinking in terms of civil rights and blacks, as I grew up there I began to recognize the difference, that if you was the same color that you had certain privileges that black people didn't have. As I grew up, and my mother and them would tell different stories about things happen with black people, and just what white people did to them, it just

Picture on the wall of Charlie Sam Daniel's home, representing childhood memories of property lost.

kind of, it, it, aaah, it just stayed with me. My father, he was about sixty-eight years old when I was born, and he was a man, of course . . . at that time—he was born in 1863 so he was born in slavery time, but he did get a education at Benedict College, and I think he finished there about maybe 1886, somewhere along in there. But, but anyway, and I say it, the way I found out the way blacks was treated and I was . . . as I say again, I didn't like it.

And then, my father, he was a churchgoing fellow, and then I began to go to church, and began to learn about what's—about the Christianity and things like that, and how people are supposed to be treated. I looked into it and I saw and I figured that really how black people was not treated fair and that stayed with me, and I said, "Once I get . . . if I get grown, I wants to do whatever I can to try to help correct this situation."

Once I got grown, of course, I was a person, I never did like to initiate a thing, but if something was going on good, I want to take a part in it. I don't like to be put in leadership's position but now I've been put in it quite a bit, but I don't seek it, but people, you know, they were trying to push me out there. So as I come up, when I was going across this, going to school, when I went to this little country school, going back across the property that my father lost, we would have to go in the woods when we got there and get some wood to make a fire so we'd get warm, and my feet, I couldn't hardly feel them then, they had gotten so cold. They'd get so frostbitten that they would kind of swell up and itch and stuff like that. Then I found out that basically the fact that blacks really was getting very little money for education, for blacks to be educated back then. That was in the 1930s. And I say again, I was just concerned about that, and I said, "Once I get grown, I want to try to do something about it."

. . . I finished school there and, of course, my sister was about two years younger than I, and so I finished the seventh grade, I'd say I reckon I was about fourteen, so my sister came along, well, she's about two years behind me, so she went ahead and finished the seventh grade in the country school. So we decided we would . . . my father and mother said they were going to send us to school down here, you know, to Rosenwald. At that time they had Rosenwald Schools, I mean for blacks, they didn't have high schools mostly for blacks in rural areas. Anyway, I think it went to about eleventh grade then, but by the time I finished they went up to the twelfth, but anyway, I just kind of waited around, and later on my sister and myself, from about five miles out, we would come to school in the buggy and tie the mule uptown, and we would walk on over here to Rosenwald, which was about a mile. You know we didn't drive the buggy all the way up to the school. But anyway, I was reading and seeing the different things happening, and once I got grown I . . . I started to cutting hair. I trained my own self to be a barber, and I worked in a shop and got my license.

So I was working at Mr. Logan's barbershop, Mr. Robert Logan's, which he was very active in civil rights. Of course, I know that there was—he would tell the story about he was the president of NAACP, and some black people were telling him that they felt he shouldn't be president or whatever. But he said, "Well, the organization, it stood for nothing but what the Constitution of the United States said," and he's just going to go along with that. Mr. Logan, really, he was my mentor as I was starting to cut hair in his shop and working and talking about civil rights, and of course that just kind of fit me and me wanting to try to do something about black peoples' situation and how they were situated. Mr. Logan got quite a few threats at his house, you know, they would throw the cross in his yard or something, and burn something in Mr. Logan's yard. So I believe some people was telling him he should leave Saluda, but he said he was born here and he planned to die here. You know, he warn't planning to move.

Those things helped motivate me to kind of push, push forward, and of course, that was a lot of things happening about in the late '40s and the '50s pertaining to lynching of black people, and I say again, I was concerned and wanted to do something about that. There were several of my people around here, who was older people than I was, was active in civil rights, so that was my cousin, Johnny Daniel, and Mr. Ernest Townsend, and Johnny Graham, which was my mother's first cousin, which they had been . . . Johnny Daniel's house had been shot in, and well, Mr. Ernest Townsend, he was very active. Of course, I don't know if anybody threatened him. And then there was another gentleman, Mr. George Attaway, they shot in his house. He was active in being a member of NAACP, and the white people, they were trying to frighten them, but they held their ground and they stood up and they didn't give in.

I remember that Mr. George Attaway, he had a son, he was a little boy, he said he remembered going to vote back in the late '40s, early '50s, and he went in and voted, and then a fool white fellow walked out behind him and said, "Well George, what you did, you're going to hate that."

And so he said, "Well . . ." His father didn't say anything, he just went on, but the fellow said he was going to hate it.

Then they later come and shot in his house, but now he didn't move or nothing. He still stayed there. He was a courageous man. There were several more people that were active in the civil rights. Of course I might can't think of their names right now, but I just remembered them right off. Mmmmh. *[There is a long pause.]*

ML: You mentioned about lynchings. Were there any lynchings locally here, or was it mostly up there in Pickens County and elsewhere, that the stories got around, or . . . ?

CSD: Well, it was none around here that I knew of, there was no lynching.

ML: Now, for instance, when the Klan would shoot into a house, do you think they were really trying to kill somebody, or were they just trying to shoot into the house to scare—to let people know that they could? That kind of thing?

CSD: I was thinking that they felt that they would shoot as trying to frighten them, but even if they shot and killed somebody, I feel they didn't care. I mean if they shoot in a window, they was calling that to frighten them or trying to make them leave or something like that, or stop doing the things pertaining to civil rights, what they were doing. But that didn't stop the people. They continued to, to, to push for civil rights.

ML: So voting was the primary thing that was contested?

CSD: That's right, that was in the early '50s. And of course, actually in the early '50s, then Mr. Logan, he started NAACP in about 1950, but then it kind of weaned off, people weaned it off . . . in the membership about '57, and when the organization went down a little bit, but then there was a gentleman, he came here, he's a Methodist minister, Reverend Roston. He was very active in civil rights, and so I would talk to Mr. Logan about the NAACP, about the organization had kind of gone down some, and he said, "Well, the people seem to not have much interest in it," and that's the reason he kind of held off in it. But this Methodist minister came, and he said that if the people wanted to reorganize the organization, he would do all he could to help reorganize it. Then he asked me would I like to serve as president, Reverend Roston did, and he said since me and Mr. Logan had started it but since I were younger, if I wouldn't mind serving. I told him it'd be fine with me, of course, quite a few things I needed to know about it, but I was willing to learn, to help carry it on because I understood what it represented. It just represented that every citizen, you know, be treated fairly, and that's what I was concerned about.

So, in 1960, I was elected president of the NAACP branch, and there was a lot of people was telling me that they didn't thought I should do that. I told them that I felt that anything was right as long as it's according to the Constitution of the United States, that I felt that I should go along with it. Then I even decided, the way I looked at it, of course, if I think something is right, I feel I'm going to take a stand on it, not to try to say that I'm mean or I want to die or whatnot, but if I take the stand that I feel is right in the sight of God, I'm going to take that stand and I'm going to stay there. Now there were some white people, they came around and would tell me, "Some people don't like what you're doing," telling me they didn't like what I was doing.

I said, "Well, what have I been doing?"

They said, "Well, that organization that you is a part of."

I said, "Well, if you're talking about the NAACP, according to my understanding it's a organization that it's only standing for carrying out the Constitution of the United States, representing the rights of all people. I don't see nothing wrong with that, but if anybody could show me what's wrong, I'd be glad to talk to anybody. If I can see what's wrong, I'll have to denounce it, but I'm sorry, if anybody want to come and talk to me, I'll be glad to talk to them about it. If they can show me where I'm wrong, I'll maybe get out of it, but if you can't do that, I plan to do more of what I'm doing. Black people has never got their rights, and the only thing it is is to see that blacks and all people get their rights. That's what I'm— If they can't show me that, I plan to still promote it."

When the schools were coming to be integrated, which my children were some of the first ones to go to what you call the "Freedom of Choice"—you know they came out with that, and my children went over to the school and they was the first to go to the schools then. That was, I believe, in 1967 or '8, somewhere in there. They got along with the children quite well, but I understand, they told me a little later, that there were some high school boys would mess with them. They were little children. They didn't tell me about it because they knew if they had told me about it, I'd have shaped them to it. But they knew . . .

ML: They just bore it.

CSD: Some things— I might go a little ahead of myself, then I might come back. But anyway, in 1968, Health, Education, and Welfare was wanting some people who got in the civil rights movement to come and testify before Health, Education, and Welfare pertaining to integrating the schools, making it a very unitary system. They could do away with segregated schools and all the schools be one school [district]. So in 1968 they selected me, the head office of NAACP, recommended, because really the field secretary, Mr. I. DeQuincey Newman, he recommended I would go to testify before Health, Education, and Welfare pertaining to integrating the schools, and which I did go there in 1968, in Washington. I remember that the—oh, I don't know if he was, you'd call him a judge, but anyway—the superintendent, he was calling me by my name, and so he told him he had to use the courtesy title to me, the superintendent calling me "Charlie," and so he had to use the courtesy title, "Mr. Daniel," which he did do that. I guess about four or five years ago, he's an attorney, Billy Coleman, he mentioned that to me, which he does some legal work for me, and he just mentioned that they told him to call me "Mr. Daniel." That was something they didn't do back then.

Of course, so often time people would say that, they called poor people "Auntie" and "Uncle," and of course they said that that is respecting, showing respect. I told them that to me it showed total disrespect, you calling somebody your aunt and uncle, because, and I tell you just like I told them, but I said, "Now show me. We're related to white people because black women was raped before they got off the ship when they was brought here as slaves, and a lot of time they say that they don't want to recognize we're related to them. Sure, a lot of this time we're kin, but they don't want to recognize that." But that's disrespect when you're saying "Aunt" and "Uncle." If you want to use a title, "Mr." and "Mrs." . . .

I remember that a white fellow that knows me, he came here when schools were beginning to be integrated, and he told me, "Charlie, you know that ain't going work, integrating schools, black boys going to school with the white girls and stuff like that."

I said, "Not going work! Why it won't work? Black women can come to your kitchen, you can rape them and get children by them, but you don't want your children to go to school with—what, you think your children is better than somebody's else? You ain't no better than no other human being God created." And I say, "Segregated schools ain't nothing but a waste of money, and it's ignorant to begin with, it was ignorant to start with. One human being want to think they more important than another."

Well, he started to walking off, and I told him, said, "Don't go, I got more for you." When you go to telling the truth, they don't want to hear it and begin to walk off and things like that. I just believe in just telling the things like they are.

ML: You have a very gentle way of speaking, but you speak the truth, firmly and gently. I can't imagine people being upset with you, with your gentle way of speaking, but you tell it like it is, and if they can't endure that, well, that's their problem. . . .

Were the changes brought about here mostly through legal means, or were there demonstrations, or marches, or was it pretty much just in the courts?

CSD: We had some, probably we did have some few demonstrations, but it wasn't much. Basically it was brought about through legal means. Of course, I was—I guess I'm using the right word—the plaintiff, in pertaining to suing that you could [not] be an at-large school board member, that it would be single-member districts. I was the plaintiff in that, and I was the plaintiff in the city council, and county council. Yes, sir, and then, as I say, I went and testified before the Health, Education, and Welfare. That was through probably legal means that they went ahead and made the unitary system, even the Supreme Court ruling in 1954 said that the segregation was illegal.

> If you force a fool
> against his will,
> he's a fool still.

There's one thing that I tell all the white people when it come to blacks' rights. Show me one right that black people got without forcing it upon the whites by suing them. There's a saying that, "If you force a fool against his will, he's a fool still." I'm saying that it was forced upon them, but I feel that even if it takes that to get your rights, go ahead and get it. But every right that blacks got, it was forced upon them, and it shouldn't be that way. It should be voluntarily that they're going to do the right thing.

I served as president of the NAACP from 1960 to 1970. Then the black community said I was kind of a little too militant. That was all right, I didn't mind that, but I didn't plan to change my way. They got somebody else to be president, which that's okay, but I was still very active in the NAACP. I served as a vice president and things like that, and on the different committees and things like that. . . .

We were always seeking to try to bring about a unified system. But they were still kind of fighting against it, but we were still pushing, pushing for it. I remember my children, they were small when the schools were first integrated, and they wanted to . . . they announced at the school that if you wanted to play ball, come back to the school, and my children were at that time about eight or nine years old, playing Little League ball, so my son, I remember him coming home that day, he was so glad, said, "Daddy, Daddy, take me back over to school. They announced that they're going to sign up for baseball."

I said, "Okay." I knew what the answer was going to be—that was what you call "Freedom of Choice," going to the white school then—so when he come, I said, "Okay, I'll take you back over there."

When I went over there, they told me, "Well, we let them come to school but we can't let them play ball."

I said, "If my son can't play, yours won't play on the field. I promise you that if my son don't play, yours won't play."

You see, I knew the law, and of course, then a little later on, they—well, at that time that was for baseball. So they got off the field and went in one of the white citizen's yard and they played a little team, so that they didn't play on the ball field. They knew if they played on the ball field that I was going straight to the courts with it. Then come football time, same thing happened. Then they said, "Well, he can't play football."

I said, "Well, if my boy can't play, you all's won't play."

Public property, you know. And so then later on, they said, "Well, we decided we going let him play."

I just think when I said, "My boy can't play, yours won't play." And so they played and they, my children, I would have to say they excelled in sports, even through high school they got scholarships, playing ball in college and things like that, basketball.

I was just believing in treating everybody fair, everybody equal. This country still don't believe in that, really, today. You have to force somebody to do something, then their heart is not with it. [There is a long pause.] There are lots of things that I feel, and which I know it would be just a much better country if everybody would just go ahead and say we're going to treat everybody fair and squarely, and we wouldn't have a whole lot of confusion.

ML: It takes some courage and leadership. I imagine your boys were sort of crushed when they found out that they weren't going to play, but then they also found out something by your witness about if they didn't get to play, nobody got to play.

CSD: Yes, sir. I tell you, even my boy, he wanted to play, and so I did take him to Columbia, he just wanted to play baseball. I took him, that's about forty-five miles away from here, I took him down there, he kind of joined the Little League, and he played down there and everything. He played a while, since he was just anxious to play.

ML: Let me go back to a couple things. You mentioned Reverend Roston, is that R-O-L . . . ?

CSD: R-O-S-T-O-N.

ML: R-O-S-T-O-N, Roston. Yes. Because when we write this out, we want to make sure we've got it right. Was he a United Methodist minister or AME or CME or . . . ?

CSD: CME.

ML: CME, yes. Tell me about your experience when you testified at HEW. I guess that was quite an experience, going to Washington to testify before that committee.

CSD: Yes, it was. Of course, I was glad to do it. I didn't mind doing it. Of course, that was the first time I rode an airplane, and then once we got to Washington, they couldn't land and kept circling and it had me a little . . .

ML: Had you a little worried?

CSD: Yes, sir, and I was wanting to get on the ground quick as possible. But it was a nice experience, and I just told them exactly how things were here in Saluda, I told them that they said that they weren't going to let Washington tell him what to do.

When [the superintendent] came back, he said, "Well, you didn't have to tell them what I said."

I said, "Well, that's what you said, wasn't it?"

ML: If you're not going to stand behind it, you'd better not say it in the first place.

CSD: That's right, yes, sir.

ML: I spoke to Ike Williams earlier in the day and he sends his regards. . . .

CSD: That's right. I remember him quite well and worked with him, yes, sir, I did.

It's one thing that my children, when they was coming up in school and whatnot, I never taught my children no type of hatred toward nobody, no race, or nothing . . . *[inaudible]*. I didn't believe in that, gonna mistreating nobody. My parents always taught me that and which I know that you shouldn't do that according to the scripture, you shouldn't do it anyway. Even my boys, when they were coming up, I told them— they were, not bragging or nothing, but they were pretty good athletes. I said, "Lord, the girls are going to like you, white girls, black girls, and all, but treat everybody like you want your sister to be treated." I couldn't teach them no form of hatred, and I just couldn't do that, yes, sir. Because I say hatred, that's what creates wars, and I hate wars. It's uncivilized. I, well, . . . you know, I can't . . . I can't . . . I have to . . . a mocking things . . . I don't think the Creator want us to fight wars. I might have to say this, that even the Bible as they know it is a version—the King James Version—but could I give Charlie Daniel's version. The Creator put me here, but I don't feel He want us to be killing each other. He want us to love. What's happening now, I can't—it's horrible, it bothers me.

ML: You mentioned about going to the Rosenwald School. Is it still standing? Is it still here?

CSD: No, sir, it's not.

ML: I believe that Delores Logan mentioned that her father had a lot to do with the founding of the Rosenwald School here. Was that right?

CSD: Her grandfather. Mr. Thomas Logan, and he was the one that talked to people pertaining to Rosenwald giving money for it, and he went around to get people to give so much money that you might build a school. Of course, something happened that was very bad pertaining to the property over there and the school, that the person who was on— Well, let me say this, they put this property up for sale, and the person who was on the school board— At the time I was just a citizen, I bidded [*sic*] on it, put it up for bids and I bidded on it, another fellow and myself, but the fellow on the school board, he bought it, and the superintendent told me, when I asked him about it, he said, "What you all bid, the gentleman who got it just bid a little more than you all." He was on the school board. He bought the property. You see . . . ! You don't do that under no circumstances. That just shows the mentality.

ML: It should be an open-bid process.

CSD: Now, he didn't supposed to bid no way. He was the one looking at the bids— and it's more than what, he said I'll give you more. But he wasn't supposed to do that. That was completely improper, but it went on through.

ML: With the loss of your farm when you were a child, was it just the debts and the Depression era? Do you think that there was . . . do you have any real facts or information about the repossession of the land and how that all came about?

CSD: I think if we would kind of search history and what happened in that time, there was thousands and millions of people really lost their property in the Depression, in '29, when the banks went broke and everything. So that had a lots to do with it, and then the price of everything went down with that. So that's what happened in that, but I can tell you really—I could tell you a story pertaining to the reason I got this land back. It was the black farmers—I don't know if you know anything about that—they sued the federal government, the Agriculture Department, because they were discriminated against, and I was a plaintiff —I hope I'm using the right word.

ML: Plaintiff, yes.

CSD: I was a recipient of some of the money that [was recovered], because I believe that if I have a right, give it to me. If you don't give it to me, if you've got rules and laws, we'll force you to do it. Which I would, and I'm going to say that is the reason even that I . . . they had discriminated, and since I was a plaintiff, as I say, I recently purchased the land back. And they told them, the FHA [Farmers Home Administration], "You got to give him priority treatment." Not only me, but this can apply to all black farmers. See, white people can get whatever money they want at the Home [FHA], but blacks, they always would come on with some type of excuse and stuff like that.

ML: So what year did you get the property back?

CSD: June 30th of 2005, *last year.*

ML: Oh, just last year! *About seventy years later.*

CSD: Yes, sir. I'm going to say, it means so much to me because ain't nobody know how bad I wanted the land, and I just thank God that allowed me to get it back in my possession, which I owe money on it . . . but it's with a barn and everything. *I just cherish it.*

ML: I'm sure you do.

CSD: Yes, sir.

ML: Anything else you think of that you'd like to share?

CSD: You know, I'm going to say that it's quite a bit more, I guess I should have maybe written some things down, but since my wife passed, that hasn't been too long, and of course, I had a lot of things kind of pile up on me, and . . .

ML: Well, you've covered a great deal. I was just asking if there was anything further that you had in mind. . . .

CSD: I just believe in telling them when they come up to try to act like they thought they were something special because God created them, letting them know you're no more than no other human being. We're all headed the same way, to the grave, and we treat everybody with dignity and respect. But, as I say, Mr. Logan and these older people, Mr. Johnny Daniel, and Mr. Ernest Townsend, and Mr. Attaway, those people, they didn't back down. They just took a stand and just stayed there.

ML: We owe a lot to them and to you in standing up. The purpose of the book is so that the current and future generations will be aware of that and it won't just fade into history and be forgotten. . . .

CSD: I can understand that. Of course now, there is something pertaining to Mr. Logan that I could tell you about how we were treated. I hadn't told that, well, really, his father owned some property, and he mortgaged the property to a white guy—back in time, blacks couldn't borrow money from the bank, there were some white people who would let them have money, you know, mortgage, but how be it— Mr. Logan's father passed and Mr. Logan wanted to take up the mortgage, but this gentleman had the connections to know that they had in mind of building a school over there next to Rosenwald School. He had the mortgage on the property. He wouldn't let Mr. Logan pay it off. So Mr. Logan decided he, well, he got a lawyer, that was back in the early '50s, to try to help him to let him pay the mortgage off, and so the white guy met him on the street and told Mr. Logan, said, "Well, I know you're suing me but I feel the white people in this county will give me the benefit of any doubt." Where the school is, Riverside—I don't know if you know where the school is, it's the school on the right down there—that was the property that the white guy wouldn't let him pay off. So he sold it to the state, the white guy did, and Mr. Logan just lost out on it. Even in the courts, his lawyer, Mr. Logan's lawyer, which he had a white lawyer, he didn't have no black lawyer, was letting them prejudice the jury, because Mr. Logan had some housing projects down there, and it hadn't been long [since] he sold the housing authority some property to build some housing projects. He brought that up in the court to prejudice the jury. Said he made enough money off of these housing projects.

Charlie Sam Daniel, who serves on the board of the Riverside Community Development Corporation, is pictured here on property previously lost from black ownership.

But I'll say this, that thank God that we have a superintendent that, this past year, helped the black community purchase the land from the school—they built a new school—so the black community controls that land now.

ML: Is the building still on it?

CSD: That's right, the building and everything. That's right, that's exactly right, and forty-eight acres of land.

ML: Wonderful. You say the black community owns it. Is it a corporation or recreation program?

CSD: It's Riverside Community Development Corporation [RCDC]—that's what it is. I'm on that board. It's for the community. Yes, sir. And we have different things there. We have after-school tutoring things and everything, but the community owns it, yes, sir.

ML: If you have time I might have you drive me down to show me that.

CSD: Yes, sir.

ML: Let me see—there was something else early on —oh! Just sort of a sidelight, but did you know Alice Pyatt?

CSD: Yes, I did.

ML: I interviewed her in Charleston a few months ago, and she spoke well about her career in education here in Saluda. She was one of the students that was expelled from or denied to return to South Carolina State because of the protests in the mid-'50s. I don't know whether you knew about that or not.

[See the interview with Alice Pyatt, "A Summer of Tears," above.]

CSD: I didn't know that.

ML: Well, she was a freshman, and her brother, Rudy Pyatt, was a senior, along with Fred Moore—who's both an attorney and a minister—and a number of others. After the Supreme Court decision on the integration of schools, the NAACP in Orangeburg applied for the black students to be admitted to the schools. The white community, the White Citizens' Council primarily, withdrew credit from blacks and fired people who were a part of that petition. So the NAACP decided that they would boycott the white businesses that had anything to do with that. They approached the student body at S.C. State and asked if they would join in, and they did, sort of undercover, but it all came to light and then a number of the key leaders were expelled. She was just a freshman, and that summer received a letter denying her readmission. She believed essentially in the purpose of it, but she sort of felt like she had been—well, that her education and her career was badly damaged by it. She overcame that, but was committed to . . .

CSD: There's one fellow that I should—he's been very active—is James Melvin Holloway, even pertaining to [buying the former] school, and he's very active in civil rights too. He's a young fellow. I didn't mention him as . . . really, he's the president our RCSDC. As hard-working and as active as he is—I guess I kind of had in mind maybe speaking of the older people, but now he's a man about fifty-five or something like that. He might be close to sixty. But he is very active in civil rights. The fellow is on the city council, he was a plaintiff in that suit, and on county council, he was a plaintiff in that, and on the school board [single-member districts]. And the recreation . . . and things like that, we've got things for recreation, too, that he's been very active in.

ML: A real champion for . . .

CSD: Yes, sir, that's right. James Melvin Holloway, yes, sir.

ML: I'll note that. . . . I think I know why you have that picture above your couch there. To me that symbolizes that young boy, going down the road to the school—across the land his daddy used to own.

CSD: Yes, sir. I went down a path and walked foot-logs going to school, and the dog followed me many times.

ML: Yes, I'm sure. I like getting folks in the context of their home and family . . .

CSD: Yes, sir. I have a son that's, well, he's going to be at the University of South Carolina. He's working in the Athletic Department. They went to Furman, two of my boys got scholarships in basketball at Furman.

ML: Oh, really! I'm going to be up there at Furman tomorrow to meet the folks up there.

CSD: And they got scholarships in basketball, and he was assistant coach there from . . . '80 to almost 1990, then he went to North Carolina State, then from there to Tessler, where he was assistant coach, and then back there to the University of Tennessee at Knoxville, which last year they changed coaches at the university, so now they want him down there in the Athletic Department at USC.

ML: Oh, wonderful!

CSD: Yes, sir, and my other son, he is a loan officer at . . . well, he trained and was with Bank of America, but right now he's working with Sun Crest Bank, yes, sir. *[He refers to a family picture.]* Well, I have six children, three boys and three girls, which basically—my baby daughter works for the State of Maryland, and she was just down and left yesterday, got back home this morning. Of course, since her mother passed, she just says she feels like she feels better if she's been down here, so that's the second time since she passed. Well, one son worked at Benedict, but he's not right now. They laid off some people. And my oldest daughter, she works for a public utility company up in Manassas. She married a guy who works for IBM, computer programmer, and then my middle girl here, she has two small children, but she is just kind of here seeing after me right now. She lives in West Columbia. Yes, sir.

ML: That's good. You need family, especially in a time of loss. It's good for them to stand by you. . . . I really appreciate you taking some time with me today.

CSD: You're welcome. . . .

Teenie Ruth Lott, a Military Tradition

Marvin Lare **[ML]:*** Today is April the 18th, 2006, and I'm in the home of Mrs. Lott. How are you today, Mrs. Lott?

Teenie Ruth Lott **[TRL]:** I'm doing fine. And you?

ML: Good. I appreciate you being willing to talk with me here today. As I mentioned on the phone, Mrs. Lott, I'm gathering the stories of the civil rights movement from first-hand accounts of people. Delores Logan mentioned your name to me and suggested that I contact you. My approach on this is very much to let people tell their story, their recollections, their experiences, in their own words. I might follow up with a few questions, but can you tell me a bit about your life and involvement in civil rights activities?

TRL: Well, I was . . . the Saluda branch of NAACP was organizing and I had been thinking about joining, and I hadn't, but one reason I did join, my mama was standing on the side of the road on Batesburg Highway, Highway 178, to catch the bus to go to Batesburg, and she got on the bus and went and sat down beside this man, so the bus driver— she knew the man—so the bus driver come and made her get up and change her seat.

Well, the man she sat down beside was mixed blood and she knew him, but my mama was real dark and she had to move. It was a hurting thing, because she paid like everybody else, but she moved. So I joined NAACP and I worked with the organization, and I never had nobody to bother me, but it was a struggle with what went on, because where we lived our white neighbors treated us like they did their [own] children. Wasn't nobody ever mean to us. My daddy was a World War I veteran, and that might have been the reason. He and my mama, they had twelve children. I'm the tenth one, and so the lady that lived on the place, was named Ruth, and she named me Teenie Ruth, so that's how I got my name.

*The interview was conducted at the Lott home near Saluda, South Carolina, on April 18, 2006.

Things haven't went like they should have been, but by we working, trying to make a change come about, they're better than they was. I was elected the first woman elected officer for the South Carolina Conference of [NAACP] Branches, as third vice president, and I served there two terms, and then I was elected president of the Saluda branch.

I had been to a convention somewhere and came home, and Nelson Rivers called and asked what was going on in Saluda. I didn't know, because the people that do the building, houses and things, the young people group had come into Saluda to work, and they had worked on one house and it was Saturday evening, they went to the swimming pool in Saluda, and they had went to the swimming pool to swim, and because it was some black students with them they would not let them swim in the pool. So I went to check to see about it, and the land where the swimming pool was, in the deed of the person that deeded it to them, it was a stipulation in there that no blacks use the pool. So we contacted them and things went on and stuff, so there were really no incident, no issues or nothing come because the people in Saluda knew they were wrong, because the county come and picked up their trash with everybody's tax money, black folks' tax money just like white folks' tax money, but black folks couldn't use the pool. And then the poorer white folks couldn't use it either. They—well, you know how you all do [laughs].

Anyway, they changed the ruling on, what was left in the deed, they dropped that, because the Lion's Club, I think, were who owned it, and so they dropped that, and so it went on smoothly that black folks could, they opened it up so black folks, all you had to do was take your membership and everything. So that worked out. But black folks still don't go over there because of the memberships, and the parents who could afford to buy the membership work out of town, and by the time they get home it's too late for them to take their children to swim in the pool, and it's bad because we have several people have got drownded [sic] going to the lake to swim, not knowing what's in the water and just got drownded. Just one of those issues.

We've had times when the Ku Klux would come in Saluda and all of these things, but I don't know nobody that they bothered. It's just a threat thing and all of that kind of stuff.

ML: What year did you join the NAACP?

TRL: It must've been like '60, maybe 1960.

ML: So it sounds like the swimming pool was sort of a community facility, but you have to join the club or something, pay dues to . . .

TRL: Yes, I think the Lion's Club who control it and everything, so you had to buy a membership to use it.

ML: That must have been quite an experience working with the statewide Conference of NAACP Chapters.

TRL: It was, because in October we have a state convention, in March we have a regional convention. The state convention was always in the state, in South Carolina, the regional convention would be in—we're in Region Five, the five Southern states—and it would move from one state to another. The national convention, well, it would go from different states where a branch was able to host it. In some places the place just didn't have big enough—like Saluda, for the state convention, well, Greenwood and Saluda cohosted one one time, but because the hotels, housing and all of that, we weren't able to accommodate the people.

So it's been a long struggle and we've come a long ways, but we still have a long ways to go, still a long ways to go, because there's a whole lot of things going on that shouldn't be going on at this late date, but it still is.

ML: What are some of those things, would you say?

TRL: As far as—Saluda now is a nice place to live, I've been here all my days, but we are kind of—it's a rare setting because Saluda County is the only agricultural county in the state of South Carolina. Okay, you've got pine tree farms, you've got chicken houses, you've got cattle farms, you've got peach trees, and in order to participate in this economic setting you've got to have a whole lot of land, and so if you don't have a whole lot of land, you're left out, because you can't have a cow on a lot, you've got to have pastures for grazing and all that kind of stuff. And then they seem to want to keep it like that, and we had two major businesses in Saluda and that was Knight's Textile Corporation and Milliken's, and Knight's closed its business down first, and went overseas because he had business in a whole lot of—Guatemala, Bangladesh, and all them places over there, so he closed the business down in Saluda. So then Milliken closed their plant in Saluda. So that means the people that live in Saluda that want to work got to drive. Now, my daughter, she lives down there, she works at Savannah River plant, it's about seventy miles that she's got to drive back and to, to work every day. So my son that lives in the first house up there, he works in Greenwood. So my other son has moved to Greenwood, so he's at home with his job. But the people in Saluda that really can make some money got to drive sixty, seventy, eighty miles. A lot of them work in Columbia, lot of them work in Greenville, Laurens—they got to drive that far to make a decent living.

And the thing about it is, the two major businesses closing, you don't see a brick on top of a brick nowhere in Saluda County where they've brought some other business in, so that people would have jobs. So you know that's a bad setting. It is, but . . .

ML: Some of the rural communities really have had a rough row to hoe.

TRL: Yes. They done a documentary on Greenwood a couple weeks ago on television, on ET television, so when Mr. Self saw that his textile business couldn't stand up under what was going on overseas and all of that, they brought other businesses in, so their people would have somewhere to work. And you notice driving from here to Columbia the structures you see going up, but when you get to Saluda, you don't see them, you don't see them.

ML: No economic development.

TRL: It really seems like there's about six, maybe seven people in Saluda that has control over the major things and decide how things going to go, and that's the way it is. And we kind of have a—what do you call it?—economic developer who's supposed to bring in development, they're paying somebody five hundred dollars to bring

Teenie Ruth Lott in her home near Saluda, South Carolina, April 18, 2006. Note the proud record of military service displayed on the wall.

business in and no business coming in yet, so I don't know why they want to give somebody the money, because ain't nobody coming in.

One time they blamed it on schools, so now we got a nice school over there. I don't know too much about what's going on because—well, I got great-grandchildren going to school over there now because all my children is out. But the school was one of the problems. The people that own businesses, they come in and see what kind of school system they had.

Housing—ain't no housing nowhere if somebody want to come in, ain't no nice house where they can stay till they get time to build them one. We don't have none of that.

It was supposed to have been water, so they brought water, get water from Newberry, but then they got some water they hoped, but then some of the poultry plants, Amick and Gentry, was having problems with the water, and they run water down, way down by Hollywood School. They didn't come through town with the water, they run the water way down through the Hollywood School area, across Batesburg Highway, and come up that way to get water to Amick and to Gentry, so they could operate their poultry plants. So there wasn't reason to say, "We don't have water enough to take care of business in Saluda," and all of that. But they got sales in the paper, got a grocery store, folks can buy groceries in Saluda. That's just about it. So anything else they need, they got to drive, and then with the price of gas, that's a strain on everybody.

ML: Yes, it really is. This is changing the subject a bit, but I notice on the wall here a number of people in the military in your family. Can you tell me who they are?

TRL: That's my son, and that's my younger son—he got killed in a car wreck about twenty years ago. That's my daughter . . . she's in the National Guard. Her daughter's in the National Guard, too, and a couple years ago when they first got ready to go to Iraq, they had both of them off, going to send both of them, her and her daughter. So when they got ready to send the second group this time, they didn't send her because she got some kind of health issues, but they sent her daughter, so my granddaughter's in Iraq. She's been over there a good while now. So the soldier there, he was in the army but he finally got out. He was in the Desert Storm thing. And this is another grandson over there that's in the navy, and he's out the navy now because he has problems with his leg. My daddy was a World War I veteran, and one of my brothers fought in the Second World War, and so I've had nephews and things in the Korean War. All the wars, I've had somebody in the wars.

ML: So there was sort of a military tradition in the family with your father being in World War I.

TRL: Yes. So it was one of them things, you try, you know, they join . . . my granddaughter was already in school and this thing, they tell them, you join up and they'll pay for the rest of your education and all that kind of stuff, and they did, but then she got, her second year she's teaching school, and then now she's in Iraq. But she's not saying anything about it because they understand what the army is.

ML: You sign up, you go where they tell you.

TRL: Yes. You're home a while, but if something come up, you just have to go fight, because that's the purpose of having an army. But the thing about it with me, I don't know what they talk about with each other, but for me, if I knew what the army was about, I would feel a heap better than I feel now, knowing that my granddaughter's over there, and if she would die, I wouldn't even know why, because I don't think many folk know the reason behind this war we're in. It's sad that we don't have no, "The reason we're over there is [thumps the table] . . . is 'x-y-z.'"

But I don't think many folk know why we're over there, because we're just over there, and got into something and didn't know the depths of what it was going to lead to, and the way it's looking, since we don't survive like other folks, and we don't know how other folk get along, and if you're going to go in somebody's else territory, you need to know how they operate things. So how you going to take advantage of them and you don't even know? And they got a whole lot of people over there, and it seem like when you listen to the news they tell you stuff, but seems like a lot of those folk that Saddam run out, they're coming back, and that's what the news says that's who's doing most of them suicide bombs and all of that. It ain't the folks in Iraq, it's the other folk coming in, and we don't know how long those folk going to keep coming, because we don't know how many it is.

So it's sad to think about with all the men, the children, hasn't even lived. Twenty, twenty-one years old, and you look at them bringing them home in caskets, man, it hurt. It hurt. And then the ones that got children, now these small children coming up, they won't ever have no daddy, and it's sad. It's sad to lose a child, but then when you lose a child and then they got little children, these children ain't going never know their daddy and their mama. It's sad to think about.

ML: Let me change the subject a little bit. Did you know Alice Pyatt, the teacher here?

[See the interview with Pyatt earlier in this volume.]

TRL: Yes, she taught my children.

ML: I see. I interviewed her three or four weeks ago, back in November I guess it was, and she's retired in Charleston now, but she speaks very fondly of her years of education in Saluda.

TRL: Being in Saluda. Yes. She was a good teacher, made a good impact on the children. Sometime teachers are teaching, the children, they don't thrive, they don't do well under everybody's teaching, but there's always somebody come in that really can put the basics, where the children don't have no problem getting it.

This one back there right behind you, the picture at the left, the poster picture, . . . the printed poster. That's our youngest daughter. She received her Ph.D. in mathematics and she's associate professor at the University of Florida in Gainesville. So two years ago she done a sabbatical and so she's doing good.

ML: Oh, that's great! Just makes you feel good to see these youngsters grow up and move along and do so well.

TRL: Yes. Her and her husband got three boys.

ML: I mentioned that Delores Logan referred me to you, but also Ike Williams asked me to give you his regards.

TRL: He did. Well, good. I worked with Ike a long time, when he was field director for the South Carolina Conference of Branches. He put a whole lot into it. He was just good at what he did. He had a way that he could get the job done. Fine fellow.

ML: I've interviewed him also, and he really told a good story about growing up in Charleston and how he came along, and was close with Reverend Newman and others.

TRL: Yes. I knew I. DeQuincey and all of them.

ML: Do you have any other reflections and memories of that period, that era. I'm focusing all the way from 1930 up through 1980.

TRL: Well, I was born in '32, and a whole lot of things went on—if you don't know, you think it's normal and that's the way things should be, but since we didn't go to town, like folks hung around on streets and stuff. My daddy had a car, but we didn't go to town unless we was going to buy something, and being out in the country where we lived there at home, and we went to the store and bought salt and sugar and ice and Kool-Aid and stuff like that, because we raised what we ate and all of that, the hogs and had our one cow, milk and stuff.

It was good. We learnt a whole lot of things. We didn't have a lot of things that other folk had, but when I got older, I found out that what you got ain't no basis on how you going to live, because all of us need food and clothing and a decent house to live in, all of us need that. But that's the problem with the integration thing, lot of folk didn't understand, and they took it as black folks trying to fight against white folks, but the white folks didn't understand. We all are human and if I stick a hole in you, red blood come out, and if you put one in me, red blood come out, regardless of what color your skin is. All our blood is red, right? And then all of us need a good house to live in, but I can't understand how these folks . . .

Now my folks come here, they were robbed of their heritage, their language, their name, they don't even know what their name was because the folk that bought them give them their name—couldn't understand nothing you're saying now, but yet I want you to come cook for me. And I still don't understand that, because I don't know what you're saying, so how I'm going to cook your food? But we have a nature of doing the thing that's right, and regardless of how we been treated, we still done what was right. And some awful things went on, but my folks still done what was right. And it leveled off, it leveled off, but if I don't know what you're saying, you might cook but I ain't going to eat what you cook. And so it's a joke told about the lady that, the Madame was going off, and she had a cook and told her, "You make me some soup." She gave her the meat to put in the pot and she said, "Well, what I'm going to put in it?" She said, "Well, you use your imagination." "Okay." So she come back, wasn't nothing in the pot but the meat. She said, "I told you to make the soup." She said, "I didn't have no 'imagination.'" She thought imagination was an ingredient [laughs]. She didn't know. She couldn't do what she didn't know, right? Said, "Well, I didn't have no 'imagination.'"

ML: Wasn't any growing in the garden or anything, huh?

TRL: So there it is. Yes, yes. Because I have a cousin that, she was like six years old, she didn't go to school, these folks asked her mama to let her stay there to play with their children, and she stood up on a box—this is in Johnson, the peach country—she stood up on a box and washed dishes at the sink, and then she's older, and then they sent her to the store to buy groceries, to buy stuff to cook. She couldn't read, and she didn't know what she was buying, so after she was about fifty years old, then she went to school to learn how to read.

Same as one of my mama's sisters there too, she's fifty years old and she went to school to learn how to read, and she got her driver's license. So my mama couldn't read, and my daddy couldn't either, but they understood our writing. They'd know which one of the children wrote it, because we all didn't write alike, they could recognize so-and-so wrote that. They knew that. But they made sure we studied our lesson, we went to school, studied our lessons, because she said, "What you got in your head, nobody can't take it out." So we all done pretty well in that area.

But, God has been good to us and I don't care how much you got, you can't eat but so much, you can't sit down in but one chair, you can't sleep in but one bed—lay in one bed, because a lot of folks on the bed ain't sleeping, they can't sleep. So you know, a lot of folk can brag about what they got, but then, too, it's ours today. Tomorrow it's somebody else's.

ML: The Bible even says that, doesn't it?

TRL: Oh, yes. It's ours today, so the best thing we can do is just do the best we can, do the best we can and go ahead.

ML: I really appreciate you spending some time with me today, and maybe you'll have some other thoughts or something to share along the way. Let me give you a page here that tells you about this project and also how to contact me.

And if you don't mind, I'll take a couple pictures of the photographs, and of you. Is that all right?

TRL: Okay.

ML: They say a picture is worth a thousand words. And your daughter here who's teaching in Florida, what's . . . ?

TRL: Thomasina Adams. That's a picture of my daddy.

ML: Your mama and daddy? A fine-looking man. He's got a full head of hair and that's more than I can say for myself *[laughs]*.

TRL: Yes. My daddy only weighed about 140 pounds. He wasn't no big old man. He lived to get about eighty-five.

I make baskets out of pine straw.

ML: Yes. Let me get pictures of a few of those too. Those are lovely. I see you're using some gourds along with the pine straw—

TRL: I saw a lady with a basket and I just didn't get what point, I found me some long-leaf pine, long-leaf straw, and started working with it, so it worked out pretty well, only don't nobody want to buy them. Folks will tell me I should go to Charleston. I said, "Well, you can buy them in Charleston, why you can't buy them in Saluda?"

ML: Yes, yes. Well, you sell these?

TRL: Yes, I sell them.

ML: How much do you ask for them?

TRL: That has a top on it, about seventy-five dollars for that one. That's another one. That's about fifteen for some smaller ones. I do a artifacts presentation, and so I made the smaller ones so I'd have something to show.

ML: Yes. Well, if you don't mind, I'd like to buy that one. And then I'd better be getting along or I'll be missing Mr. Daniel.

TRL: You haven't gotten to him yet? He was the president a long time, so he'll probably have a lot of stuff to tell you.

ML: Yes. I understand Delores's father died not too long ago. He was what, ninety-four, I think she said?

TRL: Yes. He organized the branch in Saluda.

ML: I appreciate so much you sharing with me. It's just one of those things that if we don't get these stories now, soon they'll be gone.

TRL: Right, right. Yes, we'll be gone and I think these younger folks, lot of folk don't tell their children things. They don't tell them, and they don't know. So if you don't know where you come from, you ain't got no way to figure out where you going to go.

ML: That's true.

TRL: And we all headed somewhere, and we need to have some kind of direction at which way we want to go. We need to.

ML: A number of folks that I've interviewed, their son or daughter was sitting with me when we interviewed, and I'd turn to them and ask them, "Have you ever heard this before?" And they said, "No, I never knew what he went through. I never . . ." So many people gave up a whole lot.

[See the interview with Samuel Bonds and his daughter, Sharen Mapp, in the Georgetown section above.]

TRL: Because we had, after the integration, there were these children. A white boy asked a black boy to pull his pants down and let him see his tail. Because his folks had told him black folks come from apes and things and so he assumed the boy had a tail like a monkey or something. But folks come up with all kinds of stuff, but I read my Bible and when God want a monkey, he made him a monkey. . . .

ML: Thank you so much. I really appreciate being with you today.

TRL: You're welcome.

Ernest A. Finney Jr., from Swamp to Supreme Court

Marvin Lare [ML]:* Judge Finney, I'd like you to reflect on the civil rights movement and your involvement in it across the years. I might follow up with some questions inquiring about certain aspects of it, but I'd like to see what your experiences and perspectives are that you'd like to share with folks.

Ernest A. Finney [EAF]: Basically, I graduated from law school at South Carolina State in May of 1954. That's an interesting date in time. *[He is referring to the U.S. Supreme Court decision* Brown v. Board of Education *at that time.]* I then decided that I was not going to make enough money practicing law that I could feed my family, so I went to Conway, where I became a schoolteacher. I practiced a little bit of law, and *little* being the important word, and I also waited tables. Sometime, about 1956 or '7—I don't recall when—Matthew Perry, Lincoln Jenkins, and I. D. Newman went down to the state park where they had the "wade in," I believe it is generally called. On their way back to Columbia, they stopped by my home and we had conversations, and they encouraged me that it was time for me to leave the teaching profession and become a full-time lawyer.

Moved to Sumter

EAF: Within a year or so I left Conway, and I moved to Sumter, because my survey of the state indicated that Sumter was a place that you wanted to be if you were going to be in the action. We had a great ministerial group that was supportive, we had an active and involved NAACP chapter, and there was no active practitioner in the law, no black active practitioner in the law here. I came here and the rest is history, so to speak.

*The interview took place at the law office of Judge Finney in Sumter, South Carolina, on November 16, 2004. It was transcribed by Catherine Mann, for the USC South Caroliniana Library, and Lynn Moore.

Ernest A. Finney, chief justice (retired), South Carolina Supreme Court, August 30, 2005.

Immediately after arriving here, I decided that politics was the way to get yourself involved and to be an influence in the development of the community. I ran for everything available, it looks like, for four or five years, and didn't win anything. Finally, in the election of 1972, I guess it was, I ran for the [South Carolina] House of Representatives and won that seat, in an at-large basis. Prior to that time I had run for the House. I had run for the United States Congress, as a write-in candidate against Albert Watson. I'd just run for everything, county council and various and sundry other things.

When the movement developed about 1964, with the sit-ins in Greensboro and other places, the history was changed. We had a very active NAACP chapter here. We started something called the Sumter Movement. We must remember that at that time, Sumter was the headquarters of the [White] Citizens' Council. And at the same time we had Sumter being the headquarters for James McBride Dabbs's operation—I've forgotten the name of it off the top of my head. Human Affairs Commission or something like that. So this was the center of some of the activities. One of the things that had happened just before I arrived here, a local lawyer had sued the NAACP for a hundred thousand dollars, got a verdict—I've forgotten what, it was before I arrived here—and once the verdict was announced and the appellate process concluded, he decided to donate the money to a local church. So Sumter was where the action was.

As a result of my involvement with the movement and with the NAACP, I represented CORE, I represented SNCC ["Snick"], I represented all of the unpopular organizations in that arena.

Tell me what you want to know about me.

Leaders in Sumter

ML: Who were some of the other leaders in the Sumter NAACP chapter here?

EAF: You had Bishop Frederick C. James, who is now a retired bishop of the AME Church in Columbia. You had James T. McCain, who was active with CORE [Congress of Racial Equality] and went to jail down in Mississippi. Oh . . . you've done something you never should do, and that is try to relate the people. Some of the young members were people like Reverend Ralph Canty, who served in the legislature for a while. There were a number of ladies: Irene Williams, who was a schoolteacher who lost her job because of participating in the demonstrations. You had the Reverend A. W. Wright, who was active.

[Relevant interviews with Bishop James, James T. McCain and his widow, and Irene Williams and her husband, Drefus Williams, will be found in volume 2.]

EAF: One of the dilemmas we had was, you get all these people in jail, and then the question becomes, how're you going to get them out? They were anxious to go, but they were also anxious to leave. You had the question of raising bonds. We had a man by the name of Sam Green, who was an older gentleman, who was a very conservative gentleman, but any time these young people got in jail and I needed help, he would generally come to bat and try to help us. I remember one incident where I was— remember, the movement moved around—once we had a situation where there was a bunch of people in jail and the communications had fallen apart. We didn't know how to get them out, and I called one of my associates and had them locate Sam, and Sam said, "All right, I'll be there." In a couple of hours he showed up and he had in one pocket *ten thousand dollars cash,* and he had in another pocket a *ten-thousand-dollar security bond,* and we were able to secure [their release]. So it was an interesting and rewarding and fulfilling time.

Demonstrations

ML: Were those local demonstrations that the folks were in jail for, or somewhere across the state?

EAF: Local demonstrations. In Orangeburg, that was a local demonstration. Those demonstrations were interesting. You never could tell how one was going to turn out. I was listening this morning to the news where they said Condoleezza Rice had been nominated for secretary of state, and somebody asked how would she do and what impact would that have on our president's second term, and you never know.

For example, once we had a demonstration here of about eighty-five young people who went to jail, who somebody had assured that if you go to jail, we're going to get you out. Well, they got in jail at about four o'clock in the afternoon, as a result of demonstrating without a permit, and . . . well, the bonds were not available! By five-thirty they were getting awfully antsy. Though they had gone to jail charged with one offense, a hundred-dollar bond, while they were in jail, they decided to have another demonstration. They broke up some of the furniture and they broke up some of the plates, and they—so we ended up with this eighty-five [to] a hundred kids in jail, and rather than being a hundred dollars they had increased the bond to three hundred dollars! So you never knew what was going to happen.

ML: Who provided the primary leadership and strategizing in these protests? Were you involved in that side of it as well as the legal representation?

EAF: As a lawyer you walked a very fine line, so you were careful not to put yourself in a position where the local authorities could charge you with instigating litigation for purposes of increasing your own . . . So you did not go to the public sessions. You might consult and advise the leadership, McCain and Fred James or somebody like that. *[The telephone rings.]* Excuse me. Yes, Honey?

[The recording stops, then resumes.]

ML: Okay. You were recounting some of the leadership of the movement here, and the fine line you had to follow . . .

EAF: You couldn't instigate litigation. The system would have ground you up and bumped you out if you were guilty of instigating litigation, so very seldom did, as a lawyer, did I get any involvement in what was going on, other than if somebody came in and wanted to know, "If we go to the Sumter County Public Library, what's going to happen?"

"Well, they're going to put your butt in jail. If you go to the Holiday Inn, or if you go to the dime store or put on a demonstration, you're going to go to jail. Now if you want to do it in a nice, peaceful way, we can apply to the city police department and get a permit to parade, and as long as you don't block the sidewalk or the streets, you [will be] in pretty good shape, generally."

I had to be ready. That there were going to be people—particularly in a community such as this one was at that time—you were going to have people who were going to try to agitate and try to cause a disruption, because that was in their favor. It was not only Sumter . . .

ML: White or black or both?

EAF: No, just white. You had Citizens' Council, and though they didn't do many things, they had their troops like everybody else did. For example, when the Freedom Riders came through here, there was a story told about the fact that they'd put a snake on somebody who was at the Sumter bus station. This kind of thing. When they were marching, somebody would walk past and make derogatory comments. There was an arm of SNCC and the NAACP, and you of course had Dr. King, who had troops in here who were teaching people how to be nonviolent. That's a difficult task.

I was involved in the . . . I was representing in Rock Hill, believe it or not, the only ten people who served their time. A group of students called the Rock Hill Nine, or whatever the number was, who went to jail, and when they found them guilty, though I was their lawyer they were found guilty, and they decided, "Well, we're not going to pay the fine." So they went to jail. That's an interesting sidelight to the civil rights story. I have some articles that—there were two or three girls, and the other seven or eight were males—and they worked on the chain gangs in Rock Hill.

ML: We've got some folks who are interviewing some of those folks, from up at Winthrop College. We traced down the "jail-not-bail" group.

[See the interview with Willie T. "Dub" Massey by Winthrop student Andrew Grose above.]

EAF: "Jail-not-bail" group, right. I was their lawyer. They were interesting.

ML: I imagine they took a lot of abuse on the chain gang.

EAF: I suspect they did. There was a fellow by the name of Thomas Gaither, who was a graduate of Claflin, and I'm a graduate of Claflin. Since you're a Methodist preacher, you . . . He was the leader as far as I was concerned. He had a young lady by the name of Diane Nash. I don't know whether she's still with us or not. There was a girl by the name of Smith. That would be an interesting scenario for you to work on.

We had teachers that lost their jobs in Sumter. We had one named Irene Williams. . . . I don't know how these names happen to just come back to me.

ML: Oh, they're deep in there.

EAF: Yes, they're very deep in there.

Trying Cases

EAF: Matthew [Perry] and I had to bring a lawsuit to get her reinstated in her [Irene Williams's] teaching position. There were a number of people who were hurt very seriously, economically at least, because of their participation in sit-ins. To my knowledge, we didn't lose any bond money. I lost probably eight thousand cases at the local level, but the interesting thing about it, to me, was the fact that I never had an unprofessional experience, either by a judge or by a lawyer on the other side. It was handled according to what the law was then, and the law was against us.

I remember one day that I was in Sumter in the morning trying cases, and Orangeburg in the afternoon, and Florence that evening. It was a tough time. You had, I believe it was twenty-four hours, to get your notice of appeal up. Well, when you're in court all day and half the night, you didn't get much time. But the lawyers were very professional.

ML: So the courts, within the law as it existed, they were fairly respectful and responsible in their conduct?

EAF: That was my experience.

ML: Did you have some sense of physical threat and danger in your traveling about?

EAF: Oh, yes. There was always in the back of your head . . . This was shortly after the last lynching in South Carolina. I believe it was a fellow named . . . no, that wasn't the last one, but that was one that stuck in my craw, because it was the one that occurred just as I arrived in South Carolina.

The Swamps of South Carolina

EAF: You need to remember that I came to South Carolina as a *junior in high school,* from Baltimore, Maryland. My father was a teacher at Morgan State University, and one day he came in—my mother had died so there was just Dad and I—and he came in one day and announced, "Well, we're going to Orangeburg, South Carolina." What in the . . . I had never even heard of Orangeburg! Of course by the time the word got out among my friends that I was coming to South Carolina, they explained to me that—I believe his name was Willie Earl, had recently been—this was about 1946—had been lynched up around Greenville, or somewhere in that area, and they explained to me they were going to lynch my butt, coming to South Carolina.

I never will forget that I got on the train and came motoring down here, and when we got to Florence, just before you get to Florence on the old ACL [Atlantic Coast Line] coming down next to 95, the swamp was up. They had announced already on the train that the next stop is Florence, where you change to go to Orangeburg. Well, all this water was standing there, and I just knew that Orangeburg was in the middle of some swamp somewhere. But Orangeburg grew to be a very warm place.

I sat on the front steps of Claflin—my father was then dean of Claflin. That's why we came down here—and we'd go sit on the front steps where the street that runs by State College and Claflin, and the Ku Klux Klan would parade. Those kinds of things.

ML: I spent a day up at Howard University last week, in their archives, and it was interesting that in some of the monthly reports of the NAACP, there was the lynching case, where they were suing the counties, and—let's see—there were three things that kept showing up. *Elmore v.* . . .

EAF: Voting rights case.

ML: Voting rights case. I forget what the third one was.

EAF: Teacher equalization probably was part of that. It was a tough time.

ML: So suddenly you were thrust in the middle of it as a young man.

EAF: Yes.

ML: Who were some of your biggest inspirations?

The Law Was against Us

EAF: Of course, working closely with Matthew Perry and Lincoln Jenkins. The law was against us. You leave home with that, that the law was definitely opposed to the activities that we were pursuing. It became interesting that we had to figure out a way to fit our situation to what our concept of the law [was]. Our concept of the law was not what the law had been established [as being] by the United States Supreme Court,

South Carolina Supreme Court. Every court was hooked into the old way of doing things.

ML: *Plessy versus Ferguson* just was like a pall over everything.

EAF: . . . 1897. Yes, everything. There were no rights which a citizen of African descent had to enjoy, that had to be respected, and that was the bottom line. That was the state of the law. And the law might have been—we thought it was awfully wrong, and we were successful in making changes in it, but it was a slow and grinding process.

ML: This may be the lowest point, where you just felt like despairing?

EAF *[chuckling]:* Well, there were many of those. I think that the lowest point in my individual career was when the students in Orangeburg were locked up in the stockades outdoors and they were subject to abuse, [and] the lowest point [in the movement] probably was the day that the Orangeburg massacre occurred. At that time I was chairman of the United States Civil Rights Commission, and I had as one of my commissioners Dr. Benjamin Payton, who is now president of Tuskegee. That was a very low point in my career, because the killing of those students . . . we didn't know what the details were, but we had our feeling as to the fact that they had been mistreated. That still hangs on with us when last year, year before last, when I was down in Orangeburg, one of the things we commemorated was the killing of the "Orangeburg Three." There was very little attention given to it. We got three students killed in Orangeburg, and at the same time Kent State had four, I believe it was—I don't know the exact number killed in that demonstration. Yet that became a national movement, whereas the three students who died in Orangeburg never did reach the point of impact that their lives should have justified. Of course, the school did something by naming the gymnasium [in their honor] and there's still a commemorative service, but that was probably the lowest point in my career.

ML: There were quite a number of people who were picked up and taken to CCI [Central Corrections Institute in Columbia], weren't there? Besides Cleveland Sellers?

EAF: Yes, a number of people. I don't remember the numbers. But see, I worked primarily in Sumter or Rock Hill. Did some work in Hartsville, where we brought a lawsuit to integrate the library. I did some Orangeburg work. Columbia was Matthew [Perry] and Lincoln Jenkins. We had to divide ourselves up so that there was always one lawyer available somewhere to give advice and counsel, and at least let the power structure know that there was somebody who was watching them.

ML: Were you representing the NAACP Legal Defense Fund, or were you just drawn on from time to time as needed?

EAF: I represented CORE—the Congress of Racial Equality—the real connection there was James McCain, [who] was one of their field directors. You represented anybody. Matthew and I used to tell each other stories about the fact that if a Greyhound bus had struck and killed ten people right in front of our office, we wouldn't have gotten that case, but if somebody had gotten beat by a policeman and that kind of thing ten thousand miles away, they'd end up in our office. We represented everybody, more or less.

Public Office

ML: You ran for public office innumerable times?

EAF: Yes.

ML: Did you have an overall strategy to that, or was it just to take everything that came along?

EAF: Take whatever came along. The mood of the people was such that they wanted, we needed some victories. We needed to have some winners.

My life in the political career was very interesting, very rewarding, very satisfying. When I said that I was going to run . . . when I won finally—the South Carolina House of Representatives—people would come up to me and say, "Aw, they going put you in the back row and they won't let you talk," and this kind of thing. "You're going to be just a half-weight and occupy space."

Well, I found that to be not quite true. That was the days when Saul Blatt was running the house and Edgar Brown was running the senate. Everybody just thought that everything was . . . but it was my experience that if you were prepared and if you became active and you knew what was happening, you were given an opportunity to be a player. You weren't a major player but at least you could articulate your position, which was a new thing. One of the reasons you have in South Carolina now something called the Legislative Black Caucus was the fact that as chairman of the group, I decided that we needed to have better a understanding of the rules and what was going on, and that was the basis upon which it was founded.

EAF: It was founded primarily as a study group, to know what the rules were, and to assist in exchanging ideas. It's a little different now.

ML: It sort of strategizes and takes positions. . . .

EAF: Political positions. That wasn't where we started out, but of course, everything continues to grow and prosper and tries to do something.

ML: Who were some of the white leaders that you felt like really made a difference? Supported or secretly did what they could?

EAF: I'm not going to reveal, because I don't know who is living and who's dead, and what they've done. I know that by and large, in my individual situation, they treated me professionally. When you were forty-eight hours getting in an appeal and the time said twenty-four, you didn't raise much sand about that. Because you had people who had records and if technically you were out . . . It was an interesting time. Professionally, I think they did as well as they could. Because, remember, these people had a constituency just like I had a constituency.

ML: How did you get elected at-large? Was there just that much of a strong black vote, or was there . . . ?

EAF: No. The black vote. Back in those days we could single shot. Remember that? All right. Well, I got the black vote, and there was a group of white citizens who signed a letter saying that this fellow ain't going to really be that bad and we urge you to consider him. I got probably 10 percent [of the white vote], just enough to make up the difference. I'm grateful, and I still have got copies of the letter somewhere. As you can see from the confusion here that I haven't gotten around to doing what I want to do, but I got probably 10, 15 percent [of the white vote].

ML: I'd be interested in that letter because we'd like to include in the anthology some of the original documents. We'd be glad to work with you on letters like that or other significant . . .

EAF: Oh, the documents [are here] somewhere *[waving his arm toward files and bookcases],* who knows? At Claflin they have created a Finney Library, and a Finney Auditorium, and one of these days when I go through all these desk drawers and all those books that you see up there, I'm going to turn some papers over to Claflin and probably to the law school at state college. Which *was the* law school, anyway.

The Law School at South Carolina State

EAF: You know, that was an interesting sidelight in South Carolina history. The law school at the state college produced Matthew Perry and Ernest Finney—it was an interesting time.

ML: You must have had some really powerful teachers and folks who equipped you well.

EAF: Yes, they did. Yes, they did.

ML: Who stands out? Among your teachers?

EAF: Teachers? You had a fellow by the name of T. Robert Gay, you had a fellow by the name of LeMarquis DeJarman. See—that's what you do! You ask me about who's outstanding, and there'll be somebody that I have omitted to put in the scenario. But we had good faculty. I tell everybody, when we went to school at South Carolina State, they probably had a thousand, five hundred volumes. University of South Carolina probably had a million, five hundred thousand volumes. They had teachers out the gazoo [*sic*], and they had students whose daddies were lawyers and judges, and they were well connected. But we made up our minds—one of the reasons why I drink black and bitter coffee today is the fact that our law school did not have a refrigerator in it, so you didn't get any sugar and cream. If you wanted coffee, you drank it just like it came out of the pot. It was a great time.

[For a listing of the faculty of the South Carolina State School of Law, see page 44 of W. Lewis Burke and Belinda F. Gergel, eds., Matthew J. Perry *(Columbia: University of South Carolina Press, 2004). The chapter on the School of Law was written by W. Lewis Burke and William C. Hine.]*

ML: What was your experience with some of the national folks, both like [Charles H.] Houston and Judge . . .

EAF: Carter?

ML: [Robert L.] Carter, and Thurgood Marshall and those folks?

EAF: Thurgood was . . . every time the South Carolina Conference of the NAACP had its annual meetings—I don't know where that is, probably on my son's desk . . .

ML: So Thurgood Marshall would be . . .

EAF: Oh, yes. He was an inspiration to everybody in the law, no question about that. I think the first time I met him was up in Spartanburg at an annual conference of the NAACP. You had Bob Carter, and you had Bob Ming, and you had a man from Richmond who was down here recently for Matthew's whatever that was. There was a certain collegiality and a certain spirit of esprit de corps that emanated from that group, and we did the heavy lifting.

ML: You moved in the legislature to the Judiciary Committee?

EAF: Yes.

ML: Is that what led eventually to your judgeship?

EAF: I don't know. The story was that there'd never been a black on the Judiciary Committee and the Speaker decided that it was time and I was the man, and I became a member of the Judiciary Committee. That was the most powerful committee in the house at that time. I like to say that. Everybody else says it was the Ways and Means—I don't think I'll get into that argument. It gave an opportunity to be actively involved in the mapping and the setting of the legal precedents. It was an interesting time. We didn't win many, but we were active. For example, one of the things that we fought during my early days in the legislature was the death penalty. Talk about people who were just fighting for the sake of fighting, except for the fact that the governor did veto it one time. We had our input and we actively participated in the political process, and we learned a lot about it.

ML: Who was the Speaker of the House then?

EAF: I've got it right here somewhere. Rex Carter, I believe. 1973. Officers of the House. It might have been Saul, Saul Blatt. Saul was the first Speaker I served under, and I should remember that. And Rex, I believe, was the next one.

Highest Point

ML: I asked you about your lowest points, what were some of the highest points, so far . . . ? *[Both laugh.]*

EAF: Well, I think my highest point came when I got to the South Carolina Supreme Court—when I was on it and I was chief justice—we issued a three-to-one decision called *Abbeville versus the State of South Carolina*. *Abbeville* deals with the fact that South Carolina has these school districts that are sorely underfunded and there had been a decision made by the circuit judge that said that there was *no right* for these districts to get some more of the money. The Supreme Court issued some magnanimous opinion—under which I wrote—in which it said that every child in South Carolina is entitled to a "minimally adequate education." That doesn't say a lot for a fellow who likes to be direct, but that was what we could do, and it's still going on. They haven't resolved it. That decision was probably the forefront of my career, and if somehow or the other we can get [the funding] . . . you know, we've got school districts in South Carolina where the tax base is about thirteen hundred dollars. We've got other school districts in South Carolina where the tax base is about eighty-five hundred dollars per pupil. If somehow or another we could . . . number one, you cannot expect a child who comes out of a thirteen-hundred-dollar-tax-base district to compete in the year 2020 with a student who comes out of an eight-thousand-dollar-per-pupil base. Of course, there have been some areas where they've tried to modify, but we've never articulated in South Carolina, I don't think, clearly and cogently as we could and should, an indication that we're going to educate our children, like North Carolina. Education is *not* at the top of the agenda. But that kept the litigation alive, and what's going to happen, I don't know, but at least it's a step.

ML: That brings us right down to the current issues. Besides education—of course, I'd say that's certainly the biggest issue—what do you see as being the urgent agenda? In our concluding section of the anthology, we'll have some epilogues in terms of things accomplished and agendas yet to be addressed. What do you see on both of those? The major accomplishments and also the major unresolved issues?

Regrets

EAF: I'd like to see us . . . one of the regrets I have in my life is that in the—other than the closing of the law school, we should not have let them close the law school without a fight—but as far as regrets: somehow or another that in the struggle for civil rights we left too many people behind. There are a few Ernest Finneys and there are a few success stories and there are a few . . . But by and large, we have missed the masses. Somehow or another we never got the message through to the masses of students and people that if you struggle, you might make it.

We missed too many people, and somehow or another we have . . . There have been riches and wonderful opportunities available for our young people, but too many times they have not taken advantage of it. We still have a need to get the masses. For example, I don't think that . . . I used to tell everybody when I was a judge on the circuit bench, that the American system of justice, or the South Carolina system of justice, is not perfect, but it surely is a hell of a lot better than every other system. And our system of education and economic development is not perfect. Even with the shortcomings and the moanings and groanings that we have, if somehow or another we could come together and take advantage of every opportunity we get, we could make it a lot better.

ML: The churches, I think, do a lot or try to encourage the aspirations, and public schools do, but it really is a challenge.

EAF: We've got too many families who just have no hope. Somehow or another our political leadership and . . . Every time you make one step forward, you make two steps back. The programs generally are designed and sound wonderful, but guess what? The reaction doesn't deliver. You're talking about what, forty-one million American citizens without health care? They propose something called "No Child Left Behind" and they don't fund the durn thing. What I'd really like to see, and of course, it isn't within the realm of reason, but I'd like to see us . . . What's wrong with South Carolina that every time somebody wants to run for office, what is the first thing they do? They announce they're going to run for office. What's the second thing they do? "I'm going to cut your taxes." And when you cut taxes, you're going to cut services. You've got to! So we end up where these smokers are dying and going to hell, and we have a health care system that is broken down. We have people who—how many people in Columbia last night slept in the . . . what's your coach's name?

ML: Holtz. Lou Holtz.

EAF: Lou Holtz and his wife got a shelter there. Where are the political leaders who are saying, "Let's do something about that"? I know that we can't . . . The Bible tells me we're going to have poor always, but at least we ought to have programs, and we ought to have people who are not afraid to say we're going to do better with education and economics and health care. Ain't nobody saying that today. [They say,] "Cut taxes."

ML: That cuts the heart out of communities, the sense of common . . .

EAF: You've been to California and all those places. Why've we got all these people down on the beach who're retiring down here? We must have a pretty good tax system. So we ought to make sure that the income coming in is applied in a way that does the most good *[long pause]*.

ML: Any other thoughts for today?

EAF: Not off the top of my head. You caught me cold turkey. I don't have my message ready for you this morning, Reverend *[laughs]*.

ML: I can always come back.

EAF: All right. Maybe we can get together then in Santee or somewhere like that and have an afternoon coffee time.

ML: We'll do that.

EAF: I got a little arthritis going. I don't admit that.

ML: I don't admit it, but it gets me . . .

EAF: Occasionally.

ML: Yes. I go riding in the car for a little bit and hobble around afterwards for a while, until I can get things going.

EAF: Yes, indeed. Well, I have enjoyed it and I look forward to . . .

ML: Likewise.

Gloria M. Jenkins, Birthing the Sumter Movement and the Bennett Belles

Marvin Lare **[ML]**:* Today is June the 18th, 2007, and I'm with Gloria Montgomery Jenkins at her father's home in Sumter, South Carolina. Ms. Jenkins lives in Atlanta, or near Atlanta.

Gloria Montgomery Jenkins **[GMJ]**: Good morning. I live in East Point, Georgia. Right outside of Atlanta, right at Hartsville Airport, so I hear all of the noise, and I like to joke and say I can even see what they're serving for dinner on the airplanes. I'm that close to it *[laughs]*.

ML: Okay. I appreciate being with you today. It's been some weeks since we talked on the telephone originally, and I appreciate so much your contacting me and telling me about your involvement with the "Sumter Movement." . . .

GMJ: Well, this is quite an opportunity for me and for history, getting an accurate reporting of the civil rights movement as it began and went on in Sumter, South Carolina.

One Sunday afternoon, attorney Ernest Finney, attorney Reuben Gray, Peggy White, and myself, got together and we talked about Sumter and the future of Sumter, and the segregated policies that were in effect at that time. Of course, we knew they were wrong, and we were at a point in our lives that we wanted to be community activists and make changes for the better. Peggy and I had just finished college that June, and attorney Finney and attorney Gray were relatives and new attorneys here in Sumter.

---

*The interview took place at the home of Gloria Montgomery Jenkins's father, in Sumter, South Carolina.

395

We talked about what we'd like to do, and I personally had been involved in the sit-in movement in Greensboro, North Carolina, and so it was just natural that the first thing that came to my mind was to do sit-ins, do marches and protests. They had the same ideas, so we decided that that was what we wanted to do, but we needed more people involved. We talked a while and scheduled a subsequent meeting and invited Willie Singleton, Charles Riley, who's my stepdad, Sidney Vaughn, and Nathaniel Scriven, and some other individuals. Then we started holding our meetings at Morris College, in the basement of one of the boys' dormitories, because our group had expanded, number one, and number two, it was a much more convenient location and it gave us room to spread out and invite a larger number of people.

We met there for several months, making plans and starting our protest movement, and the numbers just got too big, so we moved to First Baptist Church at the corner of Daniel and Washington. There were several well-known individuals in the community who thought we might have been moving a little bit too fast and thought we needed to just wait a while and let the future take care of itself, but of course, we didn't see it that way. So our numbers grew rapidly, and we began the picket signs, we began the marches, we began going around to the different churches holding meetings, in town as well as in the rural areas, trying to get everybody aware of what we were doing. We wanted it to spread word of mouth, but we wanted it to be accurate, so we did many, many meetings in the churches around Sumter County. And we began our marches, as I said, and individuals were being arrested, but they were kept pretty safe.

My dad, Charles Riley, was a bail bondsman for that movement, and he had things set up prior to the arrests—people who would put up bond for individuals if there were arrests made. We did the sit-ins, we did . . . this was the summer of 1963, summer and fall of '63. Emerson Brown and Frank Robinson with the Congress of Racial Equality became a part of our movement. The Sumter civil rights movement was not started by NAACP nor CORE, as the Congress of Racial Equality was called, not by any organization but by a group of individuals who saw a need, that saw a wrong and tried to right it.

We just did what we needed to do, going into Sumter Cut-Rate Drugstore, and for some reason many citizens feared that to be the worst, the dreaded spot. But ironically, now it is operated by a black pharmacist. It was a couple of months ago, anyway. But that was the spot that we were threatened most severely with axe handles and whatever else they had in mind, so everybody wanted to take on that one. They wanted to just get in there, but at the same time they were a little apprehensive about what might happen.

During that summer the March on Washington was held and Congress of Racial Equality provided funds for us to get three buses to go, but when we went to the bus station, we were told that all of the buses were booked, so Mr. Drummond, who was the bus station manager, said, "Well, go on over there to the train station. You might get you a train car for the price of those three buses." So, in fact that's what we did.

Gloria M. Jenkins at her father's home in Sumter, South Carolina, June 18, 2007.

At that point ministers in Sumter had decided that they wanted to be the spearhead of the movement, and we worked together with [a certain amount of] low-key discord, but we knew that our goal was to desegregate, so we put those things on the back burner. However when it was time to go to the March on Washington, they decided they were the ones that needed to go and that the foot soldiers needed to stay home and keep things going.

Well, the Congress of Racial Equality didn't see it that way. They thought everybody who wanted to go should go, so consequently, going back to the train station, we were able to get three passenger cars to accommodate these numbers, so when we showed up at the train station, we were told by one of the ministers who was thought to have been the leader, "Oh, well, we didn't know you all were coming to see us off!"

"We're not. We're going to the march!"

"Remember, we said you all've got to stay and remember we didn't book . . ."

"Oh, don't worry about it. We have our own three passenger cars." Of course that was a blow to their ego [laughs].

But anyway, we went on to the March on Washington and had a good trip, enjoyed the speech, and there were just mobs and mobs of people. And because of my height—I'm right at five foot or a little less—most of what I could see at that time was the belt of the person in front of me, there were so many.

When we came back, we did our letters, we did newspaper articles. Initially they were not published, but then eventually they started putting little blurbs in [the newspaper]. When the city fathers realized that these people mean business—we had no problem getting parade permits at first, which was what they said we needed in order to march downtown—but when they saw that these parades or marches were getting bigger and bigger, they decided they would not honor, they would not give us permits anymore. I guess, it looked like we were winning. We were mobilizing the people more than they wanted, so they started denying the parade permits, but creative minds come up with ways to get around things, so we did. We'd just go "window looking." . . .

ML: Just sort of individually?

GMJ: That's right. That's right.

ML: . . . two or three people together.

GMJ: . . . at a time. That's right. And Sunday afternoon we were just out for a stroll. "They came from that way. I don't know them."

"I was coming from this way. What do I have to do with them?"

"Nothin."

But we were able to say to them that we come in nonviolence. "We are able to work in these stores. We are able to work in your homes. Why deny us the right to jobs?" Which was the main focus at that point, getting better jobs, providing just a better quality of life for African Americans in Sumter and Sumter County.

That would also afford us the right to represent our peers, people who looked just like us. It's one thing to say I represent an area, which is what was intact at that time. "I represent North Main. I represent the West Liberty area." But in my way of thinking, you can't represent me if you don't—you don't necessarily have to *look* like me, but you need to *either* look like me, *live* like me, or share some of the same *burdens* and segregated policies that I share. So the Sumter Movement allowed then, the success of it, allowed African Americans to be *elected* to offices and get the jobs that we wanted.

I left the Sumter Movement in '63, November, went to Florida to work. . . .

So the movement continued, and it continued to be more successful. Laws were being changed at this point. Blacks were able to get better jobs. Or some got better jobs, some got jobs in the white retail establishments, that kind of thing. So it was very, very successful without a lot of the kinds of situations that happened in Orangeburg and in Alabama. We didn't have the beatings, we didn't have the water hose, we didn't have all of those cruel acts, and certainly we didn't have the shootings. So it was a peaceful, peaceful movement. Now verbally it may not have been as peaceful, but physically it was relatively peaceful.

I came back to Sumter in 1969, and I was hired as the first African American at the Sumter Department of Welfare, and while that was some time removed—years from the movement—it was still a successful goal of the movement. Again, because of my height, the director thought that I was a high school student, so I told him, no, that I had . . .

He said, "We only hire college graduates."

So I said, "Well, I finished college." And personally, at that point, I said, okay, these are the stumbling blocks that he's going to put up, the first one being the degree that I had.

Then he said, "Well, you'll have to take a test."

So he scheduled the test, and I think I made almost a perfect score on the test, so when I got the results and came back to him, and he had already admitted that there was a vacancy, he had nothing, no reason to deny giving me the job and not seem racist, so I was given the job and did quite well.

At the end of one year, one of the supervisors told me, "Well, we've been watching you. We wanted to see how well you would do with the job before we hired any other blacks. But you've done quite well. You've more than met our expectations."

So, of course, the next week after she made that comment, they did hire two other blacks as a matter of fact. But, you know, tribute goes to those individuals who got out there and walked with the picket signs in the hot sun and those who walked in the cool of the evening—because many people would come after they got off of work— join mass rallies and contribute that way. There were individuals who would bring food to the church just so that we would have things to eat and snack on those days. Willie Singleton was one of those persons, as well as he was one of the strategists in the movement. Reverend McCrary, and I think I gave you these names earlier.

ML: Yes, but I don't have them with me. It'd be good if I have them on tape. I have them in my notes but . . .

GMJ: Okay.

ML: But it's good to hear your own voice and all. Reverend McCrary.

GMJ: As I said, Attorney Reuben Gray, who lives right here *[pointing next door]*. And Attorney Ernest Finney, who lives two doors up that way. Peggy White, she's now Peggy White Clark, who lives in New Jersey. As I said, Willie Singleton. Nathaniel Scriven. Oh, I know I'm forgetting some names, but I can see the faces. I just can't put a name with it, but I'll continue to think about it.

But you know, most of all it bonded the citizens of Sumter. Everybody was working for a cause, and everybody was proud to be a part and wanted to see things change, so we just had a good time.

ML: Being persistent and all.

GMJ: Yeah, being persistent.

ML: You mentioned about the police and law enforcement. So they played a fairly moderating kind of role? Did you end up in jail?

GMJ: Oh, there were many . . . I was never arrested, never. But my brother, looked like he would get caught every time, and he said, "Now I want to know what you're doing. How come they don't ever arrest you?" But yes, we had many arrests.

ML: Maybe you were too small to be arrested! *[He laughs.]*

GMJ: Maybe so, maybe so. Oh, yes, we had plenty of arrests. But as I said, the bonds and things were already preset so nobody had to stay in jail any long period of time. They may have stayed overnight in some cases. It would just depend on how the police felt and whether they wanted to work expeditiously or whether they wanted to just take their time. The longer you're in jail the less you're on the street. But we did have that. I don't remember now who the chief of police was, but I think Bubba McElveen might have been the mayor. I can check that and let you know.

Sunday mornings, churches were full because they wanted to know what happened during the past week and what was the plan for the future. And the churches played pivotal roles because they were the voice, they were the airwaves that citizens were notified of what had happened or what was going to happen, or where you needed to be. So then ministers, as I said, would come and meet, and meet with the body and . . .

ML: So the original meetings were just the few of you?

GMJ: The four of us.

ML: Then it spread and became more popular and supported by the clergy and . . .

GMJ: Exactly. The clergy, the clergy and black business leaders, you know, became more supportive. There was an interesting fellow. I think his name was Jack Greenberg. I know Greenberg was his last name. A white, Jewish fellow that came to town and wanted very much to be involved and he did work with us to some degree, but there were some leaders who were so suspicious that he's a plant, he's a plant from the white community, he's sent here to find out what's going on and report back to them. But anyway, he knew that they had not accepted him for what he was trying to offer, so he left. I often wonder where he went or—you know, I might even try to find him one of these days.

ML: He might show up.

GMJ: Yes. But as I said, we did what we had to do. There were groups who were . . . everybody had their inner fear, and they knew that there were certain situations they did not want to be in for fear they could *not* be nonviolent, so there were those who wanted just to picket, and that was a rotating picket line. Nobody stayed out more than two or three hours because this was the summer. And they were brought into the church and given refreshments and allowed to cool down. If they could stay longer, they did. If not, they left and others came in. So we always had that set up and operational. Then there were those who wanted to be right in that sit-in, right in that stool in the café. Then there were those who wanted to just, "Well, I'll put up some property and work with the bond, but I don't want to get involved physically." And that was just as much of a support as getting out there marching.

ML: Everybody did what they could or what they were comfortable with.

GMJ: Exactly. And that was one thing that made it, in my mind, so successful in the black community as it relates to recruiting. Because we said whatever it is, if you can only provide water or snacks, then you are a major part just like the person walking the street. So people were made to feel comfortable doing whatever it was they thought they could do or wanted to do. So when they realized everybody was not going to be forced to get out there and walk, then that brought in other people.

We had a large number of folk who were not senior citizens by any means at that time, but they were the older—in fact, my parents at that time and maybe some of their parents if they were around—that population who had lived I'd say three-quarters or half of their life in segregated circumstances. I remember going to Sears and Roebuck in Florence and seeing the white and the colored water fountains, as well as going to a doctor's office in Sumter, and at that time blacks would have to go in the back door and whites would go in the front door, and of course, there were separate waiting rooms.

But I think overall, as white America began to realize these people have money, these people spend money, it became more feasible for them. "Hey, let me open my restaurant." Because blacks like to eat. They will spend money. So those restaurants who opened up initially saw a big increase in their economic status, and so that encouraged others to open.

The sit-ins and the marches didn't just make anybody do. It made them *think* about what to do and it made them think about what could be, and it was on those bases that they changed to allow blacks to come in. But now as far as the political scene, blacks then too became more interested in voting, and we were able to elect blacks throughout the nation in different seats to represent different things. However, it still seems today that many blacks have the perception, especially candidates when they say, "When I get in there, I'm going to change this, I'm going to change that," but they fail to realize they still have just one vote, and if they don't persuade somebody else to vote with them, then they can't change *a thing*. So that in itself causes a lot of disappointment in the black neighborhoods.

"You said you were going to go in there and change this and you haven't done a thing. You haven't done a thing."

But he has not or she has not communicated the fact that, "I can't do anything by myself." And they should never put forth that promise of what I am going to do because if you know your position and you studied that seat, then you know you've got to have other folk to help you, and if you're not able to cultivate that relationship, then you're going to disappoint your constituents because they're looking for "John Q. Black American" to change those seats from rust to white, and he can't do it by himself.

So that's the snapshot of the Sumter civil rights movement. Now, I know many stories have been written, and I read them with interest because having been one of the original four myself, I know the role that some of these individuals played, and what they're projecting is not always what happened. So my sister, Jacqueline Williams, has always encouraged me, "Write your book. Write your book." But I'm not one that likes to sit still and just do that. I need to be up and moving.

ML: That's hard to do.

GMJ: So when I read your piece in the *State,* I said, "Let me call him because I can talk, and he can write and then I'll get it out that way."

[See Claudia Brinson Smith's article for the State, "Saving the Stories of the Struggle for Equality," August 16, 2005.]

GMJ: But we were able to . . . the Nathaniel Scriven I mentioned was the primary driver for the group. Anybody that needed to go anywhere, he would always be ready to go, and that was his contribution. He would drive because he knew the area. He would drive them wherever they wanted to go. And there were individuals who would help with typing or those kinds of things, and whenever we had our mass rallies, we would always take up a collection, and that helped defray some of the cost for gas and getting food on a daily basis and that sort of thing, so we had . . .

ML: And the origins were independent of any of the national movements, the NAACP or CORE . . .

GMJ: Exactly.

ML: But when or how did they come in? Now CORE related to you, the grass roots people, about getting the train cars and that kind of thing.

GMJ: They were there with us to help with strategies, not as an organization, but two of their key people who live here in Sumter, that's Frank Robinson and Emerson Brown, they live here in Sumter so, of course, they were concerned, so they came on as individuals, and as things began to grow, if we needed something from CORE, then they would contact them and see about helping. Statistics and that kind of thing. Of course, the major piece was the transportation to the March on Washington. NAACP never came to the forefront as an organization. We knew there were members working who were members of NAACP, but they never stepped up and said the NAACP would like to do this or like to do that. At least not during my tenure with the movement, but I knew we had members . . .

ML: Now your father, actually I guess your stepfather, managed the bail bonds and those types of things, and in a lot of cases Matthew Perry and Ernest Finney represented people. I think that they were through the NAACP.

GMJ: Well, that was in later years. Later years, and maybe in other cities, but . . . because Matthew Perry was out of Columbia, I think, and Finney and Gray were right here, so I'm sure they were representing cases and things of that nature.

But people who didn't want to maybe initially be a part of that—"It might hurt this or it might hurt that business," or whatever—helped in the background. Then as they saw the masses coming and successes being achieved, then they felt more comfortable coming out and participating and doing things. And in some families it was a thing of, okay, if the wife is involved, the husband won't get involved so that there was always . . .

ML: . . . somebody at home.

GMJ: Yeah, somebody at home.

ML: Somebody to take care of the kids and take care of the property and that . . .

GMJ: Right, right. And especially if one was arrested. You know, they didn't want both of them arrested. So we had to work with those kinds of strategies as well, trying to make sure everybody was comfortable with what their commitment was, and made to feel that their commitment was just as important as the other person's out there.

ML: So valuable. That everybody counts.

GMJ: Everybody counts. That's right.

ML: Tell me about the rest of your career, too. You worked with the Department of Welfare in '69?

GMJ: I did, from '69 to '70. And I got a grant to go to South Carolina State College to get my master's in special education, and from there I went to Atlanta and I taught special ed until I retired in '92.

And I've always had that entrepreneurial side that I got from my mother, so I was operating a daycare center, and in '96 I opened a bed and breakfast and wedding facility. So I was teaching in the day care and operating the bed and breakfast, and I closed the daycare in 2005, and I went back into public education, still working with special needs children, and I'm still doing that.

But the thing I'm really enjoying is, I've been a Kiwanis since 1998, and I'm now the lieutenant governor for Region Seventeen, and I am thoroughly enjoying it. So I keep busy, still have the bed and breakfast, and out of school for the summer. . . .

Yes. And I have run for public office, unsuccessfully. I ran for city council in East Point twice, and I ran for state house of representatives twice. I led the primary against a fellow who had been in there twenty-one years, but folk didn't want to see him go out that way, so I lost in the run-off. But people have asked me to try again. I don't know that I want to get that involved. Now, if somebody appoints me to it or there's no opposition, and I don't have to get out there and do all that campaigning, sure, I'll do it. But, you know, campaigning is at a different level now. It's not comfortable or *safe* to just be out there, especially a woman.

ML: Knocking on doors and all. I can see that.

GMJ: Yes. Yes. So I don't know what my next career might be.

ML: Well, you're oriented toward service and serving others and concern for the needy and all, so I'm sure you'll find your niche. Well, let me go back to—did you attend North Carolina A&T or . . . ?

GMJ: Bennett. Bennett College. I'm a graduate of Bennett College. Sixty-three.

ML: And Bennett College, where is . . .

GMJ: Greensboro, North Carolina. Two blocks over from A&T.

ML: Okay. And so what they considered to be some of the original sit-ins . . .

GMJ: That's right. We were up there with Ezell Blair and Jesse Jackson in Greensboro.

Bennett is an all-women's college, and we had a president at that time that we thought was just as firm as a brick emotionally, and when the sit-ins started, we would sneak off campus so we could participate, and I would always get right behind Jesse Jackson and catch his coattail because he was always so big and I was little and timid. But anyway, when the first big arrest was made, there were several "Bennett Belles," quite a few Bennett Belles arrested, and the whole campus was abuzz with, "Oh, what is Dr. Player going to say? She'll probably send them home." All night we worried.

So the next morning she called us into the chapel and let us know that she knew we had been participating, and she was *very proud* of those of us who felt they wanted to, and those who were arrested. She had already sent the college nurse to the jail to be sure that they were treated right, needed no medical attention. She sent blankets, so if they were cold they would have that extra cover.

And she said, "And I've also sent their parents night letters, which means they will get them this morning, telling about the situation and how proud I am of their daughter for giving of her time and now to have been arrested, and to assure the parents that we've attended to any medical needs and their physical comfort."

And oh! That just warmed us, and it endeared her to us like never before. So we were really real proud of her. Because before that, she was a darn good administrator, but in terms of relating to the students, we didn't feel like she was approachable because of her stance.

ML: Her status.

GMJ: No, not so much her *status*, but as the way she carried herself. Very rigid and stern. And she would have been in that mode whether she was president or not, I believe. But after that we would just go up and hug her, you know, just whatever we felt, because it made a big difference.

ML: Well, that was quite a rewarding experience, and it was Dr. Player?

GMJ: Willa B. Player, who was president of the college at that time. She's now deceased, but she was a very good president. . . .

ML: You mentioned the name of your bed and breakfast. Give that to me . . .

GMJ: Rose Lane Manor. And that's in Riverdale, Georgia. It's named in memory of my mother, whose name was Rosa, and she had a wedding business named Rose Lane, so I just used that name and added the "Manor" onto it.

ML: Let me see what other questions. You went to Bennett College.

GMJ: South Carolina State is where I got my master's. Right. And when do you think you're going to print with all of this?

ML: Well, you're among the last people to be interviewed. I think I have maybe a half a dozen or a dozen at the most to be interviewed yet. I have about 140 already.

GMJ: Okay.

ML: And so I'm really closing fast, but Reverend A. C. Redd asked me back in February or so, he said, "Well, how's the project coming?" and I said, "Well, I have 80 or 90 percent of the raw material." And he said, "Well, what about the *cooked* material?" *[He laughs.]* And I had to say, "About 20 or 30 percent of it's done." . . . So it's not immediately around the corner. A project of this size, because I'm really covering the range from 1930 to 1980 . . . people who were in some kind of role of leadership or initiative—not just participants—but people like you, that were active and leaders.

Frederick C. James, Part 1

Pastor to a Movement

Marvin Lare [ML]:* Wednesday, September the twenty-eighth, 2005, and I'm visiting with Bishop Frederick C. James of the AME Church. I guess you would say "retired," but by the size, scale and busyness of this office, it looks like retirement is a purely . . . "any resemblance to retirement is purely coincidental." Is that the word for it?

Frederick James [FJ]: I expect that's a pretty apt description [chuckles].

ML: Bishop James has provided me a wealth of materials on his pastoral ministry and his involvement in community service and action. Bishop, this "Social Action Statements of the A.M.E. Church, 1960–64," is this a resolution taken to General Conference?

FJ: Yes.

ML: And adopted then as being the social action positions of the AME Church, is that a fair description, representation?

FJ: That is correct. We were pushing for the passage of the Civil Rights Bill at that time, to get it passed without the inclusion of crippling amendments. That was the threat from the people who were trying to impede it. It was at the AME Church General Conference that I was able to get this passed, so it would have the force of our entire denomination behind it.

Those photos indicate a lot of local work as well, and some meetings that I had with Martin Luther King and others in various parts of the country. I think there's a picture here of the beginning of the National Conference on Religion and Race in Chicago, in January of '63. I was part of that. Some action on the streets—I've even have a picture here where I was arrested. I was in the police car, taken to jail from the Holiday Inn sit-in. That was a very active year.

*This interview was held in Bishop James's office in Columbia, South Carolina.

ML: We'll try to include some of these in the book. Modern printing makes that easier than it used to be. If you need to keep this as the original . . .

FJ: I can really give you this package, I think. I put that together for you.

ML: Good. That's great. My approach to these oral history interviews is very open ended. . . . The emphasis is to let people set their own framework, start where they want to, and set their own parameters. That reveals so much of your own personality, and the narrative that's been going on in your head, for a few decades, I dare say.

FJ: Thank you *[chuckles]*. I like that, too. Who wouldn't like that? With that opening to me, let me say that, first of all, I appreciate very much, from what I understand to be the work that you're doing. The South Carolina Civil/Human Rights Anthology Project is just a precious, precious, precious undertaking, and I look with eagerness to see how that goes. I also appreciate your making contact with me and with us, to give us an opportunity to share a little bit in recalling some of the incidents that were so very important to us at that time, and still are very important in terms of civil and human rights, and real democracy here, as well as everywhere else it ought to be in our country, in our great country.

Roots In Freedom

FJ: I think since I was a teenager, I had a strong sense of what was right and what was wrong in human relations. I would think that it was a gift from my mother that I got the desire to cultivate human relations. That's been my concern. My father was a mechanic who died when I was ten years old, but I learned that he was very passionate about *human rights*. I found a book that he had bought written by Marcus Garvey, and he underscored some parts in it. He was a quiet man. My father was a quiet man. He was a master mechanic. He could take anything apart that was mechanical and put it back together, and was recognized as such in Florida and in South Carolina, where we . . . and in France—he was a World War I veteran. I found that he took interest in the back-to-Africa movement, some parts of it, from notes that he had scribbled in a book, although I saw also that he wrote, *"Not leaving America."* I'm not leaving America, but some of the points that Marcus Garvey and others raised and lifted up as to the discriminatory practices of our country resonated with my father, seventh-grade education. I was twenty-some years old when I first saw that. But my mother was the person who wanted to find the best in everybody and wanted to believe that there was something good in everyone, and I'm a cross between those two.

So that influenced my life, and that's why I have had the opportunity to meet and know a number of people of a number of different ethnic backgrounds, long before I went to Africa as a bishop. And I came to know the differences in people that did not run along color lines, did not run along pigmentation that was skin lines. That there were good people of all color hues and backgrounds, and that included black as well as white. And bad included all colors and backgrounds. So that gave me a restlessness to see what could be accomplished to better situations wherever I happened to be, and that was true when I was a student at Allen University, when I was a student at Bettis

Junior College, prior to being at Allen University. That was true of my experiences as a teenager, waiting tables in Columbia, or waiting tables in Washington, D.C. I always found it a challenge to find the good in a person that had nothing to do with color, even at a time when it was not really the practice to fellowship across color lines.

That led me to become active in NAACP, that led me to be active as a teenager in the attempt to register and vote, the poll tax requirement scenario—I was active in that. The requirement to learn to read a part of the Constitution—I helped try to teach people to do that. All of that, while I did not consider myself doing anything extraordinary, I was not a part of a movement as such, to me. That was the kind of thing that I needed to be doing, and I was not alone. There were others who were juniors at Allen and seniors at Allen University, and they were doing the same thing. Allen University was the forum for that kind of activity during the '40s, and even the '30s. It was the only forum that we really had in South Carolina where people could come together, could come together at the administration building and demand equal teacher's salary for equal education. To come together and challenge and demand the right to vote, begin to come together to point out the disparities and the injustices in the systems that were run by white South Carolinians.

You couldn't do that at any other place, unless it was in a church, and many churches didn't feel that, at that time, they wanted to go on record as being a fighting platform for a number of things, because jobs were involved, and then a whole lot of people in churches did not feel that the church should be so used. There were some of us who did, who believed that there was a Christian way in race relations, there was a Christian way in *all* relations.

And then I graduated from Allen, and then I went to Howard University School of Religion, at the time it was called. There again was a place of freedom: to speak, to think, to interact, to aspire, to lament wrong openly, to point fingers. Howard University has been through the years a place where African American growth and development, along with many other ethnic groups, was always welcome and always fostered and always enhanced, and the platforms there gave you an opportunity to measure, to see to what extent you have parity in terms of human rights with other people. And at our school, during the time I was there, there was instituted an official department of social ethics. One Dr. Frank Dorey was made head of that department, and I found that it was just natural for me to gravitate there whenever I had any opportunity for electives, to take them and to find a way to try to fit that into my schedule, some social ethics. So I was reading *The Rise of Capitalism,* and I was reading Richard Niebuhr right along with Reinhold Niebuhr. I think that Howard helped kind of push me in the direction of social action.

Even in New York City

FJ: When I graduated, I went immediately to Union Theological Seminary in New York, but I couldn't stay because I didn't have the money. I was victimized by a discriminatory experience with the *New York Times* in New York City. They advertised for a job from five to eleven in the evening, five in the afternoon till eleven in the evening, and I said, "Well, I could swing that." So I went down to the *New York Times,* and they eliminated the applicants for this job. It was a job working at night taking ads for advertisements in the *New York Times,* and they eliminated us down to three students, to only three applicants. One boy was from Haverford College, Haverford, Pennsylvania, other boy was from Yale, and Fred James. We took the tests of sentence structure, of spelling, of what they considered important in taking advertisements on the telephone and passing them on in the *New York Times.* They said to us at the end of the exam that they would let us know in two days, or three. And two or three days passed and no notification, five days passed, no notification, six days passed, no notification.

On the seventh day I got a call, and this person said, "Is this Mr. James?"

"Yes, this is Mr. James."

"Fred James?"

"Yes."

She said, "There is something I've got to tell you. You made the highest score in the examination for the job. The next to you was the young man from Yale, who got the job. The head of that department that was handling that job was about to hire you until he saw the photos. I don't know whether this was because he's from North Carolina, or what the reason is, but I want to sleep, and I just want you to know that you did have the highest mark."

So I said to myself, "Good Lord! In New York City, too!"

I got an invitation to come back to work at Allen University, so I came back, and to pastor, start off at a little church. So I went up to Winnsboro, they sent me up to Winnsboro, to fifty members, and a job teaching at Allen University. Both of which did not give me two hundred dollars a month. In 1947. I worked at Allen for six years. I pastored that church for three years, and then they sent me to finish building a church—somebody had laid a foundation here in Columbia, Chappelle Memorial, on the corner of Pine and Senate, or Pine and . . .

ML: College maybe? Pendleton maybe? I'm not sure how those streets come together there.

FJ: Anyway, Chappelle Memorial. I was there for three years.

The Sumter Years

FJ: Then I was sent to Sumter in 1953. In 1953 in Sumter I landed in a time and town of activism on the part of African Americans, with individuals who really were committed to moving forward. In 1953. And these were people like J. T. McCain, Luther McCain, who was there, Reverend J. Herbert Nelson, who was there, Reverend H. P. Sharper. There were some laymen who were very active, and I hate to start calling names because when you start doing that you start leaving out names.

Anyway, the NAACP was very active, and we were determined to try to advance the cause. At that time the executive committee of the NAACP was at the forefront of most of the civil rights activity in the city of Sumter, and the county of Sumter in that area, in 1953. In 1954 when the Supreme Court decision came down in May, we were more than elated with this program, so we began immediately doing what we could to implement it. We did have a stirring going on in churches all over the county, one of which got us into some difficulty.

One of the men who was taking names—we were gathering names of people who were willing to petition school systems that we may be able to use these school systems in accord with the ruling of the Supreme Court. A young man who was manning one of the tables at a major church there in Sumter was interviewed by some leaders of the White Citizens' Council, and they said—they put it in the *Sumter Daily Item,* the newspaper—that this young man, Mr. Bradley, had said that he was being forced to get the names that he was getting. They said that the members of the executive committee of the NAACP was forcing him to do these things, when the fact was we weren't forcing anybody to do anything. He was doing what he wanted to do.

We decided that we would answer that article, and we said that that is not true, we said that we know that we did not force anyone to get any petitions, to do anything, and they know, and he knows, that we did not. So we said, therefore, it appears to us that either the person who wrote this—and this is the great Mr. Shepherd K. Nash, who was a major wheel in politics in Sumter County and otherwise as well, industrial life. We said he's either fashioning his remarks to fit the Citizens' Council or for some unknown other reason, we do not know. So he sued us on that, and we got a young lawyer by the name of Matthew J. Perry. The outcome of that lawsuit was not pleasing to some of us because they finally compromised it, but some of us were not willing to compromise it. But we were very actively engaged. That was kind of a sore spot that remained from that time. That was in 1955, I believe.

One of the upshots of this was, I think it was in 1950 . . . *[uncertain]*—it might have been the year before—that I ran for city council. They got me to run for city council in Sumter. I was not elected, but I carried my ward, which was mostly white *[laughs]*. My ward was more white than black. We were very active.

I later became involved in everything that we were trying to do to push our people forward, not only civil rights protests but other kinds of community action. We later purchased an area which is—much later—called Runnymede, and we were all a part of that.

The Reconciliation Committee

FJ: But that is really ahead of—I should not mention that before I mention the year of 1963. What we did was, in 1962, we met and formed what we called a Reconciliation Commission, and we elected attorney E. A. Finney Jr. chairman of the Reconciliation Committee. Most of the African American leaders in Sumter and Sumter County were a part and parcel of this. The purpose of this was to request all of the outcomes that we fought for later in the Sumter Movement, to try to integrate the schools, to try to get jobs, to try to have opportunity to eat at public accommodations, wherever, to get better lighting in black areas, to get better representation, to get *some* representation on county boards, school boards, on other boards that affected the lives of the people. We slated every organization of any power to arrange to come before those among us who felt that arbitration and negotiation was the way to go, we decided really to give it a shot, to give it a chance. And although some of the people were skeptical from the beginning, we did set a six-month limit that we'll see if we can get anything done in six months. If it's not done after six months, we come back together again.

I've never seen courtesy like the courtesy that was afforded us by the Kiwanis Club, by the Lions Club, by the county delegation, by the city delegation, by every constituted body of leaders in Sumter. [They] gave us an opportunity to come, with the understanding there'd be no discussion, except what we present. [They said,] "So you may make your presentation, we will give you an hour and a half, but there will not be any discussion, and we will take this under consideration and get back with you after you [present] whatever it is that you want to say to us." . . . And that's what we did.

Attorney Finney was always the key man, and they would hear us, they would come in great crowds of people, many more than the constituent members of the groups, and within a month and a half we had met with everybody that we could meet with. A month passed and nothing happened. Two months passed, three months passed, nothing happened. Didn't even get back to us. Five months passed. As six months passed we had another meeting, we came back.

The Sumter Movement

FJ: We said that we see that it was nonproductive. What should the name of our group be? And they came up with the "Sumter Movement," simply because we're not getting any. And who shall we elect as chair? For some reason I forgot to duck! *[He laughs.]* They elected me the chair and we formed—we started out by first carefully trying to determine exactly what we were going after, and exactly what committees for leadership, for subordinate leadership we'd need. The third thing was a commitment that we would meet weekly. We would ask our churches, our businesses if they would permit us, if they would help us to spare the time from whatever we're doing—pastoring or whatever—to go to various parts of the county to meet, and at one time we were going every night.

Once we did that, we then organized a demonstration committee, a bail bond committee, to get our people out of jail when they exercised their right to protest. An education committee, a finance committee—we named all these committees and chaired these persons, gave them the opportunity of volunteers, but we were careful in determining who should be the leaders of those committees. At one time, I remember, we had a third of a million dollars in bail bond money, three hundred-something thousand dollars bail bond resources. We had our publicity committee, then we had our "enforcement committee."

We had a group of persons who had prizefighting expertise, who were persons who would "enforce" the observance of our picket lines. We'd tell a person three times,

"Don't come across the picket line." If, after the third time . . . we had somebody who would flatten you with one punch, and that did happen one Saturday.

To indicate how serious we were with this, a person from out of the rurals said, "Nobody tells me where I'm to shop. I'm going to S. H. Kress, I've been going to S.H. Kress for all these years, and you're not going to tell me."

So we'd tell you a second time, now after the third time, you're in danger of being hurt, so remember that.

"Aw, I'll take care of myself."

But they picked him off the street because he was out like a light, just flattened him. And, of course, they arrested him [the "enforcer"], but we had him out of jail in less than an hour. Our bail bond committee was most effective.

The upshot of that was, we closed S. H. Kress down in seven weeks. Seven weeks we just absolutely cut off. The people who were in charge of S. H. Kress, it seems to me it was [a city in] Pennsylvania, but I'm not too sure, it was some northern city, we closed that.

We began to get sympathetic understanding from some people in the Sumter community, about what we were petitioning for. We had files on persons who had abilities and capabilities to do certain work, typists, stenographers, persons who were available, and during the summer we had students from all the colleges all over the country, in the Sumter area. We had these names. These people are ready to go, not only to go to work, but to do you a first-class job. "Do you not need some better personnel in some places?" And sure enough, we placed a few of our young people, and the word got around that you've got some brilliant young black people here, and they do need to be given a chance to work.

With some leadership that was taken, the man who—Mr. Etheridge, Eldridge, Etheridge? . . . He called the merchants together and said, "We don't need to have what we find in Alabama today" and some other parts of the country. He said, "It would be so much easier and simpler, and beneficial for everybody involved if we did some things in which we had some of the leadership in doing it." And that is really, eventually what led here to what happened, especially after the Civil Rights Bill passed, which provided integration of public accommodation in 1964.

Networking

FJ: We were successful in 1963 in that particular regard. We networked with movements that were going on in Orangeburg, movements that were going on in Charleston. There was not a lot of movement going on in Columbia, but there was movement going on in Charleston, there was movement going on in Orangeburg, and some modified movement that was going on in Florence. We supported each other's efforts, we provided speakers, and as a result, we had a measure, a measure of success. But when the Civil Rights Bill passed in 1964, that provided white South Carolina a legitimate reason to change, and the more thoughtful persons, and the more thoughtful leaders, many of them, took advantage of the fact that it was then the law of the land to move forward.

I know I've rambled a lot . . .

ML: No, no, you're filling in a good bit of detail. I've talked with Judge Finney some time back, and also, of course, J. Herbert Nelson is deceased, but I had a lovely visit with Johnalee. . . .

FJ: Oh, you've met with Johnalee! She's a doll. Had he passed when you came to South Carolina?

ML: No, but if I met him, it was only in passing.

FJ: We were extremely close, we were *close*.

ML: I think he moved on to Orangeburg, maybe in the late '60s.

FJ: Yes, he did. I think it was in the latter part of the '60s. Must have been after '67 or '68. And then, of course, there in Orangeburg there was Matt McCollom. Matt McCollom was awesome. He was just a giant. Nobody was more articulate than Matt McCollom and nobody was any more focused than he was. There was the Reverend E. McKay Miller. Reverend E. McKay Miller was a Presbyterian minister in Sumter, who was also very, very, very good. He and I, and Dr. B. T. Williams [DDS], we sued the Sumter library and won, three of us, and that's listed, I think. Here we are: "Dr. B. T. Williams and E. McKay Miller turned away from the Carnegie Public Library in Sumter."

But we won this case. We sued this library. He was one of those persons that was . . . The Reverend H. P. Sharper, who left Sumter. He was pastor of First Baptist Church early on, and he went to Newark from there, and was very active, but he was president of NAACP on the state level for a while. The Reverend Dr. I DeQuincey Newman was part of our crowd. Of course, he was pastoring in the area. And then, of course, there in Orangeburg there was the Reverend Chappell M. Davis, who was very active in the program there in Orangeburg, pastor of Williams Chapel. In Charleston the leadership was the Reverend B. J. Glover, who still lives. He's living here in Columbia.

[See the interview with Benjamin J. Glover to be found in volume 3.]

ML: I've tried to locate him and I haven't been able to, but maybe you can help me. I understood he was on Piney Grove Road, in that area, but I haven't been—and maybe I just haven't pursued it adequately.

FJ *[calling to someone in another room]*: Miss Miller? *[He pauses, then speaks to Miss Miller.]* Dr. Lare wants, needs to make contact—he's been trying to contact Reverend B. J. Glover. He hasn't been able to reach him. Could you get his telephone number perhaps and give that to him to carry with him?

[He continues with Marvin Lare.]

FJ: The Reverend William Randolph was a student who is now pastoring in Sumter. He was a student at that time. And also Reverend Ralph Canty. Ralph served in the legislature for a while. Among the lay leaders in that time, of course, was Miss Modjeska Simkins of Columbia, Mr. Billy Fleming of Manning—this is in the '50s and the '60s—Mr. . . . Mr. I. S. Leevy, I. S. Leevy [Johnson]'s grandfather, in Columbia. Of course, I mentioned Mr. J. T. McCain, and you know attorney Matthew Perry. McCain of Sumter, Perry of Columbia. As I mentioned, Finney Jr. Mr. Joe [J. Arthur] Brown of Charleston was a stalwart.

[See the sidebar excerpt of J. Arthur Brown's presentation at the 1982 "South Carolina Voices of the Civil Right Movement" and the interviews with MaeDe Brown and Millicent Brown above in this volume and with I. S. Leevy Johnson in volume 4.]

White Supporters

FJ: A white person by the name of Mr. Lewis Bryan. And other white friends of the civil rights movement in the Sumter area in the '50s and '60s were these people, and not only in the Sumter area, in some other areas too, Mr. James McBride Dabbs, of Dabbs Crossroads, near Sumter—a splendid, splendid supporter, *not* a flaming liberal, but a literary giant, a thinker, a person whose heart was pure. Dr. R. Wright Spears, he and I served on the board of [the Department of] Social Services together. At the time we had a representative from each of the six congressional districts, and I was nominated and served for my district, the first African American, and he served while he was president of Columbia College, and we got some things passed.

[An interview with R. Wright Spears will be found in volume 2.]

The Lourie family, all of these, although Saul Lourie was devoted to that store alone, but at the beginning of the '50s, or it might have been 1949, when they came from St. George to Columbia, and Allen University brought Marian Anderson to Columbia, the president put me in charge of the ushers, and I decided that we needed fifty—two women and forty-eight men, but that the women would wear evening gowns down to the floor and that the men would wear tuxedos. When I went to Hope Davis, who had tuxedos for rent, and I showed up, they did not have tuxedos for *us* to rent for those Allen University boys, but—discouraged—as my last resort, I went to this new store in the middle of the block, on the same side that the Carolina Theater was on, in the middle of that block, between—I believe that that was between Washington and Hampton, on Main. I said I'm just going to walk in and see if they had tuxedos. I told him who I was and told him I was from Allen University, told him that I'm a teacher at Allen University.

"I'm in charge of ushers at the Township Auditorium for the Marian Anderson event, and we need tuxedos. Do you have any for rent?"

He looked at me from head to foot and said, "Yes, I've got some tuxedos. How many do you need?"

I said, "I need forty-eight. Do you have forty-eight?"

He said, "Yes, I've got forty-eight. I've got to take them out of the boxes. They've never been worn."

And I stood there and looked at him, and just tears came to my eyes, really. And I brought those boys down and we measured those boys up, and from that day we didn't have any assembly at Allen and at Benedict that we didn't advertise Lourie's.

But the Louries, and then of course later, Isadore, who was very young at the time, he went into politics, political life, but the Louries were always *something special.*

Senator John Land, he would come to NAACP meetings. I think he was just back from Harvard—I think he went to Harvard—just out of school, but he would come to those meetings and he dared show up at those meetings. That was really a very, very, *very, very, very,* very brave thing to do in those times.

The Reverend Dr. A. McKay Brabham of the United Methodist Church. A. McKay Brabham's heart was just as pure as gold. He was a white who supported Judge Waites Waring.

> For all the saints,
> who from their labor rest,
> who Thee by faith
> before the world confessed . . .
>   "For All the Saints," hymn, William W. How, 1823–1897

And then in Sumter there was Mrs. Rebecca Reed, a little old lady who—Weber Bryan's mother, Bryan after whom the mental health center is named here in Columbia. She was a bee in the bonnet of people who were trying to keep people out of their just desserts just because of their color. And Mrs. Anne Herbert, who was a member of Trinity United Methodist Church there. She was just back from China, where she had served as a missionary, and they would come to meetings. Then there was Mr. Earl Kirby, who was just an ordinary merchantman who said he'd take his chances and do right by all people. And then, of course, there was Dr. Roger Roff, who was a brand new, or very young chiropractor, who now I think is president of the chiropractors. These were some white . . .

ML: Dr. Roger—what was the last name?

FJ: R-O-F-F. chiropractor, of Dillon, South Carolina. Kirbys of Sumter and Herberts of Sumter, Rebecca Reed is of Sumter, Waring was of Charleston, Brabham was of Columbia, Land is of Manning, Louries of Columbia. R. Wright Spears was of Columbia. James McBride Dabbs—we said that. Lewis Bryan was, I think he was the son of Mrs. Rebecca Reed. These were people who sympathized with what we were seeking to do, to the extent that they would come out and meet with us. There were others who worked with us in various ways but they did not identify with change to the extent that we were doing it, so I'm going to . . . *[calling to the next room]* Miss Miller? Do I have another copy of that? I just want to give him a copy of that.

ML: There are so many folks that are just unsung heroes . . .

FJ: Yes, that's right. That's right. I feel really almost obligated, I'd be glad if you let it be known that I recommended that these people be given note.

I'll just put this in your package as well.

ML: That's great. Thank you.

FJ: Okay. All right. Now—you spoke of narrative. You can't get much more narrative than . . .

ML: This is fine. Are there other things before I follow up with a few questions?

Dr. Martin Luther King Jr.

FJ: Sure, by all means. I think maybe you need to also know this, before I get to your questions. In my relationship with Martin Luther King. I was listing some few things here—I personally remember Martin Luther King Jr.

In Columbia, where we planned to organize SCLC in New Orleans in 1957, at First Calvary Church. He wanted me to be a part of his leadership team. I think I would have had Abernathy's place, but I was unwilling to leave an AME pulpit.

In Frogmore, at Penn Center, where we strategized to impact the political leadership of America in 1962. In Chicago, where we organized the National Conference on Religion and Race. In Sumter, where he and Reverend Ralph Abernathy honored me with the opportunity to associate full-time in their leadership. In Cincinnati, where I presented him to deliver his world-famous speech, "Remaining Awake Through a Great Revolution," at the Cincinnati Gardens in 1964—there were ten thousand people at that, that was the night before the AME General Conference. I've got the tape in there, the first three and a half minutes, that's me. I presented him that day.

And as we walked and talked for miles between Selma and Montgomery on the march in 1965. I wasn't there the morning they got beat up at the Pettis Bridge. I was preaching that morning in Sumter, but I joined them that afternoon and caught up with them, and we marched on into Montgomery.

And on August the 6th in 1965, at the signing of the Voting Rights Act by President Lyndon Baines Johnson, in Washington, D.C., where I also received one of the pens with which that act was signed, a testimony of the accomplishments of Martin Luther King. The first one went to Martin Luther King. The second one went to Roy Wilkins of the NAACP. The third one went to Urban League—Whitney Young. The fourth one went to Walter Reuther, the labor union, and right on down the line. But the *thirteenth* one came to me, that signed the Voting Rights Bill.

These were some of the things . . .

That should be, "Remaining Awake Through a Great Revolution." I said, "*Sleeping Through a Great Revolution*"—you got to be real careful *[laughs]*.

I was not exactly outside of the civil rights movement, I must say *[chuckles]*. I was a part of it, but I always believed in trying to do a little something to make a difference, rather than just to curse everybody out. Somebody said it's better to light a candle than to curse the darkness. Is that right?

[Part 2 of this interview will be found in volume 5.]

Irene Williams, Part 1

If You Don't Have Hope

The World Is Going To Change

[As the tape begins, Mrs. Williams is speaking.]

Irene Williams **[IW]**:* . . . That is when the media and when the—well, actually, the NAACP and the black churches and whatever started talking about here it was one hundred years after the Emancipation, and we were still not able to do things like everybody else was.

Now I can go back to when I was a senior in college, in 1954. I was in a philosophy of education class at Hampton Institute. It's called Hampton University now. But the professor came in on this Monday afternoon and said, "You know, the Supreme Court has ruled that 'separate but equal' is unconstitutional. The world is going to change. Your world is changing." I have always remembered that. And of course, I graduated that May, and *[clock chimes in the background]* I wanted to . . . my ambition was to come back to Sumter County and teach in rural Sumter County. That was my ambition. My major was home economics.

So in Sumter County they were building what they called "consolidated schools." They were trying to make the schools *"equal,"* so that they could stay separate and "equal," and they brought a lot of one- and two-room schools together in a large school called Manchester School, which was built in Pinewood. It had grades one through twelve, and it was under construction. So they stopped the construction because there was this talk about this litigation and what was going to happen. And so they said they'd decided that they would *not* have a public school system in Sumter County if they had to integrate, and so when the Supreme Court had that version about "with

*The interview was conducted at the Williams home in Sumter, South Carolina, on August 6, 2006, and was transcribed by Lynn Moore.

all deliberate speed," they interpreted that as "when you want to, when you get ready to." . . .

Then they continued to build this new school in Pinewood, which is in Sumter County, about ten miles from where we are, and it was going to have a brand new home economics department, it was going to have a gym, it was going to have a business department, it was going to have just everything that schools should have. And so they continued building it, and it was to open the fall of '54, and I graduated the spring of '54.

So I came back home—well, I tried before I left Hampton—but I came home and I really pursued that application, because I wanted to teach in the school. And I got the job. I can remember that I walked—I lived on Oakland Avenue in the school district, on Main Street a few blocks from where I lived, so I remember walking up there to check on my application, and I can remember having on my hat and gloves and my seersucker suit, because I was going to ask to see if I could see the superintendent, and see what they'd decided. So I went in and they said, "Yes, you may go in to see him." And as soon as I walked in, he said—I was Sampson [then]—he said, "Miss Sampson, you can consider yourself employed. You will be the home economics teacher." Oh! I was so happy! I always remember that moment, because it seemed like my feet didn't touch the ground going back home, because I had this job. So that was in '54. Now we're talking about . . . I am rambling today.

Marvin Lare **[ML]**: Not at all, this is lovely. Just the kind of detail and the feel is what we want people to know.

IW: Okay. When the school opened, they closed all of these one- and two-room schools that were serving the colored—they called them "colored people, colored population." And they had *buses*. The students came to school on buses. And the school was located in a little town, so there were a few people who walked, but most of the students came on school buses.

Everything was just wonderful, and then I noticed that on sunny days, or days like today, the cotton would be in full bloom, and the buses would come to school practically empty, nothing but the bus driver and one or two students. It was because the students had to stay home and pick cotton. Most of them lived on sharecropping, and anyway, that was the way people made money, and that was the time to make the money, to pick the cotton.

So I taught home economics, which meant that a part of my program was to visit the homes. It was called

The Tricks of the Trade in the Land of Cotton

In Saluda County* we sharecropped. The land owners provided the land, half the fertilizer, seed, the house you lived in, the mules, and the machines, although in the 1950s there weren't many machines to speak of. The land owners would lend the tenant money for food after the crop was "laid by" [that is, it wasn't plowed anymore].

continued

*Provided by Teenie Ruth Lott of Saluda, South Carolina, whose interview is included above in this volume.

(Continued)

There was not work to do to get paid for about three months. The land owners would lend the tenant between ten and fifteen dollars a month. The tenant would pay for one half of fertilizer, provide all the labor and were supposed to receive one half of the profit from the corn and cotton produced. However, when all of the corn and cotton was sold, with one half of the fertilizer they had to pay for and the money they had borrowed during the slow months, the land owners would tell their tenants they were still indebted to them, and they had to stay to farm the land another year to pay what was owed. If the crop failed, both the land owners and tenant lost. There were people who stayed on as tenant ten or fifteen years because the landowners would say they still owed them money. It was in the '60s that we discovered a trick had been played on us all these years. Not being able to count and read, we weren't able to keep account of what we really owed. Instead of giving the sharecroppers their just due, landowners planted pine and peach trees, their land was fenced in, and cows were put on the land.

the "home project, the home experiences." So I would visit the homes in the afternoon, and they wouldn't be in a home, they'd be in the field, so I would go to the field and see the students. When it rained, the students would come to school, because they couldn't pick cotton and so they'd get to come to school. When they came to school, I would work with them on home projects, like we did things like home improvement. They would select a room that they were going to make better, and at that time, a lot of the students lived in houses that you could see sand through. When you walked in, through the floor you could see the sand, and if you looked through the ceiling you could see the sky. They papered the rooms with the newspaper, and a lot of—I would call them "my girls" because I taught only girls at that time—a lot of my girls would use, some of them would select the comic section and paper theirs. A lot of them would pick different colors or whatever, but they were creative. *[The telephone rings.]* I'll just be a moment. Excuse me. . . .

ML: If you need to interrupt at all I can just put that on pause.

IW: No, okay. No, I didn't want to talk—that's my daughter and she said my granddaughter called this morning here and left a message to call her, but they just went to California Thursday to visit another daughter, it was Lourie [the granddaughter], who is six, and her brother, Mohammad, is five. This is their first visit to California *[laughs].*

Okay. What was I? I don't know what I was . . .

ML: You were saying about the girls choosing the comics for wallpaper.

IW: Oh, yes. They would do things like they'd be creative in decorating their room and whatever, the kitchen, and so that would be something they could do at home if they couldn't come to school. And I would have, we had cooking, we had foods—we don't call it cooking, we call it "foods," but cooking is all right. Home economics was more than cooking and sewing. There were really nine areas—home improvement, whatever—but anyway, when they came we'd have things like making biscuits, so they could make them at home, and their homework would be to bring a biscuit. And oh! They just loved the sewing, because we had electric sewing machines. We had seven brand-new electric sewing machines.

Then in the afternoon I had, or at night I had, adult classes. So they were just really enthusiastic and I was *very* enthusiastic, because that was my ambition, to teach in rural Sumter County.

The reason for that is, I lived in the city of Sumter, and I went to Lincoln High School, which was right around the corner from me, and when I grew up—I grew up there and I went there from first through twelfth. My sisters and brothers went there also. They didn't have high schools in the county. Most of the schools stopped at eighth grade, or maybe tenth grade, so a lot of the people who wanted their children to finish high school would send them to live with a family in Sumter, and so my mother and father always had someone who came to live with us during the school year to finish high school. And of course, on the weekends sometimes I'd go with them home, because they lived on farms and whatever.

So I thought that that wasn't fair. I was really proud of Lincoln, and I'm not one of these people who feel that I had an education that was not up to par. I feel I got the best education possible. I wouldn't exchange it for anything. So I wanted these people who came from, who had to come and live in town just to go to school, or high school, it seemed to me to be a problem. So I wanted to teach in the rural area, because I thought that that would be where I could make my contribution, and that's why I was so elated to work in that school. Now I'm about to lose my point again.

I was telling you how I was enjoying teaching the students. Then in 1956, one of the main reasons that I chose to major in home economics was that I had a boyfriend whose ambition was to be an agriculture teacher. When we were in high school, we would talk about the need for people just learning everyday kinds of things, and there was an ag class at Lincoln that would meet out under the tree. They had a shop, a building, where they built furniture and chests and things like that, but the ag class would meet under the tree. So he said he was going to, he wanted to take agriculture and teach in Sumter County, so I said, "Ah ha! I'll take home economics and teach in Sumter County." *[She laughs.]*

He was ahead of me in school so he finished ahead of me and went to South Carolina State College, and that's where I went my first year in college. I went there to major in home ec, but most of my family members had gone to Hampton, and then this boyfriend of mine was really into schoolwork. He was not into talking to girls, or courting or whatever, which was hard to do at State at that time, because they rang a bell right after the evening meal, and when they rang that bell all the girls, the freshmen, had to go into the dormitory. You couldn't stand around on campus and talk. And then you could sign out and go to the library, and sign in the library, sign out of the library. It really was so strict! It seemed like they were just too strict, and then on the other hand, my boyfriend was really into studying and whatever, so I said, "Oh, I don't need to stay here. I need to go where I can meet some other people."

So I went to Hampton Institute my sophomore year, and I stayed there and I graduated there. But this fine young man and I continued to write, and see each other on vacations, and he graduated from State in agriculture, and he got a job teaching down in Lakeview, South Carolina, at a school called Columbus High School. Then he got drafted because of the Korean conflict, so he went into the army for two years, and then in 1956 he came by, and he was out of the army, and he said, "You know, I have a new job. I'm going to show you where I have a new job." He'd gotten a job as ag teacher at Manchester!

So I said, "Now, you know this is really wonderful. My dreams are coming true."

So in 1956 he was the ag teacher and I was the home ec teacher. So we kind of worked together with things. We had programs, we had mother-daughter, father-son banquets, we had spring balls, we went to the state fair, we did a lot of things with the students.

That continued to about '63, when all of this emphasis was put on a hundred years since Emancipation. We've got to do something about it. Also, Kennedy—John F. Kennedy—and *Jackie* Kennedy, we don't forget *[laughs]*. They were, they just seemed to be just the kind of leaders that would be needed at that time.

"You've Gotta Have Hope"

IW: White people didn't understand that people in the country, in the rural part, didn't have hope, because if you don't have hope you don't have anything. We'd always tell the students, "Now you've got to excel, you've got to get your education, you've got to do this homework, you've got to be well-dressed and well-mannered, because you will have to get other jobs. You won't be picking cotton because the cotton picker is going to take over."

"Oh, no," they said, "no machine will never take over picking cotton. It wouldn't be good enough." *[She laughs.]*

So it was during that time—we were there during the time when the cotton picker was being developed, and when we first started teaching there, rural electrification was just beginning, so there were many, many homes that had oil lamps. And then the electric co-ops would come and meet, and if you've got—the people would sign the rights to put the lines, and a lot of people got electricity. And then the tractors, people started being able to get tractors. So they were beginning, they started seeing there is something. We won't be pulling this cotton. Because cotton—first you had to plant it, then you had, you hoe it, then—No! First you had to clean the field off, clean the ditch back off. That would be to keep the *[inaudible]*. Then you had to plant the cotton, then you had to hoe the cotton, then you had to thin the cotton or something, and then you hoped and prayed the boll weevil wouldn't get it so you could pick cotton. And then you would have a little money.

So life was tied up around that, and they felt so beholding to the people who could provide these jobs for them, who were the owners of these big farms. Most people were sharecropping with a big white farmer, and they had to get this done so they could get their share of the crop. There were a few people who owned their land, and of course, they were the outspoken people. They were able to speak out, and a lot of people just couldn't speak out because they just felt beholding. They just felt that they were almost enslaved. They didn't think, they didn't see a way out. But we kept telling them, "There is a way out, and we'll get out."

I was just telling you about the '63s, and then it happened that a white girl who went to the all-white school in Pinewood won a contest by making a woolen suit. The contest was sponsored by the American Wool Council, and she won this contest and the prize was a trip to Hawaii! So the girls in my class knew this girl, Peggy . . . they all knew each other because they all worked together, but they went to separate schools, they had different opportunities. So they came to school —this is '63, fall—and said— by that time I had married this friend, you'll meet him in a little while, in '56—they said, "Mrs. Williams, Peggy won a contest by making a suit. Let's enter that contest. I want to go to Hawaii."

So I said, "Oh, sure. You can do that."

Wool cloth was rather expensive at that time and the suit had to be made out of all wool, and so I think there were seven or nine girls, I've forgotten right now the number, whose parents paid the money to buy the all-wool cloth. And we sent away to enter the contest, they sent us the application blanks. We filled in the application blanks. You had to send samples of your cloth that you were making and your pattern and all that. We went through the whole process.

They had the suits made, and the South Carolina elimination contest was going to be held at the Wade Hampton Hotel in Columbia. One day I just got a notice that I had to come see the superintendent, and I went to his office. He told me that he heard I was taking some people over to the Wade Hampton Hotel.

"No, you won't be taking them."

I said, "Well, yes, I will. They made these suits. We've been accepted in the contest."

He said, "I *forbid* you to take them!"

And I said, "Why is that?"

And he said, "Because it's against the law, because the Wade Hampton Hotel is for white people only, and you can't take colored people over there."

So I said, "Well, maybe I can't take them, but you can't stop their parents from taking them."

And sure enough, when I went back and told the parents, they agreed to it. They went up to the superintendent and asked to please let the . . . because they'd bought this cloth, and he told them he was so sorry but he just couldn't do it and if I went ahead and did it I would lose my job.

So they came back and said, "Please don't take them, Mrs. Williams. It's okay. We're sorry, and we'll just have a fashion show and whatever here. Don't take them."

And it happened that right in the time that this contest was going on was when Kennedy was assassinated in November. Yes, in November of '63.

The Sumter Movement

IW: My husband and I had been active with what was called "Sumter Movement." Anyway, it started at the beginning of '63, in January, whatever day that Emancipation

Proclamation—I think it was New Year's Day in 1863 that the Emancipation was proclaimed. So now this is 1963, in January we started. . . . I told you there was a lot of focus on a hundred years is long enough, and they started in Sumter what was called the Sumter Movement, which was a group of people who met on Sundays at churches, at different churches, and made plans as to how we would peacefully demonstrate that we needed the Civil Rights Bill passed. And of course, you know Martin Luther King was the person that we were following, because it was nonviolent. So everything had to be nonviolent, peaceable walking. So they found out that —let's see, they called it "selective buying" because the other thing—I can't think of the word. . . .

ML: Boycott?

IW: Yes, boycott, would have been considered against the law. So we started this selective buying campaign. You said you talked to Judge Finney and all of them? Finney then was just a young lawyer teaching at Morris College and all of this, and the Reverend Randolph, and—they were just so sweet. They would check everything with Finney, make sure we were doing constitutional . . . we wouldn't be against the law. So we called these things "selective buying," and that would be okay. We had placards, you'd go in front of the stores just like a boycott would, and on your sign you would say things like "Hire Negroes" or "Jim Crow is dead" or something. Things like that. And so on Saturdays my husband and I would go up there, uptown, and picket, not literally picketing but marching in front of the stores. And then every Sunday this group would meet at different churches, and from the church we would have a silent march through town, through which these people . . . Finney and all of them said you have to get a permit to march, so they'd go and get the permit from the people downtown, which they couldn't deny because we was always saying, "You can't stop us from doing it because this is our freedom . . ." What is it? It's in the First Amendment.

We did that, and then during that year, the same '63 to '64 year, they burned the church in Birmingham, those little girls got burned. So we met the Sunday after that. We'd been meeting every Sunday, and so this Sunday they asked for permission to go the courthouse steps and say a prayer. That was denied. They said we could march but you had to be silent, and could not go on the courthouse steps. So students from Morris College were ahead, and when they got down Main Street opposite the courthouse, they decided they were going to go on the courthouse steps and have their prayer meeting, which they did.

And as soon as they went up there the whole police force just came out and started dragging those students. And we were marching, walking behind, and we could see it. Then people started singing, which was against the rule. We weren't supposed to sing. We sang the freedom songs. We had "I Shall Not Be Moved" and things like that. My husband and I and Lorin Palmer's mother, Theodius, were there. Lorin was just a baby. But Dreyfus, Theodius Palmer, and myself were talking, walking along trying to decide whether or not we would start singing or not, and by the time we went up the street and crossed in front of the courthouse and we came back down the other side of the street, on which was the jailhouse, that was when the police came out and took me and Theodius. They didn't take my husband. They just took us and arrested us. We went down there. I went to the jail, and we were charged with disturbing the peace *[laughs]*.

So there was a lot of confusion. All the church bells started ringing, and of course the people who were not arrested went to tell people what happened. The people came up there, Finney and the leaders, came up to the jailhouse, and they set bond at a hundred dollars cash on a Sunday afternoon. That was just like asking you to put a million dollars cash right down *[laughs]*. But people found this hundred dollars, because I know my husband went to my father-in-law and they found money.

A lot of people who hadn't been so moved by this thing were really angry, because so many people were arrested. They paid my bond, so I didn't spend the night in jail. I got out of jail. This was on a Sunday, and on Monday I went on to school. But the students who were arrested, they wanted a court—what do you call it—a jury trial. They decided they wanted a jury trial. So they had their jury trial later, and my sister and I went up there to the courthouse, not knowing that the courthouse was segregated. White people sat on one side, and black people sat on the other. We just happened, the side we sat on was the side for the colored people, but other people came and sat on the *white* side, and *oooh!* They had a big thing about that. Somehow or another they got that straight, and the students got out of it. The lawyers argued that they were just exercising their constitutional rights at the courthouse and blah blah blah.

The thing about it, the people who were opposing civil rights didn't take a lot of time to think about what they were doing, and nor did they study what they were doing. They didn't know the Constitution would apply to everyone, and they felt that they had a right to tell people you can't do this. They really *felt* that. They felt that was their . . . and they just didn't think to realize that everybody is the same.

Well, we came— I told you earlier that I was so happy that I came through a set of teachers that taught at Lincoln, that never taught hatred. They never, they were not bitter. They were saying, "Learn this, because there will be a better day." And they made you feel if you didn't learn, you would be letting down the world. This was your responsibility to learn everything you could because pretty soon the light would come to these people who were keeping us from going different places, and everything would be fine. So we never had any—I didn't, I don't think of anybody—at that particular time there wasn't any bitterness. When people were arrested, they just let them drag them off. They didn't fight back and stuff like that.

Then they had a cultural musical series in Sumter, and they were advertising that you could come up there and buy tickets, season tickets. They were going to have these artists to come and sing or dance or whatever. So I went up there and they sold me tickets. I bought tickets for myself and my husband. I went back and I called over there *[inaudible]*, "They're selling tickets, go buy some tickets." But nobody else went. In a few days I got my check back, my money back, with a nice letter that they had mistaken me, they didn't realize that I was black, and no colored people could come.

So that made us go into selective buying even more, and we'd go around to different churches in the rural areas and talk to people and tell them, "Don't buy clothes in Sumter. Don't come to Sumter. Go to other places because we're going to make these people feel the pinch." And had things like, "When you pay your light bill, and your water bill and whatever, get your money in pennies." *[She laughs.]* So the people would have to count all the pennies. You would have the money, but you were going to make it difficult. The whole message was that—the theme was, "Freedom is the cause of God. God has made everybody equal. One person can't say they're better than the next person." That was the whole underlying theme.

So we met in churches, we had ministers talk, and we would sing [freedom] songs, so we just felt we were just driven. This was our *purpose*. We had to get this Civil Rights Bill passed, and these people who were denying us, they were just pitiful. They were ignorant. We were just so sorry for them.

A Voteless People Is a Hopeless People

[This slogan "A VOTELESS PEOPLE IS A HOPELESS PEOPLE" was printed on the hand fans provided by the Leevy Funeral Home in Columbia, S.C. according to the interview with I. S. Leey Johnson found in volume 5 of this anthology.]

IW: Another thing we did was get out the vote, because that's where the real thing was. And people were afraid to register to vote, especially rural people, because they lived on these people's farms, and they said, "You don't have time to go get a voting certificate." Plus, it was hard to get one. You had to fill out something in little writing, and they had the authority to ask you to read a passage or article from the Constitution. A lot of people couldn't read, so that would stop them. So we had these classes where we'd have them practice making the application to vote. And after school we'd go and take carloads and truckloads of people to the place to register to vote. Of course, when we got there, the white people sat in one room to register, and the blacks in another, and one man up there registering, and he would take all the people from the white side and not any from the black side *[laughs]*. It closed at five o'clock, and we didn't start doing this until after school. . . . And there were other people who worked during the day. So we'd go and say, "Look, this is not fair. You should at least take one from this side and one from that side. These people got off from work to come vote." So we had the little altercation with him, talked with this man about it.

Anyway, at the end of that school term, the school term of '64, I didn't get a contract. Everybody else got a contract, and I got a letter to come see the same superintendent again. So he told me the school trustees decided not to renew my contract, so I asked why. He said he didn't have to tell me why—it's their prerogative. There was no law in South Carolina that required teachers to have—I can't think of the word— you get it now after you teach so many years.

ML: Certificate?

IW: Oh, no, we had a certificate. It means that when you've taught so many years, then they can't fire you without giving you a reason.

ML: Sort of like tenure in . . .

IW: Yes, tenure. South Carolina had no tenure. Right. And so they didn't have to give a reason. If they didn't like you, they didn't want you, "Goodbye." So we knew that the only reason that they did that to me had to have been because of my involvement in . . . Oh yeah—I had been to the March on Washington, too, that year *[laughs]*.

The March on Washington

IW: That was interesting, because I decided I wasn't going. We went down to see the people get on the train to go to Washington because we weren't going, but when I got there—that's why I really feel that it was my calling. I feel like I was divinely led, because I got down there and it just seemed to me that I just *had* to go to the March on Washington. So my husband and my sister, the three of us were always together. . . . It cost twenty-five dollars, so they said, "Oh, we'll find the twenty-five dollars."

And the train was pulling in, and the people in charge, the ministers, and they said, "Oh, you ride over to Florence with us because all the trains from this area, the southeast area, will be making up a long train in Florence, so you can ride with us and we'll get there."

So I went on and packed my little bag, got my twenty-five dollars, and went over there and got on the train, and went to Washington. And that was— Ooooh! Did you go?

ML: No, I wasn't at that one. I was in a number of other ones but . . .

IW: That was a beautiful experience. The papers had been proclaiming it as a day of rioting, a day of . . . all kinds of things would happen, but . . . There were so many people there, when those trains came in from all over, and buses. There were people just like that *[holds her hands together]*. But everybody was quiet. And then when we got—there were people singing but there was no shouting, other than they had stars, movie stars, and people wanted to give them programs [to sign]. Then we marched down to the Lincoln monument, and that's where all those speeches were given. I was there when Martin Luther King . . . I wasn't far from the steps. Oh! It was just such a beautiful experience. And then we marched, walked back to the train, got on the train, back into Sumter the next morning, which was the first day of school.

And I was in school the first day. I'd already had my room ready, everything, but the day of the March on Washington there was a joint meeting of all the teachers from the school, so I was absent from that, but I was at school for the first day. We decided it was because I went to the March on Washington, because I was in the protest movement, because of that wool contest, because of the voting thing, that they just didn't want me to be, didn't need me to be a teacher. They were going to use me, and some other teachers also didn't get contracts from other schools, but I was the only one from my school. There were two or three others from Sumter.

Filing Suit

IW: We decided right away that we would protest. We would file a suit, which we did with Finney and—I can't think—my brother was a lawyer, too, Donald Sampson. He's not living now. What is my man in Columbia, his name now?

ML: Matthew Perry?

IW: Matthew Perry, yes. He was young. They were just young, beat-the-streets lawyers, so they were my lawyers, and they presented the . . . We had a deposition and at the deposition, they didn't . . . The way my lawyers presented the questions they found out then that is why [I had been dismissed], because they were required to answer their questions. So then the case went to Judge Hemphill in Columbia, at the federal court—it took about two years to get there, and in those two years I couldn't get a job in South Carolina, anywhere. I tried. I could not get a job. They would say, "Oh, yes, we'll send you a contract tomorrow." And the next day there would be a letter saying, "We're sorry but somebody else has that position." But the president of Morris, who was Dr. Odell Reuben at that time, came to my house and offered me a job at Morris College, and so I worked there for two years.

The case came up on the docket, and we went over there and my lawyers told me to take witnesses who could speak for me, and the principal of my school was so—he went, which was quite unusual. And several people in the community went, some of those parents. They were extremely supportive of me. They testified, and then the lawyers were saying that, they would ask them, "Was she on time? Did she not have her lessons plans?" All those things. They couldn't say anything that had to do with the business and mechanics of the job. It was just my extracurricular activities *[laughs]*. And they would say, like picketing on Saturdays: Was I required to be at school on Saturday? No. Sunday? No. It took a little while. The case went to court earlier, I guess before two years, but it took two years before the verdict was handed down, and I was offered my job back, with back pay and everything.

ML: So you were at the end of the '63 to '64 years when your contract was not renewed, and then was it maybe by '66?

IW: That was '66 to '67 I was back on the job, and it happened that the person who was in my position decided that they wanted to go somewhere else, and so there was a vacancy. And I went right back to the same school, same people, same job that I left two years ago. So that's why I know that it was, I really feel that it was divinely . . . it was just what I was supposed to do, because it just came right back to me *[long pause]*.

I was going to show you, this is the way we raised money for the Sumter Freedom Movement. Instead of sending gifts we'd say we had this donated money.

ML: So you'd give a Christmas gift in the name of . . .

IW: On behalf of, yes. That's what we called it, "The Sumter Freedom Movement."

ML: I'd like to make copies of those.

IW: And that's the letter that I wrote about the girls . . .

ML: American Wool Council.

IW: Yes, American Wool . . . And let's see. Here's the picture of my brother who ran for the House of Representatives, John Leroy [Sampson], and he is no longer living. And, let's see . . . This is an article that was in the paper at that time. We would also write letters to the editor, that was one of our strategies too. Finney . . . that's when they honored Finney. . . . Okay. This book got all tangled up because I took it when I went to visit my daughter in California. She asked me to bring it to show it to her eighth graders, because they know nothing about nothing.

ML: Yes.

IW: The contest was still going on, so I had girls to enter it, and of course, they could go. . . . But we went when I got my job back. We entered the contest and went to *the Wade Hampton Hotel!* They didn't tear it down till after we got there *[laughs].* . . .

Now this is from—they were saying that they would have a "hearing," but those people said absolutely nothing. The Board of Trustees came to the room and they just sat there behind the table, and Finney . . . *[becomes emotional]* they talked among themselves but they said [testified] nothing. And at the *hearing* they didn't do anything for but "hear," they didn't talk.

This is the article about the—it was in '65 that they had the . . . I kept this because this is where, "We will not buy at the following stores . . ." And this was just the beginning, "Kress, and Cut Rate and Lawson. Pass the word along, don't buy at those stores." But it ended up we didn't buy at *any* of the stores in Sumter. It worked, too. It worked because people did not buy.

And this I got from the March on Washington.

ML: You've been so good to keep all these materials.

IW: I didn't have them all together and they asked me to find this stuff. And this is when Goldwater ran [for president], and Johnson won. See this is what you call it, *propaganda paper.* They had something telling the people, "Don't vote for Johnson. Vote for Goldwater."

ML *[quoting from the flyer]:* "He voted against his own people and has done as much as any one man to force race mixing." So here Johnson is pictured with, Martin Luther King, Roy Wilkins, James Farmer, and . . . Was this put out by the White Citizens' Council?

IW: It must have been. It might have been by the White Citizens . . . down there, or maybe just the Goldwater campaign or something.

ML *[quoting the headline]:* "A Choice for the South. Racial Revolution Rocks America." . . .

Have you seen one of these before?

ML: No, I haven't.

IW: That was the "Application for Voter Registration." It was difficult to get a voter application. . . .

ML *[quoting the brochure]:* "Voteless people are hopeless people, Sumter Movement committee in 1964." It's got the AME Church, Reverend McGill. I would love to take these along and make copies, and I'll return the originals to you.

IW: Okay. This is the case here. The complaint. I think I have the answer, too.

ML: So was it heard by judges or by a jury?

IW: A judge. It was Judge Hemphill. . . . Robert W. Hemphill was the district judge. That's who it was *[inaudible]* . . .

ML *[quoting from court documents]*: "Heard September first, 1965; decided June 16, '66."

IW: Okay, so one must have been the complaint and that must be the answer. Okay. And to show you how supportive the people in the community were, Finney suggested that [supporters sign] petitions and here all these are! Now this is a very brave thing for people to do, to sign their name on a petition, because a lot of people lost their jobs. Lot of people worked at mills and whatever, had to go to New York and find a job and stuff like that. That was going on at the same time. There was a whole lot of . . .

[Someone enters.]

Drefus Williams **[DW]:** Hey!

ML: Hello! Hello.

DW: Is the gentleman . . . ?

IW: Yes, this is the gentleman . . .

ML: Hi. Marvin Lare.

DW: Dreyfus Williams.

ML: Nice to meet you.

DW: I'm so glad that you are. . . I'm so glad you're here.

ML: Well, I appreciate it so much.

DW: I think this story needs to be told.

ML: Well, I've even heard how you all were sweethearts from high school days.

DW: Oh, now, I didn't intend for you to get that news!

IW: I had to bring it in to show how . . . our dedication.

DW: No problem *[laughs]* . . .

[The rest of this interview will be found in volume 2.]

Lorin Palmer and Theodius Palmer, Part 1

Gloves and High Heels

[As the tape begins, Ms. Palmer is speaking.]

Lorin Palmer **[LP]**:* . . . You've spoken with Bishop James, Frederick James?

    Marvin Lare **[ML]**: Yes.

    LP: Randolph—okay, here we go, that address is 21 Wright Street . . .

    ML: Randolph?

    LP: Yes. R-A-N-D-O-L-P-H. *[She speaks on telephone.]* Reverend Randolph, this is Lorin Palmer. Would you be so kind as to call us at the funeral home? I have a gentleman with me doing an anthology on the civil rights movement, and I wanted to make sure that he spoke with you, or arranged a time when he could come and be with you. Let me try your other number as well. Thank you. *[She hangs up the telephone.]*

    Are you sure you want me as a third party when you meet people that were . . . more significant? *[She laughs.]*

    ML: Well, I want them too. But I mean, your reflections looking down the stairway [referring to photos on the walls] and all that . . .

    LP: I did integrate the schools here for elementary, which was a painful process. I can talk about that at first hand. *[There is a knock at the door.]* Come on in. Just who we want to see! Great! This is my mother!

    ML: How are you?

    LP: Do you remember?

    Theodius Palmer **[TP]**: Yes indeed, I know Marvin.

---

*The interview was conducted at Lorin Palmer's office at the Palmer Mortuary in Sumter, South Carolina, on May 22, 2006.

ML: How are you?

TP: Fine. How are you? . . .

LP: Mama, you came at the perfect time. Please sit here, Darling. Guess what he's doing?

TP: What is he doing?

LP: A book, an anthology on the civil rights movement.

TP: Really? I'm not surprised.

ML: I just can't stay out of trouble.

LP: You're not surprised? Let me take your coat. . . .

TP: Now isn't that wonderful! You know what? I might have a lapse in memory when it comes to that.

ML: Lorin was saying that so many of those things . . . it's hard to bring them out because they get buried. . . . They were painful times.

TP: Right, right.

ML: . . . Lorin was giving me contacts and making phone calls and so forth for half a dozen people or so . . .

TP: Some who're still alive.

LP: Would you kindly review those with Mother and make sure, because I know she's going to add to it as well, but tell her who I've given you so far.

ML: Okay. Dr. Agnes Wilson Burgess. Mrs. J. T. McCain. Ida Mae McCain. Irene and Drefus Williams. Frances and King David Singleton. Barbara Jenkins in Manning.

LP: She's the librarian— You were asking about the librarian at State College. . . .

LP: What about Bill Fleming? We need to send him to Marjorie, don't we? Marjorie Fleming. . . . and Delaine Funeral Home in Manning.

LP: Marjorie Fleming, yes. She's also Saunders now. You've heard about Billy? He's part of Preacher DeLaine's family. He was head of the NAACP and all.

ML: We just had a lot of the folks from [the *Briggs v. Elliott* case] in Columbia at the statehouse last Wednesday, the anniversary of the [Supreme Court decision], May 12th. There was a joint resolution of the legislature, commemorating it. They're going to make it an annual commemoration.

LP: Wonderful! Wow. I didn't know that.

ML: Yes. Judge Finney was there and spoke. . . . Let's see—you just called Reverend Randolph. What's his first name?

LP: William S. Randolph. He needs to speak with him from here. What other ministers, Mom? We want ministers, and that's what made me think about . . . Bishop F. C. James. Of course, he's already spoken with him in Columbia.

TP: Has he?

ML: You mentioned Thea Martin . . .

LP: Oh! Tell me, who was Thea's husband's name? The Presbyterian minister. Now where are they now? Do you know?

Lorin Palmer and her mother, Theodius, assisting Marvin Lare in locating civil rights activists, Palmer Memorial Chapel, Sumter, South Carolina, May 22, 2006.

TP: The last time I heard from them they were up near Laurinburg, North Carolina. He was working with some kind of poverty organization. What was that name?

Thea Martin. And her husband was . . . Well, Mrs. Burgess should be able to tell you. They were all Presbyterians.

LP: Yes, they were all Presbyterians.

LP: Did he actually go to jail and all too, or what was his role? Do you remember?

TP: His role was that he was white, and therefore it was unusual to be . . . he had to work with the black community. You couldn't work with both almost, around that time.

LP: But was he able to find out information, was he ever used as an informant maybe?

TP: Probably. He was busy. The white Presbyterian Church was not going to be very receptive to him because he was in the black community.

ML: Maybe he was on one of the national boards, mission boards or something like that, as a liaison.

TP: Yes. Let me see now, who else was around here, that's still around.

LP: Excuse me just a moment. *[She takes a telephone call.]* Mrs. McCain wants to know, is five o'clock all right with you?

ML: Yes, that'll be fine. I'll let my wife know that I'll—

TP: You're going to be late?

ML: Mrs. McCain's certainly worth it.

TP: You can leave that [door] open, let some air in.

LP: You don't mind? Okay, I didn't know.

TP: You have a card or something you want to leave with your . . . ?

ML: Yes, I've got one there in my coat.

LP: You know, I looked at him like you did, Mama. I remember him coming to Mather [Academy]. . . . He was on the board of . . .

ML: I didn't have an official relationship. I can put my cell phone number on there, too, because that's the best way to find me.

LP: What's the name of the white guy that I went to hear at the State Museum? That did a . . . was chronicling in the press the civil rights . . .

TP: Bass, Jack Bass?

ML: Jack Bass? Yes. "Ear to the Ground" *[on the business card],* that's just my moniker for my writing in retirement.

LP: Wonderful.

TP: Oh, "Ear to the Ground." Okay.

LP: Isn't that wonderful? Now, Mama, what was the name . . . from Rock Hill, that came and spoke for . . . ? He's a professor in Pennsylvania now. I have all his information. I have all the information.

ML: Is it Slippery Rock?

LP: Yes! I have all of his information.

ML: I have the name but I haven't been able to have contact with him yet.

LP: His brother, ironically, is superintendent of education or schools down in the Beaufort area, down in St. Helena. One of the schools that they're doing—when I say "they're," I mean the algebra project—had a connection with the school there that's doing very, very well, and it's outpacing Hilton Head Prep. And this is an all-black school. It's one of the ones that they didn't have the resources, but now they're really improving some things about how black children learn. Anyway, this gentleman . . . Gaither!

ML: Yes.

LP: [Thomas W.] Gaither. Gaither.

LP: Anyway, his brother . . . but you don't want to really talk with him as much. It's more the one from Slippery Rock that you want to speak with.

ML: Yes. I wonder where Slippery Rock is, because I'm going up to . . . We're going to spend a week at Chautauqua in July, and coming or going might be a good time to . . .

LP: So who else in Sumter? Are you thinking, Mom?

TP: I'm trying to . . .

LP: That's still living. We've had an onslaught of people to leave us.

ML: I interviewed Louis Fleming.

LP: Oh good!

ML: And I'm working with his daughter, Catherine . . . She's with the Modjeska Simkins Museum.

LP: Oh! How lovely! Okay.

TP: Now you remember, that's her project now. She left Humanities.

LP: I wanted to bring her back. Okay. She was so good.

ML: Catherine Fleming Bruce.

LP: That's it. Bruce. Yes. That's it. . . .

ML: I bet another name that I've just talked with . . . Eben Taylor. Remember Eben Taylor, a white Methodist minister? He's a close friend of Rhett Jackson's.

LP: Oh yes, we know Rhett.

ML: Anyhow, [Eben is] retired in Laurens. . . . I'm going up to Greenville tomorrow to interview Mayor Max Heller, who was one of the bright lights during that period, and we've done Mayor Riley and . . . I've interviewed a good many people in their nineties already.

TP: You have? Okay. We're fast getting there [laughs].

ML: Like they say, "It's better than the alternative," but of course, that's your business, too [laughs].

TP: You know, John Land's been around for a long time. He knows what must be going on.

ML: Yes, he talks about delivering kerosene and gasoline to the [black] families even during the boycott.

LP: That's exactly right.

ML: You'll think of other names, but now, when is a good time to interview you? Just for you to tell your reflections?

TP: Well, you see, I was just in the background. I was . . .

ML: I understand. With your gloves and your high heels, going to jail [laughs]. Now see, your daughter's been telling on you already.

TP: Our main thing was just that we were just trying—my husband and I were just trying to make sure that we kept the community involved. In order to do that, we had to make sure that we put our money where our mouth was, and our energies. We had to be out there when it was time to be out there, in order to make the other people come along. So . . .

LP: . . . because a lot of them were afraid to lose their jobs. Because we were self-employed, we could take certain risks. Is that what you're trying to say? That you just couldn't take if you were teaching in the school system or whatever, you'd lose your job.

TP: Exactly. And we had to make sure that we let them know that we understood that also, and provided finances, oftentimes, when it became necessary to put up front money. We also— I remember one particular instance that was really interesting to me was when we tried to integrate the First Presbyterian Church. I happened not to go to church that morning, and Perry, my brother-in-law, was still here, and he had a monitoring system that he had on top of the refrigerator. Everybody had gone to church but me and the children, who were very small. I heard the police say, "Get over to the church!" and they said, "In a rush!" And they were having a big commotion. You could hear all of this on this monitoring system. And I stopped and listened and they said, "There're some black boys from Morris College that are trying to integrate the church." So I called the sister of these Williams, Irene Williams, she was named Dorothy Sampson. . . . You ever heard that name?

ML: Yes.

TP: She was an attorney here at that time . . . female attorney here, black female attorney. So I called Dorothy, and I said, "Dorothy, they're having a big commotion up to the First Presbyterian Church and we need to get . . . the best thing for us to do is get in touch with the news." I said, "Let's get the news people down here immediately. Let's call the *Charlotte Observer* and have them here, and let's call NBC." And I said, "That's what we can do behind the scenes, is just get them in here and tell them that they're integrating the First Presbyterian Church."

The white church right across from the post office. Anyway, I've got to think, was Jack Bass . . . ? Who was at the *Charlotte Observer* at that time? It's someone that's very familiar, like Jack.

ML: Maybe Phil Grose. Phil Grose was at the *Charlotte Observer*, I think before Jack.

TP: Before Jack?

ML: And then Fred Sheheen was with the *Charlotte Observer* until the early '60s.

TP: It's wasn't Fred. Must have been Jack.

ML: Fred went with the governor's office—reluctantly. He tells in the interview I've done with him how he said he would go with the governor's office only under the condition that they dealt upfront with this race issue. Anyhow, go ahead.

TP: So we sat here and we just phoned all those offices. She had the skills for all of this and I'm just coordinating, and so I'm saying, telling who to call. And "Let's call the *Washington Post* and let's call" this and let's call that. Well, by the time they— So they took the boys to jail, and then they were going to have the hearing. David McGinnis— you know that name? Judge David McGinnis.

ML: Don't think so.

LP: Another one to contact. He'd be . . .

TP: So anyway, when they go in to have the hearing, it seems to me that it was a quick thing, like Monday morning they were going to do something. All of a sudden they decided that they needed to get this— Oh! Raymond Swartz was involved too. He's around.

ML: See, the names are coming at you.

TP: Because he was the one who was the person who was over the courts when they arrested everybody, when the Birmingham children were killed and everybody was going to march on the courthouse steps. When they arrested people, and I got arrested during that time, and when we got to court, we decided we needed to integrate the courtroom, because here it was, it was segregated. So Finney was saying, "Now listen, let's just take one thing at a time." *[She laughs.]*

ML: You were going to get them so confused . . .

TP: So anyway, Swartz, Raymond Swartz, then was the judge, and he later became a legislator, you know. My husband, when we were dealing with that, all he did was sit and look at Raymond, when they were having the hearing. And it disturbed Raymond Swartz so badly, the way he looked at him, and he was just sitting there, that he told the bailiff to tell him to stop looking at him *[laughs]*. Raymond couldn't stand for him, Bob, to just sit there and look at him like that. Anyway, they didn't stop looking at him—I remember, I just, now this is—information comes piecemeal like this.

ML: That's okay.

TP: But back to this having called the news reporters and so forth. When they got ready to have court . . . All these reporters were there, and with that, they were so disturbed, locally. "How did this happen? That they got the news so fast." So they quieted this thing very, very . . . and they soon made a decision, got some kind of agreement, . . . Anyway, they settled this matter very, very quickly. The information got to the national body of the Presbyterian Church, so some kind of agreement came about. And the president of Morris College didn't want any confusion, because, see, he didn't want any disturbance with the community and Morris College, because he was getting a lot of his money from the community, you see.

LP: Dr. Reuben at the time? Odell Rubin?

TP: Yes, I guess so. Or maybe Richardson had just gotten here. I guess it was Odell Reuben. He hadn't died at that time.

Okay. Now let me think of some other incidents that happened. My role was to go and picket every morning. I went just like I was on a job. Every morning I'd go to the First Baptist Church, this William S. Randolph's church, and . . .

LP: That's where the planning meetings were held, in the basement of the church. Back then they had a basement and they all met there.

TP: The church has been rebuilt now. But at that time, we would go every morning, pick up our pickets, and go to picket the stores. My station was always the Capital Department Store. There was a Capital Department Store—it was a nice big store then, on Main Street. We had certain places that we would picket and it was just like— my station was at ten o'clock, I would always be there. After I took Vickie, my other daughter, to kindergarten and then go to the church, and that was just a routine thing for months.

LP: Also, you got to tell him how you were pregnant with Vickie when you got arrested too. She doesn't want to talk about that.

TP: No, let me see—something else came across my mind that was very— Oh! They always thought when we first started with the picketing and so forth here in Sumter, they wanted to say that *outsiders* had come. That it was not . . . that black people knew how to control themselves and they were used to this and they were comfortable with it being the way it was. Anybody that was causing a disturbance was from the outside. Even though I lived here, I never went to town very much. I never went uptown because everything was so segregated. When I first came here, when I would go in town I wouldn't know how to act, because I would drink out of the fountains, think nothing about it, and then if I were with a friend, after we'd get back home, she'd say, "Did you know you drank out of that fountain and you weren't supposed to drink out of that fountain?" Or, "You tried on a hat and you weren't supposed to try on a hat? Or you went in the dressing room and you didn't . . ."

I was always doing the wrong thing, because I wasn't quite used to not doing that. Although I had lived in segregated places, I had been sheltered. So would therefore, didn't think very much about it. Where I had lived it wasn't as blatant. Therefore, I just said, "Oh shoot, I'm not going to go to town much here. I don't want to cause a whole lot of confusion, so . . . My husband's in business and I will just wait and do my shopping someplace else."

One Saturday afternoon, this same Williams girl, Irene Williams, who got fired from her teaching job, she and I were sitting on the porch, and we were having a discussion. She said, "You know, we need to get involved."

And I said, "Well, yes, we do."

My mother-in-law was saying, "Yes! You young people are going to have to carry this thing on. Now we just have to break these barriers here."

I said, "Okay, let's go up to town and march in front of Sumter Dry Goods, right now."

So that Saturday afternoon we went and got our pickets down to the church and went up to the Sumter Dry Goods to picket. That was one of the stores that was *not* going to give in. We picketed back and forth in front of Sumter Dry Goods. That's where that park is now, with the Rotary Club thing, there was a building there. After a while, the police came and they looked at us real hard and so forth, and she had always lived here, all her life, and she was very fair, so they were trying to see whether she was white and from the outside community. They looked at me and they didn't know me, because I never went to town very much and had been here only a short while.

Let's see, what did they do with us that day? That day they made us . . . told us that we had to do some restrictions, and we conformed. They were trying to arrest us, but we conformed to everything they said and didn't cause any confusion. We didn't talk, we didn't do anything. We just marched up and down. But they came and got a good look at us.

Then the next day, when I was marching from the church, downtown, and all these ministers, about seventeen of them, were leading the march—and this is about the Birmingham situation—and so when they kneeled on the courthouse steps, and they arrested all of the ministers, I was saying to her—she was with me that day, too—and I was saying to her, in line, "Irene, we've got to do something. We can't let them take all our ministers off. We won't have any leaders." I was very excited. That was the only thing that I was doing. That's when I had these gloves and everything.

The detective, plainclothesman, tapped me on the shoulders and said, "Come with me." And that's when they took me off to jail. Here I was. I had gone from church to there so I was in these high-heeled shoes and gloves. But the main thing, I think he had seen me the day before and out of all that crowd, he spotted me again, and so they thought we were outsiders.

ML: One of those troublemakers.

TP: Yes. So they took Irene and me, we were together that day, and they took us off to jail. Dr. B. T. Williams, who was living at that time, and some of the other men said, "Oh gosh! They got Bob's wife!" Bob, my husband, and Perry were on a funeral, so they rushed and got the news to them, and they were afraid for Bob to come up there, because he might be, you know. And he knew all the guys. Being in the funeral business, he knew every one of the police people by first names. When he got there, when they finally got him there, he came in and he was so excitable, and I was trying to keep him quiet, because he couldn't stand to see me going to jail, and I was saying, "Well, let me just go on and see what it's like." *[She laughs.]* And so they were taking me, fingerprinting me.

ML: They were trying to get you released right away and you were trying to get in!

TP: I was trying to get in *[laughs]*. And here are all of these white girls and all of them trying to do the fingerprinting, and that's about the time he walked in. I was smiling to him, "I'm all right. I'm all right."

And he was saying, "Oh no, you aren't! You're coming out of here!"

I was trying to keep him quiet, and so finally they decided to let me come on home, because I had a small child to take care of and they knew all this.

But when the detective asked me to go with him, I had—I guess it was you [Lorin], so I said to them, "Well, take her back to the house." It was right up the street here, where it happened. [I told them] to walk Lorin back down here. So some friends brought her back to the house. That was the most terrible time, that I had to leave my daughter, and she seeing me dragging off to jail!

The other thing that came about was—did you tell him about your confusion at school?

LP: Oh, we haven't gotten there yet.

[The rest of this interview will be found in volume 2.]

Appendix

In the introduction to this volume, I mention my intent to enable the reader get to know the interviewees personally, as they reveal themselves in their own words, not to bias the reader by "pigeonholing" the subject as to age, race, education, and other typical categories. I indicated that the volumes of this anthology are not "histories." They certainly contain history but are not intended to document, describe, or interpret the events except as the persons themselves describe them.

I have followed that principle, even not directly mentioning the race of the interviewee. I have sought to accommodate the interest in factual biographical information in an appendix planned for volume 3. It will provide brief biographical information on the individuals in these volumes and other key personages of the era. The reader, I surmised, could turn to that appendix for information and data on any or all of the interviewees.

I continue with that resolve; however, my friend and colleague Vernon Burton, Ph.D., recently insisted that more demographical information should be provided in each volume. He pointed out that readers may not have volume 3 in hand. Further, "Race and other identifying information may be readily available to contemporary readers, but a hundred years from now readers may well not know that Lester Bates, mayor of Columbia 1958–1970, was white and that would significantly affect their understanding of him and his role in civil rights." Spoken like a true historian. I have had to take Burton's perspective under consideration. To address this concern, I am providing the following table with relevant information on the gender, race, and primary location of those presented in this volume.

The interviewees are presented here in alphabetical order, for ease of location:

INTERVIEWEE	GENDER	RACE	REGION OF STATE*
Gloria Rackley Blackwell	female	black	midstate
Samuel M. Bonds	male	black	lowcountry
Charles H. Brown	male	black	lowcountry
MaeDe Brown	female	black	lowcountry
Millicent E. Brown	female	black	lowcountry
Septima Poinsette Clark	female	black	lowcountry
James E. Clyburn	male	black	midstate

INTERVIEWEE	GENDER	RACE	REGION OF STATE*
Charlie Sam Daniel	male	black	midstate
Bobby Doctor	male	black	midstate
Ernest A. Finney Jr.	male	black	midstate
Harvey Gantt	male	black	lowcountry
Lottie Gibson	female	black	upstate
Samuel Hudson	male	black	lowcountry
Sarah Hudson	female	black	lowcountry
Nathaniel Irvin	male	black	midstate
Frederick C. James	male	black	midstate
Gloria M. Jenkins	female	black	midstate
Teenie Ruth Lott	female	black	midstate
Willie T. "Dub" Massey	male	black	midstate
Ida Mae McCain	female	black	midstate
James T. "Nooker" McCain	male	black	midstate
Matthew Douglas McCollom	male	black	midstate
Joe McDomic	male	black	lowcountry
Beatrice "Bea" McKnight	female	black	midstate
Frieda Mitchell	male	black	lowcountry
Fred Henderson Moore	male	black	lowcountry
Johnalee Nelson	female	black	midstate
Anne Newman	female	black	midstate
Emily Newman	female	black	midstate
I. DeQuincey Newman	male	black	midstate
Xanthene Norris	female	black	upstate
Lorin Palmer	female	black	midstate
Theodius Palmer	female	black	midstate
Matthew J. Perry	male	black	midstate
Alice Pyatt	female	black	lowcountry
Lurma Rackley	female	black	midstate
Jamelle Rackley-Riley	female	black	midstate
Cleveland Sellers	male	black	midstate
Courtney Siceloff	male	white	lowcountry
James E. Sulton Sr.	male	black	midstate
Irene Williams	female	black	midstate
J. S. Wright	male	black	midstate
TOTALS	22 male, 20 female	41 black, 1 white	3 upstate, 26 midstate, 13 lowcountry

Note: *These geographic regions are very broadly drawn. The mid-state, for example, ranges from Aiken, up through Columbia to Rock Hill. The lowcountry and upstate are the broad coastal plains and the more Piedmont areas.

It should be noted that I have not set any criteria in selecting the subjects for interviews other than that they have played significant leadership roles in civil and human rights during this period. I did not set out to have a particular balance by gender, race, or geographical representation. Therefore, I offer the above table simply for the reader's reference and to assure that history does not cloud those significant factors. Similarly, the following table of interviewers is provided as summary information that may be helpful to the reader.

INTERVIEWERS	GENDER	RACE	NUMBER OF INTERVIEWS
1982 "Voices" Conference			3
Jean Claude Bouffard	male	white	1
Andrew Grose	male	white	1
Felice Knight	female	black	1
Marvin Ira Lare	male	white	25
Grace McFadden	female	black	4
Robert K. Moore	male	white	4
TOTALS	4 male, 2 female	2 black, 4 white	39

Again, the interviewers were not selected with particular bias but rather as sources and resources were available. This is described more fully in the preface and acknowledgments and the prologue at the beginning of this volume.

Similarly, the transcribers were selected as resources were available. Initially the South Caroliniana Library committed to have twenty interviews transcribed by Catherine Mann. Felice Knight, a graduate student at the College of Charleston, both conducted interviews and transcribed the text. Then I was able to secure funding and hire Lynn Moore to transcribe most of the interviews. Andrew Grose, a student at Winthrop, conducted the interview with "Dub" Massey and transcribed the text. Students at Winthrop also conducted interviews and transcribed them as described above as well. Accurate and responsive transcription is crucial to completion and publication of oral histories. I scanned some documents with character recognition software and corrected errors.

Index